W9-CBK-024

TRIAL TACTICS
AND
METHODS

TRIAL TACTICS
AND
METHODS

SECOND EDITION

ROBERT E. KEETON

Professor of Law
Harvard University

LITTLE, BROWN AND COMPANY
Boston   1973   Toronto

COPYRIGHT, ©, 1954, 1973, BY LITTLE, BROWN AND COMPANY

ALL RIGHTS RESERVED. NO PART OF THIS BOOK MAY BE REPRODUCED IN ANY FORM OR BY ANY ELECTRONIC OR MECHANICAL MEANS INCLUDING INFORMATION STORAGE AND RETRIEVAL SYSTEMS WITHOUT PERMISSION IN WRITING FROM THE PUBLISHER, EXCEPT BY A REVIEWER WHO MAY QUOTE BRIEF PASSAGES IN A REVIEW.

LIBRARY OF CONGRESS CATALOG CARD NO. 72-13326

61-X-1

Twelfth Printing

HAL

*Published simultaneously in Canada
by Little, Brown & Company (Canada) Limited*

PRINTED IN THE UNITED STATES OF AMERICA

To Betty

who, substituting intuition for legal training, read the manuscript and caused me to rewrite every sentence she thought she did not understand. If you find the meaning of any passage obscure, seek the explanation of another with intuition.

PREFACE

Two significant developments coming to fruition early in the 1970s account for most of the differences between the original and the second edition of this book: first, the Supreme Court's revision of federal discovery rules and, second, the revision of standards of professional responsibility, including those bearing on techniques of advocacy. The American Bar Association's Code of Professional Responsibility was adopted by the House of Delegates of the Association on August 12, 1969, to become effective for ABA members on January 1, 1970. A committee of the ABA achieved prompt success in urging the adoption of the code by state institutions responsible for overseeing the professional conduct of members of the bar. As a result, the ABA Code has been officially adopted in most states, and with few modifications or none.

A third development affecting some sections of this revised edition is the Supreme Court's adoption on November 20, 1972, of Rules of Evidence for United States Courts and Magistrates. As this book goes to press, the fate of these Rules remains in doubt. In any event, it has seemed appropriate to call attention to their potential application to problems discussed in this book. All references to the Federal Rules of Evidence in this book are references to those Rules as promulgated by the Supreme Court on November 20, 1972.

Apart from the numerous changes occasioned by these three developments, and some editorial changes, this second edition is essentially the same book as the first edition.

I gratefully acknowledge the proficient secretarial assistance of Jeannine Calaba in the preparation of the manuscript for this edition.

ROBERT E. KEETON

PREFACE TO THE FIRST EDITION

I

To the casual observer of lawsuits, it may seem that able trial lawyers act by inspiration and intuition. But the fact is that their reactions to courtroom situations have a sound basis in reason. The purpose of this book is to articulate the reasons for conduct that is second nature to a competent trial lawyer and to suggest rational bases for decision of the closer questions of tactics and methods that even the most competent prefer not to leave to spur-of-the-moment decision.

The fact that trial lawyers often find it necessary to make decisions quickly only accentuates the need for concern with reasoned bases for those decisions. Monday morning quarterbacking may be only fun for others, but for quarterbacks it is essential training. If one develops the habit of critical reflection afterward on the merits of the quick decisions he has made during trial, he prepares himself to meet similar situations with more assurance in the future. The experience of having faced a difficult situation teaches. But whether it teaches something of value depends on how well the experience is interpreted. The same is true of the vicarious experience of observing another in action.

Even very able trial lawyers can and do fall into some bad habits of advocacy if they do not engage in a moderate amount of self-criticism from time to time. The trial lawyer who is intent on improvement and the novice who wants to develop competence require heavier and more frequent doses of this medication.

A common basis for judgment of trial tactics, perhaps more often assumed than expressed, is that the case was won or lost. But the sequence of tactic and victory does not prove causal connection between the two. A good cause has often overcome deficient advocacy in its favor and superb advocacy in opposition. An appraisal of trial tactics and methods, to be valid and useful, must be one that will withstand analytical inquiry. The inquiry must be more than a comparison with a set of rules, even if the set includes not only the formal rules that lawyers must observe but also the unofficial rules, if they may be called "rules," that good trial lawyers observe in practice. The "how" of trial tactics and methods cannot be separated from the "why." Even the effort to make the separation tentatively, for study, is likely to produce more distortion than understanding. An intelligent choice among the range of methods available in any trial situation can be made only with understanding of the reasons each method is used in some situations and avoided in others — only with understanding of its advantages and disadvantages, potentialities and limitations.

The best method for learning these things, if competent guidance is available, is the true case method of working on an actual case. Perhaps the next best way is to simulate the problems of an actual case. That is the purpose of this book. It is a modified case study in the sense that problems are separated for discussion one by one, with relatively simple problem cases for illustration. This separation of the individual problem from its complex setting is hardly a new technique. Judicial opinions, for example, represent such a separation. It is only a small segment of the case that reaches the appellate court, and a still smaller segment that receives attention in the appellate opinion. It is common for a trial lawyer to have the feeling that the court has ignored vital aspects of his case — oversimplifying the statement of the problem — in order to give an appearance of validity to an erroneous, and incidentally adverse, opinion. The separation of problems for individual consideration in this book makes it subject to this criticism of oversimplification. The justification offered is that the total problem is invariably so complex that one can make no progress toward a reasoned solution without such a tentative assumption of a simpler problem.

The principal pattern followed in the book is (a) to identify a recurring question of trial practice, (b) to illustrate with a problem case in which the question arises, and (c) to discuss implications of the problem and considerations that should be weighed in answering it in a particular case. Perhaps the discussion should have been closed at that point, leaving you to your own solution. Instead, I have given answers of a sort, though I have felt the necessity of qualifying them more than I would have preferred. I offer the suggested answers with the realization that they will be subject to challenge. If you prove me wrong, I take comfort in the thought that you may profit by the exercise of doing so.

II

Though this book is primarily an attempt to explore trial tactics and does not purport to deal especially with ethics of advocacy, it is intended also to draw attention to ethical aspects of the total problem of choosing trial methods. Like the tactical problems, many of the ethical questions are matters of opinion, but they too are more likely to be answered satisfactorily after reasoned analysis of the implications of one decision or another. Moreover, the need for reasoned consideration is increased by the fact that the meaning of canons of ethics is often obscure and the further fact that, even when effectively enforced, the canons represent only minimum standards, less demanding than those toward which at least a substantial part of the profession is striving. There is a risk that comments on ethics of advocacy will be taken as instruction in what one can get away with, but it is outweighed by the certainty that problems of choice of trial methods are falsely presented if the ethical questions are ignored.

Though it is unlikely that a trial lawyer would object to the emphasis on tactics in this book, other readers may, on the theory that such emphasis interferes with the goal of having legal controversies decided on the merits. They may fear that discussion of the trial of a lawsuit as a series of tactical problems will degenerate into a study of the techniques of shysterism. To them I offer not an apology but an affirmation. It is true that there is danger that injustice will be done if tactical considerations are placed above all others. But this danger is not created or increased by candid recognition of tactical implications of trial methods. On the contrary, candid discussion should increase appreciation and understanding of the danger that already exists from opportunities to place tactical expediency above ethics of advocacy and above the aim of the whole judicial process — justice. Furthermore, this danger is only part of the total picture. Effective trial tactics also offer a positive contribution toward the aim of justice. In the typical case submitted to trial, what would be perfectly just is both uncertain and disputed, and the judgment of even the most earnest and competent person (juror, judge or lawyer) may be a bad judgment. The "adversary system" of trial is an effort to deal effectively with this problem of the inescapable danger of human error. An essential corollary of this system of striving for justice is that each litigant should have his case presented in the most favorable light. The system works best when both litigants have this done for them. Choosing, within the bounds of ethical limitations, the best method for presenting a case favorably is not merely the trial lawyer's opportunity; it is his duty.

III

A trial is a competition of inconsistent versions of facts and theories of law. Trial tactics and methods are aimed at persuading the jury (or the judge, as factfinder) that your version of the facts is accurate and persuading the courts that your theory of the law is sound and just. After a brief inquiry (in Chapter I) into the general subject "What makes a trial lawyer effective?"

attention is then given (in Chapters II-VIII) to situations arising during the trial itself, since the basic concern is with mastering these situations in a way that will contribute to this process of persuasion. With an understanding of the problems arising during trial, we shall then be better able to consider what should be done in advance of trial for the purpose of preparing to meet these problems effectively. This postponement to Chapters IX-XI of the discussion of pretrial preparations and procedures is not intended to disparage these subjects. On the contrary, my thesis is that you can increase your effectiveness as an advocate by thoughtful study of the problems of trials generally and of the particular problems that you can anticipate in a specific case.

IV

I gratefully acknowledge the benefits received from the criticism of the manuscript for this book by Dean Erwin N. Griswold of Cambridge, Massachusetts, and Judge Paul W. Brosman of Washington, D.C. I am also indebted to many others whose ideas may have influenced the development of mine on this subject. They include not only those whose published writings are cited in footnotes, but also the judges and lawyers with whom I have had the privilege of association, both inside and outside the courtroom. Among them, the two to whom I owe the most are Messrs. William R. Brown and Denman Moody of Houston, Texas, who served as my mentors in courtroom practice. I am grateful also to Dean R. G. Storey and Professor Roy R. Ray of Southern Methodist University for encouraging my interest in teaching, and especially the teaching of trial practice, which led to my writing this book. To one of my colleagues, Professor Richard H. Field, I am indebted for ideas on which I have drawn in revising the Preface before reprinting in 1960. None of these persons is to be held accountable, of course, if the reader finds cause to challenge any of the ideas expressed in this book.

ROBERT E. KEETON

TABLE OF CONTENTS

TRIAL TACTICS
AND
METHODS

CHAPTER I

WHAT MAKES A TRIAL LAWYER EFFECTIVE?

§1.1 Talent?

Two experienced trial lawyers may meet identical situations with wholly different methods and each achieve success. One may be dramatic and witty, while another appears equally successful with low-key methods designed to emphasize the earnestness of the appeal. Each has developed a distinctive talent for presenting the client's cause persuasively. Undoubtedly those who become the most effective trial lawyers begin with native ability to think accurately under pressure and to speak extemporaneously, but this is only a beginning. Other lawyers with less native ability may prove to be the more effective advocates because they prepare more thoroughly and give greater attention to discovering and applying the methods most suitable to their own peculiar talents and limitations.

§1.2 Sincerity of manner

Very few persons have the ability to assume effectively numerous different roles. Your attempt to assume a demeanor that is unnatural will usually result in creating the impression upon judge and jurors that you are trying to put something over on them rather than trying to persuade them to agree with a position you sincerely advance. Friendliness toward jurors is an asset unless you create the impression that you are simply trying to use their friendship. The "cracker-barrel" technique of appearing to share informally, though sincerely, in the jurors' consideration of a problem is effective unless you create the impression that you are talking down to their level by using vernacular and grammar that are unnatural for you. Timing of the development of individual points [1] to produce a dramatic climax, or any other

---

1. *E.g.*, see §§2.2, 2.6, 2.8, 2.9, 2.20, 2.26, 2.35, 2.38, 3.5–3.8, 4.6, 4.7, 5.9. See also §1.4 at n.l.

1

use of the dramatic, may deeply move the jury, if you do not overdo the matter and cause jurors to sense that you are merely putting on a show. Whatever the particular method you may be considering, avoid it if there is serious danger that it will create or contribute to an impression of want of sincerity. Use only the roles you can live.

Sincerity in the advocacy of your cause is to be distinguished from an air of confidence that it will prevail or that you are representing it adequately. Sometimes patently inadequate presentation of a case proves successful because the judge and jury feel a compulsion to protect the interests of the client who has been so poorly represented. Some lawyers make effective use of this fact by deliberately assuming the role of an underdog fighting an earnest contest against a superior adversary. You may occasionally see the interesting spectacle of two cunning trial lawyers each praising the other as the greatest advocate of all times and personally assuming the role of just an ordinary, honest plodder whose client's only hope is that the jury will protect his interests in spite of the unequal representation.

Probably you will be at your best as an advocate when you cause the judge and jury to believe that the decision you are urging them to reach is a decision you would reach yourself. Yet the Code of Professional Responsibility,[2] in one of its Disciplinary Rules, prohibits any direct statement of belief in your cause.[3] Should this rule be construed as prohibiting not only direct assertions of belief in your cause but also the kind of conduct through which, without making any direct assertion, you convey to the jury the impression that you believe in the cause you are presenting? Perhaps the general proposition that rules of conduct should not be subject to evasion by indirection points toward an affirmative answer. But quite clearly that interpretation of the Disciplinary Rule would be contrary to the prevailing practice in the courts, before and after adoption of the Code of Professional Responsibility as well as before and after adoption of earlier canons that expressed essentially the same idea.[4] It seems more consistent with the apparent objectives

2. American Bar Association, Code of Professional Responsibility (1969), adopted by the ABA House of Delegates on August 12, 1969, "to become effective for American Bar Association members on January 1, 1970," and thereafter adopted in most states as an official code of conduct governing members of their respective bars.

3. *Id.,* DR 7-106 (C): "In appearing in his professional capacity before a tribunal, a lawyer shall not:

". . . (4) Assert his personal opinion as to the justness of a cause, as to the credibility of a witness, as to the culpability of a civil litigant, or as to the guilt or innocence of an accused; but he may argue, on his analysis of the evidence, for any position or conclusion with respect to the matters stated herein."

4. See American Bar Association, Canons of Professional Ethics (1908). Canon 15, paragraph 2, was as follows: "It is improper for a lawyer to assert in argument his personal belief in his client's innocence or in the justice of his cause." The first ABA canons, including Canon 15, were adopted by the association at its Thirty-First Annual

of the rule,[5] as well as the prevailing practice, to treat it as a regulation of the form and manner of your conduct as an advocate rather than a regulation requiring that you not display, even indirectly, any appearance of commitment to your cause. Indeed, if interpreted as precluding even an indirect display of commitment to your cause, the rule could hardly be reconciled with your acknowledged duty as an advocate to bring "zeal" to your representation of your cause.[6]

§1.3 Attitude of fairness

The beneficial effect of your apparent sincerity may be lost or greatly reduced if you seem willing to use any means available, fair or unfair, to advance your cause. It is understandable that an advocate is often more intent upon winning than upon getting a fair trial, though usually the two seem to the advocate to be synonymous. An advocate's bias is expected and usually excused, though not ignored. But the advocate's methods may be viewed more critically. An appearance of desiring a fair trial — no less and no more — generally produces a more favorable and sympathetic response from jurors and judges, even though they are not surprised to see lawyers battle with every weapon available. Particularly if there is an apparent contrast between the attitudes of the opposing lawyers in this respect, the one who resorts to

---

Meeting on August 27, 1908. They were based on a code adopted by the Alabama State Bar Association in 1887 and on lectures of Judge George Sharswood, published in 1854, which also influenced the Alabama code. See American Bar Association, Code of Professional Responsibility, Preface (1969).

5. Reasons for adoption of the disciplinary rule are suggested in American Bar Association, Code of Professional Responsibility EC 7-24 (1969):

"In order to bring about just and informed decisions, evidentiary and procedural rules have been established by tribunals to permit the inclusion of relevant evidence and argument and the exclusion of all other considerations. The expression by a lawyer of his personal opinion as to the justness of a cause, as to the credibility of a witness, as to the culpability of a civil litigant, or as to the guilt or innocence of an accused is not a proper subject for argument to the trier of fact. It is improper as to factual matters because admissible evidence possessed by a lawyer should be presented only as sworn testimony. It is improper as to all other matters because, were the rule otherwise, the silence of a lawyer on a given occasion could be construed unfavorably to his client. However, a lawyer may argue, on his analysis of the evidence, for any position or conclusion with respect to any of the foregoing matters."

6. See id., Canon 7: "A Lawyer Should Represent a Client Zealously Within the Bounds of the Law." The earlier ABA Canon 15, adopted in 1908, included at the beginning of its third paragraph the following sentence:

"The lawyer owes 'entire devotion to the interest of the client, warm zeal in the maintenance and defense of his rights and the exertion of his utmost learning and ability,' to the end that nothing be taken or be withheld from him, save by the rules of law, legally applied."

methods that may be regarded as unfair [1] or contentions that may be regarded as technical or tricky, [2] rather than being founded on merits of the controversy, incurs disfavor. Judges as well as jurors may be influenced by reactions to lawyers' methods. [3]

From a long range point of view, as distinguished from concern with the immediate case only, you have an interest in avoiding customary use of methods designed to win cases on grounds that may be regarded as unfair, though legal. A reputation for this type of practice becomes a handicap to you in representing your clients in future cases, since even your more substantial contentions come to be viewed with suspicion by judges familiar with your reputation. The duty of supporting the client's cause is sometimes so forcefully stated as to support the argument that as a trial lawyer you are obliged to assert every legal claim or defense available, except those you reject on tactical grounds relating to the immediate case. [4] But the aim of the trial system to achieve justice, the interests of future clients, and your legitimate interest in your own reputation and future effectiveness at the bar compel moderation of that extreme view.

Consider the use of surprise tactics as an illustration of this problem. The Code of Professional Responsibility does not refer to the use in general of surprise tactics, [5] but clearly the use of such tactics to defeat an admittedly

1. *E.g.,* §§3.1, 3.4, 3.11, 3.17, 3.30, 4.4, 7.5, 7.12, 11.13.

2. *E.g.,* §§3.19, 4.2, 4.8, 7.7, 11.10.

3. Consider §4.14, discussing the inclusion of argumentative comment in an objection.

4. Such a construction might be placed on the first three sentences of the third paragraph of Canon 15 of the 1908 Canons:

"The lawyer owes 'entire devotion to the interest of the client, warm zeal in the maintenance and defense of his rights and the exertion of his utmost learning and ability,' to the end that nothing be taken or be withheld from him, save by the rules of law, legally applied. No fear of judicial disfavor or public unpopularity should restrain him from the full discharge of his duty. In the judicial forum the client is entitled to the benefit of any and every remedy and defense that is authorized by the law of the land, and he may expect his lawyer to assert every such remedy or defense."

But other parts of the same canon stand against this interpretation. Similarly, the Ethical Considerations and Disciplinary Rules associated with Canon 7 of the American Bar Association, Code of Professional Responsibility (1969), include forceful statements of the duty to the client — *e.g., id.,* EC 7–1, 7–7 — but along with other statements qualifying the duty to the client in view of other interests. *E.g., id.,* DR 7–101 (B):

"In his representation of a client, a lawyer may: (1) Where permissible, exercise his professional judgment to waive or fail to assert a right or position of his client."

See also *id.,* EC 7–10, 7–20, 7–36 through 7–39. Concerning tactical advantages of not asserting a right, see, *e.g.,* §§9.22, 11.13.

5. As to one particular use of surprise, however, see *id.,* DR 7–106 (C) (5), declaring that in appearing in his professional capacity before a tribunal a lawyer shall not: "Fail to comply with known local customs of courtesy or practice of the bar or a particular tribunal without giving to opposing counsel timely notice of his intent not to comply."

just claim or defense is not supportable. On the other hand, the use of surprise to expose falsification is clearly justifiable. The intermediate ground presents the timeless controversy of "means versus ends." Is it proper to use surprise tactics to defeat on a technical ground a claim or defense that you consider unjust upon grounds that you may not be able to establish? Does it make a difference whether the grounds that you consider meritorious but difficult to prove are factual or legal? It is in some such "intermediate" form that the problem of professional responsibility usually arises. Most cases are settled; in the smaller percentage going to trial, each lawyer generally thinks that the other party is at least seeking more than is justly due, if not making a wholly unjustified claim or defense. Probably the answer implicit in prevailing practice is that it is permissible to use any legally supportable ground of claim or defense, though it is a surprise move, to uphold a position you believe just, whatever the basis of your belief may be. Nevertheless, many individual lawyers practice substantially greater restraint in the use of surprise, often because of concern about taking advantage of a fellow lawyer (particularly one less experienced), as well as concern about fairness of trial methods from the point of view of the interests of the parties to the suit.

The reaction against trickery has contributed to severe criticism of surprise tactics and to a trend toward modification of rules of procedure to reduce possibilities for effective use of surprise. So long as we retain the adversary system of trial, however, no rules can be devised that will eliminate entirely the possibility of surprise. Furthermore, this characteristic is not merely a susceptibility of the system to abuse; it is also a reason for its effectiveness in achieving justice. The propriety of tactical use of surprise in trials involves competing interests. Surprise may cause an unjust disposition of a controversy because of the want of preparation for an unexpected argument of fact or law, and want of time after it is made to discover and prepare available controverting matter. On the other hand, every exposure of a fabricated claim or defense comes about through some form of surprise tactics; no one would urge a false claim that he did not think he had fabricated so cleverly as to avoid discovery. Surprise often causes a just disposition of a controversy that otherwise would have been improperly decided because of failure of the fact-finder to realize the falsification.

The extent to which either of these competing interests prevails in the formulation of rules of procedure varies considerably; in general, the opportunities for surprise tactics have been greatly reduced under the federal rules and other new rules based upon them. These rules leave much discretion to the trial judge, however, and the opportunities for surprise tactics thus vary from court to court among those operating under identical rules. A few judges have taken the extreme position of using pretrial procedures[6] to re-

6. See §11.23.

quire, for example, that each party produce all documentary evidence to be used in trial, even though it is of the type intended for impeachment against claims thought to be fabricated or deliberately exaggerated. Probably more judges consider, however, that the interest in effective exposure of fabrication should prevail with respect to impeachment evidence, and that a party should not be required to disclose this kind of evidence in advance of trial against his will.

The tactical advantages of surprise are obvious. Catching the adversary by surprise improves the chances that there will be too little time and opportunity to develop countermeasures before the harm is accomplished.

The tactical disadvantages from use of surprise are primarily outgrowths of the danger of unfavorable reaction from judge or jury to trickery in a proceeding that is intended for the discovery of truth and the administration of justice. If your surprise tactics are successful in exposing falsification by an adverse party or witness, there is no substantial danger of such an unfavorable reaction, because the ordinary person will consider your methods justified. On the other hand, if your tactics fail to expose falsification, or if they are designed not to expose falsification but to defeat the claim on some ancillary ground, an unfavorable reaction is at least possible, if not probable, and may prejudice the consideration of other of your contentions that are more meritorious.

Illustrations of the problem of using surprise will be found at several points in the book.[7]

§1.4 Perspective

To be an effective trial lawyer you must maintain perspective. Consider each trial problem in its proper relationship to the development of the case as a whole. In each instance, let your decision on whether to make a certain point — to ask a certain question of a witness, to raise a certain objection, to make a certain motion, or to use a certain technique — be guided not solely by whether you have a legally sound basis for doing so and will realize some immediate advantage, but also by your appraisal of the effect that your making the point may have upon the jury's and judge's consideration of all other aspects of the case. Likewise, let your choice of the time for raising the point be guided by the effect of timing upon the reactions of judge and jury.[1] Each of the succeeding chapters of this book concerns specific applications of this principle of perspective.

You will have the opportunity to observe trials in which the lawyers are

7. See §§2.25, 2.35, 2.38, 4.7, 5.2, 5.8, 6.9, 7.7, 7.11, 9.2, 10.3, 10.9, 11.9, 11.12, 11.23.
1. For illustrations of the effect of timing, see §§2.2, 2.6, 2.8, 2.9, 2.20, 2.26, 2.35, 2.38, 3.5–3.8, 4.6, 4.7, 5.9. See also §1.2 at n.l.

constantly engaged in bickering and jousting for petty victories, each trying to outdo the other, and each stalking triumphantly about the courtroom or assuming a dramatic pose each time he succeeds or wishes to convey the impression that he has succeeded. It is an easy habit to acquire, and always a temptation when your adversary baits you, but probably no one would seriously contend that jurors decide cases on the basis of which lawyer is the more clever at such verbal jousting. This is not to say that jurors are not influenced by such a contest between lawyers. The byplay is often damaging to one party or the other, instead of being merely immaterial to the result in the case. As a general rule, the danger of harm is greater to the party whose case has less sympathetic appeal than the opponent's. It is generally to the advantage of the defendant in a personal injury case to avoid immaterial controversies between the lawyers; sympathies being such as they are, jurors are less willing to overlook or forgive the things they do not like in the defendant's lawyer than in the plaintiff's lawyer. The defendant's lawyer should be above suspicion. Furthermore, such controversies are likely to involve remarks that go beyond the record and effectively deprive the defendant of some of the protection that rules of procedure provide for keeping out of the trial appeals to sympathy and prejudice.

§1.5 Preparation

There is no substitute for thorough preparation of each case for trial.[1] This means preparation of both law and facts. It means not only knowing and planning the presentation of your own side of the case but also knowing the other side well enough to anticipate your adversary's evidence and legal theories. It means discovering the weak points as well as the strong points of the case. In short, your aim should be to know the whole case.

One of the most commonly neglected aspects of advance preparation of a case for trial is a process that may appropriately be termed proof analysis. Sound proof analysis helps you anticipate and master troublesome problems of proof that may arise during trial. One aspect of the process is anticipating objections and developing plans for overcoming them. Thus one very important function of proof analysis is to prepare for evidence questions that may arise. But there are other functions as well. Even if your opponent raises no objection to your inartistic questions to a witness, your failure, in formulating the questions, to think through the relationship between what the witness might say and the ways you might use his testimony at other stages of trial may leave you with a weaker case than you could have developed by devising better questions. What is the relationship between an anticipated

---

1. Recurring problems you are likely to encounter in preparing particular cases are discussed in Chapter IX.

answer of the witness and one or more of the "ultimate" facts you must prove to establish your claim or defense? And how might you wish to use the answer in the course of your summation to the jury? You are better prepared to try your case well when you have directly and thoughtfully considered these questions.

You need not follow a rigid pattern of proof analysis, and with experience you may find that in most instances you need not take the time to record in your preparatory notes the various steps of analysis you use. Even with experience, however, you may find it helpful to resort to a step-by-step written analysis with respect to an especially troublesome problem. Illustrations of written forms of proof analysis that you might consider using in such instances appear elsewhere in this book.[2]

In addition to making special preparation for particular cases, you can establish some routines that will enable you to improve your performance as a trial lawyer generally. Perhaps the most significant of all routines you might establish is a practice of critically evaluating your own performance as a trial lawyer as well as the performance of others from whom you may learn. The principal purposes of this book are to help you understand the implications of trial problems and trial methods and to help you develop your faculty for critical evaluation.

A revival of interest in trial advocacy in recent decades has contributed to the development of a large and growing body of published materials.[3] It should be one of your early objectives to become familiar with publications on advocacy so you may use them to advantage both in improving your understanding of advocacy generally and in helping you resolve particular problems that you encounter.

Another routine you may usefully adopt is the building of a trial notebook in which you accumulate your own set of aids to effective advocacy. You might include notes of decisions to which you may wish to refer, references to selected articles and books, forms for pleadings, motions, and other kinds of instruments you may have occasion to use, names and information about various types of expert witnesses whom you might sometime wish to engage, forms of jury argument you have used or have seen others use with

2. See §§2.17, 4.18.

3. Selected bibliographies related to different phases of trial advocacy appear throughout A. Levin and H. Cramer, *Trial Advocacy — Problems and Materials* (1968). A very limited selection follows: M. Belli, *Modern Trials* (abridged ed. 1963); F. Busch, *Law and Tactics in Jury Trials* (encyclopedic ed. 1959-1964); I. Goldstein and F. Lane, *Goldstein Trial Technique* (2d ed. 1969); J. Kelner, *Personal Injury — Successful Litigation Techniques* (rev. ed. 1971); A. Morrill, *Trial Diplomacy* (1971); L. Schwartz, *Trial of Automobile Accident Cases* (3d ed. 1962-1971); S. Schweitzer, *Cyclopedia of Trial Practice* (2d ed. 1970).

good effect, and whatever other odds and ends you may wish to have at hand for future use.

The identification and evaluation of competing interests affecting the solution of each of the trial problems considered in this book should serve, incidentally, to emphasize the importance of preparation — the importance of not only knowing the law and facts bearing on each particular case but also understanding the implications more generally of the techniques of advocacy you use.

Chapter II

DIRECT EXAMINATION

§2.1 Aims of direct examination

For their contribution toward the ultimate aim of winning the case, these more immediate aims of direct examination deserve your attention: (1) to present evidence legally sufficient to raise each claim or defense — to complete a "record" of testimony that will support whatever legal arguments you may wish to urge in trial or on appeal; and (2) to convince — that is, to convince the factfinder (judge or jury) of the truthfulness and accuracy of all the evidence supporting the claim or defense.

Although effective direct examination is usually less spectacular, more cases are won by evidence on direct than by that on cross-examination. In the ordinary trial, the original development of all elements of the plaintiff's claim depends almost entirely upon direct examination. "Cross-examination" of witnesses called under special rules or statutes[1] pertaining to adverse parties, and in some jurisdictions to adverse witnesses, will sometimes afford opportunities for supplying essential elements of a claim, but cross-examination is less predictable than direct examination. As plaintiff's lawyer, you may plan to use cross-examination of your adversary's witnesses to support the case presented in direct examination of your own, to the end that the factfinder will be persuaded. But do not rely on cross-examination of your adversary's witnesses to supply any element of the claim that you are able to supply by direct examination of witnesses whom you can safely call to the stand as your own.[2] If during the presentation of your own case, before you first rest, you do not adduce evidence to support each element of your claim, a directed verdict or judgment may deprive you of the opportunity of cross-examining the defendant's witnesses.

1. See 3A Wigmore, *Evidence* §916 (rev. ed. Chadbourn 1970); 6 *id.,* §1892 (3d ed. 1940); Federal Rules of Evidence, Rule 611 (c).
2. See §2.2.

You may appropriately place somewhat greater reliance on cross-examination in planning a defense than in planning the development of a plaintiff's case. The defense is often a denial, rather than an affirmative assertion, and the burden is upon the plaintiff. As defense counsel, your problem is one of convincing the factfinder (judge or jury) that vital elements of the plaintiff's case are unsupported in fact, or of convincing the judge that some vital element of fact is entirely omitted from the plaintiff's proof. Also, you have the opportunity to cross-examine the plaintiff's witnesses before you call your own witnesses; if your plans to use cross-examination go awry, you have an opportunity to change plans. Even so, a shift in plans may demand more attention to discovering new sources of testimony and to conferring with new witnesses than time permits after trial has begun. With respect to an affirmative defense, it is better in your pretrial planning not to rely upon cross-examination for developing any element of the defense; at the least, you should prepare an alternative plan for developing each element by your own witnesses in the event the cross-examination does not go according to plan.

Although presenting enough evidence to go to the jury on the claim or defense is an absolute prerequisite of success in a trial, it receives and deserves less attention in the consideration of trial techniques than the aim of persuasion. Many reported decisions depend on whether enough evidence is presented to raise an issue, but they are only a very small percentage of all litigated cases. The great majority of cases are won or lost upon the persuasion of a factfinder. Legally sufficient evidence, though essential, is not enough. In practice, and in the appraisal of techniques with which this book is concerned, the aim of convincing the factfinder receives the greater emphasis.

You will rarely pause, while framing a question to a witness, to consider what immediate aim of direct examination you are serving, and how well. Yet these considerations bear heavily on the habits you develop and follow as you frame questions to a witness. If you are too much concerned with "making a record" you may fall into habits of interrogation that are detrimental to the aim of convincing the factfinder of the truth and accuracy of the record you are making. For example, if you are bent on insuring that the expression used by the witness satisfies legal requirements you may commit the error of leading the witness to such an extent that the factfinder concludes that the evidence is only the lawyer's version of the case, and not that of the witness.[3] This danger of sacrificing a more important goal to gain some immediate aim is not peculiarly a problem of direct examination but pervades all aspects of courtroom conduct.[4]

3. See §2.18.
4. See §1.4 regarding the trial lawyer's perspective.

§2.2   Choosing witnesses

Case 1. Your client, *P*, was injured by contact with *D*'s charged electric wire, while *P* was working for a building subcontractor under the supervision of *W*, foreman. *F*, foreman for another subcontractor on the job, says that *P* and *Q* were engaged in horseplay at the time of the injury, *Q* chasing *P* along some scaffolding constructed near the wire. *W*, *P*, and *Q* all say that *W* had sent *P* and *Q* on the scaffolding to get some protective materials in place before a threatening rainstorm. *W* says that he warned *P* and *Q* about the uninsulated wire, commenting that it might be swinging very close to the scaffolding in the high wind. *P* and *Q* say they did not hear *W* say anything about the wire.

What witnesses should you call?

In practically all but the hopeless cases, you will have more than one possible combination of witnesses who might furnish the evidence necessary to raise an issue regarding your claim or defense, and you will have additional cumulative witnesses [1] who might be useful in meeting the second aim of persuading the factfinder. What factors should influence your decision on which combination of witnesses to use?

In the minds of many jurors, and often in the eyes of the law, each witness is identified with some party to the lawsuit. When jurors decide what they think of the witness, they commonly credit or charge a party for it. It is unlikely that they will be so impersonal that they totally avoid allowing that credit or charge to influence, subconsciously at least, their consideration of other aspects of the case. Usually the witness is identified with the party who calls him to testify, though the average juror does not need an instruction on the right to call an adverse party in order to keep the juror from identifying such a witness with the party calling him. In addition to the practical effect on the jury, calling a witness to the stand also has significance in rules of evidence. In every jurisdiction, it is the general rule that you are not permitted to lead your own witness. [2] You may incur restrictions against impeaching by calling a witness. [3] These rules may have such drastic effect on a case that you cannot form the best judgment about what witnesses you should use without a thorough understanding of the procedural effect of calling a

---

1. See §2.3.

2. 3 Wigmore, *Evidence* §769 (rev. ed. Chadbourn 1970); Federal Rules of Evidence, Rule 611 (c).

3. 3A Wigmore, *Evidence* §§896–918 (rev. ed. Chadbourn 1970). *Contra*, Federal Rules of Evidence, Rule 607. See also Rule 801(d) (1), declaring that a prior inconsistent statement is not hearsay if the declarant testifies at trial and is subject to cross-examination concerning the statement. Does it not follow that you may call a witness who you know will testify contrary to his prior statement and then offer the

witness in your jurisdiction. You should consider this matter during the pre-trial planning for selection of witnesses.

The identification of each witness with one or another of the parties to litigation involves disadvantages that you must weigh against the advantages to be gained from using the witness. One of the most difficult problems of this character arises in the situation involving a witness who, it appears, will testify to certain facts helpful to the plaintiff and harmful to the defendant, and other facts helpful to the defendant and harmful to the plaintiff. In some jurisdictions, cross-examination is not limited to the subject matter of direct examination;[4] whenever you call the witness to the stand, your opponent may on cross-examination use the witness to develop the opposing claims or defenses in details unrelated to the subject matter of your direct examination. In such jurisdictions, it is a great advantage to have the witness called by the other party, since you may gain all the advantages of his testimony on cross-examination without being subject to the disadvantages of having called him; you may be allowed privileges of leading and impeaching the witness as to the unfavorable parts of his testimony, while the party who called him to the stand is denied these privileges. Even in jurisdictions where the scope of cross-examination is limited to the subject matter of the direct examination, there is some advantage in having the witness called by the other party; other factors being equal, the jury is more likely to identify the witness with the party who first called him to the stand, even though he is later called back for testimony on other points.

In Case 1, as P's lawyer should you call W to the stand in the trial of the case? In this case, you would not need the testimony of W in order to make a case sufficient to go to the factfinder. To you, the value of W's testimony is the corroboration of the testimony of P and Q that they were engaged in work of an emergency character, because of the impending rainstorm, and not in horseplay. Weighed against this value of W's testimony to you is the potential harm to your case by W's testimony that he warned P and Q about the uninsulated wire. It may well be that your declining to call W as a witness will not prevent the jury from hearing W's story, since your opponent might choose to call him. But the danger that the jury may accept W's testimony and base a finding of contributory negligence upon it is undoubtedly

---

prior statement not merely to impeach him but as substantive evidence? If so, the Federal Rules of Evidence enable you to make a case for the jury in some instances in which you cannot do so under the law of evidence applied in some state courts. Will different outcomes arising from different rules of evidence in state actions and federal diversity actions be permissible despite Erie R.R. v. Tompkins, 304 U.S. 64, 58 S. Ct. 817, 82 L. Ed. 1188 (1938)? Concerning the impact of this question on the choice of a forum, see §10.3.

4. 6 Wigmore, *Evidence* §§1885–1895 (3d ed. 1940); Federal Rules of Evidence, Rule 611 (b).

increased by your calling W. Conversely, the chances that the jury may accept W's testimony that P and Q were attending to an emergency task, and not engaged in horseplay, will be increased if your opponent first calls W and you bring out this information on cross-examination.[5] You may then argue that this is "admitted by one of D's own witnesses, whom he called to the stand and vouched for." These comments apply with particular force if the case is tried in a jurisdiction in which cross-examination is not limited to the subject matter of direct examination. They apply also, though in lesser degree, where the witness must be recalled by the other party for that testimony the other party desires to adduce, concerning facts distinct from those asked about on direct examination by the party originally calling him. Moreover, in the particular illustration used here, courts limiting cross-examination to the subject matter of the direct examination might conclude that the relationship between W's testimony that he sent P and Q on this task and his testimony that he warned them when he did so is such that both lines of testimony should be regarded as part of the same subject matter. Another factor you should consider is that even if, under the practice in the jurisdiction of trial, you would have a theoretical right as P's counsel to prevent cross-examination on the subject of warning, you might be foreclosed from asserting it by practical considerations concerning the jury's probable reaction to your objection.[6]

Probably the best solution to the problem is to refrain from calling W, hoping that D's lawyer may find his testimony on warning so essential to his defense that he will call W and thus give you the opportunity of obtaining the testimony you desire from W without the disadvantages of calling him. If this hope does not materialize, you might consider W as a rebuttal witness, after D's lawyer has closed his case. If the circumstances are such as to cause you to refrain from calling W originally, however, they usually would indicate also that you should not call W as a rebuttal witness. The harm from W's unfavorable testimony would be accentuated because of his position in trial, if you called him on rebuttal.[7]

It is quite possible that the same considerations that would cause you to refrain from calling W would also cause D's lawyer to refrain from calling him. This is one of the practical results of identification of a witness with a party.[8]

5. See §3.14.
6. See §4.2.
7. See §§2.6, 2.38.
8. Undoubtedly the disadvantages attached to making the witness one's own by calling him result in the court's losing in some instances information that is vital to proper disposition of the controversy. For discussion of a possible solution to this problem, see Justice Frankfurter's opinion, dissenting in part, in Johnson v. U.S., 333 U.S. 46, 68 S. Ct. 391, 92 L. Ed. 468 (1948), in which the following passage appears:

Case 87[9] is another illustration of this problem about calling a witness whose testimony is favorable in some respects to one party and in others to the opposing party. Other situations will arise in which it is clear that your adversary will not call a particular witness, but there is yet doubt as to whether you should use him. For example, in a jurisdiction where it is generally improper for the plaintiff to reveal to the jury the existence of liability insurance protecting the defendant, should you, as the defendant's lawyer, use as a witness one who has material information favorable to the defense but is an agent of the insurance company interested in defense of the case? The fact of his association with the defending insurance company is relevant because of the possible inference that interest affects his testimony; it might be held admissible despite the policy against revealing insurance coverage. Your using the witness might therefore cause such harm, because of revealing insurance coverage that would otherwise be unknown to the jury, that you should decline to call him, even though you could obtain valuable evidence from him.

Should you use an infant witness? Infancy of the witness is generally not a ground for exclusion of his testimony if, under the preliminary finding of the trial judge, the infant is able to understand the obligation of a witness to answer truthfully. Because of their known frankness, very young children often make persuasive witnesses. Because of their greater susceptibility to fancy and to being led in cross-examination, however, use of young children as witnesses usually involves more risk than use of adult witnesses. This disadvantage does not outweigh advantages of using testimony of children in all cases, but it is a factor you should weigh heavily when deciding whether to use a child's testimony. With increasing age, of course, this risk is reduced, and ordinarily you should not hesitate to use a teen-age witness of normal intelligence, whose testimony you consider reliable.

§2.3 Using cumulative witnesses

Case 2. D is defending against a claim by P for specific performance of an alleged contract under which P, acting for a meat-packing syndicate,

---

"While a court room is not a laboratory for the scientific pursuit of truth, a trial judge is surely not confined to an account, obviously fragmentary, of the circumstances of a happening, here the meagre testimony of Johnson, when he has at his command the means of exploring them fully, or at least more fully, before passing legal judgment. A trial is not a game of blind man's buff; and the trial judge — particularly in a case where he himself is the trier of the facts upon which he is to pronounce the law — need not blindfold himself by failing to call an available vital witness simply because the parties, for reasons of trial tactics, choose to withhold his testimony."

See also Federal Rules of Evidence, Rule 614.

9. Discussed in §11.21.

purchased a tract of realty from *D*, through *A*, a real estate agent. As *D*'s lawyer, you have available the following witnesses:

A, the agent employed by *D* to sell the realty, will testify that *D* specifically prohibited him from selling to the syndicate that *P* represented, saying that *D* did not mind having a heavy industry near an adjacent tract that he was retaining but did not want a meat-packing plant so located because of the odors. He will testify to an extended course of dealings with *P* over a period of weeks and to the fact that *P* represented throughout this time that *P* was acting for a group whose identity he was not free to disclose but that they were not interested in using the tract for a packing plant or for any other type of industry that would create unpleasant odors in the area.

P admits that he was acting for the syndicate throughout his negotiations but denies that he ever misrepresented the facts to *A* and says he did not know of *D*'s prohibition against selling to the syndicate.

B-1, *B-2*, and *B-3* (employees of *A*), and *C*, another person who did some negotiating with *A* on this and another tract, will testify to overhearing conversations in *A*'s office between *P* and *A*, during which the prospective use of the tract by *P*'s principals was discussed. They will corroborate *A*'s testimony.

Should you use cumulative witnesses?

In a few instances, corroboration is a legal requirement.[1] Usually the problem concerning use of corroborative testimony or cumulative witnesses is purely tactical. Calling cumulative witnesses is one of the most dangerous practices in trial technique. If they testify alike, the case is subject to the charge that the testimony is suspect because people do not observe and remember events in exactly the same way. If they differ, the case is subject to the charge that the witnesses are poor observers, or otherwise unreliable. Of course, you may answer that discrepancies on irrelevant matters merely vouch for the honesty of your witnesses and case, but you never know whether the jury will be convinced. More important, however, is the danger that contradictions on important matters will arise, especially when the witnesses are subjected to skillful cross-examination.

In Case 2, the employees of the agent, *A*, have approximately the same evidence to contribute to the defense of *D*. They will be asked to repeat, in the exact words used as nearly as they can remember, the conversation that occurred between *A* and *P*. This incident occurred months before trial. If *B-1*, *B-2*, and *B-3* answer with the same phrases when asked to repeat the conversation, their testimony furnishes *P*'s lawyer a basis for arguing that such conformity is suspicious. If they differ, *P*'s lawyer argues that they cannot all be right and that, viewing the situation in the most charitable light, they must have been so intent on their own work that none of them is able to give a

---

1. 7 Wigmore, *Evidence* §§2032–2075 (3d ed. 1940).

reliable report of what occurred, despite their natural subconscious inclinations to try to do so because of sympathy with their employer's point of view.[2] C, of course, is in a position to be a more convincing witness because of the absence of this interest of employment, although there is some indication of interest in purchase of the same tract. Ordinarily, as D's lawyer, you should not use all four of these witnesses; your decision as to which and how many will depend to a great extent upon your appraisal of what kind of impression each would make as a witness. If P's lawyer lays any predicate for urging that D is withholding evidence by not calling all four witnesses, you might conclude that the danger involved in such a charge warrants taking whatever chance there is in placing all four witnesses on the stand. An alternative is to bring them to the courtroom and prove that they are available for P's attorney to question if he desires; if P calls these witnesses to the stand they may be held to be P's witnesses even though then employed by D.[3]

As indicated in the preceding paragraph, the possibility of an argument by your adversary that you are withholding evidence is a factor favoring use of cumulative witnesses who are considered in law as being under the control of your client. Even in the absence of such a factor, however, it will sometimes be advisable to call cumulative witnesses. In Case 1, for example, P's lawyer should call P's fellow employee, Q, to corroborate P's testimony that he was attending to an emergency task with a rainstorm impending, and was not engaged in horseplay, and that W gave no audible warning about the charged wire. Although Q's testimony is cumulative in the sense that it does not add any new facts about how the accident occurred, it nevertheless contributes materially to strengthening P's case because it adds corroboration by one without the direct financial interest of P in the case. This is particularly needed by P because his testimony on one of these points conflicts with that of F (that he was engaged in horseplay), and on the other point conflicts with that of W (that he was warned). Q's position in Case 1 is therefore more nearly analogous to that of C (the customer overhearing the negotiations of P and A) in Case 2. Though his testimony is cumulative, its importance as corroboration of the testimony of the party calling him, on a point as to which there is a direct conflict in the evidence, outweighs the disadvantage of danger of conflict between the witnesses called by the same party.[4]

§2.4 Using deposition evidence

CASE 3. *P, a pedestrian, was hit at 7:00 P.M. by a delivery truck of D Produce Company, driven by S, whose regular hours of work for D Produce*

---

2. As to advisability of P's making a more severe charge against the employee witnesses, see §7.19.

3. See §2.2.

4. As to the time of calling Q, consider §2.38.

Company were 8 A.M. to 5 P.M. *D* denies that *S* was in the scope of employment and also asserts that *P* was contributorily negligent, depending primarily on the testimony of *S* to support the latter defense. *S* is still employed by *D Produce Company*. *P*'s lawyer has taken his deposition; *D*'s lawyer, though having talked with *S* in preparation for the deposition, asked no questions while it was being taken. On deposition, *S* testified that when he left *D*'s place of business at 4:45 P.M., with an order of produce on the truck for delivery to an all-night retail establishment at the edge of the city, he was told that he might go by his home to eat before making the delivery, and that he was on the most direct route between his home and the point of delivery when the accident occurred.

Should you use deposition evidence?

In order to answer this question, you must first consider the procedural rules, which vary considerably depending on the jurisdiction of trial, regarding limitations that might prohibit use of the deposition.[1] For example, in the federal practice under Rule 32 (a), the deposition of a witness other than a party ordinarily may not be used, except for impeachment of the deponent, unless the witness is unavailable to testify in person.

Once you have satisfied yourself that no procedural rule prevents your use of the deposition testimony, you are next concerned with the tactical effect of using it. Several considerations are involved. If the witness can also be called in person, what will be the effect of the testimony read from the record of the deposition, compared with the impact of "live" testimony by a witness on the stand in person? What chance is there that the live testimony might be different from that recorded in the deposition? If the deposition contains unfavorable evidence, what is the effect of offering a part of the deposition that is favorable?

Generally, the impact of testimony of a witness appearing in person is greater than that of one whose testimony is read. Whether this general rule is applicable in a particular instance will depend in part on the personality of the witness. We are often influenced as much by how a person says something as by what he says. It is impossible for the record of the deposition to reveal accurately how the witness spoke. If the manner of the witness is singularly impressive, the party depending on his testimony loses by use of the deposition instead of live testimony. If his manner is singularly unimpressive, or likely to make a poor impression, the party depending on his testimony may gain by using his deposition testimony rather than a personal appearance.

1. See 5 Wigmore, *Evidence* §1415 (3d ed. 1940); Federal Rules of Civil Procedure, Rule 32.

As for content of the testimony, there is little hope of improving it in the case of a friendly witness except by making it more complete than in the deposition. If any variance occurs, the deposition is available for impeachment; variance toward a more favorable story might well result in harm because of the unfavorable reflection on the reliability of the witness and other aspects of the witness' testimony. In short, there is a disadvantage in calling in person a witness whose favorable deposition you can use; there is little chance of improving the content and more chance of making it worse for practical purposes, especially if the deposition testimony is phrased in a manner particularly favorable to your client. Usually, however, this disadvantage of calling the witness in person will be far outweighed by the advantage of the greater impact of live testimony.

If the deposition contains unfavorable evidence, you should consider the effect of offering only a favorable part of the deposition testimony. Under rules similar to those applied to the calling of a witness in person,[2] the witness may be identified as yours if you offer parts of his deposition testimony, regardless of whether you or your adversary took the deposition. This rule is extended in some jurisdictions to the extreme of prohibiting you from leading or impeaching the witness when he is later called to the stand in person by your adversary. Accordingly, the same factors involved in determining whether to call in person a witness who will give both favorable and unfavorable evidence may affect your decision whether to use part of a deposition that contains unfavorable testimony. Also, if you decide to use the deposition testimony, you should consider introducing all of it, including the unfavorable part, for the tactical purpose of giving less emphasis to it than would be given if the other party introduced it.[3] In some courts, your opponent may compel you to offer all of the deposition relevant to the part you desire to offer in evidence.[4]

Frequently you can make good use of a deposition of an adverse party or a hostile witness. In Case 3, for example, if as P's lawyer you call S to the stand to prove facts supporting the inference that S was in the course and scope of his employment for D at the time of the accident, it will present D's lawyer with the opportunity to bring out S's testimony on all facts of the accident, by "cross-examination," in jurisdictions where the rules do not limit questions of D's lawyer at this point in trial to the subject that you opened up. Under these circumstances, if you prefer that S's story of the facts of the accident not be heard while you are proving P's case, you might offer that part of the deposition of S relating to scope of employment, rather than calling S to the stand in person. In some jurisdictions, if you offer the part of

2. See §2.2.
3. See §2.20.
4. This is true under Federal Rules of Civil Procedure, Rule 32 (a).

the deposition relating to scope of employment, D's lawyer is then allowed to introduce other parts of the deposition. Since you took the deposition, however, it may not bring out the aspects of S's story most favorable to D, or present them in the order and form most favorable to D. D's lawyer is more likely to prefer his own questions as a means for presenting S's story.

Furthermore, regardless of the scope of "cross-examination" allowed in the court of trial, you may prefer using the deposition rather than calling S in person because you know exactly what you will be offering, whereas you cannot exactly predict what S will say in response to questions while he is on the stand in person.

Against the foregoing arguments for your using the deposition of S, you should consider the possibility that offering S's deposition will make S your witness, with resulting disadvantages. If the case is being tried in a jurisdiction following this rule, you should neither call S in person nor use his deposition unless (as would rarely, if ever, be the case) you have no other way of proving scope of employment.

§2.5 Calling the adverse party as a witness

CASE 4. P suffered personal injuries and damages to his car in a head-on collision on the highway at night with a car owned and driven by D. P and D were alone in their respective cars. H, highway patrolman, investigated the accident. No depositions have been taken before trial. When interviewed by you as P's lawyer, H says that he found skidmarks and debris locating the point of impact on P's side of the center line of the highway, and that D admitted to H at the scene of the accident that the point of impact was on P's side. H says that D claimed that P's car was angling across the highway, as if P had fallen asleep, that he (D) tried to cut to the left of P's car to avoid collision, and that P's car then swung back to P's right so that D could not prevent collision.

Should you call the adverse party as a witness?

The penalties resulting from making a witness your own by calling him do not apply in most jurisdictions to calling the adverse party. Occasionally it is necessary for you, as plaintiff's counsel, to call your adverse party, the defendant, to obtain some admission from him in order to complete the plaintiff's case. You should consider seeking such admissions by pretrial procedures,[1] both to eliminate uncertainty as to whether the admission will be made and to avoid the necessity of calling the adverse party to the stand in person. Even in circumstances where there is no necessity for calling the adverse party to the stand, however, it is frequently a tactically sound move to

1. See §11.15.

call him. This is more likely to be true in cases that have not been fully developed by depositions and other pretrial procedures than in those carefully prepared by these methods.

If the defendant, your adverse party, does not know the details of your client's version of the incident on which suit is based, and if you have not committed the defendant to details of his version by deposition or otherwise, there is some advantage in calling him to the stand before your own client (the plaintiff). If you suspect that the defendant is willing to adapt his story to suit the occasion, your calling him to the stand as the first witness deprives him of the advantage of knowing before he is called upon to give his testimony what contentions he will have to meet; it affords you the opportunity of cross-examining him before he knows your theory of the case and what you are hoping to get him to admit. On the other hand, calling him first gives him the opportunity of presenting his theory of the case to the jury first, and the first impression is important. This disadvantage may be reduced because of the fact that you are examining the witness first and emphasizing the weaknesses in his version of the facts, rather than having his version presented first in its stronger light through the questions of his own lawyer. In view of such conflicting considerations as these, competent trial lawyers are not in agreement as to whether the plaintiff's lawyer should call the defendant to the stand before the plaintiff in circumstances such as those described in Case 4.

Another possibility worth considering, in Case 4, is to call the defendant to the stand after you have presented the plaintiff's theory to the jury through the testimony of the plaintiff or others, but still during your presentation of the plaintiff's evidence. By this method you lose the advantage of questioning the defendant before he hears the plaintiff's version of the incident, but the first impression on the jury is the plaintiff's version. The advantage of this procedure over declining to call the defendant at any time during the plaintiff's evidence is that the defendant's story may make a less favorable impression on the jury because it is first presented in its less favorable light, with weaknesses emphasized, by your questions as the plaintiff's lawyer. Also, the defendant's lawyer is presented with a difficult choice when you rest and it is time for the defendant's evidence. Frequently the testimony of the defendant himself will constitute the major part of his evidence. Will it seem to the jury that the defendant's lawyer has little to offer, if the defendant is not recalled to the stand? If the defendant is recalled, will objections to repetition succeed, if you choose to make them, or in the absence of sustained objections will the repetition emphasize in the minds of the jurors that your opponent has little more to add to what you have proved?

From the defendant's point of view, also, the circumstances of the case may make it tactically advisable to call the plaintiff to the stand during presentation of the defendant's evidence. If, for example, the defendant's lawyer is in possession of documentary evidence impeaching the plaintiff's testimony on a vital point, and reflecting unfavorably on the plaintiff's veracity generally, the defendant's lawyer might withhold use of the document on cross-examination during the plaintiff's evidence and call the plaintiff back to the stand near the conclusion of the case with the purpose of achieving more dramatic effect with the proof of dishonesty of the plaintiff.[2]

§2.6   Order of witnesses generally

CASE 5.   P was injured when hit by D's eastbound car while walking north across the street at an intersection controlled by a traffic light in a suburban business section, in the late evening. As P's lawyer, you have available the following witnesses:

A, who says that he was driving a pickup truck west just before the accident, entered the intersection just as the light facing him changed from green to yellow, saw P stepping off the southwest curb as A was passing directly north of him, was then attracted by the speed of D's car approaching from the west, looked into the rear view mirror extending out to the left of his cab and saw D swerving as he applied his brakes just before striking P.

B, a policeman, who investigated the accident, found a car parked too close to the corner, facing east on the southwest corner, partially blocking the pedestrian lane, and no cars parked to the rear of it. Also he found that D had traveled ten feet into the intersection before stopping. D called his attention to loose clods of dirt scattered from a point to the rear of the parked car toward the intersection. B examined D's car and found the right front fender dented and looked for dirt under the fenders and found all of them with some caked mud underneath, but he says he could not determine whether any had been recently knocked loose. P had been taken to the hospital by ambulance for examination and treatment before B arrived at the scene.

C, ambulance driver, who came to the scene on emergency call, paid little attention to anything other than getting P into the ambulance and to the hospital, found P lying with his feet about even with the edge of the intersection on the west side, and his body into the intersection, and was told by D that P had tried to get up and D had insisted that he lie still where he was.

X, an X-ray specialist who examined P, and Y, an orthopedic surgeon, who has been treating P for a hip fracture.

What factors should you consider in determining the order of witnesses?

A problem you encounter early in planning your direct examination is determining the order of witnesses. Your decision on this matter may be in-

2. Compare §§3.6, 3.7, and Case 35.

fluenced by practical factors such as the time of availability of particular witnesses whose convenience you must serve to secure their cooperation. For example, in a particular case you may find it advisable to hold your client available for a time when other witnesses cannot appear, so you can avoid delay in trial; conversely, it may be necessary to call your client to the stand early because another witness is unavailable when needed. Such factors as these influence the order of witnesses to the detriment of most effective presentation of the case; through careful planning you can usually eliminate their influence, and almost always you can reduce it.

A logical progression in the story of the case, as it develops through the testimony of the witnesses, is an asset. It aids the jury in understanding and remembering the testimony.

The opening and closing witnesses have positions of special prominence. The jury is usually more alert at these times, and especially so at the time the opening witness testifies. Most observers agree that first impressions tend to last; once an impression is formed in the mind of a juror, the burden is on the one who seeks to change it. For these reasons, it is desirable to present a strong and favorable witness as the first witness in the case. At the other extreme, the last witness occupies a special position because the memory of what he says is freshest in the minds of the jurors during their formal deliberations. It is especially damaging if that freshest memory is one of a weak witness, and helpful if it is the memory of a strong and favorable witness. Accordingly, it is usually advisable to use a strong witness first and a strong witness last, allowing other factors to govern the particular order of the witnesses in between.

This special importance of the opening and closing witnesses is but one aspect of a broader proposition that the timing of evidence may materially affect its influence upon the jury. Through careful planning, unfavorable evidence can be offered at a time calculated to reduce the notice it receives, and favorable evidence can be offered at a time that will invite special attention to it and give it greater emphasis.

The necessity of laying a predicate by one witness for some part of the testimony of another influences the order of witnesses. Your failure to consider this factor may result in delay, the necessity for recalling witnesses, and even failure to secure admission of material evidence because you are unable to get an essential witness to return for the sole purpose of proving a predicate. As *P*'s lawyer in Case 5, ordinarily you should call *P* before *Y*, the attending physician, because in examining *Y* as to his opinion concerning the nature, probable duration, and probable cause of *P*'s condition, you may find it desirable, if not necessary, to assume some facts as to which only *P* can testify — the history of his subjective complaints as well as his version of the accident. Some trial judges would receive these questions and *Y*'s answers conditionally, subject to being stricken in the event of your failure to sustain each assumption by admissible evidence offered later. In most courts, however, you cannot depend on having Y's evidence received in this way; therefore, if you call P after Y, you must carefully plan your questions so that Y's answers will be entirely dependent upon his own observations and the history he has taken, and not upon assumptions of matters that you will not prove until later.

Another illustration of the same principle is involved in the order of the witnesses X, the X-ray specialist, and Y, the attending physician. Probably Y has depended to some extent in his diagnosis and treatment upon the X-rays taken by X, and perhaps also upon the opinion of X as an expert in interpretation of the X-rays. Furthermore, if Y interprets X-rays himself, they should be available for use during his testimony so that he can point out to the jury (in jurisdictions where this is permissible) the fractures or other abnormalities about which he speaks. The X-rays must be introduced with authenticating testimony, ordinarily that of the X-ray specialist or his technician who took the X-rays, unless a stipulation makes this unnecessary. For these reasons, X should precede Y in the order of testimony.

§2.7   Order of witnesses: testimony of a party

Case 5.   (See statement of the case at the beginning of the preceding section).

At what point in the order of witnesses should you call your client to testify?

Because of the apparent logic of starting the story of the client's case with the client's version, many lawyers habitually call the client as the first witness without giving special consideration to the advisability of the plan in the particular case. This habitual practice is sound for many instances. Logical order of presentation sometimes requires that the client testify first. Also, first impressions last, and it is important to begin the case with a strong witness. Other factors may cause you to favor this plan — *e.g.,* the necessity of laying a predicate by your client for some part of the testimony of another.

In some jurisdictions, a rule of law or a discretionary ruling of the trial judge may determine the order of witnesses. In the absence of such a requirement, however, despite reasons such as those suggested in the preceding paragraph for calling the client first, calling him later is sometimes preferable. The need for a logical presentation of the theory of your case may be served by your using effectively the right to make an oral statement of the claim before any evidence is offered.[1] Then, by placing other witnesses on the stand ahead of your client, you provide your client (your most important

1. See §7.11.

witness usually) the opportunity of observing the other witnesses and the court proceedings. He may thereby become more at ease in the surroundings and less nervous when he takes the stand, so that he can state his case more effectively. Also, he is aided in avoiding unnecessary conflicts with the testimony of other witnesses. This does not mean that you can justify your client's changing his own version of the facts in order to make it coincide with the testimony of other witnesses.[2] The justification for calling the client after other witnesses is that the most truthful witness will make mistakes, particularly when subjected to skillful cross-examination. The ability of the witness to observe and to tell the facts is as much at stake as his honesty. The danger of damaging mistakes in your client's testimony is reduced when he has the opportunity to hear the testimony of his supporting witnesses and to observe the techniques of the opposing lawyer on cross-examination before he takes the stand.

A suggested solution for the order of witnesses in Case 5 is this:[3] *A*, the passing motorist; *C*, the ambulance driver; *B*, the policeman; *P*, the plaintiff; *X*, the X-ray specialist; *Y*, the attending physician. Other witnesses (such as *P*'s wife, fellow workers, a witness on life expectancy) might be used just ahead of *P*. Thus *P* has the advantage of hearing the testimony of other "fact witnesses" before he testifies, and he precedes the doctors whose opinion testimony will be based on assumptions of some of the facts to which *P* has testified. A strong witness (*A*) is used to open. The closing witness (*Y*) normally would be a strong witness, also. If, however, *Y* is a poor witness in the sense of being unable to express his testimony in a convincing way, and if you can overcome the need for using *P*'s testimony as a predicate for *Y*'s opinion evidence, it would be better to use *Y* before *P* and close with *P*.

§2.8   Order of witnesses: key nonparty witnesses

CASE 6.   *P* is a building contractor who is suing for sums claimed as extras in connection with construction of an office building, including changes in excavation through unexpected rock, changes in partitioning inside the building, changes in stone work on the exterior, changes in plumbing, and damages for delay occasioned by *D*'s refusal to act promptly and in accordance with the terms of the contract with reference to instructions concerning the changes and settlement of the resulting price differential. As *P*'s lawyer, you have available the following witnesses:

2. The danger of such abuse causes Wigmore to prefer a requirement that, if the rule of exclusion of witnesses has been invoked and a party desires to remain in the courtroom, he must take the stand first of the witnesses on his side. 6 Wigmore, *Evidence* §§1841, 1869 (3d ed. 1940).

3. With respect to the possibility of saving one or more witnesses for rebuttal after the defendant's evidence, rather than using all of them during your original presentation as in the suggested order of witnesses above, see §2.38.

P, who was on the job intermittently and conducted most of the negotiations with *D.*

S, who personally supervised the job, handled most of the negotiations with *A,* the architect, and some with *D.*

A, the architect, who is generally favorable to the owner, *D,* though he will make some admissions favorable to *P* with respect to each item in dispute.

B, a foreman who is personally acquainted with details concerning the excavation work, the difference between what was shown on the contract documents and what was encountered in excavating, and the greater difficulty in excavation that resulted.

G and *H,* who occupy positions with reference to the partitioning and stone work, respectively, similar to that of *B* as to the excavating.

J, the plumbing subcontractor.

K, P's accountant, who maintained all records as to costs incurred on the job.

At what point in the order of witnesses should you call a key witness other than your client?

The principle of reserving the client for a late point in the presentation of the case, discussed in the preceding section, is based upon his being a most important witness. This principle is equally applicable to any other key witness if he is permitted to remain in the courtroom, observe the proceedings, and hear the testimony of preceding witnesses. If witnesses are excluded from the courtroom [1] and the key witness other than your client is not permitted to observe and hear others testify, it may still be advisable for you to hold him for a late point in the presentation of the case. By doing so, you provide your adversary with less opportunity to develop from other witnesses a conflict with various aspects of the testimony of the key witness. To the extent that your adversary is able to anticipate the testimony of the key witness, this proposition has no application, for he may develop the conflict as well by laying the predicate with the earlier witnesses and pointing up the conflict when the key witness testifies. But the testimony of the key witness will cover more aspects of the case and will naturally suggest to your adversary more avenues of cross-examination of other witnesses if you place the key witness on the stand earlier.

In Case 2, the defense of a suit for specific performance of a contract to sell realty, it probably would be preferable first to call *B-1,* the employee, and *C,* the other customer who overheard *A*'s conversation with *P.* After the testimony of such number of the other witnesses as you use in presenting the case in chief for the defendant, you should call *A* as your final witness.

1. See §5.5.

In Case 6, the claim for extras on a building contract, reasons exist for your using P after some, if not all, of your other witnesses for the plaintiff. Even more danger exists, however, of material conflict between the testimony of P's supervisor, S, on the one hand, and, on the other, the witnesses B, G, H, and J, if not also the accountant, K; the inquiries will be more detailed and will concern less spectacular events. In this case, a real need exists for a logical presentation of P's theory to the court and jury at an early stage. In some jurisdictions you may accomplish this by a carefully prepared opening statement.[2] Then you may call B, G, H, and J to deal piecemeal with each of their respective phases of the case. Probably you should call A, the architect, at this point unless you omit A with the purpose of obtaining on cross-examination, after D calls A as D's witness,[3] any evidence from A that is favorable to P. Since K, the accountant, is a witness primarily as to computations of amount, a subject on which P and S will not testify to a great extent, there is less need for timing their testimony to follow K's than for timing it to follow testimony of others. Perhaps the best solution would be to withhold K's testimony until after S and P have testified regarding all of the disputed claims, tying together the previous evidence and filling any gaps in the proof of P's theory of liability, before K's evidence is presented to establish amounts. Another reason for postponing K's evidence is the possibility that some of his testimony may depend upon predicates laid in the testimony of the other witnesses. If the rule of exclusion of witnesses from the courtroom has been invoked, S probably should precede P, since S will not be allowed to hear P testify, but P will be allowed to hear S.

Obviously the problem is oversimplified in this assumed case. In a fully developed case, these considerations pointing toward calling the key witness late would be supplemented and counterbalanced by others, particularly those based on content of the testimony of each witness and the characteristics of the witnesses. In final analysis, the decision is ordinarily one requiring the exercise of discretion.

§2.9   Planning direct examination

CASE 7. As D's lawyer, you are defending against a claim for commissions under an employment contract on the ground that the work of S, another salesman, rather than P, the plaintiff, was the procuring cause of the sales in question. At your request, relayed through your client D, S writes a letter to you setting out his activities in making the sales in question. S is still employed by D in a community other than that where D resides, and where the trial is held. D has agreed with S, who draws some salary and is on a

2. See §7.11.
3. See §2.2.

lower percentage commission than *P* had been, that he will pay *S* his commission on these sales if the claim by *P* is defeated.

Should you prepare an outline of the prospective testimony of each witness? Should you advise the witness in advance of the phrasing of the questions you will ask on direct examination?

A spontaneous statement is the most convincing statement. This principle is recognized in the law of evidence by an exception to the hearsay rule. It is as surely applied by juries. *If* you could know that the spontaneous, unplanned direct examination would produce only favorable statements, you should avoid anything suggestive of a plan or outline for fear of interfering with the convincing spontaneity of the witness' testimony. Unfortunately that condition can never exist. Direct examination without planning is therefore a gamble. It may still be a gamble after the most thorough planning (as indeed to some extent is any step in the trial of a lawsuit), but at least the odds are more favorable. There may be, rarely, a combination of witness and lawyer capable of presenting effective direct examination without specific advance preparation, but preparation is necessary for most lawyers and helpful to all. The goal is a type of planning that will cause the least possible interference with the spontaneity of the testimony consistent with reasonable assurance that it will not develop unfavorably in substance. A conflict exists here between the interest in encouraging a convincing manner of testifying and the interest in assuring that the substantive content of the testimony is favorable. A compromise between these conflicting interests is necessary; the degree to which one interest is favored over the other in a particular case must be a matter of judgment in the light of the circumstances.

The early interview with the witness while the facts are fresh in his mind,[1] the written or recorded statement,[2] the investigation of law to determine what facts must be proved to support a cause of action,[3] the comparison of the witness' statement with physical facts and other expected testimony — all of these, as well as the final interview, are, in a sense, merely steps in the planning of the direct examination of the witness. In Case 7, you should take all of these steps with respect to the witness *S*, though practical factors such as expense and time required, in comparison with the amount involved in the litigation, may determine whether you allow *S*'s letter to substitute for the preferable personal interview at an early stage in the preparation of the case. As to the usual case, most lawyers would agree that planning of this type is almost indispensable. Disagreement arises as to how much farther planning may profitably proceed.

1. See §9.3.
2. See §§9.13, 9.14.
3. See §9.2.

(a) *Preparing an outline of the examination of the witness.* A jury is no doubt favorably impressed by spontaneity of answers of the witness, but they do not expect or credit spontaneity in interrogation. They know that trying lawsuits is the lawyer's business and that any good lawyer plans his work. Accordingly, it is no disadvantage before the jury that the course of interrogation reveals to them that it is carefully planned. The advantages of outlining the examination of each witness are many. Your presentation is more logical and orderly; less confusion and waste of time results; you can check your outline of the examination of all witnesses against your outline of the essential fact elements of each legal theory;[4] you are less likely to omit some vital evidence in the stress of trial; and you can more easily anticipate and provide against objections to important evidence.[5] If you have not had previous experience in trying a case of the type involved, you will usually find it worthwhile to make a detailed outline of the proposed direct examination and cross-examination of every known witness. The more experience you gain, the more of this planning and outlining you can do mentally and rapidly, without reducing it to writing.

Whether the outline is a written one or a mental one, it is not final. It is merely a tool to be used in trial, and not an invariable pattern to be slavishly followed. Variations from it will be demanded in the light of the actual developments in trial. In fact, the less you find it necessary to consult it during your interrogation, the more effective the interrogation will be.

Another advantage of outlining the examination of each witness in advance is that it enables you to open and close the testimony of the witness on the stronger points and in other ways to arrange the timing of evidence[6] for the greatest tactical benefit. For example, if you plan to offer some unfavorable evidence on direct examination,[7] such as the fact in Case 7 that the salesman *S* will be paid his commission on the sales in question if *D* wins the lawsuit, it probably is inadvisable to close the direct examination with this point. Since several sales are involved, *S*'s commission interest could logically be proved in connection with the first sale about which he is questioned, just after his testimony as to the extent of his activities in connection with that sale.

(b) *Disclosing to the witness the outline of examination.* Telling the witness exactly what questions he will be asked and in what order has the disadvantage, noted above, of interfering with spontaneity of his testimony. To some extent you can minimize this disadvantage by making the witness understand that he is not to attempt, and indeed should avoid, memory of the

4. See §9.2.
5. See §§2.17, 2.26.
6. See §2.6.
7. See §2.20.

form or order of answers or questions. When you make this kind of use of the practice session[8] with the witness before he is called to the stand, its advantages so far outweigh disadvantages that its use is fully justified.

§2.10   Preparing witnesses: unfamiliarity with court

CASE 8.   *P*, who claims that *D* committed a battery upon him, has never been involved in previous litigation, has never been a juror, and has never even been in a courtroom. His friend, *W*, who gives a version of the facts favorable to *P*, is in the same situation. *W* is not the least disturbed at the prospect of testifying and being cross-examined, but *P* is nervous about the danger of his becoming confused while he is on the witness stand.

What steps can you take to combat the disadvantages arising from a witness' unfamiliarity with courtroom surroundings and procedures?

This question assumes disadvantages from unfamiliarity with court proceedings. In a sense, naïveté about court proceedings is an advantage; one who displays skill in the art of answering cross-examination is less likely to provoke the sympathy and favorable verdict of a jury than one who appears honest but at a great disadvantage because of unfamiliarity with trial practices. The disadvantages, however, are obvious. For example, although the qualities of outstanding professional competence, integrity, and ability to express ideas persuasively in testimony are sometimes combined in one doctor, every lawyer who tries many personal injury cases is impressed by the fact that, for medical witnesses as for others, there is greater correlation between success as a witness and aptitude for answering questions on the witness stand than between success as a witness and one's professional rating as to skill, learning, and integrity. As another example, the lay witness who permits his temper to be aroused (by the deliberate efforts of the adverse lawyer to that end) may wreak havoc with his case in a fit of anger, whereas the witness with experience in such matters would have seen the purpose of the insults and increased his determination to hold his temper and answer thoughtfully. The witness who has had little or no experience in court needs some specific preparation for his appearance. The one who is nervous about the forthcoming experience (as *P* in Case 8) needs it; if there is any difference between them, the one who is overconfident (as *W* in Case 8) needs it even more, because he will be less conscious of the possibility of pitfalls and traps laid for him. Specific steps you may take to prepare the prospective witness or client for the courtroom experience include the following: (1) Tell him the general purpose and method of court proceedings, and the part played by jury, judge, lawyers, and witnesses, as well as giving more

8. See §2.14.

specific instruction concerning his own conduct on the stand.[1] (2) Inform him of rules governing his conduct while not on the stand — rules relating to separation of witnesses[2] and to conversations with jurors.[3] (3) Hold a practice session with him as to his own testimony, sometime before he is called to the stand.[4] (4) If he is one who has sufficient interest and time, arrange for him to visit the trial of other cases before he is called to testify. This will afford him an opportunity to observe the general method of court proceedings and, to some extent, the techniques most frequently employed by lawyers in examining and cross-examining witnesses. The best word picture painted for a prospective witness will yet fail to give him the understanding that he may gain if the interview between the lawyer and witness is supplemented by the witness' own observation of concrete examples of examination and cross-examination in court. He will be able to observe and avoid mistakes that he might otherwise have made. This practice is, of course, less often feasible in the case of other witnesses than in the case of the client, whose interest is sufficient to justify his devoting the necessary time to observing.

§2.11   Preparing witnesses: nervousness

How may you place a witness at ease and overcome his nervousness?

As is true of many, if not most, of the problems of trial methods, there is no guaranteed solution for this problem. It would be error to consider, however, that the problem is primarily an individual one for the witness. Rather, you can surely make your calm witness nervous by the wrong methods, and usually you can calm your nervous witness by correct methods.

Adequate preparation of the witness is a most important factor. Fear of the unknown causes nervousness. Knowledge of what is to come induces confidence and composure. Having a thorough interview[1] with the witness before you call him to testify is one effective method of reducing the chances that the witness will become nervous and confused as he testifies.

In addition to advance preparation of the witness, you should, as you proceed with your direct examination, bear in mind the interest in keeping the witness composed and at ease. It is your duty to avoid rushing the witness, to make your questions clear and direct,[2] and by all means to refrain from showing displeasure if the witness misunderstands or gets excited or confused. In short, you should yourself be composed during the direct examina-

1. See §§2.11–2.14.
2. See §5.5.
3. See §7.8.
4. See §2.14.
1. See §2.14.
2. See §2.16.

tion. The response of your witness is likely to reflect your state of composure or nervousness.

§2.12 Preparing witnesses: dress

CASE 9. *W*, a disinterested witness who acquired knowledge concerning the case in his capacity as a police officer, meets you at your request for an interview immediately before trial. He is dressed in sport clothes.

Should you talk with the witness about how he should be dressed in court?

One of your principal aims for calling witnesses,[1] that of persuading the factfinder that your client's claim is well supported factually, is best served when personalities — both yours and that of your witness — are subordinated to the testimony. As a general rule, the manner of dressing should be one that does not attract special attention. Most witnesses will dress appropriately without suggestions from you. Tact is required, of course, if you make suggestions concerning dress.

A witness who occupies some special position with which a special mode of dress is associated may and usually should appear "in uniform." Thus, in Case 9, the testimony of a uniformed officer is usually more impressive than that of one who appears in a business suit or sport clothes. As to others besides police officers, if the testimony of the witness is in any way connected with his work or observations while he was at work, and the witness is one who wears a uniform on the job, it may be preferable that he wear the uniform in court, but local custom or the preferences of the trial judge may oppose that practice. This comment applies, for example, to bus drivers. Its extension to other uniformed workers such as milk route salesmen, mechanics, and the like is more debatable. Certainly you should not ask a witness to come to court in a soiled uniform simply because his job is the type that requires him to work in greasy or dirty surroundings. The judge and jurors may take that form of dress as a mark of disrespect. On the other hand, a clean uniform with stains indicating that it has been soiled and cleaned many times provides a quick, effective, and inoffensive way of transmitting the idea that the witness knows the intimate details of his job from firsthand application — an impression that it is a part of the lawyer's job to convey, if the testimony of the witness relates to the details of his job in any way. You should be wary of advising a witness to wear such a uniform, however, if your tribunal is one in which informal dress in court is uncommon.

The foregoing instances of special dress might be regarded as an exception to the general rule that the witness should dress in a manner that does

1. See §2.1 as to aims generally.

not attract special attention. Perhaps, instead, they should be regarded as special applications of the rule, on the theory that jurors are accustomed to seeing policemen and bus drivers in uniform, and are more likely to be distracted from concentration on the testimony of such a witness by his failure to appear in uniform than by his wearing it.

§2.13 Preparing witnesses: interviewing separately

CASE 10. *P*, whom you represent, is suing for personal injuries sustained when he stopped his car behind *F*'s, as the traffic light changed to red, and was hit from behind by *D*'s car. *F* was driving his own car. *S*, his son, was in the front seat beside him.

Should you interview each witness separately (in preparation for his appearance at trial)?

When the rule of exclusion of witnesses from the courtroom has been invoked [1] and the witness has been sworn, interviewing the witness in the presence of others who have been or may be witnesses is prohibited in many jurisdictions. Some courts hold that this prohibition extends to prospective witnesses who have not been sworn. You should, of course, ascertain the extent of the restrictions applied by the court in question and abide by them strictly. Should you interview witnesses simultaneously whenever that practice is permissible and convenient, or should you interview separately even those witnesses whom you are permitted to interview simultaneously? The answer to this question will vary with the circumstances and purposes of the interview.

Normally you can obtain more accurate and reliable information on relevant facts by interviewing witnesses separately. If you interview witnesses together, the answer first given by one of them influences what the other thinks and says. If you interview witnesses together just before you call them to testify, even the methods of expression in their testimony are likely to be similar. When the similarity is noticed by the jury, or called to their attention, it supports the inference that the testimony of the witnesses is not as reliable as that of persons who have answered relevant questions each in his own peculiar way (with such variations in substance as well as form, as are consistent with the acknowledged fact that two persons observing the same incident will ordinarily differ as to what occurred). More dangerous than the inference that the witnesses have compared ideas and conformed their testimony is the possible inference that they are being guided by what you told them to say. In Case 10, one of these inferences would probably be drawn if both *F* and *S* should state, when asked to estimate the speed

1. See §5.5.

at which F was approaching the intersection before the light changed, that he "was going about 27 to 29 miles per hour." This form of expression is not normally used; when it is used by two witnesses, it appears to be the result of agreement between the witnesses or coaching by a lawyer. As a result, the jury probably would give less credence to the testimony of each, and to their testimony combined, than would have been the case if the expressions of one had been different from those of the other. Despite your cautioning each witness against adopting the expressions of the other, it probably will occur to some extent if you interview them simultaneously.

To a more limited extent, this inference that the witness is repeating someone else's ideas instead of his own may be drawn from the mere fact that several witnesses have been interviewed simultaneously, particularly if the interview occurs just shortly before the witnesses are called to testify. The likelihood that inquiry on this subject will be made during cross-examination[2] is alone sufficient to cause a preference for interviewing separately, even when the rules would permit a joint interview.

With reference to the interview conducted just before the witness is called to testify, another advantage of interviewing each witness separately is that each represents an individual challenge to your ability to judge him correctly and counsel him wisely. In Case 10 suppose, as might naturally be the case, that F, the father, is domineering and S, the son, is unduly meek. F will need to be cautioned about the danger of answering positively when the extent of his knowledge of the subject of inquiry does not warrant it, and to be advised against arguing with the opposing attorney.[3] On the other hand, S will need to be cautioned about the danger of agreeing too readily with the opposing attorney in cross-examination. It is obviously easier to impart the advice effectively and tactfully to F and S separately, rather than to have each listen to the advice you give to the other.

A different answer is frequently indicated with respect to an interview during early investigation,[4] as distinguished from an interview just before the witnesses are called to the stand during trial. Even as to the original investigation, however, separate interviews are preferable when you can arrange them with full cooperation from the witnesses.

§2.14 Preparing witnesses: content and form of testimony

CASE 11. Representing D Company, you are defending a claim by P for personal injuries suffered in a head-on collision between D Company's truck, driven by W, and a car driven by P, at a curve on a country road. D Com-

2. See §3.18.
3. See §2.14.
4. See §9.16.

pany's truck was on the outside of the curve, *P*'s car on the inside, and the principal dispute on the facts of the accident is whether *P* swung wide or *W* cut the corner. Other disputed issues include lookout, speed, and use of brakes.

To what extent should you counsel with the witness in advance regarding the content and form of testimony?

By artful cross-examination, a witness is occasionally led to suspect that discussing his testimony with the lawyer who called him was improper, and he may shortly find himself caught in a false statement that he has not talked with anyone about his testimony.[1] Another form of the same suspicion of counseling the witness is probably responsible for a reluctance on the part of some lawyers to confer with the witness in detail concerning his testimony. The suspicion doubtlessly arises from the recognition that some lawyers abuse the process by using the interview with the witness to shape his testimony to the lawyer's preferred version of the facts, rather than using it for advice and counsel to the end that the witness may present his testimony in the most favorable and convincing manner. If you do not abuse the process, conducting a thorough interview with the witness shortly before he testifies is not only entirely proper[2] but is essential to fulfilling your duty of presenting your client's case in the most persuasive fashion.

A thorough interview with the witness will include these general phases: (a) Obtaining information from the witness; (b) advising the witness about the form and manner of his testimony; (c) advising him of the anticipated cross-examination; (d) causing the witness to read his deposition and any other documents about which he may be asked during trial; and (e) conducting a "practice session" with the witness.

(a) *Obtaining information from the witness.* Usually the developments immediately before this final interview will cause you to think of additional questions you wish to ask the witness, even though you have previously obtained a thorough and complete statement. Particularly is this so if you conduct this interview at hours when the court is in recess after the trial has begun and you have had an opportunity to gain more insight into your adversary's theory and approach. If you have your principal interview with the witness before trial begins, because of the limited time available during the trial or for other reasons, you should try to make arrangements with the witness so that you can have a supplemental interview with him shortly before he testifies. The additional interview may be needed in the light of trial developments. In such an interview you can ask the witness any additional questions that have occurred to you after trial began, as well as advising him

1. See §3.18.
2. *Cf.* H. Drinker, *Legal Ethics* 86 (1953).

of any special pitfalls of cross-examination that you can anticipate in view of the trial developments.[3]

(b) *Advising the witness about the form and manner of his testimony.* Usually it happens that the witness is inexperienced in court proceedings. One of the principal functions of this interview is to familiarize him with the nature of the proceedings and the pitfalls to be avoided. The advice that you ordinarily should give the witness includes the following:

(1) Maintain an attitude of conviction[4] and fairness.[5] Without previous experience in the courtroom, the witness is likely to feel that the jury will surely believe what he has to say, regardless of the contrary testimony of others. Upon reflection, when the matter is called to his attention, he will agree that since the jurors do not know him or the witnesses who disagree with him and will testify for the adversary, they must decide who is right largely upon the basis of impressions the witnesses make when testifying. He will usually agree that his belief that he is right carries with it the duty to prepare against possible incidents during his testimony that would make an unfavorable impression on the jury, as well as preparing to tell his version of the facts in a convincing manner. The witness makes the most favorable impression on the jury when he expresses his testimony with confidence but without bias, admitting limitations on his knowledge rather than trying to answer every question in a way favorable to the party who called him.

(2) Avoid arguing with the adverse lawyer.

(3) Avoid long answers volunteering information not asked for in the questions.

(4) Be prepared for the possibility that the cross-examiner will try to make the witness angry, as a means of causing him to impress the jury unfavorably both by the way he acts and by the content of what he may say in anger, thoughtlessly.

(5) Speak distinctly and avoid dropping his voice, putting a hand in front of his mouth, or turning his back to the jury.

(6) Avoid trying to answer every question with certainty. Surely some questions will be asked, especially on cross-examination, that the witness cannot answer from his own knowledge. The adverse lawyer may try to get the witness out on a limb by coercing him into some kind of an answer. He may suggest that an honest and fair witness would answer questions asked by both sides instead of answering every question positively for the side that calls him and retreating to "I don't know" when asked by the other side. The danger that the cross-examiner will put across that idea is considerably less serious, however, than the danger that the witness will be caught in

3. See subparagraph (c) of this section.
4. *Cf.* §1.2.
5. *Cf.* §1.3.

damaging contradictions if he tries to answer without knowledge. A typical matter to which this advice applies is the estimation of speeds, times, and distances, by one who either is without experience in such estimation or did not observe closely the particular thing he is asked to estimate.[6]

(7) Avoid, during both direct and cross-examination, making personal charges against the adverse party and his witnesses; it is often harmful to one's own case to call the adverse party a "liar" or a "crook," even though the evidence clearly demonstrates this to be a fact.[7]

(8) Leave all objections to you, except as to privileged matter. A witness who himself objects to questions and tries to avoid answering them will create an impression that he is biased and unwilling to make a full and frank disclosure. An exception to the instructions against objection by the witness must be recognized as to matter that is the subject of a personal privilege — a privilege that must be asserted by the witness. If such matters are anticipated and the privilege is to be asserted either under your advice or upon the independent decision of the witness, you should be certain that you and the witness have a common understanding of the procedure for asserting the privilege. Be careful, however, that you do not undertake to advise the witness regarding an issue of privilege under circumstances in which you would be violating the Code of Professional Responsibility because the interests of the witness and those of the litigant whom you represent are in conflict.[8]

(*c*) *Advising the witness of the anticipated cross-examination.* You can profitably discuss in detail with the witness both the anticipated subject matter of the cross-examination and particular questions that may be asked. The discussion of subject matter should include possible questions on matters not to be covered in the direct examination.[9] Also, particularly if you know your adversary well, you can anticipate many of the techniques of cross-examination that might otherwise catch the witness off guard. For example, most witnesses need to be prepared for a request on cross-examination that the witness make a drawing[10] and for inquiries on cross-examination about payment of expenses[11] and about conversations between the witness and

---

6. See §3.12 for an example of cross-examination capitalizing on the willingness of the witness to make estimates.

7. See §7.19.

8. See American Bar Association, Code of Responsibility DR 7-104(A) (1969):

"During the course of his representation of a client a lawyer shall not:

". . . (2) Give advice to a person who is not represented by a lawyer, other than the advice to secure counsel, if the interests of such person are or have a reasonable possibility of being in conflict with the interests of his client."

See also *id.,* Canon 5, concerning conflicts of interest generally.

9. See §3.14.

10. See §3.16.

11. See §3.27.

others regarding his testimony.[12] Because an unprepared witness can so frequently be tripped by a question implying that a conference with the lawyer before testifying would be improper, you should advise him specifically to answer freely and honestly if asked whether he has talked with you before testifying. The same comment applies to questions as to whether he has discussed the case with others; obviously an incident that gives rise to a lawsuit is the subject of discussion between a witness and his or her spouse, for example. When the adverse lawyer hovers over the witness belligerently and asks, "Have you talked to anybody about your testimony in this case?" a denial is proof of its own falsity. You should give the same advice regarding any inquiry about payment of expenses, if the witness is one for whom you have arranged some reimbursement. You should advise him that although it would be improper for a party to pay a witness anything to testify in a particular way, the reimbursements that you have arranged are proper,[13] and he should readily admit payment of the expenses if asked. Reluctance in that respect may create the inference that more than expenses is being paid or else the witness would not have tried to hide it. Another matter about which some witnesses should be informed is that they are not compelled to give only a "yes" or "no" answer but may explain if such an answer would be misleading; on the other hand, a practice of excessive explanation will cause the witness to appear biased or evasive;[14] you should adapt the advice you give a particular witness concerning this matter to your appraisal of the susceptibility of the witness to falling into one or the other of these opposite extremes.

(d) *Causing the witness to read his deposition and any other documents about which he may be asked during trial.* Usually there is a considerable time lapse between the taking of depositions and the trial. Memory being imperfect, a person could hardly be expected to answer identical questions, on different days, in the same way. Aside from variations in the form of the answer, some variation in content is to be expected even of the most conscientious witness. Although variations of this type should not reflect unfavorably on the witness' credibility, they are often so construed, particularly after an expert cross-examiner has magnified them artfully. Accordingly, you should try to reduce to a minimum such variations in content, though not those as to form of answers. To accomplish this purpose, it is essential that the witness read over the transcript of his deposition just before trial. These comments apply with greater force to documents with which the witness is supposed to be familiar, and which have figured in some way in the circumstances of the case. If through faulty memory he misquotes one of his letters,

12. See §3.18.
13. See §9.19.
14. See §3.23.

at the least the incident supports an argument that his testimony is not entirely credible because of a poor memory. Usually there is more danger of variations of this kind than in the case of depositions, because the letters and other documents may have been prepared before any thought of litigation arose and at a time when his attention was less sharply focused on the details within them. You should undertake to anticipate what documents your witness may be shown or asked about, on both direct and cross-examination, and cause him to read them over in preparation for testifying.

(e) The "practice session." The ideal preparation of the witness includes a practice session with him, in which you ask and the witness answers questions just as if he were on the stand. No amount of advice can be as effective as this practice. Advise the witness that he is not to memorize the questions or answers and that the practice session is not intended for that purpose, but rather merely as an illustration of the general character of the experience of testifying and of some of the particular problems that may be anticipated. The values are evident. If you omit some important advice, or the witness fails to understand, there is a good chance that you will discover this fact in the practice session. For example in Case 11, you would advise D Company's truck driver W in the course of your interview that he should not attempt to give positive answers to questions concerning which he does not have positive knowledge. Suppose that in a practice session you assume the role of cross-examiner and this exchange occurs:

Q. How fast were you going?
A. About 35.
Q. Did you have good brakes?
A. Yes.
Q. At that speed of 35, and with the good brakes you had, within what distance could you stop the truck on a gravel road like this one?
A. 10 feet.

Obviously W did not understand the point of the advice. You can interrupt the practice session to point out that tests have proved that it would take much farther than W estimates, that W doubtlessly has never made any test or measurements but is making a guess, and that his guess would set him up for a line of questions showing, on his assumption that he could stop the truck in ten feet at 35 m.p.h., that he either was looking off in some direction away from the road or else did not apply his brakes when he saw the other car and the danger of collision. Similarly, in such a practice session you may clear up misunderstandings between you and the witness about what he will say, on both direct and cross-examination.

You should ask the witness every question that you may want to ask when he testifies, unless you are certain of his answer. This is not to say that the question on trial should be in exactly the same form as in the pretrial interview and practice session. But the dangers of asking during trial questions that you have not previously submitted to the witness at least in content are too great to warrant the risk. For the same reasons, you should have the witness attempt in the practice session any drawing or any interpretation of a chart or picture [15] or any demonstration [16] that you propose to have him make while testifying during the trial.

§2.15 Preparing witnesses: experts

CASE 12. Representing *D Company*, you are defending against a claim of *P* for alleged brain injury. Through pleadings, depositions, and copies of reports from *P*'s doctors, you have fairly specific notice as to the nature and extent of injury claimed by *P*. *P* and his lawyer have granted a medical examination of *P* by *N,* a neurosurgeon selected by you, and *N* is available as a witness at trial.

To what extent should you counsel with an expert witness regarding the content and form of his testimony?

The purposes of interviews with expert witnesses, immediately before and during trial, are essentially the same as in the case of lay witnesses,[1] but different emphasis warrants consideration of some special problems that arise in the case of the expert.

(a) Obtaining information from the witness. From previous preparation of the instant case, and perhaps from experience in other similar cases, you should have a reasonably accurate understanding of the subject matter of the expert testimony before the occasion arises for the final interview with the expert witness. Because of your lack of thorough knowledge of the specialty, however, there is serious danger that you will misunderstand or overlook important consequences and implications. A great part of the value of an expert to you is in advising and informing you, not only with reference to the subject matter to be covered in his own testimony but also with regard to the development as a whole of that aspect of the case concerned with the expert's field. His suggestions for cross-examination of your adversary's experts may be invaluable because of his ability, through training and experience in the specialty, to discover and expose weaknesses in your adversary's case. His suggestions as to what should be avoided in cross-examination of your adversary's witnesses are equally valuable. It is a good practice to confer with your expert and secure his approval as to all items of planned cross-examination of your adversary's experts, so that you may avoid the common error of improving your adversary's case by your own cross-examination.

15. See §§2.33, 2.34.
16. See §2.31.   1. See §2.14.

Bearing in mind this factor, in representing a defendant as well as in representing a plaintiff, you will usually find it advisable to have an interview with your experts before any witnesses are called in the trial. To the extent that, because of trial of numerous cases involving similar issues, you have become acquainted with the specialty of your experts (at least as it relates to trial of lawsuits), you will be able to reduce the time devoted to this aspect of the interview with the expert witness.

(b) *Advising the witness about the form and manner of his testimony.* Sometimes it is impossible to avoid complicated questions, and complicated answers, in dealing with expert testimony. If there is any difference, however, it is even more important to work for simplicity in the case of expert testimony than in the case of lay testimony. Titles of the expert are impressive, but they probably will be matched by similar titles of your adversary's expert. The one who tells his version in the way that makes it seem reasonable to the jury is the one more likely to triumph. The advance preparation should therefore include some tactful suggestions to the expert on this subject, if he needs it. Whether he needs such suggestions and to what extent will depend, of course, upon his individual habits of speech and his experience in testifying. Most experts are willing to cooperate in this respect but will lapse into the use of technical language unless you make a conscious effort, both in advance preparation and during the testimony, to assure that the ideas are expressed so that those not skilled in the specialty will understand them. If technical terms are used, they should be explained. It will pay dividends to spend enough time with the expert to get his ideas expressed in jurors' language, but without his appearing to condescend to a manner of speech to which he is not accustomed.

In other respects, the expert witness will usually need less counsel about the form and manner of his testimony than the lay witness, because of his broader education and experience in speaking. However, you should consider the other factors discussed in the preceding section with reference to lay witnesses.

(c) *Advising him of anticipated cross-examination.* The possible use by your adversary of various special techniques for cross-examination of expert witnesses[2] should be among the matters you discuss with your experts, except to the extent that their previous experience as witnesses limits the need for this counseling. As an example, the preparation of the expert for cross-examination involves the special problem of the anticipated hypothetical question. Effective cross-examination of an expert frequently includes a hypothetical question in which the fact assumptions are changed from those used by the expert in his own direct testimony.[3] The probability of such cross-

2. See §§3.27–3.31.
3. Reasons for the effectiveness of this technique of cross-examination are discussed in §3.31.

examination should be pointed out to the expert. Insofar as you are able to do so, you should anticipate the questions your adversary may ask and put them to your expert in the advance interview.

(*d*) *Causing the witness to read his deposition and any other document about which he may be asked during the trial.* Usually the expert will have rendered a written opinion to you or your client regarding some aspects of the case. A copy of this opinion may be in the hands of the opposing lawyer. Furthermore, if that is not true, opposing counsel may call for a copy on cross-examination,[4] and it would make an unfavorable impression on the jury to refuse the copy, even if the rules of the jurisdiction of trial would permit the refusal. It is especially important that the expert review such a written opinion, since the slightest inconsistency between his testimony and his written opinion may prove embarrassing and harmful when thoroughly exploited on cross-examination. Also, you should caution your medical witness to review carefully his records on the patient about whom he is to testify, since records may be called for during the cross-examination. It is also important that you review these records yourself, so you will be well prepared to meet anything unfavorable appearing in them and to ascertain that the favorable is not omitted from the evidence.

(*e*) *The "practice session."* In the case of the expert who has experience in testifying, a complete practice session is ordinarily not needed. As indicated in subparagraphs (b) and (c) of this section, however, the interview should include a discussion with the expert concerning particular questions to be asked on direct and particular questions anticipated on cross-examination. The most satisfactory manner of handling this discussion is simply to put the questions to the expert, with the understanding that he is to answer as he would in trial, interrupting the process, however, to advise you if he has any suggestions as to changes or additions to the proposed questions for direct examination. In the case of the expert, even more than with reference to a lay witness, the particular phrasing of questions may be of vital importance. Some of the testimony will be opinions, and the omission or addition of factors in the question may vitally affect the expert's answer. It is therefore important to consider the particular questions, as well as the general subject matter, when you are conferring with the expert regarding his forthcoming appearance as a witness.

§2.16 Framing questions

What practical rules can you use as an aid in framing specific questions?

Experienced trial lawyers invariably find it much easier to frame questions well than to tell a novice how to do it. They have developed habits of inter-

4. See §3.28.

rogation and a "feel" for what is and what is not appropriate; they find it easier to perform than to explain. This is not to say, however, that you must depend on inspiration of the moment, or what amounts almost to accidental construction of the form of your questions. Particularly as to direct examination, even if you do not have the benefit of extensive trial experience, you can anticipate accurately the subject matter that you will cover with each witness, and you can frame your questions in advance, at a time when you can consider and test each question in the light of rules such as those suggested here. In due course, that practice will help you develop good habits of framing questions, so that your phrasing of even your extemporaneous questions will tend to meet the requirements of proper interrogation. In short, the suggestions that follow admittedly can give you little help in phrasing a question during trial, because there is then insufficient time to think of a proposed question and subject it to tests such as these, modifying or abandoning it pursuant to the results of the tests. These suggestions are intended for advance preparation of specific questions and for use in developing good habits in the phrasing of questions.

(1) Ask only one question at a time, and not a question with several parts. Compound sentences are sometimes hard to understand. Answers to compound questions are worse; they are likely to be incomplete, ambiguous, or both.

(2) Avoid negatives in the question, if possible. Consider this exchange: Q — "You do not know whether Jones was there?" A — "Yes." Did the witness mean "Yes, I know," or did he mean "Yes, it is true that I do not know," or did he mean "Yes, Jones was there"? If you notice it, this doubt can be cleared by another question, and the loss is simply that of delay and a slight danger of confusion, but if you fail to call for clarification after an exchange such as this you may have lost a vital point by having the answer interpreted differently from what you yourself know that the witness meant.

(3) Make the question brief. Both the witness and the jurors must remember all of the question in order to understand it correctly.

(4) State the question in simple words — those used in everyday conversation. You want all of the jurors to understand both the questions and the answers, and this requires the use of words that the least educated among them will understand. This is not a recommendation for use of slang or bad grammar, however; that practice, unless it comes naturally with the lawyer, probably will be recognized and resented as talking down to the jury.[1]

(5) In summary, make the question clear. It is not enough that you and the witness understand each other's questions and answers, though of course that is important. Understanding by the jury is also important. The jurors are the ones whose understanding is your primary interest. They are less

---

1. See §1.2 regarding use of techniques that are unnatural.

familiar with the facts and circumstances than either you or the witness. It is no reflection on the intelligence of the jurors that simple questions are best.

§2.17   Anticipating objections to evidence

CASE 13.   *P* is suing for injuries sustained in a collision between his car and *D*'s truck. *P*'s car, after the impact with *D*'s truck, veered into *W*'s car. *P*'s lawyer, in interviewing *W*, learns that *D* paid *W* $75 for a release and that *W* tells a version of the facts favorable to *D*. *P*'s lawyer anticipates that *D* will call *W* as a witness in the trial and wants to be prepared to prove the payment of $75 by *D* to *W*, though the possibility of an objection on the ground that it was paid in compromise of a disputed claim is apparent.

What advance preparation can you make for meeting anticipated objections to your evidence?

Your case is never properly prepared until you have given some attention to anticipating objections by your adversary to the evidence you plan to offer. The following, though not an exhaustive list, are advantages that you may gain in the ordinary case by such anticipation and preparation.

(1) You can often make preparations on the law or on the facts[1] that enable you to resist the objections successfully or avoid them by alternative methods of proof. These preparations include briefing authorities bearing on the anticipated objections and investigating carefully to discover other evidence less susceptible to objection than that you first considered in support of a given point, or other evidence that supports admissibility of the questioned evidence. For example, in Case 13, it might be discovered upon careful investigation that W sustained no more than $75 damages, which fact supports the conclusion that the payment by *D* was not a compromise payment and that objection on this ground would be untenable.

(2) You can plan to prove foundations or predicates (for want of which sound objection might be urged) in due order. Often it is necessary to prove by one witness some fact that constitutes a predicate for introducing testimony of another. For example, the best evidence rule often requires accounting for an original document before you can introduce a copy. If, as in Case 23, the original was in the custody of *S* and the copy in the custody of *C*, you should call *S* to prove destruction of the original before you call *C* to authenticate the copy. Failure to anticipate the objection and provide against it (by getting an admission of genuineness in advance, or by calling *S* before calling *C*) may result in the exclusion of the document. Sometimes you may avoid the exclusion by persuading the court to receive the evidence conditionally, or the exclusion may be temporary only, in the sense that you can

1. See §§9.2, 9.5.

retrace your steps and do what you should have done earlier. You will have lost time in any event, and, if the witness is needed again and is one other than your client or his employee, you may have lost the cooperation of the witness who is too busy to come back again later. Also you will have tried the patience of the court and jury (they may blame the delay as much, however, on the one who interposes the objection).[2] You usually face a serious practical problem of getting witnesses into court when needed; the necessity of bringing one back for a second appearance in court because of an oversight in your planning seriously aggravates this problem.

(3) You can be prepared to move forward promptly, and without pause, after you have without objection introduced a question and answer to which you anticipated that objection might be made. Because you are intent on getting into evidence the matter with which you are concerned at the moment, there is a danger that you will find it necessary to pause and consider what you will prove next, after you have succeeded in getting your proof received without objection. Such a pause is often fatal, for the reason that it directs your adversary's attention to the last question and answer and is an invitation for objections. Use of this technique of smooth transition might be questioned on ethical grounds, although it is not specifically prohibited by the Code of Professional Responsibility. Probably the prevailing attitude in the profession approves its use with qualifications noted hereafter as to offering evidence of doubtful admissibility,[3] and the further qualifications that many and perhaps most lawyers would disapprove its use against an inexperienced adversary or in combination with deliberate distraction of an adversary's attention. The latter combination gives the conduct the color of deception rather than mere avoidance of any suggestion to the adversary regarding potential grounds of objection.

(4) You can prepare alternative theories for offering, for a limited purpose, evidence that may be subject to objection when offered generally. The possibilities existing in alternative theories for offering evidence for a limited purpose are surprisingly great; only occasionally will you find it absolutely impossible to secure the admission of evidence that you think may influence the jury. In situations such as Case 13, for example, it is generally assumed that the evidence of payment of $75 to W by D would be inadmissible, if it was a compromise. It has been suggested that, as P's lawyer, you should investigate to determine whether you might avoid this objection on the ground that in fact the entire damage suffered by W was no more than $75, and therefore this was a full payment though the receipt was phrased as a compromise. If this avenue of investigation is unproductive and D has called W as a witness, you might offer the evidence for the limited purpose of impeach-

2. See §4.2.
3. See §2.23.

File: Case 13   Our Client: P

Proof Analysis

Witness: W (expected to be a witness for the opposing party, D)

Item We Want to Prove: that W received $75 from D in payment for damage to W's car.

Our Alternative Plan One

Our Questions on Cross:
(1)   Did you receive money from D in return for your signing a release of claims against D for the damage done to your car when it was struck by P's car after P's car and D's truck collided?
(2)   How much?

Grounds of Anticipated Objections by D: Hearsay and evidence of a compromise.

Our Response: If Your Honor please, may I ask some further questions [preferably in the presence of the jury but alternatively out of the hearing of the jury] to lay a foundation for admission of this evidence?

Our Further Questions on Cross:
(3)   Was your car struck by P's car after P's car and D's truck collided?   (Anticipated answer: yes)
(4)   Did you have it repaired?
(5)   (If (4) is answered yes.)   What was the repair cost? (Desired answer, $75 or less.)
        (If (4) is answered no.)   Did you obtain one or more estimates of the cost of repair, and, if so, what were the amounts?
(6)   Did you receive money from D in return for signing a release of claims against D for damage to your car?
(7)   How much?

Grounds of Anticipated Objection to Questions (3) - (5): Irrelevant; immaterial.

Our Response: The answers to these questions are relevant as part of the foundation for admitting the answers to Questions (6) and (7).   (See Our Argument on (6) and (7), below.)

<u>Grounds of Anticipated Objections to Questions (6) - (7)</u>:
Hearsay and evidence of a compromise.

<u>Our Argument to the Court</u>: The amount received by W was not
a compromise payment but a payment in full of all of <u>W's</u> damages.
The rule excluding evidence of compromise in certain circumstances
does not apply to payments in full since they are not compromises.
Moreover, the hearsay rule does not apply since the fact of <u>D's</u>
payment of <u>W's</u> damages in full is an admission of fault by a
party, <u>D</u>.

<u>Further Response (if the Court nevertheless sustains the ob-</u>
<u>jection)</u>: In the alternative, without waiving our general offer
of this evidence, we offer this evidence of <u>W's</u> receipt of a payment from <u>D</u> for the limited purpose of impeaching <u>W's</u> evidence.
This evidence supports two impeaching inferences - first, that <u>W</u>
is biased because of the payment and, second, that <u>W's</u> previous
conduct in making and collecting upon a claim against <u>D</u> is prior
conduct inconsistent with his present testimony to a version of
the accident favorable to <u>D</u>. (Consider citing Federal Rules of
Evidence, Rule 408; be prepared to respond to an argument that
Rule 403 applies.)

Our Alternative Plan Two

During <u>cross</u>, ask questions (3), (4), and (5) before questions
(1) and (2) in the hope of getting out the facts as to the amount
of damage before any colloquy about compromise that might encourage <u>W</u> to say he had more than $75 damage. Also, question (1) is
very long and, if (3), (4), and (5) were asked just before it,
could be shortened to: Did you receive money from <u>D</u> in return
for signing a release of claims against <u>D</u> for the damage to your
car? A disadvantage of Plan Two, however, is that we might be
forced to disclose our purpose anyway by an objection of irrelevancy to questions (3), (4), and (5).

<u>Possible response</u>: Your Honor, I submit that the relevance
will become apparent if we may be permitted just a few more questions. [If further response is required: The answers to these
questions are relevant as part of the foundation for admitting
the answers to additional questions we wish to offer in a moment -
questions (6) and (7).]

<u>Note for Additional Investigation</u>: Can we get independent
evidence of the cost of repairs or estimates of the cost of re-
pairing the damage to <u>W's</u> car, showing that it did not exceed
$75?

ing the witness W. The theory is that W will naturally be more inclined to favor D after receiving a satisfactory settlement from him, and also that W's demanding and receiving a settlement from D is inconsistent with the aggregate of W's testimony on trial, entirely favorable to D. We need not pass upon the merits of the evidence point here;[4] in some courts the evidence would be received, and this serves to illustrate the use of the alternative theory for submitting the evidence for a limited purpose. You may be certain that if the evidence is so received, your opponent will at least fear that it is as damaging as if admitted generally, even though the court, either at the request of your opponent[5] or on the court's own initiative, instructs the jury that they will not consider the evidence for any purpose other than the limited one.[6] If the evidence is still excluded, after the alternative offer for a limited purpose, you have at least preserved a possibility of reversible error that you would have forfeited by offering the evidence only generally.[7]

The process of anticipating objections and planning to overcome them in the way suggested in this section is an illustration of what may be called proof analysis.[8] A written analysis that the defense lawyer might prepare in relation to Case 13 appears in another section.[9] The accompanying illustration shows a form of written analysis the plaintiff's lawyer might use in this instance.

§2.18   Leading the witness

CASE 14. P is asserting a claim for personal injuries sustained when he was struck by D's grocery truck at 8 P.M. Scope of employment is disputed. W, who was standing on the sidewalk and saw the accident, has advised P's lawyer that the first thing the driver of the truck said immediately after the accident was, "How will I get to the warehouse and back before the boss

---

4. See Fenberg v. Rosenthal, 348 Ill. App. 510, 109 N.E.2d 402 (1952). See also Federal Rules of Evidence, Rule 408.

5. See §4.18.

6. Is it improper, on ethical grounds, for a lawyer to offer for a limited purpose evidence that he knows the jury will consider more generally despite a limiting instruction by the court? American Bar Association, Code of Professional Responsibility (1969) does not contain any specific provision in point, though EC 7–25 declares that "a lawyer should not by subterfuge put before a jury matters which it cannot properly consider." The discretion that the trial judge has as to evidence rulings (a discretion that is broader in fact than might otherwise appear because of the "harmless error" doctrine) affords some practical protection against abuse of the technique of offering evidence for a limited purpose.

7. See §4.12.

8. See generally §1.5.

9. §4.18.

leaves?" On direct examination by *P*'s lawyer, when asked what, if anything, the truck driver said as he got out of the cab after the accident, *W* says, "He said something about wondering how he could get to the warehouse now." After additional questions, *W* still omits the element of getting "back before the boss leaves." It is apparent that this element will not be stated by *W* unless he is asked a leading question.

Should you use leading questions?

The effect of a leading question cannot be erased by objection or instruction. The vice of the question is telling the witness what the lawyer wants him to say. Having received the message, the witness can then answer a non-leading question in the desired way, even though the leading question is stricken. Consequently you may sometimes be tempted to ask a leading question deliberately, realizing that an objection to it will be sustained. The Code of Professional Responsibility does not include any provisions dealing explicitly with this practice of coaching the witness by a leading question. But more generalized provisions surely apply to the practice of deliberately asking leading questions that are known to be improper.[1] The problem of application of these provisions to the use of leading questions is complicated by the fact that rules of evidence and procedure allow leading questions under some circumstances.

---

1. See American Bar Association, Code of Professional Responsibility DR 7-106 (C) (1969):

"In appearing in his professional capacity before a tribunal, a lawyer shall not:

". . . (7) Intentionally or habitually violate any established rule of procedure or of evidence."

See also *id.*, EC 7-25, which includes the statement that "a lawyer should not by subterfuge put before a jury matters which it cannot properly consider."

If the leading question is asked for the purpose of coaching a witness, with the expectation that he will deviate from the truth if necessary in order to comply with the coaching suggestion, does this violate *id.*, DR 7-102 (A) (4), which declares that a lawyer shall not "[k]nowingly use perjured testimony or false evidence"? Whether intentionally or not, this rule may have been so drafted that it is less restrictive in relation to this question than the older canons. One might argue that the lawyer does not "knowingly" use false evidence when he does not know whether the witness might have given the desired answer even if not coached by the leading question. Perhaps it would have been easier to establish that such coaching violated old Canon 39 on the theory that it amounted to a "suggestion calculated to induce the witness to suppress or deviate from the truth." Old Canon 39 was susceptible of being construed as pertaining only to interviews with witnesses, rather than interrogation on the stand; if it did not apply to the latter, however, the prohibition against suggestions calculated to induce the witness to testify falsely might have been read into the requirements of candor and fairness expressed in Canons 15 and 22 of the 1908 Canons.

For additional discussion of the broader problem of deliberate use of any kind of improper question, see §2.23.

Although in all courts leading questions are improper as a general rule, they are permitted under some exceptions.[2] The exceptions vary from court to court; there is a great margin of variation even within the courts of a single jurisdiction, because of the discretion vested in the trial judge with respect to controlling leading questions. Usually, however, leading questions will be permitted in these circumstances: (1) questions as to preliminary matters setting the stage for inquiries relevant to the material disputed issues in the case; (2) questions as to undisputed matters, used as connectives; (3) questions that the witness has already answered (they would be objectionable as repetitious except when used as connectives); (4) questions directed to an adverse or hostile witness;[3] (5) questions on cross-examination of a witness called by the adversary, unless the witness was called under a rule or statute permitting the person who called him to interrogate him as an adverse party or hostile witness. Frequently leading questions will also be allowed (6) to a witness of limited understanding, (7) to a witness whose recollection has been exhausted but who is supposed to know additional facts material to the case, and (8) to a witness who is being asked to contradict statements previously made by other witnesses.

A question is leading if it suggests to the witness the answer that the interrogator desires. The form of the question should not be regarded as determinative and usually is not so regarded. The question may be leading, suggesting the desired answer, even though the form itself gives no cue to the answer. For example, it would be leading for you as *P*'s lawyer to say to *W,* in Case 14, "Tell the jury whether or not the truck driver said, 'How will I get to the warehouse and back before the boss leaves?'" This would also be leading: "Did he say anything about getting to the warehouse and back before the boss was to leave?" A proper question is, "What happened immediately after they hit?" Perhaps even this question is slightly leading, in an absolute sense, and surely it is leading in an absolute sense to ask, "Did the truck driver say anything?" It is leading in the sense that it suggests to the witness that the lawyer wants testimony as to the truck driver's comments rather than testimony just then as to something else that happened immediately after they collided. But questions that merely direct attention to the subject matter about which the lawyer wants the witness to testify are not regarded as "leading" in law; if such questions were not permitted, it would be almost impossible to conduct an examination on any basis other than simply asking the witness to tell what he knows about the lawsuit. Conse-

2. 3 Wigmore, *Evidence* §§769–779 (rev. ed. Chadbourn 1970); Federal Rules of Evidence, Rule 611(c).

3. Perhaps the fourth and fifth of the types listed should be considered not leading (rather than instances when leading questions are proper) since the danger of the witness' accepting a false suggestion is not present; 3 Wigmore, *Evidence* §770 (rev. ed. Chadbourn 1970).

quently, this line of inquiry is a proper way to bring out the desired testimony, and is not regarded as leading:

Q. Did you hear the truck driver say anything?
A. Yes.
Q. When did you first hear him speak?
A. He was just getting out of the cab.
Q. What did he say?
A. He said he wondered how he would get to the warehouse and back before his boss was due to leave. [4]

Aside from the restrictions of legal and ethical rules, it may be a tactical blunder to ask a leading question. [5] In Case 14, the witness fails to give the complete answer desired, omitting the element of getting back to the warehouse before departure of his boss. In most courts, you would be permitted to lead the witness, after having unsuccessfully tried by nonleading questions to get him to repeat the full statement. Would it be good tactics for you to make use of this privilege? The question is a difficult one. The effectiveness of the testimony has been greatly reduced when it is necessary for you to lead the witness in order to get it; the jury is likely to draw the inference that the purported excited utterance is really a figment of a lawyer's imagination, planted in the witness' mind but not firmly enough for the witness to remember it. Pursuing the inquiry by leading the witness may cast a cloud of suspicion not only upon this particular statement but also upon other testimony of this witness and even upon still other evidence you offer. Whether you should take that risk will depend upon how important the evidence is to the case; for example, whether you regard it as essential, in Case 14, to obtaining findings that the truck driver was driving negligently (because he was in a hurry to get to the warehouse and back before his boss's departure) or that he was in the scope of employment (the admissibility of the excited utterance on this issue might be disputed; ordinarily scope of employment may not be shown by declarations of the servant's conclusion that he was in the scope of employment; but in this case it might be urged that the statement would be admissible to show the fact that the servant was driving to the warehouse at the time with the purpose of then returning to his boss, from which fact the inference might be drawn that he was in the scope of employment).

4. On objection that the statement is hearsay, some further evidence might be required to show that an exception applies; an obvious possibility is the exception relating to excited utterances. Another possibility, if the declarant is unavailable, is that the statement was a declaration against the interest of the declarant, on the theory that the statement implied that the driver had been hurrying. If D calls the driver as a witness, use of the statement for impeachment is another possibility. See also §2.2 n.3.
5. In addition to the discussion of the problem in this section, consider §2.23.

Use of leading questions has other tactical disadvantages. If objected to, the practice will result in repeated rulings of the court sustaining the objections and perhaps reprimanding the lawyer who is doing the questioning. Although trial lawyers generally prefer to avoid objections for fear of impressing the jury unfavorably,[6] most of them consider that objections of this character, sustained by the court, are more damaging to the interrogator than to the objector, if they have any influence on the jury either way. Certainly the practice of leading witnesses causes an unfavorable reaction from the judge. Furthermore, even if no objections are being made to the leading questions, it is dangerous to assume that the interrogation is developing favorably. The legal rule against leading questions is no more than a rule of common sense; if you want the witness' own story, instead of the lawyer's, you must depend upon the witness' memory and statement of it, and not the lawyer's. This is a common sense rule that jurors are likely to apply in their judgment of the credibility of the testimony if the practice of leading is so persistent that they notice it. Adverse counsel may frame objections so as to help them reach that conclusion.[7]

§2.19   Using hypothetical questions

CASE 15.   *P* claims permanent internal injuries from consumption of spoiled canned corn. *P* has testified (over objections with reference to want of proof of causal connection) that he suffered nausea and vomiting within five minutes after consuming the food in question, was unable to eat solid foods for two weeks, and two years later is still suffering intestinal disorders. *D* contends that an interval of several hours is required, after consumption of spoiled foods, before symptoms develop, that permanent injuries of the kind alleged by *P* do not result from consumption of spoiled food, and that the evidence therefore will not support a finding that *P*'s complaints were caused by the incident on which suit is based. *P*'s wife has been allowed to testify (over objection that the statement was hearsay, self-serving, and at best a statement of opinion) that *P* stated, an hour after he had vomited, "The corn did it; when I vomited, I could tell it was the corn." *M*, the family doctor, is a witness for the plaintiff, and as *P*'s lawyer you are depending on *M*'s opinion testimony on the issue of causation.

Should you use a hypothetical question to emphasize by repetition all the favorable evidence that you can state in the question?

The hypothetical question offers the opportunity of making a "jury speech" in the form of a summary of all the favorable evidence that you have al-

6. See §4.2.
7. See §4.3.

ready produced, recalling it to the jurors' minds and pointing up its cumulative force. The tactical advantages of the hypothetical question from this point of view and the importance of bearing this factor in mind in the framing of the hypothetical question are self-evident. There are at least two precautions that you should not overlook, however, in making such use of the hypothetical question.

Do not include in the hypothetical question evidence admitted over objection, unless it is essential to a favorable answer. Including such evidence may result in making reversible error out of what otherwise would have been harmless error. In circumstances such as those of Case 15, for example, in some jurisdictions it is necessary to offer medical opinion evidence on the question whether the symptoms of which P complained were caused by the consumption of the corn in question.[1] In submitting the hypothetical question on causation to the medical witness, M, you should (unless M tells you it is an element essential to his opinion that consumption of the corn caused the illness) omit recitation of the assumption that P stated "The corn did it; when I vomited, I could tell it was the corn." Even if a higher court should later hold that the evidence of P's declaration about the corn was improperly admitted, the court might also hold that the error was harmless (that element of P's declaration about the corn having been omitted from the hypothetical question to M). But if your only competent proof of causation — your medical opinion evidence — is stated in response to a hypothetical question that includes the assumption that P made the declaration about the corn, the likelihood of reversible error is greatly increased.

For similar reasons, unless essential to obtaining the desired answer do not include in your hypothetical question a recitation of evidence that is sharply disputed. By including such evidence, you would make the expert's testimony vulnerable to the argument that his opinion is based on a false assumption and is therefore worthless.

§2.20 Offering harmful evidence on direct

CASE 16. D Company is defending a personal injury suit based upon an intersection collision. A disinterested witness, W, was driving a truck approaching very near the intersection as the accident occurred. He was not involved in the accident, and being on business, did not wait at the scene until police arrived. He was located later by D's investigation, through an interview with W's employer, after discovery that another person had seen a truck of the type and color used by W's employer. W's version of the acci-

---

1. Cf. 7 Wigmore, Evidence §2090 n.1 (Supp. 1964), dealing primarily with requirements of expert testimony in medical malpractice cases but also treating application of the principle more broadly.

dent is very favorable to *D*. *W* advises you, as *D*'s lawyer, that he has never been interviewed by any representative of *P*. Between the date of the accident and the date of trial, *W* has served six months in prison for forgery and is now on parole.

Should you offer harmful evidence on direct examination?

Should you offer harmful evidence on direct examination to avoid the more damaging effect of its being revealed dramatically on cross-examination?[1] This is one of the most difficult questions a trial lawyer faces. No rule can be devised to answer the question, but these are some of the considerations involved. Does your adversary know of the harmful evidence, or will he probably discover it? Is it directly related to the case, or is it in the nature of a smudge on the character of the witness, the proof of which by your adversary may cause some of the jurors to sympathize with your witness because of the invasion of his privacy?[2] Is it something your adversary may overlook? As indicated by the nature of these questions, the problem is in part one of outguessing your adversary and psychoanalyzing the jury.

Case 16 illustrates the problem. Suppose that *W*'s testimony on the facts of the accident is so important to the defendant that you must use it despite whatever risk is involved. Should you prove the forgery on direct examination, and if so, before the facts of the accident or afterwards? Probably the solution in this example should be not to prove it on direct examination, in the hope that it will not be proved on cross-examination, and in the belief that because of its not being directly related to the testimony of the witness about the facts of the accident, it probably will be no more damaging if brought out on cross-examination than it would have been if introduced on direct as an apparent apology for the witness. Whether this is the correct solution is at least debatable, however, and the answer might vary depending on the particular twelve sitting in the jury box and the particular adversary in the case.

Ordinarily if the harmful evidence is directly related to the issues in the case and is a matter that in all probability your opponent will inquire about

---

1. It is assumed in the discussion of the problem in the text that, under the circumstances of this problem case and in general, there is no legal or ethical duty of disclosure of harmful evidence, as distinguished from the duty not to make affirmative misrepresentations. Compare the distinction between "misrepresentation" and "nondisclosure" in the law of deceit; Prosser, *Torts* §106 (4th ed. 1971). This is an aspect of our trial system that has led to criticisms that litigation has too many of the characteristics of a game, and a duty to disclose is being recognized in some circumstances. See H. Drinker, *Legal Ethics* 76–77 (1953). Such a duty, however, is one of disclosure to the court and opposing counsel; it does not follow that there is a duty to produce the evidence before the jury, on direct examination. The tactical problem considered in this section is still presented.

2. See §3.11.

on cross-examination, it is preferable to produce it on direct examination. It can be offered at a time and manner in the course of the examination that tends to minimize it rather than dramatizing it.[3] Although your opponent probably will make additional inquiry on cross-examination, regardless of your proving the harmful evidence, the effect is likely to be less spectacular than it would have been if the direct examination had been silent on the harmful subject. Also, there is a tactical advantage in taking the position before the jury of willingness to produce all of the facts, facing frankly any unfavorable elements.[4] And, finally, you may minimize the harmful effect of the evidence by offering immediately whatever mitigating explanation is available, rather than having the harm accentuated by a determined pursuit of the matter on cross-examination for a length of time and in ways that develop a strong impression on the minds of the jurors before the explanation can be offered.

In some instances rules of evidence may stand in the way of your using this tactic of offering harmful evidence on direct in order to minimize its impact. For example, if the only ground for admissibility of the evidence you offer is that it tends to impeach the witness by supporting an inference of bias, you may be faced with an objection that you are attempting to impeach your own witness.[5] It is not a good answer to this objection that you are only trying to beat your opponent to the punch. Instead you should, if possible, develop some independent theory of admissibility.

§2.21 Proving compensation of a witness

CASE 17. Counsel for *D* in a personal injury action has obtained an examination of *P* by *N*, a specialist in neurosurgery. For his services in examining *P*, submitting his report in writing, and appearing in court to testify concerning his findings and opinion, *N* charges *D* a fee of $600.

Should you prove on direct examination the fact of payment of expenses or fees of the witness?

Basically this case presents the question, discussed in the preceding section, whether you should offer harmful evidence on direct examination. The argument in favor of offering this evidence on direct examination is based upon reducing the effectiveness of cross-examination. The payment of expenses or fees has significance, with reference to the credibility of the witness' testimony, to the extent that it supports the inference that the witness may have

---

3. As examples, see §2.9, discussing Case 7, and §3.23, discussing Case 43.
4. See §1.3.
5. See §2.2. Note, however, that this is not a valid ground of objection in some courts; *e.g.,* Federal Rules of Evidence, Rule 607.

been influenced, consciously or subconsciously, by the payment. Unless the witness commits the error of trying to hide the fact of the payment,[1] the jury usually will not draw that inference. A moment's reflection will lead most persons, even those unfamiliar with practices of payment of expert fees and expenses, to the conclusion that it is often proper[2] and necessary to reimburse expenses incurred by the witness in coming to court and to pay compensation to an expert for the time spent in making his appearance as a witness. In Case 69, if D's lawyer has reimbursed or agreed to reimburse the lay witness for his expenses, and the amount is not large, proof of the payment probably should not be offered on direct examination. Only in instances of an exceptionally large payment (or one that would seem so to a jury) is there real danger of the unfavorable inference. In other instances, there is generally no sound reason for proving on direct examination that payment of fees or expenses has been made; there may be more danger that the jury would draw an unfavorable inference from the offer of the evidence on direct examination, because of the lawyer's being overly sensitive about what ordinarily would be regarded as a routine matter in the absence of suspicious circumstances. To the extent and degree that the payment is one that the jury will regard as being large, however, there is more reason for proving on direct examination the fact of payment and explanation for it, because of considerations discussed in the preceding section.

Case 17 presents an example of this problem. As D's lawyer, should you prove on direct examination of your witness N, the specialist in neurosurgery, that N is charging D a fee of $600 for his services in examining P, submitting a written report, and appearing in court as a witness? Competent trial lawyers disagree in their views on this subject. Probably most feel that the matter of fees should not be raised on direct examination, on the theory that one should take the position before the jury that it is foolish to assert that a man of Dr. N's favorable standing in his profession and community would allow his testimony to be influenced by the receipt of a proper fee for his services. A defendant's attorney generally prefers to avoid mention of doctors' fees, since, first, this might lead the jury to think about trial expenses in connection with their finding on amount of damages and, second, the fees customarily charged for court appearances nearly always seem high to jurors.[3] Although this very fact that the fee will seem high to jurors furnishes the basis for the argument that it should be proved on direct examination to reduce the effectiveness of cross-examination on the point, that purpose may be served by other means once the opposing lawyer has made an issue of the

1. See §§2.14, 3.27.
2. See §9.19.
3. See §3.27 for consideration of the question whether a defendant's lawyer should cross-examine the plaintiff's medical witnesses regarding their charges for appearing in court.

medical fees. In most instances, at least, the doctors testifying for the opposite party would readily agree that the fee charged was reasonable.

§2.22   Proving qualifications of an expert

CASE 18.   You represent survivors of *P,* one of whose legs was severely bruised when he was caught between a building and *D*'s car, which had been left unattended on a hill, with brakes not properly set. Three days later *P* died. It is the claim of *P*'s survivors that a blood clot, formed at the site of the leg injury, moved to the heart, and caused a "heart attack," resulting in death. By agreement, an autopsy was performed in the presence of two pathologists, one employed by *P*'s survivors and the other employed by *D.* The pathologists disagree on whether the results of the autopsy support the claim of *P*'s survivors.

To what degree should you prove qualifications of an expert?

Proof of qualifications of an expert serves two distinct purposes: (1) laying the predicate for admissibility of opinion testimony of the expert; (2) persuading the jury that the findings and opinions of the expert are accurate. Some lawyers make a practice of waiving the proof of qualifications of the adversary's expert witness, if the qualifications are outstanding, on the theory that this tactical move will prevent the jury from hearing an impressive array of evidence that the expert's findings and opinion are credible. When such a waiver is offered by your adversary, you are not necessarily bound to accept it and desist from proving the qualifications of your expert; if the qualifications are impressive, you should consider asking leave of court to offer the proof so that the jury may know of the extraordinary ability and standing of the witness in his field. Ordinarily it is in the discretion of the court to grant or refuse the leave. Even if leave is refused, you have available a jury argument that although the details of the witness' qualifications have not been disclosed in the evidence, the witness is so outstanding that even the opposing lawyer admits his qualifications. Because of the availability of this argument, most lawyers decline to follow the practice of admitting qualifications of the adversary's expert witness.

Aside from the problem presented when opposing counsel offers to waive proof of qualifications of your expert, the question of the extent to which you should prove those qualifications is primarily a matter of giving to the proof the amount of time and attention that will result in the most favorable impression on the jury. Laboring over insignificant details will bore the jury and perhaps lead them to the impression that you are trying to build up the witness beyond what the facts justify. There is also a possible advantage in omitting some of the details so the witness may have something further to offer in the event your adversary chooses to cross-examine regarding his qualifications.[1] On the other hand, proof of the bare essentials necessary to make the testimony admissible fails entirely to serve the second aim of persuading the jury that the witness is competent and his testimony accurate. In most cases in which you have an expert witness, your adversary will have one also and the jury must decide which one is right. Although the content of their testimony and their methods of expression[2] will have more influence on the jury's choice between them, their respective qualifications are also likely to have weight. Accordingly, in Case 18, you should not be content with proving only the bare essential that your expert is a pathologist; to that evidence you might add proof of his professional education, particularly his postgraduate study, his writing of books or articles published in professional journals, his membership and offices in professional societies, his specialization and experience in the field of pathology, and his past practical experience directly qualifying him for solving any unusual problem presented by the case. If his past practical experience has arisen primarily in connection with other litigation, probably you should not regard it as favorable evidence; the jury may infer that he is a professional witness whose testimony can be bought for a fee, or that he is biased in favor of one group, which group includes the party calling him; under these circumstances, the question whether you should offer or instead should omit evidence of this practical experience of the witness is an instance of the question whether you should offer unfavorable evidence during direct examination.[3]

§2.23 Offering evidence of doubtful admissibility

CASE 13. *P* is suing for injuries sustained in a collision between his car and *D*'s truck. *P*'s car, after the impact with *D*'s truck, veered into *W*'s car. *P*'s lawyer, in interviewing *W*, learns that *D* paid *W* $75 for a release and that *W* tells a version of the facts favorable to *D*. *P*'s lawyer anticipates that *D* will call *W* as a witness in the trial and wants to be prepared to prove the payment of $75 by *D* to *W*, though the possibility of an objection on the ground that it was paid in compromise of a disputed claim is apparent.

Should you purposely offer evidence of doubtful admissibility?

In some exceptional instances, asking questions that are clearly improper and prejudicial is regarded as misconduct of counsel sufficient to warrant a mistrial or new trial.[1] There is a widespread attitude that it is fair practice to offer objectionable evidence so long as there is no violation of

1. See §3.30.
2. See §2.15.
3. See §§2.20, 2.21.
1. As to tactical implications of motions for mistrial, see §5.4.

these comparatively innocuous rules against misconduct of counsel. Some lawyers frankly state, and still more endorse by practice, the ethically indefensible proposition that this kind of improper question should be asked unless it is of such prejudicial character that the refusal of the trial court to declare a mistrial would be reversible error. This practice is sometimes used for the very purpose of confronting adverse counsel with the difficult choice of waiving objection by failing to make it, or else make an objection that may lead the jury to conclude that he is attempting to withhold information from them.[2] An advocate of this practice may seek to justify it on the basis that the exclusionary rule of evidence applying to the case is archaic, that the jury should have the benefit of the evidence, and that opposing counsel ought to have to pay the price of taking advantage of some technical rule of evidence. Another argument often advanced is that since the right to exclude evidence may be waived by failure to object, it is not improper to make the offer and hope that objection will be waived. Both of these arguments, and the practice of deliberate use of improper questions, seem clearly inconsistent with the Code of Professional Responsibility.[3]

Protection against the deliberate use of clearly improper questions is inadequate under existing rules of law, unless the trial judge uses his discretionary powers to deal with the practice sternly. Even aside from standards of professional responsibility, however, some limitations exist as to the advisability of asking objectionable questions, because of tactical considerations. The jury may recognize the unfairness of the tactic, especially after the court has sustained an objection to the question,[4] and may be influenced against the lawyer using the tactic. The jury's recognition of the unfairness might even occur without objection to the evidence, as in the case of a practice of continually leading the witness.[5]

If admissibility is subject to reasonable doubt, under standards of professional responsibility it is proper to ask the question if you actually wish to insist on admission of the evidence, since it is your right and duty to present the best case for your client that the facts and rules of law will support. Al-

---

2. See §4.2.

3. American Bar Association, Code of Professional Responsibility DR 7–106 (C) (1969):

"In appearing in his professional capacity before a tribunal, a lawyer shall not:

". . . (7) Intentionally or habitually violate any established rule of procedure or of evidence."

See also *id.,* EC 7–25: ". . . Thus while a lawyer may take steps in good faith and within the framework of the law to test the validity of rules, he is not justified in consciously violating such rules and he should be diligent in his effort to guard against his unintentional violation of them. . . ."

4. See §4.2.

5. See §2.18.

though it might be argued that you should first present the evidence to the court in the absence of the jury, for its admissibility to be determined, this attitude is rarely taken except when the other attorney has presented an objection to the court in advance of the offer.[6] On tactical considerations, ordinarily you should avoid offering evidence of doubtful admissibility when you represent a party (normally the plaintiff) who desires speedy termination of the case and has jury sympathy on his side, unless in your judgment the evidence is actually important to persuading the jury. This is true for the reason that the admission of the evidence over objection may result in the granting of a new trial, if either the trial or appellate court later concludes that the admission was harmful error. Might you ask the question with the purpose of not insisting upon admission of the evidence over objection? It seems best to avoid this practice, even apart from the question whether it violates standards of professional responsibility. It may be difficult to withdraw the question after it is asked. If the judge promptly overrules the objection when made and you then try to get the judge to withdraw the evidence by an instruction to the jury to disregard it, you will find it difficult to maintain even the appearance of good faith in making the offer.

If you believe that the evidence of doubtful admissibility is likely to have a strong influence on the findings of the jury in the case, you may conclude that the chance of reversal is worth taking; the decision is based upon weighing the probable value of the evidence to you in its influence on the jury against the disadvantage of possible reversal of a favorable verdict and judgment. The evidence of payment of $75 to W by D, in Case 13, presents an illustration of this problem. If admissibility of this evidence is doubtful in the jurisdiction of trial, even on the alternative theory,[7] then as P's attorney you probably should offer the evidence unless you have a very strong case without it and a client whose circumstances make it important to have a prompt termination of the litigation (and to avoid the possibility of new trial because of a decision that receipt of the evidence was harmful error).

§2.24 Proving oral statements

CASE 19. P is asserting a claim for personal injuries suffered in an intersection collision between P's car and D's truck. As P's lawyer, you wish to use the testimony of W, who had been standing on the sidewalk near the scene of the collision. Among other pertinent matters, W states that he was the first person to reach D's truck driver after the impact, and the truck driver's first words were "Where did that car come from? I didn't see it till it was right in front of me."

6. See §4.16.
7. See §2.17.

How should you prove an oral statement or conversation?

Proving an oral statement or conversation involves these separate steps:

(1) Proving that a statement was made. This is to be distinguished from testimony as to the substance of the statement.

(2) Identifying the speaker. In the usual case, no special problem is involved in proving identity of the speaker; either the witness was the speaker himself, or he knew the speaker and was present at the time of the conversation. If the conversation was by telephone, you may show identity in most jurisdictions by proving that the witness recognized the voice of the speaker.[1] If the witness did not know the speaker at the time of the conversation, you may show identity of the speaker by proving that the witness later learned the identity of the person and recognized him by appearance or by voice as being the speaker on the previous occasion. A statement of identification of the voice on the other end of a telephone line is sometimes held inadmissible because of the possibility of impersonation and lack of trustworthiness of the authentication; it may be possible to overcome this objection with evidence of other circumstances corroborating the identification by voice.

(3) Identifying a person or persons hearing the statement. If you are offering a statement against the speaker, the witness is the person hearing it and no further identification of others is required, though it may be permitted. If the statement is not that of the person against whom you are offering it, then it is sometimes necessary to prove that it was heard by the one against whom you are offering it, or by someone acting for him. In other instances, such as excited utterances, proof of the identity of the person or persons present, other than the speaker and the witness, is not required but is permitted.[2]

(4) Establishing the time, place, and circumstances. Frequently, establishing these factors will be essential to determining admissibility of the statement. Even if that is not true in the particular case, these factors may be essential to a full appreciation of the significance of the statement.

(5) Calling upon the witness to repeat the statement, or the substance of it.

To the extent that the second, third, and fourth steps are requirements for admissibility of the statement, an objection would force you to establish them before asking the witness to repeat the statement. Whether or not an objec-

1. 7 Wigmore, *Evidence* §2155 (3d ed. 1940); Federal Rules of Evidence, Rule 901(b)(5).

2. Occasionally confusion arises with respect to whether there is a need for foundation evidence that an out-of-court statement was made in the presence of the party against whom it is offered. Much of this confusion could be avoided by adequate proof analysis. The analysis should identify explicitly each particular exception to the hearsay rule upon which the proponent relies, and it should indicate the nature of the foundation required for admissibility under each hearsay exception. Concerning proof analysis generally, see §1.5. For an illustration, see §2.17.

tion is anticipated, however, it is better practice to establish these factors before offering the statement. This procedure has the effect of emphasizing the statement. The jurors' interest increases as you recreate the setting for the statement.

The order in which the first four steps in this process are stated is not a required order. For example, the fourth item (the time, place, and circumstances) may have been established first in connection with other testimony, as in the case of a witness to an accident who is being asked about an excited utterance. If there is any doubt as to whether the jury will connect the earlier evidence with the statement, however, it should be repeated just before the statement is offered. Jurors, as well as judges, are likely to consider that a statement made in the excitement of the moments immediately after the accident has a special guarantee of trustworthiness; reminding them of the time and circumstances is a part of the psychological preparation for presenting the statement itself.

The questions and answers appearing in another section [3] illustrate proof of a threat (in Case 26) made by *D* toward *P*. As an example of evidence of an excited utterance, in Case 19, the proof may appropriately proceed as follows:

Q. (Identity of the witness having already been established, and other testimony having been given by him concerning his observations at the scene of the accident) Did you see the vehicles at the moment they hit?

A. No, I heard the noise and looked around just after they hit.

Q. What did you see when you looked around?

A. The car was swinging around sideways toward a telephone pole, and the truck was still running almost straight ahead, just a little to the right.

Q. (After further questions clarifying the movement of the vehicles before they came to rest) Which vehicle was nearer to you as they stopped?

A. The truck.

Q. What happened just after it stopped?

A. I ran over to the truck to see if the driver was hurt. He was beginning to move around when I got there.

Q. What position was he in when you first saw him, before he began to move?

A. He was leaning over the steering wheel at first.

Q. How did he begin to move?

A. He pushed back from the wheel, and said something I couldn't understand because he was gasping a little, like a fellow does when he has had the breath knocked out of him.

Q. What happened just after that?

A. I told him to take it easy, and he sat there for about a minute until he got his breath, so he could talk.

---

3. See §2.31.

Q. Did he speak again when he got his breath?

A. Yes, he did.

Q. Was anybody else close enough to hear him besides yourself?

A. Some other fellows were beginning to gather around the place, but I don't believe anyone of them was close enough to hear the truck driver.

Q. Were you able to understand clearly what he said?

A. Yes, I could.

Q. What did he say? [4]

A. He said to me, "Where did that car come from? I didn't see it till it was right in front of me."

§2.25 Offering documentary evidence

CASE 20. *P* is suing on an account for materials and is faced with a defense that all of the materials covered by the account were defective. *P* delivers to his lawyer a letter received from *D*, in response to a second bill marked "overdue," in which letter *D* stated:

We have your bill in the amount of $1476. The last item (number 4) in the amount of $450, is for materials that were defective and had to be replaced after installation, as we have previously advised you. We will forward payment in the amount of $1026 if you will agree to cancel your charge for item 4 and give us an acknowledgment of payment in full of our account with you.

The introduction of a document involves these separate steps: (1) having it marked by the reporter for identification; (2) authenticating the document by the testimony of the witness (unless it has a certificate or other authenticating characteristics); (3) offering the document in evidence; (4) permitting adverse counsel to examine the document; (5) adverse counsel's objecting, if he so chooses; (6) submitting the document to the court for examination if the court so desires; (7) the court's ruling on its admission; and (8) if it is admitted in evidence, presenting it to the jury by reading, passing it among them, or other means.[1]

---

4. If adverse counsel chooses to object, the objection should be stated at this point. An objection to earlier questions would ordinarily be overruled (subject to the possibility of striking the evidence later) on the ground that they relate to the predicate and must be allowed as a means of determining admissibility of the statement itself. If adverse counsel objects to the generality of the question "What did he say?", then a leading question would be permissible, such as "Did he say anything about why he didn't avoid the accident?" Adverse counsel, if suspecting that the statement will probably be inadmissible because of its substance rather than the circumstances under which it was made, may move the court to receive the evidence out of the hearing of the jury and determine its admissibility before permitting the jury to hear it; see §4.9. The trial judge generally has discretion to grant or deny this motion.

1. See §§2.26, 2.27.

The order in which the steps are listed in the preceding paragraph is a preferred order but not the only order that is satisfactory. To avoid confusion at the time and uncertainty later as to whether you have offered a document in evidence, you should develop a customary method that you routinely follow unless you have a special reason for departing from it. The mistake most often made is the failure to offer the document in evidence after it has been identified and authenticated; another mistake frequently made is offering the document in evidence prematurely, before the predicate has been laid for its being received in evidence. The latter error merely results in delay and perhaps some confusion. The former error is the more serious, because you may find that your record is entirely lacking in essential evidence that you thought had been supplied by the document.

With reference to the marks used to identify the exhibit, the reporter customarily is willing to determine what numeral, letter, or combination will be used, and sometimes insists upon doing so. Most lawyers follow the practice of handing the instrument to the reporter "to be marked for identification," without designating what marking will be placed on it. For your own reference, however, you should keep a record of the exhibits that have been identified, noting also whether they have been received in evidence.

By advance preparation you may avoid some of these steps and the delay occasioned by pursuing them. For example, you may supply the authenticating facts by offering in evidence a stipulation arranged with adverse counsel in advance of the trial, or by offering in evidence admissions obtained by your formal requests. If a trial is to involve voluminous correspondence, it probably will be desirable to prepare a stipulation in advance to the following effect:

The instruments attached hereto as exhibits A-X are true copies of original letters, each of which was sent by the person whose name appears in the signature space and was received by the person shown as the addressee; each such exhibit may be offered in evidence during the trial of this case as if it were the authenticated original, any objection for want of authentication or want of production of the original being waived. No stipulation is made as to the admissibility of all or any part of any exhibit over objection on any other ground.

Some trial judges require that all documents the lawyers intend to offer be produced in advance in this manner so as to eliminate delays in proof of authenticating facts. Whether it is required or not, it is usually a desirable practice in the absence of some special consideration such as the fear that disclosure of the document in advance of trial may result in dishonest manipulation of testimony by the adverse party to meet what otherwise would have been presented to him as a surprise at the time of trial.[2]

2. See §1.3.

It you are offering a number of documents or other exhibits in succession, you may save time by having the reporter mark all of them for identification at one time. Also, you may have all of them authenticated by appropriate testimony relating to the group, if that is possible. For example, you may follow this practice when you are introducing a set of X-rays.

The comments in the two preceding paragraphs generally apply also to voluminous business records, except that your adversary less often knows the contents of such records and more often you will choose not to take the initiative in producing them for a stipulation as to authenticating facts in advance of the trial. It is good practice, however, to have copies available to substitute by agreement or upon motion to the court after the originals have been produced, so that the originals may be returned to their regular place of custody. Practical difficulties are involved in getting copies made after the originals are in court.

The following is an illustration of a satisfactory manner of introducing the letter in Case 20, no pretrial stipulation or admission of authenticating facts having been obtained:

Q. Mr. Reporter, will you please mark this instrument for identification (whereupon it is marked Exhibit P-7 by the reporter). Mr. W, I hand you an instrument marked for identification Exhibit P-7; do you recognize this instrument?

A. I do.

Q. Please state the circumstances under which you first saw this instrument.

A. It came to me in the regular mail at my office, in the early part of February of this year.

Q. Do you know who sent it to you?

A. Yes.

Q. How do you know?

A. I recognize the signature. Also, he referred to this letter when he talked with me a few days after I received it.

Q. Who was the person who sent you this letter?

A. It was John J. Jones.

Q. Is that the John J. Jones who is the defendant in this case?

A. Yes, it is.

P's Lawyer: Your Honor, for the limited purpose [3] of impeaching *D*'s claim that all materials involved in this account were defective, and as an admission that $1026 is due on items 1, 2, and 3 of the account, we offer in evidence the instrument that the reporter has marked for identification as Exhibit P-7. Does defense counsel wish to see the instrument?

---

3. The limitation of the offer is suggested for the purpose of avoiding the claim that by offering the letter generally, *P* would be adopting not only the implied admission that items 1, 2, and 3 were due in full but also the express statement in the letter that the materials on which item 4 was based were defective. See §2.36.

D's Lawyer: Please. (After examining the instrument) Your Honor, defendant objects on the ground that this letter was an offer of compromise of a disputed account. [4]

Court: (After examining the instrument) Objection overruled; the instrument marked P-7 is received in evidence.

D's Lawyer: To which ruling defendant excepts. [5]

(Some court reporters follow the practice of placing an additional marking on the exhibit at this point to indicate that it has been received in evidence.)

Q. Mr. *W*, I hand you the instrument marked P-7 and ask that you read it to the jury. [6]

§2.26   Referring to documents and their contents

Case 21.   *P*, having a one-family summer lodge for sale, advertises it in a pamphlet printed and distributed by a privately operated association engaged in promoting the area as a desirable place for vacation trips and summer homes. *D* writes a letter to *P* expressing interest in his lodge and asking for information. *P* replies, enclosing with his letter some snapshots, answering specific questions posed by *D*, and stating terms under which he would sell to *D*. *D* accepts *P*'s proposition by mail. Shortly thereafter, when *P* meets *D* at the lodge preparatory to closing the transaction, they get involved in a dispute both as to terms of the agreement made between them by correspondence and, also as to whether *P* made misrepresentations about the lodge in his advertisement and letter. *D* declines to go through with the transaction, and *P* sues for specific performance. The advertisement and both of the letters are attached to a pretrial stipulation stating that they may be introduced in evidence without further authentication, that each letter was sent and received by the persons indicated on the face thereof as writer and addressee respectively, and that the advertisement was authorized by *P*.

Should you, while examining a witness, refer to a given document for any purpose other than to authenticate it for admission in evidence?

Should you ask questions concerning contents of the document?

The impression you make with a document is greater as you refer to it more often in the interrogation of witnesses. Similarly, you are more likely to achieve the purpose for which you are using the document if you use it

4. *D*'s lawyer, anticipating that *P*'s lawyer would offer this letter in evidence, might choose to make this objection by a motion in limine, out of the hearing of the jury, if that practice is permissible in the jurisdiction of trial (§4.16); if not having done this, *D*'s lawyer might also consider making the objection outside the hearing of the jury, immediately after *P*'s offer (§4.10).

5. On the necessity for and advisability of stating an exception, see §4.12.

6. As alternatives, the lawyer may read the document to the jury or have it passed among them to be read; also see §§2.26, 2.27.

during your interrogation of witnesses rather than relying entirely upon your argument to the jury or judge and their study of the document. In a situation such as Case 21, it is probable that there will be some disputed issues that the courts will decide (matters of interpretation of the agreement and determination of legal rules as to what amounts to actionable misrepresentation) and other issues that will be submitted to the jury as questions of fact (whether the lodge was different from what it was represented to be in certain respects that would be material under the legal rules). The argument on law points may be renewed and developed in the trial court after verdict or even in the appellate courts, upon fully considered briefs. References during examination of witnesses are therefore relatively less significant as to law points than as to their effect upon deliberations of the jury before whom time for argument is more limited and whose time for deliberation after argument is more limited. The judge has the document available for deliberate study long after the testimony in the case is completed; jurors have it for only a short period of deliberation, during which it is more likely that they will discuss impressions gained during the presentation of evidence and arguments than that each will work from a study of the document itself. In Case 21, the significance of evidence of the state of repair of the lodge, for example, is more apparent if the representations as to that matter, appearing in the advertisement and in D's letter, are placed before the jury just before or just after the evidence as to state of repair, rather than being referred to only when the entire documents are offered and again in the course of argument to the jury. There are, however, some limitations on the manner and extent to which references may be made to the contents of documents.

A trial judge may permit the interruption of examination of a witness so that the lawyer may read excerpts from a document for the specific purpose of facilitating the jury's comparison of the document and other testimony (when the jury will be called upon to make such a comparison). Yet in practice this direct method is less frequently used than the indirect method of accomplishing this result by references within the framework of questions to the witness. Doubtlessly this is at least partially accounted for by a belief that there is less risk that an objection will be made and sustained if the latter method is used, particularly if the questions are carefully phrased. Even when the latter method is used, objections are sometimes made and sustained — usual grounds of objection being that the question is leading and suggestive or (when a comparison by the witness is invited) that it calls for an opinion or conclusion. If the questions are carefully phrased to be as inoffensive as possible in these respects, trial judges often, as a discretionary matter, permit questions that refer to the contents of documents already in evidence and thereby invite the jury to consider specific parts of the document in connection with the testimony then being given by the witness. When the trial judge will permit it, the use of such questions is tactically advantageous. They help the jury understand why you are offering particular evidence and why you claim it to be important.

A question that calls upon the witness to state the contents of a document or to interpret it, with reference to a given matter, is usually subject to sound objection upon the ground that the document is the best evidence, or that it "speaks for itself" [1] and the answer to the question would violate the parol evidence rule, or that the question calls for a conclusion of the witness. If your adversary asks such a question, it usually is tactically advisable to make an objection because of the grave risk that the witness' comments about the document will be slanted in favor of the party whose lawyer dares ask him the question. You may expect, conversely, that usually when you ask such a question an objection will be made and sustained; it is therefore doubtful that you should ask it. [2] The risk of harm from the mere fact of having your questions determined to be improper is a relatively minor consideration, however, unless your attempt to use improper questions is persistent and supports the inference that you are deliberately using unfair methods.

The prohibitions against summarizing contents of documents, or stating extracts that at least impliedly amount to interpretation, are not absolute; for example, the interests in expediting litigation lead to relaxation of these prohibitions with respect to lengthy documents. An important function of referring to a document in the interrogation of witnesses is giving emphasis to the more important parts of a document that is so long that the jury will not be likely to realize entirely its significance without having their attention focused in some manner. [3] Examination of an adverse witness is another instance in which you generally are allowed great freedom in referring to the contents of a document that is in evidence; frequently, effective cross-examination is based upon use of documents that the witness has previously prepared or approved.

A question that assumes certain content in a document not in evidence is subject to objection on the ground that it assumes matter not in evidence and is leading and suggestive to a friendly witness or misleading to an adverse witness. [4] Whether it is advisable for you to make this objection will depend upon such factors as whether the contents of the document as a whole are of the nature that it is to your advantage to force your adversary — before proceeding with the line of interrogation attempted — to introduce the document (or else to introduce a part of it, so you may make capital of introducing the balance to "bring all of the facts before the jury").

To avoid the effect of sustained objections to your interrogation, and to

---

1. But *cf.* 9 Wigmore, *Evidence* §2470 (3d ed. 1940). See also Federal Rules of Evidence, Rules 701, 1002, 1004, 1006, 1007.
2. See §2.23.
3. See §2.27.
4. 3 Wigmore, *Evidence* §§771, 780 (rev. ed. Chadbourn 1970).

avoid uncertainty in your own mind and an appearance of confusion while the trial is in progress, plan the presentation of your evidence,[5] determine in advance how much of the document to offer, and make the offer before submitting any questions dependent upon the content of the document.

Sometimes the principal function of a document in the development of the case is its usefulness in questioning witnesses. For example, a scale map or aerial photograph of the scene of an accident may be most useful as a means by which the witness may show the jury where he was located, the movement of vehicles that he observed, and other factors relevant to the cause and nature of the accident. The witness may be asked to make notations or drawings or to place markers upon the exhibit so that a diagram of his version of the accident becomes a part of the exhibit and may go with the jury to the jury room for their deliberations.[6]

Whenever you refer to a document during an interrogation, identify it by the exhibit number, so that a person reading the record at a later time will not be left in doubt.

§2.27 Emphasizing parts of lengthy documents

Case 22. P, a construction contractor, sues D (referred to as "owner" in the contract documents), for whom he was building an apartment building. Part of the contract price was paid to P in installments as the work progressed, and P is suing for the balance of the contract price, plus certain extras. D asserts that specified items of the work were not performed in accordance with the provisions of the contract and that the extras are not due because they represent variations from the contract not approved in conformity with the procedure established by the contract documents. The contract documents consist of a comparatively short "contract," which incorporates by reference certain identified "plans" (consisting of fifty blueprint sheets) and "specifications" (a 150-page document). Among the disputed issues in the case are questions whether, certain materials contemplated by the parties being unavailable except at excessive and unforeseen cost, a substitution was permissible and, if so, whether the substituted materials met the standards required by the contract. Each party claims that some specific notations on certain pages of the plans and specific provisions in the specifications, different from those relied upon by the other party, support his position.

By what means may you emphasize important parts of a lengthy document?

When a lengthy document is involved in presenting a case, as in Case 22, there is a need for emphasizing those portions of the document that are

5. See §2.9.
6. See §2.34.

especially important. Several methods are available for achieving this emphasis:

(1) Introduce in evidence only the important portions of the document. A disadvantage of this method is that the jury will not be permitted, over objection, to examine the document itself or carry it to the jury room, except in the unusual case in which satisfactory provisions may be made for obscuring the balance of the document that is not in evidence. Another disadvantage is the risk that in selecting the parts to be introduced you may overlook some parts that later you would like to rely upon to meet some unanticipated argument of your adversary or to support some newly discovered basis for upholding your client's interests.

(2) Introduce the entire document, but read aloud, immediately after the introduction, only those portions that you wish to emphasize. This method has the advantage of making the entire document available for inspection, so that the entire instrument may be taken to the jury room in jurisdictions where jurors are allowed to take exhibits with them. It is subject to objection by your adversary (on grounds that your reading only extracted portions of the document amounts to interpretive comment by you on the evidence and infringes the principle of completeness), [1] but in most instances the court will allow this method because of the saving of time over the procedure of reading aloud the entire document or allowing the jury to read it. You may increase the likelihood of such a ruling by suggesting that you will not object to adverse counsel's reading other parts of the document after you have read the parts to which you wish to call attention.

(3) Use excerpts from the document as the foundation for questions. [2] You may employ this technique in conjunction with either the first or the second of the above methods of placing the document or a part of it in evidence. The major restriction on this technique is the necessity for avoiding unreasonable repetition and leading and suggestive questions. When the document is a very lengthy one, however, this method is appropriate for presenting with reasonable clarity evidence bearing on complicated issues, and it will usually be allowed by the court as a discretionary matter.

§2.28 Offering secondary evidence

CASE 23. You represent *P Retail Company* in an action against *D Manufacturing Company* for breach of contract by refusal to deliver an order of machinery. *P Retail Company* asserts that the contract was formed by oral

---

1. See 7 Wigmore, *Evidence* §2102 (3d ed. 1940). See also Federal Rules of Evidence, Rule 107.
2. See §2.26.

acceptance by *S*, sales manager of *D Manufacturing Company,* of an order in the form of a letter to *D Manufacturing Company* from *P Retail Company,* signed by Richard R. Roe, Purchasing Agent. *S* admits receiving a letter about such machinery, but he says that he did not agree to fill the order and that the letter was destroyed after ninety days, in accordance with their custom as to orders not accepted. *C*, a clerk for *P Retail Company,* has an unsigned carbon copy of the letter.

How should you introduce secondary evidence?

Proof of secondary evidence involves these steps:

(1) Offering a description of the original (the type and nature of the instrument) — for example, in Case 23, that it is a letter of a specified date addressed to *D Manufacturing Company,* written on the letterhead of *P Retail Company,* and signed *"P Retail Company,* by Richard R. Roe, Purchasing Agent."

(2) Accounting for the original. You may do this by calling as witnesses the person or persons in whose custody the original should ordinarily be found, and proving by their testimony that it has been destroyed, is beyond the jurisdiction, or has been lost. If the adverse party is the custodian of the original, as is often the case with reference to correspondence, service of a notice to produce it, or its equivalent, may be required.[1] You should consider this requirement in planning your case, since it may be necessary that you serve this notice in advance of trial. Frequently, however, counsel is permitted to interrupt the interrogation to request that the original of the designated document be produced. If you follow this method and objection is made and sustained on grounds other than that the document offered is secondary evidence, you should try to get a stipulation that want of reasonable notice is not being asserted.[2]

(3) Authenticating the copy that you are offering as secondary evidence, or else laying the foundation for any other method you plan to use to show the contents of the original. If you are using a copy, you should produce one or more witnesses to show the circumstances under which the copy was made and custody of it from that time to the time of trial. If you are offering oral testimony as to the content of the original instrument, you may find it necessary to account for the lack of any copy of the original instrument, thus showing that the memory of the witness is the "best evidence" available.[3] Also it is necessary that the witness testify that he remembers substantially the contents of the original, at least as to the points on which he testifies.

---

1. See §11.14.
2. See §4.12.
3. 4 Wigmore, *Evidence* §1264–1275 (3d ed. 1940). See also Federal Rules of Evidence, Rules 1002–1004.

(4) Offering the testimony of the witness as to contents, or proceeding to introduce the copy[4] if you have a copy to offer in evidence.

§2.29   Using an interpreter

CASE 24.   Representing *D*, you are defending a claim for personal injuries arising from a collision between *P*'s car and *D*'s truck, driven by *W*, who was accompanied by a helper, *X*. *W* and *X* are Mexican citizens, who have lived in this country for a short period in a neighborhood where Spanish is customarily spoken, but both have worked at jobs where they talk with foremen in English. When asked whether they speak and understand English, both answer affirmatively. Their speech in English is cryptic and broken. In Spanish they speak fluently.

When and how should you use an interpreter?

The question whether you should use an interpreter is readily answered only if the witness speaks no English or if he speaks English relatively well — not in the sense of being grammatically correct, but in the sense of conveying his meaning accurately. The choice is difficult if the witness speaks broken English and his native language well.

The factors favoring use of an interpreter include these:

(1) The questions submitted to the witness on cross-examination, if not those on direct, may require more precise understanding than is true of the ordinary conversations of daily life. A shade of meaning may be important. Even though the witness speaks and understands English well enough to convey his meaning during a direct examination that you have planned and for which you have specifically prepared him, there is serious danger of confusion on cross-examination. If confusion occurs, the jurors are less likely to believe the witness dishonest than in the ordinary situation, but harm remains because of a lack of confidence in the witness' understanding of the questions and answers on direct examination, when he shows such a lack of understanding on cross-examination.

(2) A witness who speaks broken English is likely to make serious mistakes because of the difference of idioms between English and his native language.

(3) Though you may specifically prepare the witness to tell his story acceptably on direct examination, you cannot anticipate the cross-examination to the degree necessary to prepare him for the specific questions asked. The better you prepare him for the direct examination, the more marked will be the contrast between his response to the questions on direct and those on

---

4. By the steps outlined in §2.25.

cross; the contrast may cause the jury to doubt the reliability of the direct testimony.

(4) A witness of this type is usually anxious to understand English and inclined to act as if he does even when in doubt. Generally you cannot depend upon him to ask for repetition of a question that he does not understand.

Factors against using an interpreter include these: (1) Proceeding with an interpreter is a slow process at best. (2) A person experienced in interpreting for court testimony is needed; the resulting interrogation is most unsatisfactory if the interpreter does not adhere strictly to verbatim repetition of both question and answer. Impartiality and integrity are obvious requirements.[1] (3) If the witness speaks some English, the jury may be suspicious of the alleged need for an interpreter. The fact that a witness who understands English partially will have time to consider his answer, while the question is being repeated to him in his own language, may be regarded by some as an advantage to using an interpreter. It is listed here as a disadvantage for the reason that it is loaded with danger. The witness must have great presence of mind to avoid inadvertently answering directly to a question in English before the interpreter translates it, when the answer is on the tip of his tongue, and to avoid "correcting" the interpreter when the translation does not entirely satisfy the witness. Of course, such an interruption of the routine by the witness who purportedly does not understand English is calculated to have a dramatic effect upon the jury. If you decide to use an interpreter with a witness who speaks English to some extent, as in Case 24, do not play down his English-speaking ability. Instead, bring out the extent of his familiarity with English during your direct examination, with the explanation that he can get along in his work speaking English with his foreman, and in stores, and other similar contacts but that English is not used in his home or among his close friends and he does not understand it well.

If you use an interpreter, frame your question in exactly the same form you would use if interrogating the witness directly in English. "Ask him where he works" is the wrong form. "Where do you work?" is proper. The interpreter then translates the precise question to the witness, and translates exactly the answer of the witness. "He says he works at the cotton mill" is the wrong form. "At the cotton mill," is proper. If the witness does not understand the question and asks the interpreter to explain, it is not the function of the interpreter to do so. Instead, the interpreter is required to repeat exactly the translation of the witness' question — for example, instead

1. The interpreter takes an oath, in effect, that "I will truly and correctly translate the question from English to Spanish (or whatever the language may be) and the answers of the witness from Spanish to English, so help me God." See, *e.g.,* Federal Rules of Evidence, Rule 604.

of answering the witness' question according to the interpreter's understanding of the lawyer's question, the interpreter says in English, "Do you
mean now, or when the accident happened." The classic illustration of the
unreliability of the testimony if this practice of verbatim repetition is not
followed is the case in which, after a long exchange between the witness and
interpreter, the interpreter turns and says in English, "He says 'no.'"

§2.30 Reacting obviously to testimony

CASE 25. Representing *D Electric Company*, you are defending a claim
by *P*, the back of whose head touched a wire allegedly hanging low across
an alley and obscured by trees, as *P* was riding on top of a house to clear
tree branches as the house was being moved. *W*, who lives in a house adjacent to the alley at the point where the accident occurred, is called to the
stand by *P*'s lawyer, and testifies that he noticed the dangerous situation of
the wire in the trees about a week before the accident. With the expectation
that he will answer that he called the *D Electric Company* about it, *P*'s lawyer asks *W* whether he told anyone about that condition; *W* replies, "Yes, I
told these movers the day before the accident." On the next question, he tells
of a call to *D Electric Company* a week earlier, when he asked them to correct the condition because he was afraid some neighborhood boys would be
injured while climbing in the trees.

Should you react obviously to the testimony as it is given?

If you happen to be adept in dramatics, you may contribute to the effectiveness of the witness' story by your properly timed reactions to the favorable and crucial evidence, and perhaps even by antics designed to distract the
jurors' attention from unfavorable evidence or a weak witness. This type of
planned conduct, though generally not questioned on ethical grounds, is likely
to provoke an unfavorable reaction from many trial judges. Even in the absence of such a reaction, the best general rule for most lawyers is to maintain
a "poker face," during both favorable and unfavorable evidence. If you react obviously to the favorable testimony, the attention of the jury will be
drawn to your reaction, and they naturally will turn again to see how you
are taking it when something not so favorable is developed. In Case 25, if
you smile to the jury at the expense of your adversary when *W* gives the unexpected answer that he told the movers about the dangerous condition, the
jury will naturally look for your reaction when *W* next says that he told
your client about the danger a week earlier. Unless you are fully prepared
to meet that situation, it is better to keep the jury's attention focused on the
witness. Even if you are able to control your reactions to unfavorable evidence and are willing to have the jury's attention directed toward you, the
impression you create in the minds of the jurors is more likely to be that

you are a great lawyer than that you have a great case. The goal is a verdict for your client rather than recognition for yourself.[1]

Some circumstances will call for a departure from the rule against reacting openly to testimony given by a witness. For example, if a witness testifies contrary to what he had stated in conference with you, and it becomes advisable to impeach your own witness, your concealment of your indignation might be mistaken for lack of surprise. Also, if a witness is hostile to your client, there is no occasion for your hiding that hostility. The more apparent that hostility of the witness, the more readily does the jury accept any testimony from him that is favorable to your client. But it is the hostility of the witness, not your own, that you should exhibit; the jury may consider that your hostility arises merely from the fact that the witness opposes your case. If you display hostility yourself, do it only for the purpose and with the reasonable assurance that it will provoke a more evident hostility from the witness, and preferably not so much a hostility toward you personally as toward your client.

§2.31 Using gestures

CASE 26. *P* is asserting a claim for personal injuries suffered when *D* committed an assault upon him. *W*, a witness for *P*, observed the incident on which suit is based. As *P*'s lawyer you are using the testimony of *W* to prove the menacing gestures of *D*, the accompanying threats, and the fact that *D* was close enough to carry out his threats immediately.

Should you permit or encourage your witness to use gestures to convey his meaning?

For the purpose of presenting the witness' story in such a manner that the jury will understand, believe, and remember it,[1] gestures are often far more effective than word descriptions. The witness will probably be better able to express his meaning accurately, and in a way that avoids conflict and confusion as the result of cross-examination, by "showing" the jury instead of "telling" them. The jury will be better able to understand his meaning when he conveys it by a demonstration that they see than when they must depend upon interpreting the words that the witness used. The witness may indicate physical movements by his demonstration in the courtroom. He may indicate estimates of distance by comparison with the distances between objects in the courtroom, or between an object in the courtroom and an object that can be seen through a window in the case of longer distances. You may elicit estimates of short periods of time by holding a watch with a second

---

1. *Cf.* §§1.2, 1.4.

1. As to aims of direct examination, see §2.1.

hand, asking the witness to signal when to start and when to stop counting in order to fix the period equal to the witness' estimate of the length of time between two relevant events (perhaps inviting adverse counsel to observe the watch and stipulate on the time shown by it, or having another witness observe it and thereafter testify to what it showed). This is generally better than merely asking the witness to state his estimate because the average person does not have an accurate perception of short time periods in terms of seconds.

All of these methods are useful in conveying information because of the accepted fact that words are often less effective than a demonstration in conveying to the jurors' minds the "picture" that exists in the mind of the witness. The event made a "picture" impression on the mind of the witness; conveying that picture to others by words involves some loss of accuracy and vividness in his own conversion of the picture to words, and further loss in the interpretation of his words by the jurors.

A secondary aim in presenting your evidence is to make it available for the appellate court, in the event of an appeal.[2] You must do that through the record, and gestures of the witness do not serve the purpose. It is therefore necessary, if you are permitting or encouraging your witness to use gestures to convey his meaning, that you provide for converting this information into a word description for the record. It is not satisfactory to depend upon the court reporter to look at the witness and write down his (the reporter's) interpretation of what the witness has done. The reporter's eyes are usually turned to his notes as he concentrates on recording what is said. Moreover, it is not his function to make an interpretation and record it. You might make the interpretation yourself, describing the gesture of the witness. This practice may lead to sound objection by your adversary, for you are not allowed to testify as you question the witness. Also, your statements are not evidence; even in the absence of objection, there is danger that your statements would be disregarded in any subsequent dispute as to the evidence. This latter danger can be avoided by making the statement in the form of a question to the witness, asking, for example, "The distance you have indicated would be about eight feet, would it not?" Although the question is leading, the witness' affirmative answer would be evidence in the case in the absence of objection, and such a leading question would be permitted over objection in most courts, the witness having already indicated his view by gestures.[3]

Arguments over the leading character of the question and the fairness and accuracy of your statement may be avoided by calling upon the witness to give the word description of what he has first conveyed by gesture, demon-

2. §2.1.
3. See §2.18.

stration, or reference to physical objects in sight of the jury. Although it is generally preferable to call upon the witness to give the word description that is to go into the record, this will not be true with reference to witnesses who, because of ignorance, nervousness, or other reasons, are not able to express their ideas reasonably well. In your advance interview with the witness [4] you should determine whether the witness is capable of giving a satisfactory word description. It is particularly important to determine in the interview whether the witness can make a reasonably accurate estimate of distance or time before calling upon him to do so. The rule of knowing what the witness will answer before you ask a question on direct examination [5] has particular application to asking the witness to estimate distance or time, or to approve an estimate stated in a leading question, whether or not he has indicated it in other terms such as those discussed in this section. If he is not able to make satisfactory estimates of distance in feet, for example, you may ask him to make his estimates only in terms of comparison with the distance between objects in the courtroom, or to outside points; under these circumstances, you should not ask him on direct examination to convert the estimate into feet or yards, and you should caution him against doing so on cross-examination. A witness who cannot accurately estimate distance in feet conveys a more accurate and convincing story by readily admitting his inability when he is pressed on cross-examination to convert the estimate into feet.

A method of proceeding that satisfies both the aim of presenting the most convincing evidence for the jury and the aim of providing an adequate record may be illustrated with reference to Case 26. *W* is testifying with regard to the menacing gestures of *D*, his accompanying threats, and the fact that *D* was close enough to carry out his threats immediately. The examination might proceed as follows:

Q. Mr. *W*, where were you when you first learned of the incident that took place in front of the City Drug Store, last January, involving Mr. *P* and Mr. *D*? (The question is leading, but is allowed because it concerns undisputed matters that are mentioned in the testimony of this witness only as a background.) [6]

A. I was across the street in front of the hardware store.

Q. Where is the hardware store with reference to the corner of Main and Fifth Streets?

A. It is about the third door down from the corner on the east side of Main; south of Fifth Street.

Q. Where is the hardware store with reference to City Drug Store?

4. See §2.14.
5. See *id.*
6. See §2.18.

A. It is across Main, and down about two doors to the south; the Drug store is on the corner at Fifth Street, on the west side of Main.

Q. Will you step down to this blackboard, please, and draw a diagram that will show the location of the intersection, the location of the drug store, and the location of the hardware store.

A. (After drawing the diagram) That's about the way it is.

Q. Please place a "W" on the blackboard to show where you were when you first learned about the incident.

A. Right here (writing "W").

Q. You may take your seat. How did you learn about the incident?

A. I heard a loud voice across the street, up toward the corner, and turned to see what was going on.

Q. Could you understand what was said?

A. I understood the last part of it.

Q. Could you tell whose voice it was?

A. Yes, I could see that it was Mr. D. talking.

Q. Could you tell whom he was talking to?

A. Yes, I could.

Q. Who was it?

A. Mr. P.

Q. In what manner was D speaking?

A. Loud, like he was mad.

Q. What did Mr. D say to Mr. P, in that part of the statement that you understood?

A. He said, "I'll knock you clean across the street if you try to get around me."

Q. Was anything else happening at that time besides Mr. D's making this statement?

A. Mr. D was standing there in the middle of the sidewalk with his fists doubled up, and Mr. P was down this way a couple of steps with his back toward me and facing toward Mr. D. Neither one of them was moving right then.

Q. Mr. W, please step down to the blackboard again and mark the letter "P" on your diagram to show where Mr. P was, and the letter "D" to show where Mr. D was.

A. (After doing so) They were about like that.

Q. Now, please stand as far away from me as Mr. D was from Mr. P at the time when he made this statement, "I'll knock you clean across the street if you try to get around me." (After W takes his position in response to this request) Is the distance between you and me at the present time the same, as near as you can estimate it, as the distance between Mr. P and Mr. D when Mr. D made that statement?

A. Yes sir.

Q. We want to get a measurement of this distance so the court reporter may put it in his record. Do you know how long your shoe is?

A. I sure do; it's 13 inches.

Q. Will you step off the distance from you to me?

A. (After doing so) Just over five shoe-lengths — that would be just about five and one-half feet. [7]

Q. In what position was D standing when he made this statement?

A. He was standing on the sidewalk facing straight toward P.

Q. Did you observe the position of D's arms at that time?

A. Yes, I did.

Q. Show the jury by putting your arms in the same position D was holding his.

A. He had his fists doubled up and was holding them like this (gesturing).

Q. Now, in order that the reporter may get this into the record, please describe the way D was holding his arms.

A. Both fists were doubled up. He held the right one in front about his waist line, and his left fist up higher, about level with and straight in front of his left shoulder.

§2.32   Using demonstrative evidence

CASE 27. P is seeking recovery for personal injuries to the muscles and soft tissues of his body, inflicted in an automobile accident. As P's lawyer, you have available a skeleton, the use of which you are considering in connection with the testimony of M, your principal medical witness.

To what extent should you use demonstrative evidence?

The traditional way of proving a fact is by asking a witness who knows. Some trials conclude with no type of evidence having been offered other than what the witnesses say. Yet a moment's reflection will suggest to you that this type of evidence is in most respects the least convincing type of evidence you can offer. It is subject to all the frailties of human error in observation, memory, expression, and integrity. It is common knowledge that two witnesses standing side by side to observe the same event, if interrogated separately, will differ in their statements concerning what occurred. Jurors who are not already aware of these facts can usually be converted to belief in them with moderate attention to the question in the lawyer's argument. The lawyer who has more of real or demonstrative evidence than his adversary has a distinct advantage in the contest of convincing the jury. Some at least, though not all, of the chances for error are absent or reduced in the case of demonstrative evidence.

Generally you should make use of all the favorable physical or demonstra-

---

7. The following question and answer might be used as an alternative, in lieu of the two preceding questions and answers:

Q. In order that the court reporter may get a record of how far it is, I am holding the end of this tape measure at the edge of my shoe, and I hand you the other end of the tape and ask that you measure the distance to the edge of your shoe.

A. (After measurement is made) That's about five inches over five feet.

tive evidence that is available to you, and careful attention and some imagination in searching for such evidence will disclose that more is available than is customarily used in the trial of cases.[1]

The principal precautions to be observed in using demonstrative evidence relate to a constant awareness of the ultimate purpose of using the evidence.[2] Obtaining the concentrated attention of the court and jury is one of the advantages of using demonstrative evidence, but not the goal. The goal is to convey material information and convince the jury that it is accurate. You should use demonstrative evidence only if it will contribute to that goal. For example, if in a personal injury case the alleged injury relates to the bony structures, a skeleton may be useful to the medical witness in explaining to the jury the function of the injured bone and the interference with that function by the injury, his explanation being more vivid and more readily understood because it is illustrated with references to the model of the bone and to its natural place in the skeleton. On the other hand, if the injury relates to the circulatory system only, the medical witness may interest and even entertain the jury by bringing along his skeleton, but he will not have served the goal of conveying material information. Overplaying the appeal to the jury's interest, even if allowed by your adversary and the court, may develop the idea in the jurors' minds that you are trying to turn the trial into a kind of show. Though enjoying the entertainment, they may conclude that you would not use this evidence in a sincere presentation of a meritorious case.[3] If the injury, rather than being either of those suggested above, is a muscular injury without damage to the bony structures, as in Case 27, probably the danger of this reaction makes it preferable to decline to use the skeleton, even though it might have been helpful to the doctor to some extent in explaining successfully to the jury the use of the muscle and the results of impairment of that use. Models of the muscles and soft tissues of the human body are available, and it would be better in Case 27 to use a model of that type.

Demonstrative evidence calculated to inflame the passions and prejudices of jurors and to appeal primarily to sympathy may be held inadmissible,[4] and the attempted use of such evidence may result in mistrial.[5] The severity of the restraint against such evidence varies greatly among the different jurisdictions.

The guiding rule as to your use of demonstrative evidence should be: Use all the demonstrative evidence you can develop if it aids directly in convey-

1. See §9.6.
2. See §1.4.
3. See §1.2.
4. *E.g.*, see 4 Wigmore, *Evidence* §1158 (3d ed. 1940), regarding exhibition of personal injury. See also Federal Rules of Evidence, Rule 403.
5. See §5.4.

ing material information, but avoid overdoing this trial technique by the use of spectacular demonstrations that bear only a slight relation to the material issues of the case or are inconsistent with evidence rules of your jurisdiction.

§2.33 Using diagrams, drawings, and computations

CASE 28. *P* is asserting a claim for personal injuries based upon an intersection collision. *W* is one of the witnesses whom you, as *P*'s lawyer, expect to call to the stand. *W* is a police officer who came to the scene of the accident to investigate and made measurements of the length of tiremarks, the distances from curb lines, the location of debris that he took as an indication of the point of impact, and the location of each vehicle when it came to rest.

Should you call upon the witness to make diagrams, drawings, or computations on a blackboard or paper during his testimony?

Oral testimony has not only the weakness of possibilities for human error in memory, observation, and statement but also the weakness of inadequacy to convey information accurately and completely. Although any diagram made by the witness is no better than his observation, memory, and ability to draw, a diagram by one with average ability in drawing is superior to his mere statement of the information because he may more accurately convey to the jury the idea that is in his own mind. A diagram or other type of drawing has another distinct value — the preservation of the expression of the idea, so that the jury may turn back to it for study and comparison and to refresh their own memory of the testimony. These purposes would be well served in Case 28 by having the police officer prepare a diagram to illustrate his testimony. Except possibly when you are offering the testimony of a witness experienced in preparing diagrams to record data (as an accident investigator on the police force), you should never ask a witness on direct examination to prepare a drawing or diagram unless you have previously made this same request and determined that the witness is able to do it reasonably well.[1] Some witnesses are so poor at drawing, and particularly at keeping a reasonably accurate scale and relative position of various objects, that more harm than good will be done by asking that a drawing be made in the presence of the jury.[2] If you plan to use a map prepared by another during the testimony of a witness, you should show the map to the witness in the pretrial conference with him.[3] A hurried study for the first time on the witness stand may confuse the witness. Take care, however, in discussing the map

1. See §2.14.
2. See §3.16 with reference to using a drawing by the witness on cross-examination, and §3.12 for an example of using computations on cross-examination.
3. See §2.14.

with him, to prepare for the possibility that he will be asked on cross-examination if you showed him where he should place a mark on the map. A wholesale denial of talking with you about placement of the marks, by a witness uncertain about the propriety of the conference in which you properly asked him to advise you where he will place the marks if asked to do so, would be almost as damaging as proof that you actually told the witness where to place the marks.

When using a drawing, should you ask that it be prepared on a blackboard, or instead on a paper, and should you ask the witness to start from a blank, or should you furnish a scale drawing of background objects, already authenticated by previous evidence? An advantage of the drawing on paper is that you can offer it in evidence when it is completed, and, in jurisdictions where jurors are permitted to take exhibits with them, they may carry it to the jury room during deliberations. An advantage of the blackboard is that the jury can easily follow the testimony as it is given and illustrated on the blackboard drawing. A very large drawing on chart paper may be as good as the blackboard in this respect and can also be conveniently offered in evidence. Unless the witness is good at drawing, however, the blackboard may be preferable because of greater ease in erasing and changing the drawing until it satisfies the witness. With permission of the court, you may have a photograph of the drawing made for the record or for use as an exhibit at trial. Another possibility is that you use a map, aerial photograph, or chart prepared in advance to scale, asking the witness to make his markings on it. If it is large enough to be pinned to a board similar to a blackboard, a single copy may serve the purpose. If you use a small photograph or chart and it is sufficiently important to merit such attention, you should have a minimum of ten copies prepared so you can supply one each to judge, witness, and lawyers, and six to the jury (each two jurors using one between them to follow the testimony). Even if you do not follow this plan, you should have at least one extra copy available so that, if your adversary seeks to place other markings on the copy that you have used,[4] you can make the extra copy available and ask the court not to allow further markings that would deface the copy that you used to illustrate your theory.

Another illustration of this principle of using some form of demonstrative display of the testimony occurs when you wish to ask a witness to make computations. In Case 6, for example, in which the building contractor is suing for sums claimed as extras, it will be desirable to have the witness K, his accountant, record some of the figures he is reading from his records, and organize them so as to present to the jury in summary form the figures involved in the proof of damages. This may be done in advance by K, or it may be done as he testifies. Here, as in the case of the diagram, there is an

4. See §3.16.

advantage in having the computations made on a paper rather than on a blackboard, so that it can be marked as an exhibit, introduced in evidence, and carried to the jury room during deliberations. In the absence of such evidence, the jury may not remember accurately the amounts involved in several different items of extras within the single suit.

§2.34   Using photographs

CASE 29.   *P*, an ambulance driver, operating the ambulance on an emergency mission in a small town, was injured in a collision between the ambulance and a car driven by *D*, when the ambulance crossed a main thoroughfare on which *D* was proceeding. It is undisputed that the controlling law did not require *P* to stop at the approach to the thoroughfare if he was proceeding with a siren and flashing red light and that under those circumstances *D* would be required to yield the right of way. Evidence is disputed as to whether the siren was sounding, but it is undisputed that the flashing red light was operating. One of *D*'s defenses is that the approach to the intersection was so obstructed by trees and shrubbery that he could not see the ambulance, which was approaching at relatively high speed, until too late to avoid collision. The accident occurred in December. The case reaches you, as *D*'s lawyer, the following June, at which time you have photographs taken of the scene of the accident. The case is being tried in September, and you are unable to obtain any photograph of the scene taken in winter.

Should you use particular photographs?
How should you introduce photographs?

The steps involved in orderly introduction of a photograph are the same as those for any other document.[1] Variations arise only in connection with the method of authenticating the photograph. You must prove that the photograph is a fair representation of some fact material to the litigation, and even then it might be excluded on objection if the photograph includes other matters that cannot properly go before the jury.

You may authenticate the photograph as a fair representation of the scene at the time the photograph was made by using the testimony of the photographer. Usually, however, circumstances at a time before or after the photograph was taken, and not at that exact time, are the material inquiry in the lawsuit. The photographer's testimony is insufficient authentication unless he is also familiar with the circumstances at the time in issue in the lawsuit and can testify that the circumstances depicted by the photograph are substantially the same (or the same with stated exceptions, which do not make the photograph misleading). Furthermore, the photographer's testimony is

1. See §2.25.

unnecessary to the authentication if another witness is available to testify from personal observation that the photograph accurately represents the circumstances at the time material to the lawsuit. Whether you should use the photographer in such a case is solely a tactical question. Because it is general knowledge that photographs are subject to manipulation so as to make them misleading, it is worthwhile to call a reputable photographer (either amateur or professional) to strengthen the authentication, unless there is no real dispute about the fact that the photograph is a fair representation of the scene. In most situations, the accuracy of the photographs is not disputed, and the use of the extra witness is of no particular value.

Because of the fact that a photograph used in evidence is rarely one taken at the exact time material to the litigation, it will rarely be an accurate representation of the exact circumstances at the material time. With appropriate explanation offered during the authentication of the photograph, however, it is admitted in evidence unless the differences are such as to make it misleading. You should be alert for such differences. In Case 29, there is a material difference in visibility at an intersection because the photograph was taken in June and the accident occurred in December. If as *D*'s lawyer, claiming an obstruction to visibility when the accident occurred in December, you introduce without explanation this photograph taken in June, your opponent may deal a mortal blow to your case by proving that the trees shown in the picture are not evergreens and therefore do not look the same in December as in the photograph. Careless use of such a photograph might defeat your entire case because of your inability to convince the jury after such an incident that you were not trying to mislead them. It is tactically questionable whether you should use such a photograph even with explanation in advance.

When you introduce a photograph, proving the bare facts essential to authentication for purposes of admissibility is usually insufficient explanation for proper interpretation of the photograph by the jury. You may ask the witness to explain the direction toward which the camera was facing and the location of ground marks that will tie the photograph into other evidence offered in the case. Sometimes the only way you can do this satisfactorily is to have the witness show the jury, with a pointer, or by pen or pencil marks on the photograph, the objects being pointed out. Since photographs are often deceptive, and some witnesses will have more difficulty than others in locating objects accurately, you should always confer with your witness on the matter in the pretrial interview before asking him to make such a marking or explanation in court.[2]

You should consider arranging for extra prints of any small photograph

2. See §2.14.

you offer, so that judge, jurors, and the opposing attorney may each be looking at a copy of the photograph at the same time as the witness.[3]

§2.35 Using motion pictures

Case 30. Representing D, you are defending against a personal injury
claim asserted by P, one of your defenses being that P has grossly exaggerated the severity of his injury. You have available some motion pictures taken
with a telescopic lens by an experienced photographer. The pictures show a
group of workers, one of whom appears to be P, engaged in harvesting fruit,
an activity wholly inconsistent with P's claims as to the severity of his injury.

Should you use motion pictures?
If so, when and how?

The most spectacular use of motion pictures in trials is in defense against
a fabricated or exaggerated personal injury claim. Such pictures are very effective if they disclose the plaintiff voluntarily engaged in activities clearly
inconsistent with his claimed disability. For example, if the plaintiff claims
that he is unable to do any work and has done none since the date of the
accident on which suit is based, but is shown in a motion picture engaged
in heavy labor at a time between the dates of accident and trial, this impeaching evidence usually has decisive effect.

You should take account of some limitations on the usefulness of motion
pictures of a claimant's activity. If the pictures are not sufficiently clear to
identify the plaintiff positively, it is dangerous to use them. In Case 30, for
example, you should not use them if you are in doubt about identity. Even
though you are personally satisfied about identity, using the pictures is tactically questionable unless they are clear enough to identify the plaintiff or
else you have some form of independent proof to identify him in the pictures. If the jury should resolve a doubt about identity against you after you
have used such pictures, they are not likely to stop short of penalizing your
client by a more severe verdict than they otherwise would have rendered. A
similar danger is involved in using pictures that show some activity, but not
enough to be clearly inconsistent with the plaintiff's testimony. Before using
such pictures, get the plaintiff committed to testimony that cannot be reconciled with the activities shown; if he admits ability to engage in such activity as your pictures show, even though he says he cannot do so regularly,
you cannot safely use the pictures unless you have supplementary convincing
proof that they represent his regular activities.

Pictures obtained by setting a trap for the plaintiff are generally less effective than those obtained by finding the plaintiff engaged voluntarily in ac-

3. See §2.33.

tivities without inducement by any subterfuge. Sometimes juries react against the use of subterfuges as unfair tactics, [1] thereby becoming more receptive to plaintiff's explanation of the pictures as representing an isolated incident rather than what the plaintiff is able to do regularly. Consider also the possibility that plaintiff will answer the pictures with testimony that he engaged in that activity only once, the time pictured, and it made his condition much worse. You should prepare to meet any such contentions as these. If possible, have independent proof available to show that the plaintiff engaged regularly in the activities pictured. Also, try to get a positive commitment from the plaintiff on cross-examination that he never engaged in such activities so that he will be caught in a direct contradiction when he admits even the one occasion.

In some instances you can use motion pictures for other purposes than impeachment of a dishonest personal injury claimant, though you will usually encounter serious problems of admissibility with respect to other uses. A reenactment of an incident to picture your theory of the case is a very effective argument. Whether this kind of evidence should be received is subject to dispute. [2] More often you can use motion pictures for illustrative or explanatory purposes in the course of expert testimony, if the trial judge will in his discretion permit the practice. Permission is sometimes denied because showing motion pictures causes delay and often inconvenience if the courtroom was not constructed so as to facilitate showing motion pictures, and a trial judge may be concerned that motion pictures would distract the attention of the jury from the more important issues in the case. Of course, motion pictures of an incident on which trial is based would generally be admissible, but it is rare indeed that such pictures will have been taken, though this possibility increases with increasing use of television cameras. You might be able to use moving pictures instead of still photographs to disclose the physical situation at the scene of an accident. This use involves dangers of misleading, similar to those involved in the use of still photographs, and also has the disadvantage that motion pictures can not be as readily studied for detail.

If you decide to use motion pictures for any purpose, be certain that the operator of the equipment is competent. Effective pictures of a claimant engaged in physical activity inconsistent with his claim may be rendered ridiculous and perhaps even harmful rather than helpful to the defense if the operator of the projector has it operating at a speed that is obviously making the movements in the pictures more rapid than were those of the subject when the picture was taken. Also, delays and typical interruptions and dis-

1. See §9.12.
2. 3 Wigmore, *Evidence* §798a (rev. ed. Chadbourn 1970).

tractions of amateur projection may reduce or destroy the effectiveness of the pictures.

How may you authenticate motion pictures to support admissibility? The problem is comparable to that of authenticating a still photograph. It is possible to have enough testimony of the accuracy of the representation of relevant facts that no testimony from the photographer is required. For example, if in Case 30 you are offering pictures of P at work, the pictures might be produced on cross-examination of P, with permission of the court, P being asked to admit that he is the person shown in them and that they accurately represent work that he was doing at a specified time. It is always advisable, however, to have the pictures made by someone whom you can afford to produce as a witness to authenticate them, if necessary. For example, if the case arises in a jurisdiction in which it is improper for the plaintiff to reveal the fact of liability insurance and you are engaged by the insurance company, do not have an employee of the company take the pictures. Use an independent person, and preferably make the arrangements with him yourself, so that he may truthfully say, if asked about it, that you engaged him, rather than being faced with a problem in trying to avoid mention of an insurance company with whose representatives he dealt in connection with the pictures.

The fact that the pictures may be authenticated by one other than the photographer also provides an opportunity for some tactical choice as to timing of the use of the pictures. Should you offer during cross-examination of P the pictures showing his activities inconsistent with his claim, or should you offer the pictures during your own direct evidence, with authenticating testimony of the photographer? One advantage of offering them during cross-examination is that P may have less opportunity to fabricate a reasonably satisfactory excuse for his contradictory testimony if you offer them at a time when you have him on the stand under questioning; also, you may be saved the necessity of producing the photographer as a witness. You can not by this method catch P totally off guard, however, for you must secure the permission of the court to show the pictures, and that will involve disclosure to P in a general way, though perhaps not of the specific content of the pictures. Also, if the court refuses the permission, P will have even greater opportunity for fabricating his excuse during the intervening period before you offer the pictures during your evidence. From the point of view of emphasis, aside from P's explanation, there is a difference of opinion as to whether the more advantageous time is during cross-examination, when the contradictory testimony is recent and fresh in the minds of the jurors, or instead is near the close of defendant's evidence, at a point only a short time before retirement of the jury for deliberations. One possibility worthy of consideration is that you withhold cross-examination of P during the period when your adversary, P's lawyer, is offering his evidence, and then recall P for cross-examination during your evidence (assuming that the rules permit this procedure) just before you use the pictures. You could then make a request for permission to use the pictures while *P* is still on the stand. The pictures could be produced immediately with other authentication if the court refused the permission or if *P* would not admit authenticity of the pictures.

§2.36   Offering evidence for a limited purpose

CASE 31. You represent *P*, a pedestrian, making a claim for personal injuries sustained when *P* was hit by a truck driven by *S*, in the early evening. Whether *S* was at the time in the scope of his employment for *D Company* is disputed. *D Company*'s original answer contained the allegation that "*S* was told he could drive the truck to his home when he left work at 5 P.M., on the condition that he would park it in his driveway and not use it except to return to work the following morning." Subsequently *D Company* filed an amended answer omitting this allegation and stating only in general terms that "*S* was not acting in the course and scope of his employment for *D Company* at the time of the accident, but was driving the truck for some personal purpose of his own." At trial, *D Company* offers evidence that *S* was instructed to park the truck in the company garage rather than driving it home. As *P*'s lawyer, you wish to offer the original allegations of *D Company*, to support the inference that *D Company*'s latest story was concocted for trial and not supported by fact.

Should you offer evidence for a limited purpose?

Generally, evidence offered by either party may be considered by the jury for all purposes. If you wish the evidence to be considered only for some special purpose, claiming that it is inadmissible as to a different use or inference, it is important that you not offer the evidence generally, as distinguished from making a limited or special offer. This problem arises when you wish to impeach one of your adversary's witnesses by proving that he told a different story on another occasion, [1] but you do not wish the jury or court to accept either of the two stories. There is a risk that your offer of the second version, without qualification of your offer, would be construed by the court as an admission by adoption. Usually you can avoid that risk by stating to the court, at the time you offer the evidence, that you offer it for the limited purpose of impeachment. Such a statement is sometimes desirable for the further purpose of making your position clear to the jury, to avoid any risk of their misunderstanding your purpose and drawing an inference you do not intend. Another example of this problem is illustrated by Case 31; you should offer the excerpts from *D Company*'s abandoned pleadings for the limited purpose of impeachment, to avoid any claim of admis-

---

1. See §3.5.

sion that *S* was outside the scope of employment as alleged in the abandoned pleading and implied in the part of it that you offer in evidence. [2]

For an entirely different reason, a limited offer of evidence is useful in Case 13; evidence that is inadmissible for general purposes may be admissible for a limited purpose such as impeachment, and the failure to make the limited offer will preclude your claim that the court committed reversible error in sustaining an objection to the evidence. [3]

§2.37 Offering evidence of law; judicial notice

CASE 32. *P* asserts a claim on account of injuries received when the car in which he was riding as a passenger collided at night with a disabled truck, which was on the pavement of the highway where it came to rest after a wheel fell off and one end of the rear axle dropped to the pavement. In your representation of *P*, one of your claims of negligence is based on the failure of *D*'s employee to comply with a statute requiring lighted flares, visible for a specified distance, to be placed at the scene of disabled trucks of the type operated by *D*'s employee on the occasion in question.

Should you offer evidence of applicable law?
Should you move that the court take judicial notice of facts or law to avoid the necessity of offering evidence?

Customarily the court, whether state or federal, takes judicial notice of the statutes and common law of the state in which it sits, without special motion from counsel. [1] In many jurisdictions, however, it is necessary to offer evidence regarding ordinances of municipalities, rules and regulations of administrative bodies, and laws of other jurisdictions. In some instances, the evidence is supplied by the testimony of an "expert" who is familiar with the relevant law; the trend, however, is toward increasing use of motions requesting the court to take judicial notice of specific law or of the law of a specific jurisdiction relating to the case. If any part of your case depends upon foreign law, or other law of which the court does not take judicial notice without motion or proof, or if the law in question is more favorable to you than that of the forum, [2] your pretrial preparation should include appropriate planning for proving the law or invoking it by an appropriate motion. Lawsuits have been lost because of the failure to investigate conflict of laws problems and to invoke foreign laws different from

2. For an indication of the mechanics of making a limited offer, as well as an illustration of another fact situation in which the practice might be useful, see §2.25.
3. See §§2.17, 4.12.
1. 9 Wigmore, *Evidence* §2572 (3d ed. 1940).
2. The law of the forum is generally applied when the foreign law is not invoked, on the presumption that the foreign law is the same as that of the forum. *Id.,* §2536.

those of the forum, or because of the failure to investigate and invoke municipal laws different from those state laws applied in the absence of a valid municipal law to the contrary.

If the law on which you rely is of the type of which the court takes judicial notice without motion or proof, most courts do not permit the introduction of evidence of the law as such. The law is regarded as a matter appropriate for the court's charge only, and not for evidence and rebuttal evidence by lawyers during development of the case. Sometimes this is a handicap to you because you wish to have the law before the jury so they can understand the significance of evidence as it is being offered. The trial judge ordinarily instructs on the law applicable to the case only in his charge, after the evidence has been closed, but other means of getting the law before the jury at the desired time may be available. For example, if you are concerned with a motor vehicle statute applicable to special vehicles, and not likely to be known to the jurors, as in Case 32, you may be able to get the law before the jury indirectly by offering a copy of written instructions issued by D to drivers at the time of their employment, certain paragraphs of which quote the state statutes regarding placement of flares when a vehicle is disabled on the highway. Although not admissible to prove the law as such, this evidence might be received on the theory of proof of noncompliance with specific instructions issued to the drivers for safety purposes.

Courts also take judicial notice of certain well-recognized facts. As a general rule, however, unless you have specific case authority to support your request, you should not rely on a motion requesting the court to take judicial notice. If your adversary declines to stipulate the fact, it is a safer practice to prove the fact by competent evidence, even though the court may be willing to take judicial notice. You thus avoid the risk of unnecessary reversal of a favorable judgment. On the other hand, if you find after the evidence is closed that you have omitted evidence of some vital fact that is well recognized, you should consider presenting a motion that the court take judicial notice of that fact.[3] In some jurisdictions the courts may grant such a motion even when made for the first time on appeal.[4]

§2.38   Using redirect examination and rebuttal evidence

CASE 1. Your client, P, was injured by contact with D's charged electric wire, while P was working for a building subcontractor, under the supervision of W, foreman. F, foreman for another subcontractor on the job, says that P and Q were engaged in horseplay at the time of the injury, Q chas-

---

3. For consideration of other possible relief, see §5.9.

4. See 9 Wigmore, *Evidence* §2568 (3d ed. 1940). See also Federal Rules of Evidence, Rules 201 (f), 1101.

ing *P* along some scaffolding constructed near the wire. *W*, *P*, and *Q* all say that *W* had sent *P* and *Q* on the scaffolding to get some protective materials in place before a threatening rainstorm. *W* says that he warned *P* and *Q* about the uninsulated wire, commenting that it might be swinging very close to the scaffolding in the high wind. *P* and *Q* say they did not hear *W* say anything about the wire.

When should you use redirect examination and rebuttal evidence?

Though two separate problems are involved in the foregoing question, tactically there is a close relationship between the two. Each presents to you the question whether you should disclose all your evidence during the original presentation, or withhold part of it for use after your adversary's presentation. As to both problems, your first consideration is the nature of rules regarding proper scope of redirect examination [1] or rebuttal evidence [2] (the term "rebuttal evidence" being used here to signify the offering of additional evidence after you have first rested and then your adversary has presented evidence and rested), and the strictness of enforcement of any restrictive rules of this character in the court of trial. If redirect examination is strictly limited to developing matters discussed during cross-examination (or if rebuttal evidence is strictly limited to developing matters raised by your adversary during presentation of his evidence), then by withholding part of your evidence from your original presentation you run the risk that you will not have the opportunity of presenting it later, since your adversary may steer clear of the subject. In many jurisdictions trial judges are in practice very lenient regarding enforcement of rules restricting the scope of redirect examination and rebuttal evidence; even in courts in which the rules are restrictive and are enforced strictly, usually you will be able safely to withhold particular items of evidence because they relate to an important issue that your adversary is certain to face and can be regarded as properly answering some contention that you know your adversary will raise.

The principal tactical implications of withholding evidence from the original presentation are those of surprise, [3] suspense, and emphasis from timing. [4]

It is generally recognized, in relation to trials as elsewhere, that there is a tactical advantage in having the last word in the argument. This principle is given official recognition in rules granting to the party having the burden of proof the right to open and close. Some lawyers seem to seek this ad-

---

1. 6 Wigmore, *Evidence* §1896 (3d ed. 1940). See also Federal Rules of Evidence, Rule 611.
2. 6 Wigmore, *Evidence* §1873 (3d ed. 1940). See also Federal Rules of Evidence, Rule 611.
3. See §1.3.
4. See §1.4.

vantage in the examination of every witness, so that within the limits that the judge will tolerate the conclusion of the testimony of each witness is delayed by the contest between lawyers each of whom wants to ask the last question. This practice is not recommended as a goal in itself; often other more important tactical ends will be sacrificed if one persists in the attempt to ask one more question, in the hope of asking the last question. Having the last word is an advantage only if the last word is in your favor. If you do not have another question that is relevant and proper (from the point of view of tactics as well as evidence rules), you should not concoct another solely for the sake of asking the last; cases have been lost by asking one question too many.

Subject to these limitations by rules of court and by common sense, you should consider the deliberate planning of the presentation of your case, and of the testimony of your individual witnesses, with the aim of concluding the examination of each witness and the evidence in the case as a whole with a point favorable to your case. For example, assume that in Case 1, as P's lawyer, you conclude that you should call Q to corroborate P's testimony that P and Q were not engaged in horseplay and that they were not warned of an uninsulated wire by W. Should you call Q during the presentation of your original case, or should you withhold calling him until after D's primary evidence has been presented? If you withhold Q, it is improbable that D will call him for you, [5] but it is quite likely that you will thereby secure for Q the position of final witness in the case—a position of special emphasis because his testimony will be most fresh in the minds of the jury when they retire, and because the issue of conflict on the points as to which he will testify has been sharply drawn before he takes the stand. If Q is a strong witness on whom you can rely to withstand artful cross-examination, this position of special prominence will be to your advantage. If there is danger that the witness will be a weak one, either as to content of his testimony or as to manner of testifying, probably you should not take the chance of giving him this place of prominence at the conclusion of the trial.

Another tactical advantage in withholding evidence from your original presentation arises in those cases in which it appears likely that your adversary or some witness will be urging a contention the error of which you will be able to demonstrate conclusively with evidence that your adversary probably does not realize is available to you. Though you might be able to forestall the original assertion of the untenable contention of your adversary by offering your evidence first, if the circumstances indicate that an adverse witness may deliberately give false testimony on a point as to which you have conclusive proof, you may profit more by permitting him to do so

5. Consider §2.2.

before you disclose your evidence. The effect of your evidence then extends beyond the subject matter that it touches and casts a cloud of suspicion on your adversary's entire case. [6]

6. See §3.6, discussing Case 35, for a comparable situation in which D's lawyer may choose to postpone disclosing the evidence that P gave false testimony in saying he had not worked since the accident.

Chapter III

CROSS-EXAMINATION AND IMPEACHMENT

§3.1 The art of cross-examination

Cross-examination is potentially the most spectacular phase of a trial. It affords the opportunity for the most striking use of an aptitude for incisive thought and a sense of the dramatic. To excel in these, you must have native ability. If you are interested in trial work, however, it seems a safe assumption that you have this kind of ability in some degree at least. You can develop your native ability by practice and experience, just as one can develop a talent for music. But the talent for cross-examination, in this sense, is the lesser part of the secret of effective cross-examination. Nearly all effective cross-examination is planned, to one degree or another. Through adequate planning you can often achieve effective cross-examination even before you have any substantial trial experience. As you gain experience, your success in cross-examination will continue to depend on your diligence and thoroughness in preparing. This chapter concerns methods customarily used in effective cross-examination and ways of preparing to use them.

The potential aims of cross-examination may be classified into four groups: (1) discrediting the testimony of the witness being examined; (2) using the testimony of this witness to discredit the unfavorable testimony of other witnesses; (3) using the testimony of this witness to corroborate the favorable testimony of other witnesses; and (4) using the testimony of this witness to contribute independently to the favorable development of your own case.

Accomplishing one of these aims may require an entirely different method of dealing with the witness from that appropriate for another aim. A method of cross-examination designed to serve one aim may defeat another.[1] Adequate planning requires an appraisal of the relative advantages

---

1. For further discussion of the point, see §3.10.

associated with each of these aims, since this is a factor bearing on the choice of methods.

Your selection of methods of cross-examination of the witness will depend also on the type of witness you face.[2] Among other things, the age, education, and mentality of the witness are important factors. The most ignorant witness is often the hardest to cross-examine because you cannot set him up for a fall. Also, you must exercise great care to avoid creating jury sympathy for him because you are exposing his ignorance or illiteracy. Your aim is to condemn his testimony as unreliable without condemning the witness for being ignorant. If you inflict personal ridicule upon an ignorant witness, or treat him sarcastically, the jurors may think you are taking an unfair advantage of the differences in intelligence and education between yourself and the witness.[3]

Give some thought to your general attitude and demeanor toward the witness. Should you let your contempt for the reprobate be obvious for the jury to see, if you feel that way about him? Or should you be the paragon of courtesy? Usually it is best to adopt an attitude of courtesy toward the witness, for although the jurors expect you to be an advocate, they may very quickly develop sympathy for a witness whom they think you are badgering unfairly. It is quite possible to be very polite and yet convey to the jury your distrust of the witness' testimony.

§3.2 Aids to cross-examination

What aids to cross-examination can you develop during pretrial preparation?

Begin your preparation for cross-examination at the same time you begin your investigation of the case. Obviously, the kind of investigation by which you know your adversary's case and evidence as well as your own[1] is essential to the maximum success in cross-examination. Knowing what the witnesses probably will say is important not only for deciding what to ask but also for deciding what not to ask.

Thorough investigation provides the background information essential to your instantly realizing, during your adversary's direct examination, the implications of the questions and answers. Also it provides tools for cross-examination.[2] Among these tools are written statements, documents and letters written by or for the witness, depositions of the witness, information con-

---

2. With respect to distinctive problems of cross-examining particular types of witnesses, see §§3.12, 3.22, 3.25, 3.29.

3. See §1.3.

1. See §9.10

2. See §§9.4–9.14 concerning investigation of facts.

cerning actions and statements of the witness to which other persons will testify, and literature for use in cross-examination of an expert.

With due consideration for the aims of your cross-examination of each witness, the aids available, and the subjects of inquiry, you should prepare an outline (written unless your experience enables you to do it mentally without loss of effectiveness) of the proposed cross-examination of each witness whose use by your adversary you are able to anticipate. More variations from the outline are to be expected than in the case of direct examination of your own witness, but the previous consideration that you have given to problems you have anticipated will be most helpful to you during the cross-examination, even though you do not follow the outline closely.

§3.3   The decision to cross-examine

CASE 33. Representing D, you are defending against a personal injury claim by P, who has not worked since the accident on which suit is based. Whether the alleged injuries have been the cause of P's not working and whether and to what extent he is disabled are sharply disputed. P's lawyer calls P's wife W as a witness for testimony about his excellent health before the accident on which suit is based and his poor condition and continued complaints following the accident. W was not present when the accident occurred and gives no testimony relevant to any issue other than extent of disability.

Should you cross-examine each witness?

Most trial yarns concerning cross-examination tell of the brilliant cross-examination that won the lawsuit. Others tell of the inept cross-examination that lost it. Although both types of yarns are commonly influenced by a recognized license like that of the poet and fisherman, they are founded on truths.

These are some of the risks that you incur in cross-examination:

(1) Confronting a witness with a prior written statement inconsistent with his present testimony may result in proof of other facts recorded in the statement and not previously proved, or it may result in incidental disclosure of the existence of liability insurance, when its existence would have been unknown to the jury otherwise.[1]

(2) Confronting the witness with inconsistency between his testimony and that of your own witness may result in impeachment of the testimony of your own witness.[2]

(3) The cross-examination intended to show want of good opportunity

1. See §3.5.
2. See §3.6.

for observation of the facts related may serve only to demonstrate that the opportunity was good.[3]

(4) An attempt to prove or even actual proof of bad character of the witness may provoke the sympathy of the jury for the witness and the case he supports.[4]

(5) The cross-examination intended to reveal indirectly the bias of the witness by committing him to an untenable extreme may result in strengthening the direct examination.[5]

(6) The cross-examination intended to bring out matters about which your adversary failed to inquire, in the belief that the answers will be favorable to your client, may result only in more evidence favorable to the adverse party who called the witness.[6]

(7) Calling on the witness to repeat and elaborate his testimony, as a foundation for proof of prior contradictions or inconsistencies, may emphasize and strengthen the witness' testimony if he has a plausible explanation for the apparent inconsistencies.[7]

(8) Cross-examination intended to show bias from animosity associated with termination of employment may provoke sympathy for the discharged employee.[8]

(9) Asking a "why" question in the belief that the witness can have no reasonable explanation may result in his stating prejudicial arguments that would have been clearly inadmissible in the absence of the invitation by the open question.[9]

(10) Insistence upon a clear answer from an evasive witness may lead to an unexpected and unfavorable disclosure.[10]

(11) Defendant's cross-examination of plaintiff's medical expert regarding fees may emphasize plaintiff's expenses and cause a higher damages finding.[11]

(12) Cross-examination of an expert concerning his qualifications may serve only to bolster less adequate proof of those qualifications during direct examination.[12]

(13) Methods of cross-examination intended to exact disclosures from an unwilling witness may be harmful because of a jury reaction that they are unfair methods.

3. See §3.10.
4. See §3.11.
5. See §§3.12, 3.16.
6. See §3.14.
7. See §§3.15, 3.16.
8. See §3.17.
9. See §3.21.
10. See §3.23.
11. See §3.27.
12. See §3.30.

For each of the risks of cross-examination in this illustrative list, a corresponding possibility of gain is present. These are risks that you incur even though your cross-examination is carefully planned to achieve one or more of these gains. Proceeding blindly into cross-examination without an aim and a plan would involve many such risks without corresponding hope of benefit. Planning is essential to the most effective cross-examination. The plan for cross-examination need not be and should not be inflexible. Neither should the cross-examination be haphazard. Even those lawyers who use the "hop, skip, and jump" method of cross-examination (changing the subject of inquiry frequently and suddenly) [13] do so with a purpose; they hope that the truth will out because the witness does not have time to anticipate the next question and fabricate an answer other than the truth, or else that his quickly conceived untruths will be so artless that they can be exposed. Careful planning may reduce, but will never wholly eliminate, the risk of harm to your own cause by your cross-examination. The decision whether or not to cross-examine a particular witness, and to what extent and with what aims and methods, calls for appraising the advantages and disadvantages and accepting a calculated risk. This weighing of risks is something that, as a trial lawyer, you must do frequently not only with respect to crossexamination but also in determining whether to use other trial methods, and even in considering the broader question whether to litigate or settle. [14]

That lawsuits are sometimes lost in cross-examination is reason enough to beware of an unyielding rule that you cross-examine every witness. It is possible, however, that failure to cross-examine a witness may lead the jury to conclude that you concede that his testimony is correct, or that you have no way of disputing it though you might wish that you could do so. In rare instances the testimony of your adversary's witness is so favorable or so sound and undisputed that you are willing to adopt it, and you may even smile warmly as you say, "We have no questions." When you are not willing to adopt the witness' testimony, it probably is a sound rule of thumb not to release a witness without some cross-examination unless this possible inference of acquiescence in the testimony of the witness can be met successfully with an argument that either is apparent or probably will be accepted by the jury when it is pointed out in the course of your argument to them.

Case 33 illustrates a type of situation as to which disagreement will be found among competent trial lawyers. Some would apply the general rule of thumb not to release the witness without at least a few questions on crossexamination. Others would consider that it is better to forego cross-examination. In the absence of knowledge of some benefit that you may gain because of the peculiar facts of the case, the cross-examination of P's wife will merely

13. See §3.20.
14. See §9.22.

result in additional or cumulative testimony entirely favorable to *P*. The hope of having the jury discredit her testimony entirely because of her testifying to untenable extremes [15] is usually illusory. A wife may be forgiven for believing naïvely in her husband; she may even be applauded for doing so. Probably a jury would not conclude that your failure to cross-examine *P*'s wife indicates that you acquiesce in the truth and accuracy of her testimony. If *P*'s lawyer argues for such an inference, you might in reply develop the following idea:

The substance of her testimony was nothing more than to repeat some of the things her husband said. Most wives would do that for their husbands, and we do not criticize them for it. There was no need for taking her on cross-examination to show this fact; it is a matter of common knowledge.

Assuming that you have decided to cross-examine to some extent, you are also faced with a problem as to length and content of the cross-examination. Most of the individual questions discussed in this chapter are relevant to that problem, though of course not all of them will be presented in a single situation. Also, the potential use of re-cross-examination, in the event your adversary uses redirect, deserves consideration; the tactical implications in this respect are substantially identical with those involved in determining when and how to use redirect examination. [16]

§3.4 The decision to impeach

Should you attempt to impeach the witness?

Your first impulse may be to attempt to impeach every witness your adversary calls, as well as any of your own witnesses whom you may have an opportunity to impeach because of surprise testimony that is unfavorable. Before yielding to the impulse, consider whether the net effect of all the testimony of the witness is favorable or unfavorable to your client. Occasionally you will be able to elicit such favorable testimony on cross-examination that you would not want to impeach the credibility of the witness, though he was called by your adversary.

Another factor to be considered before you attempt impeachment is the soundness of your basis for impeachment — whether it will probably be a successful effort. In the trial of lawsuits, unsuccessful attempts are often worse than mere failures. The effort to impeach is itself a charge against the witness. When you fail to support it, the position of the witness in the eyes of the jury will probably be improved, both because of his ability to with-

15. See §3.12.
16. See §2.38.

stand your effort to impeach him and because of a natural inclination to sympathize with one against whom false charges are made. These comments apply with particular force to impeachment on grounds involving character of the witness.[1] Though in less severe degree, they apply also to other types of impeachment evidence. It follows that as a general rule you should not make blind inquiries, without knowledge of the probable answers or possession of facts indicating a substantial likelihood of answers favorable to you. On tactical grounds, even apart from standards of professional responsibility,[2] you should not make inquiries implying a serious charge against a witness unless you are prepared to back up your charge with satisfactory proof. The idea that the question alone will effectively plant suspicion in the minds of jurors is realistic as to charges that are true but inadmissible,[3] because as a practical matter the charge will go unanswered; it is not sound as to charges not supported by proof, because the opportunity to answer is available and usable.

Should you prove the witness' direct or indirect interest in the suit? This question arises in many forms. For example, the witness may have a share in the subject matter of the suit as such, or he may have received fees in connection with the suit, or he may anticipate incidental benefits that are contingent on the result of litigation. Generally speaking, it is advisable to prove the interest of the witness either by cross-examination or independently. If, however, the matter is so obvious as surely to be recognized by the jury, such as the relationship of husband and wife in Case 33, specific reference to it is unnecessary and may be tactically inadvisable.[4]

In some jurisdictions failure to impeach a witness on a point as to which

---

1. See §3.11.

2. Inquiries that concern any charge counsel believes to be true and and are not condemned by rules of evidence and procedure are justifiable under professional standards. The code is surely violated, however, by implication of charges known to be false, and perhaps it condemns as well those based on mere suspicion. See generally American Bar Association, Code of Professional Responsibility, Canon 7 (1969). *Id.,* DR 7-106 (C), includes the following provisions:

"In appearing in his professional capacity before a tribunal, a lawyer shall not:

"(1) State or allude to any matter that he has no reasonable basis to believe is relevant to the case or that will not be supported by admissible evidence.

"(2) Ask any question that he has no reasonable basis to believe is relevant to the case and that is intended to degrade a witness or other person.

"(7) Intentionally or habitually violate any established rule of procedure or of evidence."

Also, *id.,* EC 7-25, includes the following provisions:

" . . . a lawyer should not ask a witness a question solely for the purpose of harassing or embarrassing him; and a lawyer should not by subterfuge put before a jury matters which it cannot properly consider."

3. As to such questions, see §2.23.

4. *Cf.* §3.3.

his testimony is clear, positive, undisputed, and not improbable will result in a directed verdict as to that point,[5] leaving you no choice but to impeach if you can.

§3.5 Using inconsistent statements

CASE 34. D is defending a personal injury claim of P, a child hit by D's truck. As D's lawyer, you have in your possession a signed statement of W, a witness called to the stand by P during trial. W testifies that, according to his best estimate based on his observations from a position on the sidewalk near the point of impact, D was proceeding at a speed above 40 miles per hour, the limit according to signs posted in the zone where collision occurred. W's signed statement in your possession contains the following sentence on the first page of a two-page statement, W's signature being on the second page only: "I saw the truck just the moment before it hit the child, but looking at it from the side as I was doing, I could not say how fast it was going."

Should you confront a witness on cross-examination with inconsistencies between his testimony and his prior oral and written statements?
When and how should you use a written statement for impeachment?

The beneficial ends you may serve by confronting a witness with inconsistencies include the following: (1) emphasizing the contradiction in the minds of the jury by bringing together at one time contradictory evidence that appeared at different times during the course of the trial; the impeachment of the witness in this way casts doubt on the value of his testimony on other subjects as well as that relating to the particular subject of the contradiction; (2) upsetting the witness and thus improving your chances of obtaining admissions on other subjects.

These ends are best served by confronting the witness with *self*-contradictions — inconsistencies between the answers of the witness on direct examination and those on cross-examination, or between testimony on trial and a prior statement (sworn or unsworn, oral or written), or between his testimony on the one hand and on the other hand his pleadings, demands, or formal claims. You may serve the same ends in some instances, however, by confronting the witness with inconsistencies between his testimony and that of other witnesses.[1]

Against the potential of beneficial results from using inconsistencies, and from the timing of your use, you must weigh some risks of harm. The problem is well illustrated by the inconsistency between testimony on trial and

5. See 9 Wigmore, *Evidence* §2495 (3d ed. 1940).
1. See §3.6.

a prior written statement. The first question faced is whether any use of the statement is advisable. The fact that the witness' written statement in your possession contains matter directly contradictory to his testimony on direct examination does not necessarily indicate that you should use the statement. These are examples of the risks and disadvantages that may be involved in using the statement:

(1) If you are defending a tort case on behalf of an insurance company, but in the name of the individual defendant, in a jurisdiction where the plaintiff is not permitted to advise the jury of the insurance coverage, your use of a written statement may have the incidental effect of making it apparent to the jury that the defendant is protected by insurance. Even careful use of the statement during cross-examination involves this danger because of the jury's natural curiosity about who took the statement and the likelihood of their inferring it was an insurance adjuster. On some occasions this inference has been drawn even when it was false — that is, when the defendant was not in fact protected by liability insurance. The authentication of a statement by the testimony of an adjuster would be almost certain to result in the disclosure of insurance coverage, and authentication by another witness is by no means certain to avoid it.

(2) The statement may contain other matter that is favorable to the party who called the witness and has as yet not been proved; using the statement would probably result in proof of that matter by independent questions of opposing counsel even if that part of the statement itself should not be received in evidence over an objection.[2] If the overall effect of the statement is less favorable to your client than the overall effect of the witness' testimony, it will usually be advisable to refrain from using the statement despite the fact that it would show contradictions in some particulars. Unless the contradictions are on important matters, the value of proving them is outweighed by the harm from contributing to your adversary's case in other respects.

Closely related to the first question (whether you should use the statement) is a second one — how you should use the statement. Indeed, you must consider the various ways you might use the statement in order to reach a sound decision on the question whether any use of the statement is advisable. Two distinct methods of use are possible: (1) using the statement in cross-examination; (2) introducing the statement separately, after the witness has left the stand. It is sometimes inadvisable to authenticate a written

2. As to admissibility of the statement itself at the instance of your adversary, after you have used it in cross-examination, see 7 Wigmore, *Evidence* §§2113–2116 (3d ed. 1940). Compare Federal Rules of Evidence, Rules 107 (applying only when the statement or part of it is "introduced") and 801(d)(1) (declaring that a prior inconsistent statement, or a prior consistent statement offered to rebut an express or implied charge of recent fabrication or improper influence or motive, is not hearsay if the declarant is a witness at the trial and is subject to cross-examination concerning the statement).

statement by a person other than the one whose statement it is (for example, using an insurance adjuster to authenticate the statement is almost certain to disclose the fact of insurance coverage). This factor, when present, strongly supports the decision to use the statement on cross-examination or not at all. Also, it is usually more effective to get an admission from the witness that this is his statement than to depend on someone else's identification of his signature and of the statement. Another consideration is that the jury probably would wonder why the witness himself had not been asked about his own statement and given an opportunity to explain. This opportunity of explanation is one of the factors that has led to a requirement, in most jurisdictions, of inquiring about the statement on cross-examination to lay the foundation for its being received as a prior inconsistent statement.[3] Finally, since it is a case of self-contradiction by the witness, you probably will achieve more dramatic effect by confronting the witness than by producing the contradictory statement after the witness is off the stand and beyond the observation of the jury. In most instances you should use the statement on cross-examination rather than solely by introducing it separately. If the witness repudiates the statement on cross-examination, however, either in whole or by contending that he did not read it over and that it contains errors, you should consider authenticating the statement by testimony of a witness to the statement or of the person who took it. Ordinarily authentication by a disinterested witness to the statement is preferable to authentication by the person who took it, since the latter will almost invariably be either a lawyer or an adjuster.[4]

Assuming that you have decided to use the statement on cross-examination, you then must determine in what manner you will lay the predicate for it and produce it. Should you produce the statement and ask the witness to identify it first, as a predicate for the questions about the statement and its contents, or should you postpone production of the statement until you have asked questions about the subject matter and about the circumstances of taking the statement? In some jurisdictions decisions require that you produce the statement for inspection by the witness before you question him about the statement,[5] though this rule would not preclude your asking questions calling for the witness to present testimony about the same subject matter that is treated in the statement. In jurisdictions where this requirement is not enforced, it may be tactically preferable not to produce the statement first. Although a perfect statement[6] would include commitment of the wit-

---

3. 3A Wigmore, *Evidence* §§1025–1039 (rev. ed. Chadbourn 1970). See also Federal Rules of Evidence, Rule 613(b).

4. See §9.13 as to the practice of taking a statement in the presence of a witness.

5. 4 Wigmore, *Evidence* §§1259–1263 (3d ed. 1940). But see Federal Rules of Evidence, Rule 613(a).

6. See §9.13.

ness on all essential facts, more often the statement that is available to you in trial is, for practical reasons, less than perfect in this respect. You may jump to the conclusion that you have caught the witness in a direct contradiction only to find on rereading the statement more carefully that the witness has worked out through a loophole. One of the elements in preparation for cross-examination is thorough familiarity with the statement so that you know the loopholes and are prepared to plug them by a proper line of questions before you allow the witness to see the statement and study it.

Even though the testimony that forms the basis for impeachment was given in direct examination, ordinarily you should call on the witness to repeat it. The repetition serves the purpose of placing the contrast sharply before the jury and also the purpose of doubly committing the witness so that he has less chance for escape when the trap is sprung.

A lawyer sometimes holds the witness' statement in his hand as a means of frightening the witness (who does not exactly recall its contents) while questioning him, or as a method of conveying to the jury the impression that the statement contains certain comments as implied by the questions. This use of a statement, at least for the latter purpose and perhaps for the former, probably violates the Code of Professional Responsibility[7] and should be stopped by the trial judge if objection is made. The practice of holding the statement in view though not referring to it verbally is sometimes used when the lawyer does not want to introduce the statement itself, because of some risk of harm such as those discussed at the beginning of this section.

---

7. It would seem that deliberately conveying to the jury, by implication or innuendo, the impression that a document in your hands is a statement containing certain assertions, when in fact you know it does not contain them, would violate American Bar Association, Code of Professional Responsibility, Canon 7 (1969).

Id., DR 7–102(A) (4) and (5), declare that a lawyer shall not knowingly "use . . . false evidence" or knowingly "make a false statement of . . . fact."

Id., EC 7–25, declares that a "lawyer should not by subterfuge put before a jury matters which it cannot properly consider."

Consider also *id.*, DR 7–106(C): "In appearing in his professional capacity before a tribunal, a lawyer shall not:

"(1) State or allude to any matter that he has no reasonable basis to believe is relevant to the case or that will not be supported by admissible evidence.

"(2) Ask any question that he has no reasonable basis to believe is relevant to the case and that is intended to degrade a witness or other person.

"(7) Intentionally or habitually violate any established rule of procedure or of evidence."

Canon 22 of the 1908 Canons declared it "unprofessional and dishonorable to deal other than candidly with the facts . . . in the presentation of causes." This would seem to condemn both of the two purposes suggested in the text above for holding a statement of the witness in your hands as you cross-examine. Was the omission of this phrase from the 1969 Code intended to establish a less stringent requirement of dealing candidly with the facts?

Even this use of a statement that you do not want in evidence involves a risk, however. For example, if you attempt to use a statement in this way, your opponent may call upon you to produce the statement; if you withhold it or object to its being placed in evidence by your opponent, the jury may draw an unfavorable inference from your conduct. It might be suggested that you could evade the problem by refusing to produce the statement for your adversary to see in the absence of an agreement in advance that it can be received in evidence (with the expectation that your adversary will not so stipulate, for fear of thereby waiving objection to matters otherwise inadmissible).[8] But that attitude is more likely to cause unfavorable reaction to your methods than to your adversary's refusal to make the agreement with respect to some statement your adversary has never seen.

Usually the use of a contradictory statement in cross-examination is more effective if you are able to remember it well enough to get the witness thoroughly committed on all material points before you produce the statement, even for your own inspection (with the incidental effect of placing the witness on close guard). There is also a greater likelihood that you will catch the witness so completely off guard that the jury can see it in his demeanor or in his answers. He has less time to steel himself for the blow than when you have been looking at the statement while asking questions. Often a lawyer reads from a statement to emphasize its favorable points before identifying the statement. But you can usually get as much beneficial emphasis by reading parts of the statement after you have identified it, especially if you have remembered the statement well enough to get the witness thoroughly committed by his answers before you produce the statement and give the witness a chance to study it.

In Case 34, for example, if you produce the statement early in the cross-examination, and W has time to study it before you call upon him to explain the contradiction, he may explain by saying that in his statement ("I saw the truck just the moment before it hit the child, but looking at it from the side as I was doing, I could not say how fast it was going") he only meant that he could not make an accurate statement in miles per hour, and that he still cannot do that but can be sure that it was going over 40 miles per hour. On the other hand, if without any reference whatsoever to any statement (the content and perhaps even the existence of which the witness may have forgotten), you first ask more questions about his estimate of the speed, it may be that you can commit him to the proposition that he was not just looking at the truck from the side but had watched it for some distance, or that looking at it solely from the side he could estimate the speed accurately, or you might even commit him to a specific miles-per-hour estimate or with-

8. In a few jurisdictions, your adversary's request that you produce the document makes it admissible without any specific agreement to that effect; see §3.28.

in some stated range by pressing him for a specific range once he says it was over 40. With any of these commitments his explanation of the statement would be much less acceptable to any jury.

Generally it is also preferable, when you finally produce the statement, to ask the witness if he recalls its being taken, to ask him if it is not true that he was given an opportunity to read it (the use of this inquiry may be questionable if the statement does not contain evidence in itself that the witness read it),[9] and to ask him to identify his signature and any other handwriting or initials of his that appear in it. Also, it is sometimes preferable to ask the witness to read the entire statement rather than only the part to which you will later direct attention, in the hope that he may be led to say that he read it and approved it before signing it and still approves it now, or that the events were more recent in his memory when he made the statement and that he considered it correct when he made it.

When you have used a statement for impeachment purposes, you should also consider whether to offer the document itself in evidence. In most instances, you will be permitted, if you so desire, to offer in evidence only the part of the document in which you are particularly interested; if this rule obtains, it is usually preferable to make the offer, rather than relying solely on the reading of the statement in the course of questioning. You should consider, however, the rules of evidence in your jurisdiction as to whether by objection you can be forced to offer all remaining parts of the document pertinent to the same subject, or whether your adversary may be entitled to offer all of the remainder of the document or at least all that pertains to the same subject,[10] and if so, whether the advantage of having favorable parts of the document in evidence may be outweighed by the disadvantages of having the remainder of it in evidence. Also, you should consider whether it is advisable to limit your offer specifically to impeachment purposes.[11]

§3.6   Using inconsistency with other witnesses

CASE 35.   *D* is defending a personal injury case. *P*, the plaintiff, testifies on direct examination that he has not worked since the accident on which suit is based. As *D*'s lawyer, you have documentary proof, in the form of time records and cancelled payroll checks endorsed by *P*, as well as the testimony of the foreman, that *P* worked for a period of six weeks before he first consulted a lawyer.

9. See §9.13 as to methods of preparing the statement to show that it was read and approved by the witness.

10. 7 Wigmore, *Evidence* §§2102–2125 (3d ed. 1940). See also Federal Rules of Evidence, Rules 107, 801(d)(1).

11. See §2.36.

Should you confront a witness on cross-examination with inconsistencies between his testimony and that of others?

In deciding whether to confront a witness on cross-examination with inconsistencies you should consider the relative advantages and disadvantages of that method [1] as compared with other possible uses of the same materials. The best answer will depend to some extent on the identity and relationship of the witnesses, the nature of the evidence of inconsistency, and the reason for its significance in the case.

If the inconsistency is between the testimony of two witnesses both of whom were called by your opponent, confronting either witness with the inconsistencies serves at least the purpose of emphasizing in the minds of the jurors the fact of contradiction. The degree of benefit you realize from the cross-examination will depend upon how serious the contradiction is, but usually there is no better method of making the most of it.

Rarely will much be gained by confronting a party with an inconsistency between his testimony and that of his adversary; his answer is obvious — the adversary is wrong. It may be desirable, however, to point out the inconsistency in a manner that, without forcing the issue on the witness, gives him the opportunity to call his adversary a liar, if he is the type who might do that; usually calling another a liar is more likely to harm the speaker's cause than to help it. [2]

If the inconsistency is between the testimony of your opposing party or his witness and your client or witness, it is a two-edged sword. It may be construed by the jury as reflecting unfavorably on the testimony of your own client or witness, rather than the one you seek to impeach. If the witness being cross-examined offers satisfactory support for his own version when pressed about the inconsistency on cross-examination, the effect will be exactly the opposite of that you intended. Before pressing the witness about such an inconsistency, therefore, you should be prepared to meet this contingency with corroboration for the version of your own witness, or with other evidence tending to impeach your adversary's witness. If you have neither of these at your disposal and the inconsistency does not relate to a crucial point in the case, it is probably wiser for you to ignore the inconsistency as long as your adversary is content to do so.

The nature of the inconsistency and the reasons for its significance have an important bearing on both whether you should point it up and, if so, when. If you try to make much of obviously trivial matters you will probably bore the jury or amuse them at best, and at worst you may cause them to infer that you are trying to confuse the issues in the case rather than seeking a fair and sound disposition. [3] With this exception and that noted in the

1. *Cf.* §3.5.
2. See §7.19.
3. See §1.3.

preceding paragraph, however, the problem is primarily one of choice as to timing. If the inconsistency is one that probably reflects only upon the accuracy of the witness' powers of observation, memory, or expression, and not upon his integrity, usually the best way to use the inconsistency is to confront the witness with it on cross-examination. On the other hand, if the inconsistency probably reflects on the integrity of your opposing party or a key witness, you may make more dramatic and effective use of it by merely laying a predicate during cross-examination and introducing at a later time your convincing independent evidence of the falsity of the testimony.

Case 35 illustrates the factors that you should consider in determining which is the better use of the evidence — that is, which is the better timing. P errs in testifying that he has not worked since the accident, and as D's lawyer you have documentary proof and the testimony of P's foreman regarding a period of work for six weeks just before P went to his lawyer. This situation arises less often than defendants' lawyers would wish, but more often than careful investigation by plaintiff's lawyers would permit. Should this evidence be used on cross-examination with the purpose of getting P to admit that he testified falsely? Or should you try the case with deference and courtesy to P, recommitting him to his false testimony on cross-examination and waiting until a time near the conclusion of your own evidence to produce this positive proof of P's perjury? Generally the latter course is preferable because it will have more dramatic effect and will remain more vividly in the minds of the jurors at the climax of the trial. Against this course, however, stand other arguments: the witness will have more time to think about an explanation than if you had confronted him in the course of cross-examination and called upon him to explain immediately; the jury may, as the trial proceeds, develop an impression so favorable to the plaintiff that it is more difficult to overcome late in trial than would have been true at an earlier point; and you will have lost an opportunity for obtaining further admissions from the plaintiff while he was upset from being caught. If, contrary to the assumption in Case 35, as D's lawyer you did not have convincing and admissible proof of previous work, it would be preferable to go into the matter on cross-examination. You would thereby take advantage of the possibility that P may admit more than you can actually prove otherwise. Also, the risk of harm from proof that your suspicion was unfounded would not be so severe as if you unsuccessfully attempted independent proof rather than relying upon cross-examination of P.

§3.7 Using documents

When and how should you use documents for impeachment?

Pretrial preparation should include a careful search for documents that may be useful in cross-examination as well as for other purposes during trial.

Written statements[1] and depositions[2] are but two of many types of documents you may use in this way. The sources at which relevant documents may be found are innumerable.[3]

The choice between using any particular document on cross-examination and using it by independent offer presents essentially the same tactical considerations as those noted with respect to using written statements and using conflicts with the testimony of others.[4] Because of difficulty in locating and producing independent, authenticating testimony, when the document is a letter or instrument written or approved by the witness, usually it will be best to use the document in cross-examination rather than by separate offer. On the other hand, if the document is not one written or approved by the witness, but dependent instead upon authentication by other persons, in many cases it will be best to make a separate offer; it is possible even in the latter type of case to use the document on cross-examination, however, since the witness may admit enough to serve the purpose of authenticating it, or you may use it with the expectation of later authenticating and introducing it if the witness refuses to make the necessary admissions.

§3.8 Using depositions

When and how should you use a deposition for impeachment?

Few of the disadvantages of using a written statement for impeachment[1] confront you when you use a deposition for this purpose. The deposition is formally taken as a part of the preparation for trial of the case; it is already available, and its contents are known to the adverse lawyer. If the witness has been properly prepared by the lawyer who placed him on the stand,[2] he has reviewed the deposition testimony before testifying in the trial. This reduces the chances that he will be caught in contradictions between his present testimony and that on deposition, but it increases the effectiveness of the impeachment when the contradiction does occur. If a material contradiction occurs and the testimony on trial is more unfavorable to you as cross-examiner than that on deposition, there is rarely any occasion to refrain from proving the contradiction. Although there is no practical difficulty of authentication to support the offer of the deposition testimony separately and usually no necessity for laying a predicate by previous inquiry concerning prior inconsistent statements, the advantages of confronting the witness with the inconsistency[3] will usually make it preferable to use the deposition in cross-

1. See §3.5.
2. See §3.8.
3. See §9.6.
4. See §§3.5, 3.6, and Case 35, which involves documentary proof as well as independent testimony.
1. See §3.5.
2. See §§2.10, 2.14.
3. Compare §3.5.

examination. Of course, you might emphasize the parts of the deposition used in questioning by later offering them as evidence either generally or for the limited purpose of impeachment.[4]

In advance of trial you should have prepared some kind of outline or index of every deposition that you may have occasion to use during trial. It makes a poor impression on the judge and jury if you waste time thumbing through the deposition looking for something. Also it gives the witness too much time to think about his answer and what is coming next in the line of questioning. One satisfactory method of accomplishing this purpose of having an index is to make notations on the inside cover of your copy of the deposition, indicating the pages where testimony on a particular subject is to be found. You may accomplish the same purpose by similar notations on a separate note pad.

Whenever you use a deposition, it is desirable at some point to inform the jury of the formal manner in which the deposition was taken — under oath, before a reporter or other official, and, if the following are true, in the office of the lawyer who has called the witness to the stand and with lawyers for both parties present. If the deponent read the deposition and signed it after it was typed, you should prove that also. For impeachment purposes, the deposition is much more effective if it has been signed; this is a strong argument against waiving signature on a deposition.[5] The witness may convince the jury that the reporter misunderstood him and wrote down an incorrect answer, but the witness has little chance of explaining a contradiction on this basis if he has read and signed the deposition after it was written.

As for the time of proving the solemn manner in which the deposition was taken, the more usual practice seems to be to do this at the moment of the first reference to the deposition. An argument in favor of proving the solemnity first is that this manner of proceeding contributes to building up jury interest in what is to come, so that their attention is at a high pitch when you prove the contradiction. Perhaps that practice is usually justified, but often the delay has the same disadvantage as thumbing through the deposition to find something — it gives the witness too much time to think about what you are leading up to, and how he should answer when the critical question comes. To avoid this disadvantage, you might save the evidence of solemnity of the deposition for the conclusion of that phase of the cross-examination, and use it as a clincher, to emphasize the significance of the discrepancy after you have proved it.

4. See §2.36.
5. See §11.5.

As stated in a preceding section[6] with reference to using a written statement for impeachment, it is generally preferable that you cause the witness to repeat and become positively committed on the subject matter before producing the impeaching matter from the deposition.

§3.9 Calling on the reporter to read previous testimony

Should you ask the reporter during cross-examination to read previous testimony of the witness that apparently contradicts what he is saying on cross-examination?

If you have caught the witness in a contradiction, you emphasize it if you bring to the jury's attention the exact words previously used by the witness. The effect may extend beyond the bearing of the contradiction on its own subject matter, for the witness may be "broken down" so that he makes other admissions or the jury disbelieves other parts of his testimony. Calling upon the reporter to read the previous testimony, however, is rarely a practicable method of confronting the witness with the contradiction. Many trial judges will decline to permit the practice because of the great delay usually involved, while the reporter is searching through his notes in an effort to find the part of the testimony to which you refer. Even if the judge will permit the practice, it is questionable whether you should use it. The jury and court may grow impatient, and you will have given the witness a considerable period of time to think about the matter and be prepared with an explanation or excuse. Ordinarily it is inadvisable to ask the court reporter to go back through his notes to read previous testimony while you have the witness under examination.

Sometimes you may in some other way confront the witness with the exact words he previously used. If the contradiction is one that comes as a complete surprise to you as cross-examiner and it is impracticable to call upon the reporter to read previous testimony, you may achieve substantially the same effect by accurately repeating to the witness the substance of the previous testimony. If the witness evades the apparent contradiction by misstating what he previously said, in many courts you will be able to demonstrate this fact to the jury by having the reporter transcribe for your reading to the jury during argument the original testimony of the witness on the subject in question and also the cross-examination on that matter. If you anticipate that you will develop a contradiction during the cross-examination, you may be able to get from the reporter a transcript of previous evidence before you reach the pertinent subject matter in cross-examination. Whether this is possible will depend upon the length of the testimony and

6. See §3.5.

the timing of recesses during which the reporter would have an opportunity to transcribe the testimony you want. Expense (the reporter's charge for this service) will sometimes be a practical consideration affecting your decision whether to request that the reporter transcribe lengthy testimony. In cases involving large sums or large property interests, lawyers often follow the practice of placing a standing order with the reporter for "daily copy" of the trial proceedings.

§3.10 Inquiring into opportunity to observe

CASE 36. *P* purchased from *D* a farm located three miles from the nearest suburban residential development. *P* seeks rescission, claiming that he was induced to enter into the transaction by *D*'s fraudulent misrepresentations. One of *P*'s witnesses is *W*, former bookkeeper for *D*. *W* testifies that while sitting in an adjoining office at work, during negotiations between *P* and *D*, he overheard *D* state to *P* the following: that *D* planned to arrange for extension of utilities to another large tract owned by *D*, located one mile nearer to another residential development than the farm, and that *D* had already let a contract for construction of a shopping center and residential streets on the tract. *D* advises you, as his lawyer, that the office was so arranged that it is most improbable that *W* could have overheard the conversation unless he deliberately eavesdropped; that in response to *P*'s questions *D* did make the statement to *P* to which *W* testifies, but at the same time told *P* that the contract was let to Suburban Construction Company, a corporation, and that *D* owned the controlling interest in the corporation. *D* asserts, among other bases for defense, that his statements were not false, but made in good faith, and that subsequent changes in business conditions caused him to abandon his plans and cancel the construction contract.

Should you cross-examine the witness as to his opportunity and ability to observe matters concerning which he has testified?

Proof of poor opportunity for observation is one of the customary methods of discrediting the testimony of a witness. Ability to observe, in the sense of personal capacity, is less often an issue, but involves many of the same considerations. Whether you should cross-examine on poor opportunity or ability in particular instances will depend on the principal purpose of your cross-examination and the probable effectiveness of this method as part of the cross-examination.

Will the effort to show poor opportunity to observe be effective? Frequently more harm than good is done by cross-examination because it merely reinforces the direct testimony. This observation applies to an attempt to get the witness to admit facts showing poor opportunity to observe when the witness is not subject to effective attack on this ground. The provable circumstances as to his opportunity are more important than what the witness himself will say. The fact that the witness will insist that he had an excellent opportunity does not necessarily indicate that you should avoid inquiry on the subject; you may be able to discredit him by committing him to an extreme position [1] that is either patently absurd or clearly inconsistent with the actual circumstances proved by other convincing evidence. For example, in Case 34 the circumstances and availability of W's written statement saying that he had little opportunity to observe the speed of the truck will probably cause the cross-examination as a whole to be more effective if W insists that he had an excellent opportunity to observe the speed. On the other hand, if the actual circumstances reveal a reasonably good opportunity for observation by the witness, the fact that the witness is inclined to be conservative in his statements (that is, the type who will say only that the horse was white on the side he saw, and not that it was a white horse) does not necessarily indicate that he should be cross-examined on the subject of opportunity to observe; the effect may be only to improve your adversary's argument that the witness was entirely disinterested and careful to be fair and accurate in everything he told the jury.

Will your effort to prove poor opportunity for observation interfere with a more important purpose of your cross-examination? If, for example, your primary purpose in the cross-examination is to develop evidence favorable to you on a subject not touched in the direct examination, [2] proof of poor opportunity to observe the subject of the direct testimony might incidentally have the effect of proving also poor opportunity to observe the other subject on which the witness gives testimony favorable to you. You must weigh the advantages of weakening the adverse testimony against the disadvantages of weakening the favorable testimony. Also, if the favorable effect of the testimony on the new subject on cross-examination has been striking, it may weaken the overall effect of the cross-examination to add to it a showing of merely doubtful opportunity to observe.

In the preceding paragraph it is suggested that the selection of the primary purpose of cross-examination will influence the decision on whether to cross-examine regarding opportunity to observe. Frequently you will not be able to predict with any degree of certainty the probable success of the various routes of cross-examination open to you. Since this is true, it will often be advisable to postpone, until near the conclusion, cross-examination of the type that will probably have a favorable effect in one respect but unfavorable in another. You can then make the final decision on whether to use such cross-examination in the light of the actual development of the witness' testimony. This principle applies to any type of cross-examination that poten-

1. See §3.12.
2. See §3.14.

tially "cuts both ways." Case 36 illustrates the point. *W* is subject to potentially effective cross-examination regarding whether he was so situated as
to overhear the conversation between *P* and *D*. But, as *D*'s lawyer, you
would prefer to forego such cross-examination if *W* would testify that *D*
also told *P* that the construction contract was with Suburban Construction
Company, and that *D* held the controlling interest in that corporation; *W*
might also admit that as *D*'s former bookkeeper he was familiar with the
fact that subsequent changes in business conditions were the subject of later
conferences leading finally to cancellation of the construction contract. If *W*
would testify to these things on cross-examination, his testimony as a whole
would be more favorable than unfavorable to *D*, and as *D*'s lawyer you
would not then want to cast an unfavorable reflection on *W* by cross-examination indicating that he was dishonest or that he was an eavesdropper.
On the other hand, if as *D*'s lawyer you first try to secure admissions from
W regarding *D*'s additional statements and later decision, and *W* refuses
to make these admissions, you may then attack him by cross-examination
regarding the doubt as to his opportunity to overhear the negotiations between *P* and *D* (and perhaps regarding animosity toward *D* because of
being discharged by *D*).[3]

§3.11   Proving bad character

CASE 37.   *W*, who was a foreman for *D*, a construction contractor, is a
key witness in a suit by *P* for alleged breach of the construction contract by
use of inferior materials. As *P*'s lawyer, you discover that five years before
trial of the contract case *W* was convicted as an accomplice to an abortion
performed upon an unmarried girl for whose pregnancy *W* was responsible. Certified copies of the record of conviction and *W*'s parole after eight
months in prison are available to you.

*Should you prove bad character of an adverse party or witness to impeach
him?*

If so, should you do it on cross-examination or by independent evidence?

Evidence of bad character of a witness or party may bear directly on the
issues of the case, but more often it has no direct bearing on the issues and
is admissible merely on the theory that it affects the credibility of the witness.
The rough sense of justice in the mind of a juror often includes a principle
that mud-slinging regarding matters not before the court and jury for de-

---

3. See §3.17. In a few jurisdictions, evidence attacking credibility of the witness
would be excluded if you had first extended the subject of cross-examination to new
matter supporting your own case, on the theory that you had thereby made the witness your own. 3A Wigmore, *Evidence* §914 (rev. ed. Chadbourn 1970). *Cf.* §2.2. But
see Federal Rules of Evidence, Rule 607.

cision is improper.[1] In the legal way of thinking, the character of every witness is in issue to some extent because it affects the credibility of his testimony. Jurors, however, do not necessarily agree that any evidence of bad character that is admissible under the rules of evidence[2] is material to the case; they may regard the use of such evidence as unfair, and they may consciously or subconsciously weigh that factor against the party offering the evidence. Because of these considerations, it is usually inadvisable to offer this type of evidence if its admissibility is doubtful. Even if it is clearly admissible, you should give careful consideration to the question whether the persons sitting on the jury, as distinguished from the lawyers and judges deciding the matter of admissibility, will regard the evidence as so closely bearing on the credibility of the witness' testimony in this case that its use is justified. Such evidence is likely to have a marked effect on the jury's consideration of the case. If they regard it as bearing closely on credibility of the witness, they will be influenced to disregard his testimony and even to view with more suspicion the testimony of other witnesses called by the same party. On the other hand, if they do not so regard it, they are less likely to ignore the evidence than to be positively influenced against the party who offered it. The decision as to whether you should use such evidence therefore involves an appraisal of how directly the evidence bears on the credibility of the witness and what attitudes the jurors have brought with them into court.

In those jurisdictions where, under the circumstances of Case 37, the evidence of W's conviction as an accomplice to the crime of abortion would be admissible, the decision whether or not to offer the evidence is one as to which experienced and competent lawyers disagree. Probably the majority would decide not to use the evidence, however, unless it can be bolstered by other evidence more directly bearing on the honesty of the witness as contrasted with his adherence to other standards of conduct.

§3.12 Proving bias

CASE 38. D is defending a personal injury claim based upon a collision at the intersection of Through Street and Side Street, in a suburban area. P, who entered Through Street from Side Street on the west, with the purpose of turning left (north), relies on D's alleged negligence in proceeding south at a greatly excessive speed and failing to yield the right of way. D, on the other hand, alleges that P was guilty of causal negligence in failing to stop before entering and in failing to yield the right of way. An ordinance

---

1. Concerning jury reaction to a lawyer's methods, see §1.3.

2. There is a wide range of variation among the different jurisdictions as to admissibility of this type of evidence. 3A Wigmore, *Evidence* §§920–930, 987 (rev. ed. Chadbourn 1970). See also Federal Rules of Evidence, Rules 608–610.

gives the right of way to a car on Through Street if it is within 150 feet of the intersection when the car from Side Street enters; otherwise the car from Side Street has the right of way. *P* calls the witness *W*, who testifies that he was standing in front of a service station at the northwest corner of the intersection, observed *D*'s approach, and estimates his speed at 75 m.p.h. (in a 45 m.p.h. zone). On direct examination, *W* is not asked about his observations of *P*'s entering the highway. As *D*'s lawyer, you interviewed *W* before trial and concluded that *W* had made up his mind that *P* ought to win the lawsuit and intended to do all he could to answer questions in such a way as to help *P* win.

What methods should you use in cross-examining a witness whose testimony is greatly influenced by his bias?

Most witnesses are biased by the time they are called to testify in a case. If a witness has not been biased from his first encounter with the controversy, he probably will have been interviewed by a lawyer or other representative of each side before the trial. In addition to furnishing information himself, the witness will probably have heard enough of the claims of each party that he will have formed a definite opinion of his own as to who should win the lawsuit.

The testimony of nearly every witness, however honest and fair he may try to be, is influenced at least subconsciously by the opinion he has formed concerning the merits of the controversy. Despite this subconscious influence, the majority of witnesses with no direct interest in the lawsuit will attempt to answer fairly the questions submitted to them. If as cross-examiner you ask questions calling for information that is unfavorable to your adversary who called the witness, he answers frankly — he regards himself more as a witness for the court, charged with the duty of telling whatever he knows and is asked to tell, [1] than as a witness for one party telling only things favorable to that party. This is, of course, the attitude that a witness should have. Furthermore, aside from ethical considerations, the witness who conveys to the jury the impression that he does not have this attitude destroys or greatly reduces the effectiveness of his testimony. This self-evident truth is a key to effective cross-examination of the witness who falls in the minority group

---

1. The witness usually feels that he should not even be restricted to what he is asked to tell. Persons outside the legal profession often criticize the legal system for requiring the witness to swear that he will tell "the truth, the whole truth, and nothing but the truth," and then cutting him off sharply with objections and rules of evidence if he starts to tell the whole truth. The force of this criticism has never caused courts to establish a rule letting the witness tell the whole truth, but probably it has had some influence on the form of the oath in those jurisdictions requiring only that the witness swear to "answer truthfully all questions which shall be propounded to [him] in the cause now on trial." Compare Federal Rules of Evidence, Rule 603.

— the witness willing to frame answers for the purpose of favoring the side he wants to win. There is little hope of getting an answer from this witness that is favorable in content; the more promising aim of cross-examination is to reveal the bias of the witness.

Usually the most effective technique for accomplishing the purpose of revealing conscious bias of the witness is to pick out those subjects on which his testimony is most questionable and pursue them in detail,[2] recognizing that the anwers of the witness will be unfavorable in content and capitalizing on their extreme in this respect. Since the witness will not admit his deliberate formulation of answers in a manner favorable to the party calling him, you must expose his conscious bias indirectly. The jury must draw the conclusion of conscious bias by comparing the manner and the content of the answers the witness gives and a set of hypothetical answers that a fair witness would give. As cross-examiner, you have no opportunity to prove these hypothetical answers, or (until your argument to the jury) even to argue what they would be. By several methods, however, you may make the jury conscious of your purpose in the cross-examination, and thus invite them to consider the bias of the witness. You may elicit answers from the witness that on their face go to a patently absurd or highly improbable extreme. Having once committed the witness, you may invite the jury's attention to the unreasonableness of the position taken by questions suggestive of logical weaknesses in the extreme position. Another more obvious method of directing the jury's attention to your purpose is to clothe your question to the witness with some phrase such as "You won't even admit . . . , will you?" Ordinarily the success of this method of cross-examination will depend on the failure of the witness to realize your purpose until you have already committed him to an untenable position. It is therefore appropriate to postpone use of techniques for calling the jury's attention to the purpose until you have the witness thoroughly committed.

The types of questions as to which a consciously biased witness may allow himself to "get out on a limb" are almost as varied as the types of fact questions that may arise in lawsuits. Case 38 may be taken as an example of one such type. If as D's lawyer you judge that W is willing to color his testimony deliberately to help P, you might choose to make inquiries on other relevant issues in the case besides speed of D's car (the only important issue on which W testified on direct examination), recognizing that W will try to answer all questions against D and capitalizing on the chance that he will work himself into an inconsistency in doing so. You might proceed by asking what first attracted W's attention to either vehicle, asking for details about the movement of D's car other than its speed, establishing W's position in front of the station by a diagram drawn by W, asking for details

2. See §3.15.

about the direction and speed of P's car, and then asking whether he observed how far away D's car was when P entered the intersection, and if so, his estimate of the distance. If you have correctly judged W as a consciously biased witness, and if you have established your background data on cross-examination without making the witness realize your purpose, you may receive answers that W did observe these other matters and on that basis estimates that D was over 150 feet (the distance specified in the ordinance) back from the intersection as P entered. You may then invite the jury's attention to the patent improbability of the observations to which he has testified. Through questions you may point out that W would have had to look in opposite directions to see D and P and could hardly have observed the rapidly changing situation in both directions well enough to estimate fairly the speed of both vehicles and their relative positions when P entered. The following example is given with the realization that it is somewhat easier to develop when one writes the answers as well as the questions. Though the trial lawyer, rather than having this privilege, is forced to accept the answers as they come, and therefore can never predict with certainty the entire course of a cross-examination, the example will serve as an illustration of a type of commitment to an untenable extreme that may be possible with a witness more concerned about framing his answers to help the party who called him than about telling only the truth.

Q. What first attracted your attention to either of the cars involved in this collision?

A. It was the speed of the car coming down Through Street. As I had just stepped out of my car and was about to walk around behind it, this car was coming down Through Street like a streak of lightning and that's what caused me to watch it.

Q. Was he close enough when you first saw him that you could judge his speed?

A. O, yes, he was going at least 75.

Q. About how far away was he when you first saw him?

A. About 75 yards.

Q. Did you continue watching him long enough to form in your mind an estimate of his speed?

A. Yes, sir, I would say over 75 m.p.h.

Q. How far did he travel as you kept your eyes on him there?

A. I kept watching him right on up to the collision.

Q. Did he reduce his speed before the collision?

A. Not to amount to anything; he might have taken his foot off the gas, but he didn't apply the brakes.

Q. Were you watching him closely enough to say where he was with regard to the center line of Through Street?

A. Yes sir, he was over near the middle; his left wheels were over on the left-hand side of the street.

Q. Did you notice whether the car moved to the side any, or stayed partly over the center line?

A. He stayed about the same, with his left wheels over the center just a little.

Q. Mr. *W*, where were you at the time you were watching *D's* car?

A. In front of the service station, on the left-hand side of my car.

Q. I hand you a scale diagram of Through Street, Side Street, and the service station you have mentioned. Does this diagram appear to you to be a fair representation of that area?

A. Yes sir.

Q. I call your attention to this rectangle down here in the left-hand corner, under the heading "scale drawings"; comparing that rectangle to the width of the highway and the size of the service station, does it appear to be the right size for a passenger car of the type you drive?

A. Yes sir.

Q. Will you please draw such a rectangle on this diagram to show where your car was parked? (After *W* complies) Please write inside that rectangle "*W's* car." (After *W* complies) Now put down an "X" at the spot where you were standing, and label that "Where *W* stood." (After *W* complies) Mr. *W*, did you see whether or not Mr. *P* came to a complete stop before he drove out onto the highway?

A. Yes, he brought his car to a stop.

Q. Did you observe whether he started up quickly?

A. He made just a normal start — it wasn't any jackrabbit start if that's what you mean. He gunned it, all right, but that was when he was trying to get out of the way after he saw this other fellow speeding toward him.

Q. Did you observe closely enough to estimate the speed of *P's* car before he gunned it?

A. Yes sir, it was around 10 to 12 miles.

Q. Did you see how far away *D's* car was when *P* started into the intersection after stopping?

A. Yes sir, it was about 200 feet.

D's lawyer: We ask that the reporter mark for identification this diagram on which notations have been made by Mr. *W* (marked "D-1 for identification" by reporter). Your Honor, we offer in evidence the diagram marked exhibit D-1 for identification.

Court: The diagram is received in evidence. (Court reporter strikes "for identification" and substitutes "in evidence.")

Q. (by *D's* lawyer, continuing) Mr. *W*, you have testified that you observed *D's* car closely enough that you are willing to tell the court and jury how far away it was when you saw it, how fast it was going, and that it stayed partly over the center line all the way up to the point of collision, while you watched it the whole time, is that correct?

A. Yes sir.

Q. And also you have testified that you were watching *P's* car closely enough to tell that *P* came to a complete stop, then entered when the other car was

200 feet away and was making 10 to 12 m.p.h. before he gunned the car to try to get out of the way. Is that correct?

A. Yes sir.

Q. Mr. *W*, I'll hold up this diagram which is marked exhibit D-1 so you and the jury and court can all see it. Which direction would you have to look from point "X," where you were standing, to see *D*'s car when it was 200 feet back?

A. A little east of north, if we assume that street runs true north and south.

Q. Which direction would you have to look from point "X" to see *P*'s car starting into the highway?

A. A little east of south.

Q. You could not see both those directions with your head in the same position, could you?

A. No sir, I turned it back and forth.

Q. I ask you to help me do some figuring on the blackboard here. Do you recall how many feet there are in a mile?

A. 5280.

Q. Now, at a speed of 60 m.p.h., which is a mile a minute, let's see how many feet a car would travel in 1 second. We will divide this 5280 feet by 60, the number of seconds in a minute. (After figuring on the blackboard) Is this correct — 88 feet per second at a speed of 60 m.p.h.?

A. Yes sir.

Q. Now, you have estimated that the speed of *D*'s car was at least 75 m.p.h. when you first saw it, and that the speed was not reduced to amount to anything.

A. Yes sir.

Q. 75 m.p.h. would be 75 over 60 or 1¼ times as fast as 60 m.p.h., would it not?

A. Yes sir.

Q. Adding ¼ more to 88, that would be 88 plus 22, or 110 feet per second that a car would go at 75 m.p.h.?

A. Yes sir.

Q. And you have estimated that it was 75 yards or 225 feet away when you first saw it and that would mean it traveled a little less than that distance to reach the point of collision in front of you, as shown on the diagram?

A. Yes sir.

Q. At 110 feet per second it would take just 2 seconds to cover the distance, would it not?

A. Yes sir.

Q. So all these things about the movements of both vehicles you saw in two different directions within about 2 seconds.

A. Yes sir, I was turning my head back and forth, like I said.

Q. Do you have a watch with a second hand on it.

A. Yes sir.

Q. Please take your watch and say "go" when you start counting and say "stop" when 2 seconds have passed.

A. "Go" . . . "Stop."
D's Lawyer: Your witness.

Most witnesses will not be subject to effective use of this technique. Seldom, if ever, will you feel certain that it will be effective. If you set out with the purpose of committing the witness to an untenable extreme to show his bias and fail in that purpose, it is probable that the cross-examination will have hurt your case more than helping it; the content of the answers themselves will have been such as to strengthen, fortify, and supplement what has been said on direct examination. For this reason, it is a mistake to attempt cross-examination of most witnesses by this method. The risk involved in doing so is warranted, however, if you judge the witness to be one more concerned about answering favorably to "his side" than answering truthfully, and also as one not sufficiently clever to appreciate the purpose of your cross-examination and to conceal his conscious bias. Also, it is sometimes possible to plan the cross-examination in such a way that you may turn it to other uses if the objective of committing the witness to an untenable extreme fails. Return for illustrative purposes to the above example, based on Case 38. If *W* had answered all of the inquiries about *P*'s car by saying that he was not looking in that direction and did not see *P*'s car until just before the impact, the aim of committing *W* to an untenable extreme would have failed, and the net effect of the inquiries concerning *D*'s car and the use of the diagram would have been to strengthen *W*'s testimony. In that event, however, you might be prepared to elicit from *W* testimony to the effect that there were no obstructions to his visibility, likewise none to visibility from the position which *P* occupied in his car just before he entered the intersection, and (by expression, or by inference if express statement is precluded as an opinion) that *P* could have observed the excessive speed of *D* in time to avoid the collision if he (*P*) had observed *D*'s approach in the same way that *W* observed it.

Occasionally you may be confronted with a series of witnesses who appear to have a memorized story. In such cases, subject to the qualifications considered in the preceding paragraph, one of your best hopes of successful cross-examination is to cross-examine in detail, to demonstrate either the unnatural perfection with which the stories tally in minute detail, or else to find some vital respects in which the witnesses, when carried afield from the scope of direct examination, are inconsistent to a degree unnatural with respect to things that would have impressed witnesses honestly reporting their observations. A witness who has a memorized story is also more likely than others to be tripped by the question, "Who has talked to you about your testimony in this case?",[3] because he naturally wants to minimize the amount of contact that has actually occurred.

3. See §3.18.

§3.13 Inquiring into source of knowledge

CASE 39. D is defending against a claim for $1250 damages to P's car in a collision. P's witness, W, testifies on direct examination that he is familiar with the market value of used cars at the time of the collision and with the condition of P's car immediately before the collision, and that in his opinion it had a market value at that time of $1450; that he is familiar with the market value of wrecked cars and with the condition of P's car immediately after the wreck, and that in his opinion it had a market value in wrecked condition, immediately after the collision, of $200. As D's lawyer you have information that W was operating a salvage business at all material times, buying wrecked cars and selling parts and junk, but not buying or selling used cars in operating condition. You have available a used car dealer whose opinion is that the value of P's car before collision was $1000.

Should you cross-examine the witness regarding the source of his knowledge of matters to which he has testified?

Careful inquiry will often disclose that things the witness says as if they were his own observations are actually only repetition of what some other person has told him. If you ask a person unfamiliar with evidence rules whether he can state a fact "of his own knowledge" he may think the correct answer is "yes" if he has been informed of the fact by someone whom he considers reliable. Although courts have not adopted a philosopher's definition of "knowing," their definition is more restrictive than the ordinary layman's understanding. In the language of the courts, the witness is not able to speak "of his own knowledge" if he is merely repeating what he has been told, regardless of the reliability of his informant. His testimony that the informant made the statement, when offered to prove the truth of the matter stated, is excluded by the hearsay rule unless some exception applies. His repetition, as his own statement, of the matter he heard is excluded because of his want of knowledge of the facts stated. A showing of personal knowledge of certain facts may also be essential as a predicate for admissibility of opinion evidence. In Case 39, for example, personal knowledge of transactions in the used car market will be essential in many jurisdictions to qualification of W to give opinion testimony of the value of P's car in its undamaged state. If, as D's lawyer, you object and the testimony is excluded, the question presented in this section is not reached as such; this question nevertheless confronts you because it is one of the factors to be considered in determining whether you should object. Will your purpose of convincing the jury be better served by objecting and excluding the evidence, or instead by permitting it to come in and then, through cross-examination, exposing its weakness? [1]

1. See §4.2.

In general, if the subject matter of the questioned testimony is likely to have weight in the jury's deliberations, the advantages of entirely excluding the testimony outweigh both the risk of harm from incurring disfavor with the jury by thus withholding information from them [2] and the possibility of gain from discrediting the witness or your adversary in the eyes of the jury by disclosing on cross-examination the lack of a reliable basis for the witness' statements on direct. To the extent that you are able to impeach the reliability of the source of the witness' "knowledge" a jury will be impressed, but in the absence of the impeachment a jury is less likely than a court to consider a showing that the statement is hearsay as proof that it lacks reliability. It follows that when it is possible for you to cause the evidence to be excluded, it usually is preferable to do so rather than allow it to come in with the purpose of cross-examining to show want of personal knowledge. In Case 39, for example, if *W* would admit on *voir dire* examination [3] that he is not in the business of buying or selling used cars in operating condition and that he does not have personal knowledge of such transactions, his opinion testimony as to the value of *P*'s car in wrecked condition could be excluded in many jurisdictions because he is not properly qualified to testify on used car values. [4] If *W*'s estimate of the difference between value before and after collision is unreasonably high, [5] it would be better for you to object at the first opportunity and exclude the evidence rather than hope that the jury will disregard the $1450 estimate of preceding value merely because it is based only upon hearsay information as to used car values.

If inadmissibility of the testimony in question is less certain than in the circumstances assumed in the preceding paragraphs, there is more doubt as to the best solution for this problem. Besides the possible disadvantage in urging an objection that is overruled, the potential value of cross-examination may be greater. For example, more advantage is to be gained from cross-examination revealing want of personal knowledge in proportion to the extent to which the witness on direct examination spoke as if from personal knowledge. This is true for the reason that the disclosure of want of knowledge carries with it an unfavorable reflection on the witness generally if he has apparently tried to pass himself off as having knowledge.

2. See *id.*

3. See §4.6.

4. 3 Wigmore, *Evidence* §§711–721 (rev. ed. Chadbourn 1970). Concerning the general standard for qualification of a witness as an expert, see Federal Rules of Evidence, Rule 702.

5. If that is not the case, and other competent evidence is available to a competent opposing lawyer to prove the same damages figure, the contest on the point may produce only a petty triumph of the moment, without contributing to ultimate victory in the case. Some lawyers seek such triumphs either on the theory that the jury applauds and favors the victor's side, or else for the mere joy of triumph, small though it may be. Most competent trial lawyers consider, however, that although the jury may enjoy the game, their decision is not likely to be influenced by such factors. See §1.4.

If the circumstances are such that want of showing of personal knowledge is not a sound objection to admission of the evidence, cross-examination designed to reveal want of personal knowledge has at least the advantage of showing that the oath of the witness does not vouch for the accuracy of the facts stated; rather the accuracy of the statement depends on the reliability of the declarant. Particularly if the testimony in question is contradicted by other testimony based on personal knowledge, this cross-examination is valuable. As in other types of cross-examination, however, you should undertake it only in those cases in which there is a reasonable prospect that it will disclose lack of personal knowledge. Otherwise it may result only in strengthening the testimony by revealing a degree of personal association with the facts not disclosed in the direct examination. As a general rule, you should cross-examine as to source of knowledge only if you have a basis for reasonably suspecting, if not believing, that the cross-examination will develop information more favorable to you than to your adversary. If, in Case 39, *W* testifies to enough personal knowledge of used car transactions to qualify his opinion testimony, as *D*'s lawyer you nevertheless have a basis (in your information that *W* is in the salvage business only and not engaged in buying and selling cars) for believing that you can by cross-examination obtain admissions from *W* that his personal knowledge of used car transactions is limited, compared with that of the used car dealer whose estimate of value you wish to prove. You should ordinarily undertake the cross-examination under these circumstances. [6]

§3.14 Inquiring into new subjects

Case 40.   *P*, a man of sixty-five, is asserting against *D* a claim for personal injuries received when he was hit by a truck driven by *T*, an employee of *D*, engaged in delivering lumber to *F*'s farm, where *P* was working as a hired man for *F*, and at the particular time was helping *F* build an addition to his farmhouse. *P* asserts that he was cleaning up around a scrap pile, with his back to the approaching truck, and that the noise of a mechanical saw being operated by *F* nearby prevented him (*P*) from hearing the truck until too late; he asserts that *T*, the truck driver, was backing the truck without keeping a proper lookout, and thus hit *P*. *D* asserts that when *T* approached with the truck *F* stopped using the saw but left the motor running, that *F* was signalling to *T*, and that *T* was backing the truck in response to *F*'s signals. *P* lost a leg in the accident, and is unable to do the heavy work that he had previously done for *F*, as *F*'s hired man; nevertheless, *F* has kept him on

6. Also consider the possibility of urging, either with or without using such cross-examination, that the evidence is insufficient to support a judgment for the plaintiff. See §§4.7, 5.2, 5.3.

under the same terms as before — paying P a small cash sum weekly, fur
nishing him a small house, and allowing him eggs and garden produce of the
farm. As D's lawyer, from your pretrial investigation, you suspect that P and
F have an understanding that P will not sue F and that in return F will
keep P on as hired hand for the balance of his life under the same terms as
before; you recognize the possibility, however, that F may be keeping P on
out of sympathy for him and because P had been working for F for 20 years.
The case is being tried in a jurisdiction where an agreement such as you suspect would constitute a bar to recovery against D. F is called as a witness for
P and testifies that he was not signalling but was merely watching T approach with the truck until he saw that the truck was approaching P, whereupon he started yelling and waving his arms to try to warn P and T of the
danger. The direct examination includes no inquiries concerning F's continued support of P or any understanding between them regarding continued
support.

*Should cross-examination touch upon subjects not mentioned in direct ex-
amination?*

The possibility of independent contribution to the favorable development
of your own case by the cross-examination of your adversary's witnesses is an
important function of good cross-examination. Occasionally a witness called
by your adversary will be the only possible source of particular evidence favorable to your case. Still more often your adversary's witnesses will furnish
a potential source of cumulative evidence corroborating other evidence that
you have produced or will produce through your own witnesses.

Since cross-examination designed to serve this end of independent contribution to your own case usually involves inquiry into new subject matter
not mentioned in the direct examination, the rules of your jurisdiction concerning the permissible scope of cross-examination will affect the extent to
which you may use this method. In some jurisdictions, cross-examination,
except as to matters concerned with impeachment of the witness, is limited
to the subject matter of the direct examination; in others, no such limitation
is imposed, and as a cross-examiner you may inquire about any matters relevant to any issue in the case without making the witness your own[1] as to
that subject matter.[2] Even in jurisdictions where the scope of cross-examination is limited, the problem of this section will confront you in nearly every
contested trial; there will be matters that, though not covered in the direct
examination, are yet so related to the inquiries of direct examination as to be
within the scope of permissible cross-examination.

1. See §2.2.
2. 6 Wigmore, *Evidence* §§1885–1895 (3d ed. 1940). See also Federal Rules of Evidence, Rules 607, 611.

Illustrations, in addition to Case 40, of types of situations presenting this question are found in sections of this book dealing with the following matters: use of statements and documents on cross-examination for impeachment,[3] cross-examination as to the opportunity to observe[4] and source of knowledge,[5] proof of bad character for impeachment,[6] calling witnesses who will testify to some facts favorable to each party,[7] proof of reimbursement of expenses and payment of fees,[8] cross-examination of experts,[9] offering harmful evidence on direct examination,[10] asking a witness to prepare or add to a chart or diagram during cross-examination,[11] using cross-examination to discredit unfavorable testimony of other witnesses,[12] cross-examination as to animosity of a witness toward his former employer,[13] and cross-examination concerning the witness' talking with others about his testimony.[14]

In addition to the problem of law referred to above — whether under the rules of the jurisdiction of trial the inquiry is within the scope of proper cross-examination — you are concerned with purely tactical considerations in determining whether to open a new subject on cross-examination. Is it a subject as to which probably the answers of the witness either will be favorable to your client or else will lay the predicate for effective impeachment of your adversary's witnesses? Or, on the other hand, is it a subject as to which the particular witness on the stand will probably answer unfavorably to you? Or is it a subject that, though producing favorable answers, will probably lead to other inquiries producing unfavorable answers more than counteracting any benefits gained? Will your inquiry forfeit a bar (such as the rule in some jurisdictions excluding testimony as to transactions with a decedent, under a "Dead Man's Act") that is otherwise available to you to keep certain harmful evidence from the jury? Will the testimony on the subject finally be of more harm than benefit to your case? Will opening the matter possibly furnish proof for your adversary that he omitted, either from hesitancy about inquiring into the subject or from oversight? The competent trial lawyer views his immediate problem with a perspective that places emphasis on the most effective presentation of the entire case, and sacrifices any temporary

3. §§3.5–3.7.
4. §3.10.
5. §3.13.
6. §3.11.
7. §2.2.
8. §§2.21, 3.27.
9. §§3.27–3.31.
10. §2.20.
11. §3.16.
12. §3.26.
13. §3.17.
14. §3.18.

triumph that is inconsistent with that emphasis.[15] It follows that, although advantages to be gained by opening new subjects on cross-examination are obvious, you should observe some tactical limitations on using such cross-examination. As noted in another section,[16] you should not ask any question of your own witness on direct examination without having asked him the question previously, unless by some other means you have real assurance of what his answer will be. The risk of an unfavorable surprise answer is too great. Although this rule cannot be applied to cross-examination, the same risk of unfavorable answers responsible for the rule exists in the case of cross-examination. In cross-examination it is a risk less serious in that the unfavorable answer from your adversary's witness does not make as great an impact upon the jury as the same answer from one of your own witnesses; it is a risk more serious in that the witness, particularly if unfriendly toward you, is more likely to answer unfavorably in both manner and substance. If you can anticipate well before trial that your adversary will use the witness, you may reduce this risk greatly by interviewing the witness before trial and obtaining a written or recorded statement if possible;[17] your preparation for cross-examination is not complete unless you have attempted these steps. One significant advantage of this preparation is learning what questions not to ask.

As to a witness who declines an interview, or one your adversary calls as a surprise to you, you must base your judgment as to advisability of opening new subjects on cross-examination on your best estimate of potential advantages and disadvantages with the limited information and time you have to form an estimate. Because of the fact that the jury identifies the witness as one for your adversary, you need not refrain from opening the new subject matter merely because of the risk, even though it be a probability, that the results will be merely negative. If there is nothing in the subject matter that potentially will add independently to your adversary's case, the mere fact that the line of inquiry may prove fruitless should not deter you. On the other hand, if the new line of inquiry is one by which the jury probably will be influenced toward one side or the other, then you should be more cautious about opening it without knowing what answers the witness will give.

Though this need for caution exists, often you can think of new matters to ask about with confidence about what the witness will answer, and sometimes you will be able to think of new questions for which the witness has not been prepared by your adverse counsel. Working such virgin soil is one of the most fruitful and delightful phases of cross-examination.

Usually you will gain little, if anything, by extending your new inquiries

15. See §1.4.
16. See §2.14(e).
17. See §§9.13, 9.14.

to matters that are irrelevant either to the issues in your case or to bias, interest, corruption, skill, or source of knowledge of the witness, since as a general rule impeachment on collateral matters is not allowed.[18]

In Case 40, as lawyer for *D,* at some point in the course of preparation and trial you wish to inquire into the possibility that *P* and *F* made such an agreement as, by law, discharges all tortfeasors, including *D.* Originally you will be concerned with opening this subject matter at a time and under circumstances likely to aid you in getting to the truth of the matter if *P* or *F* or both are inclined to color their testimony to avoid the adverse effect from the arrangement between them. Although some argument might be urged for making the first inquiry at a time when the witness is before the court and jury, in the hope that he will not be prepared for the question and that any effort to fabricate an explanation would be apparent, that hope is illusory if *P*'s counsel properly prepares his case. Such preparation would involve consideration of *D*'s possible defense of compromise. Also, as *D*'s lawyer, you might be precluded by rules of pleading from raising the defense in trial without special pleadings to support it. In all probability, therefore, you will have interviewed *F* and examined *P* by deposition[19] on this subject before trial. If, on the basis of these examinations, you have concluded that you have a reasonable basis for asserting that a compromise was made, and have filed pleadings raising the issue,[20] there will be no occasion for your refraining from inquiry into the new subject of agreement between *P* and *F* after the injury. It is not a subject as to which independent harm will be done to your case if your line of inquiry is not successful in establishing such an agreement as amounts in law to a bar, unless your claim is so poorly supported by the evidence as to appear frivolous, giving the jury an idea that you are grasping for defenses. If your pretrial examinations of *P* and *F* and your investigation as to other possible sources of evidence indicating an agreement have not been sufficiently productive to remove your defense from the frivolous category, then you should not assert it and you should make no inquiries for the purpose of raising it.[21] But, under a fact situation such as Case 40, if your investigation causes you to conclude that you have a reasonable claim of agreement, though in your judgment it is very doubtful that it will be sustained by the court and jury, you will be justified tactically in making the inquiries *of F* about the understanding between *F* and *P,* by reason of which *F* is still employing *P* at the same rate. It might be suggested that this would serve as an opportunity for *P*'s lawyer to depict *F* as

18. 3A Wigmore, *Evidence* §§1000–1006 (rev. ed. Chadbourn 1970). Compare Federal Rules of Evidence, Rule 403, concerning exclusion of relevant evidence on grounds of prejudice, confusion, or waste of time.

19. See §11.2.

20. See §10.6.

21. See §7.16.

an admirable person of charitable impulses, fully deserving their commendation and confidence, thus encouraging the jury to believe his testimony on the facts of the accident. On the other hand, the same facts of F's continuing to support P also tend to support the inference that F felt that he was responsible for the accident and that D's employee was not. In view of the relevance of the evidence in this respect, as well as to a possible agreement amounting to a bar against P, probably in Case 40 you should open up on cross-examination the new subject of F's supporting P and their having an understanding on this subject.

§3.15 Asking for repetition and added details

Should you call on the witness to repeat or state more details concerning matters touched on direct examination?

It seems to be a natural tendency of neophyte trial lawyers to ask a witness on cross-examination to repeat testimony given on direct examination, interspersing here and there a few inquiries calling for greater details than were stated on direct. Perhaps one reason for the tendency is that this procedure comes naturally to one who feels a need to cross-examine but has no specific goal or plan; the only thing that comes to mind at the moment is to ask the witness to repeat in the hope that some inconsistency will develop. Though occasionally that hope is realized, usually such cross-examination serves only to emphasize and strengthen the direct testimony. In view of the obvious likelihood that repetition and elaboration of the direct testimony will improve the effectiveness of the witness' testimony in the absence of contradictions, you should not follow this procedure without some specific aim and reasonable basis for supposing that you may realize an advantage. A number of techniques of effective cross-examination involve repetition and elaboration of the direct testimony, however, and justify incurring the risk of harm by the witness' improving his testimony if you fail in cross-examination to realize the aim of the technique you have chosen.

When you have evidence of contradictions or inconsistencies between the witness' testimony on direct examination and statements made by him at other times, your first step in the effective use of such evidence is laying a firm foundation for its use — not merely such a foundation as may be required by rules of evidence to support admissibility but also such a foundation that the witness cannot formulate a plausible explanation of the apparent inconsistency. In framing the questions you should attempt to anticipate each possible excuse or explanation for the apparent inconsistency and get the witness committed to a contrary position before you point up the inconsistency;[1] otherwise, an apparently plausible excuse conceived by the witness may not only rob you of effective impeachment but also make the net effect of your

1. See §3.5.

cross-examination worse than none. This first step is essential even if you propose to offer the impeaching evidence independently rather than on cross-examination. Although the cross-examination in which you make the more detailed inquiries and call upon the witness to repeat and confirm his position serves temporarily to emphasize and not to weaken the witness' testimony, this is a part of your overall plan of giving greater emphasis to the impeaching evidence when you offer it later. With sufficient emphasis the impeachment on one point may cast suspicion on the witness personally and thus on all other things the witness has said. When you are using cross-examination for this purpose, however, it is generally not advisable to call upon the witness to repeat his entire story, or most of it; rather you should single out the points on which you have impeaching evidence available and develop them only. These points then receive the emphasis. Probably some of the jurors will develop curiosity about your purpose and an attitude of anticipation that lends further to emphasizing the importance of the impeaching evidence.

Sometimes the original testimony of the witness will be vague or ambiguous on matters as to which your adversary would prefer not to have to take a firm position. This is frequently true, for example, with reference to estimates of time, speed, or distance material to the description of an automobile accident. Each party typically has several witnesses, no two of whom would naturally give the same estimates. Both your opponent and you will be concerned that too much variation among your respective witnesses will cause jurors to think that they are poor observers and that too much conformity will cause jurors to think that your witnesses have compared ideas and reached an agreement. Conversely each of you will find the hope of proving either too much conformity or too much variation among your adversary's witnesses an inducement to cross-examine each witness in detail about his estimates of speeds, distances, and times. An added advantage of the cross-examination is that a witness rarely has the ability to observe and estimate with sufficient accuracy to avoid completely some inconsistencies within his own testimony when the examination on these matters is detailed. If you find an adverse witness who is willing to make precise statements about these matters, rather than to follow the more sensible course of keeping such statements general and acknowledging that they are only estimates,[2] you have an ideal situation for detailed cross-examination with a prospect of developing material inconsistencies that cast doubt on the reliability of other observations of the witness as well. Also, if the witness has made any precise estimate on direct examination, though not as to the particular matter about which you inquire, you are in an advantageous position to be insistent in your request for similarly precise estimates on other matters equally susceptible of observation.

2. See §2.14.

Other techniques of cross examination that involve repetition and elaboration of part of the testimony of the witness on direct examination include committing a witness to an untenable extreme as a means of showing bias indirectly,[3] developing inconsistencies when you are confronted with a series of witnesses whom you have reason to believe to be consciously biased,[4] confronting a witness with the exact words used when he is guilty of an inconsistency between his testimony at two different points within the trial,[5] asking him to add to a chart or diagram prepared on direct examination,[6] using hypothetical questions,[7] and calling upon a witness to produce documents relevant to his testimony.[8]

§3.16   Asking a witness to prepare drawings or computations

CASE 41.*   P sues for title to land on which producing oil wells are located. The dispute turns on whether a certain stump found on the ground by P's surveyor, shortly before suit was instituted, is the stump of a witness tree marked by the original surveyor, 40 years earlier. If so, P wins; if not, the survey reconstructed on courses and distances from more remote witness markers will cause D to win. P testifies that before the tree was cut down he had observed an "X" mark on it with two hacks above and two hacks below the "X," and that he would describe the appearance of the marks, at the time he last observed them about one year before suit was instituted (a short time before somebody cut down and removed the tree without his knowledge or permission), as gouged-out places where the bark was gone and the wood visible, and cleanly v-shaped as if cut by a sharp instrument, with blows toward the middle of the tree from two slightly different directions. You represent D, and your surveyor, S, advises you that after 40 years a surveyor's hackmarks would be almost overgrown and would appear only as a scar on the tree rather than a v-shaped gouge.

Should you ask the witness on cross-examination to prepare or add to a diagram, chart, map, or computations to explain his testimony?

Usually this problem arises when you are considering calling upon the witness for more detailed testimony about matters touched on direct examina-

3. See §3.12.
4. See id.
5. See §3.9.
6. See §3.16.
7. See §3.31.
8. See §3.28.

*Adapted from the hypothetical case used in a demonstration trial of a land suit reported in Institute on the Trial of a Land Suit (Southwestern Legal Foundation, Dallas, 1954).

tion;[1] the chart, diagram, map, or computations will serve to clarify the witness' testimony and you should not ask the witness to make such an exhibit unless you consider that it will then be possible for you to impeach this clarified testimony of the witness, develop inconsistencies within it, or else use it for the impeachment of more harmful testimony of another. If, however, you find apparent inconsistencies within the direct testimony or between that testimony and previous statements of the witness, usually there is no better way than using a diagram or chart for developing and demonstrating inconsistencies. Witnesses to the facts of an automobile accident, such as Case 38, are frequently susceptible to effective cross-examination by this method.[2] The use of a diagram on cross-examination is also one of the most effective means of demonstrating inconsistencies between the testimony of several adverse witnesses. In this connection it is advantageous to use markings on the diagram that are not self-explanatory, so that another witness will not be able to interpret the marks placed by a former witness. Sometimes this is impracticable; a better method of insuring that one adverse witness is not merely following the testimony of a previous one, shown by markings, is to use several identical copies of a basic diagram of the scene (prepared in advance on semitransparent paper) requiring each witness to illustrate his own testimony. The different markings placed on identical copies can then be easily compared to demonstrate material differences in the testimony; this method also has the advantage of avoiding confusion from overlapping markings on the diagram.

If your adversary has effectively used a diagram, chart or map on direct examination, it is a pictorial representation of one theory of the case, or some important aspect of it, and it will be available as an exhibit, in most jurisdictions, for the jury to study during their final deliberations. This will be a distinct advantage to your adversary unless you are able to place your theory of the case before them in similar form. Occasionally it will be possible for you to do this during the cross-examination of your adversary's witnesses, rather than during the direct examination of your own. For example, in Case 41, P's surveyor has undoubtedly prepared maps of the tract of land in controversy, and in the direct examination P's lawyer will have used one or more of these maps to demonstrate his theory of the case, supported by the surveyor's testimony. P's theory is based upon the claim that the stump referred to in the testimony is the stump of the original witness tree, and the maps made by P's surveyor have been prepared on that basis. Your claim for the defendant, on the other hand, is based on courses and distances from

1. See §3.15.

2. See §3.12 for an illustration of using a diagram and computations on cross-examination of a witness to an automobile accident.

more remote markers. When P's surveyor is on cross-examination, you may ask him to take the map used in his direct examination, assume with you hypothetically[3] that the stump is not that of the original witness tree, and place on the same map a drawing of the location of the tract of land by construction from the more remote markers. This will enable you to demonstrate clearly, upon a document that will go to the jury room, the inconsistency between the calls in title papers and the assumption that the stump is that of the original witness tree. Though some controversy may arise as to your right to "mutilate" your adversary's exhibit, most courts will grant you the right to place your markings upon it if it appears to be done in good faith and not merely for the purpose of confusion. Your adversary is adequately protected by the opportunity that he has of producing another copy of the map and seeking the court's permission to have one copy go into the record of the case, and before the jury in their deliberations, as P's exhibit with no markings on it other than those made during direct examination, while the other copy has your added markings on it.[4]

§3.17 Inquiring into attitude toward a former employer

CASE 42. P sues for breach of an apartment building contract, claiming that D used drain pipes inferior to those called for by specifications of the contract, resulting in water damage to the building because a hole allegedly rusted through one of the pipes in an upper story. As one of his witnesses, P calls W, formerly in the employ of D as a construction worker, and W testifies that he was on the job at the time the pipe was being installed, observed that the pipe was of an inferior grade, but complied with the orders given him to install it. D's defense is that the pipe was good and the hole in it appears, from laboratory examination, to have been caused by acid of some type poured into the drain in one of the apartments. D advises you, as his lawyer, that W was suspected of stealing materials from the job site; that he was confronted with the charge and then for the first time asserted that he had argued with D's foreman on the job, F, about putting in inferior pipes in the hot water heating system (not drain pipes), and that he was being framed on the charge to get rid of him. F says that all the materials used were good, and that W never said anything to the contrary until he was about to be fired for dishonesty, whereupon he made up his story about the pipes in the hot water heating system and said he was quitting. D also advises you that the value of the missing materials, thought to have been taken by W, was less than $25 and no criminal charges were filed against him,

3. See §3.31.
4. See §2.33.

though *W* admitted having materials of the same make in a cottage that he was building for himself at the time of the construction of the apartment building.

Should you cross-examine a former employee of your client as to animosity associated with termination of the former employment?

When you represent a client who employs others, you will sometimes be confronted with an adverse witness who is a former employee. Your adversary seeks out such witnesses because they frequently supply direct proof on matters as to which otherwise your adversary might find it necessary to rely on circumstantial evidence, and because their former position "inside" your client's business may make their testimony more effective. Even without prompting from the lawyers in such cases, the jurors are inclined to be curious as to whether the testimony of the witness deserves special weight because coming from a former "insider" no longer deterred, by fear of losing his job, from speaking frankly, or instead the witness' testimony is influenced by animosity toward his former employer growing out of the circumstances of termination of employment. Occasionally you may be able to make the overall effect of the testimony of such a witness more favorable to your case than to your adversary's by bringing out favorable evidence that your adversary did not anticipate when he called the witness.[1] Usually, however, the testimony of such a witness is very damaging to your client's case unless the jury infers that he is influenced by bad feelings toward your client. The witness is much more dangerous to you if he refrains from any criticism of your client or his business methods other than that implied in his testimony on facts material to the lawsuit, and if he states that he has no ill feeling toward your client and left his employment on a friendly basis, because, for example, he found a higher paying job, or one more convenient for him or better suited to his abilities. If on the other hand the witness indicates that he is at odds personally with your client, the jurors will be more inclined to discount his testimony as influenced, consciously or subconsciously, by ill will. If on direct examination the witness has testified about the cause of termination of employment, leaving an erroneous and harmful impression, there is of course no reason to refrain from going into the matter further on cross-examination either to secure some admissions inconsistent with the implications of his direct testimony or else to lay the foundation for offering independent contradictory proof.

If, as will usually be the case, the direct examination of the witness either makes no reference to the cause of termination of employmnt or else leaves an erroneous but not necessarily harmful impression about the circumstances, a more difficult problem is presented to you on cross-examination. Basically the problem is one of predicting the ultimate result of opening up the matter

1. See §3.10.

of cause of termination. After both sides of the matter have been presented, what change will have been made in the probable jury attitude toward the credibility of the testimony of this witness? Will the jury be more likely to consider that the testimony is influenced by ill feeling toward the former employer, or more likely to take the side of the employee, sympathizing with him in his loss of the job and also accepting more readily his testimony relevant to the case at hand? In short, you should not go into the circumstances of termination simply because your client's version of the circumstances would have favorable effect if accepted by the jury, or because your client's initial reaction is to want you to do so. If you open up the matter, probably your adversary will make sure that the witness presents his side of it; you must anticipate what that will probably be and whether it will have more appeal to the jury than your client's version.

Case 42 presents circumstances in which the answer to this problem is subject to reasonable difference of opinion. If you go into the circumstances of discharge, doubtlessly the question whether W was guilty of stealing from your client, D, will become an issue in the jury's deliberation, though it has no relevance to your case except as bearing on the credibility of W and of your own witnesses, such as F. You are at a disadvantage in that you have inadequate proof that W was actually guilty, and the jury will sympathize with W and react unfavorably against D unless they think W was probably guilty. On the other hand, if you do not go into the circumstances of termination, the jury may conclude that your failure to do so indicates that no unusual incident and no ill feeling was involved. Under the facts of Case 42, W's testimony will be most damaging unless the jurors consider that it can be explained by bias; otherwise the jury may conclude that the testimony of W as a disinterested witness resolves the balance between contradictory testimony of interested witnesses. Because of this fact that the existing situation with which you are faced in beginning the cross-examination is unfavorable to your client, probably you have more to gain than to lose by fighting the issue of cause of termination, and you should cross-examine on the subject.

Having decided to go into the subject of cause of termination, to what extent should you pursue it, in Case 42? Since you are not prepared to offer strong proof of W's guilt, it would be better for you to avoid bringing up the charge of stealing. Let it be brought up by your adversary, if it is to come into the case; limit your inquiries as to this subject on original cross-examination to showing by W that W and your client had some disagreement and ill feeling at the time of termination of W's employment. If your adversary goes into the matter further on redirect examination, then you may on re-cross-examination obtain the admission from W that he was building a house of his own at the time that the apartment was being constructed and was using materials of the same make as those missing from the site of the apartment job. The jury may conclude that D's suspicions and action were justified regardless of actual guilt of *W*; it is perhaps less likely that the jury would regard the matter in this light if you were the first to bring up the charge of stealing.[2] A doubtful aspect about this method of meeting the situation is the omission from the original cross-examination of inquiries about *W*'s making a claim, even at the time of the dispute just before his discharge, only with respect to defective pipes for the heating system and not the drainage system. Obviously, however, *W* would answer those questions against you. This subject is one that you should cover in the testimony of your own witnesses, and asking *W* about it probably would help none, unless you are required to ask *W* the question as a predicate for the later testimony from the other witnesses.

§3.18 Inquiring into conversations about the testimony

Should you ask the witness on cross-examination whether or not he has talked with anyone about his testimony?

Rarely, if ever, does a witness take the stand without having talked with someone about the testimony he will give. As previously noted,[1] if you prepare your case properly you will not call a witness to the stand without having asked the witness what his testimony will be on all points as to which you can anticipate he may be questioned. If you have properly prepared your case by conferring with each of your witnesses, little is to be gained by showing on cross-examination of your adversary's witnesses that your adversary has talked with each of them. Your adversary can prove the same about you; even if you represent the plaintiff and have already called and dismissed your witnesses when you first make inquiries of this sort on cross-examination of defendant's witnesses, defendant's lawyer could easily call you to the stand and force you to admit your conferences with witnesses (or perhaps accomplish the same purpose by asking in open court that, to save the time of the court and jury, you stipulate that you conferred with each of your witnesses about his testimony before placing him on the stand). If the witnesses would all answer honestly, you would gain by going into the matter of conferences with witnesses only in cases in which your adversary had conferred with witnesses more extensively or had misused the conferences to modify the content of their testimony. Many witnesses, however, unless specifically advised that a conference is proper and that they should readily admit that it occurred, will attempt to conceal its occurrence or minimize its scope; this is particularly true if the witness is bothered about whether his testimony

2. See §1.3.
1. See §2.14.

is wholly accurate. Now and then a witness will deny conferring with the lawyer about his testimony even though he has been told specifically to admit it. Particularly is this likely if the cross-examiner approaches the matter with a manner implying that a great point will be scored if the witness admits having such a conference. If you are certain that none of your own witnesses will fall for this trap, you may find it useful on cross-examination of adverse witnesses in the case;[2] if the witness falsely denies that a conference occurred, it is usually relatively easy for you to demonstrate to the jury that he has lied in this respect, supporting the inference that his testimony on other matters is not reliable, regardless of whether the conference itself was of a proper or improper type.

If your adversary has improperly used the conferences with his witnesses to shape the substance of their testimony, it is improbable that you will get any admission from them to this effect. It may be possible, however, to get admissions of circumstances supporting an inference that the conferences were improper. For example, if you are faced with a series of consciously biased witnesses, proving that their testimony is alike even in minute details[3] and that the lawyer conferred with them simultaneously, or that they were all present at a discussion of the facts of the case among themselves, may cause the jury to infer that their testimony is unreliable. When maps or diagrams are used on direct examination, questions on cross-examination about the extent of conferences between the witnesses and lawyer as to use of the maps or diagrams are frequently profitable, especially if the witness has not been prepared for such questions, or if the lawyer has misused the conference and the witness will admit enough to support the inference that the lawyer was telling instead of asking where marks should be placed.

Ordinarily a witness has also talked with other persons, as well as one or both of the lawyers, about the facts of the case or the testimony that the witness will give. It is quite natural for a person who has witnessed an accident to tell others about it and to discuss it with any other witnesses whom he knows. It is usually possible to demonstrate satisfactorily that a denial of such conversations by the witness is false.

In a tort case in which a liability insurer protects the defendant, the witness may have talked with an insurance investigator. In those jurisdictions where it is improper to reveal the fact of insurance coverage, a plaintiff's lawyer should avoid this type of question because it invites mention of the insurance

---

2. See H. Drinker, *Legal Ethics* 86 (1953), referring to this technique as a "cheap subterfuge." It is a fair, though not a necessary, inference, that a witness who will lie about his conference with the lawyer will lie about other things. This being so, is the epithet "cheap subterfuge" appropriately applied to this technique of cross-examination?

3. See §3.12.

investigator, possibly giving rise to a mistrial; a defendant's lawyer should avoid this type of question because he may have to suffer the consequences of the jury's knowing about insurance, not being allowed a mistrial when this fact is revealed in a fair response to one of his questions. In such circumstances, if you wish to prove the fact that the witness has talked with a particular person, your question should be so specific that an answer referring to the insurance investigator would be clearly nonresponsive. Even then some risk is involved; for example, if as defendant's lawyer you prove that the witness discussed his testimony with the plaintiff and the plaintiff's lawyer, it may be urged that you have opened up the matter and that it is then proper for the plaintiff's lawyer to show that the witness had also discussed his testimony with an equal number of representatives of the defendant, namely you and the investigator.

Another type of risk you incur in using questions about the witness' talking with others concerning his testimony is the risk, usually remote, of disclosure of improper conversations initiated by a representative of your own client, or one of your own witnesses.[4] Occasionally such conversations will have occurred without your hearing about them, but that is rarely true if your investigation has been thorough.

§3.19 Using trick questions

Should you use trick questions on cross-examination?

The cross-examination that extracts favorable testimony from a witness who is consciously biased is cross-examination at its best. It is often supposed, but only occasionally true, that trick questions will accomplish this purpose.

The traditional illustration of the trick question is, "Have you stopped beating your wife?" It is hardly conceivable that any witness would fail to see the trap in this question in time to protect himself, or that any jury would fail to forgive him if in the excitement of testifying he allowed the question to rattle him. But this type of question, in form only slightly more subtle, may be heard in the courtroom. These are examples: "Did you ever get the brakes fixed on that truck?" "Did you slow down to a reasonable speed after you started into the intersection?" "Did you apply your brakes after your passenger screamed?" Even if you phrase your question with sufficient subtlety that the witness does not recognize a trick or double meaning in the question, it is improbable that the jurors will hold it against the witness, or against his testimony, that he was outsmarted by a cunning lawyer; they are more likely to sympathize with the witness. The only significant advantage of the trick question is the slight chance that the witness

4. See §3.23.

will be upset and in his agitated state will be unable to maintain a fabricated story. Generally, the chance that this will occur is outweighed by the danger that the jury will react against trickery on the part of the lawyer.[1] On ethical grounds, also, the use of such questions is at least questionable.[2]

§3.20 Shifting the subject of inquiry

Should you shift the subject of inquiry on cross-examination suddenly and frequently?

The theory of the "hop, skip, and jump" method of cross-examination (shifting the subject of inquiry suddenly and frequently) is that the witness is kept so busy shifting his thought processes from one subject to another that he will not have time to formulate answers to fit some dishonest scheme, or that if he does so they will be so artless that you will be able to expose them. In practice, however, this method generally does not work effectively. The jury will have the same difficulty as the witness in shifting thought processes; in fact, their difficulty will be greater because they have less familiarity with the background of the case than does the witness. Furthermore, if you catch the witness in some inconsistency, the jury will be more likely to accept the excuse of the witness that he did not understand your questions than if you have proceeded in a logical, organized pattern of questions. Perhaps using this practice on deposition[1] is more defensible than using it during trial; even in this context it has the disadvantage, however, that you will find it difficult to use the deposition testimony later for impeachment purposes. Your use of deposition testimony for impeachment[2] is more effective if the succession of questions on the deposition demonstrates that the witness must have understood fully the line of inquiry and must have testified deliberately. As in the case of cross-examination during trial, the witness' excuse of misunderstanding is more acceptable if the question to which he was responding came out of context.

1. See §1.3.
2. Probably the trick question falls within the meaning of "chicane," which was condemned by American Bar Association, Canons of Professional Ethics, Canon 15 (1908). See also *id.,* Canon 22, requiring that the lawyer deal candidly with the facts. But what is the standard for distinguishing "chicane" from proper use of surprise tactics? Compare §1.3. And does the omission from the 1969 Code of the language about "chicane" and "candor" in Canons 15 and 22 of the 1908 Canons weaken the argument that trick questions are prohibited? Or, instead, is the argument that trick questions are improper still supported, if not strengthened, by DR 7–106(c)(1) and (2) and EC 7–25?
1. See §11.10.
2. See §3.8.

§3.21 Using "why" questions

On cross-examination should you ask the witness "why?"

When an adverse witness takes an unreasonable position, you may have to repress an urge to ask "Are you crazy?",[1] and you may be tempted to ask him "Why?" The latter question is usually as impractical as the former. The adverse party called the witness to the stand and probably, though not necessarily, the witness is sympathetic with that side of the case. Under proper questioning, however, you can limit his opportunity to help establish that side of the case by holding him to stating facts called for by the questions. If you ask him "why" he makes a certain statement, you open the door to a full explanation, which may be argumentative without being nonresponsive. In short, the "why" question removes all barriers of inadmissibility and allows the witness to state any kind of opinion, argument or inadmissible fact he chooses to state in explanation. Probably most trial judges would permit you to interrupt the answer to restrict the witness to matter that is not subject to exclusion, but your interruption of a responsive answer may be as damaging as the answer itself.

The temptation to ask the "why" question is based upon the assumption that the witness has no explanation that would seem reasonable to you, or to the jurors. If you actually have the witness in that circumstance, the question might be very effective in catching him without any explanation or with such a poor one that it will certainly be recognized as such. The risk of harm in the event that you are in error in thinking the witness cannot offer any explanation is so great, however, that it is a sound rule of thumb not to ask the "why" question.

§3.22 Using argumentative questions

CASE 38. *D* is defending a personal injury claim based upon a collision at the intersection of Through Street and Side Street, in a suburban area. *P*, who entered Through Street from Side Street on the west, with the purpose of turning left (north), relies on *D*'s alleged negligence in proceeding south at a greatly excessive speed, and failing to yield the right of way. *D*, on the other hand, alleges that *P* was guilty of causal negligence in failing to stop before entering and in failing to yield the right of way. An ordinance gives the right of way to a car on Through Street if it is within 150 feet of the intersection when the car from Side Street enters; otherwise, the car from Side Street has the right of way. *P* calls the witness *W*, who testifies that

---

1. To which question the witness replies, according to a story told by Judge W. M. Taylor, Jr., "Not really; that was just a vicious frame-up that put me in the insane asylum." 14 *The Dallas Bar Speaks* 93 (1951).

he was standing in front of a service station at the northwest corner of the intersection, observed *D*'s approach, and estimates his speed at 75 m.p.h. (in a 45 m.p.h. zone). On direct examination, *W* is not asked about his observations of *P*'s entering the highway. As *D*'s lawyer, you interviewed *W* before trial and concluded that *W* had made up his mind that *P* ought to win the lawsuit and intended to do all he could to answer questions in such a way as to help *P* win.

Should you use argumentative questions on cross-examination?

Some lawyers, regardless of the type of witness under cross-examination, customarily use the opportunity to state an argumentative question reciting the cross-examiner's theory of the case, barely nodding toward the theoretical purpose of cross-examination by clothing the statement with the phrase "Isn't it a fact that . . .?" Though this use of argumentative questions has some tactical value in aiding the jury to understand and remember the lawyer's position, it is a crude way of doing what generally can be done more effectively through other means. Long before cross-examination you have ample opportunity to present your theory of the case to the jury, at times when you are not laboring under the handicap of having to phrase the theory in the form of a question. Though you generally do not have that opportunity at all of these points in a single jurisdiction, in any trial you will have the opportunity at one or more of the times when you are examining the jury panel,[1] reading your pleadings,[2] or making an opening statement.[3] Perhaps there is value in repeating your theory as often as possible. Bear in mind, however, that the jury will be told that only what the witnesses say, and not what the lawyers say, is evidence—you may even tell them that yourself.[4] If they follow this instruction, then they are less impressed with your statement of the theory of your case, in question form, than with the answer of the adverse witness whom you are cross-examining — an answer that probably will reject your theory. Only to the extent that you can get answers from the witness that support your theory of the case, or aid in the impeachment of some part of your adversary's case, are you generally justified in continuing cross-examination;[5] indulging in further cross-examination for the purpose of stating your theories in the form of questions is more likely to be detrimental than beneficial to your case.

This is not to say that you should never use an isn't-it-a-fact-that question. Frequently this form of question is the best way of committing the witness positively, and in a way such that the jury realizes it clearly. Particularly is

1. See §7.5.
2. See §10.4.
3. See §7.11.
4. See §7.5.
5. See §3.3.

this so when the question is one that the witness should be expected to answer affirmatively. In such cases, however, the question is ordinarily restricted to some particular aspect of the facts rather than being an argumentative statement of one theory of the case. It is a question consistent with the purpose of obtaining a favorable answer from an adverse witness, even though couched in argumentative form. In this type of situation, the argumentative form helps in emphasizing for the jury that the facts involved in the question point toward your theory of the case.

If the witness is argumentative, something more can be said for arguing with him a little, although most trial lawyers would advise you not to do that generally. Actually a well-turned question is a better argument than a statement — if you are able to put your finger on the weakness of his argument with a question. The ideal is to bait the argumentative witness enough that the jury will get the idea that he is arguing while you are simply trying to get him to answer some questions of fact. Furthermore, the argumentative witness is one you may catch in an untenable extreme. For example, in the illustrative testimony previously quoted[6] with regard to Case 38, the witness in several instances makes an argumentative explanation rather than simply answering the question put to him. Although as cross-examiner you may be tempted to argue back, your cross-examination as a whole is more effective if you continue politely in your detailed questioning about what W observed, giving W as many opportunities as possible to explain in more detail, until you finally confront W with the fact that under his testimony as to speeds and distances, he would have been doing the impossible in making all of these remarkably detailed and positive observations within a period of two seconds. In so confronting W, you might ask him an argumentative question such as ,"Isn't it a fact, Mr. W, that nobody could possibly see all those things in a period as short as two seconds, and that either your memory or your observations have not been accurate?" Probably it is more effective, however, to accomplish this purpose by asking him to call "Go" and "Stop," while marking the time of two seconds by his watch, thus making your point clear for the jury but leaving W without more to say unless he chooses to volunteer more argumentative explanation.

§3.23 Demanding clear answers

CASE 43.   On behalf of P, you bring suit for damages to P's vehicle from collision with another driven by D. P's vehicle was being driven by S, P's eighteen-year-old son. W, a bystander, witnessed the accident, and his testimony on the facts of the accident is favorable to D. W, who had known S and P for years and was friendly though not intimately associated with them, had seen S drinking a bottle of beer at a drive-in restaurant a few minutes

6. See §3.12.

before the accident but says that S was not intoxicated. Your adversary, D's lawyer, calls W to the stand. During the course of your cross-examination, W testifies as follows:

Q. Have you talked with anyone about your testimony in this case?
A. I don't know what you mean; you came out to see me some time ago, if that's what you are talking about.
Q. Have you talked with anyone else?
A. This other lawyer came out to see me too.
Q. Did you talk with him just that one time, or several times?
A. Two or three, I guess.
Q. Will you recall the times and be exact for us, please?
A. Let's see — right after the accident, again about two weeks ago, and then this week.
Q. How many times this week?
A. He asked me to come to his office Monday morning, and then I just spoke to him as I came in the building today.
Q. You mean you just said "hello" to him, or did you have some discussion about your testimony in the case?
A. We talked for a minute; he had a couple of questions he wanted to ask me.
Q. Have you talked with anybody else about your testimony in this case?
A. Well, that's about all.
Q. Do you mean that is all, or have you talked with somebody else about your testimony?
A. Like I say, I think that's about all.

Should you insist on a clear answer from an evasive witness?

It is often possible for a witness to frame a seemingly plausible evasion of a single question. One of your very important tasks as cross-examiner is on-the-spot analysis of the evasive answer so that you may follow up with further inquiries that pin down the witness to one position or another on material questions. Except in the case of experts,[1] in whose testimony qualification of the answers is to be expected, an evasion usually occurs with respect to a matter as to which the witness' answer, when finally extracted, is favorable to the cross-examiner or reflects unfavorably on the witness personally. Requiring a clear answer from the witness serves not only the purpose of producing this testimony, however; it also serves incidentally the aim of revealing the witness' bias or his efforts to conceal relevant facts about which he is asked.

In determining how far to press an evasive witness for a clear answer, consider the materiality and importance of the original question asked, the nature of the answer that the witness probably will give if forced to a show-

1. See §3.29.

down, and the probable reason for the witness' reluctance to answer directly.

If the original question is not important, the principal possibility of an advantage from pressing the witness is to demonstrate his reluctance to answer your questions frankly, as supporting the inference that his testimony generally is unreliable. It is not likely that you can succeed in this aim while questioning the witness on a relatively unimportant topic, except to the extent that this may contribute toward an overall impression of evasiveness if the witness reacts similarly to other questions, including some relating to comparatively important topics.

The mere fact that the witness is evading your question on an important subject does not conclusively demonstrate that you should press him on the matter.[2] If the evasion is apparent, you have already gained some advantage from it because of the unfavorable reflection on the reliability of the witness' testimony. You may lose this advantage and may even suffer more harm if you press a witness whose evasion is caused by something other than a desire to hurt your case or favor your opponent's case. The answer, when finally extracted, may be unfavorable to you.

In Case 43 you can easily imagine possible reasons for W's evasion that, when brought out, would be detrimental to your own case. For example, suppose that S, in the excitement following the accident, cornered W, pleading with him and offering him a bribe not to tell anyone, particularly not P, that S had been at the restaurant drinking beer just a few minutes before the accident. W feels that S's drinking beer had nothing to do with the accident and that in S's subsequent conferences with W and his father about the matter he had fully realized the seriousness of his conduct in requesting W to falsify his testimony. W does not desire to reveal S's conduct, but will do so rather than lie about it if he is squarely faced with the choice. If circumstances such as these existed, even though you had affirmatively offered on direct presentation of your case for P the harmful evidence concerning S's drinking,[3] you might do much more harm to your case by pressing W for a clear answer in Case 43 to the question whether he has talked with anyone else, besides those mentioned in the assumed cross-examination, regarding his testimony in the case. On cross-examination you always face a risk that something of this character, unknown to you, will be revealed in response to your questions. It is a risk that you can reduce but never eliminate entirely by your thorough advance preparation of the case. In determining whether to press an evasive witness on a particular question during the course of cross-examination you should be wary if facts and circumstances known to you suggest possible explanations for the witness' evasion that, if revealed, would be harmful to your case. Generally, however, the mere fear of the unknown

2. See §3.29 regarding pressing an expert for a positive answer.
3. See §2.20.

should not deter you, though it is likely that in some individual case you will wish afterwards that it had. You must accept some calculated risks.

If you have determined that the risk of a harmful explanation of the witness' evasion is slight and worth taking, what means should you adopt in pressing the witness for an answer? Make your questions simple and pointed, and break down and attack item by item any qualified or conditional answers, so that you eliminate or at least reduce to a minimum the opportunities for plausible evasion. If in the face of a simplified question the witness is still evasive, you may decide to drop the matter (after the cross-examination has proceeded to the point that the evasion by the witness is apparent to the jury) on the theory that your aim of discrediting the witness has been accomplished. Other possibilities exist. For example, should you request the court to instruct the witness to answer the question? If the instruction is given, the witness might be held in contempt for failure to answer. More often, however, the instruction produces an answer. The witness cannot properly be required to answer a question that he does not understand or the answer to which he does not know, nor can he be required to give a categorical "yes" or "no" answer, without explanation, if such an answer would be inaccurate or misleading. If you have asked a question that cannot be answered categorically,[4] your request to the court for an instruction to the witness would doubtlessly be denied, with detrimental effect upon your cross-examination generally. Although you consider that your question is not of this type, if there is room for doubt about the matter it is generally better not to take the risk of asking the court for an instruction to the witness because of the possible detrimental effect of an adverse ruling by the court. Judges generally will not give an instruction to the witness unless the evasion by the witness is clear-cut, and the refusal of the judge to give an instruction you have requested may be interpreted by the jury as an indication that the judge thinks the witness is answering properly and not in the least evasively. On the other hand, if from familiarity with the attitude of the judge and from objective consideration of the manner of the witness you conclude that the judge probably will instruct the witness to answer the question upon your request, you are justified in requesting the instruction, though you incur some risk always since you cannot know the judge's reaction. Such an instruction would serve both to impress the jury that the witness is being evasive and to put him at a disadvantage if he should want to qualify his answers to your further questions.

Another technique, not involving as much risk of detriment to your cross-examination as a request to the court for an instruction to the witness to answer the question, is nevertheless designed to accomplish the same purpose generally. Let the witness complete his evasive answer, then say, "Mr. Reporter, will you read back my last question?", and then to the witness, "Will

4. See §3.19 for examples, though perhaps exaggerated for illustration.

you answer *that* question, please?" Some courts will not permit the interruption (by asking the reporter to read from previous testimony), but if permitted, this technique can be both dramatic and effective. Of course your adversary may object on the ground that the witness has already answered the question, but the judge probably will not sustain that objection if there is any doubt about whether the question has been fairly answered; the judge's attitude probably will be to keep hands off unless the witness is being clearly evasive or the cross-examiner clearly unfair.

§3.24   Responding to questions from the witness

CASE 44. *P* sues for injuries sustained when his car was hit by a rolling spare wheel and tire from a truck manufactured by *D-1* and sold by the dealer, *D-2*, to the driver, *D-3*. The spare wheel came loose from its moorings underneath the rear of the truck when the truck skidded on wet pavement, the rear end swinging around in a circle; it rolled into the path of *P*'s car and *P,* in dodging it, struck a bridge abutment, immediately after which impact there was another impact between the spare wheel and *P*'s car. One defense asserted by all three defendants is that *P* was negligent in turning into the bridge abutment, and that *P*'s negligence was a legal cause of all of his injuries. During your cross-examination of *P* on behalf of one of the defendants, the following exchange occurs:

> Q. Did you intentionally turn your car toward the right when you saw the wheel coming toward you?
> A. I wouldn't say I *turned*; it wasn't that sharp.
> Q. Did you intentionally change the course of your car, causing it to veer toward the right?
> A. Yes, I did. Wouldn't you, if you saw a tremendous truck wheel bearing down on you at high speed?

What should you do when the witness asks you a question?

Occasionally a witness will ask you a question as you are cross-examining him. If the question is one seeking an explanation or clarification of the question you have asked him, you should readily give any explanation necessary to make your question clear and unambiguous; any other attitude on your part may give your cross-examination the appearance of being more a game than a search for the truth.

If the witness' question is rhetorical or argumentative (usually such questions will be tacked on the end of the witness' answer to some question of yours) as in Case 44, the problem is more difficult. In favor of your answering the question is the fact that usually you will have at the tip of your tongue an answer that at least seems to you to be logical and convincing; your prep aration of the case has included consideration of all contentions that you think might be raised by your adversary and all questions that he might be expected to ask any of your witnesses; this has incidentally prepared you for answering any question, such as that in Case 44, that is likely to be asked you unexpectedly by the witness you are cross-examining. Another factor favoring your answering any question such as this is that it may be difficult for you otherwise to avoid the appearance, in the eyes of the jury, of evading an embarrassing question. On the other hand, a question from the witness does not remove all restraints against a lawyer's testifying rather than questioning the witness. Also, there are tactical disadvantages in answering the witness, since this may encourage more questions from him, and more interruptions and interference with the direction and purpose of your cross-examination. Furthermore, such an interchange may lead to a running argument with the witness in which he is on equal ground with you if he too is allowed to ask questions. You have a great advantage over him in the privilege of asking the questions while he must give answers; you should not surrender that advantage lightly.

Because of conflicting considerations such as those discussed in the preceding paragraph, competent trial lawyers would differ regarding the best solution to the problem presented in Case 44. Some would answer the witness' question, making of it an occasion for expressing defendants' theory that a person in the exercise of ordinary care would have realized that turning into the bridge abutment would not avoid collision with the wheel but would greatly increase the hazard. Others would prefer a course of action not involving an answer to the witness' question. In any event, you should not simply ignore the question. It is worthwhile to work out in advance a stock response to such a situation as this, which you may use unless you are able at the moment the problem arises to formulate one that better suits the particular circumstances. The following are examples of responses you might use:

(If the witness has not fully answered your last question)
Right at this moment, Mr. *W*, you are permitted to testify, and I am not. And I ask that you answer my last question. If you don't remember it, I'll ask the reporter to read it back to you.
(If the witness has fully answered and added some question such as "Wouldn't you do the same?")
Just answer my questions, please. You are testifying and I am not. I take it from what you say that you admit that you intentionally changed the course of your car toward the right. Is that correct?
(A response of more questionable propriety)
I don't know, Mr. W, I make some mistakes myself. But in any event I take

it you admit that you intentionally changed the course of your car toward the right. Is that correct?

(Either as a preface to calling for an answer to a question just evaded, or in response to a question added by the witness after a full answer to your question)

Mr. *W*, the rules of court do not permit me to testify about what I would have done if I had been there, but if you mean to ask me to state what, in defendants' view of this case, should have been done, and if your counsel and the court have no objection, I'll do so. (Then, unless stopped by objection or ruling, state defendants' theory that a person of ordinary prudence would have realized that turning into the bridge abutment would increase rather than reduce the danger).

The last of these illustrative responses has the advantage of seeming less evasive than the first two, while yet not setting a precedent for answering the witness' questions except by a statement of your contentions.

If the witness continues the practice of interrupting your cross-examination with questions of his own, you may choose to move that the court instruct the witness to confine himself to answering the questions submitted to him. Usually such a motion will be sustained if the witness has repeated the practice after being advised that it is improper. If you have answered all of the witness' previous questions, however, asking for such an instruction may place you in the light of appearing willing for the witness to ask questions as long as you have answers on the tip of your tongue, but resorting to the rules for protection when he asks an embarrassing question. In short, it is more difficult to discontinue the practice of answering the witness' questions than it is to decline to start it.

§3.25 Cross-examining female witnesses

CASE 45. *P* is suing *D* for personal injuries, including a broken neck, received in an intersection collision while riding in the front seat with his wife, *W*, driving. The case arises in a jurisdiction where *W*'s negligence bars *P*'s recovery. *W* testifies on direct examination regarding circumstances surrounding the accident, such as speed of both vehicles, direction of travel, and the status of the traffic light at the time of the accident. On cross-examination directed toward proving that the accident was caused by her negligence, *W* appears to be on the verge of tears.

How should you cross-examine the wife of the plaintiff?

In most respects, the principles of cross-examination discussed in this chapter apply equally to male and female witnesses, while under cross-examination by either male or female attorneys. However, a few special problems associated with cross-examining women deserve attention.

The rule of courtesy [1] applies with special force when a male attorney is cross-examining a female witness. The injunction against invective, name-calling, or accusation [2] applies during cross-examination as well as at other times during trial; it applies with special force when the witness is female, even if the cross-examiner is also female, though perhaps a male cross-examiner is even more likely to cause an adverse jury reaction by using invective against a female witness. Even when jurors share the cross-examiner's reaction that the female witness on the stand is dishonest or otherwise undeserving individually, at least some of the jurors are likely to think it improper for the attorney to decline to extend the courtesies customarily extended to ladies.

Another special problem of cross-examining female witnesses is the greater risk of tears and the greater risk of a jury reaction adverse to the cross-examiner if tears fall. Jurors, along with others, may be inclined to forgive and forget transgressions under the influence of sympathy provoked by the genuine tears of a female witness.

Even if you are confronted by an acting witness, who deliberately uses tears to gain sympathy, it is not likely that your pressing the witness will aid in making the jury realize the true situation. Accordingly, whether the tears are genuine or synthetic, your aim is to use methods designed to avoid them, and to avoid blame for them if they fall. Generally you will be able to do this by observing the witness carefully and separating during your cross-examination the inquiries that, by reason of the subject matter and despite your care with respect to form, are likely to provoke genuine tears or furnish an excuse for the synthetic variety. In selecting the subject matter of cross-examination, avoid inquiries that have little bearing on the decision of the case if they are the tear-provoking type. On the other hand, you need not omit important questions simply because they may be likely to cause the witness to feel such embarrassment, shame or self-reproach as to make crying likely. In Case 45, almost certainly you should ask questions directed toward showing that *W* was guilty of causal negligence. When the jurors are aware of the materiality of the inquiries, they are not likely to consider your conduct improper. If the subpect matter of an inquiry is embarrassingly personal, you may make an introductory statement to the witness, as you are about to proceed with your inquiries, reciting that you dislike to inquire into intimate personal matters but do so in order to develop facts material to the proper decision of the case. When it is necessary to go into subjects that are likely to provoke tears, continue your efforts to phrase your questions in a

1. See §3.1.
2. See §7.19.

way that reduces as much as possible the risk of causing the witness to cry.

If, as will sometimes be the case, the witness breaks into tears despite your efforts to avoid it, what course of action should you take? If the witness still appears to be in sufficient control of her emotions that she can continue answering questions, probably the best course is to continue the cross-examination without expressly taking note of the crying. On the other hand, if the crying interferes materially with her answering, you may suggest to the court that you will not object to interruption of your cross-examination for a recess if the witness desires it and the court considers it appropriate. Most lawyers prefer, as cross-examiners, to take the initiative in this suggestion rather than having the court or opposing counsel do so. The advantage is that of courteous conduct generally. One disadvantage is the danger that the jury may consider that the cross-examiner is thus confessing mistreatment of the witness; because of this possibility, some lawyers prefer to wait for the court or opposing counsel to take the initiative regarding the recess, though acquiescing when the suggestion is made.

Whenever it is necessary to interrupt your cross-examination because the witness is crying, and often when the witness cries but no recess is taken, you should consider a motion for mistrial. Generally an instruction by the court to the jury to disregard the crying of the witness would have no value; aside from the jury's realizing, with whatever assistance you may be able to give them, that the witness is deliberately seeking sympathy, your only possible remedy against crying is a mistrial. Your decision to move for mistrial or not to do so will depend upon your assessment of the development of the case as a whole.[3] Usually trial judges will not grant a mistrial on this ground unless the crying has been repeated or appears to the judge to be a deliberate play for sympathy.

§3.26 Discrediting testimony of other witnesses

CASE 41.* P sues for title to land on which producing oil wells are located. The dispute turns on whether a certain stump found on the ground by P's surveyor, shortly before suit was instituted, is the stump of a witness tree marked by the original surveyor, 40 years earlier. If so, P wins; if not, the survey reconstructed on courses and distances from more remote witness markers will cause D to win. P testifies that before the tree was cut down he had observed on it an "X" mark with two hacks above and two hacks below the "X," and that he would describe the appearance of the marks, at the time he last observed them about one year before suit was instituted (a short

---

3. See §5.4.

*Adapted from the hypothetical case used in a demonstration trial of a land suit reported in *Institute on the Trial of a Land Suit* 85–212 (Southwestern Legal Foundation, Dallas, 1954).

time before somebody cut down and removed the tree without his knowledge or permission), as gouged-out places where the bark was gone and the
wood visible, and cleanly v-shaped as if cut by a sharp instrument, with
blows toward the middle of the tree from two slightly different directions.
You represent *D*, and your surveyor, *S*, advises you that after 40 years a surveyor's hackmarks would be almost overgrown and would appear only as a
scar on the tree rather than a v-shaped gouge.

*Should you attempt to use cross-examination of the witness to discredit
unfavorable testimony of other witnesses?*

Unfavorable testimony may be discredited by independent evidence from
other sources, as well as by cross-examination of the witness who gave the
unfavorable testimony. The potential subjects of such independent evidence
are numerous; it may relate either to contradictions of the unfavorable testimony or else to impeachment of the witness who gave the testimony, on
grounds of bias, interest, corruption, or moral[1] or mental deficiency.

Whatever its nature may be, independent proof used to discredit unfavorable testimony of other witnesses is more effective if it comes from witnesses your adversary calls rather than those you call. In planning for discrediting proof, then, you should consider using witnesses your adversary
calls, unless this is precluded by rules of your jurisdiction limiting the scope
of cross-examination[2] or by practical considerations such as inability to get
any of your adversary's witnesses to state the desired facts rather than some
less favorable version. If the difference in statement is only one of lack of
the degree of certainty and emphasis that another witness whom you can
afford to call to the stand would express, you will usually profit by bolster-
ing the testimony of your own witness with admissions from a witness your
adversary has called. On the other hand, if the difference between the testimony of the witnesses is more substantial, your decision as to whether you
should go into the subject with the adverse witness must depend on your
appraisal of the probable jury reaction to your witness' testimony, neither
corroborated nor directly contradicted, compared with their probable reaction to the combination of the testimony of your witness and the less favorable testimony of the adverse witness on cross-examination. Ordinarily it
will be advisable for you to cross-examine on any subject as to which you
expect that your adversary will question the witness later by recalling him,
in the light of testimony that you offer; the risk of unfavorable testimony,
both as to substance and as to form of expression, is greater if your adversary
has time to confer with the witness and prepare him for specific inquiries
than if you cross-examine him before such preparation.

1. See §3.11.
2. See §3.14.

In Case 41, your surveyor advises you that the hackmarks made by the original surveyor 40 years earlier would not have the appearance of those described by *P* as being on the tree about which he testifies. If, as would doubtlessly be the case under the facts stated in Case 41, your surveyor also tells you that this fact is so well known and accepted among surveyors that he is certain that *P*'s surveyor would express the same views, then you should use the cross-examination of *P*'s surveyor, in addition to the direct examination of your own, to prove that hackmarks of the kind described by *P* could not possibly be those made by the original surveyor. If you use your own surveyor alone to prove this fact, the jury will be confronted with choosing between the testimony of witnesses called by opposite sides in the lawsuit, both witnesses being interested since *P* has a direct interest in the subject of suit and your surveyor has an interest in the sense that he has been employed by you in the case for a substantial fee. On the other hand, if you have obtained these facts about appearance of forty-year-old hackmarks from the surveyor called by *P*'s lawyer, it is almost certain that the jury will accept this evidence and reach some conclusion consistent with it.

§3.27   Inquiring about payment of expenses and fees

CASE 17. Counsel for *D* in a personal injury action has obtained an examination of *P* by *N,* a specialist in neurosurgery. For his services in examining *P*, submitting his report in writing, and appearing in court to testify concerning his findings and opinion, *N* charges *D* a fee of $600.

Should you cross-examine concerning payment of expenses or fees to the witness?

Frequently a witness who has not been warned that he may be cross-examined about payment of fees or expenses commits the error of trying to hide the fact of payment or minimize the amount;[1] you then have an opportunity to impeach the credibility of the witness generally by insistent questioning until the fact and amount of payment are established. Another advantage to be gained by cross-examination on this matter is that if the payment is substantial the jury may draw the inference that the witness' testimony is influenced consciously or subconsciously by the payment; it is on this theory that the evidence is relevant and admissible. In Case 17, for example, if you represent the plaintiff and opposing counsel calls a medical witness who is being paid a fee of $600 for making an examination and report and appearing in court to testify, you may choose to prove the amount of his fee and the amount of time devoted to the case (let us say three hours);

---

1. See §§2.14, 2.21, 9.19.

although medical specialists may regard this as reasonable compensation, the ordinary jury in most communities would consider it high.

Against these advantages you must weigh the possible disadvantages of cross-examination regarding payment of fees or expenses. If you represent the plaintiff, there is generally little disadvantage in going into the expert fees paid by your adversary, unless you have paid or agreed to pay your experts substantially more. The same is usually true as to expense of lay witnesses. Furthermore, in the typical case the plaintiff is more likely than the defendant to find witnesses willing to cooperate without reimbursement because of sympathy for the plaintiff's situation.

A defendant's lawyer ordinarily should not go into the matter of fees paid to experts, unless either the size of the fees of the plaintiff's experts is so greatly out of proportion to the fees for the defendants' experts as to cause the jury to be at least suspicious, or else the fees proved by the plaintiff as a part of the damages include improper elements. A defendant's lawyer must bear in mind that despite all instructions, jurors are likely to be influenced by heavy expenses when they are fixing damages, if they reach that fateful point in their deliberations. Even though the amount of the expert's fees may not be large in comparison with the damages claim, any discussion of fees leads the jury into thinking about other expenses the plaintiff must meet, including a substantial contingent fee to the lawyer. Perhaps it is too much to hope that the jurors will not have this in mind anyway, but most trial lawyers consider that the defendant's chances of a relatively low damages finding are better if the matter of expenses of suit is not raised during the trial. Of course the fees of a medical witness in treating the patient, as distinguished from testifying and counseling with the lawyer regarding the lawsuit, are part of the measure of damages and cannot be kept away from the jury; even if the amount is stipulated, the plaintiff's lawyer generally should get the stipulation before the jury on the theory that the amount of expense has weight in the jury's consideration of the severity of the injury. As the defendant's lawyer you may be confronted with circumstances in which you suspect or know that part of the fees of the plaintiff's doctor are chargeable to his time in court as a witness, or to his time in preparing reports for the plaintiff's lawyer. The fee for appearance in court and also that for preparing reports, in most circumstances, is not a proper element of the measure of damages, though uncertainty may arise if the doctor says the examination was made for purposes of considering treatment, as well as for reporting to the lawyer on the condition of the patient. In this type of situation, as the defendant's lawyer you may justify going into the fees on cross-examination with the purpose of demonstrating both that the correct measure of medical expenses is lower than claimed and also that the padding of the claim as to items that can be accurately computed supports the inference that the plaintiff's claim is doubtlessly padded much more as to items that can only be estimated and not computed.

§3.28 Demanding that documents be produced

CASE 46. You represent *D* in defending a personal injury action instituted by *P*. *M*, a medical witness for *P*, refers frequently to notes in his hands as he testifies on direct examination. The notes are on cards smaller than those ordinarily used for doctors' permanent records.

Should you call upon your adversary or the witness to produce documents relevant to his testimony?

Sometimes a witness uses documents during his testimony though they are not offered in evidence. If a witness called by your opponent is showing documents or parts of them to the jury, you should consider objecting to that procedure; likewise, if the witness is consulting the documents, even though not expressly referring to them in his testimony, you should consider objecting.[1] In the latter instance, the objection may serve the very important purpose of forcing some explanation to you as to the nature of the documents and perhaps giving you an opportunity to examine them, even though your objection is thereafter overruled. It is nearly always advisable to get access to documents the witness is using during his testimony. Through the objection you may be able to accomplish your desire while avoiding the harsh rule, referred to in the next paragraph, that a demand for production of a document makes it admissible though otherwise it would have been inadmissible. The advantages you may gain by examining documents the witness is using are considerable. You may discover that the witness is depending on notes he made after he knew of the prospect of litigation. This may cast suspicion on his testimony, particularly if he made the notes after conferences concerning his testimony. In that event you should consider offering the notes in evidence, though only for the limited purpose of impeachment[2] by showing the degree of the witness' dependence on them. Also, documents the witness is using may give you ideas and data for effective cross-examination. For example, the notes that your adversary's medical witness is using may contain notations of findings favorable to your side, which your adversary has failed to bring out on his direct examination. It is therefore good practice to seek access to the notes and records that a medical witness is using. If, as appears likely in Case 46, the witness has not brought his original records to court with him, you should consider asking that he allow you or another representative of your client to examine his original records. The pos-

1. See §4.5.
2. See §2.36.

sibilities of discovering favorable data omitted from the direct examination generally outweigh any disadvantages involved.

The practice of calling upon your adversary or a witness to produce for your inspection some document in his custody involves serious danger of harm in those jurisdictions where it is held that such an inspection makes the document admissible at your adversary's instance, even though it might have been inadmissible otherwise.[3] As noted in the preceding paragraph, you may be able by objection to gain access to the document without incurring this risk if the witness is using it during his testimony. If it is a document not being used in the testimony, however, you should not call for its production during trial unless you have ascertained its contents and would be willing for it to go before the jury, or else you are in a jurisdiction not following the rule that your demand for production bars your objections to admissibility. In most jurisdictions at the present time effective means of obtaining access to the document in advance of trial are available,[4] and you should use them in lieu of a request at trial. Even if your request for the document in trial does not bar your objections to its admissibility, it excites the jury's curiosity and may cause an unfavorable reaction against you if your adversary subsequently offers the document and you object to its going to the jury.

§3.29 Cross-examining experts: in general

How should you cross-examine an expert?

You may hear the suggestion that the best cross-examination of an expert is none. That advice was doubtlessly formulated by one who had observed attempted cross-examination of a competent expert by an unprepared lawyer. It is true that the dangers of haphazard cross-examination without planning or preparation are accentuated when the witness is an expert. He knows more about his field than the cross-examiner does. He is less hampered by rules of evidence than other witnesses since his opinions and supporting arguments are generally admissible. Frequently he is a person of unusual intelligence. Often he has experience in expressing his ideas persuasively.

Differences between the expert and the ordinary witness give rise not merely to special hazards of cross-examination, however; they also give rise to special opportunities of effective cross-examination. Rarely, if ever, is there an expert witness who is not subject to effective use of some of these special opportunities if you have studied your case carefully and made proper pretrial preparations for your cross-examination. In your pretrial preparations you should confer with your own expert[1] as a general rule (the extent of of the conference being more limited as your experience with the particular

3. 6 Wigmore, _Evidence_ §1861 (3d ed. 1940); 7 _id.,_ §2125.
4. See §11.14.
1. See §2.15(a).

type of litigation involving a certain aspect of expert testimony increases).
You should invite his suggestions concerning potential lines of inquiry that
may be fruitful in the cross-examination of your adversary's experts. Also,
you should seek his advice on the merits and hazards of the ideas that you
have conceived for cross-examination.

An expert is sometimes subject to effective cross-examination regarding interest in the case because of his employment for a fee[2] and regarding apparent bias as a "professional witness" receiving a substantial part of his in-
come from customary employment on one side of the docket in cases similar to the one on trial.[3] Occasionally the expert will be subject to effective
cross-examination regarding his qualifications.[4] Sometimes you can make effective use of an opposing expert by asking him to prepare an exhibit, or to
place additional markings on your adversary's exhibit, demonstrating your
theory of the case.[5]

The characteristic purpose for which your adversary calls an expert is to
place before the jury opinion evidence on vital issues in the case. This opinion
testimony makes the expert subject to some methods of cross-examination
that are not generally available as to other witnesses. Nearly always the expert will be subject to effective use of hypothetical questions.[6] The fact that
important aspects of the witness' testimony are opinions also leads to other
special problems. Opinions are merely estimates of probabilities or possibilities. Frequently the rules of substantive law require proof of probabilities
as distinguished from possibilities, and in some jurisdictions rules of evidence
exclude expressions of opinion as to possibilities — for example, as to conditions that may develop in the future as a result of an injury and as to possible
causal connection between conditions now existing and an impact inflicted
by the defendant.[7] In some of the jurisdictions not permitting expression of
possibilities during direct examination, however, the courts permit cross-
examination regarding possibilities as a means of probing the degree of certainty attached to the opinion of probabilities expressed by the witness. Almost certainly this type of cross-examination will be recognized as proper if
you have other admissible evidence in the case supporting your theory as a
probability; for example, if your expert for the plaintiff has testified that in
his opinion the impact inflicted by the defendant is a cause of the abnormal
narrowing of a certain intervertebral disc space, it is proper for you to ask the
defendant's expert on cross-examination if it is not true that it is possible that
an impact of the character claimed will cause such a condition, even though

2. See §3.27.
3. See §3.30.
4. See *id.*
5. See §3.16.
6. See §3.31.
7. 2 Wigmore, *Evidence* §663 (3d ed. 1940).

he has expressed the opinion that this is probably not true in the case at hand. Such a question, incidentally, is a type of hypothetical question.[8]

The fact that important aspects of the witness' testimony are opinions makes it worthwhile also to look for and develop uncertainties and qualifications in these opinions. An expert will usually admit that some questions put to him are not subject to positive answers and that under these circumstances persons qualified in the field recognize that there is always a possibility that their opinions are wrong. In developing this idea, however, you should proceed with great caution. Expert witnesses who have stated qualified opinions on direct examination have a way of stating their opinions with more conviction, rather than less, when they are annoyed by the feeling that the cross-examiner is trying to make it appear that the opinions are arbitrary guesses. This fact makes it inadvisable usually to insist that an adverse expert give an unqualified answer to one of your questions;[9] it is better to have the qualifications available for your jury argument than to press the witness until he strengthens his answer against you, as he usually will.

With respect to developing particular uncertainties and qualifications, you should exercise even greater caution. Unless you have acquired a thorough knowledge of the subject from experience in trial of similar cases, you should not attempt this without advice from your own experts; otherwise you may fall into the trap of merely giving the witness an opportunity to explain more fully than he did on direct examination why, in reaching his final opinion, he excluded the other possibilities you have identified. This is simply one aspect of the rule that you ought to know the particular subject of inquiry as well or better than the expert before you tangle with him about it; since as questioner, you are choosing the subject and can keep the cross-examination within the field on which you have especially prepared with the assistance of your own experts, it is usually feasible to follow this rule. With the advice of your own experts, for example, you may be able to develop on cross-examination weaknesses in the procedures adopted by the expert in his investigation — failure to make some laboratory tests that your own expert has used and that resulted in findings inconsistent with the conclusions reached by the witness you are cross-examining.

An expert frequently has no personal knowledge of facts of the case outside of the investigation made by him pursuant to his employment by one party to the litigation. In personal injury cases it is quite normal for the defendant's medical witnesses to be doctors who have examined the plaintiff only once or twice, and then at the instance and expense of the defendant. Obviously, it is to the plaintiff's advantage to emphasize on cross-examination both the limited opportunity of the defendant's witnesses to observe the plaintiff, as compared with that of the plaintiff's doctor who has treated him over

8. See §3.31.
9. See §3.23.

a period of time, and also the fact that when the examination was made the doctor had already been employed and was being paid by the defendant. Conversely, the plaintiff's lawyer will sometimes use a medical witness who has not treated the plaintiff over a period of time but has only made an examination at the instance of the plaintiff's lawyer. In some jurisdictions, this fact will affect admissibility of parts of the doctor's testimony,[10] and you should take this into account in determining whether to object, either with or without support of *voir dire* examination, when the first attempt is made to introduce the evidence.[11] Even if this fact does not affect admissibility, it is one that the defendant's lawyer should emphasize in cross-examining the doctor; this type of cross-examination is even more damaging when the plaintiff is using such a witness than when the defendant is doing so, for the reason that the plaintiff's obvious opportunity to consult the doctor at any time leads to the inference that his condition was not sufficiently serious to cause him to seek this consultation had there been no lawsuit. Another variation of this same principle arises when it appears that the dates of the plaintiff's visits to the doctor coincide perfectly with dates of reports to his lawyer, supporting the inference that the plaintiff went to see the doctor only when the lawyer told him to go so he could have a report on the plaintiff's condition.

The use of literature in the expert's field during cross-examination is controversial, both as to the rules of evidence applying and as to tactical considerations. If you have particular passages in such literature that you wish to use as supporting your theory of the case, generally you cannot get them into evidence through direct examination.[12] On the other hand, in many jurisdictions you can make use of them on cross-examinations.[13] The extent to which this is possible varies greatly among different jurisdictions. When you are using medical literature in cross-examination, one of the most effective methods is to get the witness committed to the authoritative standing of the particular book or of the writings of the particular author before you produce the writing itself for the expert to read and consider carefully. Sometimes you can do this by asking the witness to name the outstanding authorities in the field; it achieves much greater effect if he names your book in response to that question than if you ask only whether it is not true that your book is recognized as an authority in the field. Having established the authority of the book, you may then read selected passages contradicting his opinions, or you may hand him the book and ask that he read the marked passages. In that exceptional situation, on the other hand, in which the writings are those of the witness, it will often be more effective to

10. 6 Wigmore, *Evidence* §1721 (3d ed. 1940). Compare Federal Rules of Evidence, Rule 803(4).

11. See §§4.2, 4.6.

12. 6 Wigmore, *Evidence* §§1690–1700 (3d ed. 1940).

13. *Id.*, §1700. See also Federal Rules of Evidence, Rule 803(18).

ask him whether he agrees with certain extracted statements before advising him that the statements are extracted from his own works; occasionally such a witness is caught in the embarrassing situation of disagreeing with a passage from his own writings.[14] As to the use of particular passages from a book, whether written by the witness or another, the advance advice of your own expert is essential unless you are certain that you have a full grasp of the subject; otherwise, with limited knowledge of the field you may misconstrue the writing and get out on a limb that the witness expertly saws off by pointing out the correct construction and other passages in the book that support it.

You may hear the story of the cross-examination in which the lawyer stacks several books on the table, with titles turned away from the witness, and asks the witness if he is familiar with certain writings on the subject, including in the list many authorities that the witness will surely recognize but inserting one or two fictitious titles to trap the witness who wants to appear to know more than he does. The results are spectacular when the plan works, but in addition to controversial ethical considerations[15] there exists the possibility that the scheme will be discovered and exposed with harmful effect. Another plan sometimes used on an adverse expert, less likely to have effect on one experienced in testifying than on a novice, is merely to have the books available in plain sight throughout the examination of the witness, with the purpose of causing his opinions to be expressed somewhat more conservatively.

The list of methods of cross-examination of experts in this section is not exhaustive.[16] Generally you can meet other problems that confront you regarding cross-examination of an expert by applying the same principles you should apply to your cross-examination of other witnesses. In fact, an analysis of the suggestions presented in this section will reveal that they are merely applications of the same general principles to the special circumstances frequently arising when the witness is an expert.

§3.30 Cross-examining experts: inquiring into qualifications

CASE 47. The extent and probable duration of effects of P's injuries are major issues in a personal injury case filed by P against D. P has been under

14. See §9.8, concerning selection of experts.

15. Is this a form of "chicane," condemned by American Bar Association, Canons of Professional Ethics, Canon 15 (1908)? Does the attorney using this technique "[k]nowingly make a false statement of . . . fact" in violation of American Bar Association, Code of Professional Responsibility, DR 7-102(A)(5) (1969), or "allude to any matter . . . that will not be supported by admissible evidence," thus violating id., DR 7-106(C)(1)? Or is this a legitimate use of surprise tactics for the purpose of testing the veracity of one suspected of willingness to lie? Compare §§1.3, 3.18, 3.19.

16. See also, e.g., 2 I. Goldstein and F. Lane, Goldstein Trial Technique, ch. 16 (2d ed. 1969).

the treatment of his familiy physician, *F*, a general practitioner who does his own X-ray work and used X-rays in the diagnosis of a fracture of one of the vertebral processes. *P* was treated by *F* only, for a period of eight months after the accident, and then was referred to *S*, a specialist in orthopedic surgery, and *X*, an X-ray specialist, after *P* employed his lawyer. As *D*'s lawyer, you have obtained a medical examination by *T*, an orthopedic specialist, and *Y*, an X-ray specialist.

Should you cross-examine an expert regarding his qualifications and experience?

If the purported expert lacks qualifications essential to admissibility of important parts of his testimony, particularly his opinion testimony, it is generally preferable to raise this point by objection on the ground of insufficient proof of qualifications or else to take the witness on *voir dire* examination and demonstrate affirmatively his lack of qualifications before you make the objection.[1] This is true because of the difficulty of erasing from the minds of the jurors the opinions already expressed by the witness if you wait until cross-examination to demonstrate that they are inadmissible and then move that the court withdraw them and instruct the jury to disregard them. Furthermore, there is some danger of having forfeited your objection on the ground that the original proof of qualifications was insufficient, though not affirmatively showing lack of qualifications, and that your objection should have been made before the opinions were expressed.[2] Perhaps you should depart from this practice of early objection, however, if you have reliable information about what the testimony of the expert will be and know that you can effectively impeach it; in those rare cases in which you are able to discredit the witness completely, the damaging effect to your adversary's case is greater than when you merely exclude the testimony of the witness by objection.

Even though the witness has sufficient qualifications to make his testimony admissible, you should consider the possibility of showing that they are weak from the point of view of making his testimony credible as compared with contradictory testimony of other experts. This is the problem presented in Case 47. Whether you should cross-examine with this aim will be determined primarily by the information available to you as to weaknesses in the qualifications of the expert or factors in his experience unfavorable to the party who called him. In the absence of information indicating susceptibility to effective cross-examination, the risk is serious that your questions regarding qualifications and experience would serve only to bolster the credibility of

---

1. See §§3.13, 4.6.
2. 1 Wigmore, *Evidence* §18 (3d ed. 1940); 2 *id.*, §§486, 586. Compare Federal Rules of Evidence, Rule 103(a)(1).

the witness by supplying additional data omitted on direct examination.[3] Particularly you should refrain from questions that carry an implication of incompetency, as distinguished from merely less outstanding qualifications and experience than your own witnesses. The jury reaction probably will be unfavorable to you if you make such an implied charge when you are not prepared to prove it by satisfactory, admissible evidence.[4]

In the typical case you are unable to prove incompetency and the advantage you seek is only to prove that your adversary's experts have less impressive qualifications than your experts have. You may do this, for example, by questions calling upon a doctor to admit that he is not a member of a certain medical group in which membership must be earned by special training and experience, as distinguished from the more numerous societies to which practically every doctor is welcome if he chooses to join. Another example is the question calling upon the witness to admit that he does not purport to be a specialist in some material field. For example, if the case involves an alleged injury within the field of neurosurgery, and your adversary's general practitioner expresses opinions in conflict with those of your specialist in neurosurgery, it is to your advantage to obtain from your adversary's witness on cross-examination the admission that he is not a specialist in the field of neurosurgery and perhaps also that your witness is one of the recognized specialists in that field.[5] You may even choose to press him with a question whether the specialist's opinion would not generally be regarded as more reliable than that of the general practitioner on the specific injury alleged; this is not always a good question, however, since the general practitioner can in some cases reasonably argue that one whose practice is to consider the overall medical problem of the patient is better able to give a final judgment than a specialist, though he would give weight to the specialists' opinions.

Rarely you may be able to expose lack of qualifications by submitting a question about problems in the expert's field to which he should know the answer but does not. You should make this attempt only with the guidance of your own experts. Also, you must bear in mind that the jury will not know whether the problems are ones that the expert should answer; you must prove this fact also. You should consider also the possible use of literature[6] in the expert's field as a means of attacking his qualifications indirectly through

---

3. Your adversary may even have omitted some details with the purpose of leaving the witness more qualifications to add if you should undertake to discredit his standing; see §2.22 for discussion of other factors affecting the extent of proof of qualifications on direct examination.

4. See §1.3.

5. Some trial judges disapprove the latter type of question on the theory that it is unfair to the experts to call upon them to express their opinions as to general competency of another expert, as distinguished from their opinions as to accuracy of his conclusions in a specific case.

6. See §3.29.

proof of conflicts between his views and those of recognized authorities in the field, or through proof of his unfamiliarity with important aspects of the writings that he admits to be recognized authoritative publications.

Extensive experience of the witness regarding problems of the type presented in your lawsuit is not always favorable to supporting the credibility of his testimony and opinions. In many areas, for example, personal injury litigation has developed "plaintiff's doctors" and "defendant's doctors." Many doctors are reluctant to make any appearance in court, some appear occasionally on either side of the docket, and others appear quite frequently and nearly always on the same side of the docket, either for the plaintiff customarily or for the defendant customarily. That a doctor appears frequently as a witness in lawsuits and that he nearly always appears on the same side of the docket obviously support the inference that he is biased toward that side of the litigation. If your adversary's medical witnesses are substantially more subject to this charge than your own, then it is advantageous to cross-examine regarding the extent of experience in making examinations and reports to lawyers for use in litigation and appearing in court to testify. Also, if your adversary has first opened the subject by so cross-examining your experts, you may find it advisable to subject his experts to similar cross-examination if they are subject to the same charge, even though in less degree; in such cases, however, your cross-examination should not be detailed, and your purpose may be accomplished by a pair of questions obtaining from the witness an admission that he sees a substantial number of patients on account of injuries that are the subject of litigation and that usually in doing so he is employed by the plaintiff (or usually is employed by the defendant, as the case may be).

§3.31 Cross-examining experts: using hypothetical questions

Case 48. *P* claims injury to muscles and soft tissues of the back and to a certain intervertebral disc. It is admitted that there are no fractures. *D* obtains a medical examination of *P* by agreement or under court order; *M*, the doctor making the examination of *P*, is called as a witness for *D*, and testifies on direct examination that in his opinion *P* suffered no injury to the intervertebral disc and has fully recovered from any soft tissue injuries, except that his failure to work for an extended period has temporarily impaired the strength of muscles of his back, a condition that will be fully remedied by his gradual return to heavy work. You are cross-examining *M* on behalf of *P*.

To what extent should you use hypothetical questions in cross-examining an expert?

On direct examination hypothetical questions are generally subject to sound objection unless submitted to an expert to elicit his opinion testimony, with each element of the hypothesis being supported by independent proof.[1] In many jurisdictions the rules of evidence are less restrictive as to submission of hypothetical questions to an expert on cross-examination, in that the court may within discretionary limits allow the cross-examiner to use hypotheses not fully supported by the evidence, for the purpose of testing the expert and his expressed opinions.[2] For example, when a medical witness for a plaintiff in a personal injury case has testified to a given opinion of duration and extent of disability, apparently based largely upon the plaintiff's "subjective" complaints (as distinguished from "objective" findings of the doctor on examination), as the defendant's lawyer you may isolate each of the factors that the witness has stated as supporting his opinion, then inquiring hypothetically whether the removal of that factor would affect his opinion. It may be possible through this technique to demonstrate clearly for the jury that the opinion is based primarily upon the plaintiff's subjective complaints and that the plaintiff's claim may yet be fabricated or exaggerated, though he has an honest and competent doctor, since the doctor must rely primarily on the word of the patient in the absence of objective findings proving or disproving the patient's complaints. Similarly you may use hypothetical questions when the doctor for the plaintiff states objective findings as the basis for his opinion. You may pare down the details of complaints and findings to those to which the doctor attached significance in forming his opinion. It is then easier to demonstrate the point of conflict between medical witnesses as to the significance of given objective findings and the error in the conclusions of the adverse experts. Before attempting this use of hypothetical questions, however, you should obtain the advice of your own medical witnesses with the purpose of determining their views on the significance of various findings and the usefulness of this method in demonstrating the fallacy of the opinions of your adversary's witnesses.

Another way of using a hypothetical question on cross-examination is to submit to your adversary's expert a question in which the hypotheses are the most favorable that your evidence will support. Rarely is an expert not subject to this technique of obtaining favorable answers on cross-examination. Even those professional advocates who try to pass for expert witnesses — on the opposite side of the docket from you — may be exposed for what they are by the way they evade answering such questions. Generally, there will be a conflict in the evidence concerning many of the facts assumed by the expert in forming his opinion, as well as conflict concerning the ultimate opinion itself. Naturally the expert called by one party is likely to be one whose views on those facts, to the extent that they are ascertained by the

1. 2 Wigmore, *Evidence* §679 (3d ed. 1940). See also Federal Rules of Evidence, Rules 701–705.

2. 2 Wigmore, *Evidence* §684 (3d ed. 1940).

expert's inquiry rather than being merely assumed by him, are favorable to that party. When the expert is required, by hypothesis, to assume on the contrary that the facts are consistent with that interpretation of the evidence most favorable to the cross-examiner, it is almost inconceivable that the opinion expressed in this answer would be exactly the same as expressed on direct. At the least this technique of cross-examination serves to make the jury realize that there are some otherwise unexpressed qualifications of the expert's opinion. In some cases this technique is effective to demonstrate that the dispute is primarily one of hypotheses, rather than expert opinion; in that event, it is a technique you should use only if you have the better supporting evidence for your hypotheses. Case 48 illustrates the point. P has undoubtedly testified to a history of subjective complaints that, if true, may be most readily explained on the basis of injury of the type P is claiming. D's medical witness, though usually by implication rather than expressly,[3] has concluded that the complaints are fabricated or exaggerated and has reached his final opinion on that assumption. If by a hypothetical question you require him to assume the truth and accuracy of P's complaints, then his opinion is necessarily different. At the least, this technique probably will demonstrate to the jury that they cannot reach findings consistent with the opinion of the defendant's medical witness except upon the basis that P is a malingerer, a conclusion that the jury will be reluctant to reach without very strong proof, despite the theoretical burden of proof upon the plaintiff.

It is sometimes permissible under rules of evidence and effective as a matter of tactics to use hypothetical questions based upon the assumption of facts that are to be offered at a later stage in the trial. For example, the defendant's lawyer is generally permitted to do this, even over objection, if he represents to the court that he proposes to offer proof to support the hypothesis at a later point in the trial. This method often serves to focus attention on the importance of the supporting evidence, when it is offered. These comments would apply, for example, to evidence that certain physical conditions of the plaintiff to which a medical expert attached significance in concluding that the defendant's impact caused the plaintiff's present condition had in fact existed before the impact occurred.

Usually your adversary's expert witness is subject to effective cross-examination by this technique of the hypothetical question making assumptions favorable to the cross-examiner. Like other trial techniques, however, it has within it some danger of harm to the cross-examiner. You should be careful in framing the hypothetical questions to make them sufficiently complete that the expert witness is not able to escape the answer you seek, or evade it, through additional assumptions not inconsistent with yours (of which he may even fail to advise you). You can get help in this respect by submitting your pro-

3. *Cf.* §7.19.

posed hypothetical questions in advance to your own medical witness for criticism. Another danger in using hypothetical questions on cross-examination is that the witness may answer unfavorably to you, even upon your own assumptions; if it appears in advance that this probably will be the case, it will generally be better to avoid using hypothetical questions on cross-examination, unless you consider that you will be able to use the answers to show bias of your adversary's expert. Again, the advance counsel of your own medical witness should aid you in appraising this risk of unfavorable answers not easily shown to be biased.

Chapter IV

OBJECTIONS TO EVIDENCE

§4.1 Purposes served by objections

The most obvious purpose of objection — the primary reason for the existence of the procedure of objection — is the exclusion of improper evidence. Application of that purpose is assumed in most of the discussion in this chapter, and the focus is upon means by which you may serve that purpose while serving one or more other purposes as well, or at least not interfering with your accomplishment of other purposes. In practice, objections are sometimes used solely for other purposes than exclusion of evidence, and frequently they are used for that and other purposes jointly.

Other purposes of objection include preventing your adversary from using an improper manner of questioning (such as leading a friendly witness[1] or using an oppressive manner of cross-examining your witness[2]), preserving error in the event of an unfavorable ruling,[3] forcing your adversary to offer evidence favorable to you, as is possible in some jurisdictions in the case of objection to reading only part of the relevant portions of a document,[4] and such ethically questionable purposes as making a "jury argument"[5] or coaching the witness during cross-examination.[6]

§4.2 The decision to object

CASE 49. *P* sues *D* for damages on account of personal injuries allegedly inflicted upon *P* through negligence. The accident occurred in a small town where *P* was visiting with his parents, and *P* received emergency treatment

1. See §4.3.
2. See §4.4
3. See §4.12.
4. See §4.5.
5. See §4.14.
6. See §4.4.

from his former family doctor, M, who is still the family doctor of P's parents. P then was sent by ambulance to the city where he now resides and was treated by other doctors thereafter. At the trial of the case, P's lawyer does not call M but calls to the stand M's nurse, N. During the course of direct examination, while P is sitting beside his lawyer in the courtroom, P's lawyer asks N to recite what P said to M in her presence, at the time P was brought to M's office for emergency treatment. From your investigation as D's lawyer, you anticipate that N's answer will recite a purported declaration by P concerning the severity of the pain suffered by P between the moment of the accident and the time he reached M's office. You have also concluded from your investigation that M is honest and fair and that he had previously treated P for some of the conditions that P is now claiming first arose after the accident on which suit is based. M has refused to discuss the matter with you, however, advising you that he has been instructed by P and his lawyer not to discuss with you any treatment of P or communications between P and him.

Should you object?

The significance of your adversary's question and of the anticipated answer of the witness, as well as the significance of the various purposes that might be served by an objection, will depend on both the form and the content of the question and the anticipated answer. Some objections and the purposes associated with them are based on form alone — such as the objection that the question is leading. Other objections, usually the more significant ones, are based on impropriety of the subject matter of inquiry. Regardless of the character of the question and the basis of the objection available, ordinarily you should not object if you are reasonably certain that the answer will be neutral or favorable to you, unless you anticipate that it is preliminary to the offering of materially harmful matter that you can exclude if you object in time. More frequently, however, the immediate answer anticipated is unfavorable; otherwise your adversary probably would not ask the question. It is to your advantage to exclude the unfavorable answer, and often to accomplish some other purpose also by the objection; your problem is one of appraising those advantages as compared with any disadvantages that may arise from the objection.

Often your objection will serve to call special attention of the jury as well as the court to the unfavorable evidence you seek to exclude, thus tending to emphasize its significance. Natural curiosity will cause a juror to speculate privately and perhaps also to share the speculations with other jurors regarding the excluded matter. Frequently the question will have given enough of a clue that jurors surmise the nature of the excluded evidence. They may even surmise something worse than the excluded evidence.

Jurors know that they are not supposed to consider this excluded matter in their deliberations, but being human they may let it affect them, consciously or subconsciously. If the jurors engage in such speculative consideration of excluded matter, the added emphasis given to it by your unsuccessful effort to keep them from considering it may cause it to be more damaging than if you had permitted it to come in without objection. This danger is often exaggerated, however. Most jurors conscientiously try to follow the rulings of the trial judge; it is the exceptional juror who conceives it to be a duty to do justice according to the juror's own peculiar ideas rather than according to the rules stated by the judge.

This disadvantage of emphasis to the evidence you have attempted to exclude is more apparent and dangerous if your objection is overruled. In this situation the jurors are in effect told specifically by the judge that it is proper that they consider the evidence; your unsuccessful objection having called it particularly to their attention, it is almost certain that they will consider it and give it more weight than if you had made no effort to exclude it. One of your problems is to anticipate the probable ruling of the trial judge upon your objection and give that factor consideration in determining whether to object.[1]

Other disadvantages of objection are primarily associated with the possibility of an unfavorable reaction of the jury to the practice of making objections. Will they view your objections as an attempted use of technical rules[2] to keep them from knowing the whole story as the basis for their findings? Some rules of evidence are based on the theory that the jury cannot be trusted to render a fair and impartial verdict if the excluded information is known to them. Such rules are not necessarily indicative of a judicial concept that jurors are incompetent or untrustworthy, but only that they are human and should be protected insofar as possible from influences that experience has indicated are calculated to impair human judgment. The courts might have set up similar rules to protect trial judges from such influences but for the fact that this is not feasible since the trial judge in many instances must hear the evidence alleged to be objectionable in order to pass on whether or not it is proper. Nevertheless, many jurors will eventually draw from your persistent objections either the inference that you do not trust the jurors or else the inference that you want to hide everything from them that you can and let them hear only your own side of the case. Either inference is likely to influence the jurors against you and your case.

In some instances you can avoid the danger of unfavorable jury reaction to the practice of making objections by presenting objections in an advance motion,[3] and less often by arranging for objections out of the hearing of the jury after your adversary has asked the objectionable question.[4] When

1. See §4.11.
2. See §1.3.

3. See §4.16.
4. See §§4.9, 4.10.

neither of these practices is feasible, the danger of unfavorable jury reaction to objections should cause you to exercise care with respect to what you say and how you say it in objecting but is not so great as to warrant your waiving important objections. Jurors have seen and heard enough about trials, whether it is accurate information or not, that they expect some objections on the part of lawyers. They are not likely to react unfavorably unless your objections are frequent as compared to your adversary's few or your objections are often unfounded. The possibility of unfavorable reaction is also balanced by the possibility that the jury will blame the lawyer asking the questions rather than the one objecting if the objections are consistently sustained by the court. As against the possible inference that the objecting lawyer is hiding something and not trusting the jury, there is the possible inference that the lawyer asking questions ruled improper by the court is attempting to win by violating the rules. The jurors' respect for the court and for fair dealings may turn them against the lawyer who tries to get by with as much as possible.[5] Also, aside from respect for the court's rulings, jurors may upon independent consideration reach the conclusion that the objectionable question is unfair. For example, your objection to leading questions[6] serves the purpose of appealing to the jurors' sense of fairness about allowing witnesses to tell their own stories in their own words, as well as appealing to the court to stop the practice. These factors cause most lawyers to consider that a sustained objection, if it harms anyone, is more likely to harm the side of the lawyer who asked the question, though an overruled objection is more likely to harm the side of the objecting lawyer. For this additional reason, you must consider the probable ruling of the trial judge on your objection when you are deciding whether to make it.[7]

In general, these disadvantages of objecting should cause you to refrain from making objections that you have little reasonable hope of upholding and objections to questions that you anticipate probably will not lead to admission of evidence that is harmful to your case. But they should not cause you to waive sound objections to admission of evidence that probably would have practical weight against you, or to questions that would furnish you a basis for exposing tactics of your adversary supporting a mistrial[8] or a basis for an appeal to the jury against your adversary's use of methods the jury may regard as unfair. The sections immediately following this one deal with application of this general rule to some particular situations that arise frequently in trials.

In addition to reasons discussed above for withholding objection, another very important factor may indicate that you should not object in some in-

5. See §1.3.
6. See §4.3.
7. See §§2.23, 4.11 for other applications of this proposition.
8. See §5.4.

stances when you have a sound objection available. Permitting the objectionable evidence to come in may be the key to admissibility of other evidence that you wish to offer.

If your adversary offers evidence that could be excluded by objection, you may then be free to offer additional evidence that would otherwise have been excluded.[9] By opening the subject matter, your adversary invites evidence in rebuttal and cannot successfully complain of its admission. In considering the advisability of objection you must therefore take into account the possibility of your offering retaliatory evidence that you could not otherwise use; if its effect will more than counteract the objectionable evidence offered by your adversary, refrain from objecting.

Dead Man's Acts present an illustration of a situation in which you should withhold objection to open the door for retaliatory evidence. Questions addressed to the disqualified witness by the lawyer for the representatives of the decedent may forfeit the protection of the statute.[10] When you are representing the surviving party, rarely if ever should you object under such circumstances, since the testimony of the witness as a whole will be favorable toward your own case, though the answers to some individual questions asked by the lawyer for the representatives of the decedent might be unfavorable. This is so clearly true in the usual case that the lawyer for the representatives of the decedent should never open the subject in examining the survivor and probably would not do so except through inadvertence or ignorance of the rules of evidence involved.

In Case 49 your adversary (P's lawyer) asks N to recite statements made in her presence by P to M concerning pain suffered by P before he reached M's office. You may be able to exclude these statements as hearsay, though some dispute might exist as to applicability of the exception in favor of declarations of pain.[11] Even if you could exclude the evidence by objection, however, it may be more advantageous to your client's cause, in a jurisdiction having a physician-patient privilege, to permit it to come in and then urge that the submission of this question on behalf of P bars the assertion of a privilege that P may otherwise have had to exclude evidence as to communications between P and M, and as to former treatment as well if that, too, is covered by the privilege.[12] The problem is one of more nearly balanced considerations than in the illustration concerning a Dead Man's Act, and your decision may depend on the scope of the privilege and your considered estimate of the probable value of M's testimony, perhaps unwillingly given even after the court's ruling that the privilege has been forfeited, as compared with the harm from N's testimony.

This problem whether you should urge a sound objection may be one of

9. 1 Wigmore, *Evidence* §15 (3d ed. 1940).
10. See 2 *id.,* §578.
11. 6 *id.,* §1722. See also Federal Rules of Evidence, Rule 803(3), (4).
12. 8 Wigmore, *Evidence* §§2388, 2390 (rev. ed. McNaughton 1961).

balanced considerations in other situations also. This is true if you consider that you may be able to impeach the witness effectively as to his answer to the objectionable question. It is also true of the question whether you should object to the scope of cross-examination of a witness whom you have called, in a jurisdiction where the scope of cross-examination is strictly limited. If the new subject of inquiry by the cross-examiner is one on which the testimony of the witness will be unfavorable to you, you should consider the relative value of being able to treat the witness as an adverse witness on this point of inquiry, with greater freedom as to the manner of examination,[13] and whether or not under the law of your jurisdiction it is necessary to the preservation of this right that you object to your adversary's cross-examination beyond the scope of the direct examination.[14] Against this possible advantage of objection you must weigh the fact that the dangers of an unfavorable jury reaction to an objection, as such, are somewhat greater when you are objecting to a question asked during cross-examination of a witness whom you have called to the stand than when you are objecting to direct examination of a witness called by your adversary. This question of advisability of objection because of the improper scope of cross-examination is one that you should anticipate and consider in determining whether or not to call a witness whose testimony on some points will be unfavorable to you, though favorable in other respects.[15]

§4.3 Objections to the form of questions

CASE 14. *P* is asserting a claim for personal injuries sustained when he was struck by *D*'s grocery truck at 8 P.M. Scope of employment is disputed. *W*, who was standing on the sidewalk and saw the accident, has advised *P*'s lawyer that the first thing the driver of the truck said immediately after the accident was, "How will I get to the warehouse and back before the boss leaves?" On direct examination by *P*'s lawyer, when asked what, if anything, the truck driver said as he got out of the cab after the accident, *W* says, "He said something about wondering how he could get to the warehouse now." After additional questions, *W* still omits the element of getting "back before the boss leaves." It is apparent that this element will not be stated by *W* unless he is asked a leading question.

Should you object to your adversary's questions in leading or otherwise improper form?

Every lawyer asks some improperly leading questions, inadvertently if not by design. With some adversaries, you could spend a major part of the time of trial on your feet objecting to their leading questions. So long as you at-

13. See §2.2.
14. 3A Wigmore, *Evidence* §914 (rev. ed. Chadbourn 1970).
15. See §2.2.

tack only the improper questions, your objecting each time will result in repeated rulings by the court in your favor; if there is any jury reaction to the continued objections under these circumstances, it probably will be more unfavorable to the questioner than to you.[1] Furthermore, if you do not object, your adversary may succeed in leading the witness into much more favorable testimony than otherwise would have been given, and this may happen without the jurors' having realized that it is the lawyer's story they have heard, with the witness simply acquiescing. Your objection also serves the purpose of calling to the attention of the jury this unfair method by which your adversary is obtaining favorable testimony. The major vices of the leading question — coaching the witness and getting something before the jury that they might not otherwise hear — are already accomplished before the opportunity to object to the leading question arises. Your reasons for objecting are not so much related to exclusion of the anticipated answer as to restraining the further use of leading questions and calling to the jury's attention the use already made and its bearing on the credibility of the evidence.

Assume in Case 14 that *P*'s lawyer decides to use a leading question to produce the purported statement of the truck driver, immediately after the accident, that he wondered how he could get back to the warehouse before his boss's departure. The leading question to refresh the witness' memory, after nonleading questions failed to produce the desired testimony, might be permitted over objection, within the discretion of the trial judge.[2] Even if your objection as *D*'s counsel is overruled, however, it will serve to emphasize for the jury the fact that the witness could not recall this statement on his own and that this fact casts doubt on the credibility of this item of evidence. Probably this advantage outweighs any possible disadvantage from making an objection that is overruled, or giving further emphasis to a matter that *P*'s lawyer obviously intends to emphasize for the jury anyway. Furthermore, the court may as a matter of discretion sustain your objection and effectively prevent *P*'s lawyer from producing the desired evidence. Your adversary's question serves to advise the jury of the content of the alleged statement, but the jury will be less inclined to give it any weight if the court instructs them not to consider it; also, your adversary will be prevented from making use of the statement either to serve the purpose of raising a fact issue on scope of employment not otherwise raised or for argument bearing upon the fact issue. These factors lead to the conclusion that as *D*'s lawyer you should object if *P*'s lawyer asks the leading question in Case 14.

As against an adversary who persists in asking leading questions, the generally preferred practice is not to object to every such question but to call the

1. See §4.2.
2. 3 Wigmore, *Evidence* §777 (rev. ed. Chadbourn 1970). See also Federal Rules of Evidence, Rule 611(c). And see §2.18.

matter to the attention of the court and jury by periodic objections pointing out that the practice is being followed continuously and that the jury should be allowed to hear the witness tell his own story instead of hearing the lawyer's version of it. After the practice has become persistent, you may also request and obtain an instruction by the court to your adversary not to lead the witness. Rarely does a trial judge impose any penalty on your adversary for further leading questions (though he has the power to do so not only by contempt proceedings but also by means more directly affecting the litigation — for example, by declaring a mistrial[3]). Such an instruction aids you, however, in impressing the jury that your adversary is not giving the witness the opportunity to tell his own story. The extent to which you state in your objection what is intended as an argument to the jury about the unfair practice of leading will depend partly upon the attitude of the trial judge. A judge who customarily is strict may disapprove the use of the objection as an argument to the jury;[4] in such courts, however, the need for the argument will not be as great because the judge probably will effectively restrain your adversary from leading his witnesses. On the other hand, if the judge is lenient, though there may be no effective restraint against your adversary's leading questions, you will doubtlessly be permitted to express your reason for objection more fully with the purpose of calling the jury's attention to the practice. Following is an example of an objection that would be appropriate in a court moderately lenient regarding argumentative comment:

Your Honor, I have indulged counsel by sitting quietly while he has been leading his witnesses, but I submit that he has carried the practice to the point that his witnesses are not being called upon or permitted to tell their own stories. It may be necessary for me to impeach and contradict some of this testimony, and I therefore want the court and jury to hear what the witnesses themselves would say. I object to the last question as leading, and I ask that the court instruct counsel not to lead his witnesses.

Another instance in which it is sometimes wise to object to questions on the ground of form is the case of a question calling for an answer regarding knowledge, as a preliminary fact supporting admissibility. For example, when evidence of custom is being offered, a witness who is asked to state whether or not he is familiar with the custom regarding a specific matter will usually reply by stating what he thinks the custom to be, rather than answering "yes" or "no" to the question. If you consider that there is reasonable hope of getting the witness to admit that he is not familiar with the practices of others generally, but only with the practices of a few individuals, so that his idea

3. See §5.4.
4. See §4.14, which considers also the ethical problem involved in this use of an objection.

of what the custom is would be based upon insufficient knowledge to make it admissible, you should object (if you desire the evidence excluded) or else move that the court instruct the witness to answer the question only "yes" or "no." If, on the other hand, you know that the witness will testify so as to qualify himself, your objection or request for the instruction, though sustained, would serve no useful end; it would be better under these circumstances to refrain from objecting and develop by cross-examination any weakness in the degree of familiarity of the witness with the custom.

§4.4 Objections to the manner of cross-examination

CASE 50. *P* sues *D* for personal injuries sustained in an intersection collision. You represent *D*. In a part of the cross-examination of *D*, your adversary proceeds as follows:

Q. (While looking at a memorandum) Now, Mr. *D*, it is a fact, is it not, that you made a statement right after the accident that you did not see Mr. *P*'s car until it was right in front of you?

A. I don't remember *that*.

Q. You are not able to say, then, one way or the other, whether you saw Mr. *P*'s car before it was right in front of you?

A. Yes sir. I saw him before that.

Q. You just said you don't remember, and now you say you do remember that you saw him.

A. If I said I don't remember whether I saw him, I want to change my answer — I meant I don't remember saying I didn't see him before he was in front of me, because I did see him before.

Q. (Advancing closer to the witness and pointing an accusing finger at him) I remind you that you were under oath when you answered my question. Do you now wish to change your answer?

Should you object to your adversary's manner of cross-examining your witness?

Several possible objections may be available because of the *manner* of cross-examination of a witness, as distinguished from the subject matter of the questions. At various times you may object that the cross-examiner is being unfair with the witness, is using an oppressive manner, is arguing with the witness, or is asking a question that is repetitious, ambiguous, confusing,[1] or duplicitous.

These objections are addressed to the discretion of the trial judge, and you should use them only when there is a reasonable basis for hoping that the judge will sustain them. They are sometimes used for ethically questionable,

1. See §3.19.

if not indefensible, purposes such as giving the witness time to think, calling his attention indirectly to a trap for which he may be falling, or indirectly suggesting a good answer. Of course, more harm may be done by the jury's realization that the witness is being coached[2] or given time to think than by the less favorable answer he would have given otherwise; whether that is true will depend upon how well the witness is able to take care of himself and how well the lawyer conceals from the jury his real purpose in objecting.

Even when you are considering an objection for the legitimate purpose of avoiding oppressive or misleading cross-examination, it is better not to make it if the witness is able to take care of himself. If your adversary is mistreating the witness, the jury probably will be sympathizing with the witness. If the substantive content of your witness' testimony is not being weakened and your witness is not responding with angry or sarcastic answers, you may as well let your adversary have the freedom to err; you may finally object, but not until you are certain that your adversary has gone so far that the court will sustain the objection and thus convict your adversary in the presence of the jury of trying to take unfair advantage of the witness. On the other hand, if you consider that your witness is becoming angry, emotionally upset, or confused, you should object promptly for the purpose of stopping the practice before your witness harms your case. Case 50 presents a situation in which the witness, D, may be unfairly confused and intimidated by the cross-examiner's interpretation of his answer,[3] and the threatening manner your adversary uses when D tries to clarify what he meant by an answer that he phrased in an unfortunate way. Probably the better course of action is to object in this situation unless, as would rarely be the case, the witness is one who is almost certain to take care of himself by pointing out that he is not trying to change the substance of his testimony but only to clarify his meaning on a point as to which there apparently was a misunderstanding.

§4.5 Objections to methods of using documents

Should you object to your adversary's methods of using or presenting contents of a document?

Occasionally your opponent will make use of a document in the course of examining a witness, exhibiting the document to the jury but not offering it

2. See §1.3.

3. "I don't remember *that*." The witness may have intended to imply that he did not say that he failed to see P's car until it was right in front of him, an implication that would appear more clearly in the longer expression, "I don't remember ever saying any such thing as that." D's answer is unfortunately susceptible to the construction "I don't remember whether or not I made the statement," though not fairly susceptible to the construction used by the cross-examiner, "I don't remember whether or not I failed to see him until he was right in front of me."

in evidence. You have a sound objection to this use of the document, and if the document is inadmissible, ordinarily you should make the objection. If the document is admissible, you may force your adversary to put it in evidence by stating that you have no objection to its being received in evidence but object to its being displayed without being introduced. An advantage of forcing introduction of the document in this way is that it avoids uncertainty in the record for appeal as to what was before the jury — a matter that may be important in avoiding a claim that inspection of the document supplied some omission that you assert is fatal to your adversary's legal theory, or a claim that it may have included something that made harmless an error of the court in overruling one of your objections at another point in trial. The burden is generally on the complaining party to produce a record that supports his contention, uncertainties in the record being resolved against him.[1]

Forcing the introduction of a document by making such an objection has disadvantages in that the document may contain more details than those displayed to the jury and may actually supply some otherwise fatal omission, or may give the jury a chance to study it during their deliberations, which would not have been possible had it not been introduced.

If the witness is consulting documents but not expressly referring to them in his testimony, usually you should object. There is little disadvantage to be feared; the jury surely will not react unfavorably to your efforts to find out what the witness is using in his testimony against you. Advantages are apparent. If the documents are of a type not properly usable by the witness, your objection will be sustained and the testimony against you may be materially affected. Even if your objection is overruled, you may gain valuable information for use in cross-examination.[2]

The interpretation by the court and jury of documents that have been introduced into evidence is frequently a matter of great concern to the lawyers. Though the interpretation as such is generally a matter of law for the court, parts of the documents may be material as background circumstances bearing on fact issues submitted to the jury, and in some circumstances the jury will be called upon to determine the true agreement between the parties, considering the document in the light of the circumstances. It is usually possible for competent counsel to place contentions before the jury regarding material contents and interpretation of the documents through planned use of permissible methods,[3] but the temptation to attempt other methods is often too great to resist. Any selective reading from a document implies interpretation. Naturally you can anticipate that the implied interpretation will be unfavorable to you when an opposing lawyer or witness is doing the selective read-

1. See generally 1 Wigmore, *Evidence* §§17–21 (3d ed. 1940); Federal Rules of Evidence, Rule 103.
2. See §3.28.
3. See §2.26.

ing. Although you should avoid objections to permissible methods of accomplishing this indirectly — objections that would be overruled — it is generally advisable to urge any sound objection you may have to methods used by your adversary to present contents of documents. This may not be true, however, if you do not want the document itself before the jury because of some objectionable parts and prefer to acquiesce in the informal reference to excerpts from it instead of causing your adversary to offer the document, whereupon you would find it necessary to object again.

If your adversary calls upon a friendly witness to explain a document that is in evidence, obviously the anticipated explanation will be against you, and the witness will be likely to include in the statement his own alleged understanding and interpretation, which he could not state over your timely objections. The chance that it will be so unreasonable or extreme that you can take advantage of that fact to impeach the witness is generally remote; even though you see that prospect under the circumstances, usually the chance is not worth taking and your conclusion should be in favor of making your objection.

Should you object to your adversary's reading of excerpts from a document that is already in evidence?[4] Though this would not always be a sound legal objection, in some circumstances the rules of evidence support the objection and make it possible for you to force your adversary to read other portions of the document relating to the same subject matter and favorable to you.[5] If you have such a sound objection available, the choice is one of means of emphasizing that portion of the document favorable to you. Probably greater emphasis is given when you force your adversary to offer it by making the objection than would be achieved by your making the offer later.

§4.6 Objections of lack of foundation

CASE 51. In a personal injury suit that is being tried in a rural community, P's lawyer calls to the stand W, who testifies that he practices medicine in a nearby city. Without offering any evidence of qualifications of W as a heart specialist, P's lawyer asks W to recite his expert opinion as to whether the strain associated with the impact inflicted by D, whom you represent, was in reasonable probability a cause of P's abnormal heart condition.

---

4. Compare §2.27.

5. 7 Wigmore, *Evidence* §2102 (3d ed. 1940). Compare Federal Rules of Evidence, Rule 107 (concerning the right to force your adversary to "introduce" other parts of writings or of a recorded statement a part of which your adversary has "introduced"); Federal Rule 32(a) (4) (concerning the right to force your adversary to "introduce" other parts of a deposition, a part of which your adversary has "offered in evidence" or "introduced," the two concepts apparently being used interchangeably).

Should you object because of want of proof of foundation for admission of evidence offered?

When and how should you offer evidence in support of your objection?

The validity of an objection sometimes depends upon a factfinding on some preliminary matter. In Case 55, for example, validity of an objection to the doctor's opinion based in part on hearsay and self-serving statements of *P* to him may depend upon whether *P* went to the doctor, *N-3*, solely to prepare the doctor to testify or instead went also for treatment. Under some decisions, findings on preliminary facts are solely within the province of the judge, and the judge's findings cannot be disturbed on appeal if a reasonable person could have reached those findings upon the evidence before him. Under others, preliminary factfindings by the judge are followed by instructions to the jury to consider the evidence only if they find the preliminary facts. Still other decisions hold that the trial judge may consider only whether the evidence raises an issue on the preliminary fact, rather than making a finding himself, submitting the matter to the jury with appropriate instructions if the issue is raised on the preliminary fact.[1]

Regardless of the procedure by which the issue is decided, and whether ultimately by judge or jury, insofar as urging the objection is concerned it is to your advantage to produce all the evidence available in support of your objection. The pursuit of a potentially valid objection should not blind you to your more important aim of winning the entire case, however.[2] Weigh the chances of its being sustained and the advantages therefrom against the risk of harm from the anticipated evidence concerning the preliminary fact issue and from the effort before the jury to keep something from them.[3] If it is obvious that the facts constituting the foundation for admission of the evidence exist and can be readily proved, your objection, though sustained, probably will serve no useful purpose. In fact, it may serve only to emphasize the harmful evidence and to invite further harmful evidence in the proof of the preliminary facts. Lack of proof of sufficient expert qualifications to render an opinion admissible[4] is an example of this problem. Objecting to want of proof of medical qualifications when those qualifications actually exist emphasizes both the opinions, which are originally excluded but finally received, and the standing of the expert whose qualifications your adversary fully proves in meeting your objection.

If you have decided to urge an objection, you may also have a choice regarding the time of offering your evidence on the preliminary fact issue. This will not be the case if the judge's decision on admissibility is final; in that

1. 9 Wigmore, *Evidence* §2550 (3d ed. 1940). See also Federal Rules of Evidence, Rule 104.

2. See §1.4.

3. See §4.2.

4. Compare cross-examination concerning qualifications, §3.30; see also §3.13 on lack of proof of personal knowledge.

situation you must offer your evidence promptly, before he rules. On the other hand, if the ultimate decision on the preliminary fact issue will be made by the jury and it is the judge's duty to submit the evidence to the jury with instructions regarding the preliminary issue, then your decision on the timing of your controverting evidence should depend upon your best judgment as to when it will have greatest effect upon the jury. Usually you should offer the evidence at the first opportunity, at which time you can interrupt your adversary's proof and present your own theory on the preliminary issue before the jurors have formed an impression that may be difficult to change. Sometimes, however, you might find it preferable to withhold your evidence until a later time — for example, a time near the conclusion of all the evidence in the case. Usually the latter procedure will not be feasible because of your desire to reserve the conclusion of your evidence for more vital matters that you wish to emphasize. Also, you may hope that by offering the evidence at the first opportunity your evidence will be so conclusive on the preliminary issue that the judge will hold that no issue is raised for the jury's consideration on the point and that the objection should be sustained by the court as a matter of law.

Another factor that merits consideration is whether you should ask the court to hear the evidence on the preliminary issue, both that offered by you and that offered by your adversary, out of the presence of the jury.[5] Frequently this will be to your advantage; it may avoid clouding the issues before the jury with evidence on ancillary matters, and it may prevent the jury from hearing evidence on the preliminary issue that might tend to turn them against your client and influence their decision on primary issues in the case. Also, since there may be no need for repetition before the jury of this evidence on preliminary issues even if the objection is overruled, you may avoid the jury's hearing the preliminary evidence, regardless of the ruling; in such circumstances trial judges are less reluctant to grant the request for hearing outside the presence of the jury since not as much duplication of testimony and loss of time will be involved as when repetition of all the testimony will be required if the objection is overruled.

Having concluded that you will offer evidence in support of your objection, you will find it possible in most instances to produce some, if not all, of the desired evidence by questions to your adversary's witness on *voir dire*. Admissions obtained from your adversary's witness are obviously more persuasive to the factfinder than the same testimony given by your own witness. Furthermore, with the admissions from your adversary's witness, you may be able to present such a conclusive array of evidence on the preliminary facts supporting your objection that the objection must be sustained as a matter of law — no reasonable difference of opinion as to the preliminary facts being possible under the evidence.

5. See §§4.9, 4.10.

Generally you should not request permission for *voir dire* if you are reasonably certain that the witness will testify to facts constituting the foundation for admission of the questioned evidence. Lawyers sometimes use *voir dire* as a means of exposing supposed weaknesses in the qualifications of an expert before he has an opportunity to make a strong impression on the jury with his testimony. The rules permitting *voir dire* do not contemplate its use for this purpose,[6] however, and if your adversary attempts this use the court probably will sustain your objection that he is trying to use the *voir dire* for cross-examination of the witness.

If there is doubt in your mind regarding the existence of facts constituting the foundation for admission of the evidence called for by your adversary's question, you should consider requesting the court to permit *voir dire* rather than simply objecting for lack of proof constituting foundation for admissibility of the evidence. This method has the advantage that you may be able to develop the want of foundation better by controlling the questions and putting them to the witness before he hears the grounds of objection than by stating what foundation proof is lacking, thus giving your adversary and the witness specific notice of what they need to develop to meet your objection.

In Case 51, if *W* actually is qualified as a heart specialist and *P*'s lawyer has merely overlooked proving this fact in the midst of trial, your objection would serve no useful purpose to your client's cause but would be a help to *P* both in emphasizing the opinion evidence to which you objected and the doctor's qualifications proved in support of it. On the other hand, if *W* is not a specialist but a general practitioner, you may reasonably choose to object and take the witness on *voir dire*. His opinion will generally be held admissible though he is a general practitioner and not a specialist, if he is willing to testify that he is sufficiently familiar with the subject to form a reliable expert opinion. Your examination should be directed toward bringing out his limitations as compared with those of specialists in an effort to obtain an admission that he does not assert that his opinion would be that of an expert.[7] Even if you fail in your effort to get an admission that would make his opinion testimony inadmissible, however, you will have placed before the jury evidence indicating weaknesses in the qualifications of the witness and in the reliability of his opinion as compared with those of a specialist whom you intend to call.

§4.7 Objections of insufficiency of evidence

CASE 52. *P* brings suit on an accident insurance policy including coverage for medical and hospital bills. *D Insurance Company,* whom you represent,

6. 2 Wigmore, *Evidence* §485 (3d ed. 1940); 5 id., §1385.
7. See §3.30.

defends on the grounds that P did not suffer an "accident" within the meaning of that term as defined in the policy and in the alternative that part of the medical and hospital bills included in P's claim were attributable to the treatment of a diseased condition of P's body not associated with an accident. P's lawyer offers proof that an accident caused P to enter a hospital and proof of the amounts of the medical and hospital bills, but without any showing that all charges were reasonable and that the services for which each charge was incurred were made necessary by the accident.

Should you object because of insufficiency of the evidence?

At whatever point the proof of facts material to any case may begin, it is then conceivable that the initial evidence is immaterial because not supplemented by enough other evidence to make a case or defense sufficient to go to the factfinder. Obviously objection on that ground must be overruled as a practical matter; otherwise the judge would find it necessary to hear much evidence twice — once in the form of an offer of proof to meet an objection, or to preserve error with respect to an adverse ruling on objection, and then again before the jury after a final decision to overrule the objection. It follows that insufficiency of evidence is usually asserted by a motion for directed verdict [1] or some other form of motion seeking a final judgment. [2] In some instances, however, the lawyer who asserts that the evidence is insufficient will have the option of raising this contention by an objection to proffered evidence. For example, if your adversary is offering parol evidence to vary the terms of a written document under circumstances inconsistent with the parol evidence rule, should you object to admission of the parol evidence or should you permit it to be received in evidence, later asserting that the parol evidence is insufficient to support a claim for variance from the writing? This problem may also be encountered in some jurisdictions with respect to hearsay evidence, medical evidence of causation based on possibilities rather than probabilities, proof of a fact by circumstantial evidence (each item alone being apparently too remote, but perhaps sufficiently material when considered with all the circumstances), and, under facts such as those of Case 52, with regard to proof that expenses incurred were reasonable and were made necessary by the incident on which suit is based.

An important factor you should consider in meeting this problem, whatever the nature of the evidence may be, is whether under the authorities of your jurisdiction a failure to object to the evidence will constitute a bar to the contention of insufficiency, [3] as distinguished from merely a bar to the

1. See §5.2.
2. §5.3.
3. This problem may arise when your adversary offers testimony of a medical witness based on possibility rather than probability. See generally 7 Wigmore, *Evidence* §1976 (3d ed. 1940).

right to keep the jury from hearing the evidence. For example, under the circumstances of Case 52, do the decisions in your jurisdiction hold that a failure to object to the evidence of the amount of hospital and medical bills is a bar to the contention that the evidence is insufficient to raise a fact issue as to whether they are reasonable amounts made necessary by the alleged accident on which suit is based, or do the decisions recognize that you may urge this contention of insufficiency for the first time after the evidence is closed?

As against a careless adversary, waiting until the last opportunity to raise the contention of insufficiency — "lying behind the log"[4] as it is frequently referred to — has the advantage of giving your adversary less opportunity to cure his omission, particularly if the decisions of your jurisdiction permit you to raise the point for the first time so late in the trial that there is no possibility of reopening the evidence and curing the omission.[5] As against an adverse party (or witness) whose honesty you doubt, waiting until the last opportunity to raise the point also has the advantage of giving him less guidance regarding the minimum to which he must testify. This practice allows him less opportunity for improvisation to supply omissions and improves the chances that he will in some respect, especially with your encouragement on cross-examination, adopt positions inconsistent with later improvisations. From the point of view of achieving justice, the existence of rules permitting one to take this advantage of a lawyer's careless omission to prove facts supporting a client's claim is subject to serious criticism; the existence and retention of these rules may be accounted for by fear that changing them would also abolish one of all too few methods available to defeat a dishonest claim. Whatever the justifications may be, rules of this type exist in some jurisdictions with respect to each of the illustrations of insufficiency of evidence referred to above. As the lawyer urging the theory of insufficiency, you lose the advantage of these rules if you object to the evidence at the first opportunity and thus coach your adversary on the legal requirements, or cause your adversary to return to more careful study of the authorities concerning what is needed to make a case. There are some disadvantages to withholding objection, however, aside from the danger of forfeiting the contention of insufficiency. Unless your tactics pay off with some disclosure that the case against you is dishonest, or with commitment of adverse witnesses to positions that would make it impossible for your adversary to make a case on new trial without some retractions, a trial judge may be inclined to grant a new trial when your contention is finally made, rather than entering judgment for your client. Also there is the disadvantage of loss of the opportunity of terminating the trial at an early stage, because of a favorable ruling on the crucial point of law that you might raise by way of objection. The relative weight of these advantages and disadvantages will depend upon individual circum-

4. As to surprise generally, see §1.3.
5. See §§5.2, 5.3, 5.9.

stances, and especially upon your confidence or lack of complete confidence in the integrity of the adverse party and his witnesses. The possibility that their interest in the litigation will induce exaggeration, and less often outright fabrication, frequently makes it more advisable to withhold objection if that practice will not result in a forfeiture of the contention of insufficiency. When you choose this method, you should be particularly diligent in your analysis of the testimony of adverse witnesses for the purpose of finding points on which you may commit them to positions inconsistent with the omitted facts that you fear they may try to supply later.

Unless by allowing your adversary to introduce inadmissible evidence you may hold him to a forfeiture of an objection to more important evidence that you wish to use,[6] there is generally no reason for withholding objection to any harmful evidence when the circumstances of the case disclose no danger of your adversary's curing the insufficiency by other evidence after the objection is made. When, for example, both parties are represented by counsel of competence and integrity, and through discovery processes and voluntary disclosures each lawyer knows the contentions and the evidence that will be offered by the other, there is no reason to postpone an objection founded on the parol evidence rule.

Occasionally you may successfully meet an objection for want of proof of supporting facts essential to admissibility by asking that the court receive the evidence conditionally, upon your representation that you will offer the supporting evidence later in the trial. Frequently a trial judge will permit this practice when the testimony of one witness does not establish enough to make the evidence admissible and must be supplemented by that of another. One item of circumstantial evidence alone may seem too remote to warrant admission, but reasonably material when considered with other evidence to be offered later. When evidence against you is received conditionally, you should take care to renew your objection and ask that the evidence be stricken, if at the close of the evidence your adversary has not offered the necessary additional evidence. Otherwise, you will be barred from asserting a sound objection.[7]

§4.8 Objections of want of pleadings

Should you object on the ground of want of pleadings to support the evidence?

Reform of systems of pleading[1] in recent decades has greatly reduced the area of sound objections to evidence for want of pleadings to support its ad-

---

6. See §4.2.

7. 6 Wigmore, *Evidence* §1871 (3d ed. 1940); Federal Rules of Evidence, Rule 103(a) (1).

1. See §10.1.

mission. If pleadings are expected to serve the purpose of sharply defining the issues, omission of an issue from the pleadings may result in its being resolved automatically against the party with the burden of pleading that issue. Evidence pertaining only to omitted issues and not to any that are raised by the pleadings can be excluded as irrelevant. Under the present federal rules, however, and those of many states patterned after the federal rules, pleadings may disclose very little as to the nature of the specific issues to be tried. Under these rules, an objection to evidence on the ground of want of pleadings to support its admission is rarely sound. In some jurisdictions, however, it is still expected that the pleadings will define and give specific notice of the issues to be raised in trial, though permission to amend is more freely granted than in earlier times; in these jurisdictions, the objection to evidence for want of pleadings to support its admission is still available. Should you use it?

Usually the end result of an objection to evidence for want of support in the pleadings, even if the objection is sound and is sustained, will be an amendment of the pleadings and a renewal of the offer, at which time the evidence will be received. The legal maneuvers will have done no good for the objecting party under these circumstances, but may have caused harm by emphasizing the evidence finally received and perhaps contributing to an unfavorable reaction of the jury against a "technical" objection.[2] If, however, the new issue not indicated by the pleadings is one on which you are not prepared for trial, you should make the objection. It is quite likely that the trial judge, in his discretion, will either refuse leave to the other party to amend his pleadings or else will grant you a continuance[3] if he does allow the amendment, thus giving you an opportunity to prepare for trial on the new issue as to which you were surprised. As a general rule, therefore, you should make the objection of want of pleadings only if the nature of the particular evidence offered, the circumstances of the offer, the rules of procedure under which the case is being tried, and the anticipated attitude of the trial judge are such as to indicate that you have reasonable hope of excluding the evidence entirely or obtaining a continuance or postponement of trial to give you an opportunity for further preparation. Otherwise, the chances of reversing the trial judge's ruling are remote, and affirmative harm to your own client's interest by the unsuccessful objection is probable.

§4.9 Objections to generality of questions; motions to hear testimony "in chambers"

CASE 53. *P* sues *Davis Plumbing Company*, your client, on account of personal injuries sustained while *P* was engaged in construction work, together

---

2. See §§1.3, 4.2.
3. See §§5.8, 11.21.

with *W-1* and *W-2*, all in the employ of *S*, a subcontractor on an industrial building. *P* was hit by a falling pipe wrench. *Davis Plumbing Company* was another subcontractor on the job and had employees at work on plumbing in an upper level. The case arises under the laws of a jurisdiction where *Davis Plumbing Company* is not protected from common law liability by compensation statutes. *Davis Plumbing Company* contends that the wrench was properly placed beside one of its employees and was carelessly dislodged by another worker, employed by someone else. An investigator for *Davis Plumbing Company* shortly after the accident interviewed *W-1*, obtaining a written statement; when asked about any conversation immediately after the accident, *W-1* said that as he and *W-2* reached *P* and found the wrench beside him and a gash on his head, *W-2* said, "Some fool *Davis* man is mighty careless with his tools."

In the trial of the case, *P*'s lawyer calls *W-1* to the stand, and during the direct examination, after laying the predicate for offering an excited utterance by *W-2*, asks *W-1* to repeat the statement that *W-2* made.

Should you object to the generality of a question?
Should you move that the court hear testimony "in chambers" to determine its admissibility?

One of the reasons for examining witnesses by detailed questions and answers, rather than by simply placing each witness on the stand and asking him to tell all he knows about the case, is to provide an orderly means by which objections to improper evidence can be raised and ruled upon before the evidence is heard by the jury. Usually the questions asked by your adversary will indicate to you whether the answer is likely to contain objectionable evidence. In some instances this will not be true, either because of the generality of the question or because of uncertainty about the expected answer to a question that would ordinarily be regarded as specific.

If your adversary should ask the witness to tell all he knows about the accident on which suit is based, you would have a sound objection to this general question on the ground that it does not afford you the opportunity of objection to improper matter before it is stated in the presence of the jury.[1] Usually it is inadvisable to allow the examination of your adversary's witness to proceed in that manner; it is too difficult for you to anticipate whether objectionable matter may be included in the answer. You should urge your objection to such a general question.

In some instances even a less general question will confront you with basically the same problem of uncertainty as to whether the answer will contain inadmissible matter, even though the question does not necessarily call

1. 3 Wigmore, *Evidence* §767 (rev. ed. Chadbourn 1970).

for inadmissible testimony and is therefore not objectionable unless it be on the ground of failure to restrict the witness specifically to admissible matter. Under such circumstances it is much less likely that the trial court would sustain an objection. Furthermore, if the objection were sustained, the result might be to cause your adversary to use a specific question that implied the existence of the inadmissible fact; you are in relatively poor position to complain of such a question after you have objected to a previous question as not being sufficiently restrictive concerning the matter of inquiry. Some procedure other than objection is needed to meet this situation. Generally the best available procedure is to request that the court hear the answer of the witness out of the presence of the jury to determine its admissibility, thus avoiding any reference to the matter in the presence of the jury if it is held inadmissible. Since the jurors may react unfavorably to your asking that they be excluded from the courtroom or that the judge hear the witness outside their presence, a better phrasing of the request, if you are not able to state it outside the hearing of the jurors, is to ask that the judge hear the matter "in camera" or "in chambers," or that he hear counsel "at some length" on the question, or that he allow you "to present authorities to the court."

Case 53 illustrates the problem.[2] The statement made by *W-2*, "Some fool *Davis* man is mighty careless with his tools," would be excluded in some jurisdictions as an opinion and conclusion, and not the type of statement to which the exception to the hearsay rule for excited utterances applies.[3] The circumstances under which it was made were those typical for application of the exception for excited utterances, and your objection on behalf of the defendant is not to the question as such but to the particular answer that you anticipate the witness will give. An objection to the question on the ground that it calls for the witness to recite a statement of opinion would not be sound, and of course the hearsay objection appears to be met by the circumstances raising the exception for excited utterances. If you postpone objection until after the answer of the witness, the harm of the jury's hearing the answer will already be done. Under these circumstances, you should move that the court hear the matter apart from the jury and determine admissibility before the jury hears it. Although it is rare that you can reverse the trial judge for abusing his discretion by allowing such improper evidence to be heard in the regular manner rather than complying with your request, particularly if he thereafter sustains the objection and charges the jury to disregard the answer of the witness,[4] usually the trial judge will grant such a request for hearing apart from the jury. If the judge refuses your request, you might

2. See §2.24 n.3 for another illustration.
3. 6 Wigmore, *Evidence* §1751 (3d ed. 1940).
4. See §4.15.

next request an instruction to the witness that he not repeat any expression of opinion or conclusion in his answer; this is generally an unsatisfactory procedure, however, because of the possibility of a loose interpretation by the witness of what is an expression of fact and not an opinion or conclusion, or because of comments that may be made if the witness is in doubt as to what he should answer in the face of the instruction.

Occasionally a fact issue must be decided before the admissibility of evidence is determined. If the circumstances are such that this fact issue is determined by the judge, it is often advisable to request a hearing of the evidence on this fact issue apart from the jury to avoid introduction or prejudicial matter during the proof on that fact issue.[5]

Though the motion to hear evidence outside the presence of the jury and predetermine its admissibility is appropriate in Case 53, you cannot use the procedure indiscriminately. Obviously, the trial judge should not tolerate the delay of hearing evidence twice unless there is reasonable justification for your fears that your client might otherwise be irreparably harmed. Also, such delays might annoy the jurors (who are notably impatient about trial delays anyway) and thus contribute to an unfavorable jury reaction to your making objections.[6]

§4.10 Making objections out of the jury's hearing

CASE 20. *P* is suing on an account for materials and is faced with a defense that all of the materials covered by the account were defective. *P* delivers to his lawyer a letter received from *D*, in response to a second bill marked "overdue," in which letter *D* stated:

We have your bill in the amount of $1476. The last item (number 4), in the amount of $450, is for materials that were defective and had to be replaced after installation, as we have previously advised you. We will forward payment in the amount of $1026 if you will agree to cancel your charge for item 4 and give us an acknowledgment of payment in full of our account with you.

Should you make your objection out of the hearing of the jury?

In some instances you will prefer that the jury hear your objections; this is true, for example, when you are objecting to leading questions[1] or to oppressive or argumentative questions.[2] It is arguable in Case 20 that it is better for the jury to hear your objection that the letter was an offer of compromise; if the objection is overruled and the letter goes before the jury, you

5. See §4.6.
6. See §4.2.
1. See §4.3.
2. See §4.4.

want them to consider from the time of their first interest in the letter that it was an offer of compromise. On the other hand, if you urge that contention in an objection that is overruled in their hearing, will it not appear to the jury that your contention that it was a compromise offer has been overruled? If your objection is sustained, you would prefer that the jury never hear that word "compromise." In this case, as in most instances when you are invoking an exclusionary rule of evidence, you would prefer that the purpose of objection be accomplished without your taking the risk of unfavorable jury reaction to the practice of objection as such [3] and the risk of harmful inferences concerning excluded matter. It is very difficult to state the basis of an objection without making known to the jury enough of the very thing you are trying to keep from them that they will either surmise the rest or surmise that something still worse is being concealed from them. This danger affects both your choice of phrasing and your decision as to whether you should make the objection outside the presence of the jury.

Generally the court will grant a hearing outside the presence of the jury if the evidence in question is likely to have weight in the jury's deliberations and the objection could not be freely discussed without disclosure of the questioned matter.

Disadvantages of making such a request [4] are that it will arouse the curiosity and speculation of the jurors, they may reach an unfavorable inference as to what the facts probably are, and your emphatic indication of a wish to keep something from them is more likely than a mere objection in their presence to cause them to react against the methods you are using. If the evidence is of a type that probably would influence the jury's deliberations, however, these possible disadvantages are outweighed by the advantage of avoiding any statements in the presence of the jury by yourself, your adversary, or the court, from which the jury might infer the substance of the objectionable evidence. Some judges permit or encourage the practice of stepping near the judge's bench to make objections when it is especially important that the jury not hear them. You should not adopt that practice, however, unless you know that the trial judge permits it, since some trial judges sharply disapprove. Also, if you adopt the practice, take care that the court reporter notes your objection in the record of trial in the event it is overruled. Insofar as the probable effect on the jury is concerned, there is little difference between the method of retiring the jury from the courtroom while the objection is presented and presenting it to the court in whispers while they watch intently from the jury box and strain to pick up a word here and there; the advantage of the latter method is merely that of saving time and causing less inconvenience.

3. See §4.2.
4. Even though you request a hearing "in chambers" as suggested in §4.9.

If you are able to anticipate well in advance that your adversary will be offering a particular item of objectionable evidence, you should consider making an advance motion at a time when it will not be necessary for you to disclose to the jury that you are urging an objection to evidence.[5]

§4.11 Making objections that you know the court will overrule

CASE 54. *P* is asserting a claim for personal injuries. *D*'s lawyer offers in evidence hospital records regarding hospitalization of *P* on an occasion before the alleged injury on which suit is based. *D*'s lawyer asserts that the hearsay statements of doctors and hospital attendants, included in the records, are admissible under a statute of the jurisdiction of trial. As *P*'s lawyer, it is your position that the statute authorizes admission of certain parts of the hospital records but not the hearsay statements. The trial judge, after full argument on this point in other cases, has ruled that such hearsay statements are admissible under the statute.

What should you do when you know that an objection would be overruled by the court?

Frequently you know in advance what the ruling of the judge will be on an objection that you are thinking of making. You may know this either from previous rulings of the judge in the case on trial or from other knowledge of the opinions of the judge regarding specific points of evidence law. You should take account of the possibility that the judge's ruling in your case may differ because of effective advocacy or because of distinguishing factors between the point of your proposed objection and the judge's known views. If after full consideration you conclude that the judge will overrule your objection, the disadvantages attached to making objections[1] should cause you to refrain from objection unless your aim is one other than the usual aim of possible exclusion of harmful evidence. The other aim most frequently applicable is the preservation of error, to support your motion for new trial and your appeal in the event of an adverse result in the trial court. How significant is that aim in your case and how well will it be served by your objection?

Your first problem is one of knowing the rules of evidence of your jurisdiction and the rules followed by your appellate courts in determining whether an error in admitting evidence warrants reversal or is instead "harmless error." Rarely will you gain anything by objection if the trial judge's ruling will not be reversible error under the appellate decisions in your jurisdiction — or, more precisely, under the predicted decision of the court of last

5. See §4.16.
1. See §4.2.

resort on your point. It is often impossible to predict with any degree of certainty what that decision would be. In such cases, the choice as to whether you should object involves weighing the disadvantages of objection against the chance and value of a reversal of the trial judge in the event the final judgment of the trial court is adverse. Your appraisal of the chance of reversal depends on your study of previous appellate cases to discover the rules developed there and your reasoned prediction concerning the applicability of those rules, or other rules the court might now adopt, to your facts. Your appraisal of the value of a reversal depends on your assessing the effect of extension of the litigation, the costs of retrial, and whether upon retrial you would be likely to achieve a better result; for this appraisal you need not only a thorough knowledge of your case but also a thorough understanding of the local situation in which it must be tried.[2]

Case 54 illustrates the problem of this section. If in your considered judgment, first, the rulings of the trial judge on the evidence point are in conflict with the probable appellate ruling, second, the nature of the hearsay statements is such that they are likely to influence the jury's decision on the facts, and, third, the delay and expense of appeal and retrial would not be prohibitive from the point of view of your client, then you should object for the purpose of preserving error. On the other hand, if because of other appellate decisions or the phrasing of the statute, or because of the relative insignificance of the hearsay as bearing on the probable result of the jury's deliberations, you consider a reversal highly improbable, or if expense or delay makes appeal impractical for your client, you should keep quiet rather than aiding your adversary by adding emphasis to the evidence with an objection that you know the trial judge will overrule.

§4.12   Preserving error on evidence rulings

Case 54.   (See statement of the case at the beginning of the preceding section.)

What should you do to preserve error when the court rules adversely on an evidence point?

In many jurisdictions it is not necessary to the preservation of error that you except to the court's adverse ruling on your objection to evidence.[1] In the absence of an affirmative indication of acquiescence, it is assumed that you do not acquiesce in the ruling. Many lawyers nevertheless follow the custom of remarking "Exception," "Note my exception, please," or other

2. Compare §5.4.
1. 1 Wigmore, *Evidence* §20 (3d ed. 1940); Federal Rules of Civil Procedure, Rule 46.

words to that effect, following an adverse ruling by the court. Expressions of this sort are often used for the purpose of concluding the matter without the appearance of acquiescence, rather than with the thought that such an expression is essential to the preservation of error. If you use an exception for this purpose, be careful to avoid a manner of expression disrespectful toward the court.

When evidence is erroneously admitted, the record necessarily shows the exact testimony upon which you must base your argument of harm. If no formal exception to the adverse ruling is required, no further immediate action is necessary to the preservation of error in the admission of evidence. There are, however, additional requirements that you must meet before the erroneous ruling will result in a reversal of an adverse judgment.

Reversals of trial court judgments because of erroneous rulings in relation to evidence points are now comparatively rare. Many rules of evidence allow the trial judge to admit or exclude evidence as a matter of discretion. Furthermore, even when the trial court abuses discretion or is allowed none, appellate courts are reluctant to reverse because of an error in admitting or excluding evidence. If not actively searching for a way to hold that a claim of error in an evidence ruling is barred or that the error is harmless, they are at least receptive to such suggestions in the argument of the lawyer who seeks to sustain the judgment of the lower court. The net result is that in practical effect the trial judge has much more discretion on evidence points than a study of the rules of evidence alone would disclose.

In many jurisdictions, exclusion of evidence is not reversible error if any valid theory supports the ruling even though the objection to the evidence stated in the trial court was a general objection or a specific objection on some other ground.[2] If your excluded evidence is admissible for some special purpose, though not generally, you must advise the trial court of the special purpose for which you offer it in order to preserve error.[3] Conversely, admission of evidence is not reversible error, even though the evidence is not properly admissible for general purposes, if some sound theory of admissibility for a special purpose can be found by the offering party and the objecting party did not move for an instruction that the evidence not be considered except for that limited purpose.[4] Because of the failure of some courts to observe the distinction between subsequent use of evidence similar to that objected to and subsequent use of evidence to explain or rebut that objected to,[5] you may incur a risk of having your claim of error barred if you cross-examine or offer other evidence concerning the matter you sought to exclude.

2. 1 Wigmore, *Evidence* §18 (3d ed. 1940). Compare Federal Rules of Evidence, Rule 103.

3. See §2.36 as to offering evidence for a limited purpose.

4. See §4.18.

5. See 1 Wigmore, *Evidence* §18 (3d ed. 1940).

It is the general rule, however, that you do not forego relying on a previous overruled objection by cross-examining or offering independent evidence to explain or rebut the objectionable matter. The risk of forfeiture can be reduced by your pointing out to the court before your cross-examination or rebuttal that you are offering it subject to and without waiving your primary contention that your objection should have been sustained.

If you do not make a new objection to each new question asked, even though it presents precisely the same law question as a previous objection, it may be held that the error of the court in overruling your sound objection is harmless because essentially the same evidence was received elsewhere in the trial without objection.[6] Obviously continued objections to a series of questions on the same subject matter will become tedious and boring to the jury. This difficulty is the more pronounced because of the fact that the adoption of the previous objection by simply saying, "Same objection," when the new question is asked, is not always a safe practice; it, too, may result in a forfeiture of your sound objection on the theory that you did not make the ground of objection sufficiently clear. Particularly is this so if there is reason for distinguishing between the questions, some of them being subject to the objection and others not.

One method of meeting this problem is to make your objection clearly and fully when the first objectionable question is asked, securing the court's ruling[7] and then stating to the court a request in substance that it be understood that you have the same objection to each other question that counsel asks on the same subject, without the necessity of your repeating the objection each time. You may also include in your request a statement of the reason you find it necessary to make the request, so that if the court denies your request either with or without the intervention of opposing counsel, the jury will understand the reason for your persistence in repeating objections.[8] For example, if the court has overruled your first, fully explained objection, and the next question asked is of the same character and appears to be leading to still more on the same point, you might make a statement as follows:

Your Honor, it is obvious that some additional questions raising this same point of law will be asked. In the absence of some special arrangement it might be asserted that I have forfeited my objection if I do not renew it by stating it fully each time a new question is asked. In order to avoid boring the court and jury with such repetition, may we have an understanding that I have the same objection I have

6. *E.g.,* State Highway Dep't v. Hollis, 106 Ga. App. 669, 672, 127 S.E.2d 862, 865 (1962). But *cf.* 1 Wigmore, *Evidence* §18 at n.18 (3d ed. 1940 and Supp. 1964).

7. See §4.13.

8. As to whether it is ethically proper to include such statements for the purpose of influencing the jury, see §4.14.

stated to the last question, as a running objection to each question raising the same point and to the whole of this line of questioning, without the necessity of my objecting again to each question?

If this request is granted, then your remaining problem is merely that of watching the questions carefully to insure that you are not overlooking some other valid objection to a particular question in addition to that you have preserved without repetition. It is also advisable, after opposing counsel has stepped aside to some other line of questions not subject to the objection and then returns again to the objectionable line of questions, to point out again that your "running objection" applies.

Sometimes the court, either because of the opposition of your adversary or independently, will not permit such a "running objection." In that event, you might request that the court permit you to adopt by reference the previous full statement of your objection, so that you can limit your subsequent statements of the objection to a few words, such as this: "Same objection, Your Honor, as previously stated in full." Unless you have permission of the court to do this or the rules of practice in your jurisdiction clearly permit it, it is not a recommended practice. Even with the permission of the court or the authorization of specific rules of your jurisdiction, you must take care that you make your statement of the objection clear. You might, for example, have two or three different subjects of repeated objections within an entire trial; if so, it is necessary to phrase your references so the trial judge could not reasonably misunderstand which objection you are adopting by reference.

If you use either a "running objection" or an adoption by reference, it is important that you make your full statement of the objection in a form that will be entirely apt as an objection to all of the questions to which you apply it by reference. That is, if your full statement is read into the record at the point where you state "Same objection," it should fit perfectly. If it does not, there is again a danger of forfeiture. Because of the difficulty of making a single statement of grounds of objection that will fit perfectly as the objection to numerous questions, it is sometimes not feasible to use either the "running objection" or the adopted objection.

In Case 54, if you decide to object[9] and D's lawyer has chosen to offer several different records, one at a time, each containing some hearsay statements of the objectionable type, make your objection in full when the first record is presented. Probably you should not at that time ask for the running objection; await counsel's offer of another record and then ask that it be understood without full repetition that you have the same objection to this record as was made to the previous one. Point out the specific statements that you claim to be hearsay; otherwise, your objection that the record contains hear-

9. See §4.11.

say might be regarded as too general. In the circumstances of Case 54, a "running objection" is not the best procedure because of this need for pointing out specifically the parts of each document to which you are objecting. In order to avoid accentuating the harm from admission of the hearsay, consider asking the court to hear the matter "in chambers." [10] If through investigation and discovery you have anticipated your adversary's offering of these records, you should be fully prepared to identify the objectionable parts of each separate document. If you are not adequately prepared to do that, you should consider asking for a recess while you examine all of the records to be offered.

In most jurisdictions you cannot successfully complain of a ruling sustaining an objection to a question during examination (direct or cross) and thereby excluding evidence, unless the answer of the witness appears in the record or its substance is stated or is apparent. In the absence of such a record in an offer of proof (or "bill of exception" — terminology varies), the court is unable to determine whether the error in the ruling is material and harmful. Since the jury is not allowed to hear the answer, the process of completing the offer of proof involves delay in the trial; usually the question will be one of several on the same general subject, to all of which the objection extends, and a jury recess or retirement of several minutes will be required. Sometimes trial judges insist that the offer of proof be completed later to avoid taking the jury's time, and sometimes lawyers voluntarily make this suggestion for similar reasons, perhaps in concern over the possibility that some of the jurors will be displeased about the delay and may react unfavorably against the lawyer who asks for it to complete the offer of proof. The practice of postponing the completion is more often inadvisable from the point of view of the lawyer making the offer of proof, and you should not follow this practice unless the judge is insistent. The matter of completing the offer may slip your mind as you are occupied with the many other immediate problems during trial, and perhaps this will occur even though you have taken the precaution of jotting down a note as a reminder. There is always the possibility that in completing the offer you may persuade the judge that the evidence should be admitted; you may even conceive and develop some alternative theory [11] for its admission as you are in the process of completing the offer of proof. Also, if the matter is postponed, even though the evidence is finally admitted it may then come in out of order and lose part of its effectiveness. If the exception is worth preserving, the better practice usually is to complete the offer of proof immediately after the objection is sustained. In doing so, include in your offer a clear statement of any alternative theories on which you offer the evidence.

10. See §4.9.
11. See §2.17.

Difficulties in preserving error and securing a reversal because of an erroneous ruling on admission or exclusion of evidence emphasize the importance of directing your efforts primarily toward development of the evidence so as to secure a favorable verdict rather than to preserve reversible error. [12]

§4.13 Dealing with the court's failure to rule on your objection

What should you do when the court fails to rule on your objection?

Occasionally a trial judge will fail to respond to an objection or motion made during a trial. Sometimes this occurs as a result of the judge's remaining silent as he is considering the objection, the silence being interrupted by a further question or comment by your adversary or the witness that diverts attention from the objection. Sometimes it occurs as the result of diversion of attention by some comment or question raised by the judge.

If the judge remains silent and the witness answers the question to which you objected, you may have no ground for error. The burden is upon you to secure a ruling by the judge upon your objection, and his silence may not be interpreted as equivalent to overruling the objection. You should obtain an expression that indicates his ruling.

If the question is never answered because of some diversion, there may be no point in your pressing for a ruling on the objection. The failure of your adversary to secure an answer to the question makes the point immaterial to you unless in your view the question itself has caused harm. In that event, you may either request an instruction to disregard the question [1] or move for a mistrial. [2]

If you are confronted with a situation in which the witness is proceeding with an answer to the question after the judge has failed to respond to your objection, it is proper for you to interrupt the witness with a request that the witness be instructed to withhold his answer until the judge has ruled upon your objection.

§4.14 Using an objection as an argument to the jury

CASE 55. *P* sues *D* because of head injuries. *P* has been treated by *F*, his family doctor, and *N*, a specialist in neurosurgery, from the date of the accident until the date of trial. Their opinions are sharply contradicted by those of your medical witnesses, *N-1* and *N-2*, both specialists. Shortly before trial, *P* goes to *N-3* for an examination preparatory to use of the testimony of *N-3* in the trial of the case. *N-3* takes an extensive "history" from *P* regarding his

12. See §1.4.
1. See §4.15.
2. See §5.4.

complaints. When *N-3* is testifying on direct examination by *P*'s lawyer, he is asked to state the opinion regarding *P*'s condition that *N-3* has formed after taking into consideration the history recited by *P*.

Should you use an objection as an argument to the jury?

Using a frivolous objection as a vehicle for expressing some argument to the jury is a practice condemned both by rules of procedure and by professional standards. On the other hand, expressing serious objections in a manner calculated to appeal to the jury as well as the court is generally regarded as a proper practice,[1] and clearly it is proper to give attention to phrasing objections in such a way as to avoid causing an affirmatively adverse reaction by jurors. Obviously you may give argumentative comment such relative emphasis in your statement of a serious objection that your statement is subject to the same criticism as a frivolous objection used for making an argument. The distinction is primarily one of degree, and great differences of opinion exist regarding such practices. These differences are reflected in attitudes of trial judges regarding argumentative comment in the trial generally, as well as in relation to objections. Some trial judges favor and practice limiting the lawyers strictly to questions and the bare essentials of statement of grounds of objection when objection is made; others favor and practice considerable leniency in this respect. Before judges who do not enforce strict limitations so as to discourage the use of argumentative comment, the lawyer whose adversary uses argumentative comment is without remedy other than retaliating in kind, or else somehow causing the jury to become aware of the practice in the hope that they will regard it as unfair. If by comparison one lawyer appears to the jury as an artist in cunning and the other an honest plodder, they may admire the artist but they will be more inclined to believe the plodder.[2]

Within the limitations imposed by the trial judge and by professional standards, what factors should determine the nature and amount of argumentative comment included in your objection? In this respect, a distinction may be made between objections aimed at exclusion of certain subject matter and those aimed at form or manner of questioning.

The typical grounds of objection to form of questions or manner of ques-

---

1. It was rather difficult, to say the least, to reconcile this practice with the provision in American Bar Association, Canons of Professional Ethics, Canon 22 (1908), that a lawyer should not "introduce into an argument addressed to the Court remarks or statements intended to influence the jury or bystanders." However, this provision was not carried forward into American Bar Association, Code of Professional Responsibility (1969). Can this practice be reconciled with the provision in *id.,* EC 7–25, that "a lawyer should not by subterfuge put before a jury matters which it cannot properly consider"?

2. *Cf.* §1.3.

tioning, as distinguished from subject matter of the questions, are based upon ideas that appeal to the ordinary layman without any background of experience in the administration of justice. This is true, for example, of objections that your adversary is leading the witness[3] or is cross-examining in an oppressive manner or with misleading questions.[4] In such instances, explanation of your ground of objection serves not only to make the legal point clear but also to convince the judge and the jury that the objection is entirely reasonable and fair.

Most of your objections made for the purpose of exclusion of subject matter that you think would prejudice the jury against your case afford no opportunity for such argumentative comment. You would prefer that the jury not have any indication whatsoever as to the nature of the evidence being excluded, and you can hardly make an argument for the fairness of application of the exclusionary rule to your situation without some reference to the nature of the evidence being excluded. Your purpose is to get the point of the objection before the court while attracting the least possible attention of the jury. Though you may explain and argue more fully if you have the opportunity to do so out of the hearing of the jury, your statement of the ground of objection within the hearing of the jury will be the least that will serve to advise the court clearly of your basis for objecting. You can make good use of special phrases that have a specific meaning to the judge because of his familiarity with the rules of evidence, but little meaning to the average juror. If you intend to rely upon an adverse ruling on your objection by the trial court as a ground of appeal, you should make your objection sufficiently explicit that the appellate court will not take the position that you did not clearly advise the trial court of the contention that you make on appeal as to grounds of inadmissibility.

Though most objections aimed at exclusion of evidence present no occasion for using any argumentative comment, some will. Many of the exclusionary rules of evidence are based upon either unreliability or else irrelevancy or immateriality of the proffered evidence. The reasons that lead the courts to develop and apply those rules do not always appeal to jurors, particularly when the information is being kept from them by the operation of the rules. But sometimes those reasons will appeal to jurors, and, subject to such limitations as are imposed by professional standards and the attitude of the trial judge toward argumentative objections, you may profitably express them in urging the court to sustain the objection. This would be true, for example, of an objection in Case 55 by which you seek to exclude a medical opinion based upon self-serving complaints made by the plaintiff to a doctor whom he has consulted for the purpose of preparing him to testify as a witness in the case.

3. See §4.3.
4. See §4.4.

The advisability of making the objection is subject to dispute, even where its applicability is not limited by a rule making the evidence admissible if the doctor is consulted for treatment (or advice concerning treatment) as well as for testimony; [5] the exclusion of the opinion can generally be avoided by the use of hypothetical questions and your objection may only emphasize those opinions when finally received. If you decide to make the objection, however, the reason for the existence of the rule is likely to appeal as much to jurors as judges — unsworn statements of a litigant, to a doctor whose favorable testimony he is seeking, lack a sufficient guarantee of reliability, and an opinion based upon such statements is no more reliable than the statements.

§4.15 Requesting an instruction to disregard

CASE 56. *P* sues for personal injuries sustained in a collision between his car and one owned by *D* and driven by *A*, while working for *D*. Suit is against *D* only, *A* not being joined as a party. *A* was charged in a municipal traffic court with the misdemeanor of careless driving, entered a plea of guilty and paid a fine of $10. *A* claims that he was not guilty of careless driving, but that he did not know anything about court proceedings, did not have advice of counsel, and entered the plea only because he was told by the prosecuting attorney that by pleading guilty he would get the minimum fine of $10, whereas if he were tried and found guilty he might be fined as much as $200; after talking with *D* about it immediately after returning from court to his work, *A* went back to the court and with the court's permission withdrew the plea of guilty. As *D*'s lawyer, it is your opinion that the admission of careless driving, by plea of guilty, is inadmissible as against *D* (regardless of admissibility as against *A* if he were a party).

Should you move for an instruction to the jury to disregard an improper question or answer?

Most objections are made against the question before an answer has been stated in the presence of the jury. The failure to make your objection at that time may result in forfeiture of the objection unless the question on its face did not give notice of the inadmissibility of the responsive answer. [1] If the question does not disclose the probable or desired content of the answer, there is generally no occasion for seeking an instruction to the jury to disregard the question. This is the case, for example, if the question is "What did Jones say?", and the hearsay objection is sustained. On the other hand, if

---

5. See 3 Wigmore, *Evidence* §688 (rev. ed. Chadbourn 1970).

1. 1 Wigmore, *Evidence* §18 (3d ed. 1940). See also Federal Rules of Evidence, Rule 103(a)(1).

your adversary's improper question has enough information within it to advise the jury expressly or by implication of the content of the anticipated answer, or if your adversary during cross-examination of one of your witnesses asks a question that contains in itself an implied charge that it was not proper to place before the jury, you should consider moving that the court instruct the jury that the question constitutes no evidence whatsoever and is to be disregarded by the jury. This motion is often referred to as a motion to strike; it is preferable, however, to request a specific instruction to disregard, since the jury may not be as much impressed by a statement that the evidence is "stricken from the record" as a statement to them that they will not consider it for any purpose.

Whether you choose to make this request should depend upon your judgment as to whether that additional emphasis on the matter will probably cause more thought to be given to it by the jurors and more harm to be done to your case, despite the instruction, than if only the objection were made. This in turn will depend on the nature of the improper matter and how much is disclosed by the question. If the question alone serves to disclose to the jury the evidence that you are trying to exclude, you should generally request the instruction; the value of a specific statement by the court to the jurors that they shall not consider it outweighs any disadvantage of emphasis. On the other hand, if the question is probably not sufficiently specific for the jurors to infer what the evidence is, you may prefer to avoid any instruction by the court to the jury. If you seek the instruction, you should seek only an instruction to "disregard the last question," or some similar instruction phrased in general terms. If the court instructed the jury in Case 56, for example, to disregard the question concerning A's plea to the charge of careless driving, when the question had been only "Were you asked in traffic court whether you were guilty of careless driving?", it probably would have been preferable from defendant's point of view to have no instruction.

If you were unable to anticipate an objectionable answer to an apparently proper question, either because the answer was nonresponsive or for other reasons that may exist despite careful preparation of your case, you should move for an instruction to disregard the answer rather than merely objecting to the answer. Without the instruction, the jury may not catch the significance of the court's "objection sustained." With this motion and instruction, the jurors' minds are directed to the subject with greater emphasis; if you consider that the harm from the jurors' hearing the evidence would only be accentuated by the additional emphasis of an instruction and cannot be removed, you are without effective remedy unless the harm is so severe as to support a mistrial. A motion for mistrial [2] based upon an in-

2. See §5.4.

admissible answer is not often sustained, however, unless it appears that clearly inadmissible evidence was deliberately offered through the device of an apparently innocuous question.

§4.16 Advance motions to exclude anticipated evidence

CASE 56. (See statement of the case at the beginning of the preceding section.)

Should you present an advance motion for exclusion of evidence that you anticipate your adversary will offer?

Your protection against improper questions is inadequate if you are confronted with an adversary who deliberately asks such questions, for the purpose of calling inadmissible matter to the attention of the jury before you have an opportunity to object and prevent it, and a trial judge who will not deal with that practice sternly. The hope of reversal by an appellate court because of improper questions is usually illusory; as a practical matter the discretion to control the conduct of counsel is generally vested in the trial court, and the appellate court is loathe to find an abuse of that discretion.

To the extent that you are able to anticipate particular objectionable questions that your adversary may ask, whether seriously contending that they are proper or only using the contention as an excuse for stating a talking question that gets the matter before the jury, some courts will permit and consider motions made in advance of the offer of the evidence. You may thereby prevent the offer from being made in the presence of the jury until the court has first heard and passed on the admissibility. For example, in Case 56, if you are certain that P's lawyer knows the traffic court incident and intends to bring it up during cross-examination of A, claiming that A's plea of guilty in the traffic court is admissible, you should make an advance motion to the court, out of the presence of the jury, and preferably at the beginning of trial. In this motion you should advise the court of the nature of the evidence question presented and request either a ruling at that time upon your objection or else an instruction by the court to your adversary not to offer the evidence within the hearing of the jury without having given you an opportunity to present your objection and obtain a ruling out of the presence of the jury.

Whether your motion is granted or denied, it serves at least the purpose of advance notice to the court and your adversary concerning your contention that the matter is so prejudicial that its coming to the attention of the jury even in the form of the question only will cause irreparable harm. Your adversary is thereafter in poor position to use a talking question designed to tell the jury the critical information before you can make an objection and then claim that the injection of prejudicial matter was not deliberate. Even if the court will not consider an advance motion of the character suggested here, your aim may be partially accomplished by notice to the court and counsel, in advance of the offer of the evidence, of your contention regarding its irreparably harmful character. You may give this notice either in writing or orally in court, out of the hearing of the jury. Both your chances of dissuading your adversary from asking the talking question and your chances of obtaining a mistrial [1] if he uses it are improved by such an advance motion or advance notice.

You may use this method of advance motion to the court, also, in relation to objectionable documentary evidence that you know your adversary intends to offer. You may ask the court either to exclude the entire document or to exclude specified parts of it to which you object.

§4.17 Replying to your adversary's objections

Should you reply to your adversary's objections?

The answer to this question will depend to a great extent on the practices and preferences of the trial judge before whom you are trying your case. Some judges customarily rule immediately upon an objection, not expecting any reply from the other lawyer; others prefer that the opposing lawyer respond to all but routine objections. In addition to the customary practices of the trial judge in this respect, a number of other factors bear on the question whether you should reply to your adversary's objection.

Sometimes you will recognize the soundness of your adversary's contention when it is called to your attention. Since your aim is to win the case and not merely to vindicate yourself by upholding every question you ask, [1] you should not urge, either expressly or implicitly, that the court overrule objections when you consider that doing so probably would be reversible error. You have had the opportunity to study your case more thoroughly than the judge, and despite the judge's greater experience in considering evidence points generally you may be better able to assess the risk of reversible error on specific points that you have briefed. In such circumstances, if the trial judge overrules an objection and you do not wish to take the risk of reversible error, you may generally avoid it by withdrawing the question. Though the court might decline to permit the withdrawal, that reaction is so rare that the customary phrasing of the withdrawal of a question in most localities is not in terms of a request to the court to permit it but in terms of a statement, "I withdraw the question." Your frequent use of this practice, however, might give the appearance of bad faith in asking the ques-

1. See §5.4.
1. See §1.4.

tions. Your withdrawal of a question, either before or after a ruling by the court, waives any error that the court may have committed against you by sustaining an objection. The practice of withdrawing questions after the court has sustained the objection has little, if anything, to recommend it. If you do not choose to preserve your point of error, merely let the matter pass without further comment after the court's ruling.[2]

If the question you ask is one that you consider proper and material, and one as to which you would prefer having the witness' answer before the jury instead of a possible point of error to use as a basis for new trial in the event of an adverse result, express your contention unless it is already apparent to the court that you seriously urge, despite the objection, that the question is proper. Usually your insistence on the question will be assumed by the court. It is often a mistake to make an argument. If the court appears inclined to exchange views with your adversary on the merit of the objection, it is best for you to remain quiet and let the court argue for you. It is conceivable that the court may think of some arguments that you had not considered, or may express them better; also you may gain an insight into the court's thinking and into the matter of choosing the points for emphasis and those that may better be left undeveloped in the event you are called on for argument. Do not interrupt a judge who is arguing for your side of the matter merely because you see a vital point that the judge is not expressing and is apparently overlooking. If you fail to follow this advice, you may find on interrupting the argument that you merely divert the judge's attention from finding weaknesses in your adversary's argument to finding weaknesses in your own.

If you misjudge the need for reply to your adversary's objection, and in the absence of your reply the court sustains it, you are then at a disadvantage in the court's consideration of the matter but you may nevertheless ask that the court permit you to present your answer to the objection made by your adversary and your reasons for considering the question proper. Ordinarily the court will grant such a request, though of course you then have the laboring oar as a practical matter since you must persuade the court to modify a ruling already made.

§4.18 Requesting limiting instructions

CASE 13. *P* is suing for injuries sustained in a collision between his car and *D*'s truck. *P*'s car, after the impact with *D*'s truck, veered into *W*'s car. *P*'s lawyer, in interviewing *W*, learns that *D* paid *W* $75 for a release and that *W* tells a version of the facts favorable to *D*. *P*'s lawyer anticipates that

---

2. Your failure to make some form of showing of the answer that would have been given by a witness generally forfeits your point of error, §4.12.

D will call *W* as a witness in the trial and wants to be prepared to prove the payment of $75 by *D* to *W*, though the possibility of an objection on the ground that it was paid in compromise of a disputed claim is apparent.

Should you move for an instruction that evidence not be considered except for a limited purpose?

In general, when you assert that evidence is admissible for some limited purpose only, you are precluded from asserting the error of the court in admitting it generally if you fail to move that the evidence be received for the limited purpose only. [1] Your adversary has no burden of calling to your attention the limited purpose for which the evidence is admissible; indeed, your adversary may conceive the limited purpose for the first time after trial is completed, and with the aid of exhaustive consideration of authorities. Very often such an exhaustive analysis will disclose some alternative theory for admissibility of the evidence for a limited purpose. [2] This rule barring complaint on appeal by the objecting lawyer has a counterpart in the rule that the lawyer offering the evidence cannot complain successfully of its exclusion if it is admissible for only a limited purpose and was not offered for that purpose. [3] The combined effect of these rules is that the party against whom the trial judge rules has the burden of calling to the trial judge's attention any limited purposes as to which the rules of evidence vary from those concerning admissibility of the evidence for general consideration. This burden has tactical implications for both the lawyer offering the evidence [4] and the lawyer objecting to the evidence.

When you decide to object to evidence that your adversary has offered generally, and it may conceivably be admissible for some limited purpose though inadmissible for general consideration, should your original objection refer to admissibility for a limited purpose? Generally it should not. If the court sustains your objection, the burden will be on your adversary to make the offer for the limited purpose. In the absence of an offer for the limited purpose, your adversary will not be able to reverse the trial court because of exclusion of the evidence. Your referring to the limited purpose for which the evidence may be admissible under these circumstances would have done your client no good but perhaps considerable harm through suggesting to your adversary a theory under which the evidence might be admissible.

After your objection to admissibility generally has been overruled, how should you proceed in meeting your burden of pointing out a distinction between admissibility of the evidence generally and for limited purposes?

1. 1 Wigmore, *Evidence* §13 (3d ed. 1940). See also Federal Rules of Evidence, Rules 103, 106.
2. See §2.17.
3. See §4.12.
4. See §2.17.

You are concerned with preserving your basic position that the evidence is not admissible for any purpose; usually you can do this by stating to the court, as a preface to any request for limiting instructions, that you make your request in the alternative and without waiving your primary contention that the evidence is not admissible for any purpose. You are still confronted with the tactical problem of avoiding the suggestion of theories of admissibility that your adversary may not think to develop, either at the time of trial or in subsequent briefing on appeal or motion for new trial.

One method of meeting this problem, permissible in many jurisdictions, is stating to the court that, to avoid any contention of forfeiture of your objection on the theory that the evidence may be admissible for some special purpose though not generally, you request that the court give an instruction to the jury that the evidence shall not be considered by them as bearing on a specified issue in the case — the issue as to which it is harmful to you and as to which you contend it is inadmissible. For example in Case 13, if under the decisions of your jurisdiction you consider that there is substantial danger that the evidence that W collected $75 from D on account of W's damages will be held admissible on the theory of impeachment (of the aggregate of W's testimony at trial implying that D was in no way at fault, or the aggregate of D's evidence as a whole), then as defense counsel you might ask that the court instruct the jury that D's payment of $75 to W in compromise of the claim for W's damages is not to be considered by the jury as bearing on the question whether D was negligent.

The other alternative would be to request an instruction by the court to the jury that this evidence is not to be considered by the jury for any purpose other than the limited one of giving it whatever weight, if any, they think it deserves for impeachment purposes.

The advantage of the former type of request is that it may preserve the error of the court's permitting the evidence to be considered on the vital negligence issue, even though you have not anticipated some limited purpose that is not mentioned by your adversary but might be sustained under some theory developed later. The disadvantage is that it calls to the jury's attention your recognition of the relevance of the evidence to the very issue on which you are seeking to avoid their considering it. Ordinarily this disadvantage is sufficiently serious to make it inadvisable to use this procedure.

The second possible procedure — that of requesting an instruction that consideration be limited to whatever bearing, if any, the evidence has for limited purposes for which you fear it may be admissible — has the disadvantage of forcing you to anticipate *all* limited purposes for which your adversary might later establish that the evidence was admissible, and also the disadvantage of disclosure to your adversary of all the theories that you seriously fear, including perhaps some that your adversary had not yet considered. As to anticipation of *all* purposes, consider the effect of your requesting a limitation to consideration for impeachment of W's testimony, if later the courts should hold that the evidence was also admissible for the impeachment of the aggregate of D's contentions as a whole, since D's making the payment is inconsistent with his insistence that he was not at fault.

Though your choice among methods will vary with circumstances, usually the disadvantage of your impliedly admitting to the jury that the evidence is relevant to the vital point as to which you seek to avoid their considering it will make it advisable for you to choose the latter method of requesting an instruction on limitation rather than the former. In Case 13, for example, request an instruction that impeachment is the only purpose for which the jury may consider the evidence, rather than an instruction that they shall not consider this evidence as bearing upon the negligence issue.

In the preceding discussion of Case 13 it has been assumed that it is your judgment that there is substantial danger that the evidence that W collected $75 from D on account of W's damages will be held admissible on the theory of impeachment. If your judgment is to the contrary, and it is also your considered judgment that the evidence is not admissible for any other limited purpose, then make no request for limitation whatsoever. Since either type of request discussed above has some disadvantages, you should not incur the risk of harm unless you consider it necessary to being reasonably certain that you have preserved reversible error. This principle also applies if the objectionable evidence is not sufficiently material to warrant urging that its admission is reversible error, or urging that the admission of this evidence should be treated by the appellate court as one of several factors combining to deprive your client of a fair trial, even though it would not alone be regarded as reversible error.

The process described in this section of, first, considering the possibility that evidence that is inadmissible for general consideration may nevertheless be admissible for one or more limited purposes and, second, planning your method of dealing with the problem at trial is an illustration of what may be called proof analysis.[5] A written analysis that the plaintiff's lawyer might have prepared in relation to Case 13 appears in another section.[6] The accompanying illustration shows a form of written analysis that the defense lawyer might use in Case 13.

§4.19 Interrupting to object

Should you interrupt a question or answer to make your objection?

Your adversary, if not abusing the privilege, is entitled to the courtesy of an opportunity to state a question to a witness or an argument to the court

5. See generally §1.5.
6. §2.17.

File: Case 13   Our Client: D

Proof Analysis

Witness: W (expected to be a witness for our client, D)

Evidence P May Offer: that W received $75 from D in payment for damage to W's car.

P's Question to our Witness, W, on Cross:
(1)   Did you receive $75 from D in return for your signing a release of claims against D for the damage done to your car?

Our Response: Objection, Your Honor.

Our Further Response (if the Court inquires about our grounds or overrules our first general objection):   Hearsay and evidence of an offer to buy peace and compromise.

Our Additional Response (if the Court overrules our objections on the above grounds):   Your Honor, in the alternative and without waiving our position that this evidence is inadmissible for any purpose, we request that the Court instruct the jury that under the law they are not to consider this evidence for any purpose other than the limited one of giving it whatever weight, if any, they think it deserves for impeachment.

Notes:
(1)   Do not speak of impeachment of W. The evidence might also be admissible for impeachment of the aggregate of all of D's evidence on the theory that not only is W's claiming and accepting payment inconsistent with W's present testimony but also D's paying W is inconsistent with D's present position.
(2)   If, after our general objection, P offers the evidence for a limited purpose, seek a hearing out of the presence of the jury, if feasible, to make the following response: Your Honor, we take the position that the evidence is not admissible even for a limited purpose. Whatever slight relevance, if any, it might have for any limited purpose that P's counsel might suggest is far outweighed by its tendency to confuse and mislead, and to result in unfair prejudice of the very type that the rule protecting compromises is designed to prevent.
(3)   If after an offer by P for a limited purpose the Court admits the evidence without explicitly giving a limiting instruction, consider requesting a special instruction as stated under Our Additional Response above.
(4)   Consider presenting a motion, out of the presence of the jury before we call W, asking the court to rule on admissibility of this evidence. Disadvantage: P may not even offer it. Advantage: we can argue more freely - for example, as in Note (2) above - out of the hearing of the jury.
(5)   Should we present such a motion as is referred to in Note (4) even before calling D for fear that P's attorney will raise this issue in cross-examining D? Should we use such a motion for the additional purpose of protecting against any suggestion that the payment on D's behalf was made by a liability insurer for D?

without interruption. Even when your adversary is abusing the privilege, the most effective response from the point of view of favorably impressing the court and jury is generally the courteous response. In the exceptional situation in which your adversary is stating matter in the presence of the jury that you are seeking to exclude as improper, an interruption is advisable. If you do not interrupt, the prejudicial matter is before the jury and the harm already done before the court has an opportunity to rule upon it. If you do not make a practice of interrupting your adversary on other occasions, most trial judges not merely condone but approve interruptions designed to avoid the jury's hearing prejudicial statements before the court has an opportunity to pass on whether they are improper. This proposition applies equally to your adversary's talking question (that is, a question revealing implicitly the prejudicial matter) and the witness' improper answer (for example, an answer that is nonresponsive, or one that contains inadmissible matters not indicated by the question, or one that is begun before you have time to consider the question and state your objection).

§4.20 Phrasing objections

How should you phrase your objection?

The first question you must consider in phrasing an objection is whether you want to indicate some ground or grounds of objection or instead merely to communicate to the court the fact that you object. Practices vary widely in this respect, not only among jurisdictions but also among courts within a single jurisdiction and among different counsel practicing before the same court. Some trial judges prefer that counsel practicing before them merely indicate the fact of objection in most instances. Before a judge who prefers this practice, you may simply say, for example, "Objection," or "We object," or "I pray Your Honor's judgment."

Before any trial judge, however, there will be circumstances in which you will need to state your objection more fully. You may usefully think of a full statement of objection as consisting of three parts — the introduction, the identification of the rule or rules of evidence invoked, and explanatory comment.

Many different forms of introduction are commonly used, and there is no prescribed pattern. These are examples:

Objection.
Objected to as . . . .
Objected to on the ground that . . . .
Your Honor, we object on the following ground: . . . .
May it please the Court, the defendant objects for the reason that . . . .

Although the one-word form of introduction to your objection serves the purpose from the point of view of legal requirements, most lawyers and judges prefer the addition of one of the customary phrases of respectful address to the court, as a matter of courtroom etiquette. Also, the added moment of time that passes as you state such an introduction to the objection may give you an opportunity to formulate a better organized and more effective statement of the substance of the objection. A more important aspect of the introduction of your objection concerns the objection on multiple grounds. When you have several grounds, it is desirable, for reasons of clarity, that you state them separately. It may have been true at some time past that a clever lawyer could jumble together several grounds of objection and effectively conceal one good ground among other insufficient grounds, purposely getting his objection overruled and injecting reversible error into his case as insurance against an unfavorable jury verdict. The attitude of modern courts toward such tactics and toward reversal on evidence points generally [1] is such that this procedure is now tactically imprudent as well as probably improper under professional standards. The reaction against such methods has gone so far that there is often danger of the court's disregarding a sound ground of objection included in a statement that is merely poorly organized and expressed, and not deliberately jumbled. For the purpose of avoiding this danger and expressing your objection in more persuasive form, you might consider closing your introduction with the phrase "on the following grounds," then numbering your grounds of objection as you state them.

It is helpful to have at the tip of your tongue, for use when you have no time for deliberation, a customary phrasing for your statement identifying each of the more common objections that you may have occasion to invoke. This greatly simplifies your problem of extemporaneously stating those objections the occasion for which you are not able to anticipate and prepare specifically. [2] Illustrations of forms that you might use are given below. They should be regarded only as guides and not as patterns to be followed strictly.

Generally you should supplement the forms of objection given below with a brief statement showing application of the rule of evidence to the facts at hand. This is needed both to help persuade the trial judge and to avoid a claim later that the trial judge who ruled against you had not been advised specifically of your objection because of the generality of your statement. Furthermore, if there is any doubt as to the applicability of your objection, you should consider adding some comment as to qualifications and exceptions to the general rules expressed in these forms. For example, the general hearsay objections included here do not deal with the exceptions and qualifications that account for the principal difficulties in application of the hearsay rule.

1. See §4.12.
2. See §§4.16, 9.2.

To the extent that you are able to anticipate points that will arise in trial your advance preparation should include a study of authorities and preparation for argument to the court on your own and your adversary's objections. When argument is to be heard, if the trial judge does not on his own initiative send the jury out of hearing of the argument, you should consider requesting that this be done.[3] Other sections of this book concern the presence of the jury as a factor influencing your decision to object or not[4] and, if so, the phrasing of your objection.[5]

Although objections on irrelevancy and immateriality are included in the forms below, they are rarely worth making. Frequently the only sound argument in favor of such an objection is the saving of time that will otherwise be spent on collateral issues. The trial judge's fear that the evidence offered may later prove to be relevant and material on some theory, though he may not see it at the moment, usually causes him to overrule such objections unless the party objecting also reasonably urges that jurors are likely to give the evidence undue weight or are likely to be confused by it, or that it is of a prejudicial or inflammatory nature, calculated to influence the jury to render a verdict based upon sympathy or prejudice. Though the statement that the evidence is inflammatory or prejudicial is thus an important part of some objections, the fact that it is inflammatory or prejudicial is alone not a sound ground of objection; the most effective competent evidence is often of that character.

An objection on the ground of "incompetency" of evidence is not included in these forms. The grounds of incompetency are so many and varied that an objection that the evidence is incompetent, without statement of a specific reason, is too general to advise the court of the true ground asserted. You may sometimes use such an objection, however, when the ground of objection would be obvious to anyone trained in the law and you prefer not to state it in the presence of the jury. If the court sustains the objection, your general objection has served its purpose (in most jurisdictions the ruling cannot be reversed if any sound ground can be found for sustaining it, though that ground was not stated[6]). If the objection is overruled, you may then ask the court to hear you out of the presence of the jury,[7] or accomplish that purpose indirectly by requesting leave to present authorities for the court's consideration.

The following are forms for the more common objections. You might use forms such as these for those parts of your objections concerned with identification of the rules of evidence invoked:

3. See §4.10.
4. See §4.2.
5. See §4.14.
6. See §4.12.
7. See §§4.9, 4.10.

ACKNOWLEDGEMENTS

The acknowledgement on the document is irregular on its face because of
— want of a seal or other evidence of the authority of the person purportedly taking the acknowledgement.
— want of evidence of the authority of the person who took the acknowledgement, it being purportedly taken outside this jurisdiction by one whose authority must be affirmatively shown.
— failure to comply with the statutory requirements, namely . . . .

AFFIDAVITS

The affidavit offered is mere hearsay, the affiant not being a witness at this trial (or hearing) when it was made.

AMBIGUITY (*see* UNCERTAINTY)

ANCIENT INSTRUMENTS

The instrument is not shown to be an ancient instrument within the meaning of that term in law since
— there is no competent proof of its age.
— there is no competent proof that it comes from proper custody.
— it shows on its face alterations and blemishes.
— it fails to appear on its face to be free from suspicion, and in fact the alterations upon it raise reasonable suspicions regarding authenticity, if not compelling the conclusion that it is not authentic.

ASSUMING FACTS NOT PROVED

The question assumes facts not in evidence, namely . . . .

AUTHENTICATION (*see also* BOOKS AND RECORDS)

The instrument offered has not been properly authenticated because of
— want of competent proof of its execution.
— want of competent proof of its delivery.
— want of competent proof as to the identity of the person who prepared it and the circumstances under which it was prepared.

BEST EVIDENCE RULE

The evidence offered is not the best evidence;
— the original writing has not been accounted for.
— the books offered are not books of original entry.
— the purported explanation for failure to produce the original writing is inadequate and fails to establish any competent excuse for nonproduction of the original.
— the preferred secondary evidence, a carbon copy made at the time of the original writing, has not been accounted for, and it is not shown that the oral evidence offered is the best available under the circumstances.

— the original writing speaks for itself, is the best evidence, and cannot be varied by attempted oral interpretation.

BOOKS AND RECORDS (*see also* AUTHENTICATION AND BEST EVIDENCE RULE)

The instruments offered are hearsay;
— neither the requirements of common law nor those of statutes for admissibility of records have been met.
— no witness has testified to personal knowledge of the purported transactions recorded.
— at most the evidence shows that the witnesses produced had incomplete knowledge of the purported transactions, and at least their testimony must be supplemented by testimony of someone knowing other vital facts to support admissibility of the documents.
— the person who furnished the data has not been produced, but only one who recorded matter that was purely hearsay as to him.
— the person who furnished data for record has been produced, but he did not make the record presented here and whether these are records of data he furnished does not appear by competent evidence.
— it is not shown that the entries in these books were made in the regular course of business.
— the entries disclose, by the nature of the subject matter and content, that they were not made in the regular course of business.
— the entries, by their substance, show that they were made for use in litigation and not in regular course of business as that term is used in the law of evidence.
— the recitations identified (by the offer, or by objection) are not the type that may be received from books and records, but instead are
— hearsay.
— opinions and conclusions.

COMPROMISE

The question is improper because it relates to a matter involving an offer to buy peace and compromise a disputed claim.

CONCLUSIONS (*see* OPINIONS)

CRIMINAL OFFENSES

The matter is incompetent because
— the person accused was acquitted of the charge.
— it relates not to a conviction, but merely to a charge, which is wholly denied and not proved.
— the charge was only a misdemeanor and had no relation to veracity.
— the date of the conviction is too remote, being (*specify number*) years before this date.

DEAD MAN'S ACTS

The question calls upon the witness to testify regarding a transaction with a decedent, as to which he is disqualified to testify under the Dead Man's Act.

DISQUALIFICATION BY VIOLATION OF ORDER FOR SEPARATION OF WITNESSES

We move that the witness be disqualified from testifying (and that his testimony already given be stricken from the record, the jury being instructed not to consider it for any purpose) because the witness has violated the court's order for separation of witnesses by

— remaining in the courtroom when X and Y were testifying.

— discussing with X the testimony that X gave in trial.

DOUBLE QUESTIONS (*see* UNCERTAINTY)

HEARSAY.

The question invites the witness to state hearsay information rather than restricting him to statement of facts upon personal knowledge.

The question does not limit the witness to stating what he knows from personal observations, and it allows hearsay.

That part of the answer regarding what X told him is hearsay and not within any exception to the hearsay rule. We move that it be stricken and that the jury be instructed not to consider it for any purpose.

IMMATERIALITY (*see also* IRRELEVANCE AND RELEVANCE OUTWEIGHED)

The matter is immaterial to any issue in this case. Both from the point of view of time and from the point of view of unnecessarily confusing the real issues in the case with evidence on immaterial matters, it is improper to impose upon the court and jury as well as parties by raising such collateral matters.

— Further, the subject is one of an inflammatory and prejudicial nature, designed to invite the jury to reach a verdict on the basis of sympathy or prejudice instead of unbiased findings on the facts.

— (*see* added statements under RELEVANCE OUTWEIGHED; similar statements might be used with an objection of immateriality).

INTERPRETATION OF AN INSTRUMENT (*see* BEST EVIDENCE RULE AND PAROL EVIDENCE RULE)

IRRELEVANCE (*see also* IMMATERIALITY AND RELEVANCE OUTWEIGHED)

The matter asked about is irrelevant to any issue in this case.

MEMORANDA IN AID OF TESTIMONY

The witness is testifying from a memorandum rather than from knowledge and memory, the memorandum being one that is not properly usable for this purpose. (A motion to strike and a request for instructions to disregard answers already given may be added.)

NONRESPONSIVE ANSWERS

We move that the answer be stricken and that the jury be instructed not to consider it for any purpose. It is not responsive to the question. (Any other ground of objection might be added — such as, that the answer is a statement of opinion, or hearsay.)

OPINIONS AND CONCLUSIONS

The question calls for (or the answer is) an opinion and conclusion;
— the witness has not been shown to be an expert.
— it is upon a matter that is not a proper subject of opinion testimony, even if expert qualifications are shown; it invades the province of the jury.
— the basis for the opinion has not been shown.

PAROL EVIDENCE RULE

The evidence offered is incompetent under the parol evidence rule;
— it relates to negotiations before the integration of the agreement in a written contract.
— it is an effort to vary the terms of an unambiguous writing by parol evidence.
— the instrument speaks for itself and cannot be varied by oral interpretation.
— though the evidence relates to alleged negotiations subsequent to the written agreement, there is no evidence of independent consideration to support a modification of the written agreement.

PERSONAL KNOWLEDGE (*see* HEARSAY)

PLEADINGS

The evidence is inadmissible for want of any support in the pleadings, which do not raise any issue as to which the evidence offered is relevant and material.

PREJUDICE (*see* IMMATERIALITY AND RELEVANCE OUTWEIGHED)

PRIVILEGE [8]

The question invades the field of confidential communications between
— husband and wife.
— client and attorney.
— patient and doctor. [9]
The question is one that the witness cannot be compelled to answer because of the privilege against self-incrimination, and that privilege is hereby invoked. (Reference to state and federal constitutional provisions is often added.)

REAL EVIDENCE

The exhibition of the injury (or weapon, etc.) would have little probative value, if any, and it is designed to be prejudicial and inflammatory in nature

8. Note that the privilege must be asserted by or on behalf of the one to whom it belongs. 8 Wigmore, *Evidence* §2196 (rev. ed. McNaughton 1961); Federal Rules of Evidence, Rules 501–510.

9. A statutory privilege, not as prevalent as the others illustrated. 8 Wigmore, *Evidence* §2380 (rev. ed. McNaughton 1961). Compare Federal Rules of Evidence, Rule 504, recognizing only a psychotherapist-patient privilege.

and to appeal for sympathy and prejudice rather than for fair findings based upon facts.

RELEVANCE OUTWEIGHED (*see also* IMMATERIALITY AND IRRELEVANCE)

Even if this evidence be considered relevant, its probative value is outweighed by the danger of
— unfair prejudice.
— confusion of the issues.
— misleading the jury.
— undue delay and waste of time.
— needless presentation of cumulative evidence.

REPAIRS AND OTHER REMEDIAL MEASURES

The matter asked about relates to subsequent repairs of an instrumentality allegedly involved in the incident on which this suit is based, and is therefore inadmissible.
The matter asked about relates to remedial measures instituted after the incident on which the suit is based and is therefore inadmissible.

REPETITION

The question is repetitious. It has been asked and answered (several times) and we object to further repetition (in the interest of time).

REPUTATION

The matter is incompetent because
— it does not concern reputation for (lack of) veracity.
— there is no competent evidence that the witness knows the reputation of X for truth and veracity in the community in which X resides.
— the witness offers to testify only that he would not believe X, and not that X has a reputation for lack of veracity.

SEPARATION OF WITNESSES (*see* DISQUALIFICATION)

SCOPE OF EXAMINATION

The question is not within the scope of proper
— cross-examination. It has no relation to matters touched on direct examination, and counsel must call the witness as his own if he wants to go into this matter.
— redirect examination. It is not responsive to anything in the cross-examination.

STATUTE OF FRAUDS

The question calls for parol evidence of an alleged agreement that must be in writing under the Statute of Frauds, and Section ___ of that statute in particular.

UNCERTAINTY

The question is ambiguous and uncertain in its meaning. We ask that it be clarified to avoid misunderstanding.

This is a double (or multiplicitous) question, containing two (or more) distinct parts that should be separated so the witness, and the court and jury, can be certain of counsel's meaning.

The question is confusing; there is doubt as to what is being asked and danger if not probability of misunderstanding.

The question is too indefinite and uncertain to indicate clearly what is being asked and to insure that it is interpreted in the same way by the court and jury as well as the witness and counsel.

The answer indicates that the witness is uncertain. Since he does not know, we move that his answer be stricken and that the jury be instructed not to consider it for any purpose.

Chapter V

MOTIONS DURING TRIAL

§5.1 Aims of motions during trial

The term "motion" is sometimes used in a broad sense to include all of the requests addressed to the court by a party seeking some ruling or action. Generally a request made before the beginning of trial is made in writing and designated formally as a motion for a particular purpose. As to such motions, the rules of procedure for a jurisdiction, and often the local rules of particular courts, contain special requirements concerning the purposes for which they may be used and the form, time, and manner of presentation. Tactical problems associated with such motions made before trial are discussed in Chapters IX, X, and XI of this book.

Requests to the court for rulings during trial are more often made orally in open court but are occasionally made in writing, either because of requirements of rules of procedure or for the purpose of clarity or emphasis. The requests made in writing are usually designated formally as motions. This is often true of the oral requests as well, but many of the oral requests are not customarily referred to as motions, though basically that is what they are.

Some of the customary trial motions, in the broader sense of that term, are primarily associated with problems falling within the scope of other chapters of this book, where they are discussed. This is true of requests that the court permit the use of an interpreter in the interrogation of a witness,[1] permit completion of the record or the offer of proof as to excluded evidence,[2] receive evidence for a limited purpose,[3] take judicial notice of law or facts,[4] or exclude evidence.[5]

1. §2.29.
2. §4.12.
3. §2.36.
4. §2.37.
5. Chapter IV.

216

Other kinds of requests to the court for some action during trial, overlapping or beyond the fields of other chapters, will be discussed in this chapter. These may be grouped, according to the aims of the requests, as follows: (1) those designed to terminate the trial by a final order favorable to the moving party (motions for directed verdict[6] or the equivalent, and motions for judgment[7]); (2) those designed to terminate the trial because it will be impossible for the case to be fairly considered by the jury in view of incidents during trial (motions for mistrial[8]); (3) those designed to insure the fairness of trial processes (motions for separation of witnesses and exclusion from the courtroom,[9] and motions regarding arrangements for preservation of a record[10]); and (4) those designed to promote favorable development of the moving party's theory of the case (motions for leave to amend pleadings,[11] motions for leave to withdraw an announcement of readiness for trial,[12] motions for leave to reopen the evidence,[13] motions for leave to take a voluntary nonsuit,[14] and motions requesting leave to open and close[15]).

§5.2 Motions for directed verdict

CASE 57. *P*, a building contractor, sues *D*, for whom he was constructing a building, upon several different claims for extras under the contract. The claims total $20,000. As *D*'s lawyer, it is your position that *P* is not entitled to recover on any of the items because he failed to comply with the requirements of the contract for written approval by the owner (*D*) and architect of any modifications of plans, as a prerequisite to claims for extras. *P* asserts and offers evidence aimed at showing that the requirements of the contract for advance written approval were waived. At the close of *P*'s evidence, it is apparently *P*'s theory that he has raised a fact issue on waiver as to every item in his $20,000 claim; it is your opinion that his evidence probably raises a fact issue supporting waiver as to one item of $150, but not as to any of the remaining claims.

Should you move for a directed verdict?

The function served by the motion for directed verdict under the federal rules and those of many states is served also by procedures of slightly dif-

6. §5.2.
7. §5.3.
8. §5.4.
9. §5.5.
10. §5.6.
11. §5.7.
12. §5.8.
13. §5.9.
14. *Id.*
15. §5.10.

ferent form, variously called motions for instructed verdict, motions for peremptory instruction, motions for involuntary nonsuit or dismissal, and demurrers to the evidence. The discussion in this section refers generally to any form of motion that is made during trial but before the case is submitted to the jury, requesting a ruling by the court that the evidence is insufficient to raise fact issues upon which findings could be made to support a judgment for the opposite party, other than for such relief as is conceded by the moving party.

Under the rules in some jurisdictions, your motion for directed verdict, or its equivalent under other form and terminology, is a prerequisite to successfully contending after verdict that a judgment should be entered for your client notwithstanding an unfavorable verdict.[1] In these jurisdictions you may not obtain a judgment for your client by withholding your contention of insufficiency of the evidence and raising it for the first time after the verdict is in and the jury has been discharged. The most that you may obtain by originally raising the point of insufficiency after verdict is a new trial. On the other hand, in some jurisdictions it is possible under the rules to obtain a judgment by raising the ground of insufficiency of the evidence for the first time after verdict.[2] Where this is possible, the use of the motion for directed verdict has the disadvantage of disclosing your contention in time that the opposite party may succeed in curing the omission after obtaining permission to reopen the evidence.[3] Though the deliberate entrapment of a careless or unskilled adversary by delaying the assertion of insufficiency of the evidence is questionable under both professional and tactical[4] standards, it is a practice sometimes used.

With reference to the evidence considered in determining after verdict whether a judgment should be entered for the party against whom the verdict was rendered, a distinction is made in some jurisdictions between the motion for directed verdict at the close of the plaintiff's evidence and the motion for directed verdict at the close of all the evidence. There is some authority for considering only the evidence offered before the motion was made, and nothing received thereafter, in determining whether judgment should be entered for the defendant as the trial court should have done when the motion was made; the obvious injustice in final disposition of the cause, if sufficient evidence was actually available and was not offered because of some oversight, misunderstanding, or difficulty, supports the cases approving consideration of all the competent evidence upon a motion for judgment

---

1. Vanderbilt, *Minimum Standards of Judicial Administration* 247–249 (1949).
2. *Id.*
3. See §5.9.
4. See §1.3.

after verdict or upon appeal.[5] A companion rule to the latter view is that in most jurisdictions a motion for directed verdict at the close of the plaintiff's evidence is not a prerequisite to consideration of a motion after verdict for judgment notwithstanding the verdict, even though a motion for directed verdict at the close of all the evidence may be a prerequisite as noted in the preceding paragraph. Nevertheless, the possibility that the insufficiency of the evidence originally offered by the plaintiff will be cured on his rebuttal, or by his cross-examination of your witnesses, makes it advisable generally to urge a motion for directed verdict at the first opportunity if you expect to urge one at any time.

As a general rule, if as the defendant's lawyer you consider that you have grounds for a directed verdict, it is advisable to make two motions — one at the close of the plaintiff's evidence and one at the close of all the evidence — to avoid any possibility of forfeiture of your contention. The federal rules and those of some states contain provisions that, at least arguably, make it imperative that you move for directed verdict at the close of all the evidence, even though you have presented a motion for directed verdict at the close of the plaintiff's evidence, urge only the same grounds, and know that the court will overrule the new motion. This is true because the provisions for the judge's carrying the motion undecided until after verdict and for a new motion after verdict for judgment in accordance with the motion for directed verdict refer only to the motion at the close of all the evidence and not to the motion at the close of the plaintiff's evidence.[6]

Following a practice of filing a motion for directed verdict in all cases is not recommended. One who develops a reputation for that practice has greater difficulty in persuading a judge to take his motion seriously when he does have one that he thinks sound. If you have substantial grounds, however, the danger of forfeiture of a basis for judgment notwithstanding the verdict makes it advisable normally to present the motion even though your grounds are doubtful. Usually you can anticipate the grounds and prepare your motion in advance of trial, thus avoiding any need for a lengthy delay that might cause unfavorable reaction from the judge or the jurors (who, of course, should be out of the hearing of the proceedings when you are presenting a motion for directed verdict). One way of handling this situation, which is particularly useful in those jurisdictions where you may use a substantial amount of time in preparing the motion because it must be in writing and specify the grounds, is to prepare an "open-end" motion in advance of trial, placing your formal conclusion of the motion on a separate sheet of paper so that you may insert additional grounds if some appear that you had not anticipated. If the rules require that the court's ruling

5. See 9 Wigmore, *Evidence* §2496 (3d ed. 1940).
6. Federal Rule 50(b).

also be reduced to writing before further proceedings, you might follow the same practice with respect to the order, leaving blank the recitation of the ruling granting or denying the motion, but completing all the formal parts of the order. This procedure has advantages over stipulating that the motion and order may be later reduced to writing (even where rules permit such a stipulation), because of the danger of misunderstandings or oversights and consequent incompleteness or inaccuracy of the record.

Occasionally the evidence offered will present material fact issues on only one of several claims, or for only a limited amount as compared with a substantially larger claim. If such a state of evidence exists at the close of the plaintiff's case, you should as defendant's lawyer consider making a motion for directed verdict segregating the particular issue for consideration by the jury[7] or a motion making concessions, for the purpose of the motion only, as to the limited fact issue. Unless a motion of the latter type is provided for specifically by rule, statute, or decisions, however, the better practice is to request an advance ruling by the court that concessions offered solely for the purpose of the motion will not be binding except as to consideration of that motion. The usefulness of this procedure is illustrated by Case 57. Under your theory of the case no fact issue is raised to support any judgment for the plaintiff above $150. If you decline to offer evidence on the other issues involving large sums, however, and the trial or appellate court finally passing on the matter rules against your theory, your tactics will have proved very costly. Rarely in practice will you have such confidence in your legal theory, contested by your adversary, that you are justified in declining to offer evidence that would be important to your client's interests if your theory were held erroneous. In Case 57, it would be to your client's interest to avoid the expense of presenting lengthy evidence on the larger issues in the case, but a motion for directed verdict on the entire case is obviously not sound. The concession of the $150 item in a motion for directed verdict (or the segregation of that item by a motion conceding that it should go to the jury, if that type of motion is recognized in your jurisdiction) is a good solution to your dilemma, and in the extreme circumstances of this case you should consider it even if you will not be permitted to limit the concession to application only in connection with your motion.

In jurisdictions where the filing of motions for directed verdict by both parties has the effect of forfeiture of jury trial,[8] you must consider the pos-

---

7. After the close of all the evidence, such segregation may be sought by objecting to the submission of all issues except the one on which it is conceded a fact issue is raised by the evidence. Also compare the possibility of such segregation of claims under summary judgment procedures. See §11.23.

8. Federal Rule 50(a) explicitly rejects this doctrine, which had appeared in some earlier federal as well as state cases.

sibility that your adversary may file a motion and the question whether you would wish to have the case decided by the court rather than the jury.

§5.3 Motions for judgment after verdict

CASE 58. *P* sues *D* for personal injuries suffered when *P* was hit by a spare wheel dislodged from *D*'s truck as it skidded out of control on icy pavement and collided with a utility pole. The spare wheel rolled 200 feet along the street and onto the adjacent sidewalk before striking *P*. *P* asserts that *D* was negligent in the manner of operating the truck and in failing to render effective first aid to *P*. As *D*'s lawyer, you move for a directed verdict at the close of *P*'s evidence, and again at the close of all the evidence, asserting that *D* was not negligent in the manner of operating the truck and that *D* owed no duty to *P*, either as to the manner of operating the truck or as to rendering first aid. Your motions for directed verdict are overruled. The jury find, in a special verdict, that *D* was not negligent in the manner of operating the truck but that he was negligent in failing to render effective first aid to *P*; they also find that *P* was not negligent.

What form of motion for judgment should you present after verdict?

Frequently both parties to an action, or several parties to an action involving more than two parties, will have conflicting theories regarding the judgment that should be entered after verdict. The terminology for the motions available varies, but every contention for judgment falls within one of three groups: (1) In this group are motions contending that the general verdict or findings in answer to special interrogatories support a judgment for the moving party. These motions are generally referred to as motions for judgment on the verdict. (2) In this group are motions contending that the only proper judgment is one for the moving party, notwithstanding the verdict, either because the verdict is not supported by evidence, or because the findings are immaterial under the moving party's legal theory. There is more variation in terminology regarding these motions. Such a motion is usually referred to either as a motion for judgment notwithstanding the verdict, a motion for judgment non obstante veredicto, or a motion for judgment in accordance with the motion for directed verdict. (3) In this group are motions contending that one or more findings in answer to special interrogatories should be disregarded because not supported by evidence and that upon the basis of other findings within the verdict judgment should be entered for the moving party. The occasions for using this form of motion are less frequent than those for using the other types, and of course do not arise unless special interrogatories have been submitted to the jury. No standardized terminology has been adopted for this form of motion; it may be referred to as a motion to disregard specified findings and thereafter to enter judgment upon the verdict.

The importance of distinguishing among these three separate types of motions lies in the fact that the failure to use the correct motion may result in forfeiture of a right to entry of a favorable final judgment, as distinguished from an order for merely a new trial, at the termination of a successful appeal. In the absence of an appropriate motion of either the second or the third type referred to above, in some jurisdictions the appellate court upon concluding that the jury verdict or some special finding within it is not supported by evidence can grant only a new trial and not a final judgment for the appellant.[1] If you have a serious contention of the second or third type, therefore, you should in such jurisdictions present the appropriate motion even though you are already aware of certainty that the trial judge will overrule it. Also, you should make it in a form that will avoid any possibility of a holding that your motion was too general and thus bars your urging some point on appeal. The tendency of the courts is to look through form to substance, holding that the clear presentation of your contention is sufficient even though you designate your motion improperly; even so, proper designation is better practice and aids in making your contention clear.

In Case 58, as *D*'s lawyer, you contend that the evidence will not support a judgment for *P* and that your motions for directed verdict were sound. After verdict, you should urge this contention again by a motion for judgment notwithstanding the verdict, or a motion of this type under other terminology. One doubtful point with respect to that contention is the possibility that *D* should be held liable if he was negligent in the operation of the truck. (Must *P* be a foreseeable plaintiff under the authorities of your jurisdiction?). That doubt is resolved by the jury finding that *D* was not negligent in the manner of operating the truck. You should therefore present a motion for judgment based upon this finding. You are faced, however, with a finding of negligence on another ground — failure to render aid. You should present a motion urging that this finding be disregarded as immaterial on the theory that *D* had no duty to render aid, especially in view of the finding of no negligence as to operation of the truck. Your motion (or motions, if it is the practice in your jurisdiction to state these separate grounds for judgment in separate motions) in Case 58 should therefore include both the second and third of the three types of bases for judgment referred to in the first paragraph of this section.

It is generally held that a correct judgment should be sustained even though an incorrect reason for entering it was indicated in the judgment or the record. This principle is not necessarily applicable, however, to a con-

1. Vanderbilt, *Minimum Standards of Judicial Administration* 250 (1949).

tention raised for the first time on appeal that a verdict should have been directed below for the appellee, or that one or more findings in a special verdict should have been disregarded below so as to sustain the trial court judgment on a theory not followed by the trial court. You should therefore consider making a motion or motions for judgment urging each of the three types of contentions listed above, when these contentions are reasonably supported, even though it is apparent that the court will grant the motion on one particular ground (usually as a judgment upon the verdict).

Though usually the points raised in a motion for judgment notwithstanding the verdict have already been denied by the trial judge in his action upon a motion or motions for directed verdict, the chances of obtaining a favorable ruling are not so small as is generally true when you are calling upon a judge to reverse his own rulings. This is true for the reason that trial judges are inclined to overrule motions for directed verdict when in doubt. They commonly do so with the purpose of receiving a jury verdict that may dispose of the case without need for a ruling on the close question of law. Also, the verdict may make possible a final disposition of the case in one trial even if the holding of the final authority on appeal is against the motion (a situation in which a new trial would have been necessary if the motion for directed verdict had been erroneously granted).

§5.4 Motions for mistrial

CASE 59. *P* sues *D* on a claim for compensation for services as manager of a garage catering to trucking firms. Both parties agree that the employment contract was oral, and *P*'s compensation was to include a bonus of 20% on the amount by which sales and service charges for each period exceeded costs of products sold and wages paid to employees performing the services. A credit customer went into bankruptcy and a $2500 loss was suffered on account of his bill. *P* claims that this $2500 loss is to be borne entirely by *D*; *D* claims that it is to be deducted from the sales figure before computing the difference between sales and costs on which *P*'s bonus is computed. *D* tenders *P*'s compensation in accordance with his theory, and *P* sues for the additional $500.

P testifies that it was expressly agreed between *P* and *D* that *D* would handle collections and bear all credit losses. *D* testifies that there were no credit customers at first, and that as to each customer allowed credit *D* first asked *P*'s approval, clearly indicating to *P* that he would share the risk as it affected his bonus, and that *P* agreed.

You represent *P*. On your cross-examination of *D*, you ask about his agreeing to handle all collections. *D* replies: "I agreed to handle collections, but not to stand all credit losses. When *P* says I was to stand credit losses it's just a question whether you'll take my word or that of an ex-convict."

P is forty-five years old, had been convicted of a felony, assault to murder, at the age of twenty-two, and has lived an exemplary life since being released under a pardon at the age of twenty-five. Assume that evidence of the conviction is inadmissible in your jurisdiction.

Should you move for mistrial?

Occasionally some improper and prejudicial incident during trial will make it impossible to insure a fair consideration of the case free from prejudice and unfair influence. The party harmed by such an incident has the right to a new trial. The terminology for the procedure by which this right to a new trial is asserted varies; it will be referred to here as a motion for mistrial. The following are examples of such incidents: (1) false or inflammatory answers of jury panel members, or inflammatory comment by counsel, during interrogation of the panel; [1] (2) misconduct of a juror as in talking with a witness during trial; [2] (3) improper comment by the trial judge, particularly in a jurisdiction where comment on the evidence by the judge is prohibited; (4) deliberate injection of improper matters during examination of witnesses; [3] (5) improper argument of counsel. [4]

In any situation raising the possibility of mistrial, you should also consider other procedures designed to remedy the harm. For example, if an opposing attorney or a witness injects improper matter during the testimony of the witness, you should object to the question or answer, as the case may be. If that objection is erroneously overruled, no further immediate action on your part is essential to the preservation of that error (unless in your jurisdiction it is necessary to "except" to the ruling). If the objection is sustained, however, and it is your contention that this ruling alone does not cure the harm done, then you should consider moving for an instruction to the jury to disregard the matter, [5] or moving for mistrial, or both. The motion for an instruction to the jury to disregard the improper matter is discussed in Chapter IV [6] since its most frequent application is in connection with objections to evidence. The principles there discussed apply equally, however, to the circumstances of matter improperly injected into the case at times other than during examination of witnesses.

It is generally held that if an instruction to the jury to disregard the improper matter would cure the harm, then no ground for mistrial exists. The remedy of mistrial is not available if the less drastic remedy of instruction would be effective. The theory of the mistrial is that the harm is irrep-

---

1. See §§7.4, 7.5, 7.6.
2. See §§7.8, 7.9.
3. See §§2.23, 3.25, 4.2, 4.3, 4.12, 4.13, 4.15, 4.16.
4. See §§7.12, 7.15, 7.19.
5. See §4.15.
6. See *id.*

arable; if that is so, an instruction about the matter cannot repair the harm and may only accentuate it by calling further attention to the prejudicial matter. It follows that a request for an instruction to disregard the improper matter should not be a prerequisite to a motion for mistrial, though some courts so regard it. The safer practice is to move for an instruction to disregard unless you consider that the instruction probably will accentuate the harm. If you do not move for an instruction to disregard the matter, you should consider including in your motion for mistrial a recitation of the fact that you refrain from asking an instruction for the reason that it would serve only to accentuate the harm done.

Obviously the primary consideration in determining whether you should move for a mistrial is your opinion as to how well your client's theory of the case has been presented and received in the trial as a whole, up to and including the incident that furnishes the basis for the possible motion, as compared with how well the case probably would be presented and received in a new trial. Even though the particular incident may have an unfavorable bearing, if the progress of the trial as a whole has been better than could be expected on new trial, you probably should not make the motion unless you know it will be overruled, in which case you may make it as a means of preserving a point of error as insurance. If you have effectively exposed a self-contradiction on the part of your adverse party or one of his principal witnesses, the impact upon the jury may be much greater than will be possible in the next trial, when the witness will be better prepared for the incident than when he was caught unexpectedly. Even the effect of the prejudicial matter itself may be uncertain. In Case 59, for example, is the jury more likely to react adversely to D because of his unfair injection of the remote conviction (particularly after an instruction by the court that it was improper and should be disregarded), or on the other hand is the jury more likely to resolve the conflict in testimony against P because of his being an ex-convict?

You should take into account also the relative advantages and disadvantages to your client from the delay, expense and inconvenience of an additional trial. Extending the period of uncertainty and expense has disadvantages to both sides, but usually they will be so much greater to one party that the delay is relatively an advantage to the other.[7]

7. With reference to the ethical implications of making your choice upon the basis of advantages of delay, there is no general condemnation of dilatory tactics by standards of professional responsibility. Probably the prevailing attitude is that dilatory tactics are wrong when used solely to delay a just cause but quite proper when used to delay a cause considered unjust but hard to prove as such. See H. Drinker, *Legal Ethics* 82–84 (1953). See also American Bar Association, Code of Professional Responsibility DR 7–102 (1969). In *id.*, DR 7–102(A) (1), it is stated that a lawyer shall not "delay a trial . . . when he knows or when it is obvious that such action would serve merely to harass or maliciously injure another."

In cases involving very important or numerous disinterested witnesses, it is often more difficult to secure their cooperation with reference to appearances in a second trial than in the first, since these appearances invariably involve inconvenience to the witnesses and irritation at the necessity of appearing a second time.

The foregoing factors bear on the question whether you really want a new trial. Other questions are involved. Ordinarily the failure to present a motion for mistrial when the grounds therefor arise results in a forfeiture of any right to urge that a fair trial has been denied in any respect because of those grounds. In Case 59, for example, you should move for a mistrial at the time of *D*'s injection of the improper matter, or at least within reasonable time thereafter and before the submission of the case to the jury. Generally, you are not allowed to wait and see first whether the jury will return a verdict in your favor regardless of the improper matter. You may get such a "free ride," as a practical matter, by the court's overruling a good motion for mistrial; some trial judges are inclined to overrule all such motions made after the trial has proceeded for an appreciable time, with the purpose of reconsidering after verdict if the verdict is adverse to the party asserting the motion. Also some decisions permit this "free ride" when improper matter is deliberately injected, on the theory that no litigant should be permitted to profit by such deliberate practices.[8] This reaction may be expected, in exceptional situations, even from courts ordinarily requiring a prompt motion for mistrial. For example, the motion may not be required of one who represents an impecunious client (usually, but not necessarily, the plaintiff) to whom speedy justice is of great importance and to whom the cost and delay of a new trial makes it undesired. The aim of preventing an unscrupulous person from taking advantage of these circumstances by deliberately injecting improper matter, knowing that the disadvantages of delay to the opposing party will preclude his lawyer's moving for a mistrial, supports a rule permitting the motion to be made for the first time after adverse verdict, at least when it appears that the improper matter was deliberately injected. You should consider this possibility in Case 59. One of the important factors in determining whether or not you should present a motion for mistrial is to know the status of the law of your jurisdiction as to whether you may safely wait and hear the jury verdict before making the motion.

Since the prejudicial matters possibly forming a ground for mistrial are likely to be things that you have not anticipated, you may be confronted in trial with an unexpected situation presenting law questions (regarding the right to mistrial and whether you must make your motion immediately) as

---

8. Concerning deliberate injection of improper matter generally, see 6 Wigmore, *Evidence* §1808 (3d ed. 1940).

to which you are not thoroughly familiar with the authorities of your jurisdiction. If this occurs, and you consider it possible that your later investigation of authorities will support the motion, and if you would not be disappointed to have the court grant your motion because of practical considerations, such as special interest in speedy termination of litigation, then you probably should move for mistrial. The principal qualification is that you should avoid making or arguing the motion in the presence of the jury, if possible. Such a motion, if understood by the jury, is dangerously like admitting that you think they are against you, an admission that could hardly fail to have effect on any who are then undecided. Another qualification to the proposition that you should move for mistrial when in doubt is that you should avoid making such motions on frivolous grounds, since that practice would probably cause both the trial and appellate courts to view less seriously a motion upon borderline grounds in the same case, or even in another case if you develop a reputation for such motions.

§5.5 Motions for separation of witnesses

Should you move that witnesses be separated and excluded from the courtroom?

In all jurisdictions some provision is made for the exclusion of witnesses from the courtroom, except when testifying, and for other measures designed to prevent one witness from being influenced consciously or subconsciously by hearing what another says in court or elsewhere. The procedure used for this purpose is variously called separation, exclusion, or sequestration of witnesses. It is often governed by specific statutes or rules, and in some areas the procedure is referred to as invoking the rule of separation, or merely by the shorthand expression, "invoking the rule." The extent of discretion of the trial judge and the degree of restriction placed upon the witnesses varies considerably. In general the witness is ordered to remain outside the courtroom except when he is called to testify, and to refrain from discussion of his testimony or the facts of the case with anyone other than the lawyers in the case. [1]

It is an interesting fact that in some localities, in nearly all cases contested on the facts, one party or the other requests separation of witnesses, and often both parties desire it because neither wholly trusts the other party and his witnesses. On the other hand, in other areas the procedure is used only in exceptional cases. This variation in practice reflects a difference of opinion among lawyers regarding the advisability of invoking the procedure. Separation of witnesses has great advantages to you when you hope by cross-examination to break down the testimony of any of the adverse

---

1. As to conferring with a lawyer, see §2.14.

witnesses. Techniques of cross-examination used against one witness are much less likely to be effective against another who has been present during the examination of the first. Your chance of exposing deliberately fabricated testimony is greatly improved if you have the opportunity of examining the several adverse witnesses separately, none hearing the examination of another. For example, your chance of developing, during cross-examination, conflicts in details not developed on direct examination [2] almost totally disappears if witnesses are not effectively separated.

It is undoubtedly also true that the testimony of honest witnesses may be affected by the extent to which they have heard others testify. They are naturally influenced by the ideas and forms of expression used by others — inclined to be more conservative in their expression of differences and more positive in points of agreement. Also the adverse effect of unfamiliarity with courtroom procedures may be reduced by the witness' remaining in the courtroom and observing the proceedings during the testimony of others. [3] Whether such factors as these are in favor of or in opposition to your moving for separation of witnesses and exclusion from the courtroom depends upon the relative effect that they would probably have upon your own witnesses and upon your adversary's witnesses.

Another factor you should consider is the application of the order of exclusion to witnesses whose testimony might be given much more expeditiously if they have heard preceding testimony of one or more others. For example, if you plan to use an expert, you may choose to have him hear all of the testimony of given witnesses so you can call for his opinion on the basis of that testimony and without the necessity of stating long hypotheses in your questions. [4] Particularly if it is the adverse party whose testimony you want your expert to hear, this method may be preferable because of the expert's opportunity to observe the party as well as what he says. If you follow this plan, you should insure that your expert hears all of the relevant testimony, to avoid the claim that the basis for his opinions is incomplete or uncertain.

The rules of procedure generally allow for exceptions to the rule of exclusion, at least in the discretion of the trial judge. As already noted, experts may be permitted to remain in the courtroom to enable them to hear testimony that is to be used as a foundation for their own testimony. An exception is also generally made for experts whose presence the lawyer desires for consultation. The parties to a case also are customarily excepted from the order of exclusion, and this exception applies to a designated representative of a corporation or association, as well as to individual parties.

2. See §§3.12, 3.15.
3. See §2.10.
4. The question in which you ask the witness to base his opinion on testimony he has heard is, of course, a form of hypothetical question. See generally §§2.19, 3.31.

§5.6 Arranging for proceedings to be reported

Should you arrange for a reporter for proceedings for which reporting services are not provided?

All jurisdictions have provisions for the reporting of at least part of the proceedings in the more important trial courts. These provisions often do not extend to some of the trial courts dealing with smaller claims, or in the more important courts to certain proceedings such as interrogation of the jury panel, statements and arguments or summation of counsel to the jury, and proceedings in chambers or out of the presence of the jury during jury trial. As a matter of course, the courts customarily permit the reporting of the additional proceedings by the official reporter, whenever arrangements are made with the reporter by one of the lawyers; in some jurisdictions, no special permission from the court is required, and no motion to the court is expected. In case of doubt, however, you should request leave of the court before you call upon the official reporter to report proceedings that he is not required by law to report, or before you call upon any reporter to report proceedings in a court that has no official reporter. It is customary for the reporter to make a charge for his services in such reporting, and ordinarily this charge is not taxable as costs.

The difficulty of preparing, for consideration on motions for new trial or on appeal, a satisfactory record of proceedings not reported verbatim is usually sufficient reason to warrant the comparatively small expense involved in arranging for reporting of the proceedings. If a point of error is based upon the proceedings, the verbatim record will generally be less expensive to prepare, as well as more accurate and useful, than a record prepared by other means. The possibility that something might occur during the proceedings that will support your assertion of a point of error strongly indicates that you should arrange for reporting services. Often an incidental effect of the arrangements is to cause an adversary who is inclined normally to make use of inflammatory and improper comments to be more cautious about staying within bounds.

In jurisdictions where summations or arguments to the jury are not reported without special arrangements, most lawyers representing the party against whom arguments based on sympathy or bias might be effectively made (usually the defendant) follow the consistent practice of arranging for reporting of the arguments of the opposing lawyer. Some also arrange for the reporting of their own arguments to avoid any claim that otherwise improper arguments of the adversary were invited by the arguments of the complaining lawyer.

§5.7 Amending pleadings during trial

Should you move for leave to amend your pleadings during trial?

Under the federal rules and those patterned after them, the occasions for considering amendment to pleadings will be rare if you have properly prepared your case in advance of trial. The pleadings in those jurisdictions are of such general character[1] that ordinarily only your failure to anticipate a major issue in the case, or your misunderstanding the burden of pleading, would lead to a need for your filing an amendment to support a theory you desire to urge at trial. It is possible, of course, for issues to arise unexpectedly in trial despite careful preparation, as in the case of unanticipated evidence on cross-examination supporting some theory favorable to your client.

In those jurisdictions where the parties are expected to plead in detail, the pleadings being used to define the issues in the case and give notice of contentions to be urged, greater need for trial amendments is apparent. It is in these jurisdictions that an omission from the pleadings is more likely to have serious consequences. A lawyer faced with such consequences sorely needs the amendment. It is unfortunately true that these jurisdictions are often the ones in which trial amendments meet with less favor. A trend toward allowing trial amendments has been established, however, and most of the trial judges given discretion in the matter allow them freely, particularly in the absence of indications that the other lawyer is actually surprised and unprepared to meet the issue raised by the amendment.

If the rules of procedure in your jurisdiction permit the filing of trial amendments and you can satisfy the conditions prerequisite to leave for an amendment, it is usually advisable to seek the leave. The problems in connection with which the need for amendment may arise are varied. For example, it may arise when you offer evidence and your adversary objects on the ground of want of pleadings to support its admissibility;[2] or when you seek a special issue, interrogatory, or instruction in the court's charge to which your adversary objects on the ground of want of pleadings to support its submission;[3] or when you move for judgment[4] and your adversary contends that your pleadings do not support a theory you urge.

You should consider offering a trial amendment when you recognize the possibility that the pleadings do not support one of your theories and that your adversary may be withholding his contention to that effect with the purpose of raising it so late in the trial that you cannot cure the omission. In this connection, the federal courts and those of some other jurisdictions apply a rule that pleadings are treated as if amended by operation of law when issues are tried without objection. You must recognize the possibility, however, that your adversary may successfully urge that the issue was not tried because he considered your contentions and evidence as bearing upon

1. See §10.1.
2. See §4.8.
3. See §6.8.
4. See §5.3.

a theory expressed in your pleadings and not a separate theory that you did not plead. Since evidence is often relevant to more than one independent ground of claim or defense, this danger is a material one and supports the practice of seeking leave for amendment of your pleadings when you are in doubt as to their sufficiency, even though your adversary has not objected. The disadvantage of this practice is that it may suggest to your adversary a contention that will be troublesome to you, particularly if there is doubt as to whether the court will grant you leave to amend or danger that the court would grant your adversary's motion for withdrawal of his announcement of readiness, on the ground of surprise and unpreparedness to meet the new issue presented by your amendment.[5]

§5.8 Seeking a continuance based on surprise

Should you move for leave to withdraw your announcement of readiness for trial because of surprise?

Interests in the efficient administration of justice compel the courts to look with disfavor upon the delay and the duplication of effort and expense incident to granting new trials. In many situations, those interests yield to the more important interests in fair disposition of the controversy. It is nevertheless true that injustice may be done in individual cases because of the refusal of the courts to allow the period of litigation to be extended. One of the situations presenting this possibility is that arising when counsel is surprised by some issue of law or fact raised during trial. The surprise may occur because of inadequacy of preparations for trial, in which case the courts generally grant no relief unless it is quite probable, and not merely possible, that material harm will be done and that an injustice will result because of the lawyer's ineffective representation of the client. If you should find yourself unprepared because of your failure to anticipate an issue, however, particularly in your earlier years of practice when the trial judge is more likely to be sympathetic regarding your shortcomings, you should consider urging a motion for leave to withdraw your announcement of readiness for trial and for continuance or postponement to allow you time for preparation. Such a motion is also appropriate and even more likely to be granted when you have been caught by surprise under circumstances of excusable failure to anticipate and prepare for the issue. A clear example is the case of injection of issues not covered by the pleadings but allowed under trial amendment of the pleadings.[1] In urging such a motion, when it appears that your adversary has deliberately used surprise tactics,[2]

5. See §5.8.
1. See §5.7.
2. See §1.3.

you should emphasize the element of surprise since it has material bearing on the reaction of the ordinary judge to the question of fairness, as between the parties, of granting the motion.

The disadvantages of the motion for leave to withdraw an announcement of readiness for trial are those associated with delay of litigation[3] and are ordinarily outweighed by the advantages of time for further preparation if the surprise issue is one of material importance. There is, of course, the added disadvantage of difficulty in relations with your client because of the risk that he will blame you for delay, but this is less serious than the consequences of clear failure to develop his case properly.

The order that the court makes when granting a motion of the type considered in this section may be either a continuance of the case until a later date, at which time the trial will be commenced anew, or a recess of hours or days, the trial being resumed before the same jury and without beginning anew. Generally, it is preferable that you seek the former order because of the danger that the jury will hold you responsible for the delay and may also be less inclined to rely upon evidence that you present after a change in or addition to your theories during trial, occasioned by the surprise matter.

§5.9 Seeking leave to reopen the evidence; taking a voluntary nonsuit

CASE 60. *P* sues *D Trucking Company* for personal injuries sustained when, as he was walking across a street intersection at night, he was struck by a speeding truck. After hitting *P,* the truck swerved into a lamp pole, and the driver fled from the scene. You have obtained pretrial admissions that the truck was owned by *D Trucking Company* and was regularly driven by *T,* who had been assigned to deliver a load out of the city earlier in the day and was scheduled to be back to the company lot shortly before the time the accident occurred. *D Company* denies that *T* was the driver, contending that *T* had returned the truck to the lot and it was thereafter stolen. *T* is suspected of driving the truck at the time of the accident, but other witnesses have given statements supporting an alibi, and because of want of sufficient evidence, no criminal charges have been filed. *T* voluntarily left the employ of *D Company* two weeks after the accident. As *P*'s lawyer, you have undertaken to obtain *T*'s deposition. He has declined to answer pertinent questions, asserting the privilege against self-incrimination.

Under the case decisions of your jurisdiction, it is your theory that evidence that the truck was owned by *D Trucking Company* raises a "presumption" that it was driven by a servant in the scope of employment, which presumption will disappear only after *D Trucking Company* produces as witnesses all persons in its employ at the time of the accident, or accounts for them

3. See §5.4.

by unavailability, and establishes by the testimony of those produced that the truck was not being operated by a servant in the scope of employment. At trial, you offer the admissions but have no other evidence on the identity of the driver or on scope of employment. You rely upon the presumption. In the course of argument on the defendant's motion for directed verdict, the court indicates disagreement with your theory of presumption and states a view that the motion for directed verdict is sound.

Should you move for leave to reopen the evidence?
Should you take a voluntary nonsuit?

You may sometime find after resting your case, as many lawyers have found during their early trial experience, that you have omitted some important evidence, either through oversight or because of your interpreting decisions as to the need for the evidence contrary to the interpretation urged by your adversary. You may realize through your own initiative that there is a gap in your proof, recognizing the problem as you are preparing for trial of the case (as in Case 60), or you may realize that there is a gap as you develop the case in court, or you may be jolted into the realization by a sound motion for directed verdict urged by your adversary. If it appears to be in the interest of fair disposition of the case upon the merits, the trial judge usually will be inclined to exercise such discretion as he has in favor of allowing you to withdraw your announcement that you rest and to reopen the evidence and cure the omission. Usually you should move for such an order by the court if there is any hope of producing evidence that would cure the omission, since ordinarily no harm will be done by the effort, even if it fails. You should consider using this procedure even though you regard the grounds for directed verdict as unsound and the court indicates an intention to overrule the motion for directed verdict. There is no reason for taking a chance of reversal that you can avoid without incurring other disadvantages in the process of avoiding it. Your purpose is not to prove that your theories of law are better than your adversary's, or that your judgment is better, but to insure a final disposition on the merits for your client. You should not be stubborn to the point of gambling your client's interests unnecessarily on your own opinions of the law.[1]

In exceptional situations, disadvantages weigh heavily against your using all possible witnesses in the hope of supplying an omission, even when you have indications that the court considers the motion for directed verdict sound. Case 60 presents a problem of this nature. On the issues of identity of the driver and scope of employment, your only known hope for favorable evidence, as distinguished from the presumption you urge, is to get a direct admission from *T* or some admission of circumstantial evidence from other

1. See §1.4.

employees of *D Company*. If you call any of them as witnesses, however, there is danger that you will be held bound by their testimony[2] contrary to the presumption you urge; particularly is this danger present in the case of *T*, who is no longer in the employ of *D Company*, and as to whom it is less likely that you would be permitted to use a rule or statute concerning hostile witnesses. If the views of your adversary and the court regarding your alleged presumption are sound, your case is probably hopeless. On the other hand, if you are correct about the law, your case will be certain to go to the jury (though it may be necessary to appeal and get a new trial first) unless your adversary calls and persuades *T* to testify fully; in that event, you will at least have your opportunity to obtain a direct admission or admission of enough circumstantial evidence to raise your issue. These factors indicate that you should stand on your position and not ask leave to reopen the evidence in these circumstances.

Should you take a voluntary nonsuit without prejudice on the merits (or its equivalent, referred to variously as a motion for dismissal without prejudice, discontinuance, or non prosequitur)? This is not always possible under the rules of procedure. In some jurisdictions the plaintiff has a right to take a voluntary nonsuit without prejudice at various stages of trial,[3] the extreme being any time before judgment or verdict, subject only to his paying all costs of court. In other jurisdictions, this is permitted only with leave of court or by agreement, in the absence of which the dismissal would be with prejudice on the merits. If the period of limitations on the claim has not expired, so as to make the filing of a new suit impractical, the delay of starting the litigation over again will be more acceptable than a final adverse judgment because of your failure or inability at the time to prove existing facts that are essential to make a case. In the circumstances of Case 60, there would be an advantage in taking the voluntary nonsuit in the hope that before another trial you would have been able to develop some affirmative evidence on the issues of identity of the driver and scope of employment, and there might be an additional advantage of filing the new suit in a different jurisdiction where the presumption you urge is more clearly applicable (if that choice exists, you should have considered it, of course, in your original selection of the forum[4]). You should weigh these possibilities against your client's interest in getting promptly a favorable decision in the appellate courts on your theory of presumption. The decision you reach will depend greatly on the degree of your confidence in your legal theory.

If you find that you have omitted evidence that, though not essential to your presenting a case, you wish to offer for purposes of persuasion, you

2. See §2.2.
3. Vanderbilt, *Minimum Standards of Judicial Administration* 251–254 (1949).
4. See §10.3.

may have another opportunity to present it on rebuttal, after your adversary has closed his evidence.[5] This may also be true when there is a dispute as to whether the evidence is necessary for making a case, if the court has not sustained a motion for directed verdict; in some jurisdictions, however, the alleged error in overruling the motion for directed verdict is considered upon the basis of evidence produced before the motion was presented, and without consideration of evidence offered later.[6]

Ordinarily reopening your evidence will not be feasible unless the evidence you omitted is comparatively important. As a tactical matter, it probably is not a point on which you desire the special emphasis it would thus receive. Also, you will find the court less inclined to grant such a motion when you wish to offer evidence for purposes of persuasion than when you wish to cure an omission so you will have a case sufficient to go to the factfinder.

§5.10 Seeking the right to open and close

CASE 61. *P Utility Company* institutes proceedings for condemnation of land owned by *D*. As *D*'s lawyer, you contend that the condemnation proceedings are invalid, and you claim a substantially higher valuation for the land than that urged by *P Utility Company*. In your jurisdiction, fact issues in condemnation cases are subject to jury trial.

Should you move for leave to open and close?

Customarily the right to open and close summations or arguments to the jury and to open the evidence is given to the party with the burden of proof on the case as a whole.[1] This is a very valuable right from the point of view of tactics, because of the obvious advantages of getting your theory of the case before the jury first and last. Usually the answer to the question who has this right is clear and not subject to being affected by tactical maneuvers. It is therefore the exceptional case in which the problem of affirmative action to secure the right is raised. Case 61 is such an exception if we assume (with support in some authorities[2]) that *P Utility Company* has the burden on the condemnation case as a whole, and therefore has the right to open and close, but that *D*, the landowner, has the burden upon the issue of value of the property condemned. In such circumstances, by conceding as *D*'s lawyer that the condemnation proceedings are valid, you could eliminate all issues

---

5. See §2.38.
6. See §5.2.
1. See generally 6 Wigmore, *Evidence* §1866 (3d ed. 1940).
2. *E.g.,* Fort Worth & D.N. Ry. v. Johnson, 125 Tex. 634, 84 S.W. 2d 232 (Comm'n App. 1935).

from the case other than the issue of value, thus leaving the case as one in which D has the burden on the case as a whole and entitling D to open and close. Your decision will depend on how confident you are regarding your contention that the condemnation proceedings are invalid, and how seriously your client prefers his land to compensation for it (the compensation usually being more generous than he could receive in a private sale, at least where jury trial of condemnation cases is permitted, since in most localities juries are inclined to resolve doubts in favor of the landowner and against the condemnor). It is usually extremely difficult to establish invalidity of condemnation proceedings, in view of the recognized discretion of the condemnor with regard to the particular site or route chosen for a structure or right of way. In most cases the sound decision would be to concede the validity of the condemnation proceedings and seek leave to open and close, in the hope that the tactical advantages would improve your chances of obtaining very favorable findings on the issue of value.

CHAPTER VI

THE CHARGE

§6.1 Preparation of the charge

Although the charge to the jury is the *"court's* charge," the lawyers can and should play a vital role in its preparation. At the least, each lawyer has an opportunity to present requested instructions or questions and to present objections to the charge as finally given by the court. Many trial judges customarily invite or expect more active participation by the lawyers in the original preparation of a tentative charge. This is especially true in jurisdictions where the charge is prepared in writing. Often this participation takes the form of preparation of the entire tentative charge by one of the lawyers or by each lawyer's preparation of that portion relative to his or her claims or affirmative defenses.

Regardless of the extent to which the trial judge permits or expects participation by the lawyers in preparation of the charge, full preparation of your case requires thorough consideration to the charge both from the point of view of instructions or questions that you will ask to be submitted and from the point of view of possible objections to those that may be given by the court or requested by your adversary. This consideration is a part of your preparation of the law of your case,[1] and you should complete it in advance of the beginning of trial (at least until you have acquired sufficient experience in the type of case involved that you will not need to consider authorities regarding most aspects of the charge). There is rarely time for satisfactory briefing of any point after the trial begins.

§6.2 Form of the charge

The types of charges used in jury cases may be divided into three major groups: (1) general charge; (2) general charge supplemented by special in-

1. See §9.2.

237

terrogatories; (3) charge requiring a special verdict.[1] Spurred by the influ-ence of the federal rules, use of the second form of charge is increasing. Since the rules authorizing it commonly provide that it shall be used only at the discretion of the trial judge, the extent to which it merits your consideration will depend in many instances upon the attitude of the individual judge be-fore whom your case is being tried. In some of the jurisdictions not recog-nizing the second form of charge, the trial judge may in his discretion use either the first or the third form. A minority of jurisdictions leave determina-tion of the form of the charge to the litigants.[2]

Aside from these fundamental differences in the form of the charge, the variations in detailed application among the different jurisdictions are great. It is generally advisable and often necessary, rather than relying on general sources, to study local rules, statutes, decisions, and form books or pattern jury instructions as you consider the charge. Despite all the variations in de-tail, however, there are certain fundamental tactical principles of general application, and these are the subject of the present chapter.

The particular form in which an instruction or question is phrased may materially affect the verdict. Obviously different shades of interpretation may mean the difference between a verdict for one party and a verdict for the other on a close question.

The relationship between the phrasing of instructions or questions and the phrasing of testimony may be a significant influence on the verdict. As a question is related more directly in the minds of the jurors to a statement made in the testimony, the verdict is more likely to be based upon the jury's judgment of the credibility of the witness and less upon their interpretation of the conflicting implications of statements of one or more witnesses.

The clarity of the question or instruction is another matter of form that may have material bearing on the verdict. Particularly for the interests of the party whose case has more sympathetic appeal, it is vital that the charge be phrased in simple and clear form to avoid misunderstanding by the jury. This factor is one of special importance because of the tendency of lawyers and judges to make the charge complicated by numerous qualifications and exceptions and by the use of legal terminology that is familiar to judges and lawyers but not to jurors. The definitions of legal terms used in the charge are inadequate to meet this problem since they are generally complicated themselves. It is difficult for one not familiar with the terminology to carry in his mind, as he reads an instruction or question, the meanings given to the special terms by definitions stated elsewhere in the charge. The written charge is somewhat better than the oral charge from this point of view, since a conscientious jury may at least refer to it and study it.

1. See Vanderbilt, *Minimum Standards of Judicial Administration* 237–243 (1949).
2. *Id.*

§6.3 The advocate's perspective concerning the charge

Rarely is a specific phrasing of an instruction or question required. Instead, the requirements of law may be satisfied by any number of different forms of expression. Within the limitations of the legal requirements there is a broad field for discretion of the trial judge and for advocacy by the lawyers with regard to the judge's exercise of that discretion. The borderlines where the legal requirements impose limitations on that discretion are frequently uncertain. From these factors arises a necessity for balancing the chances of reversible error in the form of instruction or question that you prefer, on the one hand, against, on the other hand, the improvement in your chances of obtaining a favorable verdict by the use of that particular form, in lieu of one that is approved by authorities or accepted by your adversary, and the improvement in your chances of obtaining a new trial if the court refuses to use your form. Even though you think you are right in your position, it is folly to insist upon the letter of your supposed legal right if by doing so you do not materially improve your chances of obtaining either a favorable jury verdict or a new trial in the event of an adverse verdict.[1] If the form of instruction or question submitted by your adversary is clearly within bounds permitted by the authorities and there is doubt as to whether your preferred form is also within those bounds, the temporary "victory" of persuading the trial judge to use your form may turn out to be your undoing because your form is held erroneous on appeal. You should not take this risk unless the chances of a jury verdict favorable to your client are in your judgment materially better under the form you prefer. If you think they are materially better, your decision must turn on balancing the advantages of the improvement in your chances of a favorable verdict against the disadvantages of increasing the risk that a new trial will be granted against you after you obtain a favorable verdict. If your preferred form of instruction is clearly proper, there is no disadvantage in insisting upon it, other than that of personal reaction of the trial judge. If either of the forms being considered would comply with legal requirements, advantages are solely in the influence of the particular form upon the probable verdict. If conformity of your opponent's proposal to legal requirements is doubtful, the advantage of a possible ground of error and new trial is added in the event the judge adopts your opponent's form rather than yours.

§6.4 Limitations on value of case authorities

Case decisions approving or disapproving particular forms of instructions or questions may be quite misleading. Differences in facts between a re-

1. See §1.4.

ported case and your own and differences in the contentions urged by the lawyers in the reported case and those urged or to be urged in yours may materially affect applicability of previous decisions to your own case. Rarely does a court do more in an opinion than hold the questioned form proper or improper under the given facts and in the light of the specific contentions urged by the lawyers. An instruction that is proper in one case, because of conceded facts, may be wholly improper in another because those facts are in dispute under the evidence. An instruction that is upheld in one case against specific objections may have been subject to other objections that counsel in that case did not raise either from oversight or because of tactical considerations. It is dangerous to assume accuracy of the proposition, which you will often find lawyers arguing, that a given instruction is proper because it was approved in some previous case.

§6.5 Considering all possible interpretations of the evidence

When you are considering the proposed phrasing of questions or instructions to the jury, you should consider all potential theories of fact that might reasonably be reached under the evidence. You should test the questions and instructions that you request, and those that the court proposes to give, from this point of view to insure that they do not fail to take into account some of the possible interpretations of the evidence under which you would be entitled to judgment. This is especially important in the preparation of a charge requiring a special verdict, since a favorable judgment generally must be based upon specific favorable findings. Omitting to inquire of the jury whether they will make some of the possible findings that would be favorable may therefore result in loss of a case that you might otherwise have won. Conversely, it will help you find errors that make the charge unduly favorable to your adversary if you test it by considering what finding would be made by the jury under various possible interpretations of the evidence.

§6.6 Disclosure of the legal effect of jury findings

When a charge requiring a special verdict is used, the extent to which the charge discloses to the jury the effect of their answers to specific questions is an important factor. Under a minority rule the jurors are instructed to find their answers according to the facts without regard to the effect of their answers, and the lawyers are not permitted to state directly the effect of the answers during their arguments. The charge sometimes indirectly discloses the effect of the answers, or contributes readily to a realization of the effect by the arrangement of questions, by the phrasing of particular questions, or by implications of instructions accompanying the questions. For example, if the damages questions are predicated on affirmative answers to other issues (the jury being told to answer the damages questions only in the event of affirmative answers to certain other issues), it is obvious to any juror that the plaintiff will not recover unless the issues referred to in the predicate are answered affirmatively.[1] From the point of view of the lawyer representing the party whose case has less sympathetic appeal (usually the defendant) it is important to examine the charge carefully for indirect disclosures of the legal effect of answers.

§6.7 Objections compared with requests

In your preparations regarding the charge, you should consider distinctions between the legal and tactical effect of objections, on the one hand, and requests, on the other. Rules of procedure sometimes make a distinction between the two as to form, time and manner of presentation, and effectiveness to preserve error committed by an adverse ruling.[1] There are also differences between the two from the point of view of tactical use. Because of the great latitude for discretion[2] in the phrasing of issues or instructions without violation of legal limitations, objections are often wholly ineffective in circumstances in which a well-phrased request might be favorably received by the trial judge. Furthermore, a judge generally is more receptive to argument for a better form of instruction or question than to mere objection to one that has been proposed. The objection may be considered primarily from the point of view of determining whether the charge as it stands is legally erroneous, rather than from the point of view of determining whether it can be improved. Merely objecting is a less constructive form of criticism of the charge than supplementing the objection with a proposed form of instruction or question that meets the objection.

§6.8 Your adversary's objections and requests

Consider fully all objections and requests made by your adversary. It seems to be a natural tendency to take issue with the opposing lawyer's proposed modifications of the charge, and particularly to defend one's own requested instructions or questions. A better approach is to concede everything that you can without agreeing to materially unfavorable changes. If the change proposed by your adversary probably will influence the verdict, or if there is serious danger that it will, then the advantage to be gained by keeping the charge as you prefer it may warrant taking the risk of reversal if your opinion on the point of law involved in the objection should be con-

1. *Cf.* 7–18.
1. *E.g.*, Federal Rule 51. *Cf.* Federal Rule 49(a).
2. See §6.3.

trary to that of the court of final authority on the point. On the other hand if, viewing the objection as impartially as you can rather than from the point of view of argument, you have any doubts about the point of law raised by the objection, and if the change proposed by your adversary in all probability will not affect the verdict of the jury, let the change be made. The duty of avoiding reversible error in the charge is not solely that of the court; it is also your duty to your client to insure that a favorable verdict for your client is not set aside because of your stubborn refusal to agree to a change in the charge that should have been made. Though the doctrine of harmless error generally prevents reversal for an error in the charge that deprives your adversary of only a theoretical right and in all probability would have had no influence on the verdict in the case, still the risk of reversal, small though it may be in jurisdictions applying that doctrine, is one you should not take except when you gain some advantage that warrants it.

If your adversary makes an objection on the ground of want of pleadings to support an issue or instruction, consider the advisability of requesting leave to amend your pleadings.[1] If your adversary makes an objection on the ground of want of evidence, you should consider filing a motion for leave to reopen,[2] though the trial judge is likely to view that type of motion with less favor than a motion for leave to amend pleadings.

§6.9 Time of objections and requests

The time of presenting requests and objections may have material effect on the court's response to them. The rules of procedure generally prescribe a final point beyond which you may not present requests or objections. Many trial judges will expect to receive at least your requests, and sometimes also your objections to your adversary's requests, substantially in advance of the time limit provided by the rules. Obviously, your requests receive more favorable consideration when you comply with the wishes of the trial judge in these matters rather than wait until he has completed a tentative charge and then assume the burden of persuading him to revise it.

It is customary in most courts, and a requirement in some, that you present a copy of your requests to your adversary at the time you present the requests to the court for consideration.[1] This practice makes it necessary

1. See §5.7.
2. See §5.9.
1. Also, it is generally improper under professional standards to present requests to the court without a copy to your adversary. See American Bar Association, Code of Professional Responsibility DR 7–110 (1969). In general, *id.,* paragraph (B), prohibits a lawyer from communicating with the judge in an adversary proceeding unless, if the communication is written, "he promptly delivers a copy of the writing to opposing counsel or to the adverse party if he is not represented by a lawyer" and, if it is

that you consider the effect of presenting your theory of the charge before the evidence is closed. If your adversary has not correctly anticipated your requests, the resulting notice of them before the evidence is closed may cause an improvement in the presentation of the opposing case through additional evidence on issues previously overlooked or given inadequate consideration.[2] The choice as to timing of your requests will therefore involve a weighing of conflicting factors in some cases. The trial judge usually has a decided preference about the matter, however, and that preference ordinarily should control your timing of the disclosure of your requests and of your objections to the proposals of your adversary.

§6.10 Negative instructions

Negative instructions are frequently of questionable value. This is not to say that you should never request negative instructions but only that you should be very cautious about doing so. If you request negative instructions, phrase them to avoid arousing the minds of the jurors to consideration of the very things they are designed to exclude from consideration. For example, in relation to the damages issue in a death case, an instruction that says in effect that the jury will consider "the following elements of damages, and none other" (then listing the proper elements) is preferable from defendant's point of view to one that says "you will not take into consideration the survivors' loss of love and companionship of the deceased, the despair and loneliness of the bereaved, or the empty chair at the family fireside." It is obvious that the latter type of instruction may result in a higher damages finding rather than lower. Even jurors who try to comply with the instruction are likely to feel that they should grant a generous measure of compensation for the properly considered elements of compensation, since so many real consequences are uncompensated.

§6.11 Instructions on damages

An instruction on damages is generally more favorable to the plaintiff if broken down into numerous separate elements. This is true because of the added emphasis given to the damages question and the likelihood of a higher total when elements of damages are computed separately and added together than when a single figure is estimated. This idea is expressed in the saying among trial lawyers that "the cash register rings more when it rings twice."

---

oral, "upon adequate notice to opposing counsel or to the adverse party if he is not represented by a lawyer." See also H. Drinker, *Legal Ethics* 198 (1953).

2. As to use of surprise tactics generally, see §1.3.

Separation of damages elements has other advantages from the point of view of the plaintiff in those jurisdictions using a charge requiring a special verdict. If there is an error in an instruction on one of the elements of damages in a general charge, it may be impossible to determine what part of the damages finding is clearly not influenced by the error. The plaintiff may be allowed to rely upon the finding after deduction of the maximum that the jury might have allowed for the improper item under the erroneous instruction and the evidence (for example, when future medical expenses have not been properly proved but are allowed by the instruction, the maximum figure for such expenses referred to in the evidence would be deducted from the finding, and the verdict for the remainder allowed to stand, in some jurisdictions). At best, the plaintiff may be required to suffer a remittitur that probably is in excess of the amount actually allowed by the jury for the erroneous item. On the other hand, if separate findings on the different elements of damages are required by the charge, then if the inclusion of a particular damages finding in the judgment is error, it affects only that element, leaving the plaintiff with a recovery of the remainder rather than a new trial, at least when he prefers that disposition. Also, if there is grave doubt about any element from the legal point of view, the trial judge may submit it to the jury separately and avoid the necessity of a new trial in the event the appellate court disagrees as to whether the element of damages is a proper one. As the plaintiff's lawyer you are faced with a difficult tactical problem if the questionable element is, in your opinion, one that may support a substantial finding but probably will not be allowed by the court of final authority, though you find some support for its allowance. If you urge the inclusion of the element, even in a separate question to the jury, it may conceivably result in a lower finding on other damages issues since the jury will be somewhat influenced by consideration of the total they think they are awarding the plaintiff, including the questionable item. If the questionable item is later held improper, your net recovery is less than if you had never urged its inclusion in the charge. On the other hand, of course, the total recovery would be increased by the inclusion of the questionable item if it should later be held proper. Your choice must be based upon assessment of the probable amount of the additional finding and its effect on other findings, together with your best judgment as to the probable ruling of the court of final authority on the propriety of the questionable element.

CHAPTER VII

THE JURY

§7.1 The jury as a factor in trial tactics and methods

The decisive issues in the majority of litigated cases are fact issues. Though few cases go through the entire process of litigation without serious contest on some law points, the answers to most questions of law involved in the typical controversy will be indicated clearly by precedent, which is usually though not always controlling.[1] On the other hand, not only are jurors not bound by precedent but also they are not even allowed to know officially of fact findings in previous trials that may have presented analogous issues. Decisions on issues of fact are less predictable and more subject to the influences of effective advocacy than those on issues of law. Compromise settlements dispose of the great majority of even those controversies that cannot be resolved before the filing of suit. The fact that uncertainty is typically greater as to issues of fact than as to issues of law leads to greater difficulty in settlement of disputes involving serious controversy on fact issues than in settlement of those involving only law issues, with the result that in the cases reaching trial the facts are typically more in dispute than the applicable law.

In view of the place of fact issues in litigation, your thoroughly understanding the applicable rules of law is but the beginning of your preparation for being an effective trial lawyer. This is not to say that command of the rules of law is unimportant or that it does not deserve all the attention it customarily receives, and more. But being a trial lawyer involves another ingredient as well — call it what you will — the art, science, or skill of effective advocacy on fact issues.

Most fact issues, though not all in any jurisdiction, are subject to being submitted to jury determination upon timely request of either party. The

1. *Cf.* B. Cardozo, *The Nature of the Judicial Process* 34, 112, 149–167 (1921).

effect of having a jury becomes a major consideration both in determining whether to request jury trial[2] and in determining appropriate tactics and methods of advocacy during trial. This book is concerned primarily with methods directed toward persuasion of the factfinder (jury or judge), and the title of this chapter, taken in a broad sense, might embrace nearly all of the subject matter of the entire book. Distinctive problems encountered in specific aspects of trial are discussed, however, in other chapters. This chapter concerns problems associated with counsel's role in the selection of the trial jury, relations with the jury during and after trial, and methods of persuasion both during argument to the jury and during the trial generally.

§7.2 Requesting jury trial

Should you request a jury trial?

Customarily, statutes or rules of procedure require affirmative action on the part of one desiring a jury trial to have the case placed upon the jury docket; cases are assigned to the nonjury docket in the absence of that affirmative action.[1] Time limits for making the request for jury trial vary, and in most jurisdictions the trial judge has discretion to grant requests made too late to entitle the requesting party to jury trial as a matter of right. The attitudes of individual judges on this matter vary, but in general there is a tendency to grant a request for jury trial though made late, if it does not appear that the request is being made for the purpose of delaying trial. Nevertheless, in the early stages of development of the litigation you should consider the question whether jury trial is preferable from the point of view of your client. Unless the other party requests a jury, your failure to make a request has the effect of choosing nonjury trial, a choice you should make deliberately and not merely from lack of attention to the question.

The desirability of jury trial may sometimes influence your choice of a forum,[2] since the scope of jury trials varies in the different jurisdictions. For example, in cases involving application of principles of equity, no jury is available in some jurisdictions except for advisory purposes, in others a jury is available in certain circumstances or for limited issues, and in one jurisdiction (Texas) fact issues bearing on equitable relief are determinable by a jury as a matter of right, upon demand by either party, to the same extent as fact issues bearing on relief of the type granted at law.[3]

It is generally considered that a jury is more likely to be subject to sym-

2. See §7.2.
1. See, *e.g.,* Federal Rule 38.
2. See §10.3.
3. *Ex parte* Allison, 99 Tex. 455, 90 S.W. 870 (1906).

pathetic appeals than a judge,[4] though there are doubtlessly individual exceptions to this proposition. The general acceptance of this idea is a major factor in accounting for the fact that juries are customarily demanded by the plaintiffs in negligence cases, and in other cases by the party whose circumstances have greater sympathetic appeal. This custom has become so prevalent that it is followed as a routine in most areas. Other factors that may have an important bearing on the advisability of requesting a jury in a particular case include the following points of difference between jury and nonjury[5] trial: fewer new trials are granted in nonjury cases;[6] litigation is concluded more promptly by nonjury trial;[7] the danger of misunderstanding of the issues, particularly in very complicated cases, is more serious in the jury trial;[8] and probably the results of jury trial are somewhat less predictable than those of nonjury trial.[9]

Although the existence of a dispute on a material fact issue is essential to proper submission of the case to a jury, the fact that under your theory of the case there is no fact issue does not necessarily mean that you should not request a jury. The point at which this determination of existence or nonexistence of a fact issue has been traditionally determined is by motion for directed verdict after the plaintiff rests or after both parties rest. Your choice of jury or nonjury trial will be made much earlier, but will be primarily influenced by your preference as to whether judge or jury should consider the fact issues in the event the judge disagrees with your position that your client is entitled to judgment as a matter of law; other factors mentioned above, such as the effect on speed of disposition of the litigation, may also have a bearing. In many jurisdictions it is now possible to raise your contention of lack of a genuine dispute on a material fact issue by summary judgment proceedings[10] in advance of ordinary trial setting, regardless of whether the case has been placed on the jury docket at the instance of your adversary or yourself, or remains on the nonjury docket. If you contemplate urging a motion for summary judgment and the time limitation on a request for jury trial permits you to await the decision of the trial judge on that motion before filing a request for jury trial, it is generally preferable to postpone requesting jury trial. (In some jurisdictions, however, as in federal courts,[11] this is not feasible). At the least, a request for jury trial displays a lack of confidence in your motion for summary judgment. There is less danger of the request being so interpreted,

4. See §8.4.
5. Nonjury trial is discussed in Chapter VIII.
6. §8.2.
7. §8.3.
8. §8.5.
9. §8.6.
10. See §11.23.
11. Federal Rule 38.

and more reason for making the request though you contemplate using a motion for summary judgment, in those jurisdictions where the request for jury trial must be made earlier to avoid forfeiture.

§7.3 Selecting jurors: in general

What factors should govern your selection of jurors?
What methods should you use in selection of jurors?

Each lawyer has some voice in the selection of the trial jury, though it is negatively expressed through the exercise of challenges for cause and peremptory challenges. Except as to trials in a rural community (where local counsel may be associated if you do not practice in the community regularly), you will normally not have the benefit of personal acquaintance with members of the jury panel, and your choice must be based upon the limited knowledge that you are able to gain from independent investigation of the jury panel (when that is permissible and feasible),[1] from the interrogation of the jury panel,[2] and from your observation of the panel members during the interrogation.

Since you must assimilate very rapidly all of the information that you gather during the interrogation of the panel in preparation for exercising your peremptory challenges (or "striking the jury list," at the conclusion of the interrogation of the panel), it is important to have some system of notations, unless you have such an exceptional memory that you do not require notes. You will not have sufficient time to write ordinary long-hand notes of all the relevant information. Furthermore, a private code of notations is useful to avoid disclosing to anyone who may see your notes, including panel members, your appraisal of panel members and whether or not you intend to strike them. Probably you will find it helpful also to keep your notes in the form of a chart representing the seating of the panel members if they are examined while seated together in a group. This system aids in association of names, faces, and other information and facilitates appraisal and comparison of the different individuals when you come to the usually difficult problem of deciding on your last strike. Such a system may also be useful if you wish to memorize enough information to aid in a personal appeal to individual jurors.[3]

It is rarely easy to decide which members of the panel to eliminate in exercising your peremptory challenges. Usually it will be obvious that a certain individual or individuals should be stricken, but it is also usual

1. See §7.4.
2. See §7.5.
3. See §7.15.

that there will be many more about whom you have some doubt and among whom you have difficulty in choosing in the use of your remaining challenge or challenges. Under the procedure followed in some instances you are required to challenge or accept each panel member at the time he or she is examined; if this practice is followed, you must be careful to avoid exhausting your challenges too soon. Even when you are permitted to exercise your peremptory challenges after the interrogation of all panel members is completed, however, you should be actively engaged in the task of reaching a tentative decision on your strikes as the interrogation is proceeding.

You will find it easier to come to a satisfactory final decision on this problem if you make a tentative decision at the earliest possible moment, and then test it and reconsider it as the interrogation proceeds. Obviously you must be careful to use your tentative decision as only experimental and not permit it to have any greater weight in your final choice than the factors that accounted for it deserve. For example, if your tentative decision as to which of three or four doubtful persons you should eliminate with your final strike is based primarily upon physical appearance, you should be engaged in the reconsideration of that decision as further information is developed about each of these individuals, giving your tentative selection no greater weight in the determination of your final selection than the factor of appearance itself deserves.

In addition to making your final decision more satisfactory, this process of constant consideration of your strikes during the interrogation of the panel has the advantage of enabling you to turn in your jury list to the clerk promptly after the conclusion of the interrogation. When this must be done in the presence of the panel, as is often the case, delaying substantially longer than your adversary in the striking of your list may make an unfavorable impression on those who remain as the trial jury. Some of them will note the difficulty you have in deciding whom to strike; each may wonder if he is one of those you were doubtful about but had to take because you were even more anxious to get somebody else off the jury.

The limited time available for your appraisal of individuals on the panel makes it necessary to rely to a great extent upon the assumption that attitudes of particular individuals on the panel conform to those usually held by persons of similar background. The weight you should give to this assumption will depend upon how extensively the person has been examined by the trial judge, or you, or your adversary during the interrogation and how well you are able to appraise his individual characteristics. In the typical interrogation conducted by the court without direct questions by lawyers, you must rely very heavily on the assumption of normal attitudes and reactions, whereas you are better able to consider the panel members as individuals when lawyers extensively question each member of the panel.

The following discussion concerns factors that deserve consideration in your appraisal of the panel members as potential jurors. These factors often conflict with one another, and you must determine case by case the relative weight you will give to each, though some general guiding principles are suggested. These factors will include all those relating to the subjects suggested for consideration in formulating questions to be submitted to the panel,[4] the primary importance of the interrogation being the disclosure of information useful in the selection of the trial jury. Although the discussion of interrogation is organized according to subject matter, the discussion in this section is organized in terms of specific questions you may ask yourself with respect to each panel member whom you are considering. In addition to the factors appropriate for interrogation, other factors are considered here — factors that would be inappropriate for questions to the panel or to individual members. As to factors concerning which you cannot safely question panel members, you must depend upon your observations during the interrogation or upon independent investigation.

Does the juror have interests in common with those of either party to the litigation? Are they members of the same group in racial, social, political, occupational, religious, or other affiliation?

Does the juror have interests in common with those of any of the key witnesses? Or with any of the lawyers?

Is the juror a member of a group, individuals within which characteristically have some attitude or prejudice that would influence the reaction to the evidence and issues in your case?

Is the juror related to or personally acquainted with any of the parties, witnesses, or lawyers? If so, how closely, and favorably or unfavorably?

Has the juror heard about the controversy, and if so, what influence will that have?

Has the juror already formed an opinion on the controversy?

Has the juror had any previous experiences in other legal controversies that might influence the deliberations?

Is the juror one in whose thinking the interests in strict adherence to the judge's instructions on the law will receive special emphasis, or one who is more likely to be influenced by sympathy to shape findings to support a desired result?

Is the juror one who will probably weigh evidence carefully or one who will make snap judgments or be influenced by bias or prejudice?

All of the foregoing questions are aspects of the broader question whether the juror brings to the case some attitudes or feelings that probably will produce a bias toward one party or the other.

Has the juror had experience in some special field of work or learning

4. See §7.6.

that is involved in the controversy? A juror who has had such experience is likely to bring to the case some ideas that will have a bearing on the deliberations. It is natural for such a person to take the point of view of the party whose work and experience is more like his own. In addition to this danger of bias, however, such experience has importance in other respects. Regardless of which way such a person reacts to the evidence, his ideas are likely to carry weight with other jurors because of his special experience. Also, there is serious danger that such a person will relate his own experiences during jury deliberation, giving rise in some jurisdictions to the possibility of a new trial because of jury misconduct. These factors may work to the advantage of either party to the litigation. In general, the risk of harm from taking such a juror is less to the party whose work and experience is more nearly like that of the juror, because of the normal inclination to take the point of view of the person whose work is similar to one's own. For this reason, most lawyers representing a plaintiff in a damages suit based on negligence of the defendant's truck driver generally prefer not to have truck drivers on the jury. Sometimes, however, the juror with experience in a special field of work involved in the litigation proves to be the most critical of the conduct of the party, employee, or witness within his occupational group.

Is the juror one who would be likely to lead and influence others on the trial jury to accept his views, or will he acquiesce readily in the view prevailing among the others? Will he be merely a "seat warmer" or will he be a principal in the deliberations? Will he be likely to compromise, or is he one who might be stubborn and hardheaded (in views against you) or determined (in views favorable to you)? Some lawyers hold to the one-juror verdict theory — that the verdict is usually determined by the ideas of one strong-willed and influential juror and that it should be your primary aim in selecting the jury and in conducting the trial to ascertain which juror is the one and to direct the development of the case toward influencing that one. Although this theory may be somewhat exaggerated, it has within it the element of truth that in every case some, and usually the majority, of the jurors will not play a significant role in the deliberations but will merely go along with one or another of the leaders in the group. This is an important factor in the selection of the jury because, in taking on a jury a person about whose attitudes you are in doubt, you incur greater risk if that person is a leader rather than being one who probably will acquiesce in the prevailing view among the other jurors.

Have you offended the juror by interrogation intended to disqualify him for cause or interrogation otherwise indicating your suspicion of him?

Is he accustomed to big-figure or little-figure thinking with reference to money? Some lawyers consider that a personal injury plaintiff with a clearly meritorious claim is likely to get a higher verdict from persons who deal in their work with large figures than from those accustomed to living and thinking on a lower scale economically. White-collar workers, in particular, may be exposed to big-figure thinking without having personal interests that strongly influence them toward a point of view favorable to the defense. The prevailing view, however, is that a person who deals with big sums is usually "defendant-minded" because of his association with businessmen and their point of view, and is less likely to agree to a high verdict than the average laborer. If there are seriously contested issues of liability, as well as amount of damages, from the plaintiff's point of view the reasons are stronger for preferring the laborer to the businessman or white-collar worker.

§7.4 Selecting jurors: investigating the panel

Should you investigate the jury panel?

The extent of the opportunity for investigation of a jury panel varies greatly not only between jurisdictions but also between different courts within a single jurisdiction. You should familiarize yourself with the procedures for selection of the panel members in your jurisdiction and with the local practices in your particular court. Although corrupt practices with respect to selection of jury panels are relatively rare, it is obvious that failure to discover the use of such practices might easily make the most careful preparations in all other respects fruitless. Furthermore, even when no corruption is involved in the methods of selection of the panel, your knowing the particular manner of selection that has been or may be used aids you in your interrogation of the panel members, in the intelligent use of your peremptory challenges, and in determining whether to waive any irregularities of procedure of selection or to insist (by motion to quash the panel, challenge to the array, or other appropriate procedure) upon strict compliance with prescribed procedures. In some courts a "pick-up jury" may be used, or individual members may be added to the panel by the "pick-up" system; obviously, such a system of selection of the panel is not likely to produce a representative cross-section of the citizens of the community and is particularly subject to abuse by the officer who summons the individual panel members. In view of the practical difficulties of ascertaining whether the method of selection was free of abuse, favoritism, and selection from groups likely to be biased, it is generally advisable to resist the use of that procedure unless you have complete confidence that the choice of panel members was not harmful to your client's interests.

Sometimes it is possible to investigate individual members of the panel to a limited extent, though the identity of the individual members is generally not known far enough in advance of the time of selection of the trial jury to permit extensive investigation. You should always consider the possibility of previous contact between individual jurors and your client. If you represent an individual, your client will probably remember such contacts. If you represent a business concern whose records are so arranged as to facilitate checking on accounts or contacts with individual customers, you should arrange for such a check to be made. For example, if you represent a public utility, or a large department store, it is advisable to check your client's records to assure that you do not unwittingly accept on your jury a person who has had some disagreement or unpleasant experience in relations with your client. In smaller communities, jurors who are not known to you will undoubtedly be known to other persons from whom you are able to obtain confidential information; if you are to try a case in a community where you are not known, your lack of sources of such confidential information is one reason for engaging local counsel.

Although much of the information obtained by independent investigation could be more easily obtained by interrogation of the panel at the beginning of trial, independent investigation of the individual members of the panel to the extent this is permissible and feasible is more satisfactory for several reasons. (1) Certain types of information, though quite relevant to exercising your peremptory challenges, cannot safely be inquired about during your interrogation of the panel.[1] (2) Your adversary has at least equal opportunity to benefit from the interrogation that is feasible. (3) You are not restricted to considering the answer of the panel member about such things as bias; you may ascertain by independent investigation the existence of bias that the panel member does not recognize or would not admit. Without independent investigation, however, you are not entirely at the mercy of the panel members with respect to dishonest answers, since it is sometimes possible to obtain a mistrial[2] or new trial when dishonesty of the answers deprives you of a fair opportunity to exercise a peremptory challenge so as to exclude a panel member who is actually undesirable.

§7.5 Selecting jurors: interrogating the panel

How should you participate in the interrogation of the jury panel preparatory to selection of the trial jury?

The potential usefulness of the interrogation of the jury panel varies with the scope and manner of the interrogation. In some instances the judge alone addresses questions to the jurors, lawyers being given only the opportunity to suggest to the judge questions that they want him to address to the panel as a whole or to individual members. At the opposite extreme is the practice of interrogation by counsel of each panel member outside the presence of other panel members; this practice is usually reserved for serious criminal

1. See §§7.5, 7.6.
2. See §5.4.

cases but is sometimes available upon motion in civil cases as well. A method more frequently used in civil cases, but likewise providing great leeway for the lawyers to determine the scope and content of the interrogation, is the practice of examination of the jury panel in a group, each lawyer being permitted to address questions to individual members of the group as well as to the group as a whole and being permitted to make such statements to the panel regarding the nature of the case as may reasonably relate to the questions properly addressed to the group or individuals. Some of the suggestions in this section are usable only in jurisdiction where this procedure is practiced; others have broader application. To determine whether particular practices may be used in a given case, you must consider both the rules of procedure of your jurisdiction and the local practices in the particular court, since the trial judge generally has discretion to control the scope and manner of interrogation to a marked extent.

The fundamental aim of the procedure of interrogation of the panel is to provide information upon the basis of which the lawyers may present challenges for cause and may intelligently exercise their peremptory challenges (three each in most cases in federal courts[1] and often more in other courts). As the extent of participation of the lawyers in the procedure of interrogation is increased, there is also an increase in the possibilities of using the procedure for the incidental purpose of commencing the process of persuasion of those jurors who will finally determine the fact issues. If the lawyers are permitted to make statements to the panel regarding the nature of the case, as a background for questions to the panel, the form and content of these statements may have a material influence on the jurors' first impressions concerning the merits of the controversy. The questions asked by the lawyers and the manner of interrogation may also have an influence on the jurors' original ideas about the controversy itself and about the lawyers. Their impressions of the lawyers may have a marked influence on their consideration of the evidence and contentions offered, though jurors do not customarily decide cases according to which lawyer they like better. One aim of your methods during interrogation (including such matters as memorizing the names and data concerning jurors and conversing with them on these subjects without referring to notes[2]) should be to develop a favorable inclination toward your client's case and a friendly feeling toward your client and toward yourself as a means of securing favorable consideration of your client's case. The interrogation of the panel is both a basis for selection of the trial jury and a part of the process of persuasion of the trial jurors. Not only from the tactical point of view, however, but also from the point of view of adherence to professional standards, your efforts to create and

1. 28 U.S.C. §1870.
2. See §7.15.

maintain friendly feelings should not descend to the level of undue solicitude for the comfort or convenience of the jury.[3]

Frequently the trial judge will advise the panel, before interrogation by either counsel or the judge, of the purpose of asking personal questions of them. If such an explanation is not made by the court and the lawyers are permitted to interrogate the panel directly rather than through the court, you should consider making a brief explanation to the panel of the purpose of your inquiries. Although many lawyers customarily make statements of this type, there is great variation in the content. Some prefer to limit such a statement to no more than saying in substance, "Before asking any questions I want to explain to you that my purpose in doing so is to get better acquainted with you, and I do not intend to pry into your personal affairs." Others prefer a fuller statement that the purpose is to obtain information for use of the lawyers and parties in the selection of the trial jury. Such a statement may be embellished with reference to the fact that the rules provide for this procedure with the purpose of making it possible to select the most impartial and unbiased jury possible, which is no less and no more than each party deserves. Jurors are apt to realize that they are being looked over, whether they are so told or not. Some are sensitive about this fact and may be easily offended, some are amused, and most accept it as a necessary and proper part of the trial process. If the length of your questioning of a panel member or the nature of your questions discloses that you suspect that he may be biased against your client, he will be a very unusual person if it does not offend him at least slightly. He will be likely to view your suspicion as a fear that he would be unfair, or else a fear that he would be unbiased whereas you want only jurors who are biased — in your favor. In either case, you are off to a bad start in the process of persuading him. If you realize after already asking the questions that they have indicated to the juror your suspicion, this is a factor you should consider in exercising your peremptory challenges.[4]

Not infrequently preliminary questions indicate a doubt as to whether a witness may be disqualified for cause — for example, on account of bias. In such circumstances, you wish to ask detailed and searching questions in the hope of disqualifying him. There are limitations on how insistent your questioning should be, however, because of the practical certainty of offending him and the risk that some of his answers may disclose unfavorable matter before the panel as a whole. Also, there is danger that other members of the panel may react unfavorably because of a feeling that you are unfairly attacking the panel member, or trying to get an unfair advantage by excluding

3. American Bar Association, Code of Professional Responsibility EC 7–36 (1969). See also §7.13.

4. See §7.3.

him. Conversely, if it develops either in your questioning or that of the trial judge or your adversary that a member of the panel is biased in your favor, insistence on retaining him, though involving little risk of reversal of the trial judge's discretionary ruling in your favor, involves a substantial risk of causing other jurors to feel that you are out to win your lawsuit by any methods needed, fair or unfair.[5] Such a reaction is not probable if you succeed in persuading the trial judge to rule in your favor, but it is a real danger if the judge rules against you.

Once you enter upon a detailed inquiry in an attempt to disqualify a panel member for cause, you are generally committed to excluding him from the jury as a practical matter; that is, if you do not succeed in disqualifying him for cause, you probably will feel compelled to use one of your peremptory challenges, not only because of the bias or other ground of disqualification that you suspected, whether you proved it or not, but also because you probably will have alienated him by your extended questioning.

If you suspect that a panel member is disqualified upon a ground that involves matter you do not want the entire panel to hear, you should consider making a request to the court to permit interrogation apart from other panel members. Making such a request has disadvantages, however. You should not make it in the hearing of the panel or the individual member you desire to question (unless that is unavoidable) because of the unfavorable situation that would exist if the request should be refused, and further because of the danger of unfavorable reaction on the basis that you are hiding something. The danger of this latter reaction exists regardless of whether the request is made in the hearing of the panel as a whole, and whether or not it is phrased as a request for hearing "in chambers,"[6] since the panel members see and hear enough to realize generally the purpose of the separate inquiry.

If your adversary asks any questions of a general nature to the panel as a whole and receives less response than should be expected, or if he asks an ambiguous or misleading question, consider making further inquiry on the subject yourself. A general inquiry, by the defendant's lawyer in a personal injury case, about previous claims[7] is an illustration. As the plaintiff's lawyer you should consider more detailed inquiry if the defendant's lawyer asks a very general question on this subject and receives less response than should be expected. Some panel members are inclined to be reticent about mentioning their personal experiences and may remain silent when a general question is asked, particularly if their experience was with a relatively minor claim or their association with the claim was relatively remote. Failure of the panel member to mention such matters involves danger of a mistrial[8]

5. See §1.3.
6. Compare §4.9.
7. See §7.6 (f).
8. See §5.4.

or a new trial after a favorable verdict for the plaintiff. The plaintiff's lawyer, in most courts in which lawyers interrogate the panel, is allowed under these circumstances to state that since the inquiry has been made by the defendant's lawyer, it is important that every panel member search his memory and so state if he has had any experience to which he thinks the question might possibly apply. If your adversary's question is ambiguous or misleading, you may prefer to ask for a clarification from your adversary rather than merely proceeding to reemphasize the matter by your own questions.

Generally you should phrase your questions so they call only for very brief answers without explanation. Usually the question calling merely for an affirmative or negative answer is best. Questions that call for comment by panel members involve danger of statements in the presence of other potential jurors that may influence them. Because of the more striking effect of such comment when it is unfavorable to the questioner than when it is favorable, the danger of harmful comment is more severe than the possibility of favorable comment. Furthermore, if the comment is favorable it may provide a basis for mistrial or for the court's quashing the panel at the instance of your adversary.

§7.6   Selecting jurors: questions used in the interrogation

What should be the subject matter of questions you submit to the jury panel directly or through the court?

Regardless of the form of the jury interrogation and the extent to which lawyers are permitted to ask questions directly rather than through suggestions to the court, one of the steps of complete preparation for trial is considering the questions to be submitted to the jury panel or to individual members. Those questions are affected by the identity, status, and background of the parties to the particular case, and by the nature of the controversy, and will therefore require independent consideration for each new case, though certain types of questions are appropriate in all cases.

This section concerns subjects you should consider in selecting the questions to be asked of the panel in a particular case. The extent to which these subjects are covered and the detail and number of questions asked will be influenced by the form of interrogation. It is generally impractical to arrange a very lengthy interrogation by suggestions to the court, but if you are permitted to ask questions directly you have more freedom and may include all of these subjects in your questions if you choose to do so. Further discussion of reasons for the importance of these subjects appears in the section concerning factors that should govern your exercise of peremptory challenges.[1]

1. See §7.3.

(a) *Status in the community of each member of the panel.* Obviously the more information you have about each individual the more accurate your appraisal is likely to be. On the other hand, there are practical limitations on how much you can ask. Questions concerning occupation and residence are generally acceptable, and the answers are often quite indicative of the social and financial status of the person. Even if they are not, further inquiries involve the danger of offense to the person questioned and disfavor on the part of other panel members because of a feeling that unnecessary prying is involved. Many lawyers customarily inquire about marital status, and the question whether a panel member has children may provide pertinent information in a case involving children as parties or witnesses. Questions on family relationship of panel members to other persons than those directly connected with the case are not generally asked except in rural communities, where such questions may produce useful information or may be used for the purpose of establishing something in common with the panel member to promote friendly feelings. It is generally inadvisable to ask questions about racial background, though of course you should note the racial background of a panel member, as indicated by physical appearance and speech, when it may be a significant factor in the exercise of your peremptory challenges. Religious and political affiliations may be important to your selection of jurors, but inquiries on these subjects must be very discreet to avoid offense; the danger of offense generally makes it inadvisable to ask questions on these subjects unless the background of the parties to your case and the nature of the fact issues involved make them exceptionally important to you.

(b) *Relationship or acquaintance with persons participating in the trial.* The degrees of relationship by consanguinity or affinity that support a challenge for cause vary, statutory provisions affecting the question. It is obvious that even though relationship is not so close as to constitute a ground for challenge for cause, it is one of the factors likely to give rise to bias. You should consider asking about any relationship or acquaintance and the extent of association with not only the parties and lawyers in the case but also witnesses. A juror's decision might well turn on the interpretation or acceptance of the testimony of a witness other than one of the parties, and previous association with that witness might materially influence the decision. If each party knows in advance of trial the identity of all witnesses the other intends to use, it is not likely that there will be any good reason for refraining from inquiry about acquaintance with witnesses. If you are not certain of the identity of all the witnesses the other party proposes to use (as will usually be the case), the incidental tactical effects of the disclosure merit consideration in determining whether to ask that your adversary disclose the identity of his witnesses during interrogation of the panel.[2]

2. See §7.7.

(c) Knowledge or hearsay information concerning any matters relevant to the controversy. The strictness with which the courts customarily enforce a requirement of want of previous knowledge or hearsay information about the case is influenced by the practicability of finding jurors who have heard nothing whatsoever about the controversy before being called as prospective jurors. Except with respect to controversies that have received newspaper publicity, it is unusual that any member of the jury panel in a large city will have heard of the controversy, and the trial judges are inclined to excuse readily panel members who have heard anything about the case. On the other hand, in smaller communities it is often very difficult to find jurors who have not heard of the controversy in at least a general way, and trial judges are inclined to allow jurors to remain on the panel if they indicate that they can and will put aside what they have heard and reach their verdict solely upon the basis of the evidence received under the rulings of the court. The scope of your questions about previous knowledge of the case will be influenced by other factors as well as consideration of the probable attitude of the court toward excusing panel members. It is inadvisable to ask a panel member to relate in the presence of other panel members what he has heard about the case. If the matter related is unfavorable, there is danger of influence on other panel members to the harm of your own cause. If it is favorable, there is danger of mistrial.[3] If it does not appear desirable to question the person outside the presence of other panel members,[4] it is important to phrase the questions so as to limit answers generally to "yes" or "no" without calling for explanation.[5] For example, you might request of the panel member: "Without telling what you heard about the case, please state whether or not it has any bearing on which party is right as to any disputed facts, or as to who ought to win the case." It may be advisable also to ask whether the panel member has formed any opinion about the case, at least tentatively, on the basis of what he has heard. The extent to which you make inquiries of such a panel member will also be influenced by your judgment as to whether, considering what he has heard and all other factors, the panel member is favorably or unfavorably disposed toward your case. If you feel certain that he is favorably disposed to your own cause, you should avoid detailed questions and ask only whether the panel member feels that he can put aside anything he has heard and decide the case strictly on the basis of the evidence he hears during trial; leave it to your adversary to make more detailed inquiries if he chooses. On the other hand, if you fear that he is probably inclined to favor your adversary, you will want to disqualify him for cause if possible. If you are in doubt as to the attitude of the panel mem-

3. See §5.4.
4. See §7.5.
5. *Id.*

ber, you may be able to induce your adversary to undertake the more detailed questioning by limiting your questions so as not to indicate your
doubts, and perhaps to give the appearance of confidence that the panel
member would be a satisfactory juror to you; such situations present a contest of wits[6] between counsel, each not knowing whether the other has some
information concerning the panel member other than that disclosed during
the interrogation.

(d) Existing opinion. Inquiries concerning existing opinion present problems essentially the same as those concerning knowledge or hearsay information about any matters relevant to the case. Usually an inquiry concerning
existing opinion is made in connection with those concerning knowledge or
hearsay information and after a panel member has indicated that he has
heard something of the controversy.

(e) Bias. In a broad sense, nearly all of the inquiries during the interrogation of the panel are directed toward revealing bias through the disclosure
of facts with which bias is normally associated. Rarely will a person be willing to make a direct admission of bias, and when one does admit bias he is
likely to add an inflammatory statement that may influence other panel
members one way or another. Many lawyers and judges customarily ask a
direct question about bias during the interrogation of the panel, but when
they do so it usually is in some form deliberately phrased to reduce the danger of inflammatory comment — preferably a form calling for only an affirmative or negative answer. For example, you might include in the question
a statement that the panel member is not being asked to tell his private views,
or to state which party he favors if he does, but only to state whether or not
he has at this time a leaning toward one side or the other, either because of
the identity of the parties, or something he has heard, or the nature of the
claims, or any other reason he might have. Similarly, the panel members
might be asked to state, without saying what their reasons may be, whether
or not for any reason any one of them feels that he would rather see one of
the parties win than the other, regardless of which it may be.

Some lawyers representing a corporation or insurance company against an
individual ask whether the panel members have any bias against corpora-

6. For an interesting answer to the blanket assertion that a trial should not be a
battle of wits, see the concurring opinion of Justice Jackson in Hickman v. Taylor,
329 U.S. 495, 516, 67 S. Ct. 385, 396, 91 L. Ed. 451, 465 (1947), wherein he states:
"Discovery was hardly intended to enable a learned profession to perform its functions either without wits or on wits borrowed from the adversary." But is this apt
comment concerning discovery problems applicable also to the method of interrogation discussed in the text? As to ethical implications the latter, at least when used
against a less competent adversary, might be attacked as a form of implied misrepresentation and not merely nondisclosure. Compare §2.20 n.1.

tions (or insurance companies), or feel on the other hand that they can give the same fair trial to a corporation as to an individual. On rare occasions, a member of the panel will respond to that question by admitting bias, but when the question is used it is ordinarily intended primarily as a way of exacting a promise from the jurors who finally constitute the trial jury that they will be fair. Whether such questions serve any good purpose is doubtful. Most lawyers prefer as a general rule to omit such questions for fear that discussion of the subjects may emphasize them and increase rather than diminish the danger that they will influence the jurors. On the other hand, experienced trial lawyers generally favor some questions of this type on other subjects. For example, if you must try a case against an opponent who knows nearly all the jurors personally, you may ask whether they feel that they can give you and your client equal consideration and a fair trial, despite the fact they are personally acquainted with the lawyer on the other side. Such a question is ordinarily used with no expectation of a negative reply but in the hope that the jurors who are finally selected to serve on the jury may be induced to make an effort to avoid bias if not to lean over backwards to be fair to the strangers in their midst.

(f) *Experience or participation in some way in other controversies, particularly any involving similarity to the case on trial.* If the case on trial involves a personal injury claim of some type, persons who are engaged in work sometimes involving defense against such claims are obviously likely to be biased in favor of the defense, and those who themselves have had claims of some type are likely to be biased in favor of the plaintiff. In jurisdictions where the fact of liability insurance coverage cannot properly be revealed to the jury over the defendant's protest, persons who have had previous claims are undesirable jurors from the defendant's point of view for the added reason of danger that they will realize and cause other jurors to realize that an insurance company is defending the case in fact, or even to think that is so when it is not. Plaintiff's lawyers quite frequently ask the panel members whether any of them are or ever have been defendants personally or employed in any capacity in connection with defense against personal injury claims of any type. Defendant's lawyers almost invariably ask whether any member of the panel has ever had a claim of any type himself, and often the question is extended to whether any member of the immediate family has ever been either a party or a witness in a case based on personal injuries. As a plaintiff's lawyer, you should consider further inquiry if your adversary has asked a very general question of this type without affirmative response.[7]

Some lawyers customarily inquire about the association of any panel mem-

7. See §7.5.

bers with other litigation, either as jurors, parties, or witnesses, even though not of a similar type to the case on trial. This inquiry may reveal important information, such as the participation of the panel member as a juror in a trial in which a verdict exceptionally favorable to one side or the other was reached, or after which extensive investigation of alleged jury misconduct occurred, or in which other incidents occurred that might influence the individual in the current trial.

(g) Experience in a special field of work or learning that may be involved in some way in the evidence. If, for example, your case grows out of the operation of a certain type of machinery by one of the parties or a servant of one of them, persons whose work involves the operation of similar machinery may be objectionable to one or both parties.[8]

(h) Reaction of individual panel members to particular situations or problems that are expected to arise during trial. In a contested divorce case, for example, it is important to know whether the juror approves of the law that makes the ground relied upon in the case an adequate basis for divorce. In an action for damages dependent upon a statute (for example, a statute imposing liability on one who sells intoxicating drinks to another who, acting under the influence of the intoxicants, injures a third), it may be material whether the prospective juror approves the statutory policy.[9] Such questions as these are asked for the purpose of supplying information to the questioner for use in exercising peremptory challenges. Other questions concerning the reaction of panel members to situations that are expected to arise in trial may be asked with no expectation of obtaining information but for the purpose of influencing the reaction of the trial jurors when that situation arises. For example, some lawyers who anticipate that they will make many objections to evidence during trial ask panel members if any of them would hold it against the client or allow it to influence their findings if a lawyer should make objections to evidence. As in the case of questions concerning willingness to give a corporation a fair trial,[10] the advisability of using this question is debatable. Another question sometimes used involves less risk of harm, but also less hope of any benefit in the usual case; a lawyer desiring to assume the role of underdog[11] may ask whether the members of the panel feel that they can disregard the difference in ability of the lawyers, deciding the case for the party whose claim is supported by the evidence, though he may not be represented by the better lawyer.

8. See §7.3.

9. The propriety of such questions is subject to dispute in jurisdictions where the jury is instructed to return a special verdict without regard to the effect of their answers: §6.6.

10. See §7.6 (e).

11. See §1.2.

§7.7 Selecting jurors: disclosing identity of witnesses during the interrogation

CASE 62. On behalf of *P*, you bring an action against *D* on account of injuries sustained in a head-on collision between cars operated by *P* and *D* respectively. You intend to use as witnesses in trial *P*, *S* (*P*'s adult son who was asleep in the back seat of *P*'s car when the accident occurred, and escaped injury), *M-1* and *M-2* (medical witnesses), *X* (X-ray specialist), *T* (a motorist who was trailing *P* at the time the accident occurred, and left his card with *P*'s son before leaving the scene of the accident), and *W* (wrecker driver who reached the scene shortly after the accident and will give favorable testimony concerning the positions of the vehicles and markings on the highway). You are also considering the use of *H* (highway patrolman) as a witness, but his testimony is unfavorable in some respects and it is your tentative plan to omit *H* during presentation of your prima facie case, calling him on rebuttal if *D*'s lawyer does not call him. You suspect that *D*'s lawyer has been investigating and arranging for expert evidence to support a possible defense of unavoidable mechanical failure of the steering mechanism on *D*'s car, causing it to fail to respond when *D* tried to turn sharply. It is *D*'s contention that *P* was apparently asleep at the wheel and his car was veering to *D*'s side of the highway and that *D* started to cross to *P*'s right and then tried but was unable to cut back sharply when *P* apparently waked up and jerked his car back to his own right side. You do not know whether *D* intends to urge mechanical failure or simply lack of sufficient time to make the car respond. Assume that discovery processes available in your jurisdiction have been inadequate to disclose for you either the identity of the experts whom *D* has consulted or the nature of their findings.

During interrogation of the jury panel should you request disclosure of the identity of witnesses your adversary intends to call?

If your adversary makes such a request, should you comply?

Even though you have carefully prepared your case and have made use of available discovery procedures to reduce to a minimum your uncertainty as to what evidence and what contentions your adversary will present, there will usually be some remaining doubt in your mind as to whether your adversary will call certain witnesses, or whether you know of all of the witnesses whom he may intend to use. The interrogation of the jury panel affords an opportunity to call upon your adversary to make a full disclosure of the identity of all of the witnesses who are to be called during the trial, on the theory that you wish to ask whether any member of the jury panel is acquainted with any of the witnesses.[1] If the disclosure is made in re-

---

1. See §§7.3, 7.5, 7.6.

sponse to your request, you have a better opportunity to prepare for meeting contentions urged by your adversary, to protect against surprise, and to prepare specifically for cross-examination of each of the witnesses he names. A disadvantage of making such a request is that it is likely to lead to a similar request for disclosure of the indentity of all of your witnesses. In Case 62, for example, you would prefer to avoid this because of doubt as to whether you will call *H*, since you hope that your adversary will do so. Even if you are unable to maneuver him into the first commitment as to *H*, however, that disadvantage is probably outweighed by the advantages to you from disclosure of the identity of *D*'s other witnesses.

In many jurisdictions the rules of procedure do not specifically provide for a compelled disclosure of the identity of witnesses during the interrogation of the panel or through pretrial procedures. Under rules granting the trial judge great discretion as to pretrial hearings, he may cause the disclosure of identity of witnesses, though many of the trial judges having that discretionary power do not exercise it generally. Similarly, in exercising discretion with respect to interrogation of the jury panel, a trial judge may cause disclosure of identity of witnesses at that time, in view of the relevance of jurors' acquaintance or relationship with witnesses.

Even if the trial judge will not coerce disclosure, a refusal to make the disclosure upon request has disadvantages that usually outweigh the advantages of withholding names for purposes of surprise[2] or in the hope that the other party might call certain witnesses whom you intend to call if he does not.[3] If it later develops that one or more of the jurors selected to serve on the trial jury have been closely associated with one of your witnesses, your refusal to disclose the identity of the witness and allow your adversary to inquire about acquaintance with him will have deprived your adversary of a fair opportunity to exercise peremptory challenges and may result in a mistrial[4] or new trial. Even if no juror on the trial jury has ever known any of your surprise witnesses, there is still a possibility of unfavorable reaction on the part of the jury to your tactics of withholding information that your adversary needs to make a complete interrogation of the panel. Your adversary whose request for disclosure of identity of witnesses you have refused may contribute to the development of this reaction by appealing to the panel members for protection, in view of your refusal to disclose the identity of your witnesses. As part of this appeal, your adversary may ask whether each member of the panel feels that, in the event some witness is called who happens to be his friend or acquaintance, he can and will put aside completely any personal feelings and consider the testimony as if it had come from a total stranger.

2. As to surprise tactics generally, see §1.3.
3. See §2.2.
4. See §5.4.

The potential disadvantages of your refusal as *D*'s lawyer to disclose identity of your witnesses probably outweigh advantages in Case 62; your best course of action as *D*'s lawyer is to disclose the names of witnesses you intend to use. If in doubt, you may hedge to some extent by naming only witnesses you know you will call, pointing out that you are unable to say just what witnesses you will call since you do not know exactly what *P*'s claims will be until the evidence comes in. Similarly, you might suggest that there were witnesses to the accident whom you may call if *P*'s lawyer does not, and that you cannot be certain what witnesses you will call until you have heard *P*'s evidence. You should bear in mind, however, that partial disclosure in a case in which jurors may later conclude you were not in real doubt involves the danger of an unfavorable reaction by the jury to your tactics as trickery. [5]

§7.8 Responding to a juror's conversational initiative

CASE 63. In a personal injury case, you call a doctor to the stand as a witness. At the recess, after his testimony is concluded, one of the jurors approaches the doctor, indicating a desire to consult him professionally with reference to medical treatment of the juror's wife.

What should you do when a juror wants to talk with you, your client, or a witness during trial?

Although it is improper for a juror to talk with anyone about the case on trial, except with other jurors during their deliberations, conversations on the other subjects are not generally prohibited as such. As a means of protecting the integrity of the judicial proceedings, however, the Code of Professional Responsibility imposes a strict prohibition against any conversation during trial, regardless of subject matter, between a juror and a lawyer or any other person whom the lawyer causes to act. [1] The practical interpretation of the prohibition varies with different conditions in particular courts. For example, prohibitions against conversations on subjects other than the case on trial are often less strict in rural communities than in cities, because jurors in a rural community are likely to be personally acquainted with persons on both sides of the lawsuit. Reserve is more unnatural in a

---

5. See §1.3.
1. American Bar Association, Code of Professional Responsibility DR 7–108 (1969). *Id.*, paragraph (B), declares:
"During the trial of a case:
"(1) A lawyer connected therewith shall not communicate with or cause another to communicate with any member of the jury.
"(2) A lawyer who is not connected therewith shall not communicate with or cause another to communicate with a juror concerning the case."

rural community where people know each other generally and are accustomed to chatting whenever they meet. The practical need for restrictions against conversations during trial is at least as great and perhaps greater under these circumstances. Undoubtedly the most satisfactory method of meeting this problem is for the court to impose a strict prohibition against conversations on any subject during trial and to advise the jurors of this prohibition so that jurors do not initiate conversation and thereby place others (whether parties, witnesses, or lawyers) in the embarrassing and difficult situation of being obliged to cut off the conversation though fearful of offending a juror.

Regardless of whether an instruction against conversations has been given to the jurors by the court, your reaction to the situation when a juror initiates a conversation will depend partly upon the degree of restriction customarily enforced by the judge of the court in which the case is being tried. If the judge permits conversations between jurors and other participants in the trial, so long as they do not relate to the case, should you shun a juror or cause your client or witness to do so when the juror takes the initiative? The Code of Professional Responsibility, dealing only with the lawyer's position and not that of the client or witnesses, states that both before and during the trial a lawyer connected with a case "shall not communicate with or cause another to communicate with" a juror.[2] The phrase "concerning the case," which appears in the paragraph applying to a lawyer *not* connected with the case,[3] is omitted from the paragraph applying to a lawyer who *is* connected with the case,[4] thus implying in the latter instance a prohibition against communicating on any subject. If you even permit rather than "cause" your client and witnesses to adopt a less strict view, it is imperative that you caution them that any conversation should be carefully kept away from subjects concerning the case on trial. In most circumstances it is better to advise your client and witnesses to avoid having any conversations with jurors if at all possible. A person can usually avoid conversation without offense to the juror by stating in substance that though he would otherwise gladly talk with the juror he feels that he should not do so at this time since it might be considered as having some bearing on the case and that you cautioned him that the rules of procedure prevent him from discussing the case with any of the jurors individually during the trial. So long as he phrases his comment in such a way as to make it plain that he is not implying that the juror was knowingly acting improperly in raising the subject, it is not likely that the juror will be offended, and it is quite likely that the juror will respect and approve the attitude of fairness.[5] If the trial

2. *Id.,* DR 7–108(A) and (B).
3. *Id.,* DR 7–108(B) (2).
4. *Id.,* DR 7–108(B) (1).
5. See §1.3.

judge's customary restriction extends to all conversation other than a greet-
ing of "Good morning" or the like, you may use and advise others to use
the same type of explanation to the juror for declining to talk with him on
any subject if he attempts to initiate conversation.

Most lawyers agree that if, as in Case 63, a juror approaches one of your
witnesses when there is a restriction against any conversations, it is preferable that you interrupt to explain rather than leaving it to your witness
to explain to the juror that the rules of procedure prohibit such conversation
even though it is about a matter unrelated to the case and would have no
bearing upon it. Obviously you are the one who should know about the
rules rather than your witness; it would seem more natural to the juror for
you to make the explanation, and your greater experience and preparation
for meeting such a situation should equip you to make the explanation with
less chance of offense to the juror. If a conversation has proceeded to a point
that would violate the restrictions before you learn of it, you should report
the conversation to your adversary and the trial judge. [6]

§7.9 Responding to a juror's misconduct

*What action should you take regarding misconduct of a juror during
trial?*

Some trial judges follow the commendable practice of instructing the
trial jury, immediately after their selection, against such things as (1) discussing the case during the trial, even with other jurors before retiring for
their deliberations after receiving the court's charge following conclusion of
the evidence, (2) talking with the parties, witnesses or lawyers on any subject during the trial, and (3) visiting any physical scene involved in the
case. If the trial judge does not give these instructions on his own initiative,
you should consider requesting that they be given. They serve to reduce the
chances of embarrassment or offense to jurors who might innocently initiate
a conversation if not so instructed. Such instructions also serve to reduce
the possibility of improper conduct that you do not discover or the true nature of which you are unable to prove, and to reduce the possibility of mis-
trials or new trials after conduct that was innocent but is nevertheless condemned by the court as a means of protection against improper conduct. A
request for such instructions should be made out of the hearing of the jury
or else phrased very carefully so as not to offend the jurors by creating the
impression that you do not trust them; the former procedure is preferable
generally, even if it means a slight delay in the timing of the instructions.

As a part of the preparation of your client and witnesses for trial, you
should inform them of the nature of the restrictions against conversation

6. See §7.9.

with jurors, as they are enforced in the court where your case is to be tried.[1] It is also advisable to suggest a means of breaking off inoffensively any conversations initiated by a juror and to suggest that any such matter be reported to you promptly.

The forms of jury misconduct most likely to come to your attention during the course of the trial, rather than by specific investigation after trial, are communications between jurors and a trial participant and visits by jurors to the scene of an accident or other incident involved in the case. If some communication during trial is initiated by a juror with you or your client or your witness, you should consider reporting it promptly to the trial judge and your adversary. If the communication is improper under the restrictions in effect in the court where the case is being tried, not only is it your duty as an officer of the court to report the matter[2] but also it is wise to do so in the protection of your client's interests. If the fact of the communication becomes known to your adversary for the first time after you have received a favorable verdict and it appears that you knew of it and failed to report it, the risk of mistrial or new trial is generally serious. On the other hand, unless the communication involves serious misconduct, a mistrial is less likely when the incident is reported promptly to the court and your adversary.

If the communication is between a juror and someone associated with the adverse party in the case, you are faced with the choice of determining whether you wish a mistrial[3] or other remedial action. Ordinarily you forfeit any possible complaint by failing to seek relief promptly after you are informed of the incident; you are not permitted to withhold your complaint in the hope of a favorable jury verdict and then raise it after verdict if your hope does not materialize.

The duty and advisability of reporting misconduct that comes to your attention and the necessity for seeking relief promptly are generally the same for other forms of misconduct as for communication between a juror and a participant in the trial. In the case of a juror's visit to the scene of an accident, for example, if you fail to raise the point when it first comes to your attention you risk forfeiture, and if you fail to report it to your adversary and the court you violate your duty as an officer of the court and increase the risk that your adversary will first learn of it after a verdict favorable to you and will then be granted a new trial.

In making a report of a juror's misconduct that has come to your attention, you should be prepared for the possibility that your adversary or the court will suggest that the juror involved be excused, the case proceeding

---

1. See §§2.10, 7.8.

2. American Bar Association, Code of Professional Responsibility DR 7–108(G), EC 7–32 (1969).

3. See §5.4.

with a smaller number of jurors, if that practice is permissible in your jurisdiction. Usually it will be to your disadvantage to agree to the excuse in that the juror's initiation of conversation with one of your witnesses tends to indicate that he is favorably impressed at least with that witness and his testimony. Against that disadvantage you must weigh the chance that the trial judge will grant a new trial if you do not make the agreement. In some jurisdictions, the trial judge has discretionary power to excuse jurors up to a certain number without consent of the parties. Under those circumstances it is generally advisable to seek retention of the juror, since your doing so is not likely to increase the risk that a mistrial or new trial will be granted; if the trial judge thinks the situation can be fairly handled by excusing a juror, he will be likely to adopt that course over your opposition, rather than granting a new trial.

The most drastic remedy available in case of jury misconduct is the declaration of a mistrial or granting of a new trial. In addition to questions of law as to whether the misconduct is such as to support a motion for this remedy, you should also consider factors such as the effect of delay and expense of retrial and whether the overall development of the case has been as favorable as it probably would be on new trial. The misconduct frequently is indicative of favor of the individual juror toward one party or another; in Case 63, for example, communication with the doctor implies that the juror is favorably impressed with the doctor and his testimony. To a limited extent, this may also indicate the probable reaction of other jurors. As a general rule, if the jury misconduct is of this type, implying that the juror involved is favorable to your opponent's side, it is advisable to seek a mistrial or new trial unless delay and expense are prohibitive from your client's point of view.

§7.10 Interviewing jurors after verdict

What interviews should you have with jurors after verdict?

The propriety of posttrial interviews with jurors, aimed at improving one's jury techniques in future cases (by discovering factors that accounted for the verdict in this case), is a disputed matter.[1] The propriety and need for interviews for the purpose of protecting your client's interest in the immediate case depend to a great extent upon the nature of the grounds of jury misconduct recognized in your jurisdiction and the admissibility of testimony of jurors themselves concerning alleged misconduct. In jurisdictions where the opportunities for establishing jury misconduct are most extensive, many trial lawyers interview or arrange for another representative of the client to interview each individual juror as a customary part of the

---

1. See H. Drinker, *Legal Ethics* 84 (1953). See also American Bar Association, Code of Professional Responsibility DR 7–108(D), EC 7–29 (1969).

handling of a case. In these circumstances, there is often a race between the parties to interview the jurors after verdict. The losing party seeks to develop evidence of jury misconduct and the winning party may seek statements negating jury misconduct or may seek to persuade jurors not to answer any questions of the opposite party concerning their deliberations unless subpoenaed and required to do so in open court. If the grounds of jury misconduct recognized in your jurisdiction are extensive, a prompt attempt to interview jurors after verdict is essential to the best representation of your client's interests for the same reasons that prompt investigation of a case [2] after the dispute arises is essential.

§7.11   Opening statements

How detailed should you make an oral or written statement that you present to the jury before the evidence?

Rules of procedure customarily provide for either reading of the pleadings to the jury, statement of the pleadings, or an opening statement of contentions or of prospective evidence, and sometimes for a combination of reading or statement of the pleadings and an opening statement. Whatever the form of the statement, by written pleadings [1] or orally, the problem concerning the detail to be used in the statement arises. In some courts, either by rule or by the trial judge's exercise of discretion in the matter, the statement must be limited to one of general outline or summary of contentions. In others, it is permissible to recite in detail the evidence that you expect to prove by each of your witnesses.

If a detailed statement is permitted, is it tactically wise for you to use it? This is a controversial question. [2]

One extreme is represented by those lawyers who prefer, in making an oral statement, to name each witness who is to be called in presenting that side of the case, summarize the testimony that each witness is expected to give, and note an outline on a blackboard during this statement so that it may be kept before the jury and referred to throughout the trial. This method has the advantage of presenting an organized statement of all the favorable evidence at the first opportunity, making a convincing argument early in the trial and making it possible for the jurors to understand the importance of evidence as it is received, rather than leaving them to recall and realize the significance of particular evidence only after other connecting evidence has been received. There are disadvantages to this pro-

2. See §9.3. As to encouraging jurors not to talk with the opposing party or his representatives, compare §9.17.

1. See §10.4.

2. As to other opportunities for placing your theory before the jury at an early stage of trial, see §§2.7, 2.8, 2.19, 3.22, 7.5.

cedure, however. Material variations between the opening statement and the evidence actually given in trial are extremely harmful. On the other hand, the ability of the lawyer to anticipate and state with complete accuracy the testimony of all of the witnesses may create suspicion that they have been coached to testify as the lawyer desires. Also, impeachment or contradiction of any part of the testimony makes the impeachment doubly effective when the lawyer who offered the impeached testimony has made an emphatic commitment by reciting it during the opening statement. It follows that you should not use a detailed opening statement of this character unless you have developed the case by deposition and other discovery procedures during pretrial preparation so thoroughly that you know of the availability of contradictory evidence or impeachment evidence and can avoid vulnerable positions. Obviously you should make the effort to avoid vulnerable positions regardless of your use of the detailed opening statement; using such a statement merely emphasizes and increases the harm that may result. Another disadvantage of the detailed statement is its inconsistency with the use of surprise tactics. The risk of unfavorable reaction by jurors to surprise tactics is increased if you use a detailed statement as a trap for your adversary by deliberately omitting the material elements you introduce later as a surprise.[3]

The opposite extreme in views concerning the degree of detail of the opening statement is that it should be no more than the minimum statement appropriate under the federal system of pleading, unless more is required by law. Some lawyers take the slightly less extreme view that it should be a statement of the "facts" of the case, as distinguished from evidence, no references being made to the testimony of individual witnesses or even to the evidence supporting each of the alleged facts, regardless of the source of the evidence. This method has the advantage of minimizing the harm from unanticipated developments in the evidence, by avoiding commitment in advance; when another theory is more consistent with the evidence as it develops in trial than the theory based on the anticipated evidence, and the other theory would be equally favorable to the client's cause, the lawyer is not faced with the reduction of chances of jury acceptance of the alternative theory because of the more obvious shift of theories in trial. On the other hand, this method fails to take full advantage of the opportunity to prepare the jury for understanding the significance of each item of evidence as it is received during trial and to make the most persuasive argument at the early point in trial.

Most lawyers prefer a practice between these extremes, designed to make use of the opportunity for a persuasive summary of the contentions to be supported by the forthcoming evidence but at the same time to avoid state-

---

3. As to surprise generally, see §1.3.

ment of the prospective testimony of individual witnesses, so as to reduce the risk of harm from variations from the anticipated testimony of either one's own or adverse witnesses. If the statement must be made within the pleadings because rules of procedure permit only the reading of the pleadings, it will generally be less detailed than an oral statement. Most lawyers prefer even in using an oral statement to avoid tying particular facts or contentions to the testimony of named witnesses.

§7.12 Argument to the jury

Everything you say and do in the presence of the jury throughout the trial is a part of your jury argument, in a broad sense, whether you intend it to be or not. The importance of fact issues in determining the result of litigation [1] makes it imperative that, with respect to every method and technique throughout trial, you give major consideration to its contribution to the aim of persuading the jury to accept your version of the facts. You should make no motion, no objection to evidence, no statement of any type, even when you are primarily addressing the court, without considering the impact it may have on the jury. Even in those instances in which professional standards or rules of law impose restrictions against adding to your statements to the court matter intended to influence the jury, [2] they leave you free to use this test of potential influence on the jury as a negative guide — that is, as a guide to what you should not say in the presence of the jury.

Efforts directed toward persuading the jury culminate in the argument to the jury, or summation as it is sometimes called, after the conclusion of the evidence and before the jury deliberations. The most effective argument is one that is made without notes. But the importance of assuring that you do not omit discussion of important aspects of the case by oversight makes it essential that you use notes to some extent, unless you have an exceptional memory. Rarely is there justification for relying on the notes so closely as to read the argument, however. Most lawyers find that the most effective means of preparing for the argument is to prepare an outline or even a full statement of the argument in advance, thinking through each problem that should be treated and how it should be treated in the argument, then discarding all except a very brief outline for reference during the argument. [3] As your experience in trying cases increases, you will be able to rely more upon going through this process mentally, without reduc-

---

1. See §7.1.
2. Compare §4.14.
3. There is a popular saying among trial lawyers that a good lawyer has three arguments in every case — the one he plans to make, the one he makes, and the devastating argument he thinks of afterwards.

ing your proposed argument to writing, except in terms of an outline of topics. The argument is so important, however, that the time required for full advance preparation of your argument in your earlier cases will be well spent, if you do not then allow your prepared argument to be your strait jacket rather than your tool.

In considering your jury argument during preparations, apply these tests to it: Does it make the jury *want* to find for your client? Does it tell the jury *how* to find for your client? It is a rare person indeed who would overlook the first of these objectives, but the latter objective is too frequently overlooked or given inadequate consideration, particularly when the charge is not one calling only for a general verdict but rather for answers to a large number of individual questions, either supplementary to a general verdict or as a special verdict. Even when only a general verdict is required of the jury, attention to the matter in argument may be needed to reduce the risk of irregularities in form, mistakes with respect to elements of damages, or other misunderstandings. Even if jury argument by counsel precedes the court's charge, you usually have a fairly accurate idea of the specific problems that the jury may face in applying the charge to the evidence. Your own and your adversary's requests to the court and your knowledge of the law and the fact issues raised by the evidence can guide you generally in this respect, and most trial judges simplify the matter by providing the lawyers with at least a general statement of intentions with respect to the charge and sometimes with a copy of the specific interrogatories, if interrogatories are to be submitted.

Most lawyers develop some customary forms of argument useful in situations that are often repeated from one trial to another. Allowing your argument to become stereotyped has disadvantages. It generally results in less effective delivery of the argument. Also, it allows your adversary to know in advance what you will say, and to embarrass you by making some of your arguments or cutting you off from them by making them for you and answering them in advance of your own argument. On the other hand, it is helpful to have at your fingertips a stockpile of potentially useful arguments from which you can select readily in finally putting together your argument in any particular case. As you are preparing for trial practice, keep a lookout for good arguments and illustrations that you might use when facing problems that arise in trials frequently. [4]

If you are just entering trial practice, you will find it useful to study jury arguments being used by successful trial lawyers. Although most appellate records do not contain reports of the arguments, some do, and a study of the arguments in the light of the entire record can be very helpful. You may also

---

4. Notes about effective forms of argument are among the many items you might appropriately include in your personal trial notebook. See §1.5.

profit by listening to arguments in the trial courts in cases tried by successful lawyers. Listen with the purpose of analysis and evaluation of the argument, and note for your own future reference the significant conclusions
you draw.

For reasons similar to those discussed in connection with "open-end"
questions to an adverse witness, [5] it is generally inadvisable to pose questions to your adversary during your argument. You should not do so unless you are absolutely certain that your adversary cannot possibly develop
a satisfactory answer. If, however, you can conceive the type of question
that meets the test of being both relevant and unanswerable, you may use
it with good effect, since your adversary is loathe to ignore it, for fear of
the harmful inference from silence, and may spend valuable time trying
unsuccessfully to answer it.

Generally you should be careful during your argument not to make
statements of fact that are beyond the record. Such statements are ordinarily
improper from the legal point of view, and when deliberately employed,
are violations of professional standards. [6] The doctrine of invited argument
makes argument beyond the record inadvisable from the tactical point of
view, also, for the lawyer whose client's circumstances do not have sympathetic appeal. Every improper argument invites a response that otherwise
might have been improper. In such an exchange, the lawyer whose client's
situation has sympathetic appeal has a decided advantage. This proposition
applies not only to making statements of fact beyond the record but also
to drawing inferences that invite a response that might otherwise have
been improper.

Unless the trial judge will deal with the practice sternly, [7] the means of
protection against argument beyond the record are usually inadequate for
the lawyer representing the party whose circumstances have less sympathetic appeal, even though there is a possibility of unfavorable jury reaction
to unfair tactics. [8] For those who prefer not to respond in kind to statements
that go beyond the record, or who consider such response tactically inappropriate in particular circumstances, one of the customary ways of meeting
the practice is calling the jury's attention to the unfairness of going beyond the record, reminding them that nothing either lawyer says in argu-

5. See §3.21.

6. American Bar Association, Code of Professional Responsibility DR 7–106(C)
(1969):

"In appearing in his professional capacity before a tribunal, a lawyer shall not:

"(1) State or allude to any matter that he has no reasonable basis to believe is relevant to the case or that will not be supported by admissible evidence.

"(2) Ask any question that he has no reasonable basis to believe is relevant to the
case and that is intended to degrade a witness or other person."

7. Compare §4.16.

8. See §1.3.

ment is evidence, and calling attention to the obligation of jurors to decide the case according to evidence. With the aim of presenting an attitude of complete fairness before the jurors, you may elaborate this argument with a statement inviting the jurors to disregard your own argument if it does not conform to the evidence and to be guided by the evidence, suggesting also that your argument is intended only as an aid to jurors in sifting and weighing the evidence.

If you have the burden of proof on the case as a whole generally you have the right to open and close the jury argument[9] and often have the choice of dividing as you see fit the total time allotted to you for the two arguments combined. As a tactical matter should you reserve a major part of your time for the closing argument under these circumstances? The closing argument has a special importance because of the lack of any opportunity for your adversary to respond to it[10] and the fact that it remains freshest in the minds of the jurors as they retire for deliberations. There are disadvantages to giving it a major part of your time, however. Jury arguments are generally too long, from the point of view of jurors. Jurors are tired by the time of the closing argument, and you will lose their attention in a long argument unless you have unusual ability as a speaker. You make your opening argument when they are fresher, and it should be the more thorough. Also, jurors may consider that saving most of your time for your closing argument is taking an unfair advantage[11] of a right given you for the purpose only of answering any new matter raised in your opponent's argument. All factors considered, it is generally preferable to make your closing argument much shorter than the opening, even though it may be permissible to reserve a major part of your time for closing. If you are adept at including dramatic or emotional appeals in your argument you can use them most effectively in a closing argument, and one which is relatively brief.

With respect to any of the individual problems considered in this and other sections[12] concerning argument to the jury, a primary consideration is sincerity in what you say. Just as you adopt habits of courtroom demeanor that are suitable to your own personality, so likewise your most effective form and type of argument to the jury will depend in part upon your own peculiar abilities and limitations. Some lawyers can make effective use of dramatic arguments; others appear only to be transparent actors when at-

9. See §5.10.

10. One of the customary arguments by the lawyer who does not have the right to close refers to this lack of opportunity to answer the closing argument and suggests to the jury that they recall the evidence while listening to the closing argument, as "the evidence will be my client's answer to any argument opposing counsel may make."

11. See §1.3.

12. See §§7.13–7.19.

tempting the same form of argument. Pointed appeals to sympathy are at least theoretically prohibited; even when trial judges fail to control argument effectively it is wise to avoid direct appeals to sympathy. Not only do they involve serious risk of reversal of a favorable judgment because of improper argument but also there is some risk (the degree depending upon the character of the particular jury) that the jury will consider the argument as a plea for a gift rather than a plea for justice.

As it is true of your courtroom demeanor generally, [13] so is it true of your argument that the most important single factor is that it have the ring of sincerity. If you can skillfully add touches of the oratorical or dramatic, your argument may be the more effective, but you should not use any technique at the cost of making your argument seem insincere.

§7.13 Complimenting the judge and jury

Should you compliment the judge and jury?

Some lawyers customarily begin their arguments to the jury with compliments to the jury, judge, or both, perhaps including some references to willingness to submit the controversy to their judgment, confidence in the fairness of their deliberations, and appreciation of their unselfish sacrifices or even patriotism in serving on the jury. The extent to which such an argument may be effectively used will depend upon the apparent sincerity with which it is made [1] and also upon the attitudes of the particular jurors to whom it is addressed. If they see through it as just one of your lawyers' devices for trying to influence them, it will fail to serve its purpose. It may even harm your cause, since some jurors resent that type of appeal. Many lawyers consider, however, that it unlikely that jurors will resent the compliment, even though they may doubt the sincerity of the expression or the purity of the motive. Moreover, there is a risk that jurors will expect the courtesy of a few complimentary remarks and may note their absence, particularly if the opposing lawyer includes some remarks of this kind. The Code of Professional Responsibility is not generally understood as prohibiting such expressions as are consistent with courtesies customary in the community, but it does condemn more extreme solicitude. [2]

§7.14 Waiving argument

Should you waive argument?

Some observers contend that jurors are rarely influenced by the argument of counsel to the jury, their minds being made up before the argument be-

13. See §1.2.
1. See §7.12.
2. American Bar Association, Code of Professional Responsibility EC 7–36 (1969). See also §§7.5, 7.15.

gins. Although that may be true in some instances, they are surely a minority of the seriously contested cases. Among the factors that make argument of counsel very important to the decision in many cases are the jurors' misunderstanding or lack of understanding of the issues, lack of such grasp of the whole case as to realize the significance of every item of evidence when they hear it or to recall it when later they hear connective evidence, doubt or uncertainty in the jurors' minds in close cases and their susceptibility to persuasion by an effective argument, and disagreement among jurors' original views, entailing argument during their deliberations that may be strongly influenced by the arguments with which the lawyers have armed their respective advocates among the jurors. It is difficult to determine whether these and other factors would work to the advantage of one party or the other in a particular case. Usually you should not agree to a mutual waiver of argument of counsel to the jury in a case in which you have the real (as distinguished from merely theoretical) burden of persuasion. Even if you consider that the burden of persuasion is primarily on the opposite party and that the probable initial attitude of the jury after hearing the statement of the nature of the case and contentions of the parties, by pleadings or opening statement, is favorable to your client, waiving argument is likely to be a gamble on the jury's full understanding of the case and their reaction to the waiver of argument. Most lawyers decline to waive argument unless absolutely convinced that it is to the client's best interests. Under any other circumstances, the losing lawyer is likely to be left with a sense of personal responsibility for the loss because of failure to make use of the opportunities for advocacy provided by the law.

In some jurisdictions, by waiving argument the party who does not have the right to open and close may be able to cut off the opponent's closing argument, the theory being that the closing argument is only a rebuttal. Such a possibility may exist either as an absolute right or as a matter within the discretion of the trial court. In either case, it is conceivable that you may use a waiver of argument effectively in a case in which your adversary has the right to open and close the argument and reserves the main argument for the closing.[1] Usually waiving argument for this purpose is not a sound tactic since it places the case before the jury with an unanswered argument for the opposing side. There is also danger that jurors will construe your waiver of argument as a confession of weakness. If you try to avoid that construction by some comment to the effect that you waive argument because the opening argument requires no answer, or that the evidence is your answer to the opening argument and you therefore waive your argument, that comment alone may well be construed by the court as an argument that the other party is entitled to answer in the time reserved for the closing argument.

1. See §7.12 regarding this practice.

§7.15 Appealing to individual jurors

Should you make a personal appeal to individual jurors?

The traditional requirement of a unanimous verdict still exists generally for some cases, though exceptions have been made in many jurisdictions for verdicts by a prescribed majority (for example, five-sixths). Regardless of whether the requirement is for unanimity or only a substantial majority, it is obvious that a vote without discussion among the jurors would rarely produce a verdict except in the simplest cases. It is also clear that in any discussion of competing ideas the influence of some jurors will be much greater than that of others.[1] Sometimes a single juror of strong will and influence determines the verdict by persuading all the others to accept his or her point of view. Although some consider this "one-leader jury" typical, rather than exceptional, most observers hold to the view that a typical jury will contain more than one but not ordinarily more than three jurors who are leaders in the deliberations. Other jurors tend to follow one of these leaders, surrendering any views they may have developed earlier. It is normal that the deliberations will proceed from considerable variation of views among these leaders, through a process in the nature of negotiation and compromise, to a verdict that all or the required majority of jurors will approve. This normal process of compromise is to be distinguished from an agreement to be bound by a majority vote — an agreement that in most jurisdictions is recognized as misconduct vitiating the verdict.

What is the best method of gaining the support of these leaders on the jury? Should you address all of your appeals to the entire jury, should you make personal appeals to all of the individual jurors to the extent that is possible, or should you attempt to pick out the leaders and make personal appeals to them? A major part of your jury appeal must be directed toward the entire jury because of the limited opportunity for individual appeals. This approach is tactically sound. You may err in picking out the individuals who are the probable leaders on the jury. Also, it is possible that a few of the jurors will react unfavorably to the personal appeal, although this is not a normal response unless the appeal is very clumsy. Moreover, the leaders on the jury may disagree; the final verdict is then affected by the extent of the original following of each of the leaders as well as the personal strength and influence of each. The combination of these and other factors, including the difficulty of formulating individual appeals that are both ethically and tactically proper, accounts for the fact that many trial lawyers customarily make no particular effort to direct any appeals to individual jurors. On the other hand, a trial lawyer who develops the ability to make such appeals shrewdly, without overdoing them, may substantially improve his effectiveness.

1. See §7.3.

In those jurisdictions where lawyers are permitted to question the panel directly rather than through suggestions to the court, the first opportunity for singling out jurors for individual attention arises at the time of interrogation of the jury panel. In such a jurisdiction, when you are representing the defendant you will have some length of time, as the plaintiff's lawyer is questioning the panel, to associate faces of jurors with names and other information about them. If you have a very good memory you may memorize enough that without referring to notes you can call the individual panel members by name and ask questions indicating familiarity with the other information disclosed during the interrogation by the lawyer for the other side. Even if you have only an average memory you may find it possible, with practice, to do this with the assistance of a good system of notes worked out in advance. Keeping notes in a chart form, representing the seating arrangement, is helpful. Even if you find it impossible or impractical to memorize all of the names, you can at least pick out those whom you consider the probable leaders on the trial jury, giving special attention to them. This method has the advantage of complimenting them by the added attention. If you choose to follow this method, avoid wasting your time on panel members who obviously will not serve on the jury because your adversary will exercise his peremptory challenges to exclude them; as a matter of fact your special attention to any juror may cause your adversary to consider more carefully whether he should strike that juror. Another precaution that you should observe if you single out the potential leaders for special attention is that your questions to them should not be such as to make them think you are giving them special attention because you suspect that they may be biased against you.

If you use the practice of memorizing and calling all jurors by name, avoid doing it in a way that makes it appear to be merely a display of your ability. Jurors will be impressed by the display, but they are not likely to bring in a verdict for your client simply because they think you are brilliant, and you may even be contributing to your adversary's effective use of the "underdog" role.[2] One aim of memorizing names and other data and using them in interrogation is to provoke a friendly feeling from each juror — a natural response for most people to a friendly attitude on your part. You want the juror to feel that you have sufficient interest in him personally to recall his name and other information about him, and not merely to feel that he is a pawn in your game. As a matter of fact, most lawyers who use this method find it to be an effective way of appraising the jurors — becoming well enough acquainted with them to make the most intelligent use of peremptory challenges at the close of the interrogation of the panel. The mind that otherwise might be passively engaged in transmitting information to note paper for later consideration after the close of the interrogation is actively engaged in

2. See §1.2.

learning everything possible about the individuals on the panel. This point is so clearly sound that you need not hesitate to state to the jury, if your adversary makes some remarks about your memorizing jurors' names, that this is your way of getting acquainted with jurors. If your adversary has asked the rhetorical question whether you will hold it against a party that his lawyer cannot call them by name, you may reply with a similarly rhetorical question whether they will hold it against your client that you happen to prefer this way of getting acquainted with jurors.

In some jurisdictions, calling individual jurors by name during the progress of the trial, outside of the time of interrogation of the panel, is considered improper. Where that view does not prevail, some lawyers use such devices as calling the name of the juror most distant from the witness in asking that the witness speak louder so that jurors may hear, and calling names of individual jurors and referring to their individual backgrounds in arguing the case. The latter device is particularly risky, even if not condemned as improper argument; it encourages consideration of personal experiences and increases the risk of improper discussion and consideration of those experiences during jury deliberations.

It is possible to make personal appeals even without calling individual jurors by name. You can shape the presentation of the case so as to appeal to the individual jurors whom you expect to be the probable leaders by using analogies and illustrations in the evidence and argument that would normally appeal to persons with their background. As a minimum, you should test your proposed presentation from the negative point of view. Will it probably be received unfavorably by particular jurors because of their background, and if so, can you use another presentation that will not involve similar risk of unfavorable reaction, particularly among the probable leaders on the jury? For example, if your case involves evidence that one of the parties to a collision of two automobiles had done a limited amount of drinking shortly before the accident, in determining the extent to which you emphasize that aspect of the evidence you should consider the known or probable attitudes of the leading jurors concerning driving after drinking; you should also consider this factor in your selection of jurors to the extent permitted by the number of your challenges and the need to exercise them for other reasons.

§7.16 Asserting multiple theories

CASE 64. *P* sues for personal injuries sustained in a highway collision. *P* was making a U-turn on the highway in a dense fog. He did not see *D*'s approaching car until too late to avoid collision. *D* was proceeding from the direction that *P* originally faced, in the direction toward which *P* was turning, and did not see *P*'s car until too late to avoid collision. The accident occurred at night, both cars had their lights burning, and neither had fog lights. Both were on pleasure trips.

Should you assert several theories of claim or defense?
Should you assert inconsistent theories?

You will find two extremes among conflicting approaches advocated in regard to asserting several distinct theories of claim or defense. One is to assert every conceivable contention, insure that none is overlooked, and concede nothing — don't give an inch. The supporting theory is that you can never tell what contention may appeal to a judge or jury, or may be unexpectedly supported by trial developments, and furthermore since decisions are often compromises you should make your demand extreme to allow more room for compromise without serious impairment of your client's interests. The opposite approach is to limit your contentions to the bare minimum — a single theory of the case, if possible. The supporting theory of this approach is that you can get better results by maintaining an attitude of sincerity[1] and a clear-cut position free from uncertainty, ambiguity, and demonstrable weaknesses. Neither extreme can be a completely satisfactory answer to the problem.

If you represent the plaintiff and your alternative theories lead to different results with respect to which one or more among a number of persons will be responsible to your client, it is generally advisable to join all of them in your suit.[2] Subject to that qualification, when you have several distinct theories available, even if all of them are reconcilable, it is doubtful that you should assert them from the point of view of persuasion. When a person tells six reasons for his doing something, it is a natural reaction to wonder what is the seventh and real reason that he knows is not worthy of mention. You may encounter this reaction from the judge and the jury when you urge six reasons for giving you a judgment. When you have a perfectly sound theory, is your assertion of five more theories an implied admission of fear that the main one is not sound? Undoubtedly, the person to whom the argument is addressed takes more seriously your main ground if it is the only one you assert. This proposition reaches the extreme when you depend upon one decision alone to support your position on the law, and it accounts for the saying among trial lawyers, "Beware of the lawyer with one book." As a fixed rule of asserting only one theory of claim or defense — the one you consider to be your best[3] — this method falls down because of the fact that your reaction to the merits of various theories may not be the same as that of others. It sometimes happens that a court upholds a legal theory that you

1. See §1.2.
2. See §10.2.
3. As to appraisal of potential theories of law, see §9.2.

considered hopeless, and probably even more often a jury finds facts more favorable to your client than you expected or on a different theory from your
expectations. When you have more than one possible theory available under
your appraisal of the facts and law, you must weigh the interest in emphasizing the theory you consider best against the competing interest in asserting
others that the judge or jury might consider best, contrary to your own
views. [4]

A theory reasonably supported by evidence may have disadvantages because of its giving argumentative support, by analogy, to some theory available to the other party. This is especially true of negligence cases, and is
illustrated in Case 64, discussed below. [5] Also, a theory reasonably supportable
may result in disclosure of some particular evidence that would be harmful
to your client's cause in other respects, if that theory should fail. For example, if your client is a liability insurance company, in a jurisdiction where
plaintiff is not permitted to show the fact of insurance coverage, and you
have evidence that a settlement was made with the plaintiff by an adjuster,
asserting the defense might win the case, but if it fails, harm probably will
be done to your client's cause, since disclosure to the jury of the fact of insurance coverage usually can not be avoided in the course of the evidence on
the purported agreement between the plaintiff and the adjuster. One possibility you should consider is asserting the settlement theory by a motion for
summary judgment. [6] You may take the plaintiff's deposition, get him committed to as many facts as possible in support of your settlement theory, and
present a motion for summary judgment based upon the deposition, pleadings, and admissions that you have secured under the discovery procedures.
This practice would be possible in the federal courts and those of many other
jurisdictions. This is not a completely satisfactory answer to the problem in
that the motion is not good, and an exception to an adverse ruling on it
would be worthless on appeal, unless you have enough admissions to reduce
the question to one of law. If you do not have a good chance of reducing the
issue to one of law, the summary judgment procedure may be disadvantageous not only because of the wasted effort and time but also because of
the fact that you will have disclosed your theory fully, giving your adversary
ample opportunity to patch up any holes in the plaintiff's case, if it can be
done. If only a fact issue is raised by your evidence, you are faced with the
difficult choice of forfeiting a possible defense or risking harm to your presentation of others, unless you can prevail upon the court to sever the issues for
trial. [7]

Another factor affecting the decision regarding assertion of more than one

---

4. Compare Case 72 and §10.6.
5. Also see Case 40, §3.14.
6. See §11.23.
7. See §11.22.

theory is that the various theories will often involve some inconsistency. In earlier times, there was little opportunity for the trial lawyer to assert inconsistent theories of fact or law, but at present most jurisdictions freely permit the practice. Some limitations on alternative assertions still exist, especially when elements of estoppel are present because the adverse party changes his position materially in reliance on one's assertion. Much confusion and conflict exists in the decisions concerning alternative contentions and doctrines of election of rights and election of remedies. You should therefore carefully consider the authorities of your jurisdiction if you are concerned with asserting alternative theories. If the decisions permit you to urge alternative theories of the type you are considering, you may nevertheless find it tactically inadvisable to do so because the effectiveness of your argument on each of your theories is reduced by the presence of the other theory in your argument. It was noted above that the assertion of several consistent reasons for requesting a specific judgment may reduce the strength of your best argument; for stronger reasons, this is true when your different reasons are inconsistent, one being based upon the assumption that another is not sound. You can and should avoid inconsistency in your own argument by adopting the best theory as your primary position, suggesting another as one that might reasonably be applied though not the one you advance. Even with this precaution, the fact remains that each of your theories is less forcefully presented because of the other.

Sometimes the distinct theories considered will bear only upon the extent of recovery, dealing with different elements of damages or different factual theories as to amounts supportable under a particular element. With respect to distinct theories of this kind, the arguments in favor of asserting both or all are stronger. Some lawyers consider that asserting every possible claim is the best practice, since compromises are frequently made in the disposition of a controversy, whether by settlement between the parties or by agreement among jurors or judges with conflicting reactions. Others suggest more caution, taking the position that you should urge only claims that you can reasonably hope to support, with the purpose of resisting compromise and adopting the attitude that you ask not a penny more than your client deserves and your client should receive not a penny less than you ask. The usual practice in this respect is a compromise at least to the extent of urging claims based on factual theories that would not be overturned by the courts after favorable jury findings, even though it appears very doubtful that the jury will make such findings.

The comments of the preceding paragraph would apply either to consistent theories or to those inconsistent theories as to which no election is required of the party (as in the case of factual theories on the extent of damages under a given element of the legal measure, the jury making the election by their factfinding).

If the distinct theories available, supporting different relief, are so inconsistent that the party must make an election, a different problem is presented. For example, in a case based upon fraud, the victim has an election in many jurisdictions among a variety of forms of relief. Some are based upon affirmance of the transaction and retention of what the plaintiff has received. Others are based upon disaffirmance and restoration of the former status.[8] Usually the action for deceit will involve a fact question on the amount of damages, regardless of whether the out-of-pocket or loss-of-bargain measure of damages[9] is applied. The value to your client of these respective remedies in damages, or in some other form of relief, will depend on such factors as the nature of the transaction, what change in his position has occurred, whether restoration of the former status is possible from his point of view and whether it might be more valuable to him than a money judgment, and the nature of the evidence of damages and the probable finding on damages. Since a choice between the inconsistent theories is required, the problem is merely one of weighing their respective advantages and disadvantages.

Case 64, a personal injury action, illustrates some of the problems of asserting multiple theories, either on behalf of the plaintiff or in defense. With the background facts of Case 64 before you as P's lawyer, you might consider several possible grounds of negligence against D — for example, making a pleasure trip in such dense fog; failing to keep a proper lookout; driving too fast under the circumstances. All of these different theories of negligence are consistent, and you might assert all of them. It is readily apparent, however, that the first two have disadvantages other than merely detracting from the emphasis on the third; if the jurors conclude that D was negligent in the first two respects, it is quite likely they will also conclude that P was negligent in the same respects. By urging D's negligence on these grounds, as P's lawyer you would be doing more harm than good to your case as a whole, because of the support you would thus lend to D's theories of defense. If the evidence will support your third theory, you should avoid the first two and concentrate on the third. If you are in a jurisdiction where contributory negligence is a complete bar, the first two grounds offer little hope of recovery by P.

From D's point of view, the defense of unavoidable accident might be urged. Inconsistent with that defense, but consistent among themselves, are several possible theories of negligence — making a pleasure trip in such dense fog; failing to keep a proper lookout; making a U-turn under circumstances of such poor visibility. Obviously, the last is the best of the three theories from the tactical point of view, if the evidence will support it. If as D's lawyer you are doubtful about securing a favorable finding on that ground, as usually would be true, should you assert the other grounds of negligence as well (assuming, for the moment, that at least one theory of

8. W. Prosser, *Torts* §105 (4th ed. 1971).
9. See *id.* at §110.

negligence is to be asserted and not merely unavoidable accident)? Your choice may be influenced by the law of your jurisdiction as to whether contributory negligence is a complete bar. If not, you would prefer to avoid at least the first theory of negligence (which applies equally against D) and probably the second also (though you might argue a difference between P's and D's positions as to lookout, since P should expect traffic moving directly down the highway whereas D had less reason to expect and discover in time traffic moving across the road in a U-turn). If contributory negligence is a complete bar, the only reason for omitting these defenses is that of interference with emphasis upon other defenses. Though the matter is subject to dispute, probably most trial lawyers would consider that you should assert at least the additional theory of negligence as to lookout; probably you should not urge the mere fact of going out on a pleasure trip in the fog as negligence, since that contention comes with poor grace from a party who deliberately did that himself.

As to the choice of urging only negligence, or only unavoidable accident, or both, even more disagreement would be found among experienced trial lawyers. Probably a majority would urge both theories, at least to the extent of seeking inclusion of both in the court's charge, though adopting one or the other as the primary position in argument on the facts before the jury. The choice as to which theory you should emphasize, in representing D, would depend upon the specific evidence available and your best judgment as to which a jury would be more likely to accept. In this connection, when jurors are declining to award a recovery to the plaintiff in a personal injury case, they generally would prefer to place their decision upon a theory of unavoidable accident, if specific findings are required of them, rather than upon the ground of fault on the part of the plaintiff.[10]

§7.17 Arguing for a claim of unliquidated damages

CASE 65. *P Company* sues *D Company* for breach of a contract by which *D Company* agreed to manufacture and deliver to *P Company* periodically over a two-year term a large quantity of special parts that were to be used by *P Company* in the manufacture of industrial machinery. *D Company* performed for a period of eight months and then, in breach of the contract, refused further deliveries. *P Company* was forced to close down its plant three weeks later and was unable to get substitute parts for a period of six months.

As plaintiff's lawyer, how should you treat unliquidated damages claims in your argument?

Some arguments on unliquidated damages must be limited to figures supported by affirmative evidence, as in the case of an issue of market value of

10. Compare §7.19.

property. Dealing with the conflicting evidence under these circumstances, and presenting an argument in support of the higher figure claimed by the plaintiff, presents basically the same problems as argument on any other issues as to which conflict in the evidence exists. Frequently on the damages issue there is an added difficulty, however, in presenting the matter in such a way that the jury will clearly understand the basis upon which you arrive at the figure claimed and will clearly remember that exact figure; a variety of possible findings is open to the jury on an unliquidated damages issue, as compared with a simple choice of affirmative or negative as to most other questions before them. Furthermore, the basis of finding urged is more speculative, particularly in personal injury cases; in the case of pain and suffering, the figure argued is reached without any specific estimate in the evidence as a guide to the jury.

These distinctive features warrant special attention to your method of argument on damages questions. They cause most lawyers to favor a detailed explanation of the process by which the requested figure is reached, and argument for a computed figure rather than for a general round figure. In a claim for lost profits because of breach of contract, as in Case 65, rather than arguing for a round figure somewhat above what you may expect to be found under your evidence, select a precise figure that you can reach by computations supported by evidence offered. Typically, the evidence would show the profits realized during normal operations before breach and losses or reduced profits during the period affected by the breach, including consideration of the special costs of shutting down and reopening the plant and the detrimental effect on goodwill and sales potential. You should also consider possible recovery of interest as an element of damages. You should plan the development of your evidence and argument as a unit; you may use figures that are in evidence for computations you place on a blackboard during your argument in many jurisdictions, though you may not need this procedure if you have had the computations reduced to paper by a witness and offered in evidence as an exhibit.[1] Whichever time you present the computations, they lend strength to your argument if they are properly prepared. Though assumptions are involved in the argument, the final result seems less arbitrary when computed than when assumed in general terms, and furthermore the process of computation is likely to arouse more interest.

The same method is usable in personal injury cases, as in Case 66. Whether or not the charge as to damages calls for separate jury findings on different items,[2] it is generally advantageous to argue them separately. Thus, the computations discussed in your argument would include separate items for medical bills past and future, loss of earnings past and future, pain and suffering

---

1. Compare §2.33 as applied to Case 6.
2. See §6.11.

past and future (if blackboard computations of damages for pain and suffering are permissible in your jurisdiction), and any other items allowed within the measure of damages. As to items of future damages, in most jurisdictions you should in your computations recognize a discount in some form because of the instruction that the jury is to find what sum "if paid now in cash" would fairly compensate for the loss.

Another problem of arguing unliquidated damages is the choice between exaggeration with the purpose of leaving room for jury compromise and on the other hand taking advantage of the favorable psychology of asking only for what you can support with argument that you consider will appeal to reason.[3] Though there is disagreement on the subject, probably the majority of experienced lawyers favor the latter approach. You encounter this problem even though you choose to detail and specify your items of damages and to use mathematical computations or other methods of showing the jury the way in which you reach the figure for which you ask. Your computations are based upon an assumed figure for the smallest unit (as, for example, the figure you choose to argue for one day's pain and suffering, or one month's loss of future profits); in the choice of this figure, at least, and perhaps also in the choice of other figures used in the process of computation, you express your decision on the problem of exaggeration.

At what point in the argument should you discuss damages? Most lawyers prefer placing the discussion of the damages question after discussion of questions bearing on liability. That is a logical way of arranging the argument; the charge is generally arranged with at least the questions of the primary case and often the defenses as well before the instructions or questions on damages. Also, most lawyers prefer in representing a plaintiff to place the damages discussion at a climactic point in the argument, generally near the conclusion. If the rules of procedure permit it, some lawyers prefer to argue comparatively little on the damages issue in the opening argument of a personal injury case having sympathetic appeal, reserving the major part of the discussion of damages for the closing argument. This approach has the disadvantage, however, that jurors may regard the use of the rebuttal time for an argument that is basically new as taking unfair advantage of the right of closing, or as leaving the jury the responsibility of weighing the argument with more caution because of the lack of fair opportunity for defense counsel to answer it.[4]

§7.18 Arguing against a claim of unliquidated damages

CASE 66. *P* sues *D* for personal injuries. *P*'s evidence supports the inference that his injuries are permanent and that he will suffer a loss of earning

3. See §§7.16, 10.5, 10.6.
4. See §7.12.

capacity, medical expenses, and mental and physical pain in the future, as well as during the period before trial.

As defendant's lawyer, how should you treat unliquidated damages claims in your evidence and argument?

Cases occasionally reach trial with no real dispute existing as to whether liability will be imposed and only a dispute as to amount of damages. In most cases reaching trial, however, there is a genuine dispute and uncertainty as to liability and not merely as to amount of damages. As the defendant's lawyer in such cases, it is primarily your position that no amount should be awarded against your client. You may logically avoid any discussion of the evidence bearing on the amount of damages by adopting and expressing the attitude that it is immaterial. What factors should you consider in determining whether you should present a contest on the damages issue, other than your claim of no liability, during the evidence and in your argument? In the cases of admitted liability, and in those others in which it appears desirable to discuss evidence bearing on amount, in what manner and to what extent should you urge your contentions for a smaller sum than the plaintiff claims?

The position that the evidence on amount of damages is immaterial because of want of liability is so natural that there is danger that discussion of evidence bearing on amount may lead the jury to infer that you are not really as serious in your claim of no liability as you try to appear. This factor and the difficulties of determining exactly what to argue lead many lawyers to adopt the rule of arguing only that the question of amount of damages is immaterial because the liability questions should be determined against the plaintiff and in favor of the defendant.

Few lawyers carry this principle of treating the damages issue as immaterial to the extreme of refraining from attention to the damages question during the evidence. At least you should cross-examine the plaintiff regarding his testimony bearing on the amount of damages if effective cross-examination appears to be possible. Probably the danger of an inference that you impliedly concede the importance of the damages issue is not so great when you are cross-examining as when you are pointedly arguing the damages issue as such; it is natural that you take every opportunity to demonstrate that the adverse party is guilty of exaggeration or error. If you effectively impeach the testimony of the plaintiff bearing on the amount of damages, that also contributes generally to defeating his claims on the fact questions determining liability. The question whether you should offer independent evidence to rebut the plaintiff's testimony is more doubtful. For example, should you in a personal injury case seek a physical examination of the plaintiff by a doctor of your choice so as to have available at trial some medical testimony to contradict that offered by the plaintiff, in the event the usual difference of views among doctors exists?[1] One of the disadvantages of using this testimony is the added emphasis it gives to the question of damages and the danger that the jury will infer that you really think it necessary for them to pass on that issue despite your contention of no liability. On the other hand, completely ignoring the question of amount of damages during the evidence, during the argument, or at both times, involves serious danger that in the event liability questions are resolved against your client the damages finding will be materially higher than if you had devoted attention to developing weaknesses in the plaintiff's contentions on damages. If some of the jurors are originally convinced of the soundness of your position, and give in to a compromise, they probably will insist upon a compromise reducing the amount of damages urged by jurors most favorable to the plaintiff. The extent to which they are successful in this, and even the original amounts insisted upon by those most against you, may be affected by your failure to offer contradicting evidence and to make use of your greater familiarity with the case to develop the strongest possible argument against the amount the plaintiff claims and for the lowest possible figure. The relative importance in a particular case of these competing interests will depend to a great extent upon your judgment as to the probabilities of findings on the liability questions and the extent to which the plaintiff's damages evidence is excessive.

The form of the charge affects the problem. If special interrogatories or issues are being submitted to the jury, they will usually include one or more separate questions on damages. Sometimes these questions are predicated on those relating to liability, and the jury does not reach them if they find for the defendant on the questions determining liability.[2] If this form of charge is used, the effect upon the problem of defendant's argument on damages is essentially the same as if a general charge is used. As the defendant's lawyer you may if you choose simply take the position that the jury should not reach the question of damages. On the other hand, in some jurisdictions the damages questions are submitted without predicate, and the jury is expected to answer them regardless of their findings on other questions in the case. Usually in such a situation there is no basis for arguing a finding of "none" to the damages issue, though the desirability of a phrasing of the issue that would permit such an argument is a factor you should consider in formulating your requests and objections to the charge. If the argument of nonliability is unavailable as to the damages question, or its use is inadvisable because of directing attention to the effect of the answers,[3] the choice is one

1 See §11.20.
2. See §6.6.
3. See *id.*

of wholly ignoring the damages issue or else discussing amount in at least general terms, if not specifically. This practically forces you to discuss the amount of damages to some extent.

If you argue a specific amount (other than an argument that the finding should be "none" in those cases in which the form of the charge and the nature of the evidence give you reasonable support for such an argument), the choice of the exact figure is most difficult. If you choose a figure too low, you are likely to cause a jury reaction that you are being entirely unreasonable, which reaction will impair the effectiveness of your argument on other questions as well as this one. On the other hand, as you raise the figure to avoid that possible reaction you may be raising the damages finding. Sometimes a jury will find a lower figure than you would dare argue under the evidence. This is especially true because of the inclination of jurors to compromise both as to differences between their respective views and as to doubt about questions affecting liability (in the latter case, by finding so as to support a judgment for the plaintiff but reducing the amount). This difficulty of selecting an amount to argue usually supports a decision to refrain from stating a specific amount, except in cases in which you can reasonably argue that the answer should be "none," and perhaps also in cases in which the only real issue is amount. Even in the latter type of case, most lawyers favor not setting a definite figure in the defendant's argument in a personal injury case. Another situation in which you should argue a specific amount is the rare case in which the plaintiff's lawyer, after making an argument based on computed damages, challenges you to point out any error in his computations and to tell the jury what you think they ought to find if you do not agree with him. Allowing a challenge to go unheeded is likely to cause a very unfavorable inference by the jury.

A method of argument frequently used is to point out weaknesses in the argument of the plaintiff's lawyer on the amount of damages, leaving to the jury the question of a specific figure. Some lawyers prefer to add a statement that the reason for doing so is that it is impossible in the nature of things to discover and offer evidence that would show an exact figure, though the argument of the plaintiff's lawyer may have been designed to leave the opposite impression, and that under such circumstances the matter will be left to the judgment of the jurors. If the plaintiff's lawyer has used mathematical computations, nearly every computation will involve at least one and perhaps more assumed figures; by building up an argument as to the number of these assumptions that you can reasonably contest, you may effectively challenge the validity of the result without the necessity of substituting another specific computation and specific amount in your argument. If, on the other hand, the plaintiff's lawyer has not used a mathematical computation to reach the figure advanced, then you may call attention to that fact. In doing so, however, you run some risk of inviting special attention to any supporting theory the plaintiff's lawyer may advance in his closing argument.

If the plaintiff's lawyer fails to argue damages in his opening argument to the jury after the close of the evidence, or does so in only very general terms, you should consider moving to require a full opening of the matter or a restriction of the plaintiff's closing argument on damages to matters fairly within the limits of rebuttal to the defendant's argument.[4] If such a motion is not feasible, it is usually preferable to make your answering damages argument as defendant's lawyer in similarly general terms. If you suspect that the plaintiff's lawyer intends to make a fuller argument on damages in closing,[5] perhaps using computations at that time, you may call attention to your lack of opportunity to answer anything the plaintiff's lawyer may say in the closing argument.[6]

§7.19 Charging moral turpitude

CASE 67. In a suit involving a dispute over the location of the boundary line between tracts of land owned by P and D in a thinly settled rural area, P claims that the boundary is fixed by a certain large tree that, at the time of trial, admittedly has some hackmarks on it. P, age thirty-two, testifies that he first saw these marks, purporting to be surveyor's marks, when he was twelve years old. W-1 and W-2 testify, when called on behalf of D, that they had camped during three successive summers at the site of this tree, which stood out as much larger than other timber, and that they first saw the hackmarks the third summer, only eight years before suit, at which time they particularly noticed the marks because they appeared freshly cut. W-1 and W-2 also produce pictures of their fishing catches during the three summers. The picture for the third year shows the hackmarks on the tree in the backgrounds of the picture; the hackmarks cannot be seen in the pictures for the preceding years, the angle of the pictures and shadows being slightly different, however.

Should you expressly charge adverse witnesses or parties with lying, cheating, or other conduct involving moral turpitude?

An express charge of fraudulent conduct[1] in connection with the lawsuit is a stimulant to the reaction of jurors. The jurors who agree that it is justi-

---

4. See §7.12.
5. See §7.17.
6. See §7.12 at nn. 9, 10.
1. Such a charge is improper, under standards of professional responsibility, unless the lawyer believes it to be justified by the evidence. See American Bar Association, Code of Professional Responsibility DR 7–102, 7–106 (1969), particularly at DR 7–102(A) (5) and 7–106(C) (1) and (2). The discussion in this section is based on an assumption of evidence justifying a charge of fraudulent conduct.

fied are fortified in their own discussion of the case with other jurors during deliberations; with the prodding of t.w. frankly expressed charge of lying, cheating, or the like, they are less likely to temper their own views in deference to the doubts or disagreement of others and more likely to urge them vigorously. On the other hand, if any jurors consider the charge unjustified, it is quite likely that they will adopt more extreme opposing views because of sympathy for the one they think unjustly charged. Compromise verdicts are less probable if the issue of fraudulent conduct is sharply drawn than if the issue is merely one of honest disagreement on the facts, because each juror is more likely to feel impelled by principle to hold out for what he believes. A primary consideration in determining whether to make a frank and express charge of lying, cheating, or other conduct involving moral turpitude is whether the "all-or-nothing" approach is to the best interests of your client.

A second factor that affects the question of advisability of express charges of deliberate misconduct is the general reluctance to find a person guilty in the face of reasonable doubt. Though there is generally no legal requirement in civil cases of proof by more than a preponderance of the evidence, jurors are inclined to apply such a requirement informally with respect to any charge of deliberate misconduct. Furthermore, jurors are inclined to decide cases on a basis that does not imply a finding of misconduct, if by doing so they can reach (or think they can reach) the result they desire. This tendency is illustrated in a jurisdiction using the special verdict by the inclination of jurors to find unavoidable accident in preference to finding that the plaintiff's negligence was a legal cause of the accident, when the jurors are agreed that the defendant should win the case. In view of these tendencies, you need stronger supporting proof for pitching your appeal to the jury solely on a charge of deliberate misconduct. As a general rule, if you can present to the jury, as supporting the result you desire, a theory that does not involve expressly or impliedly a finding of misconduct of the opposing party, it will improve your chances of obtaining a favorable jury verdict. Of course you may do this by taking the primary position that the opposing party was guilty of misconduct, while suggesting as an alternative a theory supporting your desired result without a finding of misconduct. Most lawyers consider that suggesting such an alternative, when the factual situation supports it, is a desirable practice.[2] Unless the evidence to support your charge of deliberate misconduct is strong, it may be preferable to adopt the theory not involving a finding of deliberate misconduct as your primary position. Particularly if the adverse party or witness against whom the charge must be made is a woman, men serving on

2. See §7.16.

a jury are likely to have the feeling that as a lawyer you should not make an express attack on her character when it is unnecessary to do so. [3]

Most lawyers consider that as a general rule, even though it is your primary position that an adverse party is guilty of deliberate lying or other misconduct, it is tactically better to marshal the evidence indicating guilt in such a way that you make your opinion and contention plain but leave the conclusion to the jurors rather than yourself using epithets such as "liar" or "thief." This proposition is supported by the theory that jurors generally feel that a lawyer should not make unnecessary attacks on character. Jurors who firmly believe the charge to be supported by the evidence are not likely to change their votes because they disapprove the use of epithets, but there is serious danger that the lawyer's unfavorable impression on the jurors who are in doubt might adversely affect the chances of their consenting to a verdict that apparently conforms with the charge expressed in the epithet. An attack made in a reasoning way is less likely to arouse an emotional reaction among the jurors, whether it is one basically favorable or one basically unfavorable.

Though it may be inadvisable to make express charges of deliberate misconduct, that practice is to be distinguished from specific argument that the witness' testimony is subject to the normal influences of bias. One method of pointedly arguing this proposition is the use of catch phrases in the references to the witness during argument — the "$5000 witness" for an expert who receives a $5000 fee that seems very high under the circumstances; the "two-second witness" for one who said he saw so many different things within that period of time. [4]

In Case 67, [5] the evidence would support three different factual theories that would be equally favorable to the defendant with respect to the question whether the tree is a true boundary monument: (1) that P was honestly mistaken about the identity of the tree or the time when he saw the hackmarks; (2) that P deliberately lied about the date when he first saw the hackmarks, but honestly believed the marks to be those of the original surveyor; (3) that P deliberately lied about the hackmarks and that he cut them himself when he realized eight years before the time of trial that a boundary suit might arise in the future. As D's lawyer, with no more evidence to support the third theory than that indicated in the problem case, you should not urge such a charge. It is a most serious charge, one the jury would be reluctant to adopt without more proof, and one that some of the jurors might feel very strongly is not only unnecessary but unfair without

3. Compare §3.25.
4. See §3.12.
5. See also Case 2, discussed in §2.3.

more proof. Probably the best method of using the evidence would be to marshal it in such a way as to demonstrate that P in fact did not see the hackmarks twenty years ago and that they were placed there only eight years ago, stating specifically in the jury argument that it is immaterial who placed the marks on the tree and why P is wrong, and that you therefore will not argue the point. The material fact is that the tree is not a genuine boundary monument, the hackmarks having been placed on it only eight years ago, as demonstrated by the evidence of disinterested witnesses. By this method, you use no epithet or express charge of deliberate misconduct, but you have obviously left the way open for the jurors to draw either the second or the third of the inferences, so as not to weaken the stand of any juror who in the deliberations may adopt one of those positions.

CHAPTER VIII

THE NONJURY CASE

§8.1 Scope of the chapter

Basically, the tactical problems involved in trying a case before a judge are the same as those involved in jury trial; the solutions suggested elsewhere in this book as to jury trials are generally applicable in nonjury trials also. This chapter concerns respects in which nonjury trials tend to differ from jury trials. These distinctive characteristics may affect your choice of methods of presenting a case; also, they have an important bearing on the choice between jury and nonjury trial [1] when you have a choice.

§8.2 New trials

Nonjury trial is more often finally conclusive than jury trial; new trials are more frequently granted in cases tried before a jury. This is true both because of greater possibilities of error in the conduct of a jury trial and because of greater difficulty in proving that an error in a nonjury trial warrants the granting of a new trial.

An increase in chances for error in the jury trial is apparent from the addition of several procedures not required in the nonjury trial—the selection of the jury, the charge to the jury on the law applicable to the case, the summation or argument of counsel to the jury, and the deliberations of the jury. Also, problems arising during the development of the evidence in the presence of the jury increase the risk of reversible error.

The treatment of objections to evidence illustrates both the greater likelihood of error in jury trials and the greater difficulty of showing that errors in nonjury trials were harmful. Many trial judges follow the custom in nonjury trials of withholding ruling on all objections except those as to which the correct ruling is very clear. This practice of "taking objections

---

1. See §7.2.

with the case" has the advantage of permitting the judge more time to study doubtful questions, thereby reducing the chances of erroneous ruling. This practice also greatly reduces the possibilities of *reversible* error because of a presumption on appeal that the trial judge did not consider inadmissible evidence unless the record clearly shows that he did. The burden is upon the objecting party to call the objection to the attention of the court again after the evidence is closed and to secure a specific ruling upon it if no such ruling is made at the time the objection is presented. A slightly different presumption — that the trial judge's decision was not materially influenced by consideration of the inadmissible evidence — is sometimes invoked even though the trial judge has specifically overruled an objection during trial.

The trial judge usually has sufficient discretion in this matter of withholding ruling on objections to give him power to misuse the device as a means of insuring affirmance of the judgment that he considers proper, without due regard for a fair opportunity for appeal. A similar opportunity for misuse of the trial judge's power, with reduction in the chances that one who deserves a new trial will get it, arises from the judge's full realization of the legal effect of his findings of fact and the greater opportunity for making findings to achieve a desired result rather than determining the result upon the basis of findings reached without regard to their legal effect. Fortunately, these abuses are exceptional. When they occur, however, an individual litigant has less adequate means of protection against an arbitrary decision in a nonjury case than in a jury case. In view of the discretion and power vested in the trial judge, the protection against these abuses lies primarily in the selection of judges of competence and integrity.

The method of dealing with factfindings in the nonjury case involves special danger for a careless lawyer in that all findings are generally presumed on appeal in favor of the judgment unless specific findings have been made or the complaining lawyer has pursued prescribed procedures for requesting them.

Another feature of the handling of factfindings is that unnecessary new trials may sometimes be avoided by the trial judge's making specific findings on issues that may be material under some legal theory advanced by the parties, even though immaterial under the theory adopted by the trial judge. In this respect, however, trial judges are generally reluctant to make findings on controverted fact issues, when the necessity for doing so does not exist under the theory of law considered sound by the trial judge; this attitude is doubtlessly an outgrowth of the general principle of avoiding decision of moot issues. For the purpose of reducing the chance that a new trial will be necessary (for want of some essential factfinding) if the appellate court adopts a different legal theory from that of the trial court, the use of special interrogatories or special issues submitted to a jury is better than the use of special findings by a judge; the jurors are expected, if they can agree, to answer all fact issues submitted to them, even though some of the fact issues may appear to be moot. The trial judge is likely to consider it better practice not to resolve disputed issues of credibility that he considers immaterial to the proper result.

§8.3 Speed of trial

A nonjury trial is more expeditious than a jury trial. When the separate factfinding body is being used, many time-consuming procedures are employed for the purpose of selecting qualified jurors, advising them of court procedures, advising them of the background of the case and the contentions of the parties, instructing them on the law applicable to the case, and protecting and preserving the impartiality of their deliberations. Each of the following points of difference may have substantial effect upon the speed of trial.

(1) The use of time devoted to interrogation of the jury panel in the jury trial is avoided in the nonjury trial. This is a very substantial factor in the normal length of trials in jurisdictions where lawyers are allowed to examine each member of the jury panel.

(2) The reading of pleadings or making of opening statements, one or both of which are used in jury trial to acquaint jurors with the general nature of the controversy, may be avoided in the nonjury trial through the judge's study of the pleadings in advance of trial. In jurisdictions where the pleadings are very general, the judge may desire introductory statements by counsel, but they are generally much less lengthy than those made before a jury.

(3) Consideration of objections to evidence is much more time-consuming in the jury trial. The jurors are often retired from the courtroom while the judge hears arguments on objections to evidence — time that the judge may save, if he is finding facts as well as law, by the procedure of withholding ruling on objections until the evidence is all in. At that time, he may find some questioned evidence immaterial because he considers that fact issues to which it relates are taken out of the case by other findings, or because even taking the questioned evidence into consideration on material fact issues he would find it outweighed by contradictory evidence.

The realization by the lawyers that the chances of reversible error on account of an evidence ruling are greatly reduced in the nonjury trial[1] has still more effect on the length of trial because of the reduced incentive for objection and the reduced number of objections urged. Another reason that lawyers make fewer objections in the nonjury trial is that there is the pos-

1. See §8.2.

sibility in jury trial of keeping the factfinders (the jury) from hearing inadmissible evidence that might prejudice them, whereas in the nonjury trial the judge must hear it either to determine admissibility or in permitting counsel offering the evidence to complete his record or offer of proof[2] to support his claim of error in the exclusion of the evidence.

(4) Submission of the case at the conclusion of the evidence is much simpler in the nonjury case, since the troublesome problems of preparation and objection to the court's charge are avoided. Also less time is generally taken in summation or argument on the facts in a nonjury case than when the case is tried before a jury. This may be partially accounted for, however, by the fact that nonjury cases frequently depend primarily upon law points rather than fact questions.

(5) Nonjury trials may be interrupted and more easily resumed, when unexpected occasions arise, without the necessity for beginning trial anew, thereby losing the time devoted to the incomplete trial.

(6) Since the possibilities of reversible error are less serious in the nonjury case,[3] the possibilities of extended delay in termination of the litigation because of new trials are reduced.

(7) Nonjury dockets are usually less crowded than jury dockets. Usually nonjury cases reach trial setting more promptly. The opposite may be true of the dockets in some individual courts, however.

As a result of the more rapid progress of the trial, there is generally less opportunity for such matters as conferences with your own witnesses during the progress of the trial, planning of cross-examination of your adversary's witnesses, and countering unexpected developments. There is accordingly more need for completing all preparations before the case is called. In the more lengthy trial, whether before judge or jury, the recesses at noon and periods before morning sessions and following afternoon sessions are usually very busy periods of attention to such matters as these.

§8.4 Bias and sympathy

Is a judge less likely than a jury to be influenced by bias and sympathy?

Since both judges and jurors are human, any generalizations about their behavior may be entirely inaccurate as to a specific judge or a specific jury. In an absolute sense, however, no decision of either a judge or a jury could be entirely free of subconscious influences of background, interests, and attitudes. It has been the aim of our system of justice to reduce the effect of those factors to a minimum. The question whether this has been more

2. See §4.12.
3. See §8.2.

nearly accomplished in the jury or in the nonjury trial is one as to which difference of opinion exists.

The leveling effect of numbers drawn from different groups in the community to form the jury is a factor pointing toward the conclusion that the danger of decisions based on bias is less serious with a jury deciding than with a single judge doing so. A jury of twelve (or fewer, if permitted) will include representatives from a number of different groups, with different backgrounds, so that bias of one may be balanced by that of another, whereas no such balancing factor is available when one person alone, acting as judge, makes the decision. What we know of the deliberations of jurors, behind doors forever closed against direct observation by judges and lawyers, indicates that it is rare indeed that twelve persons agree unanimously in their original views on the material fact issues in a case, as they begin their deliberations. Consider an issue of damages in a personal injury case as an example. Ideas of the jurors as to an appropriate damages finding, aside from issues bearing on liability, sometimes vary to such a degree as from $2,500 to $25,000. Although it is generally held to be misconduct for the jurors to agree to average their respective ideas and be bound by the result as their unanimous finding, it is not misconduct to agree upon some intermediate figure after deliberations; otherwise unanimous verdicts, required in many jurisdictions, could never be reached. In such a case, for example, a verdict of $15,000 might be agreed upon, the exact figure depending upon the number, determination, and persuasiveness of the jurors contending for opposing figures. It is obvious that if one individual had been deciding the case, the chance that the same verdict would have been reached is remote. It is true that it is likewise improbable that two juries hearing the same evidence would reach the same findings, but the probable percentage of variation would surely be greater if decisions were being made by individuals rather than groups. Perhaps it is improper to compare the decisions that would have been reached by individual jurors with the decision that would have been reached by an individual judge. Extreme variations are less likely in the case of the judge because of his experience and training. Nevertheless, if you practice in a populous community, trying cases regularly before several different judges, you will develop a working knowledge of the eccentricities of the judges — that *Judge A* is very lenient in his requirement as to proof of grounds for divorce and *Judge B* very strict, that *Judge C* is favorably inclined toward granting injunctions and *Judge D* opposed to them, that healthy *Judge E* is skeptical of all back–injury claimants and arthritic *Judge F* very sympathetic (or that long-suffering *Judge F* is impatient with one who says he cannot work when his back hurts, and *Judge E* is very sympathetic toward those unfortunates not blessed with such health as his), and so on with respect to every recurring type of case. To the extent that you have a choice with respect to the forum in which your case will be tried, this kind of information about the differences among judges will be a part of the basis for your reasoned choice.[1]

Pointing to the opposite conclusion — namely, that the judge's decision is more likely to be free of bias than that of a jury — is the fact that judges generally are persons qualified by temperament, training, and experience for the function of weighing contradictory evidence and deciding disputes. The jury will doubtlessly include some whose temperament does not suit them to this function and rarely will include any with specific training or experience in deciding disputes.

The form of bias most feared by a lawyer representing a defendant in the typical negligence case of poor individual versus corporate defendant is sympathy. In most other types of cases, the situation of one of the parties has materially greater sympathetic appeal than that of the other. A jury is generally more likely to be influenced, or likely to be influenced more materially, by a feeling of sympathy for one party than is a judge. That this opinion prevails among lawyers is attested by the fact that less effort is directed toward appeals to sympathy in nonjury cases than in jury cases, and by the fact that jury trial is generally chosen by the party whose situation presents the greater appeal to sympathy. The training of judges in a system of administering justice according to law regardless of station in life, and in a system in which the law of each case is considered from the point of view of its overall operation, and not solely its operation between the parties before the court,[2] doubtlessly contributes to a background more favorable to earnest effort to put aside sympathy and decide according to facts and law. It is a grave error, however, to assume either that judges are not subconsciously influenced by sympathy or that jurors will deliberately disregard facts or instructions on the law because of sympathy for one party. Appeals to sympathy may provoke an unfavorable reaction from jurors; it is generally better tactics to avoid pointed appeals to sympathy as such because of the danger of this reaction[3] as well as the impropriety of such appeals legally and ethically. On the other hand, it would be poor tactics in a nonjury case to ignore the availability and significance of relevant evidence that would be likely to provoke sympathy.

Political considerations sometimes give rise to differences in danger of bias as between judge and jury. Neither the procedures for selection of juries nor those for selection of judges insure freedom from the influence of political affiliations. The extent to which freedom from such influence has been accomplished with respect to judge as compared with jury varies in different localities and is affected not merely by the differences in methods of

1. See §10.3.
2. Cf. B. Cardozo, *The Nature of the Judicial Process* 33–34, 103 (1921).
3. See §§1.3, 7.12.

selection but also by the interest of responsible persons in maintaining independence of the judiciary and impartiality in the selection of jurors.

§8.5 Erratic findings

Is the risk of erratic verdicts greater than the risk of erratic factfindings by judges?

Many of the conflicting considerations relevant to the comparison between judge and jury as to bias[1] apply equally to this question whether jury or judge is more likely to make erratic factfindings. On the one hand, the judge's background and training better suit him for the task. On the other, the exchange of ideas and balance of numbers are some protection against whimsical or erratic notions of jurors. If the judge, deciding the case alone, gets off on a tangent, there is no restraint on him other than the loose one that he must not go beyond the bounds of reasonable inferences from the evidence, the appellate court indulging all presumptions in favor of his findings since the trial judge saw and observed the witnesses in person. This same restraint is exercised by the trial and appellate judges with respect to the jury verdict, of course. In addition erratic jurors are restrained by fellow jurors.

The danger of miscarriages of justice because of misunderstanding is more apparent in jury trials than in nonjury. Especially if the issues are complicated and the evidence is lengthy, the possibility of misunderstanding by a jury may become serious. This difficulty is partially due to the complicated instructions often given jurors, and to that extent it may be reduced materially by the use of clearly phrased interrogatories submitting specific questions of fact for their decision. With even the best possible charge, however, the availability of more satisfactory methods for the judge to refresh his memory and study portions of the testimony after hearing a lengthy case gives the judge a clear advantage over the jury in deliberation. Also, his greater familiarity with the legal issues involved and his education, superior to the average of the jurors, better equip him to understand complicated evidence. On the other hand, realization of the legal implications of facts may be a handicap in the task of attempting to find facts impartially. The judge cannot put out of his mind the relative results to which different factfindings will lead as he is weighing the evidence; to the extent that the jurors do not either realize or think they realize those effects, jury trial avoids this handicap to a sincere effort to find the facts as they are.

The greater ability of the judge to understand complicated evidence, both because of his superior training and experience and because of his opportunity of studying the record, has an effect on methods of developing the

1. See §8.4.

evidence. The greater details of explanation needed for a jury, unfamiliar both with the technical facts involved in a case and with the litigation process, may be only boring and irritating to a judge. Even in the nonjury trial, however, you should present your evidence with the purpose of making it clear and understandable to one only listening to it, and not with the expectation that the judge will read over and study it, unless he has indicated in advance that he prefers that method of considering the case.

§8.6   Predictability of results of trial

Are results of nonjury trials more predictable?

Both jury and nonjury trials terminate frequently in results that come as a surprise to at least one of the lawyers, and occasionally to both. If there is a difference between jury and nonjury trials in this respect, it is one of degree only and arises from the fact that usually something is known of the predilections of the trial judge and of his probable reaction to the case on the basis of decisions in other cases that might be considered analogous. There are never two cases exactly alike, and a prediction on this basis may prove wrong, but there is at least a better chance of accurate prediction than in the case of twelve separate jurors whose inclinations vary and are often entirely unknown. In a rural community the lawyers may be personally acquainted with most or all of the jurors, but even then the jury verdict is probably less predictable than the decision of the judge, who is also generally well known personally. There is considerable support for the view that judges are more likely to compromise a case than a jury, both by inclination and because their understanding of the legal issues of the case gives them greater opportunity to do this. On the other hand, a jury verdict is also likely to be a compromise unless the strong personality of one juror results in a "one-leader jury."[1]

1. See §§7.3, 7.16, 7.17.

Chapter IX

PREPARATION FOR TRIAL

§9.1 The problem of preparation

Preparation for trial is never finished until the trial is over. Even then preparation for the prospect of a new trial may be indicated. The time in the courtroom is only a part of the time that, as a careful and thorough lawyer, you must devote to a case during the days it is on trial; you must give attention to such matters of preparation as conferring with witnesses and considering the legal and factual aspects of developments that vary from those you anticipated in your advance preparation. During the period before trial, adequate preparation will require your periodic attention to a case despite your most thorough investigation of facts and law immediately after the case reaches you. Circumstances bearing on the case are changing as the date of trial approaches. In many cases damages will depend partly upon developments during this period. Issues of liability may be directly affected by changing circumstances — for example, by developments supporting waiver or estoppel. Still more important in the average case is the indirect effect that developments during pendency of the case may have upon the availability and the attitudes of witnesses.

The fact that preparations must continue through the pendency of the case is no reason for relaxing your efforts directed toward the fullest practicable investigation of facts and law well in advance of trial. On the contrary, if you delay investigation you may in the end devote much more time and energy to the case with much less satisfactory results. You can increase your effectiveness as a trial advocate by beginning your preparation early and continuing it diligently.

In the sense of preparing *yourself* for effective trial advocacy, this entire book is devoted to the subject of preparation for trial. With more specific reference to the preparation of individual cases, each of the two following chapters[1] is devoted to some aspects of this broad problem of trial preparation, and other problems of preparation are treated in preceding sections concerned with subjects to which the preparations relate — selecting witnesses[2] and evidence,[3] planning the order of your witnesses[4] and your examination of each,[5] planning cross-examination,[6] considering potential objections and planning for the time and manner of presenting those you decide to use,[7] choosing between jury and nonjury trial,[8] and considering the theories you will urge and the arguments you will make to the jury.[9] The present chapter is devoted primarily to advance preparations out of court, with particular emphasis upon *investigation* of law and facts.

§9.2 Aims of investigation of law

As your experience in litigation increases, your need for detailed investigation of law with respect to each case decreases. Though it is dangerous to assume without investigation that a new case will be governed entirely by rules of law that you have already mastered, it is possible to reduce greatly the time you commit to investigation of law when you are able to draw upon a background of trial experience. The type of investigation described in this section is a thorough one, parts of which you may omit in reliance on your existing knowledge as your experience increases.

The primary and most obvious aim of your investigation of law is to ascertain the substantive rules that will govern your case, or the competing rules that might be asserted by each party if there is doubt about the rule applicable to some phase of the case. Your study of the rules and the authorities available to support your adversary's interests is as important to your preparation as your study of those supporting the interests of your own client. This is true not only because of the necessity of advising your client concerning the question whether he should compromise or litigate the case[1] but also with respect to advocacy during the trial. Urging wholly untenable propositions interferes with your advocacy of those more tenable; your more tenable propositions lose emphasis in the mass, and the

---

1. Chapter X, Pleadings; Chapter XI, Proceedings Before Trial.
2. See §§2.2, 2.3, 2.5.
3. See §§2.4, 2.19–2.28, 2.32–2.37.
4. See §§2.6, 2.7, 2.8, 2.38.
5. See §§2.9–2.15, 2.29, 2.31.
6. See §§3.1, 3.2.
7. See §§4.1, 4.16, 4.20.
8. See §7.2.
9. See §§7.12, 7.16.
1. See §9.22.

judge who has found you wrong in one contention may be inclined against you on another when there is doubt.[2] You therefore need to test each of your legal theories by constructing the best arguments you can against it, and comparing them with the arguments that you would use to support it. If, in doing so, you find that the theory that you were considering is plainly insupportable, abandon it for the sake of improving your chances of success on those with a better basis. As to those theories that you retain for use, your anticipation of the response of your adversary and your planning for meeting that response will obviously improve the effectiveness of your advocacy during the trial.

Your study of the substantive rules applicable to your case should culminate in an outline of the facts required for establishing each legal theory upon which either you or your adversary may rely. This outline is a guide for developing the evidence, and it should note any law that you must prove or of which you must ask the court to take judicial notice, typical examples being foreign law and municipal ordinances.[3] Your outline will be useful to you throughout the litigation — in preparing your pleadings, your statements or arguments to the jury, your plan of evidence, your requests and objections to the charge, your motions during trial and after verdict, and your briefs and arguments in the higher court if either party appeals. With extensive experience in a particular type of litigation, this outline may become so well known to you that you no longer need to put it in written form for each new case. Even the experienced lawyer uses at least a mental check list, however, to avoid oversights.

In addition to ascertaining the substantive rules that may be applied to your case, you may be serving a number of other purposes in your law investigation. These other matters also deserve your attention, though they are relatively less important to the outcome of most cases than ascertaining the substantive rules within which your case will be developed.

You may study reports of cases similar to yours for the purpose of noting types of evidence developed. Often such study will suggest avenues of fact investigation that you might otherwise have overlooked. As an example, you may find indications of the type of expert evidence used by the parties, perhaps revealing to you a field of inquiry that you would otherwise have overlooked for lack of familiarity with the subject matter of the expert testimony. In this connection, if you find very similar cases tried by lawyers whom you know to be competent, it may even be worthwhile to take the necessary time to examine the records of those cases on file with the appellate courts to get more detailed ideas about the development of the evidence.

2. Compare §7.16.
3. See §2.37.

You must consider both substantive and procedural rules in deciding what parties to sue,[4] in what forum,[5] and for what relief.[6]

You can anticipate in advance of trial many of the evidence points that will arise. This is not so often true of points relating to the form of questions and the manner of examination, unless your adversary is notorious for his leading or argumentative questions, or sidebar remarks, and your aim is to plan for keeping them within control or otherwise meeting them. As to issues relating to the exclusion of evidence, however, you can anticipate most points that will arise both by way of objection to your evidence and by way of your objection to evidence offered by your adversary. Having anticipated these points and briefed the authorities relating to them, you are prepared to urge your contentions with forceful argument; to give advance consideration to the phrasing of your objection;[7] to present an advance motion on evidence points to prevent prejudicial matters from coming before the jury even in the form of questions;[8] to request a limitation on your adversary's evidence if your objection to admission generally is overruled;[9] to offer your own evidence on alternative theories if a general objection is sustained;[10] and to develop evidence on preliminary facts[11] bearing on admissibility of either your own evidence or evidence that you expect your adversary to offer.

Calling a witness to the stand makes him your witness normally, with some disadvantages through operation of rules of procedure as well as other practical disadvantages.[12] You should consider these rules of procedure for your jurisdiction in connection with your selection of witnesses.

The customs and rules of procedure for preparing the court's charge vary from jurisdiction to jurisdiction, and from court to court within a single jurisdiction. In some instances, the trial judge prepares the charge without inviting assistance of counsel; in others, the trial judge expects the lawyers to prepare the entire proposed charge, leaving him only the task of granting, refusing, or modifying their requested charges. Regardless of the method followed, however, you should be prepared to discover and argue against any parts of the charge that are improperly unfavorable to your client. Usually, you must do this on fairly short notice and in short time. Ob-

4. See §10.2.
5. See §10.3.
6. See §10.5.
7. See §4.20.
8. See §4.16.
9. See §§4.12, 4.18.
10. See §§2.17, 4.12.
11. See §4.6.
12. See §2.2.

viously, you can do it better if you have anticipated the problem by preparing a proposed charge in advance, as you would prefer it, with authorities to support your position, and another as you would prefer it if you represented the adverse party, and with a study of authorities that might be urged to support it. Nearly every judge is receptive to suggestions from the lawyers regarding the charge, even if the judge customarily prepares it himself. This is particularly so if your suggestions are in the form of specific requests rather than objections only [13] and in a form that is supported by specific authorities that you can cite.

Both the form and content of your pleadings will be influenced by your investigation of the law. Though you will determine the general form on the basis of rules you already know except perhaps in your earliest cases, you may find it necessary to do some research as a basis for considering the propriety of particular allegations that you might consider using, or your adversary might attempt to use, for tactical purposes. [14]

At whatever point in the trial the judge may be called upon to make any ruling, you will meet the situation more effectively if you have anticipated the point and prepared yourself in advance by investigation of the law on the issue. The attempt to anticipate and brief all issues that will arise, unless you are already thoroughly familiar with the law applicable, is one of the aspects of thorough preparation for trial. This does not mean that you should take the time to prepare written arguments on all points; that is not feasible. It does mean that at least you should have notes available from which you can make your argument in organized and persuasive form, though extemporaneously, and that you should consider the advisability of a written memorandum or "trial brief" on more important and controversial points. In some areas, it is customary to prepare a trial brief for submission to the court; that practice has the disadvantages of disclosure to your adversary that may interfere with any planned use of surprise, [15] but otherwise is a recommended practice whenever it is feasible from the point of view of the time (both legal and stenographic) it takes.

§9.3 Priorities in early preparations

Should you give priority to fact investigation or to law investigation in your early preparations?

Unless you have had much experience with other cases of the same type, and often even then, your initial interview with your client about the facts

13. See §6.7.
14. See §10.4.
15. See §1.3.

of his case will raise in your mind some questions of law to which you do not know the answers. Frequently the answers to those questions will determine the scope and nature of the fact investigation needed. If you proceed with the fact investigation first, you may find that in part your efforts have been in vain, because the matters investigated prove to be immaterial when the answers to the questions of law are known. This factor indicates that solution of the questions of law before undertaking detailed fact investigation is preferable.

On the other hand, as you proceed with the fact investigation new fact disclosures may make some of your thoroughly investigated legal theories immaterial and may suggest new legal theories that might be asserted either by you or your adversary. These new possibilities in legal theories may also require further study of the law and may suggest new subjects for both legal and factual investigation.

Your two investigations — on the law and on the facts — should proceed simultaneously, the scope of each being influenced by the results of the other. Should either receive priority?

If it were possible to anticipate all of the avenues of fact inquiry needed to support any legal theory you might later assert, or to meet any legal theory that your adversary might later assert, then clearly you should give priority to the fact investigation because of the advantages of completing this investigation while facts are fresh in the minds of witnesses, before the influences of time and discussion have affected their views of the facts, and before your adversary has interviewed them. Truth may be eternal, and facts may not change, but facts do not prove themselves, and factfindings must be made by people with human failings. Furthermore, unlike judges who are expected to investigate the law independently and may reach quite proper conclusions without the aid and even despite the obstructions of counsel, jurors are forbidden to make independent investigation of the facts; it is almost certain that they will fail in their job of making findings that conform to actual facts if those facts have not been discovered and proved by one of the lawyers. In most cases, facts are more easily discovered when they are fresh. This is true not only because witnesses remember more but also because their memory is less confused by reflection. The ideas of the most conscientious witness will undergo some modification as he thinks about and discusses the facts of the case with others. The observations and attitudes of others influence his. He is more than human if his own desire or conviction that one party should prevail in the controversy fails to influence his views as to the facts of the case, and to greater and greater extent as time dims his memory of those facts. Your problem of discovering the facts is less difficult if you see the witnesses early. Furthermore, if your adversary has interviewed them first, you face the added difficulty of the influence of that interview and the priority in time of any statements taken from the witnesses in the earlier interviews. The period of early investigation is a crucial point in the tactical development of litigation.

There are disadvantages to giving priority to fact investigation. It is impossible to anticipate all the legal points that may affect the scope and importance of investigating certain aspects of the facts. You must also take account of limitations of time. Trial practice, though it requires some of the greatest skills, is not the most lucrative law practice. One reason this is true is that it is so time-consuming. Perhaps you will wish to believe that every case you handle demands your best in time and energy; you may be advised that you should not take a case unless you can give it your best. Unless we say that "your best" is qualified by an implied condition — "the best that you can reasonably do under the circumstances" — the advice is visionary. Rarely is a trial lawyer able to devote enough time to preparation of a case that he will feel that there is nothing more that he would do if he had the time. Furthermore, thorough investigation often involves the use of services of others, and incurring expenses that must be borne eventually by the client; the feasibility of incurring expenses will depend on the amount involved in the case and the materiality and probable success of the investigative efforts. In view of these considerations, it becomes important to avoid wasteful investigation of facts that will not possibly be relevant under the theories of law applicable to the case.

Weighing these advantages of priority to the investigation of law against those of priority to early fact investigation, your decision will depend upon individual circumstances. In most negligence cases, however, forming the greater part of contested litigation, the issues of law will be fairly simple and you will know the answers to them at the beginning; though you will require some further study of individual problems of law, and perhaps some supplementary fact investigation because of the conclusions reached in that study, your initial emphasis should be upon the fact investigation.

Neither your investigation of law nor your investigation of facts should be regarded as final at any time before conclusion of trial. This is true both because you will not have discovered all of the facts existing at the time of your investigation and because subsequent events may be material. Rarely will the issue of litigation be such that no intervening circumstances could form the basis of material evidence in the case, and perhaps raise new legal theories.[1] Also, as you use discovery processes after suit has been filed and anticipate more accurately the evidence and theories relied upon by your

---

1. See §9.1.

adversary, you will doubtlessly find that you have overlooked some matters that bear further investigation.

§9.4 Interviewing your client

The interview, as that term is used in this section, refers to the occasion or occasions when an attorney or other representative of a party first goes into the facts systematically with the party. This is not necessarily the first contact.

The initial interview may be one that somebody else conducts, though the purpose is to initiate preparations for a trial in which you will represent the client. For example, if in a negligence case you are representing a defendant on behalf of a liability insurance company, an investigator for the company may have conducted this interview long before you heard of the case. The interviewer may look to you for guidance, however, and if you represent the plaintiff you, or someone under your immediate supervision, will conduct the interview ordinarily.

Though the subjects of discussion[1] and the details of this interview will vary widely according to the type of case and the stage in development of the controversy at which you conduct the interview, the fundamental purposes that will determine those details remain constant, and it is these purposes that we now consider.

(1) Get your client's own version of the controversy as he tells it without prompting, with his irrelevant comments and important omissions, and including any ideas he may volunteer about legal aspects of the matter.

(2) Get from him also a more complete version of all the relevant facts he knows, including those he will state in answer to your questions, as well as those he volunteers.

(3) Get from him the names of all potential witnesses whom he can identify, including the group he is most likely to omit, namely, those who probably will be witnesses against him.

(4) Arrange to obtain from him, or otherwise put in safekeeping, all documents and real evidence accessible to him that may have some bearing on the controversy. If you anticipate that it will be necessary to authenticate the documents during trial with proof of custody and absence of modifications, there are advantages in leaving them always in the custody of your client so that it will not be necessary for you to be a witness.

---

1. For helpful lists of questions that are useful in personal injury cases, see *e.g.,* 1 I. Goldstein & F. Lane, *Goldstein Trial Technique* §2.48 (2d ed. 1969); 1 L. Schwartz, *Trial of Automobile Accident Cases* xvii (3d ed. 1968); 1 S. Schweitzer, *Cyclopedia of Trial Practice* §§63, 65, 81 (2d ed. 1970).

(5) Arrange to obtain from him all possible leads to the discovery of other documents and real evidence that may have some bearing on the controversy and that may be accessible through your efforts though not accessible to your client.

(6) Get a memorandum or statement in permanent form as to all matters dependent upon his memory as to which he may be called upon to testify. You should obtain at least a summary statement in writing or by recording at the time of the first interview. Some lawyers prefer to record the interview, if that procedure is not disturbing to the client. Whether or not you take a written or recorded statement at the time of the interview, it will be helpful to have the client prepare for you a thorough memorandum of all material points that he can think of, doing this at his leisure over a period of days, and adding points to it as they occur to him. The resulting memorandum often includes details or even points of major significance that he has forgotten to mention in his interviews with you. It is well to advise him that, throughout the period that the case is pending, whenever anything occurs to him that he thinks might be material, he should make a note of it so that he will not forget to bring it to your attention.

(7) Ask the client questions that will bring out the weak points in his case as well as the favorable. A certain amount of tact is required in this respect, of course. Usually you can accomplish your purpose by explaining to the client that you and he must be prepared for contentions that may be raised by the opposite party, and you therefore want to ask him in some detail questions of the type that may be expected to come from the lawyer on the other side.

§9.5 Methods and leads for fact investigation [1]

Merely asking a person the right questions does not insure that you will get from him the information you seek, even if he has it. Few people are willing to tell all they know to anyone who asks; more often, the person you are interviewing will hold back until you have gained his sympathetic interest, so that he wants to be helpful. If you are intent on rushing through your task, you can pursue every known method for finding leads and still have indifferent results because you have not taken the necessary time with persons who could have aided you if they had wanted to do so. It is the experience of competent investigators that they sometimes get their most valuable tips during a second or third interview, after friendly relations have been established.

---

1. For a very limited selection of books on fact investigation, among other aspects of trial advocacy, see §1.5 n. 3.

You can discover many leads for investigation in your interviews with persons whom you see as prospective witnesses — persons whom you expect to have some firsthand knowledge of facts material to your case. In your interviews with your client and with each other witness, you should be as much concerned with obtaining information regarding leads to other sources of admissible evidence as with obtaining information on the admissible evidence that the persons you are interviewing can furnish. You will see some persons with the sole aim of finding leads to admissible evidence. Experienced investigators have developed a number of standard methods of locating witnesses, because experience has indicated that they are most likely to be productive. You should treat the methods referred to below as merely suggestive, however. In any individual case, you should seek other sources of information as well; use your imagination to reconstruct the circumstances of any incident that bears on your case, and use your knowledge of people and their habits to guess what persons were there to observe and how they can be found, or who might possess some documentary or real evidence that would be material. This imaginative approach has been responsible for development of many of the standard methods in the list that follows.

(1) Encourage everyone you interview to tell you all he has heard about the case or about any incident or circumstance material to the case. Hearsay is a most productive source of leads, though a hearsay statement may itself be quite inaccurate. Not infrequently you will find that a witness with only hearsay information is more willing to volunteer it than the person who has personal knowledge and fears that he will be called to testify.

(2) Leave your card with each person whom you interview and ask him to call you if he thinks of anything else about the circumstances that he omitted mentioning, or if he hears something new.

(3) Search for and develop demonstrative and documentary evidence.[2]

(4) When you are representing a claimant, give special attention to identifying all potential defendants, so that your choice as to which one or more you shall sue will be the best. If a vehicle is involved, you should check public records as to registration and ownership of the vehicle, with a view toward discovering any relationship of the driver to another legally responsible party. Also, consider the possibility that the driver was engaged in employment as a servant of another, even though using his own car. Known presence in the vehicle of tools used in his employment may lead to such disclosures. If a business entity is involved, give careful attention to correct identification of that entity. Sometimes closely associated business enterprises may be operating under the same or related management but

2. See §9.6.

under arrangements such that suit against the wrong one would be fatally defective. Information on corporations is available from the office of a state official; you should ascertain whether the corporation is a local or foreign one, and if foreign, whether licensed to do business in the state. Information on the identity of service agents designated by foreign corporations is also available from the office of a state official. Most jurisdictions provide for some statutory form of registration of assumed names, at least in the case of noncorporate enterprises not registered with the public official keeping records of all corporate licenses to do business in the state. Other sources of information are public utility records and telephone and city directories; information obtained from these sources may be incomplete or inaccurate from the point of view of correct identification of the legal entity involved, and you should always check it against other sources of information. Both for this reason and also as an additional source of information, you should consider using discovery processes[3] either before or after instituting suit; this is usually the surest way of ascertaining whether your original information from other sources is complete and accurate. Some particularly dangerous pitfalls to be avoided are the possibility that there are two separate entities of the same name or very similar names, that a change of entities by incorporation or dissolution may have occurred after the date of an incident on which suit is based, or that a vehicle or other machinery involved in an accident may have been owned by one but leased to another either with or without a "loaned servant."

(5) Consider the financial responsibility of the potential defendants. A perfect case of liability may be practically worthless because of your inability to collect a judgment from the defendant. This is especially true in states with liberal exemption statutes as to property subject to levy of execution. In most states financial responsibility laws afford both protection and a source of information regarding insurance coverage or other financial responsibility of defendants in suits based upon operation of motor vehicles. Other sources of relevant information in any case are public records regarding ownership of realty, personal property subject to *ad valorem* taxation, and motor vehicles, and concerning interests in corporate and other enterprises subject to public control. Often credit reports can be obtained from various credit agencies, disclosing relevant information on financial responsibility. Such a report is frequently not exhaustive, however, and you should use it as an aid to determining financial responsibility rather than as a final determination.

(6) Consider official files that may provide information relating to some phase of your case. State, federal and local governments maintain a

3. See Chapter XI.

variety of official files that may prove to be sources of useful information not only in the typical negligence case based on an automobile collision but also in many other types of cases.

(7) Personally observe as many as possible of the physical objects and scenes that are material to the case. In an accident case, for example, go to the scene of the accident yourself and study it thoroughly. This study not only increases your own understanding of the facts of the case but also may provide you with new ideas and leads for investigation.

(8) If your client or his adversary has employed other persons who may have had some association with circumstances relevant to the case, consider in particular former employees of both parties, since they may be inclined to speak more freely and more critically of the former employer than others would.[4]

(9) If you are defending a personal injury claim, consider using the records of claim index bureaus that will usually be accessible to you and may help you acquire information about previous claims and previous medical history. Since most personal injury claims that reach litigation involve liability insurance, information from index bureaus will be available through the insurance company and usually will have been obtained in the course of investigation before the matter is turned over to you. To a more limited extent, information about previous claims and medical history can be obtained from official files of bodies administering workmen's compensation and from court records, military service and Veteran's Administration files, hospital records, and records of drug prescriptions. Some of these sources are accessible only with the claimant's consent.

(10) Consider court records as a source of information concerning a party or witness to the suit. Convictions of a party or witness may be admissible for impeachment.[5] Records of previous civil litigation may also disclose useful information.

(11) Consider potential sources of scientific evidence material to issues in your case. Following are illustrations[6] of types of issues as to which scientific evidence has sometimes figured prominently: nature, extent, and cause of personal injuries (medical); location of properties (surveying); authenticity of photographs and freedom from distortion and touching; identification or association of a defendant with incidents on which suit is based (laboratory examination of paint marks, clothing fragments, etc., in a hit-and-run driver case, gunpowder tests, fingerprints, blood tests); veracity

4. See §3.17.
5. See §3.11.
6. See also §9.6.

("lic detector" tests);[7] intoxication (breath and blood tests); presence of poisons in foods (chemical analysis); existence of defects in machinery or other products (defective metals causing critical failure of automobile part, defective glass causing "exploding" beverage bottle); means of contact with sources of electricity (laws of physics as to "arcing" of current without contact); manufacturing methods (effectiveness of nonhuman "inspection" devices). This list is merely suggestive. As scientific advances are made, additional opportunities for effective use of scientific evidence will arise. Obviously, you cannot become familiar with all the scientific fields potentially involved in cases that you may handle, though your preparations are simplified as your knowledge of the sciences increases. Since you will be an amateur in a foreign field, however, you will need the guidance of an expert within the field. You may find it helpful to make use of a good public library as a starting point to get ideas as to sources of available evidence when you recognize the possibility of using scientific evidence in a case, but you cannot rely on that method as an accurate way of determining whether scientific evidence can be useful in the case. The better method is to seek out the experts for consultation and advice, as well as for potential witnesses. If you are uncertain about the stage of development of a science that might be relevant to some issue in your case, frequently the most expeditious approach to the problem is through consultation with scientists in educational institutions.

The following additional suggestions relate particularly to cases based upon an accident:

(12) Check for wrecker drivers, ambulance drivers, and news reporters who may have been at the scene.

(13) Check police records.

(14) Examine all photographs taken at the scene of an accident for the purpose of identifying persons who appear in them so that you may interview them if you have not already done so.

(15) Canvass the neighborhood of the scene of an accident to find persons who may have seen it, and those who went to the scene afterwards and may provide useful information on physical circumstances and on conversations by the parties (perhaps including some admissible declarations), and also information on identity of persons who saw the accident.

(16) Go to the scene of the accident on some succeeding day, at the same hour that the accident occurred and observe passing traffic with the purpose of discovering the identity of persons who customarily pass at that hour of the day and may have observed the accident or may have come upon the scene immediately afterwards. This method is sometimes useful also in

7. See 3A Wigmore, *Evidence* §999 (rev. ed. Chadbourn 1970).

identifying the driver and passengers in a vehicle referred to by other witnesses but not identified by them.

§9.6 Types of demonstrative evidence

The available types of demonstrative evidence vary greatly with the type of case as well as the peculiar facts of the individual case. The following is a suggestive list, intended as a point of beginning in considering kinds of evidence to look for and develop. You should also consider the admissibility of the contemplated evidence in the jurisdiction of trial; some of the types of evidence listed below are held inadmissible in particular instances because of concern that their use may distract the minds of jurors from fair consideration of the issues before them.

This list includes not only matters described by the term "real evidence," but also such things as documents and photographs, since they may be offered as exhibits and have the characteristic of independence from some of the human errors affecting testimony.[1] This is one of the characteristics making demonstrative evidence particularly persuasive.

(1) Documents — letters, statements, contracts, telegrams, former pleadings in this or other lawsuits, transcripts of evidence in previous proceedings, accounts, sales slips, orders, and other business records. You should consider the possible sources of evidence of this character carefully, both from the point of view of finding evidence useful to your own case (for example, in the form of admissions of the adversary) and also from the point of view of ascertaining what evidence of this character may be available to strengthen your adversary's case or weaken that of your client. If your case involves correspondence between the parties, examine all of the correspondence for items that you may use and for items that your adversary may use against you. In searching for documents possibly useful in cross-examination of a witness or party, consider not only documents signed by him but also those that he has adopted by reference or approved orally or by separate writing. Your preparations for use of documentary evidence should include attention to the means of authenticating the evidence when you use it (by pretrial stipulation, or admissions concerning authenticating facts, or developing evidence necessary to establish them).[2]

(2) Physical evidence of identity of an actor or a weapon used in a relevant event — fingerprints, footprints, blood tests, powder burns, photographs, bloodstains, false teeth, personal effects, jewelry, laboratory tests of clothing, hair, blood, etc.

(3) Evidence of physical surroundings of the scene of an event — photographs[3] (including aerial photographs, color photographs), maps, charts, models, diagrams. You may increase the effectiveness of models and maps by asking the witness to use some special devices in explaining his testimony — *e.g.,* colored pins to indi-

1. See §2.32.
2. See §2.25.
3. See §9.7.

cate the positions of the witness, other persons, and objects not on the map, and scale model objects such as cars involved in a collision, to clarify and illustrate the witness' testimony.

(4) Evidence of physical condition and personal injuries — X-rays, photographs, moving pictures, exhibition of an injured member, manipulation of an injured member, series photographs (showing changes of condition over a course of time, and perhaps taken in color in the case of burns or other skin conditions more accurately shown by color films), laboratory tests of the medical practice (blood, urine, stomach contents, stools, electrocardiograms, electroencephalograms, myelograms, spinal fluid tests, etc.). Witnesses may use models effectively to explain their testimony; a medical witness might use a skeleton, for example, in a case involving bone injury or a plastic model of the heart, brain, kidney, or other organs, when injury to one of them is involved.

(5) Evidence of the manner in which an accident occurred — small objects involved in the accident (a carpet on which plaintiff alleges he slipped; a waxing machine and the wax used on a floor; a handcar that struck the plaintiff; a piece of metal that was driven into his body; a shoe that was worn as the plaintiff was dragged for a distance with the shoe scraping); diagrams drawn by the witness as he tells his story (either drawn on a blackboard, which will not be introduced in evidence as an exhibit, or on a paper, which may be introduced in evidence and carried to the jury room).

(6) Other possibilities — The possibilities for demonstrative evidence are almost unlimited. In many instances, it will be possible to conduct an actual experiment in the courtroom. Bottling companies frequently present an experiment, for example, in cases involving a claim of explosion of the bottle from excessive internal pressure. Bottles are taken from the production line of the defendant bottler and subjected, in the courtroom, with specially designed equipment, to tests of internal pressure and breaking pressure of the bottles, with the purpose of demonstrating a large safety margin. Another type of experiment that is occasionally used is the "lie detector."[4] In an appropriate case, a bold lawyer with absolute faith in his client and in the expert tester might challenge the opponent to submission to lie detector tests, with notice that he will undertake to prove the request and refusal[5] if the adversary declines.

§9.7 Preparing photographs for use in trial

How should photographs be prepared for use in trial?[1]

Frequently, your investigation will disclose the existence of photographs of scenes material to some issue in the case, taken before your association with the case. For example, officers investigating motor vehicle accidents

4. See 3A Wigmore, *Evidence* §999 (rev. ed. Chadbourn 1970).

5. Obviously there is a serious problem of admissibility of this evidence. Compare, however, the proof of a request by the defendant that the plaintiff submit to a physical examination and the plaintiff's refusal to do so.

1. For a comprehensive treatment of this problem, see C. Scott, *Photographic Evidence* (2d ed. 1969).

frequently take pictures; also, some professional photographers in cities make a practice of going to scenes of major accidents to take pictures before vehicles and debris are moved and tire marks are obscured, knowing that they will be desired by one or both parties when claims based upon the accidents are being considered. Occasionally an amateur photographer will also take pictures. The possibility that such pictures have been taken is one of the matters that you should investigate in each case. If the pictures have been taken by officers or by professional photographers customarily going to accident scenes, a record of identifying data probably will have been made already. If such a record does not exist, however, you should obtain the data from the photographer for your own files, preferably with a notation by the photographer certifying the accuracy of the data, to insure that he would be able to use it to refresh his memory if it should be necessary or desirable to use his testimony with reference to the photograph at a trial months or years later.

In recording data concerning photographs you should include the identity of the photographer, the date, time, and position from which the photograph was taken, the direction toward which the camera was facing, the identity of others present either assisting or observing the photographer's work (persons whose testimony might be used to authenticate the photograph if the photographer should be unavailable), and notation of important things shown in the photograph. Since some of the data may be interpretive in nature, it is quite likely that this record concerning the photographs would not be admissible in evidence, even when vouched for by the photographer under oath at trial; furthermore, the notations standing alone are hearsay and would ordinarily be excluded from evidence upon objection. To avoid interference with the usefulness of the photograph as evidence, because of the inadmissible data, it is preferable to have the data recorded separately rather than on the photograph, only an identifying symbol being placed on the photograph for purposes of reference in the data sheet. Numbering the pictures in the order in which they were taken is one satisfactory method of doing this. Another reason for preferring the separate record of the data is that you may wish to offer the photograph without producing the photographer and with authentication by a witness who testifies that it fairly depicts a scene that he observed.[2] You may not wish to have all of the identifying data in evidence, aside from the problem of admissibility. Another advantage of the separate recording is that you may then make better use of the pictures for interviews with other witnesses, recording their comments by reference to the identifying numbers. Also, separate recording of the identifying data gives you greater flexibility for using the photographs.

2. See §2.34.

It is a good practice to have your pictures examined and identified by statements of other witnesses besides the photographer, as a protection against the unavailability of the photographer and anyone assisting or observing his work.

You should also consider having photographs specially made for your use in trial. With reference to motor vehicle accidents, photographs taken after a lawyer is in the case are generally not as useful as those taken immediately after the accident; they fail to show the positions of vehicles and markings on the road that might have been preserved by earlier pictures. Nevertheless, they are often useful in demonstrating such matters as visibility from specified points of approach to the intersection, the presence of obstructions, and relative positions of traffic signs and other objects. You should arrange for such pictures to be taken at a time when the scene is as nearly as possible like that at the time of the accident, and you should study the pictures carefully before using them, to insure that they are not misleading or distorted;[3] the danger of misleading pictures is particularly apparent with reference to showing such matters as obstructions to visibility, since the position of the camera and the perspective in the pictures has so much influence on appearances. Also, devices such as special lenses and filters may cause a picture to give a completely false appearance.

If you have one or a few particularly important photographs, you should consider having enlargements and extra copies made to facilitate study by the jurors and judge during your use of the photographs in trial.[4]

You should consider using color photographs because of the additional detail they show and the additional interest they create.

§9.8 Preparing expert testimony

What factors should govern your search for expert testimony and choice of expert witnesses?

How many experts should you use?

In most cases, in preparing for trial you should consider using expert testimony; by far the majority of cases ligitated at the present time involve some form of expert testimony.[1] Having found certain issues in your case

3. See *id.*
4. See *id.*
1. Illustrations in §9.5(11) of types of scientific evidence frequently employed will serve to demonstrate the need for carefully considering the development of expert testimony in your preparations for trial. Other types of "expert" testimony frequently used include testimony on valuation (of vehicles, real estate, stocks, or any other thing involved in the measure of damages) and estimation of speed of a vehicle (from seeing it in motion, and less often from observing marks afterwards).

on which expert testimony might be used, what factors should govern your choice of a particular expert or experts who can qualify in that field? If the matter of "expert" testimony is one as to which most people can qualify, and many of the witnesses who will be called in the case for other purposes can be used, you probably will not seriously consider employing special witnesses. In such circumstances, you may even make the most effective presentation on the point by using cross-examination of one of your adversary's witnesses placed on the stand for another purpose,[2] if you are reasonably assured of a favorable answer.

If the expert testimony that you are considering relates to a point as to which only persons with special training will qualify, it is more probable that you will find it necessary to employ one or more experts specially for the litigation. In some cases, however, experts will be among the persons whom you would naturally interview and consider as potential witnesses because of their familiarity with some of the relevant facts in their expert capacity. This is true, for example, of the typical personal injury case from the point of view of the plaintiff's lawyer. The medical experts who have treated the plaintiff before he comes to you may not be the exact ones whom you would select if you had your choice, but it is ordinarily advisable to use them unless manifestly incompetent or unfavorable to your client in their findings and opinions. The expert chosen by a lawyer is more likely to be regarded as the lawyer's expert, and his testimony is more likely to be regarded as an argument of an advocate. The family doctor's opinions generally carry more weight with a jury than the opinions of another doctor to whom the plaintiff was sent by his lawyer, and this is often true despite great disparity in their respective professional qualifications.

Qualifications of the expert in his field are important, both as bearing on his competency and as a bearing on the probable effectiveness of his testimony before a jury. If other things were equal (as they never are), the jury would presumably favor the testimony of the witness with the more impressive qualifications when there is a conflict between experts. From the point of view of aid to you in preparing your case, however, the expert with the most impressive qualifications is not necessarily the most useful. Whenever expert testimony has material bearing on the issues in a case, you will need a competent expert as adviser (regarding methods of meeting your adversary's case[3] and development of your own[4]). It is generally more practical to have one expert engaged as both adviser and witness.

2. See §§3.14, 3.31.
3. See §§3.29–3.31.
4. See §§2.15, 3.31.

The ability of the expert to express his views persuasively is a matter of major significance. It is unfortunately true that the most competent experts are not necessarily the best witnesses. Sometimes an expert who is especially competent will be so conscious of the need for hedging and qualifying his opinions in the interest of scientific accuracy that his testimony is devoted more to qualifications of his opinions than to forceful expression of his best judgment in the matter. Characteristics of personality wholly independent of professional competency also materially affect the ability of the expert to state his views persuasively.

Experience of the expert as a witness has both its favorable and unfavorable aspects. One who is experienced is usually better able to express his views in conformity with rules of court procedure, is more at ease, and is better able to take care of himself on cross-examination, as well as needing less of your time and effort in a preparatory conference.[5] On the other hand, the fact that he is frequently called as a witness may cause an unfavorable inference that he is prepared to sell his testimony for a price, or that his views are otherwise biased.[6]

Another factor that has both favorable and unfavorable aspects is the extensive writing of professional books or articles in professional journals. The fact that he has done this writing may weigh heavily with the jury as they assess the relative qualifications of experts on opposite sides of the case, and it may indicate competence both as a witness and as an adviser. On the other hand, the witness who has written extensively is often subject to effective cross-examination by the development of contradictions or inconsistencies between statements made on the witness stand and those appearing in his writings. Experts are notoriously conservative in their expressions in professional writings; that degree of conservatism may interfere with acceptance of their opinions by a jury, even though only probability and not certainty is the most that is required so far as the legal test is concerned. Furthermore, unless the witness is a very unusual person, he will either have written some things at another time with which he now disagrees, or he will fail to recognize some quotations from his own writings when read to him on cross-examination, and will insist on some modification, or he will use such different forms of expression that seeming inconsistencies arise.

Expenses involved in using expert testimony frequently bear consideration, contrary to the interests of most effective development of the case. Expenses also have a bearing from the point of view of effect upon the jury. It is inadvisable ordinarily, from the tactical point of view as well as that of economy, for a defendant to expend sums for expert testimony that

5. See §2.15.
6. See §§3.29, 3.30.

are sizeable in comparison with the amount of the claim. Jurors do not generally think in terms of "a million dollars for defense but not a cent for tribute"; rather, a very large expenditure is likely to cause them to infer that this must be a rather serious claim and that the defendant recognized that the jury might decide for the plaintiff unless the case was defended with everything available. If either party has expended for expert testimony sums that will impress the jury as being unreasonably large, the jury may draw the inference that the payment influenced his testimony; this inference may be aided by proof of the amount of the fees[7] (and perhaps also by descriptive references to the witness during jury argument — e.g., the "$5000 witness"[8]).

With respect to the number of experts used, there is often an advantage in having more than one, particularly if their fields are very specialized and the issues in the case may overlap more than one specialty, as in medical testimony. It does not follow that the party with the most experts has the advantage, however. One of the disadvantages is that of expense, both from the point of view of economy and from the point of view of favorable inferences by the jury. Another disadvantage is that of using cumulative witnesses generally — the serious danger of contradictions among them.[9] This danger is especially apparent in the case of experts because of the possibilities of cross-examination upon hypothetical questions[10] and upon points not directly relevant to major issues in the case (which can generally be done on the theory of testing qualifications). These factors of expense and danger of contradiction combined make it generally advisable to use only one expert unless the issues in the case overlap more than one specialized field, in which case you might use one expert in each field. If you engage more than one expert, your unexplained failure to call them all to the stand may result in an unfavorable inference as to what the testimony of those not called would have been.[11]

§9.9 Developing alternative theories

Should you prepare distinct theories of claim or defense, though they are inconsistent?

In considering what preparations you should make for asserting several different theories of claim or defense, whether they are consistent or inconsistent, you should take account of different factors from those applying

7. See §3.27.
8. See §7.19.
9. See §2.3.
10. See §3.31.
11. See §2.3.

at other stages of litigation. Other sections of this book concern the advisability of pleading several distinct theories of claim or defense [1] and the advisability of actively asserting several distinct theories before the jury during trial. [2] In your preparation of both facts and law you should consider every theory that you can identify. In the typical case, you are likely to conclude upon thorough consideration that some of your original theories are obviously not supportable. Others you will appraise as being good, and still others will be doubtful. The ideal is to develop your factual and legal preparations for trial upon the doubtful theories as well as those that you consider good, though limitations of time and expense will usually force you to give less attention to some and emphasize others. Insofar as preparations are concerned, the limitations on number of distinct theories of claim or defense that you develop are primarily those of time and expense.

§9.10. Anticipating your adversary's evidence

Why and to what extent should you look for evidence supporting your adversary's case?

To develop an effective plan for competition of any kind you must anticipate your adversary's resources and the ways he will use them. In a lawsuit, the resources include the potential evidence. Some illustrations will demonstrate the importance of your appreciating the potential evidence available to your adversary.

Your client may be lying to you. Or he may be grossly, though honestly, mistaken. Never accept your client's story at face value. This does not mean that you are to insult him by saying during your initial interview that you must check on everything he says; it does mean that you should do the checking before you go to trial, and preferably before you file pleadings on his behalf, unless because of your own extensive association with the client you are willing to stake your own reputation on his being right. If you do not follow this rule, you will sooner or later find yourself in the embarrassing predicament of having a client's falsifications exposed to your surprise during trial. If you are not sufficiently concerned about the integrity of your client to investigate for yourself, you do not deserve the gift of deliverance from a fellow lawyer representing the other party. Your adversary may be kind enough to notify you in advance of trial of the character of your case, but your adversary has no obligation to you to do so. Furthermore, your adversary may be concerned that your client will fabricate plausible explanations if he is tipped off to the availability of proof

1. See §10.6.
2. See §7.16.

that he is lying; under such circumstances your adversary may conclude that the lawyer's duty to protect a client's interests demands secrecy rather than disclosure to you for the purpose of saving you from embarrassment. To protect yourself against such an experience, which if often repeated will be professionally damaging despite your good faith, you should investigate your own client's story as thoroughly and with as great skepticism as if you were representing the opposite party and seeking some evidence to discredit it.

A second reason you should search for evidence that supports your adversary's case or discredits your own is to aid you in the planning of your own case. You can then discard those theories of fact and law that you have initially considered but have found to be hopelessly defeated by evidence that your adversary is certain to find and offer. Also, you will be prepared to treat with caution those theories as to which uncertainty exists; whether you should discard them also will depend upon the availability and strength of safer theories of supporting your client's interests. If you do assert them, you will be better prepared for the contradictory or counteracting evidence offered by your adversary, and you will be able to plan your presentation tactically to emphasize the favorable and avoid emphasis on the unfavorable. You should interview each witness thoroughly on all aspects of the case, from both your point of view and that of your adversary. Then you may decide intelligently what witnesses to call, [1] bypassing those who are subject to cross-examination more damaging than the value of their direct examination to your case. You will be prepared to offer on direct examination unfavorable evidence that may be de-emphasized in this way, [2] to use cross-examination of your adversary's witnesses for the development of your own case, [3] and to know when not to object because the question opens a subject on which you can produce more favorable testimony than your adversary. [4]

An appreciation of the evidence available to your adversary and the identity and probable testimony of each witness your adversary may use will also aid you in preparing to meet the opposing case effectively. By anticipating the identity of each of your adversary's witnesses, you can prepare your plan for cross-examination. [5] By anticipating particular items of evidence, you can consider in advance the advisability of objections and the form and timing (perhaps in advance, out of the presence of the jury [6]) of those you choose to make.

1. See §2.2.
2. See §2.20.
3. See §3.14.
4. See §4.2.
5. See §3.1.
6. See §4.16.

From these examples, it is evident that what you know of the contentions and supporting evidence of your adversary influences most of your decisions on immediate tactics in trial. You are not fully prepared to try the case for your client until you have investigated each aspect of the facts as if you were to try the case for the opposing party.

§9.11 Engaging independent investigators

Should you do your own investigation or use an independent investigator?

In every populous community, and within access to all rural communities, individuals or associations offering their services as private investigators are available. You must consider the relative cost to your client of using these investigators or instead making the investigation yourself. The greater percentage of the business of most such private investigators is connected with personal injury claims — claims for workmen's compensation benefits or for damages for personal injuries sustained in industrial or vehicular accidents. Typically the defendant is a large business, or else is protected by insurance, or both. Much of the investigation for the defense is done by independent investigators before the case ever reaches the hands of the lawyer who will try it; a larger company may have its own private staff of investigators. Either arrangement is generally chosen in preference to investigation by the lawyer because the charges of the investigators for their time are generally less than those of the lawyer, who is more highly trained. Most experienced trial lawyers find it impossible in the representation of defendants to do their own investigations without reducing unreasonably the volume of business they are able to handle and thereby either reducing their total fees or else making their fees for each case prohibitively high. On the other hand, lawyers representing the plaintiffs under contingent fee contracts receive larger fees per case on the average and, finding it feasible to do their own investigation or have it done by a younger associate, usually prefer this over employing an independent investigator. Furthermore, it is generally not feasible to use an independent investigator under such circumstances because of the client's lack of cash and the doubtful propriety of the lawyer's paying or guaranteeing payment of the expenses if he knows that the client will be unable to meet his liability for the expenses unless the lawsuit is successful.[1] These factors usually deter-

1. See American Bar Association, Code of Professional Responsibility, Canon 5 (1969), and particularly the following provisions under Canon 5:
DR 5-103(B): "While representing a client in connection with contemplated or pending litigation, a lawyer shall not advance or guarantee financial assistance to his client, except that a lawyer may advance or guarantee the expenses of litigation, including court costs, expenses of investigation, expenses of medical examination, and costs of obtaining and presenting evidence, provided the client remains ultimately liable for such expenses."

mine the answer to the question who shall do the investigation, regardless of other considerations.

There are advantages in doing investigations of your own. You are more familiar with all of the issues in the case than anyone else. An independent investigator working on the case after you have come into it will be looking to you for guidance and direction. Regardless of his good understanding of your theories about the issues, and even if he makes excellent reports to you on his findings, you will not know your case as well from reading his reports as you would have known it from doing the investigation yourself. You will not have had the personal meeting with witnesses. Also, the investigation may not have been as good because of the investigator's lack of the detailed knowledge that you possess as to all issues, legal as well as factual.

To the extent that you decide to use subterfuges in investigation,[2] it is generally necessary to employ an independent investigator, either because your identity would be known in advance so as to make the subterfuge impossible or because the subterfuge would later be disclosed when your identity became known to persons interviewed under the subterfuge.

When a need for investigation in a distant community arises, it may be appropriate to use an independent investigator for that part of the investigation, even though you are doing most of it yourself. Another possibility is to refer the matter to a lawyer in the other community, either for personal attention or for referral to a local independent investigator.

§9.12   Using subterfuges

Should you use subterfuges in your investigation?

The Code of Professional Responsibility does not deal specifically with the use of subterfuge in investigation.[1] It is generally considered a permissible practice within reasonable limits, and it is often justified on the basis

---

EC 5–8: "A financial interest in the outcome of litigation also results if monetary advances are made by the lawyer to his client. Although this assistance generally is not encouraged, there are instances when it is not improper to make loans to a client. For example, the advancing or guaranteeing of payment of the costs and expenses of litigation by a lawyer may be the only way a client can enforce his cause of action, but the ultimate liability for such costs and expenses must be that of the client."

Compare §9.19 n.1. Perhaps the quoted code provisions do not rule out the possibility of employing an investigator on a contingent fee contract. Also they do not rule out (at least, not clearly so) a plaintiff's lawyer's payment of expenses with no expectation of reimbursement until final disposition of the claim, if he believes the plaintiff will recover on the claim. Perhaps they do not even rule out such payment when the plaintiff's lawyer recognizes that the claim may be unsuccessful.

2. See §9.12.

1. Probably the use of a subterfuge in investigation does not constitute "deceit" or

that it is a practical necessity in discovering falsification by the adverse party or his witnesses. It would be a violation of the Code, of course, for you to use subterfuge as a means of directly interviewing an adverse party who is represented by a lawyer.[2] Doubtlessly, the spirit of the Code may be violated by some uses of subterfuge in interviewing other witnesses, but the absence of an absolute prohibition leaves some area, not clearly defined, in which the use of subterfuge to interview persons other than the adverse party is proper. For example, if as defendant's lawyer in a personal injury case you suspect that the plaintiff is engaging in activities inconsistent with his claim, it is generally considered proper for you (or another person acting under your instructions) to interview under subterfuge (such as preparation of a credit report) persons with personal knowledge of those facts. The justification offered is the necessity for using subterfuge if the plaintiff's falsification is to be discovered without tipping him off. If you do not use subterfuge, he will undoubtedly learn of your interview and will then be warned to guard his activities more closely unless he has chosen the more commendable course of revising his claim (a course that is often more practical from the point of view of his realizing the most from the claim).

In addition to the ethical problem involved in using subterfuges in investigation, the danger of tactical disadvantages deserves your attention. If the fact of your using a subterfuge is disclosed during trial, it may cause an unfavorable reaction on the part of the jury. This danger is particularly apparent if your investigation by subterfuge fails to achieve the aim of revealing falsification by the adverse party. Subterfuges are often used for obtaining information that would otherwise be unavailable, even though it may not directly involve falsification by the adverse party or a witness; this danger of unfavorable reaction indicates, however, that you should be very cautious about using a subterfuge for a purpose other than one leading directly to disclosure of falsification. If you do succeed in exposing false testimony, the typical jury is willing to forgive, as justified, methods to which they might otherwise have reacted adversely.

Another purpose for which investigation by subterfuge is sometimes used is checking the accuracy and truthfulness of statements of a witness the use of whose testimony you are considering as part of your own presentation. Usually it would be embarrassing at the least, and perhaps also damaging to your relationship with the witness, if he should discover that you are checking his story rather than taking his word for it. Even if the witness passes the test, he may resent the fact that you were not willing to accept him on his own word.

"misrepresentation," proscribed by American Bar Association, Code of Professional Responsibility DR 1-102 (1969).

2. *Id.*, DR 7-104(A) (1).

§9.13 Taking statements

What are the characteristics of a good written statement?
How should a written statement be prepared?

Written statements of witnesses may serve many different purposes. At the time you take a statement, it may not be apparent for which, if any, of these purposes, you will need the statement at a subsequent time. For this reason, when you are preparing a statement you should consider its desirable characteristics for every possible purpose, though its usefulness for a particular purpose may be paramount in your thinking because it appears that it is most likely to be used for that purpose. These characteristics represent the ideal. Usually, some compromise short of this ideal is indicated by practical difficulties, such as lack of complete cooperation of the witness or inability to anticipate accurately the future development of the controversy.

Each of the following lettered subsections concerns a separate purpose for which written statements may prove useful. To facilitate comparison and cross-reference between these subsections, only one series of numbers is used for the list of different characteristics of a statement, not all of this series of numbers being used under each lettered subsection.

(*a*) *To avoid misunderstanding between you and the witness.* The primary characteristic of the statement serving this purpose is:

(1) Clarity. Clarity is best accomplished by using simple forms of expression; misunderstandings are more likely to arise when you attempt to translate the witness' story into a more sophisticated style. If an expression used by the witness is ambiguous to you, however, translate it to another form of expression, as well as recording that used by the witness, then calling the different expression to the witness' attention to insure that it expresses his meaning.

(*b*) *To serve as the basis for trial preparations.* Often the investigation will be made by someone other than the lawyer who has the primary responsibility for the trial of the case, and the lawyer's only factual basis for preliminary preparation and planning may be the file of statements of witnesses and memoranda of the investigator. Ideally, as the lawyer responsible for a case you will interview the witnesses personally in your early preparations and not merely at the time you are preparing them for appearance as witnesses,[1] but it is frequently impractical to arrange this. Under such circumstances, the danger of misunderstanding is far greater than when you yourself take the statement. Misleading statements may completely destroy the effectiveness of your planning. The characteristic of clarity of the statement is therefore even more important to the usefulness of the statement for your

---

1. See §2.14.

trial preparations if you did not take it yourself. The following are other characteristics important to the usefulness of the statement for preparations:

(2) Inclusion of the complete story of the witness on all points as to which he might be questioned, and not merely the favorable aspect of his story. A statement containing most favorable recitations of fact is not necessarily a good statement. A good statement is one that says what the witness would say in person, if he were present. A statement with recitations more favorable than what the witness will say is a vicious trap for the lawyer who must prepare his case for trial without benefit of personal interviews.

(3) Inclusion of complete information as to where and how the witness can be located — his full name, address, occupation, names and addresses of one or more close relatives who do not reside at the same address and through whom he could always be located if he should move or change jobs.

(4) Inclusion of a supplementary memorandum, not part of the statement itself, but containing observations of the person taking the statement concerning the witness, his age, status, characteristics, interest in the litigation directly or indirectly, and other factors bearing on his testimony and the impression he probably would make as a witness in trial; if any unfavorable aspects of the witness' story are omitted from the written statement, they may be referred to in this memorandum.

(*c*) *To serve as the basis for settlement appraisal.* [2] In the appraisal of the relative chances for winning or losing and the probable amount or value of the judgment, the characteristics of the most useful statement include (1) clarity and (2) completeness, discussed above. Obviously a sound appraisal of the probable outcome of trial is difficult, and sometimes impossible, if the statements relied upon do not have these characteristics. The fourth characteristic discussed above — preparation of a supplementary memorandum by the interviewer — is also a material aid to the usefulness of the statement in settlement appraisal.

(*d*) *To refresh the memory of your own witnesses immediately before trial.* Again the first two characteristics discussed above — (1) clarity and (2) completeness — are important to this use of the statement. [3] Closely related to these is another —

(5) Use of the witness' own words and methods of expression. A statement written in this form will naturally recall more to the witness than one written in a different literary style. Furthermore, refreshing a witness'

---

2. See §9.22.

3. The third characteristic (inclusion of identifying data) and the fourth (preparation of a supplementary memorandum) are relatively unimportant to the usefulness of the statement for refreshing the witness' memory, though important for other purposes discussed above in subparagraphs (b) and (c).

memory with a statement written in words not customarily used by the witness is likely to confuse him. He must either translate it to his own customary way of talking or else he must in his testimony use words that he does not customarily use, in either of which events confusion while on the witness stand is possible and often probable.

(e) *To impeach a hostile or adverse witness.* Even though a person may appear to be friendly at the time he is giving a statement, you should take his statement with the thought in mind that he may have a change of heart before trial. When that happens, an impeaching statement can provide valuable ammunition, though you must weigh against the advantages to be gained from using it the possible disadvantages, such as incidental disclosure of insurance coverage in a jurisdiction where the plaintiff is not permitted to advise the jury that the defendant carried insurance.[4]

The characteristics of a statement that you use for impeachment may materially affect the result in a case since it is quite likely that the statement so used will be seen by the jury before the trial is over. In view of this importance of the matter, each of the characteristics referred to in the preceding discussion of other uses of a statement is reconsidered here as it bears on use of the statement for impeachment, and other desirable characteristics are added.

(1) Clarity is as important here as with reference to other uses discussed above. An ambiguous statement increases the chances that the witness can materially change his testimony and yet not be effectively impeached.

(2) As to completeness of the statement, there is a conflict with interests mentioned above. For purposes of the preparation, settlement appraisal, and refreshing the memory of your own witnesses, the more complete the statement is, the better it proves to be. For those uses, the inclusion of some irrelevant or immaterial details has no important disadvantage — merely a loss of time being the cost. When you wish to use the statement in trial for impeachment, however, too much length and detail intereferes with emphasis upon contradictory points. Suppose, for example, that you catch the witness in only one material contradiction; if the statement is one page long, that contradiction seems more significant than if the statement is fifty pages long. On the other hand, your chances of catching the witness in further contradictions are improved, of course, if the statement is longer. In general, the statement is in best form for possible use for impeachment if it contains recitations on each material point as to which he may be called upon to testify, those recitations being as brief as they can be made while yet committing the witness to a firm position and giving him no leeway for changing his testimony without contradicting the statement. A statement meeting this

4. See §3.5.

specification is probably not as satisfactory for other uses discussed above as would be a more lengthy statement.

Competent trial lawyers have widely varying opinions as to the advantages and disadvantages of including the unfavorable aspects of the testimony of a witness when you anticipate that you may wish to use the statement for impeachment, and as to the ethical propriety of omitting the unfavorable. The Code of Professional Responsibility is not explicit on this matter.[5] Some consider that it is permissible to omit unfavorable matter and that it is preferable to do so in order that you may offer the statement in evidence in its entirety when you use it for impeachment, without qualification of the offer to avoid damaging admissions[6] and without facing the need for offering only part of the statement and objecting if your adversary offers other parts. Others consider that the unfavorable should be included, even from the tactical point of view. Otherwise the witness will testify to the fact that he told the interviewer many other things, but the interviewer left out everything that was against him; this may effectively discredit the statement. Inclusion of the unfavorable aspects of the story as told by the witness when he is interviewed does not prevent his falsely testifying later that he also mentioned other unfavorable things not included by the interviewer, but it does reduce the chance that such a charge by the witness will be given weight by the jury. By closing the statement with a comment that it includes everything that the witness can think of that he considers material to the controversy you can further reduce the risk that the witness will persuade the jury that unfavorable matter was omitted.

(3) Identification data included in the statement primarily for your use in preparing for trial are also helpful in establishing the authenticity of the statement if the witness attempts to repudiate it when you are using it for impeachment.

(4) The supplemental memorandum prepared just after you have taken a statement will sometimes be useful in connection with your cross-examination. If there has been any substantial revision of the statement in the course of taking it, or any reluctance on the part of the witness to sign it, or special circumstances in connection with the witness' checking the accuracy of the statement, and your memorandum records these details, you will be well armed to remind the witness of these matters during cross-examination, and you may obtain enough admissions to aid you in establishing the authenticity of the statement and the fact that it fairly represented the story of the witness at the time it was taken.

5. See generally American Bar Association, Code of Professional Responsibility DR 7-102 (1969).
6. See §2.36.

(5) Phrasing of the statement in the witness' style of speaking is very important to usefulness of the statement for impeachment. A document written in six-syllable words, purporting to be the statement of a two-syllable witness, is not likely to be very effective for impeachment, before either a two-syllable juror or a six-syllable juror. A statement in question and answer form, recorded and later reduced to writing, or taken down by a shorthand reporter and reduced to writing, has distinct advantages over the narrative statement in this respect, since the exact words used by the witness are thereby established.[7]

(6) Inclusion of inconsequential details that the witness mentions is often helpful to use of the statement for impeachment, particularly if they are matters that seem important to the witness, though erroneously so. In cross-examination, before producing the statement, you may ask the witness about such matters, and probably will obtain the same answers as appear in his statement. You thus build a background of authenticating data, convincing the jurors of the genuineness of the statement as against arguments that it merely represents a record of what the lawyer, or other person taking it, wanted the witness to say or induced him to say.

(7) Favorable conclusions expressed by the witness may be helpful if the witness changes his testimony and you then seek to use his statement for impeachment. Even if the conclusions are inadmissible as primary evidence, they may be admissible for the limited purpose of impeachment when the witness changes his testimony in a manner inconsistent with those conclusions. Pointedly including many favorable conclusions expressed by the witness and no unfavorable conclusions, if he expresses unfavorable ones also, is a practice of doubtful propriety both tactically and ethically; as in the case of the omission of unfavorable factual recitations, the witness may convince the jury that the statement is not a fair record of his views because it was unduly edited by the interviewer.

(8) Corrections help to authenticate a statement, when they have been carefully made and the witness has been asked to initial each. Some interviewers follow a practice of deliberately making at least one error on each page so that the witness will observe it in reading over the statement, and with corrections made, will have his initials on every page. The presence of these corrections is also impressive evidence that the witness probably read the entire statement carefully before signing it.

(9) Signature by the witness is very important to use of the statement for impeachment. If the statement has not been signed, there is too much danger that the witness will say he did not look over it to see what the interviewer wrote down and that the things written down are not the same as

7. See §9.14.

what he said. A recitation in the witness' own handwriting, just above his signature, that he read the statement before signing it, and that it is true, is an added help. Some interviewers use another similar device — writing questions at the end of the statement and getting the witness to write in "yes" in a blank after each, using such questions as "Have you read each page of this statement before signing it?" and "Is every statement made on these three pages true and correct?"; this procedure is not quite as effective as a recitation in the witness' own handwriting from the point of view of usefulness of the statement for impeachment, but it is much more likely to be feasible with a witness who is skeptical or reluctant about giving a statement.

If the witness refuses to sign a statement, the next best thing is to read it to him and get him to approve it orally. For some strange reason, witnesses who refuse to sign will sometimes even write "O. K." on a statement, which gives it as much value as a signed statement once the written "O. K." is established as being that of the witness.

(10) Postscripts to a statement give special emphasis to the matter in the postscript. If there is some particularly vital point in the witness' story, as to which there is special concern about the possibility of a change in the witness' attitude, you might omit the point from the original statement and ask the witness to add it as a postscript, in his own handwriting.

(11) Witnessing of the statement by an observer other than the interviewer increases its usefulness for impeachment. It may prove necessary or desirable in trial to authenticate the statement with the testimony of the observer. If there is no observer, the person taking the statement (ordinarily a lawyer or adjuster) must give the authenticating testimony when the statement is repudiated by the witness or other reasons exist for not introducing it with the witness' own authenticating testimony. As a matter of tactics, it is generally better to call some other observing witness rather than to offer the testimony of a lawyer or adjuster.[8] Code provisions relating to a lawyer's testimony in a case that he is trying cast doubt on the advisability of his testifying on such a point as this, even though it might be considered a "formal matter" not within the prohibition of the Code.[9] A non-lawyer adjuster, and probably even the adjuster who is also a lawyer, is not controlled by these Code provisions. However, in jurisdictions where the plaintiff is not permitted to advise the jury of insurance coverage, there is the great disadvantage that the appearance of the adjuster as a witness is almost certain to result in disclosure, either directly or inferentially, that insurance is involved. It is diffi-

8. See §3.5.
9. See American Bar Association, Code of Professional Responsibility DR 5-101, 5-102 (1969).

cult to avoid this even if a disinterested authenticating witness — a bystander to the interview — is used. The ideal is to have the statement witnessed by some disinterested person of official standing — for example, a court reporter or clerk.

§9.14 Recording interviews

Is a recorded interview preferable to a written statement?

Advances in design and production of portable recording equipment have made it feasible to use recorded interviews in many circumstances in which mechanical difficulties or expense were formerly prohibitive. Which is preferable, using a recording device or taking a written statement?

The witness may answer the question for you by being willing to make one form of statement but not the other. Some people refuse to give a written statement while being willing or even pleased to have their comments recorded. Others decline to have the spoken word recorded but are willing to make a written statement.

The record of an interview is usually more complete and accurate when you use recording equipment. Recording is a faster way of obtaining a record than preparing a written statement, with the result that you take somewhat less time with each witness, or you obtain a more thorough and accurate report of the interview, or, more often, a combination of these occurs. The recorded interview also has the advantage of preserving the exact words used by the witness, and the inflections of his voice. Ordinarily you would have the recording transcribed for convenience in study, but you should preserve the recording itself for purposes of authentication in case of attempted repudiation and also because of the greater effectiveness of the playing of the recording in some trial situations.

The written statement has the advantages of aiding you and the witness in avoiding misunderstandings. When you take a statement by recording, it may happen that you will not realize until you play it back or have it transcribed that you and the witness misunderstood each other at some point in the interview; such misunderstandings are likely to be cleared up when you reduce a statement to writing at the time of the interview.

Editing is more difficult in the case of the recorded interview. This is an advantage in that it reduces the chances of successful evasion of an impeaching statement on the ground that it was unfairly edited. It is a disadvantage in that it may result in the inclusion of so many expressions of inadmissible and unfavorable matter as to interfere with the effective use of the statement. Of course, editing is still possible in the case of the recorded interview. One way you can develop an edited record is by first interviewing the witness "off the record" before you use the recording equipment, then limiting your recorded questions to the desired inquiries. Probably, the inference that the purpose of such editing was to produce an unfairly favorable statement is more likely to be drawn in the case of the recorded interview, however, than in the case of a written statement, as to which considerations of length of the statement and time required for taking it are available to explain the editing consistently with fair recording of the witness' story.

§9.15 Giving the witness a copy of his statement

Should you give a witness a copy of his written statement?

If a witness requests that you give him a copy of his statement at the time you interview him, it is only fair that you honor his request, and you may find it necessary to do so in order to get his cooperation in making the statement. If he does not request a copy of the statement, the customary practice is not to give him one. If you do give the witness a copy of the statement, your adversary probably will discover that fact sooner or later and may succeed in obtaining it or a copy of it. Your adversary then has not only the advantage of knowing the contents of your file but also the advantage of some saving of time in establishing what the testimony of the witness will be, though of course a knowledge of the product of your interview is no substitute for a careful independent interview. The indications of your interests and possible contentions (implied in the subject matter of the statement you took and the emphasis you gave to particular subjects) will doubtlessly aid your adversary in anticipating your case. These disadvantages of giving the witness a copy of the statement are not as significant now as formerly, because of the changes toward broader discovery rules, but even under the most liberal discovery rules you may be able to protect from your adversary's scrutiny those statements taken by you or by another representative of your client.[1] Furthermore, some experienced trial lawyers, though doubtlessly a minority, favor leaving a copy of the statement with the witness and encouraging him to give it to any representative of the opposite party who interviews him, thus making it possible for the witness to decline to make any additional statement without creating the appearance that he is partisan.[2]

Suppose the witness comes to you at a time subsequent to the interview but before trial and requests a copy of his written statement. When you are confronted unexpectedly with a request of this type from a witness, without time to give consideration to the nature of the statement and to the motiva-

1. The leading case treating this question under the original Federal Rules was Hickman v. Taylor, 329 U.S. 495, 67 S. Ct. 385, 91 L. Ed. 451 (1947). However, the discovery rules have been substantially revised since that decision. See especially Federal Rule 26(b).
2. Compare §9.17.

tion that lies behind the request, you may be unprepared to make the important decision whether to comply with it or not. Though you may get only limited help from this procedure, it generally is advisable to talk with the witness in some detail about why he is prompted to ask for the statement, pointing out that you ask merely that he testify to what he knows about the case, without leaning to one side or the other, and seeking to discover from the witness whether the adverse party or one representing him is behind the request and how closely the sympathies of the witness are aligned with the adverse party at the time the request is made. Usually a witness does not make such a request unless prompted by the adverse party or someone representing him. Also, it is improbable that the witness will make the request unless he is considering testifying to matters that may be inconsistent with the statement. If you give him a copy of his statement under these circumsances, it is likely that he will place it in the hands of your adversary. If the witness is one whose integrity you doubt and whom you probably would not call as a witness at trial, your decision should usually be to withhold the statement. This has the effect of giving you greater protection against his falsification, because of his fear that he may be contradicting the statement and exposing himself to possible perjury charges. If he has the statement to study, he will have a better opportunity to fabricate his story without contradiction of the statement, the extent to which that is possible depending upon how thorough the statement is.

If you do not comply with the request of the witness to see or obtain a copy of his statement, that fact may be proved in trial, and the jury may react unfavorably to your position. Also, it will doubtlessly cause the witness to be unfriendly toward your client and you, and you cannot thereafter expect him to cooperate in making himself available to appear as one of your witnesses. This latter factor will usually indicate a decision to comply with the witness' request if he is one whom you intend to call and if he is insistent in the request. You may be able to satisfy him, however, by the compromise measure of allowing him to see the statement without taking a copy of it. After the matter is explained, he may sympathize with your desire to prevent your adversary from obtaining a copy of the statement taken by you, and he may agree that it is not fair that your adversary have a copy of the statement you took unless you have a copy of the one your adversary took. If his request was prompted primarily by fear that you were holding the statement over his head, your willingness to let him read it and your explanation of reasons for desiring that he not take a copy may meet with his approval; he may even prefer your procedure because he then does not have the problem of either making the statement available to the other lawyer or else explaining to the other lawyer why he will not produce it. Another possibility is to give him a copy with the suggestion, if he has not made a statement for the other side, that he may give this copy to them with the undersanding that he will not make any additional written statement. A witness is often receptive to this suggestion because of fear that the second interviewer wants his statement in writing merely for the purpose of trying to get him crossed up, so as to nullify the effectiveness of his testimony.

§9.16 Interviewing witnesses separately or together

CASE 10. *P*, whom you represent, is suing for personal injuries sustained when he stopped his car behind *F*'s, as the traffic light changed to red, and was hit from behind by *D*'s car. *F* was driving his own car. *S*, his son, was in the front seat beside him.

Should you interview each witness separately?

The dangers of the influence of each witness upon the other, which make it disadvantageous to have several witnesses with you at once as you conduct the final interviews preparatory to their testifying,[1] also cause disadvantages with respect to original interviews. The practical limitations of time will more often force a decision to conduct original interviews with more than one witness simultaneously, however. Many of your original interviews will be exploratory; you do not know whether the persons will be usable as witnesses for either party until the interviews have developed. Also, if the witnesses are related, as in Case 10, or otherwise closely associated, it may be awkward to request separate interviews. Such a request directed to a husband and wife, for example, might cause them to be suspicious of your intentions and to guard their statements to you for fear of contradictions between them. Some interviewers follow the practice of interviewing such witnesses together informally, then taking a statement from one in the presence of the second, and concluding by having the second sign a postscript adopting the statement of the first either entirely or with such reservations and additions as are consistent with differences in their knowledge and observation of material facts.

§9.17 Advising witnesses not to talk

Should you advise your client and witnesses not to talk with the adverse party or his representatives?

The Code of Professional Responsibility prohibits a lawyer from talking privately with an adverse party who is represented by legal counsel, without

1. See §2.13.

the consent and approval of his counsel.[1] Though not directly bound by the Code, liability insurance companies defending personal injury claims generally recognize such a limitation against their interviewing a claimant. It is sound practice to advise your client of this limitation against direct interviews with him by representatives of the adverse party, instructing him not to talk with them about the case but only to refer them to you if they approach him improperly or without knowledge that he is represented by counsel. Allowing your client to talk with them in your absence involves a number of disadvantages. Obviously, there is a possibility of their using such an interview for the purpose of developing impeaching material. If your client's story is subject to impeachment, and particularly if your client is deliberately withholding anything from you, you will want to know in advance of trial, rather than being embarrassed in trial by the disclosure that you are sponsoring a falsified claim. By forcing any representative of the adverse party to interview your client in your presence (or else forego the interview), you improve your chances of learning about it in advance of trial if your client is withholding any information from you. For other reasons, also, you may profit from knowledge of the exact inquiries that representatives of an adverse party wish to submit to your client; they may suggest his theory of the case or suggest leads for investigation that you had previously overlooked. Against the disadvantages there would be little advantage in allowing your client to discuss the facts of the case with representatives of the adverse party; unless your client is very clever and well informed about the legal implications of the matters of inquiry, he will reveal more than he will learn for you. Also, the possibility of any unfavorable inference because of his refusal to talk with a representative of the opposite party is extremely remote — there is more danger of an adverse reaction against the party whose representative was attempting such an interview.

A somewhat different problem is presented as to your client's talking with the adverse party, rather than one of his representatives. No ethical considerations stand in the way of such conferences. If the case arises out of business relationships, it would be quite natural for the parties to discuss the matter, even after both have engaged lawyers. Your client's absolute refusal to discuss it when approached by the opposite party might, when proved during trial, create the suspicion among jurors that your client was afraid to talk without having his lawyer at hand to tell him what to say and keep him from saying anything that might harm his claim. An alternative that is probably better than advising your client not to discuss the case with the opposite party under any circumstances is to caution him that if the opposite party initiates discussion, he may be doing so for the purpose of obtaining

1. American Bar Association, Code of Professional Responsibility DR 7–104 (1969).

information. You should also advise your client to make a complete memorandum in writing of what each party says in any such conversation, for your use and for his use in later refreshing his recollection if the conversation should become material to any issue in trial. The possibility that such a conversation directly between parties, and without counsel present, may result in their agreement to settle should not cause you to oppose it; when settlement is to the best interests of the client, you should favor it. As for protection of your fee for services rendered before such a settlement is made, this should be provided in the terms of your original employment contract if the protection is needed and feasible, rather than by disapproving direct negotiations between the parties.

The Code of Professional Responsibility does not prohibit conversations with witnesses other than the adverse party,[2] except that probably some persons not nominally parties are to be treated as if they were parties (for example, the manager of that aspect of a corporate party's business that is involved in the litigation). Is it ethically proper and tactically sound to advise a witness other than your client not to discuss the case with the opposing party or his representatives?

From the point of view of tactics, you may gain some advantages by persuading a witness to follow such advice. To the extent that you can keep witnesses from talking privately with the opposite party or his attorneys, you increase your adversary's difficulties of preparation and your own chances of superior preparation. Your adversary must then take depositions to discover the testimony of the witnesses, thus disclosing to you everything learned from them, filling any gaps you may have left in your interviews with the witnesses and at the same time not disclosing all that you have learned from them unless your adversary's questions are so inclusive that they cover every question that the witness discussed with you. The refusal of the witness to volunteer information places even a most competent adversary at a disadvantage, since it is practically impossible to anticipate all the matters on which the witness might be able to testify; the help of the witness in volunteering additional information that he thinks might be material is important. In addition, the advantages, suggested above, of causing your client not to discuss the case with your adversary outside your presence also apply in the case of other witnesses; if your adversary is forced to interview them in your presence, by deposition or informally, you are more likely to learn in advance of any basis for impeachment of the witnesses and of the direction of inquiry and probable theories that your adversary is preparing or considering (if you do not allow him to mislead you by inquiries designed for that purpose).

2. See American Bar Association, Code of Professional Responsibility DR 7–104, 7–109 (1969).

The nature of these tactical advantages demonstrates that the practice of encouraging witnesses not to talk to the opposing party or his representatives is opposed to the interests of full and fair development of the facts. Primarily for this reason, the practice has been held to be ethically improper,[3] though it is at least doubtful that this view prevails in all jurisdictions. Even if the practice be considered ethically proper, however, it would sometimes prove to be tactically disadvantageous. Your efforts to conceal facts from your adversary may lead to the suspicion that unfavorable facts exists or you would not be using these means of concealment. Your adversary may buttress this inference and argument by proving during trial that the witness talked freely with you and refused to talk with your adversary. Another inference to be drawn from this proof, which is perhaps even more damaging, is that the witness is not impartial and disinterested, but an advocate for your side. The jurors are therefore likely to judge his testimony by standards applied in considering testimony of interested parties rather than those applied in considering testimony of wholly disinterested witnesses. How much more effective is the witness' testimony when he is able to say that he has told the same facts to anyone who had an interest in the matter and asked him, than when he must admit that he refused even to discuss the facts with one lawyer!

Another factor that doubtlessly has great influence in causing some lawyers to favor the practice of asking witnesses not to discuss the case with the opposing lawyer is the fear that the witness will give a written statement that weakens his testimony. Even without direct contradictions, the substance of his story may be weakened by change of emphasis. Furthermore, a clever interviewer may persuade the witness to make and sign a statement without taking sufficient care to study the statement carefully to insure that what the interviewer has written down correctly expresses what the witness means and that the statement does not carry any implications contrary to his views. This danger may be reduced, if not eliminated, without the witness' refusal of an interview, however. You may advise the witness to discuss the case with the adverse party or his representatives but not to make any written statement about it and not to allow his interview to be recorded. Undoubtedly this advice is ethically proper. Also, a jury would normally be willing to accept that attitude as a fair means of protecting against the possibility of overreaching by an interviewer, and they would not be so likely to take it as an indication of bias on the part of the witness. Some lawyers, though distinctly a minority, favor going even further by giving the witness a copy of the statement so he may furnish it to the opposite side as a summary of what

3. American Bar Association, Opinions of the Committee on Professional Ethics and Grievances, Opinion 131. See also H. Drinker, *Legal Ethics* 86 (1953).

he knows about the matter, refusing to make any further written statement to either party[4] If you advise the witness against giving any written statement, you should also advise him that reading over and orally approving a written statement has essentially the same dangers as signing it, since he may later be compelled under oath to admit that he read it over and approved it, thus giving it virtually the same force for impeachment as if he had signed it.

The type of witness involved and the nature of his association with either or both of the parties to the case bear upon the question whether you should request that a witness not talk with the opposing party or his representatives, or not give a written statement. For example, if the witness is a personal friend or close acquaintance of the adverse party, such a request probably would be fruitless and might alienate the witness as well as causing him personal embarrassment; furthermore, his compliance with the request would be even more difficult to explain, on a basis other than bias, than in the case of a witness not acquainted with the other party before the incident on which litigation is based.

§9.18   Giving notice

CASE 68. *P*, a passenger riding in the back seat of *W*'s car, was injured when the car was struck from behind by a truck owned by *D Trucking Company* and driven by *S*. *P*, whom you have never known before, is referred to you by a former client. *P* asks you to represent him under a contingent fee contract. Your investigation discloses that *D Trucking Company* has liability insurance with *X Insurance Company*, and that *P* has a good claim on the facts.

Should you, before you file suit, notify the adverse party of your client's claim and of the fact that you represent him?

If so, at what stage in your handling of the claim?

In a few exceptional situations, notice of a claim within a specified time is a legal requirement. For example, many municipalites have charter provisions requiring notice to a specified municipal official regarding personal injury claims against the municipality; similar provisions are sometimes made by statute. Usually these provisions contain special requirements as to form and content of the notice. Sometimes there is doubt about the validity of a special notice requirement of this character, but obviously the better practice is to comply unless you are confident of invalidity and have some special reason

---

4. See also §9.15.

for noncompliance. Another example of a notice requirement frequently encountered is that applying to a claim based upon a contract containing a provision for notice; insurance policies usually contain some form of notice requirement (which, however, may be modified or affected by decisions or by statute[1]), and other contracts often contain such requirements. Your first step in considering whether you should give notice to the adverse party, and in what form, is to study the basis of your claim and determine whether notice is required by the terms of any agreement or by law, and if so, what are the provisions as to form and content of the notice.

Even when notice is not required for the protection of the claim of the client, lawyers sometimes give notice to the adverse party in order to protect the lawyer's interest in a claim that he is handling under a contingent fee contract. The preferred form of such a notice, and the extent of protection afforded, are affected by local variations in law. Local form books usually contain appropriate forms in common use in a given jurisdiction.

Another purpose of notice to the adverse party and his lawyer is to assure that the lawyer and other representatives of the adverse party know of your representation so that they will not approach your client without your approval.[2]

Even when notice is not required by agreement or by law, and is not needed for the protection of a lawyer's contingent interest or for protection against interviews with the client by representatives of the adverse party, it is nevertheless customary to give notice to the adverse party before filing suit. This custom is based partly upon courtesy but also upon the hope that litigation may be avoided through the adverse party's willingness to make a satisfactory adjustment of the matter without resort to litigation. If your client's interests can be protected by legal means without resort to litigation, it is your duty to avoid the unnecessary litigation.[3] The notice customarily given for this purpose is preferably not constructed as an argument, or as an indictment of the conduct of the party to whom it is addressed, but is a brief and simple notification of your representation of your client in regard to his claim against the other party and an invitation to him to communicate with you about the matter if he is willing to make amends without resort to litigation. If the other party is already represented by counsel with respect to the claim on which you propose to sue, you may either send a copy of your letter to his counsel or else address your letter to his counsel alone. Ordinarily an original notification does not threaten litigation, and a

---

1. See generally R. Keeton, *Insurance Law* §7.2(a) (1971).

2. See §9.17 regarding advice to your client not to discuss the case with representatives of the adverse party.

3. *Cf.* American Bar Association, Code of Professional Responsibility EC 7–7, 7–9 (1969). Also, see §9.22.

second letter is sent to advise that suit will be filed within a short time if satisfactory compensation for the claim is not made promptly.

With reference to personal injury claims against persons covered by liability insurance, as in Case 68, the customs observed vary from those followed in other types of litigation. In most areas, the lawyer representing the plaintiff customarily sends only one letter of notification. It may be addressed to the insurer, with a copy to the individual defendant, or vice versa. Often it states that suit will be filed within a specified number of days unless the writer is approached for the purpose of making a satisfactory adjustment of the matter.

At what stage in the handling of a claim for a plaintiff should you notify your adversary of the claim and of your representation of your client? From the point of view of protection of a lawyer's contingent interest in the claim, the earlier notice is to be preferred; usually in claims of the type handled under contingent fee contracts the adverse party already knows of the claim before a lawyer is engaged by the plaintiff, and there is no reason for delaying the notice of your entering the case and your contingent interest in the claim. Frequently, with respect to other types of cases, however, and occasionally with respect to claims handled under a contingent fee contract, the interests of the client demand that you withhold notification until after you have completed all of your investigation. It is preferable, of course, not to accept a case until you have gone far enough in your investigation to assure yourself that you will not later prefer to withdraw from it — to ascertain that the claim is genuine and one that you will wish to handle. It is important to go further and complete the investigation, if possible, before you give notice of the claim and of your representation of the client, because of the advantages to the one who investigates and interviews witnesses first.[4] Unless the potential defendant already knows of the claim and has engaged counsel or else has its own personnel to represent it, as in the case of an insurer, it is ordinarily preferable to withhold notice until you are fully prepared to file suit and to try the case as promptly as it can be brought to trial.

§9.19 Reimbursing and compensating witnesses

CASE 69. *P* sues for personal injuries sustained in a collision at an intersection controlled by a traffic light. Each party claims that he entered with a green light. *W*, who lived in the neighborhood at the time of the accident, tells you, as *D*'s lawyer, that he was walking in the same direction that *D* was driving and that *D* entered on a green light. Before the date of trial, *W* moves to another location, 300 miles from the place where the case is to be tried.

4. §9.3.

Should you arrange for reimbursement of expenses of your witness?
Should you arrange for compensation for your witness' loss of earnings during time spent conferring with you and appearing in court?

In some instances these questions will be answered for you by the client's lack of cash to pay the expenses of witnesses, the impropriety of your bearing them yourself or making any contingent arrangement with the witness, and the doubtful propriety of your advancing a cash payment if you may not be reimbursed unless your client wins.[1] Fortunately, in such cases, your client is usually one whose circumstances have sympathetic appeal so that the witnesses are willing to cooperate to avoid expenses and time lost from work, while at the same time being available when needed for trial. On the other hand, if your client is financially able to bear expenses, the extent to which you should arrange for reimbursement of expenses and compensation for time lost from work is often a delicate problem.

Statutory provisions for witness fees are outmoded in many jurisdictions, and they are often practically disregarded. Even where they have been modernized in terms of a dollar of comparatively current value, statutory fees may be inadequate compensation for the loss suffered by individual witnesses. It is clearly improper to make any payments to a witness, other than an expert, above reimbursement of expenses he incurs and reasonable compensation for loss of time.[2] The serious danger involved in making even a proper payment is that it will affect the jury's appraisal of the credibility of the testimony of the witness. The fact of the payment is clearly admissible, and it may lead the jury to question good faith if it is large.[3] On the other

1. Compare §9.11 n.1. That section is concerned with the expense of investigation, as to which a contingent arrangement might be proper. Clearly, a contingent arrangement as to expenses or fees of a witness is improper. American Bar Association, Code of Professional Responsibility DR 7–109 (1969). See H. Drinker, *Legal Ethics* 86 (1953).

2. American Bar Association, Code of Professional Responsibility DR 7–109 (1969). *Id.,* paragraph (C), provides:
"A lawyer shall not pay, offer to pay, or acquiesce in the payment of compensation to a witness contingent upon the content of his testimony or the outcome of the case. But a lawyer may advance, guarantee, or acquiesce in the payment of:
"(1) Expenses reasonably incurred by a witness in attending or testifying.
"(2) Reasonable compensation to a witness for his loss of time in attending or testifying.
"(3) A reasonable fee for the professional services of an expert witness."
Distinguish this problem of propriety of voluntary reimbursement from the questions whether such expenses are taxable as costs and whether the witness can require reimbursement as a condition to an effective subpoena or under an agreement that the litigant declines to honor.

3. See §§2.21, 3.27.

hand, if the payment is reasonable in amount and clearly not in excess of the loss and expenses really suffered, jurors are not likely to draw any unfavorable inference; it is more likely that they will consider it only fair to the witness that he not suffer financially because of his appearance in a case.

Less practical difficulty is encountered in connection with expenses than with payment for lost time from work. Whether a witness will actually lose pay depends on the nature of his job. If he is able to readjust his working hours, or if he does not lose pay when he is off work to appear as a witness, it is generally inadvisable, even though it may be permissible, to compensate him for the time he spends in court or preparing or awaiting his appearance. If he actually suffers a loss of pay, however, it is much less likely that the jury will draw any adverse inference from the fact that you arrange for reimbursing the lost pay. Compensation other than reimbursement for loss is proper in the case of an expert witness who is engaged in rendering professional services in appearing as a witness.

In a situation such as Case 69, it would be impossible in most instances to secure the attendance of *W* without reimbursing his expenses and compensating for any lost pay, since he is beyond the normally effective area of a subpoena. The choice will usually be one of bearing these costs to get the advantage of his appearance in person, or else using his testimony by deposition, or not at all. As a disinterested witness corroborating *D*'s testimony that he had a green light as he entered the intersection. *W*'s testimony is of great importance. Though you might choose the deposition if *W* does not make a favorable personal appearance,[4] ordinarily you should arrange for *W* to appear in person, reimbursing his expenses to the extent that reimbursement is proper in the jurisdiction of trial.

§9.20   Using subpoenas and tenders

Should you subpoena witnesses?
Should you tender witness fees and expenses?

The subpoena is available to compel an unwilling witness to appear and testify. As a matter of tactics, however, you will rarely choose to use it for that purpose. The experience of trial lawyers has demonstrated that the witness who comes unwillingly often causes more harm than good to the side calling him. Even without changing the basic content of his testimony about the case, he can change the emphasis, the manner of expression, or the degree of certainty with which he expresses it and make a material change in its effect on the jury.

Circumstances will sometimes justify your using a subpoena to compel an

4. See §2.4.

unwilling witness to appear and testify, despite the risk of adverse effect upon his testimony. This is the case, for example, if some part of the testimony of the witness is required for your case or defense and is not available elsewhere. The same is true if you consider that the witness possesses such integrity and such conviction regarding the matters on which he may be interrogated, either by you or by your adversary, that his unwillingness to come and his personal hostility toward you for forcing him to come will not affect his testimony. As a matter of fact, his testimony may carry greater weight under these circumstances than if he would come for you willingly, because his attitute rebuts the possible inference of interest in your client's winning.

Another instance in which you may safely use the subpoena against an unwilling witness arises when he has custody of a document but no knowledge as to other facts on which his testimony might be damaging to you. In such a case, a *subpoena duces tecum* may be used to compel him to bring the document into court. Also you may find a *subpoena duces tecum* useful as to an admittedly adverse witness, or even the adverse party, having custody of documents that you wish to have in court.[1]

If none of these exceptional situations exists, you are faced with weighing the need for the testimony of the witness against the danger that his testimony as a whole will take an unfavorable turn because of his hostility toward you when you force him to come against his will. It is no answer to this problem that the subpoena comes from the court; the witness will undoubtedly find out from your adversary that you instigated the process, if you do not advise him yourself. The better course is to advise the witness yourself, stating to him your reasons in the hope that he will appreciate the necessity for your calling him as an aid in proper disposition of the controversy.

Witnesses often are willing to come, realizing their duty to do so as citizens, though they find the experience unpleasant because of the necessity of giving testimony unfavorable to a friend, neighbor, or business associate, or of giving testimony that reflects unfavorably on the character of some other person. Such a witness may desire that you subpoena him to avoid the appearance that he is volunteering. Under these circumstances, you may also find it advisable to prove by a question to him during your direct examination that he was served with a subpoena to come to court as a witness.

You may find a subpoena useful if you fear that the witness will be unwilling to appear at the time of the trial setting because of personal inconvenience, though not unwilling to give his testimony. In this situation, you have a choice in many instances between using the subpoena and using a

1. Compare §11.14.

deposition. Against the advantages of greater effectiveness of the testimony of the witness in person you must weigh the same danger referred to above — that of influence on the witness' testimony because of his personal hostility at being compelled to come against his will at a time that is inconvenient for him. The rules regarding use of depositions when a witness is within the subpoena jurisdiction of the court vary, and in some instances you cannot use the deposition unless you have used reasonable diligence to procure the appearance of the witness, through subpoena, and the witness has failed to appear.[2]

Another advantage of the subpoena is to support a motion for continuance[3] because of the absence of a material witness. Usually it is necessary to show that you have used reasonable diligence to secure the attendance of the witness, and that his absence was not anticipated in time to take his deposition (except that in some jurisdictions you may obtain at least one continuance even though the deposition is available, on the ground that the testimony of the witness is vital, his appearance in person will probably affect the weight given his testimony, or additional matters are likely to arise that could not be reasonably anticipated at the time his deposition was taken, and that he probably will be available at the next trial setting). Obviously the best method of showing diligence to secure attendance of the witness is to show that you have had him subpoenaed, and a failure to show that may result in a finding of want of due diligence. Some lawyers make a practice of issuing subpoenas to their witnesses as a part of the routine of preparation for trial and as a protection against being put to trial in the absence of vital witnesses. A disdvantage of this practice is that the officer's returns are placed on file among the papers in the case and the subpoenas have the effect of disclosing to your adversary the identity of witnesses whom you intend to use, if he checks the papers on file.[4]

A subpoena is sometimes essential to taxing as costs the fees and expenses paid to the witness. The extent to which this factor deserves weight in your decision regarding use of a subpoena depends upon the amount involved as compared with the effect of the subpoena upon development of the case. Usually the only disadvantage in using a subpoena for this purpose is that of advance disclosure to your adversary of the identity of your witness, since you are able to satisfy your witness, by explaining your reasons for using a subpoena even though he is willing to come voluntarily. You may avoid the disadvantage of disclosure to your adversary by having the subpoenas issued only as the witnesses are needed; you may even arrange for a subpoena to be

---

2. See *e.g.*, Federal Rule 32(a) (3) (D).
3. See §11.21.
4. See §9.21.

served just shortly before the witness takes the stand, having the witness available for the service by an officer at the court house.

In some jurisdictions, a subpoena once issued in the case is valid and effective for subsequent terms of court. If you rely on such a subpoena for a later term of court, however, you should insure that the witness is notified in some way, formally or informally, of the date and hour at which he is expected to appear.

It is generally recognized that arranging for a witness to be subpoenaed in the case does not make him your witness; he becomes the witness of the person who calls him to the stand during trial. Accordingly, you may sometimes choose to subpoena a witness though you are in doubt as to whether you will actually use him in trial. You should bear in mind, however, that your adversary will be allowed to prove that you had the subpoena issued for the witness, and even though he suffers the disadvantage of rules making the witness his own, the jury will not be as likely to hold him responsible for the witness in their deliberations[5] when it is shown that you required the witness to be present.

The subpoena for appearance at trial is not generally an effective means of obtaining information from a witness who refuses to talk with you privately. After the subpoena has been issued, you still cannot compel the witness to talk with you privately, though occasionally he is more willing to do so. You can compel him to answer questions on the stand, but the risk of unfavorable answers is ordinarily too great, even if you are given the benefit of treating him as a hostile witness under special rules. A better means of dealing with such a witness is by a subpoena for deposition in advance of trial. Though there is some conflict on the matter, it is generally held that he does not become your witness, even as to the testimony on deposition, merely because the deposition was taken at your instance;[6] rather, that matter of whose witness he is, if relevant at all,[7] will be determined by who offers his testimony at trial. Again, however, the fact that the deposition was taken at your instance may have some influence on the jury's attitude toward the witness and his testimony. This question will be affected by the extent to which it is apparent whether you were taking the deposition as one for discovery of the testimony of a hostile witness or as one for preservation of the testimony of a witness with the apparent purpose at the time of having it available for your use.

A tender of witness fees and expenses is necessary in some jurisdictions to

5. See §2.2.

6. 3A Wigmore, *Evidence* §912 (rev. ed. Chadbourn 1970).

7. See §2.2. See also Federal Rules of Evidence, Rules 607, 611, 801(d) (1), drastically reducing, if not eliminating, the legal (though not the practical) significance of making a witness "your own."

the effectiveness of the subpoena,[8] and in such cases you should make the tender as a routine. Note also that an additional tender may be necessary to the effectiveness of the subpoena beyond the original day of attendance. You should also consider any local customs with respect to tender of witness fees. If the fees and expenses are inadequate to reimburse the witness for his actual loss, consider as well the propriety and advisability of tendering the additional amount necessary to full reimbursement.[9]

§9.21 Checking papers on file in your case

As to most papers filed in any cause, you will have received either a notice of the filing or a copy of the instrument itself. In some instances, however, rules do not require service upon the attorneys in the cause. It is therefore important that you check the papers on file in your case to insure that you are familiar with all of them and any developments they represent. You should do this not only in advance of trial, as a part of your preparations, but also during trial to keep yourself advised of any additional papers filed. For example, it is not generally necessary that your adversary notify you in any way of the issuance of subpoenas to witnesses at his instance; to keep yourself advised as to potential witnesses for your adversary, you should check the papers during trial for information on any subpoenas he may have had issued.

In cases involving great numbers of parties, rules frequently relieve each party of the necessity of serving pleadings on each of the other numerous parties in the case. Usually some arrangement is made among attorneys, as a matter of mutual convenience, to give notice to each of the filing and contents of additional pleadings. Even though such arrangements have been made, it is a good practice to check the official files of the court to insure that you have copies or know the contents of all pleadings filed. Another instance in which such a check is needed is the situation involving third-party pleadings to which your client is not a party. The existence and contents of such pleadings may be material to the development of your own case. For example, you may be able to anticipate more accurately the contentions and evidence of your adverse party when you know the issues raised between him and a third party to the suit, since it is likely, though not necessarily true, that the contentions he urges against you will be consistent with his position in the third-party proceeding.

Having assured yourself in advance of trial that you have copies or know the contents of all papers on file in your case, you should recheck the plead-

---

8. 8 Wigmore, *Evidence* §§2201, 2202 (rev. ed. McNaughton 1961).
9. See §9.19.

ings shortly before trial to insure that your own pleadings are adequate for your own intended uses,[1] and to see whether your adversary's pleadings contain any allegations that you may effectively use as judicial admissions or lack any allegations necessary to support all of the evidence that you expect your adversary to offer and all of the instructions or interrogatories that you expect your adversary to request in connection with the charge.

Another matter as to which you should check the official papers in advance of trial is the filing of depositions. If the depositions are likely to be used during trial (whether or not they were taken primarily for discovery purposes), you should also check the depositions as to compliance with any formal requirements. In some jurisdictions, even formal objections may be raised to deposition evidence for the first time when it is offered at trial, and your failure to discover and arrange for the correction of some formal defect of a deposition on which you rely might cause exclusion of important evidence. In most instances, however, formal defects must be raised in advance of trial, though objections to admissibility because of the subject matter of the evidence may generally be raised when the evidence is offered.[2] The time for objections as to formalities associated with taking the deposition is sometimes determined by the date of filing of the deposition, thus requiring your attention to checking the official files periodically, if notice to you is not required by the rules. Though the better procedure, and that followed in the federal courts, requires objections to form of questions to be made at the time the deposition is being taken, in some jurisdictions these objections may be made after the deposition is filed; this is another instance as to which a check on the official files may be important to you — either to determine whether sufficient time has elapsed since filing of the deposition to preclude objection by your adversary, or to determine the time of filing of the deposition for the purpose of computing the date by which you must file objections if you wish to do so.

§9.22 Considering settlement

What should be your position regarding settlement?

In the usual course of development of litigation, the problem of possible settlement will confront you whether or not you initiate negotiations. The question sooner or later arises in nearly all cases except those in which the parties have developed such animosity toward one another that neither is interested in making the concessions necessary to a compromise. It is one of

1. See §10.1.
2. See, *e.g.,* Federal Rule 32(b), (d).

your duties to your client to advise settlement of a controversy whenever, in your judgment, settlement would promote the interests of the client.[1] Conversely, it is one of your duties to advise against settlement, though your client may be inclined to favor it, when you consider that it would be against his interests. Your duty is not that of determining whether settlement is to be made, however; rather it is the duty of appraising the factors that your client should consider in making that determination, giving your client the benefit of your appraisal and leaving to his judgment the question whether to settle upon a specific proposal of the adverse party or to make a specific proposal to the adverse party. If your client insists on settlement, though you think he should take the risks of litigation, that is his right. If he prefers to settle, though you think he would stand to gain by litigating, you should advise him fully of your views and reasons for them but yield gracefully to his decision if he disagrees with your conclusion.

The extent to which you have responsibility in the process of your client's considering settlement in a particular case depends upon the type of case and the nature of the relationship with your client. Though the final decision is his, in nearly every case he is less familiar with the processes of litigation than you are and less able than you to detach himself from the circumstances for objective appraisal of the risks and the probable results of litigation. You are therefore normally better able than he to reach an objective appraisal of the case and of the advisability of settlement. Frequently your client will recognize these facts and will depend entirely upon your judgment concerning settlement and upon your representation in negotiations.

In some instances, negotiations for settlement are conducted by the parties directly, in which case you act only as an adviser to your client with respect to the negotiations. More often, however, the lawyers conduct the negotiations. You and your adversary may conduct the negotiations on a tentative basis, with the understanding that any conclusions you reach will be submitted to your respective clients for approval or disapproval; this is the usual method of negotiating. Occasionally, however, one or both lawyers are authorized to bind their respective clients.

Opening settlement negotiations often presents a problem. Since settlement negotiations are a normal part of the process of handling litigation, an invitation to the lawyer representing the adverse party to discuss settlement of the claim is not ordinarily construed as a confession of weakness or lack of confidence. Nevertheless, there is such fear of that reaction, particularly as between those who have dealt with each other little, that you may observe

---

1. *Cf.* American Bar Association, Code of Professional Responsibility EC 7-7, 7-9 (1969).

lawyers pretending indifference toward the question of settlement while each knows that it will finally be discussed and anxiously hopes the other will raise the subject for discussion. There is a similar reluctance on the part of many lawyers to name the most reasonable terms they would recommend or to which their clients would agree. As in any other type of negotiations, the question whether you may get directly to the point or must first engage in "horse trading" depends entirely upon the individuals involved and their degree of confidence in each other. If you prefer to dispense with the wasted motion of a period of jockeying, you will find that you can establish a satisfactory relationship with some lawyers for negotiating on that basis, whereas with others you must expect no serious effort to determine the possibilities of settlement until the date of trial is at hand. With an adversary of the latter type, you may reduce the possibilities of settlement by making your best proposal early in the development of the controversy, since your adversary will expect further concessions. Another factor you should consider is whether the trial judge is one who becomes an active participant in negotiations at a pretrial hearing, or as the case goes to trial, and actively encourages each party to make concessions not previously offered.[2]

Some lawyers prefer to wait until the jury is selected before making their final and most serious effort at settlement, on the theory that the variation in character of juries is material to appraisal of the probable results of trial. The question whether the parties wish to postpone settlement efforts until the last moment is simply a question of what risks they are willing to appraise as best they can. The probable result of litigation becomes clearer as the time of final decision approaches, even up to the point immediately before the verdict is returned, determining the facts, or a judgment is rendered, determining law points in dispute. On the other hand, the intervening developments as trial approaches and proceeds may be either favorable or unfavorable; it is usually impossible to say which party will be favored by delay, in the sense of anticipating developments that change the appraisal of probable results of litigation. It is often as reasonable to settle in the early stages as later; usually, if a case is to be finally settled, both parties benefit by an early settlement because they avoid the disadvantages of uncertainty and increasing expenses. It is not a sound practice, however, to consider settlement before a thorough initial investigation of both facts and law. In unusual cases in which the investigation would be very expensive, an exception to this rule might be warranted. But ordinarily you should undertake to give advice concerning settlement only after you have the benefit of a thorough investigation of both facts and law.

Settlement value of a disputed case is not susceptible of precise determina-

2. See §11.23.

tion, and no satisfactory rules for fixing settlement value can be stated. The breaking point between the terms under which it would be better for the client to have the case tried and those under which it would be better for the client to have the case settled will always be a matter of opinion. Every factor that might affect the result of litigation is a factor that you must weigh in a settlement appraisal — for example, all evidence available to each party, all legal theories potentially applicable to the case, procedural rules with potential influence over the result, and the imponderable personal factors arising from the fact that the entire process of litigation is an intensely personal process, despite our relatively successful efforts to administer justice under general and stable standards ("under law"). In addition to factors that may affect the result of litigation, delays and expenses of litigation are often important considerations.

Advantages to both parties of avoiding uncertainty and expense are doubtlessly major factors in accounting for the high percentage of settlements. In final analysis, any appraisal is only a calculated guess about the settlement value of the case.

Chapter X

PLEADINGS

§10.1 Aims and systems of pleading

Concepts of the function of pleading in the litigation process have undergone significant changes in the history of Anglo-American law,[1] and the different systems of pleading in effect within the various American jurisdictions at the present time reflect very different expectations.

The federal system of pleading, adopted with the rules in 1938, supplemented by the concise forms attached to those rules as an appendix, is the outstanding illustration of a system assigning to pleading a relatively minor role in the litigation process. By reason of the influence of the federal rules themselves, and of the men and concepts responsible for their adoption, the use of this system of pleading has spread to many state jurisdictions; further extensions are to be expected. Under this system, it is contemplated that pleadings will serve to invoke the jurisdiction of the court and to indicate only in very general terms the subject matter of the suit and the nature of the cause of action. This system vests great discretion in the trial judge, however, and in actual practice pleadings are frequently used to serve some of the additional functions contemplated by systems requiring more detailed allegations. This is particularly true in the federal courts, where practices are likely to be influenced in any particular district by the procedures of the state within which that district is located. The judges are generally persons trained in the state procedures and the practicing bar consists mostly of lawyers regularly appearing in the state courts as well as federal courts. There is a tendency for the lawyers to use, and the judges to permit, the same procedures in both state courts and federal courts within the state; the federal system of pleading being the more elastic, generally, the tendency is therefore to use the state methods of pleading in the federal courts. The tendency is never so strong as to make the procedures essentially identi-

1. C. Clark, *Code Pleading* §§4–12 (2d ed. 1947).

354

cal, since the federal rules do not contemplate forcing an unwilling lawyer to plead in detail; furthermore, there are individual variations from this tendency because of the fact that the federal district judge has sufficient power and discretion to resist it if he so desires, regardless of the willingness of lawyers on both sides of a case to follow the state practices.

For our purpose of considering trial tactics and methods, the primary importance of the differences among systems of pleadings arises from the extent and degree that pleadings are required or expected to serve one or more of the purposes discussed below, in addition to the function of notice in general terms of the nature of the claim.

Pleadings may serve the purpose of narrowing the scope of the controversy and defining the issues to be tried. Such pleadings must be in detail, the degree of detail varying with the extent to which it is expected that the issues be narrowed. For example, in some jurisdictions a general allegation of negligence is objectionable, and the pleader may be required to specify particular acts and omissions alleged to constitute negligence; likewise, in some jurisdictions, a general allegation of injury is objectionable, and the pleader may be required to specify the parts of the body alleged to be injured or even the medical diagnosis alleged. Omission of a particular ground of negligence, or a particular claim of injury, under such a system may result in the exclusion of evidence upon objection for want of support in the pleadings,[2] or in refusal to submit a charge or special issue or interrogatory,[3] whereas these objections are rarely sound and still more rarely useful[4] under a system of pleading on the federal pattern. In the federal system, it is contemplated that discovery and pretrial procedures will serve the functions of narrowing the scope of the controversy and defining the issues.

It is often said that pleadings should serve a notice function. To some, the "notice function" implies notice only in a general way of the assertion of a claim or defense and of its subject matter. To others, the "notice function" implies the more detailed notice of the specific legal theories to be asserted, the nature of the supporting evidence, and the legal issues to be urged — in short, a definition of the issues as conceived by the pleader. When the term is used in the former sense, it is fairly descriptive of the federal system of pleading; when used in the latter sense, it is fairly descriptive of code or other systems requiring detailed pleadings.

Pleadings may serve the function of revealing or raising the contention of want of a material fact issue, so that the trial judge may enter a final judgment upon the pleadings without hearing evidence. The general demurrer serves this function in some jurisdictions now, and formerly did in

2. See §4.8.   3. See §§5.7, 6.8.
4. *Cf.* §4.8.

others.[5] The extent to which the demurrer practice *reveals* the want of a fact issue depends entirely on how fully the point is argued rather than upon the form of the pleading itself. The reduced favor of the general demurrer stems largely from the fact that it allows the demurring lawyer to conceal the grounds until it is either too late or too costly for the opponent to cure the omission or irregularity. In many jurisdictions, various forms of procedure requiring specification of reasons for urging that the opponent's pleading does not state a cause of action or ground of defense have been substituted for the general demurrer; some procedures for exception to the pleading and for motion for judgment upon the pleadings are of this type. The summary judgment procedure,[6] which provides for consideration of other matters in addition to pleadings in determining whether there is any genuine, material fact issue, is growing in favor and may eventually supplant the more restrctive procedures based upon the pleadings alone. Because of the availability of the more adaptable summary judgment procedure, the provision in the federal rules for a motion for judgment on the pleadings[7] is seldom used in practice.

Thus far, we have been considering the aims and functions of pleadings generally, as they have influenced and are reflected in the many different pleading rules in the various states and federal courts. From your point of view as an an individual lawyer, preparing pleadings in a particular case, your aims include these: (1) stating a legally sufficient claim or defense; (2) providing support for every theory that you may wish to urge — to support all the evidence you may wish to offer, all the theories you may wish submitted in the charge to the jury, and all the theories you may choose to urge in motions for judgment; (3) making a statement that is designed to convince the jurors of the merits of your client's position;[8] (4) conforming with and contributing to your overall plan of developing the case in the most favorable manner. Your consideration of these potential aims of your pleading will influence the decisions you reach concerning the tactical problems of pleading, including those discussed in this chapter and any others that may arise. These different aims sometimes come into conflict with each other, necessitating a compromise or choice between them.[9]

§10.2 Deciding whom to sue

CASE 70. *P*, a child, was hit by a tractor operated by *E*, who was clearing timber from an oil well site. As the lawyer engaged by *P* and his

5. C. Clark, *Code Pleading* §78 (2d ed. 1947).

6. See §11.23.

7. In Federal Rule 12.

8. This aim does not merit attention in jurisdictions where the pleadings are not read or stated to the jury.

9. *E.g.*, see §10.4, concerning how detailed the pleadings should be.

parents, you investigate and conclude that *P*'s status on the premises and *E*'s manner of operation of the tractor were such as to support a negligence action against *E* and his master. *E* was a permanent employee of *Tractor Contracting Company*, a foreign corporation and owner of the tractor. *E* and the tractor were on the site pursuant to an agreement between *Tractor Contracting Company* and *Drilling Company*, which latter company had a foreman, *F*, on the site, and is also a foreign corporation. One of your witnesses says that *F* remarked after the accident, "It may look like I was careless, but it was mainly *E*'s fault."

Whom should you sue?
Should you join multiple claims in the plaintiff's pleading?

The first consideration in determining whom to sue is careful investigation to insure that you know the identity of all potiential defendants [1] and the legal requirements [2] as to which ones must be included in your suit. You should always consider whether it is necessary to join a spouse, to appoint a guardian *ad litem* for a minor or other legally incompetent defendant, or to allege the capacity or capacities in which you sue a party when such matters as trusts and guardianships are involved. Sometimes your investigation will disclose several possible defendants, under circumstances in which the law gives you a choice of suing only one or some of them. You will make that choice on the basis of tactical considerations.

Some fact situations will give rise to doubt as to which one of several persons or legal entities is legally responsible for the wrong committed against the plaintiff. For example, a possible "loaned servant" situation may raise a fact issue as to which of two or more legal entities was the master of the individual wrongdoer (the individual wrongdoer is theoretically responsible, but usually judgment-proof; as a practical matter, you need his master as a defendant so that your judgment will be collectible). This circumstance that a fact issue determines which of several potential defendants is legally responsible presents a dilemma for you in some jurisdictions, because of lack of adequate provisions for joinder of all potentially responsible parties in one suit. In an increasing number of jurisdictions, however, it is now possible for you to join all such parties in one suit, asserting liability against them alternatively. When permitted, generally you should follow that practice if there is doubt as to which of several parties is responsible; exceptions to this general rule are considered below.

In a situation of alternative as distinguished from joint liability, an unsuccessful suit against one of the potential defendants generally does not

1. See §9.5.
2. See §9.2.

bar a separate proceeding against another of the potential defendants. If, therefore, it is impossible to gain personal jurisdiction over all potential defendants in one court, you may consider suing first the preferred defendant, with the purpose of proceeding against the other in a different jurisdiction if the first suit is unsuccessful. This plan involves not only the disadvantage of delay and duplication but also the disadvantage that the findings in one suit are not controlling in the other, and it is conceivable that inconsistent findings, both unfavorable, will be reached. That is, in the loaned servant situation, it might be found in the suit against each employer that the employee was not acting as the servant of that employer at the time of the accident, even though the circumstances are such that he was necessarily acting as the servant of one or the other. This possibility is one of the factors making it preferable, in a situation of alternative liability dependent upon a fact issue, to join all potential defendants. Another factor favoring joinder is that each defendant, in self-protection, is likely to aid the development of your case against the other. [3]

Relative financial positions of the potential defendants, and the relative effect of their respective positions from the point of view of jury appeal, often affect the decision on joinder of defendants. In the typical situation of a tort committed by a servant in the scope of his duties for a large business, most lawyers in representing the plaintiff would prefer to have the suit proceed against only the large business, for fear that the presence of the individual servant as a party defendant might be likely to cause more sympathetic consideration of his contentions or a more conservative verdict as to damages. This factor is usually outweighed, however, if joinder would affect jurisdiction or venue. Another situation in which it is outweighed by factors favoring joinder is that existing when the suit is based upon negligent operation of a vehicle covered by liability insurance and there is at least doubt as to whether the driver was acting in the course and scope of employment and as to whether other circumstances exist that would support a judgment against the owner of the vehicle. Since the insurance policy typically (though not always) has an omnibus clause affording insurance coverage to the driver operating the vehicle with the permission of the owner [4] a judgment against such a driver is collectible despite his insolvency. You should join him if there is any doubt as to legal responsibility of the owner, even though the driver is a penniless individual and the owner of the vehicle is a large business.

If one of the potential defendants is insolvent, or if for any other reason a judgment against him could not be collected, this is a factor against in-

---

3. *Cf.* §§10.10, 11.22.
4. R. Keeton, *Insurance Law* §4.7 (1971).

cluding him in the suit, though it may be outweighed by contrary considerations as indicated above. Particularly if you are concerned with a situation of alternative liability, it is preferable not to make the insolvent person a party. His presence in the suit reduces your chances of obtaining a judgment against another defendant who is solvent. A jury is likely to be more reluctant to find for the solvent defendant when he is the sole defendant than when he is one of two. In the latter situation, though being persuaded that the plaintiff should recover, they may fail to realize that one defendant is insolvent and may conclude that the insolvent defendant should be held solely responsible. Also, there is danger of cooperation between the defendants through a so-called "gentlemen's agreement" [5] with the purpose of causing the judgment to be imposed on the party who is already insolvent and can thereafter secure a discharge in bankruptcy at little cost.

In a situation of either joint or joint and several liability the prosecution to judgment of a suit against one defendant may affect proceedings against other potential defendants. [6]

Another factor affecting desirability of joinder of more than one of the potential defendants is the effect upon either jurisdiction or venue. Frequently the state courts are preferable to the federal courts from the point of view of the plaintiff, and occasionally the reverse is true. [7] A plaintiff's lawyer who prefers the state court may, by joining the resident servant as a codefendant, prevent removal to federal court by a nonresident master (or other joint tortfeasor), in the absence of a "separate and independent claim or cause of action" against the nonresident. [8] Conversely, a plaintiff's lawyer who prefers the federal court may find it necessary to omit a resident defendant in order to preserve complete diversity of citizenship to support federal jurisdiction. The joinder or omission of a defendant may have similar effects upon venue in some jurisdictions.

Joinder of parties may affect the scope of issues in the case and the admissibility of evidence. [9] Whether this factor favors joining or omitting certain parties depends upon the nature of the additional issues and evidence. On the one hand, it is generally in plaintiff's favor to keep the issues in a case as simple and limited as possible. On the other hand, the added evidence may be of a character incidentally having some favorable influence on other issues in the case.

5. *Cf.* §§10.10, 11.22.
6. W. Prosser, *Torts* §48 (4th ed. 1971).
7. See §10.3.
8. See 28 U.S.C. §1441(c).
9. See Case 56, discussed in §4.15.

Occasionally you should join a party for the reason that it might otherwise be necessary for you to call him to the stand, making him your own witness, [10] whereas if he is an adverse party you will be able to secure the same needed testimony from him without becoming responsible for other parts of his testimony; you might also present more effective testimony because of the absence of restrictions such as that against leading your own witness. These factors may be outweighed by the probability that the person whose testimony you need will become more hostile toward your client and yourself and will give testimony that is less favorable both in form and in substance.

Applying the foregoing principles to Case 70, you should sue both *Tractor Contracting Company* and *Drilling Company*. It is very likely that *E* is insolvent. Also, there appears to be doubt as to whether both companies are responsible and (in view of the "loaned servant" problem) doubt as to which one if only one is responsible. If you wish to prevent removal, you might do so by joining *E* only, and you might omit *F* insofar as this consideration is concerned; this is probably true under the present removal statute even though the evidence would support a finding that *E* was free from negligence and *F* was guilty of negligence. [11] Aside from removal, however, there is another important reason for joining *F*; his presence as a party may affect the admissibility of the testimony that he said, "It may look like I was careless, but it was mainly *E*'s fault." In some jurisdictions a stronger case for admissibility can be made if *F* is a party, on the ground that it is an extrajudicial admission by *F* of his own negligence but cannot be treated as an admission of his employer because made outside the scope of authority. [12] An argument might be made for its admissibility even though *F* is not a party (*e.g.*, for impeachment if *F* is a witness), but the case for admissibility is stronger if *F* is a party. The basis upon which the evidence is admitted might be material also with respect to whether the court may consider it in determining whether there is sufficient evidence to support a factfinding of negligence of *F*; if this statement were admitted for the limited purpose of impeachment, for example, the court might disregard it in determining whether the plaintiff had offered evidence sufficient to go to the jury on the issue of *F*'s negligence.

10. See §2.2.

11. See 28 U.S.C. §1441(c).

12. See 4 Wigmore, *Evidence* §1078 (3rd ed. 1940). But *cf.* Federal Rules of Evidence, Rule 801(d) (2) (D), declaring that a statement is not hearsay if it is offered against a party and is "a statement by his agent or servant concerning a matter within the scope of his agency or employment, made during the existence of the relationship . . . ."

Another common example of the joinder of claims of the alternative type involving more than one defendant is the interpleader action in which inconsistent claims are being made against the plaintiff by two different parties. In addition to the advantages of disposing of all claims in one suit, the interpleader proceeding frequently offers the advantage of obtaining reimbursement of attorneys' fees as well as any court costs incurred.

§10.3 Choosing a forum

What forum should you choose?

In most cases, as plaintiff's lawyer you have a choice among several forums. Usually there are many courts with potential jurisdiction over the subject matter. Your first consideration is whether it is possible in each court to acquire jurisdiction over the person of each of those who are potential defendants, or else in rem jurisdiction over property that will be sufficient to afford the relief you seek. Even after you consider this limiting factor there will ordinarily be more than one court left to choose from, and an opportunity of choosing upon the basis of considerations of tactics and convenience.

Similarly, as the defendant's lawyer you will sometimes have a choice of forums, although less often and generally with less range of choice than that you have as a plaintiff's lawyer. The choice you have as a defendant's lawyer comes about by reason of the possibilities of removal to federal court or change of venue either within a state system or within the federal system.

Your choice among courts within a single jurisdiction will involve no basic differences of procedure or law and will be influenced primarily by personal factors, relative condition of the dockets in the various courts, and relative convenience of location.

Great differences may exist with respect to the character of the juries available; for example, the basic attitudes of a jury of farmers and local merchants in a rural community will contrast sharply with those of a jury composed primarily of laborers in an industrial area. A custom of relatively high verdicts on unliquidated damages claims appears to exist in some areas, generally the industrialized areas, as compared with other areas within the same state. Also the extent to which each of the parties is known in either community may be of material importance,[1] particularly if either court is located in a small community in which most persons

---

1. Compare Horace Greeley's statement: "He will not like to bring it [the action] in New York, for we are known here, nor in Otsego, for he is known there." Cooper v. Greeley, 1 Denio 347 (N. Y. 1845).

who might be chosen as jurors would be acquainted with the parties, the witnesses, or the lawyers.

Differences between individual judges may have a significant bearing on your choice of a forum. They may be particularly material in federal courts or those of other jurisdictions in which the trial judge has great discretion. Even if the discretion of the trial judge is limited, however, the known views and attitudes of the judge may be important factors. For example, if you know of previous rulings by the judges on points analogous to some involved in your case, you would ordinarily prefer the court of the judge who has ruled more favorably from your point of view, rather than taking your case through the other court and into the appellate courts to establish your point.

The condition of trial dockets in different courts within the same jurisdiction usually produces a material difference as to the probability of early trial. Although efforts are constantly made, through both legislative and administrative processes, to equalize the case loads of different courts and to make it possible for all cases to be tried promptly, nearly every jurisdiction has some courts in which cases must customarily remain on the docket awaiting trial two or more times as long as in others. Shifting population and business activity create differences in this respect despite earnest efforts of competent personnel; remedial action almost invariably lags considerably behind these changes.

Obviously, if personal factors and docket conditions are evenly balanced, you will choose the forum most convenietly located for presenting your client's case. This may not be the court nearest your client's and your own residence. You must consider such factors as convenience for your important witnesses whose voluntary attendance you may rely upon and the area within which subpoenas from the court will be effective if you have need of the personal appearance of witnesses who may be reluctant to appear voluntarily.

Greater variations exist when there is a choice between courts of different jurisdictions — those of different states, or state and federal courts. All of the differences that you are likely to encounter as between courts of the same jurisdiction are present, and in addition there are many more because of differences of procedural law and occasionally even differences in the substantive law that will be applied to your case.

Divorce litigation is an obvious example of differences of substantive law — a situation that has given rise to a considerable practice of shopping around for the most desired forum. [2] Outside the field of divorce

2. Such shopping for a forum can be justified if there is a bona fide intent to change domicile, even though the possibility of quick and easy divorce is a factor in

litigation, conflict of laws rules often effectively prevent shopping around for a forum with desired substantive law by providing for application of the law of a certain jurisdiction regardless of the forum of trial, but the rules are not intended to make that proposition universally true, and disagreement concerning the rules expands the area within which shopping for a forum of desired substantive law is practiced.

The rule of *Erie R.R.* v. *Tompkins*[3] has been described as one aimed at causing the trial result, insofar as it is determined by rules of law, to be the same as if the case were being tried in a state court of the state in which the federal court sits.[4] It would fall short of that aim if the only material differences in law applied were those of "procedural law" as that term has been narrowly defined in decisions developing the *Erie* doctrine. The differences are undoubtedly somewhat greater. If, for example, you have a decision of an intermediate court of the state in your favor, and the matter has not been passed on by the highest court of your state, the federal court would ordinarily be a better forum for you since it is generally considered that in reality federal courts are less likely than your highest state court to overrule, distinguish, or decline to apply the rule of your intermediate state court decision. Conversely, if there is an intermediate state court decision against you, you would prefer the state forum, other factors being equal, since you have a better chance there of finally winning your point in the highest court of the state, if not in the lower courts.

When your choice is between courts of different states, differences in law applied by each forum as its own "procedural law" may be directly determinative of the controversy, since the term "procedural" has broader meaning in this connection than in connection with the *Erie* doctrine. Furthermore, even those rules that are procedural in the narrow sense of the *Erie* doctrine may have substantial effect on the litigation. For example, there are areas in which the difference between juries customarily available in state and federal courts is so marked that it would be mockery to assert that the probable verdict would be the same in both courts. Differences in procedure for selection of the jury panel contribute to this situation. Other matters as to which there are frequently important differences include the question whether an issue is appropriate for trial by jury,[5] procedures for

---

the formation of that intent. But obviously a serious ethical problem is presented to the lawyer advising a client who, the lawyer knows, has no such bona fide intent. See H. Drinker, *Legal Ethics* 80–82 (1953).

3. 304 U.S. 64, 58 S. Ct. 817, 82 L. Ed. 1188 (1938.)

4. Guaranty Trust Co. v. York, 326 U.S. 99, 109, 65 S. Ct. 1464, 1470, 89 L. Ed. 2079, 2086 (1945).

5. See §7.2.

attack upon jurisdiction, discovery and pretrial procedures, rules of evidence,[6] form of the charge,[7] types of relief available,[8] procedures for obtaining new trials and the general attitude toward granting new trials, and appellate jurisdiction and procedures.

§10.4 Determining degrees of detail

CASE 71. *P* sues *D* for damages because of personal injuries sustained in a head-on collision between cars driven by *P* and *D*. The principal issue in dispute is whether the point of collision was on *P*'s or *D*'s right-hand side of the highway. As *P*'s lawyer, you have learned that *D* was in a garage to get his car greased a few hours before the accident and requested a brake adjustment. "Brakes pull to left" was written on the service ticket and then scratched off. The garage foreman says he remembers the incident, that *D* told him the brakes pulled to the left, that he told *D* that he could not assign anyone to work on the brakes until afternoon, and that *D* said he could not wait for the car that long. On deposition before trial, when you ask *D* the condition of the brakes on his car, he replies, "Excellent shape; they had never given me any trouble."

How detailed should your pleadings be?

Although the degree of detail you use in the preparation of your pleadings will be limited by the rules of your jurisdiction (some rules contemplating very concise pleadings and others contemplating various degrees of greater detail), in every jurisdiction some latitude remains for your preference. What factors should determine how detailed you will make your pleadings?

In jurisdictions where pleadings are read to the jury, or a statement paraphrasing them is used, the pleadings afford an early opportunity for a thoroughly considered jury argument. This is a function of pleadings easily lost in a mass of legal phrases, which may have been intended as a shorthand summary of facts. For one trained in the law, accustomed to writing legal briefs and making oral arguments on the law, and accustomed to thinking of his facts in terms of satisfying legal requirements for a cause of action or ground of defense, it is quite natural in drafting pleadings to make liberal use of legal terms. Jurors may be impressed by the formal language, but when they consider whose client is right they are less inter-

---

6. See *e.g.*, §2.2 n.3, suggesting an instance in which a rule of evidence may be outcome-determinative rather than merely "procedural" in the *Erie* sense.

7. See §6.1.

8. See §10.5.

ested in the legal description of the alleged wrong or defense than in whether under the facts it is "fair" that the defendant be required to pay the plaintiff. It should be your purpose, therefore, to state the circumstances in a way that will appeal to a person's sense of fairness. This purpose requires more than a statement of legal conclusions, such as that the defendant was negligent, or that he was guilty of a breach of contract, or that he defrauded the plaintiff. This purpose is best served by a full statement of the factual circumstances, just as you would tell the story if you were explaining to a person outside the courtroom why your client should be awarded the sum for which you sue, or why your client should not be held liable for the sum for which the other party sues.

With few exceptions, the rules of pleadings make no requirement that the defendant plead the facts supporting denial of the allegations of the plaintiff's prima facie case, as distinguished from those supporting an affirmative defense. In some jurisdictions, however, the defendant may include allegations of the basis for the denials. If the pleadings are read or stated to the jury, you may use such a "talking denial" for the purpose of making a persuasive statement of what otherwise might be a mere statement that what the plaintiff says is not so. For example, if the defendant is charged with negligence in the manner of manufacture of an article, an alleged defect of which caused the plaintiff's injuries, the defendant's answer might include a summary description of the process of manufacture, emphasizing particularly the safety measures used to insure that defective articles are not released.

In the pleadings of either the plantiff or the defendant, the ideal statement is not a full statement of all the evidence, even if that were permitted. If you use any statement beyond the barest outline, you should take care to make it sufficiently general to allow for variations in the evidence, rather than making it so specific as to point up minor conflicts and to restrict your evidence and the chances of jury agreement on a favorable version of the facts. For example, is it not better to rely on an allegation that the defendant failed to swerve to avoid the collision, rather than to assume an unnecessary burden by alleging the direction in which he should have swerved, as to which there is more chance of disagreement? You should avoid exaggeration, since a demonstration of numerous exaggerations in your pleadings leads to the impression that all of your representations to the jury are to be viewed with suspicion and reserve. This is not to say that you should not adopt and assert the position most favorable to your client when reasonable difference of opinion is possible; going beyond that to an extreme not reasonably supportable by evidence is the thing you should avoid.[1]

1. *Cf.* §10.5.

The interest in making a full statement of the facts to convince the jury of the merits of your client's position at the earliest opportunity in trial sometimes comes into conflict with the interest in overall development of the case in the manner most favorable for your client. You may find it preferable to omit unnecessary allegations to avoid advising your adversary of certain evidence, the value of which depends in part upon surprise.[2] In Case 71, you might be tempted to tell the jury of the defendant's outrageous conduct at the first opportunity, by pleading specifically (by amendment after the deposition) that the defendant requested a brake adjustment, telling the garage foreman that his brakes were pulling to the left, and that the defendant then declined to wait for the adjustment, because he was in a hurry, and recklessly drove his car upon the highway with dangerously defective brakes. If you do so, however, D is forewarned and more likely to be prepared with a satisfactory explanation if (as you suspect in view of his deposition testimony that the brakes had always been in excellent shape) he is willing to let his interest in the lawsuit influence his testimony. Cross-examining D on the matter during trial, and then producing independently the garage foreman and the service ticket if D denies the conversation about his brakes pulling to the left, would be a more effective use of the contradiction.[3]

In jurisdictions where allegations of specific grounds of negligence are required upon objection by the opponent but a general allegation is sufficient in the absence of objection, it is usually better to use the general allegation in the absence of objection (or certainty that objection would be made if you used a general allegation). The advantages of the more detailed statement are outweighed by the greater leeway for developing the evidence and charge without restriction by specific pleading. The general plea affords greater freedom in framing special interrogatories to the jury, or charges on specific grounds of negligence, in the light of the testimony as it actually develops during trial; it does not limit you to grounds as you conceived and plead them on the basis of what you anticipated the evidence would be. Frequently you will rely upon your cross-examination of the adverse party and his witnesses to develop evidence of negligence, and you are rarely able to anticipate their testimony with complete accuracy, even though you have taken depositions in advance of trial and have thoroughly prepared your case. Furthermore, as to a witness whose testimony you have not taken in full by deposition before trial, you may prefer to have the opportunity of cross-examination under circumstances such that he does not know exactly what are your factual theories on negligence; if you have alleged your grounds specifically, your adversary probably will have

2. See §1.3.
3. See §§3.5–3.7.

considered each of those grounds carefully in interviewing witnesses before calling them to the stand.

In jurisdictions where allegation of specific acts or omissions constituting negligence is required, how many such grounds should you allege? Many lawyers who handle a considerable volume of negligence cases in such jurisdictions develop a list of fifteen or more grounds that they include in nearly every case of negligence in the operation of a motor vehicle, and other lists for various other types of negligence cases that fit a pattern. Such lists are undoubtedly useful as suggestions for grounds of negligence that you should consider. There is disagreement as to the advisability of including such numerous grounds in your pleadings. There are some advantages in doing so. It helps to protect against being caught at some point in trial with unduly restrictive pleadings that will not support some theory you wish to urge in view of the way in which the evidence has developed. It provides some leeway for changes of theory, with minimum harm, if the evidence develops in an unexpected way. Sometimes this practice is used as a means of avoiding clear disclosure to the adversary before trial of the exact grounds to be emphasized.[4] Disadvantages include the loss of an opportunity to use this part of the pleading in presenting to the jury your theory of the case; it will be obvious that the other party was not guilty of all the grounds of negligence alleged in such a "shot-gun charge," and the pleadings therefore not only fail to contribute to developing a conviction among jurors that your basic theory of the facts is sound but may even interfere by causing confusion. The conflict of ideas on this point is basically the conflict as to whether it is better advocacy to ask only for what you can firmly support by credible evidence and reasonable argument or instead to ask for more than you can hope to receive on the theory that a compromise is to be expected.[5]

§10.5 Framing the prayer for relief

What relief should you request?
For what amount should you sue?

In the majority of cases, the object of suit is a money judgment, and your primary problems in drafting the prayer in the plaintiff's pleadings are those concerning the amount you seek and the extent you choose to itemize. You should also consider many other forms of relief, however.

---

4. See §1.3 as to surprise tactics generally. If surprise tactics are generally accepted, still the deliberate use of insupportable allegations to conceal the true basis of claim might be condemned as a form of misrepresentation in the face of a legal duty to disclose the true basis of claim.

5. For additional discussion of this conflict, see §§7.16, 10.5.

Ancillary relief of garnishment, sequestration, or attachment may be available either before or after judgment. Costs of suit are generally recoverable, and occasionally attorneys' fees will be included in the recoverable items, though the usual rule is to the contrary. You should also consider the possibility of obtaining one or more of the many forms of equitable relief. The differences as to availability of particular remedies among different courts with potential jurisdiction over your case may affect your choice of a forum.[1] With the addition of declaratory judgment as a form of relief, there is now little chance that you will not be able to find in the procedural law of some accessible jurisdiction a recognized procedure for securing any form of relief for which the situation of your client creates a need and justification.

In determining what relief you should seek in a particular case, you should consider the possible application and effect of the doctrines of res judicata, estoppel by judgment, and merger of the cause of action into the judgment. In some circumstances you will have a choice of placing in issue only part rather than all of the disputed interests arising out of a given fact situation; in others, failure to seek additional forms of relief will result in loss of any opportunity to obtain those forms of relief. The trend of procedural reform has been toward requiring disposition of the entire controversy in one suit in one forum, and in most situations that will be in the best interests of both parties as well as those of the public in avoiding unnecessary duplication and wasted effort in the administration of justice.

With respect to the prayer for a money judgment, for what amount should you sue? Should your prayer be itemized? You may answer these questions readily in cases involving fixed amounts, such as suits on notes, accounts, or other contracts for payment of a specified sum. Frequently the same is true of quasi-contract cases involving a service or property that has a readily ascertainable value, and occasionally the same is true in negligence cases involving property damage. You will often encounter uncertainty concerning the valuation of damage to property, however, and injuries to person invariably involve great uncertainty. If the damages for which you sue are ascertainable with certainty, padding the claim by naming higher figures than those that you can prove not only is ethically questionable[2] but also is obviously poor tactics, because your adversary's exposure

1. See §10.3.
2. Deliberately overstating the claim is not to be unqualifiedly condemned on ethical grounds, however. For example, some trial lawyers justify overstatement of a personal injury claim as a means of allowing for possible, though improbable, changes for the worse between the date of filing suit and the date of trial; others resort to the broader and perhaps more questionable argument that (as in the case of salesmen's puffing) nobody is misled by overstatement of damages claims.

of this padding naturally leads to suspicion that your evidence may be exaggerated, too. If it is possible to add extra items to the claim rather than to exaggerate the amount of any one item above what it is possible to establish, some lawyers favor the practice even when adequate evidence to support the extra items is lacking. This is one expression of the idea that anyone passing on a disputed claim will be inclined to compromise it, and that it is both ethically and tactically proper to inflate your claim within reasonable limits so as to leave more room for compromise without cutting into the amount you actually hope to recover. Estimates of damages for personal injuries provide an even greater field for operation of this principle. There is great disagreement among experienced lawyers regarding this point. Many take the opposing view that, although you should seek the maximum that you think a jury is likely to find, ordinarily you will get better results if you stay within that maximum and never ask for more than you can support by credible evidence and sincere, reasoned argument. By doing so, you give those jurors who agree with you a figure to stand on, whereas exaggeration on your part leaves them the problem of finding a figure they can support by reasonable argument against the disagreement of others; since most verdicts are reached after some initial disagreement and argument, it is better to choose a figure that you point toward throughout the development of your case, thereby planting in the minds of jurors who agree a line of argument and supporting evidence that will come readily to their minds during the jury deliberations. If you exaggerate your claim, on the other hand, so that even your sympathizers realize that you are asking for too much, you leave them to work out their own argument, for which task they are less adequately equipped than you both by training and by degree of familiarity with the facts of the case.

Probably the majority consider that the better approach is to determine before drafting your pleadings the form of your damages evidence and argument and to plead the exact figure your proof and argument will show. You may itemize your argument in considerable detail,[3] computing separate amounts for medical bills, loss of earnings in the past, future medical bills, loss of future earning capacity, and various separate periods of pain and suffering. Customarily, the allegations of damages in the pleadings are not broken down into computations, as in the argument. Even in jurisdictions where more detailed pleadings are used and a lawyer may make extended allegations of each item of damages in a separate paragraph if he chooses, most lawyers prefer not to itemize beyond stating a separate figure for each of the items listed above, omitting the daily or other smaller figures and computations by which they reach the total for the item.

3. See §7.17.

The practice of pleading the specific amount you expect to support by evidence has the disadvantage of limiting you if the evidence develops in trial so as to support more than you had anticipated; subject to discretion of the trial judge, often you can practically neutralize that disadvantage by amendment, however. The amendment, if made known to the jury, may be subject to the criticism of being an afterthought or grandstand play instead of a genuine claim, but the lawyer for the defendant is generally reluctant to argue the matter for fear that the argument might be interpreted as an implied admission that there is a basis in the evidence for the jury's accepting the amended figure or something near it.[4]

§10.6   Choosing a theory or theories

CASE 72.   P sues D Railroad for personal injuries sustained when P was knocked from a trestle by a train. P had gone out to get part of his fishing line that had caught on the trestle, and he saw the train approaching after it was too late for him to reach a place of safety. As P's lawyer, it is your conclusion that the case decisions in your jurisdiction will support a recovery against D Railroad, though P is regarded as a trespasser, if you can obtain findings of fact to support the last clear chance theory. Your investigation discloses evidence to support findings of ordinary negligence against D Railroad and also findings necessary for the last clear chance theory.

Should you limit your pleadings to a single theory of claim or defense?

From the point of view of having a basis in your pleadings to meet any contingency of trial, alternative pleadings are very advantageous, and they are freely permitted in most jurisdictions at the present time. Tactically, however, alternative pleadings may be a handicap. It is advantageous to have a single theory to emphasize in every phase of the trial. To the extent that you assert several theories, consistent or inconsistent, or even allege inconsistent theories in the alternative though adopting one as your primary position, you weaken your primary contention.[1]

Although the factors bearing on assertion of inconsistent theories during trial point strongly toward the plaintiff's adopting a single theory and have the same though less pronounced tendency for the defendant, still you should be less reluctant about stating alternative and inconsistent theories in your pleadings than about urging them at trial. In most instances jurors give little attention to the pleadings. Furthermore, the jurors

4. *Cf.* §7.18.
1. See §7.16.

are more inclined to dismiss alternative statements in pleadings as just "lawyer's talk" than they are to dismiss an equivocal position with respect to development of the evidence or of argument to the jury.

As a general rule, if there is danger of forfeiting an alternative theory by omitting it from pleadings and any reasonable likelihood that you may have occasion to assert it even though you hope for development of the case along other lines, it is preferable to include your alternative allegations. On the other hand, if you have reached a firm conclusion during preparations that it would be tactically inadvisable to assert one of the potential theories, you should omit it from the pleadings to avoid the argument that your position at trial is a retreat and a confession that your case is not as strong as you claimed before the evidence was heard. Also, the addition of the theory that you do not expect to rely upon might affect the development of evidence by your adversary, by opening the door to contentions that otherwise would be immaterial.

In circumstances such as those described in Case 72, you might decide to try the case solely on the theory of last clear chance, conceding that P was negligent in placing himself in a perilous position and urging that D thereafter was guilty of actionable negligence. This approach has several advantages — first, reducing the harmful effect of unfavorable facts by disclosing them before the defendant can do so with greater emphasis and effect,[2] second, omitting a contention (of P's freedom from negligence) that probably will be recognized by the jury as unreasonable and may cause them to view less favorably the better theory of last clear chance, and, third, reducing the danger of a special verdict of negligence against both parties and findings against last clear chance (a verdict that jurors might regard as a compromise favorable to the plaintiff in their ignorance of the effect of their answers, particularly in a court where direct argument on the effect of answers in a special verdict is prohibited). Having made the decision during preparations to rely upon the last clear chance theory only, your including in the plaintiff's pleadings the plea of ordinary negligence would create a handicap. It would open the door to the defendant's pleading and proving contributory negligence, whereas if you plead only last clear chance, that defensive pleading would be irrelevant and the evidence supporting it likewise irrelevant, except to the extent it may bear upon the last clear chance issue.

§10.7 Rebutting anticipated defenses

CASE 73. P makes a claim against D *Company* for personal injuries sustained when P was walking across a street at an intersection and was hit

2. *Cf.* §§2.20, 10.7.

by *D Company*'s truck. An agent representing *D Company* took a release from *P* two hours after the accident, leaving with *P* a check for $100. *P* did not cash the check and claims that he was in such pain at the time of signing the release that he did not understand what it was; independent investigation that you have conducted before accepting employment for *P* tends to confirm *P*'s story.

Should you anticipate defenses and rebut them in the plaintiff's original pleading?

In the preparation of any pleading, whether you represent the plaintiff or the defendant, one of the steps in the process of doing the task in the most effective manner is a study of your own pleading from the point of view of your adversary's contentions. Such a study helps you avoid effective impeachment of your claims or defenses because of overstatement, inaccuracy, emphasis upon vulnerable points, or inadvertent admissions expressed or implied in your pleading and thus readily available for your adversary's use as judicial admissions. In testing your original pleading for the plaintiff in the light of the defenses that you anticipate, you should consider the possibility of improving your tactical position by anticipating defenses and rebutting them in advance.

This problem involves many of the considerations that you encounter in deciding whether to offer harmful evidence on direct examination.[1] As in the case of harmful evidence, there may be tactical advantages in bringing up the question of the defense yourself, at a point and in a manner that avoids unnecessary emphasis upon it. In jurisdictions where pleadings are read or stated to the jury near the beginning of the trial, your referring to the defendant's affirmative defenses and rebutting them before your adversary has a chance to make a statement on the point may reduce the effect that the opposing statement might otherwise have. This principle does not apply to the type of defense that probably will not be referred to in the defendant's pleading — one supported by a mere denial of the plaintiff's pleading. Your referring to such a matter in the plaintiff's pleading would unnecessarily complicate your statement of the plaintiff's theory, and your reference to the contradictory contentions would weaken your statement. The potential usefulness of such anticipatory allegations may also be restricted because of the trial judge's disapproval of this method of pleading; generally, he has sufficient discretionary power to prevent this practice if he disapproves it.

Using allegations regarding an anticipated defense has other implications distinct from those in common with offering harmful evidence on

1. See §2.20.

direct examination. The fact that the plaintiff pleads that a defense is not sound may affect the burden of proof. It has been held (contrary to the prevailing view) that although the burden of proof on the issue of contributory negligence would otherwise be on the defendant, if the plaintiff pleads freedom from contributory negligence in his original pleading, he assumes the burden of showing freedom from contributory negligence.[2] Another factor bearing on the use of such anticipatory pleadings is the possible tactical advantage of pleading in rebuttal, if that is permitted. On the theory that there is a tactical advantage in having the last word, some lawyers prefer to omit any reference in the plaintiff's original pleading to any affirmative defenses if they have a factual theory of rebuttal or confession and avoidance that probably will appeal to the jury. In Case 73, you might conclude that the circumstances surrounding the purported compromise are of this character. Furthermore, if the issue is a very doubtful one under the evidence and decisions, you may prefer, as the plaintiff's lawyer, to omit reference to the matter in the hope that the defendant will not assert the defense of settlement. The defendant's lawyer might well reach that decision if the damages are small and liability is doubtful, for fear that asserting the compromise would disclose insurance coverage, or that if the plea of compromise is not sustained the jury might react unfavorably to the attempt to settle the claim while the plaintiff was still in pain and penalize the defendant by a high verdict. On the other hand, considering from another perspective this same possibility of reluctance on the part of the defendant's lawyer to urge the compromise, you might choose to refer to it in the plaintiff's original pleading to increase the chances that the issue would be urged so that you might place the inflammatory evidence before the jury. However, your adversary might counter your move by admitting that the purported compromise was ineffective and moving to strike the allegations concerning it from the plaintiff's pleading as no longer material in view of the admission.[3]

§10.8 Omitting affirmative defenses from the initial answer

CASE 74. *P Insurance Company* sues *D* and *X* for a declaratory judgment of no policy coverage with respect to an accident in which a trailer owned by *D* and towed by his car collided with a car in which *X* was a passenger, causing serious injuries to *X*, who is making claim against *D* and *P Insurance Company* as *D*'s alleged insurer. The company asserts as grounds for denial of coverage (1) that the trailer was not specifically insured and was

---

2. See, *e.g.,* Hatch v. Merigold, 119 Conn. 339, 176 A. 266, 96 A.L.R. 1114 (1935).
3. See §10.15.

not the type covered by a general provision for coverage of trailers and (2) that the policy condition concerning prompt notice was violated. You are employed by *D*, who did not realize that his policy extended to the trailer and did not give notice of the accident to *P Insurance Company* until a friend suggested that he do so three weeks after the accident. *D* advises you he telephoned *P Insurance Company* to report the accident and explained his delay and that on subsequent occasions he had several conferences with *A*, claims agent for *P Insurance Company*, about policy coverage, and does not specifically recall any mention of any ground for denying coverage other than that the trailer was not the type covered by the policy. *D* also advises that he waited two months before employing a lawyer because he felt sure that he was right about the trailer after reading over the policy and that he got the impression that *A* agreed, but merely had to get approval from his home office before admitting coverage. *D* says, however, that he cannot be sure that *A* did not refer to the late notice as a basis for doubt as to coverage, though he knows that the character of the trailer was the primary subject of discussion.

Should you omit affirmative defenses from your initial answer with the purpose of amending before trial?

The rules of pleading in some jurisdictions require that the defendant in his answer admit or deny each allegation in the plaintiff's original pleading, or express a sound excuse for failing to do so; this is the requirement in federal courts,[1] for example. On the other hand, in some jurisdictions the defendant is permitted to file a general denial (or the equivalent under other terminology) of all of the plaintiff's allegations, even though he actually does not dispute many of the allegations. In jurisdictions of the latter type, lawyers sometimes follow the practice of preparing an answer containing only such a general denial and filing it immediately upon employment and before careful study of the case. Even in the jurisdictions requiring specific admission or denial of each allegation, it may be possible to file a temporary answer without thorough study of the case, leaving till later the consideration of affirmative defenses. Whether this practice is possible depends upon your confidence that the answer may be amended either as a matter of right or because leave of court is customarily granted. You should not follow this practice if there is uncertainty about your freedom to amend. Even when time is too short for careful study of the case before the date answer is due, it is usually possible and preferable to obtain, by motion, an extension of time within which you may answer.

1. Federal Rule 8 (b).

Should you file a temporary answer, containing only denials and no affirmative defenses, if freedom to amend before trial is assured? The first problem is whether the affirmative defenses possibly available are worth asserting.[2] If they are, there is an advantage in presenting your entire pleadings in your original answer. If you wait until the last possible moment or until a time comparatively near to trial to add affirmative defenses, your answer is subject to attack on the basis that the added defenses represent afterthoughts conceived either in grasping for straws or in an effort to muddy the waters. Delaying the assertion of affirmative defenses until the filing of an amended pleading also has the effect often of causing them to receive greater attention from your adversary. It is natural for him to assume that you have some special plan in mind, which he must prepare more carefully to meet. Another reason for preparing your full answer originally is that in the press of other work there is danger of your reaching trial without having prepared and filed your contemplated amendment far enough in advance to be used in view of customary limitations on the filing of amendments near the time of trial.

The advantages of filing the complete answer originally may be outweighed by other factors in some circumstances. One such factor is uncertainty regarding the extent to which you will be able to obtain admissions from the adverse party or his witnesses to support an affirmative defense that you are considering. In Case 74 you may be considering a plea of waiver, election, and estoppel to assert delayed notice because of the reference only to another ground of denial of policy coverage in all of the negotiations between P Insurance Company's claims agent, A, and your client, D.[3] D's testimony is too weak to establish the defense. You probably will prefer not to raise either of the points in trial unless you can get enough admissions from A to raise at least a fact issue. Your chances of obtaining the admissions from A may be reduced if you plead waiver, election, and estoppel and thereby insure that your advesary will advise A of the assertion of the defenses and the fact that he will doubtlessly be asked about facts bearing on them when his deposition is taken. Your chances of obtaining frank answers uninfluenced by A's full realization of their effect are greater if the particular inquiries concerning the subject matter of his conversations with D come as a surprise to him.[4] If the privilege of amendment is freely available, it would generally be better in circumstances such as those of Case 74 to omit the pleas of waiver, election,

2. See §10.6.
3. See generally R. Keeton, *Insurance Law*, §§6.1, 6.8(a), at pp. 343-345, 430 n.24 (1971).
4. As to surprise generally, see §1.3.

and estoppel until after you have taken the deposition of *A* and then file the amended answer with the pleas included if the testimony is sufficiently favorable to support them.

§10.9 Counterclaiming

CASE 75. *P* sues *D*, your client, for damages because of injuries to his person and his car incurred in a head-on collision with a car owned and operated by *D*. *P* was thrown from his vehicle and sustained two vertebral fractures, a broken leg and head injuries that he claims to be permanent in character. *D* suffered a broken left arm that has satisfactorily healed before trial. *D* carried collision and hospitalization insurance but not liability insurance.

Should you file a counterclaim with your answer?

In many jurisdictions the rules of procedure provide that certain counterclaims are "compulsory" in the sense that failure to assert them in the action in which your client is the defendant will result in their being barred.[1] As to such a compulsory counterclaim, your first problem is determining whether the possible counterclaim has sufficient merit to be asserted for its own sake. If so, however, it may still be inadvisable to assert it because of its potentially adverse effect on a larger and more important primary claim. The assertion of the counterclaim normally will expand the field of evidence and argument to new matter that may be either favorable or unfavorable in its incidental effect upon the primary claim. This factor of effect on the defense of the primary claim also bears upon your decision as to whether you should assert permissive counterclaims in the same suit or withhold them for possible assertion separately.

Some lawyers consider it advisable to counterclaim as a defense tactic whenever there is the slightest basis for doing so. This practice has the advantage of bringing to the attention of the jury the fact that the defendant has also suffered damage from the transaction on which the suit is based. Also, the psychology of claiming that justice demands that you be awarded something the opponent is unjustly withholding from you is more suitable to a stirring jury presentation than the psychology of merely trying to retain something you already have.

There are distinct disadvantages to the counterclaim as a defensive weapon, however. In the usual case of unliquidated damages, either in a contract action or in a tort action such as Case 75, you are confronted with a severe tactical problem in fixing the amount of your counterclaim. The

1. See, *e.g.*, Federal Rule 13.

plaintiff's damages usually will be higher than those the defendant might reasonably claim, and if you exaggerate in your counterclaim and fix the damages high, you give the plaintiff a useful jury argument. The plaintiff's lawyer can point out the proof showing that the plaintiff's damages were considerably more severe than the defendant's, then point to the defendant's counterclaim and the amount alleged, whether you argue that amount or not, and draw the deduction that you surely would not justifiably argue that the plaintiff is entitled to less than double that amount, or triple it, or whatever proportion might be justified by the comparison of the proof of damages in the case. On the other hand, if you place the amount claimed in your counterclaim at a figure too low, the jurors (aided by the plaintiff's lawyer) may realize your reason for doing so and discount your sincerity in urging the counterclaim. Unless they think the plaintiff is protected by liability insurance, they may also react unfavorably to your seeking the "pound of flesh" from one who has already suffered severely.

In jurisdictions where the special verdict is used and the jurors are not to be told directly the effect of their answers, the presence of the counterclaim may make them realize the significance of issues they otherwise might not know, and it may cause them to consider the case more on the basis of the result to be achieved than on the basis strictly of the facts. This attitude on the part of the jury is detrimental to the interests of the client whose case has less sympathetic appeal — usually the defendant. The obvious example is the typical collision case, such as Case 75, in which the jury may not realize the effect of contributory negligence. Particularly, they may not understand that it is a *complete* bar, where that is true. They may be less reluctant to find that the plaintiff was negligent if his claim alone is in suit than if you have counterclaimed against him and they think they may be awarding some amount of damages against him by finding him negligent.

§10.10 Filing a third-party claim

CASE 76. *P* sues *D* for personal injuries suffered by *P* when *P*, while walking across a street in a pedestrian lane, was hit by a car owned by *D*. *D* had parked his car on a hillside, where it remained until hit by *X*'s car after *X* dodged a child running into the street. *P* alleges that *D* was negligent in leaving the car on the hillside without engaging the parking brake. From your investigation, representing *D*, you conclude that the evidence would raise issues of fact as to negligence of *X* in the operation of his car and that, with favorable factfindings, *D* would be allowed at least contribution from *X*, and perhaps indemnity, under the law of your jurisdiction.

Should you file a third-party claim with your answer?

The typical third-party claim, such as might be urged in Case 76, asserts a cause of action over against the third party in the event of liability of the original defendant to the original plaintiff. That cause of action might be one for either indemnity or contribution, and you must consider at the outset the law of your jurisdiction as to the existence of such a cause of action and whether it may be asserted in the same action. If you resolve these questions favorably, an obvious advantage of the third party proceeding is to determine all related issues in one trial. Leaving the third-party claim for assertion in a separate suit may result in your client's having the burden of proving his own liability to the plaintiff as well as the third party's liability over to him, since the third party is generally not bound by the findings of the original action to which he was not a party.

The presence of the third party in the case may be a distinct disadvantage in defending the primary claim, however. The double position taken by the defendant (that he is not liable to the plaintiff, but if he is, that the third party is liable over to him) weakens the emphasis and force of his defense,[1] in addition to whatever effect the additional evidence and argument of the third party may have upon the case. Also, in many cases there is a very severe practical danger of cooperation between the plaintiff and a third-party defendant, openly or *sub rosa* under a so-called "gentlemen's agreement." The plaintiff's best case is against the original defendant; the way is obviously open for an agreement between the plaintiff and the third party to help each other against the defendant, by exchanging information and investigation files and by coordinating the development of their evidence and arguments in the case. Even if circumstances of the case are such that danger of that type of cooperation does not exist, the presence of the third party in the case and the attention devoted to issues between the third party and the defendant may well lead the jury to conclude that this is the real dispute in the case and the reason the case has not been settled without trial, the plaintiff's claim being inferentially conceded.

Though there is a sharp division of opinion among experienced lawyers concerning this point, probably the majority consider that the disadvantages of interference with the defense of the primary claim make it advisable not to assert the third-party claim in the same suit if it is legally and practically possible to assert it by a later independent suit.

§10.11 Verifying pleadings

When and how should you verify pleadings by affidavit?

Although rules of procedure often prescribe some penalties for filing plead-

---

1. *Cf.* §§7.16, 10.2, 10.6.

ings or making allegations in bad faith, they do not generally require verification by affidavit. Many exceptions to that general rule are prescribed by rules, decisions, or statutes, requiring verification of particular types of allegations, and in some instances requiring verification of the entire pleadings. Unless you have all such requirements of your jurisdiction committed to memory, at least with respect to the particular type of case you are concerned with, when preparing your pleadings you should always consider such requirements to insure that your pleadings are not insufficient for want of verification. The penalties attached to failure to verify pleadings vary; under some decisions the insufficiency of your pleadings may be pointed out by your adversary at such a late stage in trial or appeal as to make it impossible for you to avoid harm by amending your pleadings to include the verification.

Form of the verification sometimes presents a dangerous pitfall. An affidavit on information and belief is sometimes held insufficient in the absence of specific authorization for that type of affidavit. As an extension of this doctrine, an affidavit purporting to be based upon knowledge but stating facts that obviously could not be known to the affiant may be held insufficient. Affidavits signed by an attorney himself, rather than by the client or by another who has actual knowledge of the facts from personal observation, may be condemned on this basis in the absence of specific authorization by rule or statute. Occasionally it will be necessary to use affidavits of more than one person because no one has personal knowledge of all the matters that you wish to allege. Another important precaution as to form is that if you incorporate by reference any matter that is required to be verified, you must phrase the verification so that it clearly applies to the incorporated matter.

§10.12 Pleading law

CASE 32. *P* asserts a claim on account of injuries received when the car in which he was riding as a passenger collided at night with a disabled truck, which was on the pavement of the highway where it came to rest after a wheel fell off and one end of the rear axle dropped to the pavement. In your representation of *P*, one of your claims of negligence is based on the failure of *D*'s employee to comply with a statute requiring lighted flares, visible for a specified distance, to be placed at the scene of disabled trucks of the type operated by *D*'s employee on the occasion in question.

Should you plead the law?

Rules of pleading are based upon the theory that the pleadings should be a statement of the facts or some form of short-hand characterization of the facts, the law applicable to those facts being judicially known. As a general rule, it is not necessary to plead the law. Some exceptions exist. For example,

it is often necessary to plead municipal ordinances, administrative regula-
lations, or special legislative acts. In some jurisdictions, you must allege these
special laws in detail, as a part of your basic pleading; in some, you may
file a separate motion to invoke judicial notice of laws of which the court
does not take judicial notice without special motion.[1]

Although allegations may sometimes be stricken from pleadings on the
ground that they are conclusions of law,[2] which ground would surely apply
to a recitation of the law as such, trial judges frequently permit such allegations within the scope of the discretion allowed them under pleading rules.
In these circumstances, is it tactically advisable to recite propositions of law
in your pleadings?

In jurisdictions where special verdicts are used and the jury is required to
consider factfindings on specified questions without regard to the effect of
their answers upon the verdict, the lawyer representing the client whose
situation has the lesser sympathetic appeal (usually the defendant) should
avoid reciting the legal effect of facts. For example, he should avoid concluding an allegation of contributory negligence with the statement "by
reason of which contributory negligence the plaintiff is wholly barred from
any recovery herein." Such an allegation would be a perfect tool for the
plaintiff's lawyer to use in making it plain to the jury that a finding of contributory negligence would be fatal to the plaintiff's case (a fact that jurors
often do not realize independently of being educated by the plaintiff's
lawyer on the point). Conversely, allegations disclosing the effect of facts
might be useful to the party whose client occupies the position of greater
sympathetic appeal, though these allegations might be stricken upon appropriate motion by the opposite party.[3]

Often a rule of law is a part of your convincing statement of your case
from the point of view of a layman's consideration of it.[4] This is particularly
true if the rule of law is one that laymen generally do not know. Case 32
provides an example. It is to the plaintiff's advantage in such a case that his
pleadings include a recitation of the statutory requirement as to placement
of flares near a disabled truck of the type in question, since the details of
these requirements will not be known to laymen generally, even though the
fact that some such requirements exist may be generally known. If pleadings
are either read or stated in summary form near the beginning of the case,
the inclusion of these details will help plant the plaintiff's theory of the case
in the minds of the jury from an early point in the trial.

1. See §2.37.
2. See §10.16.
3. See §§10.15, 10.16.
4. See §10.4.

§10.13 Incorporating by reference

Should you incorporate material by reference?

In jurisdictions having a system of detailed pleadings, rules of procedure generally make specific provision for incorporation by reference, in the interest of abbreviating pleadings. It is usually permissible in contract cases (and because of the practical difficulty of anticipating all the problems that may develop, it is advisable) to attach a copy of the contract documents to your pleading as an exhibit, incorporating them by reference so as to supply any deficiencies that might otherwise exist in the pleading. Since you will probably not wish to read the whole exhibit to the jury in jurisdictions where pleadings are read, it still is advisable to plead specifically the gist of the particular provisions on which you expect to found your case, unless rules or decisions in your jurisdiction indicate that such specific pleading would have the effect of restricting your theories of action or defense to those specified.

Provisions for incorporation by reference generally extend to the use of this practice for the incorporation of other pleadings in the case, at least if they are not superseded. For example, in a multiple-party suit, one party may adopt certain paragraphs of the pleadings of another; likewise a party may be permitted in one pleading to adopt certain paragraphs from another of his own pleadings. This practice is often useful in meeting some technical requirement of pleading without unduly lengthening a document. You should use it with caution, however, and generally you should avoid it unless the adopted paragraphs, if quoted verbatim in the new pleading at the point of reference, would need no revision of phrases to make them perfectly applicable. If verification of pleadings is required, the verification must be so phrased as to make it clearly applicable to the adopted allegations. If you are adopting something prepared for another party, you should examine it very closely to avoid any undesirable admissions. If the statement that you are considering adopting contains important fact recitations in a jurisdiction where pleadings are read to the jury, it is generally preferable to repeat the allegations since the jury will not be likely to realize fully the significance of a recitation of adoption by reference.

§10.14 Pleading to the court only

CASE 77. *P Insurance Company* carried $50 deductible collision insurance on *X*'s car, which was damaged in a collision allegedly due to the negligence of *D*; the company paid *X* $780 on a loss of $830 and has engaged you to proceed against *D*, in a jurisdiction permitting suit in the name of *X*, for the use of the company, without disclosing to the jury the interest of an insurance company.

What should you do about allegations that you wish to include in your own pleading but prefer that the jury not hear?

Whether or not the pleadings are read to the jury in your jurisdiction, your pleadings may come to the jury's attention in some incidental manner. Parts of your pleadings may be offered by your adversary as judicial admissions, or parts of your superseded pleadings may be offered in evidence by your adversary as extrajudicial admissions. Pleadings may be incidentally referred to during interrogation of the jury panel, during examination of witnesses, or during argument to the jury. In some instances, you will find it essential or desirable to include in your pleadings allegations, addressed to the court, that you do not want the jury to hear. In Case 77, for example, it is desirable, though usually not essential, that your pleadings disclose the beneficial interest of your client, *P Insurance Company*, rather than that they indicate only that judgment should be for *X* in the event of successful prosecution of the suit; disclosing this interest to the jury, however, particularly if *D* was not insured or if the fact of his being covered by liability insurance is not disclosed, would be likely to reduce your chances of obtaining a favorable jury verdict. Even though the rules of procedure of your jurisdiction do not make specific provision for this situation, it may be possible to accomplish your purpose of including the allegation without forfeiting your right to prevent disclosure to the jury of the fact that a collision insurer is beneficially interested in the claim. If the rules or decisions of your jurisdiction clearly permit the practice, you may include in one paragraph of your pleadings the recitation of the interest of *P Insurance Company*, prefacing that paragraph with a statement that it is addressed to the court only, not to the jury, and that you move that the fact of the beneficial interest of the insurance company not be disclosed to the jury. If there is doubt about whether the court will grant the motion, it is better that you not include this matter in your principal pleading in the case, since that probably would increase the chances that the entire paragraph, including your prayer for secrecy, would get before the jury to your detriment; a separate motion disclosing the beneficial interest of the insurance company and requesting nondisclosure to the jury would be less risky.

§10.15 Keeping allegations of other parties from the jury

CASE 78. As *P*'s lawyer, you sue *D* for personal injuries suffered by *P* in a collision between cars of *P* and *D*. *D* counterclaims against *P*. As a defense to the counterclaim, *P*'s insurer, *Liability Insurance Company*, represented by another lawyer, pleads a release obtained from *D* by one of its adjusters, acting in *P*'s name but without *P*'s personal participation in the transaction.

What should you do about another party's allegations that you prefer that the jury not hear?

If the pleadings of another party contain references to matters that you wish to prevent the jury from hearing, you should first consider a motion to strike the allegations (or the equivalent of such a motion under other terminology and procedure).[1] In some situations, however, the allegations of another party, whether adverse to your client or not, may be proper and not subject to a motion to strike and yet improper for jury consideration under your theory of the case. Also, entirely proper allegations might necessarily lead to evidence that is improper for jury consideration under your theory of the case. Assume that Case 78 arises in a jurisdiction where as a general rule the fact of liability insurance cannot properly be disclosed over objection and that P did not personally participate in the alleged settlement between D and P's insurer, *Liability Insurance Company*. As P's lawyer, you cannot prevent the lawyer for P's liability insurance company from asserting the defense of compromise, but the evidence to support the defense would be very damaging in the trial of your case. If, as might well be true under the assumed facts, D's counterclaim is frivolous in view of the perfect defense of compromise, you might succeed in a motion to strike the counterclaim; this would be a case in which the pleadings of D contain no prejudicially improper matter within themselves but would lead to the introduction of evidence of a very damaging character and with no materiality to the issues bearing on P's claim against D (if the compromise by P's insurance company without P's participation does not affect P's claim, which appears to be a sound rule).[2] Another possibility of relief from the situation would be a motion for severance of P's claim from D's counterclaim for trial.[3]

§10.16 Motions to strike

CASE 79. *P* sues *D Grocery Company* for injuries sustained when *P* slipped on a decayed, damp vegetable leaf while walking in the aisle near the vegetable counter. *P* asserts that the decayed leaf was so nearly the same color as the floor that she was not negligent in failing to observe it and that it was dropped there by an employee of *D Grocery Company*, or in the alternative, had been left there for such length of time after being dropped by a customer that *D Grocery Company* was negligent in failing to remove it. *P*'s pleadings allege that the customary practices of *D Grocery Company*

1. See §10.16.
2. See R. Keeton, *Insurance Law* §7.10(a) (1971).
3. See §11.22.

in cleaning were inadequate, that *P* learned after the fall that another customer had fallen under like circumstances just a week before *P*'s fall, and that *D Grocery Company* changed the cleaning schedule after *P*'s fall so as to clean twice as frequently as before.

Should you seek to have improper parts of your adversary's pleadings stricken out?

The procedure by which you may request that improper parts of your adversary's pleadings be stricken is generally referred to as a motion to strike, a special demurrer, or an exception to the pleadings. In many jurisdictions you may advance such a request on the theory that the allegations objected to are legal conclusions rather than statements of fact. Where leave for amendment is liberally granted, such an attack on the pleadings usually serves no end other than delay, unless there is an actual lack of factual support and therefore a hope of final disposition of the case by a judgment during the pleadings stage,[1] or else you wish more definite pleadings to give you better indications of your adversary's theories or to limit the possible scope of his proof.[2]

Another ground available in some jurisdictions for striking allegations from a pleading is that the allegations are evidentiary. If an amendment by substitution of nonevidentiary allegations is allowed, you gain little by urging such a ground unless the allegations are not supportable by admissible evidence. If admissible evidence is available, striking the allegation from a pleading merely affects the time and form in which the jury first hears the harmful matter; only if these factors would affect the influence of the harmful matter on the jury is the objection to the pleading worth making. Even if the allegations are not supportable by evidence, in some situations it might be preferable to allow them to remain in the pleading with the purpose of supporting your argument that your adversary's proof is nothing like his claim.

Allegations within a pleading may be stricken because they concern a subject matter as to which evidence will be inadmissible, the subject matter also being of a type likely to appeal to sympathy or bias. This ground is often extended to subject matter as to which evidence will be of doubtful admissibility, on the theory that the jury should not be biased by hearing the allegations before the court hears and passes on the admissibility of the evidence offered at trial. You gain a substantial advantage by having such allegations stricken. There is a disadvantage in inviting your adversary's attention to your contemplated objection to evidence, since it may cause him to give more

1. See §10.17.
2. See §10.18.

careful consideration to alternative theories of admissibility,[3] but that disadvantage is generally slight compared to the advantage of avoiding the harm already done by the allegations in the pleading if you should be successful in excluding the evidence. In Case 79, you may succeed in excluding evidence of the previous fall of another customer as lacking materiality or as contravening an auxiliary policy of evidence law (such as avoiding unfair surprise or confusion of issues),[4] and you may succeed in excluding evidence of the change in the cleaning schedule as incompetent because of the policy of encouraging remedial action without fear of its affecting pending claims.[5] By bringing the points up in advance of trial, you may increase the likelihood that *P*'s lawyer will develop the evidence so as to come within an exception or qualification to each of these rules. On the other hand, if you do not object in advance, the reading of the pleadings may substantially harm your client, even if the court thereafter excludes the questioned evidence; it is therefore better to urge that the allegations be stricken from the pleading. An alternative possibility, though not generally provided for specifically by the rules, is to request the court at least to require the deletion of these allegations in the reading of the pleading to the jury, or in any oral statement to the jury, until after the court has heard the evidence in chambers (or otherwise out of the presence of the jury) and has passed upon its admissibility.

§10.17   Asserting failure to state a claim or defense

CASE 80.   *P* asserts against *D* a claim for personal injuries sustained by *P* when his car ran into a sharp depression at the site of a wooden bridge on a rural road, the bridge having broken down from the weight of *D*'s heavily loaded truck crossing it. The case arises in a jurisdiction requiring that the pleadings specify acts or omissions alleged to constitute negligence, and the only types of such acts or omissions alleged against *D* in *P*'s pleadings are those concerned with failure to stop and provide for approaching drivers, including *P*, some means of warning of the defective bridge. Under your theory as *D*'s lawyer, *D* was merely the first victim of the wrong of unknown persons who allowed a camp fire to spread to some of the supporting timbers of the bridge, weakening though not destroying them, and *D* had no legal duty to warn others.

---

3. See §2.17.

4. See 2 Wigmore, *Evidence* §§441–465 (3d ed. 1940); Federal Rules of Evidence, Rule 403.

5. See 2 Wigmore, *Evidence* §§282, 283 (3d ed. 1940); Federal Rules of Evidence, Rule 407.

Should you by pleading assert the want of any material fact issue or the insufficiency of your adversary's pleadings to state a claim or defense?

The procedures for asserting the insufficiency of your adversary's pleadings to state a claim or defense vary considerably among the different jurisdictions; general demurrers, exceptions, and motions for judgment on the pleadings are examples of procedures available for this purpose. By whatever name or procedure the point is raised, the possibility of its use raises basically the same tactical problem.[1]

The great advantage in raising a contention of insufficiency of pleadings to state a claim or defense by a procedure available during the pleadings stage of litigation is the possibility of final and favorable disposition of the controversy without the delay and expense of a full trial. Another possible advantage is that of forcing more complete disclosure by your adversary of his theory of the case. Ordinarily, this latter advantage is far outweighed by the disadvantages of educating your adversary on the details of your legal and factual theories, including your contentions and supporting authorities with respect to requirements that your adversary must meet to make out the asserted claim or defense, and the further disadvantage of unnecessary and fruitless expenditure of time and effort. Furthermore, using discovery procedures is generally a more effective means of learning your adversary's probable contentions and probable supporting evidence. It is sound practice to refrain from urging the contention of insufficiency of pleadings to state a claim or defense unless it deals with an omission that your adversary probably cannot cure — an omission that is therefore likely to lead to a final judgment in your favor without full trial. If the omission or irregularity of your adversary's pleadings is, on the other hand, one that is probably due to oversight or difference of views as to the requirements for supporting the questioned claim or defense, it is usually better to forego raising the point during the pleadings stage. Ordinarily, this will not forfeit your right to assert the same point by some other means during trial, as by a motion for directed verdict at the close of the evidence, or perhaps even later.[2] A point based upon your adversary's oversight or misconstruction of the requirements for a claim or defense, when the evidence to support the omitted requirements is available, is rarely good for anything more than harassment or delay, in view of the prevailing interest in proper disposition of controversies on the merits.[3] To the extent that such a point has potentialities of more decisive

---

1. Compare the problem of using summary judgment procedure to assert want of any genuine fact issue material to correct disposition of the case, §11.23.

2. See §§5.2, 5.3.

3. *Cf.* §5.9.

use, however, you can more readily realize them by surprise[4] at later stages of litigation[5] than by raising the point during the pleadings stage.

Case 80 illustrates the problem. There is a conflict of authorities as to whether one in D's position, whose vehicle has figured in the creation of a traffic hazard without negligence on his part, has a legal duty of reasonable care to warn others. It is your theory, as D's lawyer, that no such duty exists. If you are correct in your theory, what will be the result of your asserting it at the pleadings stage of the litigation? Will it not be probable that P's lawyer will reconsider his legal theories and the authorities more carefully, improving his chances of avoiding application of your theory by changing his own theory to some other charge of negligence — such as operating the heavily loaded truck over a bridge that D knew or should have known would not sustain the weight? The whole approach of P's lawyer might be changed from reliance solely on the lack of warning to emphasis on D's residence in the area, frequent use of the bridge, knowledge that fire had reached the supporting timbers, and other factors pointing to the conclusion that D was a joint tortfeasor in the breaking of the bridge, and is liable to P both on this ground and also on the ground that this wrong gave rise to a duty of care to warn, in the violation of which he committed a further wrong toward P. Only if there is no substantial possibility that P's lawyer might discover evidence to support such a theory, or some other theory better than that expressed in the pleadings (as, for example, assuming the duty of warning by entering upon the task, then failing to do it effectively), would it be serving your client's interests to urge the error of P's legal theory at the pleadings stage. If you wait till a later stage to assert your theory, you might, for example, secure admissions from P's witnesses on cross-examination that would be inconsistent with later attempted proof for P that the bridge was so damaged by the fire that D should have known it would be unsafe for his loaded truck; when your theory is finally asserted by motion for directed verdict or motion for judgment *non obstante veredicto*, the chances of a successful revision of P's theory of action will be reduced.

§10.18 Objecting to vagueness

CASE 81. P sues D for personal injuries suffered in a collision between their cars. P's pleading describes the injuries only as "serious and disabling

---

4. As to surprise generally, see §1.3.

5. For example, by motion for directed verdict, §5.2; by motion for judgment *non obstante veredicto*, §5.3; by objection to evidence on the ground of want of supporting pleadings, §4.8; and in some jurisdictions by motion for judgment on the opening statement.

injuries to his body generally, and his back in particular, causing damages of $100,000."

Should you object to allegations in your adversary's pleadings on the ground that they are vague and indefinite?

A primary factor affecting the question of this section is the nature of the rules of pleading in your jurisdiction — whether detailed pleadings or only general pleadings are contemplated by the rules.[1] If general pleadings such as those of the federal system are used in your jurisdiction, an objection that a pleading is too vague or indefinite is not upheld unless you show that it is so indefinite that you are unable to answer. The motion for more definite statement under the federal rules[2] is not intended for use as a demand for clarification of claims beyond that necessary for your preparation of a proper responsive pleading. If you wish greater clarification for trial preparations, you may use the discovery processes to accomplish that purpose. On the other hand, under many of the state systems in which pleadings are expected to serve in some degree the purpose of clarifying and defining the controverted issues for trial, an objection to the generality or indefiniteness of allegations is sound. The procedures by which this objection is made in the various jurisdictions include a motion for more definite statement, a motion seeking a bill of particulars, and an exception to the pleadings. In such jurisdictions, is it tactically advisable to urge this objection?

The availability of effective discovery processes will affect your decision. If such processes are not available, you may be compelled to use the attack upon your adversary's pleading as the only practical means of learning what you wish to know about your adversary's theories, or approaching that goal as nearly as possible. Even if discovery processes are available, the attack on the pleading may be useful to you in addition to or in lieu of discovery processes. It is often a less expensive and time-consuming technique, but it is generally less effective than careful and thorough use of discovery processes in achieving a full disclosure of your adversary's theories and of the evidence likely to be available to support them.

The attack upon generality of a pleading may also serve the purpose of placing limitations upon the evidence that your adversary will be permitted to offer and the issues covered in the charge. Usually these advantages make it advisable to urge the point of improper generality of the pleading, even though you may also plan to use discovery processes to insure full preparation for any theory your adversary may assert.

1. See §10.1.
2. Federal Rule 12(e).

There are disadvantages in raising generality of a pleading. If pleadings are customarily read to the jury, or if the opening statement is primarily a summary of pleadings, the amended pleading prepared to meet your objection may make a somewhat greater impression on the jury because of the added details. Your adversary may be forced into more careful and adequate consideration of the theories of action and the supporting evidence. Usually these disadvantages are of relatively slight importance compared to the additional information you receive concerning your adversary's case and the additional limitations imposed on your adversary's development of the case at trial under more specific pleading.

Allegations of negligence provide an example for application of these principles. If the rules of pleading in your jurisdiction require, upon demand of the opponent, specific allegations of acts and omissions relied upon as constituting negligence, most trial lawyers agree that it is to your advantage to demand the specific allegations. You may thus limit the grounds of negligence your adversary relies upon during trial and reduce the risk of surprise.

Another illustration is provided by Case 81. Under the general pleading of injury it is quite possible that you may be surprised at trial by proof of some type of injury or incapacity that you had not anticipated; this possibility exists even despite your careful use of discovery processes, since there is always a possibility of a claim that some effect of the injury was observed for the first time after your discovery processes were used.[3] Suppose, for example, P claims at trial that since the time his deposition was taken — and you examined him in detail regarding injuries — he has observed a loss of hearing, and it is steadily growing worse; suppose also that he has medical testimony to support the causal connection between the accident on which suit is based and the loss of hearing. If you require more specific pleading of injuries in a jurisdiction where detailed pleadings are contemplated by the rules of practice, this evidence probably will be inadmissible without such an amendment of his pleading as serves to give you notice and an opportunity to prepare to meet the new claim. On the other hand, if you make no objection to the general pleading of injuries, you might receive no notice of the claim of loss of hearing until evidence is offered at trial, at which time it might be impossible either to secure a continuance because of the surprise or to prepare adequately to meet the issue without a continuance.

3. The amended federal discovery rules substantially reduce this risk, though not eliminating it, by providing explicitly for supplementation of responses. See Federal Rule 26(c).

Chapter XI

PROCEEDINGS BEFORE TRIAL

§11.1 Purposes of taking depositions

The purposes for which you may take depositions fall into two general categories — recording of testimony and discovery. Your specific aim in recording the testimony may be to enable you to use in trial testimony that would otherwise be unavailable because of the witness' illness, location beyond the effective area of subpoena of the trial court, or unavailability for some other reason. In some circumstances your aim may be to enable you to use deposition testimony in trial even though the witness is readily available to testify in person if called, or it may be only to preserve testimony as insurance against loss through death or other change in circumstances between the date of deposition and the date of trial.

In some jurisdictions, including the federal courts,[1] specific provisions are made for taking depositions for each of these general purposes and for taking depositions either before or after institution of suit. At the other extreme, statutes and rules of some jurisdictions do not include discovery as a recognized aim of depositions; in the absence of a broader authorization by rule or statute, it is generally necessary to rely upon limited and cumbersome equitable procedures for taking and preserving testimony. It is often possible, however, to use for discovery those deposition procedures authorized by statute or rule to serve other ends, though it may be necessary to do so on theory of recording testimony for use in trial or to preserve it against loss by death or other unavailability of the witness.

§11.2 Deciding whether to take a deposition

CASE 82. *P* sues *D* for $2500 on an alleged oral contract regarding

1. Federal Rules 26–32, 37.

P's services in promoting a special athletic event. *P* was given an expense allowance during the four-week period of his services but was paid no other compensation. The athletic event was a greater success than had been anticipated, and *D* collected proceeds of $25,000 above expenses. *P* claims that *D* agreed to pay him, in addition to his expense account, 10 percent of the profits from the event after payment of all expenses other than compensation for promotional services, and that *D* estimated when talking with *P* that this amount would be $500. It is *D*'s position that he agreed to pay *P* the smaller of the two figures, $500 or 10 per cent of the profits after payment of all expenses other than *P*'s compensation. According to *D*, the other expenses include compensation of $500 each to *D*'s wife, *W*, and two children, *C-1* and *C-2*, ages eighteen and twenty and members of *D*'s household, for their "secretarial services" in connection with the event.

Should you take the deposition of a particular witness?

Though one of the recognized purposes [1] for taking depositions may be the primary motivation for taking a particular deposition, no deposition can in fact serve one purpose only under the prevailing rules of admissibility of deposition testimony. The deposition taken primarily for discovery purposes has the incidental effect of preserving the testimony of the witness, as a defendant's lawyer occasionally realizes to his dismay when he takes the plaintiff's deposition about an unwitnessed accident and the plaintiff then dies before trial. Likewise, the deposition taken primarily to preserve testimony has the incidental effect of discovery; not even the lawyer toward whose client the witness is friendly, much less the other lawyer, knows exactly what the witness will say under fire. Frequently the usefulness of the deposition for these different purposes presents conflicting considerations regarding the advantages of taking a deposition; the deposition giving an advantage to one party with respect to one of the uses will give the other party advantages with respect to the other use. Sometimes, particularly in the case of a disinterested witness whose testimony is favorable to each party in some respects, the deposition will be useful to both parties both for purposes of discovery and for recording of the testimony. The advisability of taking a deposition will depend upon weighing predictions as to these relative advantages to each party.

The primary usefulness of the deposition of your own client or a favor-discovery. You want to know what he will say so you can appraise your adversary's case and your own. If you get him committed on all material matters, you know that he will take the same position in trial or that you can impeach him with his own deposition testimony if he changes. Also,

---

1. §11.1.

you may obtain information to aid you in developing other impeaching evidence and to aid you in preparing to meet his testimony with that of your own witnesses.

The primary usefulness of the deposition of your own client or a favorable witness is the preservation of his testimony, insuring its availability in the event of his death, illness, or unavailability at trial for any other reason. For example, a key witness may go into the armed forces or move to a distant community, from which the expense of bringing him back to the trial might be prohibitive even if you could locate him and persuade him to come. Also, you may want the deposition of a favorable witness other than your client to protect against the hazards of defection by faulty memory, unexplainable changes of heart, the influence of a clever adversary, and in some cases against the possibility of the influence of "greenback salve" (less often in the pure form of bribery than in more subtle forms that may be legally permissible but nevertheless clearly affect his financial interests). Other incidental advantages of taking the deposition of your own witness, or having it taken by your adversary, are the experience that the witness thus receives in answering lawyers' questions and the better understanding and appreciation he then has of the procedure for placing a witness' story before a tribunal. Unless you advise the witness [2] of the differences between the deposition procedure and procedures for taking testimony during trial, however, he may get some erroneous impressions that will cause him to be more confused and ill at ease at trial than he might have been with no previous experience in testifying.

The usefulness of a deposition of your own client or a favorable witness is ordinarily more than counterbalanced by the usefulness of the deposition to your adversary for discovery. Ordinarily you should not initiate the taking of a deposition of your own client or witness unless he is ill, feeble, or planning to move beyond the jurisdiction, or his testimony is absolutely essential to your making out a case. Conversely, it is ordinarily to your advantage to take the deposition of the adverse party and his witness. If your client is a plaintiff whose testimony is essential to making out a case, however, as in a personal injury case based on an unwitnessed accident, and he is in serious condition and has dependents to whom the case would be important in the event of his death, it is imperative that you take his deposition despite the disadvantages of fully informing the opposing lawyer.

It is ordinarily to your advantage to take the deposition of the adverse party or his witnesses, usefulness for discovery outweighing the advantages to your opponent except in some cases of probable unavailability of the

2. As to conferring with the witness before trial, see §2.14.

witness' testimony at trial — the same exceptional cases in which it is advantageous for you to take the depositions of your own client and witnesses. It will be advisable to take the deposition of the adverse party more often than that of any adverse witness other than the party; one important reason for the distinction is that you have an opportunity to interview the adverse witness privately to discover what his testimony will be, whereas you are prohibited by the Code of Professional Responsibility from interviewing the adverse party, except with the consent of his lawyer.[3] If an adverse witness other than a party will not talk with you privately, however, the choice is practically limited to taking his deposition under subpoena or else doing without the benefit of knowing what he would say.[4]

Expense may be a significant factor, particularly in smaller cases. The costs of originals of depositions are ordinarily taxed as court costs, though that is not usually true of copies ordered by lawyers for their convenience in preparation. The probability of victory in trial is therefore a factor in determining the effect of expense on advisability of taking depositions. Of course it is conceivable that your judgment on that probability may be quite different in the light of the information developed on deposition.

The operation of a "Dead Man's Act" is sometimes a very important factor. It may be important as bearing on whether the death of one party would seal the lips of the other, making it impossible for the latter to meet his burden of proof unless depositions taken before death are recognized as defeating the operation of the statute. Also, in some jurisdictions a deposition of the surviving party taken by the lawyer for the estate of the deceased upon subjects covered by the disqualification is held to bar the assertion of the disqualification of the survivor.

Since your taking the deposition of one witness often leads to action by your adversary regarding depositions of other witnesses in the case, you should consider whether your initiating depositions may lead to other depositions that otherwise would not have been taken, and if so, whether development of the entire group of depositions is to your disadvantage, even though it would be to your advantage to have a particular one. In such situations, you may find it better to wait patiently, taking advantage of the chance that your adversary may fail to initiate depositions.

In most jurisdictions, taking the deposition of a witness does not make him your witness. If this rule does not prevail, you must consider the practical disadvantages[5] of making the witness yours.

In Case 82, if you represent P and P has potential successors to whom this $2500 claim would be important if he should die, you should give

---

3. American Bar Association, Code of Professional Responsibility DR 7–104 (1969).
4. *Cf.* §9.20.
5. See §2.2.

serious consideration to taking *P*'s deposition; *D*'s lawyer would be more inclined to attempt to prepare for trial without *P*'s deposition than would be true if *P*'s testimony was not absolutely essential to making a case for *P*. This factor of possible effect of *P*'s death weighs heavily if *P* is aged, or in poor health, especially if the docket of the trial court is so heavy that an extended delay before trial is to be expected; otherwise, this factor is not of controlling importance. Unless expense of the depositions is prohibitive, which would depend upon length of inquiries and the basis of the reporter's charges, it would be to your advantage as *P*'s lawyer in Case 82 to have the depositions of *D*, *W*, *C-1*, and *C-2* for discovery purposes, *D*'s being the most important and the one to which you might limit your discovery proceeding if expense is a major factor. You must also consider the possibility that *D* will be unavailable at the time of trial. This possibility gives rise to a distinctive problem because of the effect of the "Dead Man's Act" in some jurisdictions. Since the burden is on *P*, if death seals the lips of *D* and a statutory disqualification seals the lips of *P*, *P* will lose his case; in jurisdictions where the taking of *D*'s deposition, or the taking of *P*'s deposition by lawyers for *D* (or for *D*'s estate, if the deposition is taken after *D*'s death), would prevent the assertion of this disqualification of *P*, this would be a factor in the decision of either lawyer regarding depositions. It might be an important factor if *D* is in poor health and the case is pending in a court where trial will be delayed materially by a crowded docket.

§11.3 Timing of depositions

CASE 83. *P sues D Bus Company* for personal injuries suffered by *P*, a passenger, when the bus operated by *B*, a bus driver in the employ of *D Bus Company*, collided with the rear end of a car operated by *C* as the latter stopped at the edge of an intersection controlled by a flashing "caution" light. *C* stopped suddenly to avoid collision with a car that proceeded on the intersecting street through a flashing "stop" light at high speed, the identity of the speeding car and driver being unknown. The accident occurred late at night, and there were no other passengers on the bus and no other known witnesses to the accident. The case is filed in a court where jury cases are generally tried about eighteen months after being filed, a crowded docket preventing earlier trials.

At what time during trial preparations should you take the deposition of a particular party or witness?

Once you have decided to take a particular deposition [1] during preparations for trial, the status of the trial docket of the court determines the

---

1. See §11.2.

question of time if the docket is current and prompt trial is probable. In courts where cases are customarily tried as soon as they can be prepared for trial, it is essential that you take depositions at the earliest opportunity to avoid being forced to trial before you have completed your preparations. In many courts, however, the backlog of untried cases on the docket results in a customary delay of months or even years beyond the time that the case could be ready for trial. In such circumstances, is it better to take depositions promptly after the case is filed, or is it better to postpone them until a time nearer the date of probable trial?

The purpose for which you are taking a deposition affects the problem. If you are taking it to preserve the testimony of a witness who is seriously ill, obviously you should take it at the first opportunity. If you are taking it primarily for discovery, there is more doubt.

In personal injury cases, defense lawyers often prefer to delay the taking of the plaintiff's deposition until a date near trial in order to have the benefit of the plaintiff's deposition testimony with respect to a longer period of recovery and activity. Although this may be a sound practice in some cases, more often it is better from the defendant's point of view to take the plaintiff's deposition as soon as possible. If you wait, the plaintiff has more opportunity to learn about your theory of the case and to modify his testimony to meet it if he is willing to do so deliberately or may do so subconsciously. Taking the deposition early gets him committed on facts concerning liability; you may meet the later need for more up-to-date information on the extent of his recovery by a supplementary deposition or other discovery processes. The slight addition to time and expense devoted to the case is generally justified. Another reason for taking the deposition promptly is that you then have more time to investigate claims made in the deposition, to develop any matter that may be available to contradict or impeach his testimony, and to weigh the advisability of attempting to compromise the case[2] rather than trying it.

Another reason often relied upon in delaying the deposition of an adverse party or witness is the desire for completion of all practical investigation before the deposition is taken, so that the lawyer taking it for discovery purposes will be better informed as to matters concerning which it will be wise for him to question the adverse witness or party. The extent to which this reason is valid will in turn depend upon the extent to which questioning of an adverse party or witness on deposition should be influenced by what you know from your own investigation.[3]

Although the conflicting considerations that bear on the question of time for taking a deposition lead to disagreement among competent law-

2. See §9.22.
3. See §11.9.

yers, it is probably a majority view that the interests of your client are best served in most cases by taking depositions promptly and preparing the case fully at the earliest opportunity, though it may be months or years before the case can be tried in view of a crowded court docket. Case 83 is typical of situations in which these conflicting interests are present. Most lawyers representing *D Bus Company* would prefer to take *P*'s deposition early. Likewise, most lawyers representing *P* would wish to take the deposition of *B*, the bus driver, at an early time, to get him committed concerning the circumstances of the accident and to learn what his version is. Whether or not *C*'s deposition should be taken and, if so, the time of taking it, either by *P*'s lawyer or by *D*'s lawyer, would depend upon *C*'s willingness to talk freely and to commit himself by written statement or some other means besides merely unsworn oral statement. From *D*'s point of view, the danger that *C* will cooperate with *P*, and *C*'s greater reluctance in talking with *D*'s lawyer for fear that *D*'s lawyer intends to bring a claim over against *C*, would generally indicate that *D*'s lawyer should take *C*'s deposition promptly if *C* is not willing to make a written or sworn statement regarding the circumstances of the accident.

The timing of one deposition with reference to other depositions in the same case may be important. Obviously a dishonest witness or party is greatly aided in constructing his testimony so as to accomplish his dishonest purpose if he has the opportunity to study the testimony of others before he testifies. Even the witness who is only inclined to a little "fudging" or exaggeration may be influenced by hearing the testimony of others before he testifies. For these reasons, it is generally wise to avoid allowing depositions of your witnesses to be taken substantially in advance of those of adverse witnesses. Lawyers frequently meet this problem by arranging for the depositions to be taken on the same date, one immediately after the other, with neither witness hearing the other, and the order of their testifying being determined by some method of chance. [4]

§11.4 Preparing a deponent

Should you confer with the witness before his deposition is taken?

If the deposition of your own client is to be taken, you should confer with him as fully as if he were about to testify in trial. [1] The availability of the deposition for use at trial makes it almost as important as his testimony on the stand; any changes in his testimony would be harmful because of the unfavorable inferences about the credibility of his testimony generally as well as the credibility of the particular answers he changed.

4. *Cf.* Federal Rules 26(c) and (d), 30(a).
1. See §§2.10, 2.14.

If the deposition is that of a witness whose testimony is expected to be favorable to your client's cause but who is not related to or associated with your client, some argument might be made for requiring your adversary to make all arrangements with the witness for the deposition, avoiding direct communication with him yourself concerning it. The position of the witness as entirely disinterested would be better maintained in that way. On the other hand, a series of friendly communications between your adversary and the witness may affect his testimony subconsciously, if not by deliberate choice, and the want of your counsel concerning court processes and lawyers' tactics may make his manner of telling his story less effective, just as is true of testimony at trial. These factors generally outweigh the advantage of remaining aloof from the witness at the time a deposition is being arranged. If the witness is really your witness — one whom you intend to call and whom you do not expect your adversary to call, and whose deposition your adversary is taking for discovery or you are taking to preserve his testimony — you should confer with him as you would in preparation for his testifying in person at trial. You should hold the conference regardless of whether your adversary approaches the witness to make the arrangements for the deposition or you make the arrangements with the witness, either because you are taking the deposition or because you have entered into a waiver of formalities for a discovery deposition at the request of your adversary. In either case, the fact of your conference with the witness before his deposition is not likely to add much to the risk that the jury will disregard his testimony at trial as biased, since you expect to call him and confer with him in preparation for his appearance in trial. On the other hand, if his testimony should be less favorably developed as a result of your failure to confer with him, this might materially harm your case, since you would not benefit much, if any, by more favorable testimony at trial than he gave on deposition.[2]

With reference to the conference with one of your witnesses in preparation for his deposition, you should consider the possibility of inquiries on objectionable subjects or in objectionable form.[3] If you anticipate a dispute during the deposition regarding objections, it is best to advise the witness so he will not be surprised and upset when it occurs. Also, with respect to an objection of privilege, you may need to have him prepared to assert the privilege himself, if he wishes to do so, rather than relying on you to assert it.[4]

2. See §2.4.
3. See §11.11.
4. See *id*. Note, however, that you should not advise a witness concerning an issue of privilege if there is a conflict of interest between the witness and your client. See §2.14 n.8.

If the witness whose deposition is being taken is adverse, you may still profit by a conference with him in advance of his deposition, though your purpose in the conference should be to determine as accurately as possible what his testimony will be. This information aids you in deciding what questions you should ask and what questions you should avoid. Frequently it is impossible to arrange such a conference. You are precluded by the Code of Professional Responsibility from having a private conference with the adverse party, represented by counsel.[5] Though you are free to interview other adverse witnesses, they frequently refuse to talk. With those who will talk, however, the conference aids you in developing the testimony more favorably; even though your primary aim in taking a deposition may be discovery, it still is advisable to develop the evidence as favorably as possible, short of omitting inquiries that would disclose additional information you desire and do not have. Such an advance conference is particularly important with respect to preparation for the deposition of a witness who has no personal interest in the controversy and willingly tells what he knows without reference to whom it harms or aids. Often the testimony of such a witness contains elements favorable to each party, and in the conference before deposition he may willingly volunteer information favorable to your client for which you would not have asked if you had been taking the deposition without the benefit of the previous conference.

§11.5 Waiving formalities

Should you waive formalities in connection with a deposition?

By far the greater percentage of depositions are taken under waiver of at least some of the formalities provided by the rules; insisting upon compliance with all formalities rarely affects the taking of the deposition in any way other than increasing the time devoted to arrangements and the inconvenience to each of the lawyers. Occasionally, however, a waiver of formalities mkes it possible to obtain a deposition rather than missing it because of the departure of a witness before time for compliance with formalities,[1] or makes it possible to obtain a deposition orally rather than by written interrogatories. Even in such cases, it is the practice of a majority of lawyers to cooperate in obtaining depositions and to agree to taking them orally. Any advantage gained by insistence on formalities would be gained on a basis other than merits of the controversy.[2] In the

5. American Bar Association, Code of Professional Responsibility DR 7–104 (1969).

1. Note, however, that Federal Rule 30(b) provides for taking depositions on "reasonable notice," which may be rather short notice if the deponent is about to leave the jurisdiction.

2. As to the problems of professional responsibility involved in taking advantage of or declining to assert such formal requirements, compare §1.3.

overall practice, the position of the lawyers may be reversed on the next occasion, and reciprocity may be expected. Of course, if substantial additional expense is involved, as in the case of taking an oral deposition at a community distant from that where the lawyers' offices are located, waiver is often denied in the absence of an offer by the party desiring the deposition to bear the expense.

The signature and oath of the witness are to be distinguished from formalities such as notice of the intention to take the deposition, commission to the officer taking it, subpoena to the witness, and the manner of preparing and returning the record of the deposition. Undoubtedly the oath and signature of the witness give the deposition materially greater force for impeachment purposes[3] in the event of variance between the testimony at trial and that on deposition. If you attempt to impeach a witness with an unsigned deposition, which he has not read over after the record was prepared by the reporter, the witness may take the position that he did not say what the reporter wrote down. The witness is sometimes correct, reporters also being human. Whether he is correct or not, however, the impeachment is much less effective than it is if he has read over the deposition, has changed any parts that he contends are incorrect for any reason, and has signed it. For these reasons, many lawyers make a practice of insisting that an adverse witness read and sign his deposition, though they customarily waive formalities concerning arrangements for taking the deposition and for having the record of it returned and filed. It is preferable, of course, to have the deposition read and signed promptly after it is taken, rather than immediately before trial, so that you may have advance notice of any changes the witness makes.

§11.6 Choosing oral or written questions

Should you take the deposition orally or instead by written questions?

It is generally possible for you to take any deposition by written questions, if you prefer that method. If you prefer an oral deposition when your adversary insists upon taking a deposition by written questions, a practical remedy usually exists in cases in which the witness is readily accessible; your adversary's taking the deposition by written questions does not prevent your taking the deposition of the same witness orally, in the absence of an unusual rule or protective order.

In every jurisdiction there are limitations by rule or statute, or provisions for protective orders, regarding the taking of oral depositions. The limitations may prescribe the area or distance from the trial court within which the witness must be located if his deposition is to be taken orally,

3. See §3.8.

or they may give full discretion to trial judges to enter orders imposing such limitations in the interest of avoiding unreasonable expense or other unfairness.[1] It is possible, regardless of distance and circumstances, to take a deposition orally by stipulation of the parties.

If the witness is one whose testimony you intend to use during trial, you are generally able to develop his testimony much more satisfactorily in an oral deposition than in one taken by written questions. You are able to clear up any misunderstanding of questions with little or no harm when you take a deposition orally, but a misunderstanding may be fatal to the usefulness of testimony taken by written questions. On the other hand, it is also very difficult to cross-examine by written questions, and this disadvantage to your adversary may indicate in some instances that it is to your advantage to take the deposition by written questions.

Usually a deposition is taken by written questions only if the witness is located at a considerable distance from the community where the lawyers and the court are located. In such instances, it may be necessary for you to correspond with your witness to make arrangements for his deposition. You may wish to send him a copy of a written statement that he has previously given you so that he may refresh his memory regarding events that occurred months or years previously. If you do so, however, bear in mind that all of your correspondence may find its way into the deposition through answers of the witness on cross-examination. Write your correspondence in such a way that it will not harm your case if this should occur. The same precaution applies to your oral communications with any witness preparatory to having his deposition taken, or to his testifying in trial; in such cases, however, exact quotation is not so likely as in the case of your written communications.

If the deposition that you wish to take is that of an adverse witness, an oral deposition is far more satisfactory than a deposition by written questions because of your better opportunity to protect against evasive or ambiguous answers. When you take a deposition by written questions, you have no opportunity to follow up the evasive answer with additional questions that force the witness to a positive commitment on the point.

When you take the deposition of an adverse party or witness, usually you do so for discovery purposes as well as to get the witness committed to firm positions that will be useful either as admissions or for impeachment if he changes his story. When you take a deposition for discovery, many of the leads for questioning will develop from answers to questions you ask; it is practically impossible to obtain satisfactory discovery depositions by written questions.

---

1. See, *e.g.,* Federal Rules 26(c), 45(d).

If the witness whose deposition you are taking is located at a great distance from the community where your practice is centered and it is not feasible to have the witness come to that community for the deposition, it is often possible either by stipulation or under rules or court order to have the deposition taken orally rather than by written questions. It may happen that each lawyer will engage associate counsel in the community where the witness is located. This is not a completely satisfactory answer to the disadvantages of a deposition by written questions, however, because of the practical difficulties of having another lawyer take a deposition for you in a case that you are otherwise handling entirely by yourself. Added expense is another disadvantage. If you decide to engage associate counsel for such a deposition, advise him fully of your theories of the case as a whole, as well as what you hope to develop from the particular witness, so that he will be prepared to meet any unanticipated development of the evidence. If, as is frequently the case, he practices in a different jurisdiction, inform him also of any special practices to be followed in connection with the manner of taking the deposition — particularly such matters as whether objections to form of questions must be made when the deposition is being taken.

§11.7 Demeanor of the lawyer during oral depositions

The written record of a deposition never reveals the entire picture. The expression with which words are spoken often conveys meaning that is lost in the written words. This is one of the reasons that live testimony is generally more satisfactory than deposition testimony as evidence during trial. [1] The written record captures enough, however, that you should conduct yourself during a deposition with the fact in view that the record of the deposition may be used as evidence in trial; you may be performing before the judge and jury when you are participating in a deposition. In general, therefore, the principles governing your demeanor during trial [2] should govern your conduct during depositions.

Probably most lawyers adopt a more friendly attitude toward an adverse witness during a deposition taken for discovery than during examination at trial. The theory supporting this practice, aside from the natural increase in feelings of hostility as the climax of litigation approaches, is that a friendly atmosphere will appeal to the witness' finer instincts and cause him to testify more freely. That is not necessarily an advantage, since his greatest favor to you, as the adverse lawyer, would be to get out

1. See §2.4.
2. See §§1.2–1.4.

on a limb with hostile, unfavorable statements that you can impeach. Furthermore, your adversary probably has cautioned him, before you start taking his deposition, that your true attitude is more purposeful than friendly. Despite the warning to the witness by your adversary, most lawyers consider that you obtain more satisfactory depositions for discovery purposes with a friendly manner than with a hostile one. Nevertheless, there comes a point in the deposition when it may be necessary to press the witness relentlessly in the face of evasion. An ambiguous or evasive answer may be worthless for discovery purposes, and it is nearly always worthless for impeachment purposes.

It may also be necessary sometimes to curtail your natural desire to win the approbation of your fellow lawyer on the opposite side of the case. The problem of length and detail of your questioning presents an example. [3]

§11.8 Detail and length of depositions

When you are taking a deposition primarily to record testimony for use as evidence during trial, in most respects you should proceed as nearly as possible in the same manner as you would in examining the witness at trial. One important difference is that the probable unavailability of the witness at the time of trial forces you to give more attention to assuring that you do not omit any significant question, since you will have no opportunity to recall him. Other differences arise from the fact that the jury will not have the opportunity to see the witness at trial if only this deposition testimony is used. Ask him more questions about himself, as a means of getting the jury acquainted with him. Take particular care that you do not accept his use of gestures and vocal inflections to convey his meaning; aim at requiring that all of his meaning be expressed in the words used.

For discovery purposes, you need a very thorough deposition. You are often confronted with the temptation to reduce the length of your questioning to avoid personal disapproval of your fellow lawyer on the opposite side of the case. For motives of self-interest, as well as more laudable ones, you should generally remain on friendly terms with an adverse lawyer [1] and should willingly agree on waivers of formalities and other courtesies. [2] In practising this commendable spirit, however, a lawyer taking a deposition for discovery purposes (and particularly a young lawyer) is often subjected

---

3. See §11.8.
1. *Cf.* Code of Professional Responsibility EC 7–10, 7–37, 7–38 (1969).
2. *Cf. id.*, EC 7–38.

to pressure for reducing the length of the deposition.[3] A good deposition
for discovery is a thorough one. Obviously you must bear in mind the
time and expense involved in lengthy depositions, and you must consider
whether the case warrants the time and expense. If it does, there is no reason to stop while you still have an unanswered, material question in mind.
You should also take into account the possible use of the deposition at trial
and the fact that prying into irrelevant matter that serves no purpose other
than to harass or embarrass the witness may backfire against you when your
prying is made known to the jury at trial. Even if your questions are all
relevant, insinuations may be made at trial about how many questions you
asked on the deposition, its length being shown to the jury by your adversary to support the argument that you spent a whole day asking questions
and then could not trip the witness in more than one or two minor matters
that are not really material. The risk is usually worth taking, however. The
force of all such insinuations and argument is wiped out by one clear-cut
lie that you can prove against the witness because of the additional questions you made him answer. If the witness is telling the truth throughout
his testimony, the risk is worth taking because of the value of the additional
information you gain.

You should avoid long individual questions during depositions for the
same reasons that you should avoid them in an examination during trial.[4]

§11.9 Subject matter of deposition questions

In jurisdictions where the only purpose of taking depositions specifically
recognized in the rules of procedure is the recording of testimony and no
provision is made for depositions to be taken for the specific purpose of discovery, questions that are irrelevant to the issues in the case as limited by
the pleadings are generally improper. In practice, however, the difficulties
attendant upon submitting a dispute about relevancy to a court for decision usually cause lawyers to waive objections based only on irrelevancy
except in extreme cases. In the federal courts[1] and those of most of the states
where specific provision is made for taking depositions for discovery purposes, it is not a sound objection to a question on deposition that does not
call for admissible testimony, if it may reasonably be expected to lead to
the discovery of admissible evidence.

---

3. You may hear it said that those just out of law school or otherwise inexperienced
in trial advocacy take interminable depositions, including many foolish questions,
whereas the more experienced lawyers make their depositions short and to the point.
If you fall into line, your adversaries may love you more than your clients should.

4. See §2.16.

1. Federal Rule 26(b).

In a deposition that you are taking primarily for discovery purposes, you should not tie the scope and subject matter of your questions closely to your own theory of the individual case or to the facts as indicated by your investigation file. Organizing your questions around your own investigation may have the incidental effect of disclosing to your adversary, by the nature of your questions, the outlines of your own investigation. Such organization of your questions may even disclose to an observant witness, as the questioning proceeds, something of the scope and nature of your own investigation; if the witness is dishonest, a possibility that you must at least consider in the proper representation of your own client, this disclosure helps him avoid the type of fabrication or exaggeration that you might be able to prove against him. A factor that is probably more important than either of these in the average case is that organization of your questions around the information disclosed by your investigation tends to divert your mind from potential lines of inquiry other than those that your investigation has suggested. Some lawyers advocate that you never study your own investigation file in preparing to take the deposition of an adverse party or witness. That advice is exaggerated for emphasis and is not consistent with common practices, but the purpose it implies is sound — to conduct the questioning of an adverse witness so that your own questions are not limited by your investigation and so that your questions do not enlighten your adversary or his witness as to the scope and content of your own investigation. It is particularly revealing if you consult your investigation file during the deposition, as a reminder to yourself regarding the questions you want to ask (unless you do so with the purpose of creating some false impressions to mislead your adversary and his witness, an ethically questionable device that very few persons could use successfully, from the strictly tactical point of view). It is best to leave a confidential investigation file in a safe place in your office, rather than to subject it to the risks of scrutiny by others, of being lost or mislaid, and of being "read" through your questions.

You may need some form of reminder of subject matter to insure that you do not overlook important matters during the deposition. Having ruled out carrying the file with you for this purpose, we must find some other form of reminder. Probably the most satisfactory is a memorandum sheet on which you note only in general terms the subjects that you should cover on the deposition. In your earlier cases you may want to consider more fully the exact questions and the exact phrasing. You may even write them out in advance to be available for reference. With experience, you will find that your memorandum outline prepared for one case will be satisfactory for other cases of similar type, with few changes, and you may eventually develop an outline committed to memory that will serve your purpose of a check list. In preparing such a list for your earlier cases you may find it helpful to study depositions on file in similar pending cases and to study the entire records in similar cases tried and appealed.

In the chapters on direct and cross-examination are several illustrations supporting the proposition that in each case there will be some subjects about which you had best not ask a particular witness, regardless of relevancy to the issues in the case.[2] You should consider the disadvantages of such inquiries since almost anything you ask on deposition that is relevant may under some circumstances be admitted in evidence during trial.[3] The risks of harm giving rise to practical limitations against asking certain questions are generally reduced, however, when it is your adversary who introduces the matter before the jury, even though you may have been the one who originally made the inquiry. For example, asking on deposition about matters that reflect on the character of the witness, when you wish to discover exactly what the witness will say about some aspect of his past, then giving further consideration to the problem before introducing the evidence during trial, does not involve the same risk of unfavorable jury reaction as asking such questions in trial;[4] if you decide not to offer the evidence in trial, the jury will not know about your questions unless your adversary offers them, in which case jurors are not likely to blame you.

Another limitation on the subject matter of questions during deposition is that you should not ask questions disclosing impeaching evidence in your possession when advance notice to the witness would reduce the effectiveness of the impeaching evidence. Surprise is frequently essential to the most effective disclosure of the dishonesty of a witness.[5] A question telling the witness that you know of his dishonesty and how you propose to prove it may enable him to construct an excuse or at least to improve his position before the jury by admitting his error before you prove it and adopting the position that he has reformed, so as to increase your adversary's chances of persuading the jury to believe the witness' testimony in other respects.

§11.10 Form of deposition questions

Questions on deposition, like those during examination of a witness at trial,[1] should be simple and clear. A deposition that you may use later for impeachment serves its purpose much better if it is clear to the jury that the witness was not confused or misled and must have understood the questions and intended the obvious meaning of his answer. Deposition testimony

2. See §§2.20–2.23, 2.33, 2.34, 3.4–3.6, 3.10, 3.11, 3.13, 3.14, 3.16–3.18, 3.28–3.31.
3. Cf. Federal Rule 32.
4. See §3.11 as to asking such questions during trial.
5. See §1.3.
1. As to questions during trial, see §2.16.

offered during trial for any other purpose is more effective if the jury can easily understand it.

The usefulness of the method of sudden and frequent shifting of the subject matter of the questions on deposition is a subject of disagreement, but there is more reason for using this technique on deposition than during trial.[2] Especially is this true if you use more detailed and orderly inquiry after the skipping technique has served its purpose of obtaining initial answers from a witness who might have concealed information or modified his answers with more time to anticipate each question in an orderly series. The sudden shifting of subject matter makes that particular part of the deposition less useful for impeachment in trial than testimony in response to orderly questioning, in which the jury can easily follow the train of thought and in which it is apparent to the jury that the witness was not confused by quick and frequent changes of subject. The witness is likely, however, to stand by the original answer he gives during your use of this method on deposition, if you question him more fully later during the same deposition. You can use that part of the deposition containing the logical sequence of questions and answers for impeachment if the witness later changes his story before trial. The principal disadvantage of using the device of sudden and frequent changes of subject in this way, supplemented by more detailed later questioning in the deposition, is the greater length and cost of the deposition both in time and in expense.

The matter of form of questions on deposition is affected by rules of your jurisdiction with respect to the time within which objections to form must be made. Under the federal system, objections that could be obviated if made at the time the deposition is being taken are barred if not made then.[3] On the other hand, in some of the states it is possible to raise objections to the form of the question for the first time after the deposition has been filed, or even when used in trial. If you are taking a deposition for use in trial in such a jurisdiction, you should try to get a stipulation that objections to leading questions and other objections to form must be made at the time of the deposition; frequently it will be to the advantage of both parties to make such a stipulation when both are taking depositions. If you cannot obtain such a stipulation, then you should take special care to keep your questions in clearly proper form; otherwise you may lose valuable evidence at trial on purely formal grounds.[4]

2. As to using this technique during trial, see §3.20.

3. Federal Rule 32.

4. Compare, however, the risk of unfavorable jury reaction if your adversary makes "technical" objections in the presence of the jury, §§1.3, 4.2.

§11.11 Objections to deposition questions

What action should you take with reference to objections to a deposition or to individual questions?

Some objections to deposition testimony are seasonably made if first presented at the time the testimony is offered at trial, many variations existing as to the particular objections that do not fall within that rule. In general, the objections that are barred if not made in advance are those relating to formalities for taking the deposition and matters of form of questions and answers. For example, in federal courts objections to irregularities with respect to disqualification of the officer taking the deposition are barred unless objection is made before the taking of the deposition begins or as soon thereafter as the disqualification becomes known or could be discovered with reasonable diligence; objections to irregularities in the taking of the deposition and objections to the competency of the witness or competency of the evidence are not barred unless the ground of objection is one that might have been obviated or removed if objection had been presented at the time the deposition was taken; objections to leading questions are barred unless made at the time the deposition is being taken, because these are objections that might have been obviated if made at the time; if the deposition is being taken by written questions, objections to the form of the questions are barred unless served within the time allowed for cross or other questions and within five days after service of the last questions authorized; objections to the manner of completion and return of the deposition are barred unless a motion to suppress is made with reasonable promptness after the defect is, or with due diligence might have been, ascertained.[1] The federal rule has thus been worked out so that the objection procedure is as simple as possible, objections of substance being left to the time of trial but objection at an earlier time being required with respect to matters that could be obviated. Not all state rules have been so carefully planned; it is generally true, however, that objections to form must be made at some time before trial.

Even though under the rules of your jurisdiction you may make your objection for the first time when the deposition testimony is offered at trial, it will sometimes be to your advantage tactically to make it at an earlier time. When deposition testimony is being offered, you can usually prevent the reading of any objectionable question in the presence of the jury by interrupting the offering of the deposition testimony just before the objectionable question is reached, rather than after it has been read. You may accomplish the same purpose by a motion before or at the beginning

1. Federal Rule 32.

of trial.[2] This latter practice has the advantage of reducing any risk of harmful jury reaction because of the practice of objecting.

Objections on the ground of privilege present a special problem. As a general rule, such an objection is forfeited if not claimed, by or on behalf of the person for whom the privilege exists, when the first question on the privileged subject matter is asked.[3] Thus, it may be necessary that the objection be made before questions are answered on deposition, and it may be necessary for the witness, rather than a lawyer, to assert a privilege that is personal to the witness. Generally, when it is to the advantage of your client that the privilege be asserted, it will be a privilege that is personal to your client, or else personal to a witness who is favorable to your client. The possibility of questions concerning such privileged matter should be included in the subjects of your conference with the witness before the deposition[4] so that he is prepared to assert the privilege without detailed explanation from you during the deposition. However, you must not undertake to advise a witness, regarding an issue of privilege, in violation of the Code of Professional Responsibility.[5]

Even when your objection is on grounds other than privilege, sometimes you will prefer that the question not be answered because the answer will supply information that will serve your adversary's purposes though it is not in form to be admissible in trial. This is particularly true of depositions that your adversary is taking for discovery purposes. For example, in jurisdictions where deposition inquiries are limited to matters relevant to the issues in the case, as indicated by the pleadings, you may have an objection of irrelevancy to some of your adversary's "fishing expedition" questions. Since no officer of the court qualified to pass on objections (under the prevailing practice) is present as the deposition is being taken, your only possible means of preventing your adversary from obtaining the information he desires is to keep the witness from answering. You can do this by interrupting the questioning to state, for the record of the deposition, that you object to the question for stated reasons and that either you are instructing the witness not to answer or else (if your relations with the witness require it) that you are advising the witness that he need not answer unless he prefers to do so. Generally it is better for the refusal to come from you than from your witness, since it is upon a lawyer's ground; the refusal initiated by the witness involves more danger of a jury reaction that the witness is

2. See §4.16.
3. See, *e.g.*, 8 Wigmore, *Evidence* §§2196, 2241, 2242, 2268–2273, 2327–2329, 2340, 2388–2391 (rev. ed. McNaughton 1961); Federal Rules of Evidence, Rule 511.
4. See §11.4.
5. See §2.14 n.8.

consciously trying to make his testimony favorable to one side instead of merely relating the facts as he knows them. Objections made in this manner as the deposition is taken can generally be brought to the court for ruling by motions in advance of trial, regardless of whether the rules of procedure make special provision for such motions. Generally the initiative as to such motions is taken by the lawyer who desires the question answered, since the other lawyer is content to let the matter rest with the objection stated and the answer refused.

Unless there is either a requirement for making the objection when the deposition is taken to avoid forfeiting it or else a reason such as those discussed above for making it to prevent the witness from giving the answer, it is generally preferable not to make objections when the deposition is taken. Making an objection then has the disadvantage of advance disclosure to your adversary of your theory of objection. Also, it has the disadvantage of being in your way if, at trial, you choose for tactical reasons not to make the objection that you stated in the deposition, or if you choose to make additional objections that you did not make at the time of the deposition. Using the opportunity of studying the deposition testimony carefully to decide when and where to make your objections, you can generally improve your statement of the objections and your choice as to whether to make particular objections. Although it is not necessary that objections reported in the deposition be read at trial, probably it would come to the attention of the jury at the least that you had made them, because of the skips during the offering of the deposition.

§11.12 Cross-examining on deposition

Should you make use of your right of cross-examination when your adversary takes a deposition?

If your adversary's purpose in taking a deposition is discovery and the witness is your own client or a favorable witness whom you expect to call in person at trial, you are helping your adversary if you cross-examine on matters about which your adversary failed to inquire. It may be to your advantage, however, all things considered, to ask such questions. If they are of a type needed to clarify some part of the witness' testimony because it is misleading in the incomplete form, you may prefer to ask the questions to avoid a possible inference by the jury that the supplementary testimony offered for the first time at trial was the product of ingenuity exercised after the deposition had been completed, rather than fact. If there is a prospect that the witness will be unavailable at the time of trial, you may wish to ask the additional questions to insure completeness of the testimony in the event it is necessary to use the deposition instead of having the witness present in person. But unless you have some such special reason for asking questions of the witness, the best cross-examination upon deposition is no cross-examination. Rarely will it be to your advantage to ask many questions of your own witness whose deposition is being taken by your adversary.

If your adversary is taking the deposition of a witness with the apparent purpose of recording it for use in trial, then obviously your cross-examination should be more extensive and should be directed toward development of weaknesses that will limit the effectiveness of the testimony before the jury. In general, your cross-examination should be guided by the same considerations as if you were cross-examining the witness in trial. Some differences exist, however; for example, you may want to withhold examination on some subjects because of your intention to use them as surprises during trial.[1]

If your adversary is taking by written questions a deposition apparently intended for use during trial, cross-examination is most difficult, particularly if you have never had the benefit of an interview with the witness. The principal subjects of inquiry may be determined generally by the considerations that would govern your decision in cross-examination of the witness in person, except that you should be more cautious about asking questions of doubtful value. The risks of doing more harm than good by your questions are increased because you have less direct control over development of the cross-examination and no opportunity to adapt it in the light of answers to your earlier questions.

On the other hand, certain special questions may often be useful if your adversary has had to communicate with the witness from a distance. For example, you may ask the witness by one of your cross-questions to attach to the deposition all written materials that have come to him in connection with the taking of his deposition or the preparation for it, and all written statements or other materials that he has examined or has had read to him or discussed with him in preparation for the deposition. You may also ask that he relate the substance of any oral communications with him regarding his deposition.

After a deposition by written questions has been returned, review the testimony carefully with a view toward taking a supplementary deposition to submit any additional questions you wish to have answered. Sometimes such a supplementary deposition is not very usable, however, since the witness may be regarded as yours[2] for the purpose of questions that you offer from any deposition other than the one used by your adversary in originally presenting the testimony of the witness.

1. As to use of surprise generally, see §1.3.
2. See §2.2.

§11.13 Using discovery processes generally

Should you use discovery processes to compel disclosures by your adversary and his witnesses?

Should you make voluntary disclosures to your adversary?

The advantages of using discovery processes are obvious. One aim of your pretrial preparation is to know the opposing lawyer's possible theories and evidence as well as if you were preparing to represent the opposing party.[1] Greater knowledge and understanding of the opposing case increases your opportunity for successful defense against that case and for improved presentation of your own. You should not use discovery processes indiscriminately, however. As you make greater use of processes for compelling disclosures by your adversary and adverse witnesses, you must anticipate that your adversary will be inclined to apply against you the same and any other available techniques for compulsory disclosure. If for any reason you prefer to use surprise tactics[2] during the trial of a particular case, you should be more cautious about using available discovery procedures unless you are confident that the information that you propose to use for surprise is privileged or otherwise protected against compulsory disclosure under the law of your jurisdiction. This is not to say that you should altogether avoid using discovery procedures simply because you plan a surprise for the adverse party. You may likewise be surprised. Your choice is one of appraising relative risks. Generally, your client's best interests will be served by your learning all that you can about the facts of the case, accepting any disadvantage of improvement of your adversary's preparation and using procedures for compulsory disclosure if you need them to gain full information. In smaller cases, of course, factors of time and expense may impose practical limitations inconsistent with the interest in most thorough preparation.

The nature of discovery processes available greatly varies, depending on the jurisdiction in which your case is pending.[3] Knowledge and understanding of the law of your jurisdiction in this regard is important to determining not only whether and with what methods you will attempt to compel disclosures by your adversary and his witnesses but also what disclosures you will make voluntarily to your adversary. Although there may be a certain sadistic satisfaction in confronting your adversary with as many obstructions as possible to his preparation,[4] and a possibility that your

1. See §§9.2, 9.10.
2. See §1.3.
3. See §§11.1, 11.14, 11.15, 11.20.
4. Compare §1.3 as to the problems of professional responsibility involved in using or declining to use this approach.

adversary will prepare less adequately in view of those obstructions, it does not necessarily follow that it is to the best interests of your client that you adopt this attitude. Reciprocity may be expected, with greater expense to both clients and poorer preparation by both lawyers because of the additional attention both lawyers must give to the case. If an attitude of obstruction becomes known to the court and jury during the trial of the case, as it might, it is likely to affect their reactions, particularly if there is a noticeable difference between competing lawyers and parties in this respect. From this point of view, it is generally advisable to disclose, upon request by your adversary, anything that you clearly can be obliged to disclose under the applicable discovery rules.[5]

Voluntary disclosures are often made, sometimes even without an inquiry or request for information, in the interest of improving the chances of satisfactory compromise of the controversy without trial.[6] If you have evidence the value of which is substantially affected by its surprise use, however, disclosing it may damage your client's interests unless you benefit by similar frankness of your adversary.

§11.14 Securing production of documents or objects

CASE 84. *P* sues *D Company* for compensation under a contract of employment of *P* as a sales representative for *D Company* in a specified geographical area. There is a dispute as to the terms of the contract. *P* asserts that he is entitled to a commission upon all orders of customers within the area, including those forwarded directly to the company after the date *P* started working the area; *D Company* contends that he is entitled to a commission on only those orders forwarded through *P* or by customers approached by *P*. As *P*'s lawyer, you have only *P*'s estimate and information regarding a few specific transactions, and you do not have complete information on all orders forwarded directly to the company by customers within *P*'s geographical area.

What methods should you use to secure production of documents or objects?

Although in practice documents and objects are more often produced by agreement than under compulsion, certainly the availability of compulsory processes frequently accounts for the willingness of a party to produce them voluntarily. These compulsory processes include the following: a *subpoena duces tecum* requiring appearance and production of the documents or

5. *Cf.* §11.20.
6. See §9.22.

objects[1] at trial; a *subpoena duces tecum* in connection with a deposition; a bill of discovery under equity principles or a modified form adopted by decision, rule, or statute; and a motion for discovery under Federal Rule 34 or under rules or statutes of some of the states. In some jurisdictions, inherent power to require disclosures is recognized by decisions, but discovery under those decisions is generally more limited in scope and less expeditious in procedure than when authorized by court rules or statutes. Your first step in determining what method to use to compel production of a document from an unwilling adversary is to consider the authorities of your jurisdiction concerning the extent to which these various methods are recognized and the regulations and limitations attending each.

These procedures for compelling production of a document are to be distinguished from a notice to produce it. The latter is a notice from a party, rather than the court, and ordinarily (though perhaps not if the document is in court) it may be ignored by the party to whom it is addressed without penalty other than that it affects admissibility of secondary evidence and may prevent a later offer of the original document to contradict the secondary evidence.[2] If you want the document itself, for reasons such as comparison of handwriting or study of changes upon its face, or incompleteness of secondary evidence, the notice to produce the document is inadequate for your needs. If the document is in the hands of a third person other than your adversary and not under your adversary's control, the notice to produce will be ineffective, since it is directed only to an adverse party.[3] A request to a third person for an original document, however, sometimes serves the purpose of laying the foundation for secondary evidence.[4]

If you have secondary evidence that you would find as satisfactory as the document in the hands of your adversary, a notice to produce may be more satisfactory than compulsory processes. For example, it is generally more satisfactory than a *subpoena duces tecum*. The notice to produce may be served on the lawyer and will be effective if either the lawyer or client has custody, under the prevailing view, even though the document may be located beyond the territorial jurisdiction of the court,[5] whereas the *sub-*

1. Though there is doubt in some jurisdictions as to the possibility of requiring production by *subpoena duces tecum* of an object other than a document, Federal Rule 45(d) makes specific provision for production of objects that may be evidence. See also Federal Rule 30(b) (5), which provides that the notice for taking the oral deposition *of a party* may be accompanied by a request under Rule 34 for production of documents and tangible things at the taking of the deposition.

2. 4 Wigmore, *Evidence* §1210 (3d ed. 1940). See also Federal Rules of Evidence, Rules 1003, 1004.

3. See 4 Wigmore, *Evidence* §1208 (3d ed. 1940).

4. *Id.,* §§1211–1213.

5. See *id.,* §1208.

poena duces tecum in some jurisdictions has more limited effectiveness. The *subpoena duces tecum* is ineffective if the document is not within the control of the one on whom it is served; there is conflict as to whether a *subpoena duces tecum* served on a party is effective when the document is then in the custody of another but subject to control of the party served.[6] Also, there is conflict as to the effectiveness of the *subpoena duces tecum* if the document is outside the territorial jurisdiction of the court issuing the subpoena.[7]

In the event you first realize during trial the need for certain documentary evidence, your choice as between a *subpoena duces tecum* and a notice to produce may be influenced by the time required for each to be effective. An instanter subpoena is effective as soon as it can be served upon the custodian of the document; the delay that might be required for such service would depend upon the circumstances and might be affected by subpoena dodging. There generally is no specified time for the effectiveness of the notice to produce, reasonable notice being required.[8] If the document is in the files of the opposing lawyer or party in the courtroom, the notice may be given in the course of trial and will be effective immediately. On the other hand, if the document is elsewhere, reasonable time to produce it will be allowed before your secondary evidence will be admissible.

In some instances neither the notice to produce nor the *subpoena duces tecum* from the trial court will be effective because the document is in the hands of a third person, not associated with the adverse party, and is located outside the jurisdiction. In such cases, you should consider the possibility of taking the deposition of the custodian, under *subpoena duces tecum* in the foreign jurisdiction. In some jurisdictions a *subpoena duces tecum* is not available in connection with depositions, and in some its usefulness is limited, though it is available, because of limitations on taking depositions for discovery purposes. Particularly such limitations would affect discovery of documents that are inadmissible but might lead to discovery of admissible evidence. Under Federal rule 45 (d) and under the practice in some states, a *subpoena duces tecum* may be issued in connection with a deposition. This is often an effective means of obtaining access to desired documents or objects (the federal rule expressly extending to things other than documents). Disadvantages are that such a subpoena is generally effective only as to a witness who has custody of the documents or objects; uncertainty as to the identity of the person having custody or as to the location of the documents or objects is a problem; and in some instances, efforts to

6. See 8 *id.,* §2200 (rev. ed. McNaughton 1961).
7. *Id.*
8. 4 *id.,* §1208 (3d ed. 1940).

gain access to them may be thwarted by changes of custody and location.[9]

If your efforts to gain access to a document or object are prompted not by desire to meet the requirements of the best evidence rule but rather by purposes of discovery, the notice to produce is not useful. The subpoena for production of the document or object at trial is also generally unsatisfactory because of the need for examination well in advance of trial and for attention to additional investigation and trial preparations based upon your study of the documents or objects. Furthermore, procedural law limits the effectiveness of the *subpoena duces tecum* to those documents within the control of the witness, and the subpoena for production of the documents at trial may be wholly ineffective because the custodian of the desired documents or objects is beyond the jurisdiction of the court. In jurisdictions where a *subpoena duces tecum* may be used with a deposition, it has greater value for discovery purposes than the subpoena at trial, but under given circumstances it may be less effective than other discovery procedures.

The equitable bill of discovery had severe limitations because of ponderous procedural requirements that made it necessary in effect to go through a complete suit for discovery purposes only. Also, its use was limited to discovery of evidence affirmatively supporting a party's contentions; discovery of the evidence that the adverse party probably would use to support his position was not a recognized aim.[10] Where the equitable bill of discovery is still available, it generally involves vestiges of these procedural limitations despite modifications by statute and rule.

In the federal courts and those of other jurisdictions having provisions for discovery similar to that under Federal Rule 34, this is generally the most efficient and satisfactory method of compelling production of desired documents or objects. Generally you can deal with attempted evasion more effectively under Rule 34 than under a *subpoena duces tecum*. Unless an independent action is filed, however,[11] Rule 34 discovery is available only against parties. Thus, it is necessary to file an independent action or to resort to one of the other procedures when the document or object is not within the control of the adverse party.

The right of "inspection" under Rule 34 is often more satisfactory than that under a deposition with *subpoena duces tecum* because the document remains only in the custody of the witness under the latter procedure, or in the custody of the reporter or other court official if it is attached to the record of the deposition. Under Rule 34, on the other hand, provisions may

9. But *cf.* Federal Rule 30(b) (6), establishing a procedure for taking the deposition of "a public or private corporation or a partnership or association or governmental agency."

10. 6 Wigmore, *Evidence* §1846 (3d ed. 1940).

11. See Federal Rule 34(c).

be made as to time, place, and manner of inspection. Thus, for example, you might arrange for an inspection by a questioned documents examiner. There is at least a possibility that you might also arrange such things as chemical analyses and experiments, whereas they could not be required by use of the *subpoena duces tecum*. The federal rule makes no specific provisions for chemical analyses and experiments but does extend specifically to inspection, copying, testing, sampling, photographing, measuring, and surveying, and might be construed broadly to include chemical analyses and experiments.

Another respect in which there may be a material difference in a particular jurisdiction between proceeding under a discovery rule and using a *subpoena duces tecum* with a deposition is the effectiveness of each to require production of documents or objects that are within the control of a party but beyond the territorial jurisdiction of the court. There is a conflict as to the effectiveness of the *subpoena duces tecum* for this purpose.[12] Under Rule 34, a party may be compelled to produce such documents or objects. Similarly, if the documents or objects are scattered in location or in the custody of numerous persons, all of whom are subject to the control of the party, a single request for discovery might serve more effectively than numerous depositions, each with a *subpoena duces tecum*.

If you do not have adequate information concerning the description of the document or object that you wish to examine and must obtain information on that subject by deposition, you may choose to issue a *subpoena duces tecum* requiring the witness to produce such documents or things as you can describe, in the hope that your entire purpose will be satisfied with completion of the deposition but with the purpose of filing a request for discovery using the descriptive information obtained during the deposition if not all documents or objects you desire have been produced. The discovery request is generally treated as a procedure for requiring production of documents and things known to exist and not as a fishing expedition for the possibility of documents or things not known to exist. This fishing, if appropriate, can be done under other discovery procedures, especially depositions.

§11.15 Obtaining information from the adverse party

What methods should you use for obtaining information from the adverse party?

Federal Rule 33 and similar provisions in some states establish a procedure for "interrogatories to parties" as a method of compelling disclosures by the

12. See 8 Wigmore, *Evidence* §2200 (rev. ed. McNaughton 1961).

adverse party (in addition to depositions, requests for admissions, discovery requests or motions, and exceptions or motions relating to pleadings). In the practice under the federal rule, the interrogatories are customarily delivered to the adverse party through his attorney, and the adverse party answers under oath in writing rather than answering orally before an officer as in the deposition procedure. The deposition is therefore more advantageous in that it does not allow time for deliberate preparation of the answer to questions you may ask, whereas the answers to the interrogatories will be carefully considered by the adverse lawyer as well as the adverse party and will doubtlessly be phrased, within limitations of the obligations of the oath and rules, in the manner most favorable to the adverse party. For this reason depositions are ordinarily preferable to the procedure of interrogatories, unless the greater expense of depositions is a material consideration. Of course, both interrogatories and depositions may be used in the same case. Ordinarily, however, interrogatories are not needed after a thorough deposition and are not used before a deposition, since they would disclose in advance the major lines of inquiry and thereby give the party time to prepare his answers.

A disadvantage of the deposition is that in some jurisdictions an offer of a part of the deposition at trial opens the way for your adversary to offer other parts at that point in trial, or to require you to do so; in jurisdictions where this is possible, you might serve a request for admissions after taking the adverse party's deposition with the purpose of offering in evidence the admissions by request rather than those made in the deposition.

If the adverse party is a public or private corporation or a partnership or association, the interrogatories under the federal rule may be served upon any officer or agent, "who shall furnish such information as is available to the party." By an amendment of Rule 30, a similar provision now applies to depositions.

The federal rules in original form did not make any specific provision for using the answers to interrogatories as evidence during trial, but the amended rule states that answers to interrogatories may be used in trial to the extent permitted by the rules of evidence.

Interrogatories are more useful than a request for admissions if your information is incomplete; that is, interrogatories are more suitable for discovery purposes. On the other hand, the request for admissions is generally more suitable for the purpose of committing the adverse party to admissions for your use in trial, since you can phrase the statement as you prefer it in requesting the admission and it is more difficult for the adverse party to thwart your efforts with an evasive or ambiguous answer.

Each of these procedures is generally so much more useful in obtaining information from the adverse party than exceptions or motions relating to pleadings in the case [1] that the latter are generally used only as a means of obtaining information concerning what contentions the adverse party will assert in trial, as distinguished from information as to evidence that may be available to support those contentions.

§11.16   Requesting admissions

Should you request admissions?

Every lawsuit involves many undisputed facts and circumstances. Some of these you will prefer to prove by testimony as a part of the persuasive development before the jury of your theory of the case. As to those facts, you may refrain from seeking any stipulation or formal admissions by your adversary, since they might interfere with your plan for developing the evidence through the witnesses. Unless reference to stipulated facts is essential to logical presentation and understanding of the testimony, it may be prevented by objection that the evidence is immaterial in view of the stipulations — an objection as to which the trial court has discretion. Only in exceptional situations is such an objection worth making; [1] only in exceptional situations should you give any substantial weight to the risk of such an objection when you are deciding whether to seek admissions. As a general rule, it is to your advantage to obtain as many admissions as possible in advance of trial so as to reduce the expense, time, and inconvenience of proving matters not actually in dispute. Using formal requests for admissions also helps you avoid surprise. It gives you a means of requiring your adversary to confirm your view that certain matters are undisputed, or else to put you on notice by a denial. If the procedure of a formal request for admissions is not available, you may in part serve the same objectives by making an informal request for stipulations.

In jurisdictions providing a procedure for formal requests for admissions, it is good practice for the plaintiff's lawyer, in particular, to include a request for admissions in the routine of his preparations for trial. Requesting admissions to establish that the defendant is the right party for you to sue is important because of the danger of misunderstanding with respect to the correct identity of the party or parties who should be sued. [2] This is particularly true if closely associated business entities are involved; it is sometimes necessary to sue several parties to insure that you have the right one included. Similarly, there may be doubt, for example, as to

1. See §10.18.
1. See §11.19.
2. Compare §§9.5(4) and 10.2.

what employer a person was representing in committing a tort against the plaintiff, or doubt as to the party liable because of contractual arrangements that may create an independent contractor relationship or may amount to a lease of equipment possibly affecting tort liabilities.

Another purpose often served by a formal request for admissions is to obtain admission of facts that you could prove only by the testimony of an adverse party or witness whom you do not wish to call to the stand. [3]

A request for admissions with respect to documents often eliminates the necessity for tedious proof of facts constituting the foundation for admitting documents in evidence [4] and eliminates the need for calling a custodian as a witness in trial, if his testimony is not required for other purposes.

Though a request for admissions is very useful as to truly undisputed and vital facts, you gain little if anything by indiscriminate requests for admission of matters that are not especially important. Many undisputed facts are material to issues in the case because of forming the background circumstances but are not practically appropriate for the subject of a request for admissions because of the certainty that they will not be disputed, the necessity for including them in the testimony of some of the witnesses by way of explanation of other matters as to which dispute may exist, or the unnecessary expenditure of time that would result from your pursuing the formal procedure, simple as it may be. Abusing the use of the procedure by excessively lengthy and detailed requests has not only the disadvantage of waste of time in preparing the requests but also the danger of retaliatory harassment by similar requests from your adversary.

Another limitation on the extent to which you should use the request for admissions is the effect upon potential use of the subject matter as a surprise during trial. [5] For example, in Case 35, you should not make a request for admission of the fact of engaging in work inconsistent with the deposition testimony of the witness, since you use that fact more effectively by way of surprise, either on cross-examination or by offering independent evidence. [6] Using a request for admissions may also affect indirectly your opportunity for using tactics of surprise, since it may influence your adversary to counter with a request for admissions or other discovery procedures, forcing you to disclose information that otherwise your adversary might not have obtained before trial. [7]

In jurisdictions where the disqualification of a witness under a "Dead

3. See §2.5.
4. See §2.25.
5. As to surprise generally, see §1.3.
6. See §3.6.
7. See §11.13.

Man's Act" is precluded by taking his deposition, you should consider the risk that a request for admissions would likewise preclude assertion of the disqualification.

§11.17   Form of requests for admissions

What should be the form of your request for admissions?

Rules concerning requests for admissions generally contain certain formal requirements but leave to the lawyer's individual preference the matter of form of the recitation of the facts as to which admissions are requested. Some lawyers customarily phrase the request in the form of questions: "Do you admit that . . . ?" Probably a majority prefer a phrasing in terms of statements such as the following:

> You are requested to admit the truth of the following statements of fact, pursuant to Rule X, under the terms of which these matters will be deemed admitted if you do not serve a response in accordance with that rule on or before . . . 1. That . . . 2. That . . . (reciting a single fact in each paragraph).

The latter form is generally better for the purpose of making each statement of fact clearly understandable, and it is also better for use in introducing the matter before the jury. When the fact is admitted by failure to respond properly or in due time, it is better to be able to read the statement as an admission rather than reading a question and explaining that the answer is deemed to be "yes" under the court's ruling, although no answer or a different answer was given by the party. You should take care, in addressing the request, to insure that you name all parties correctly and that you correctly designate all the different capacities of any party who is in the suit in more than one capacity.

With respect to the individual statements, keep them as simple and precise as possible. A complex statement involving several different elements is likely to be false because of only one of the several elements, furnishing an excuse for either a denial or else explanatory comment that weakens the effectiveness of the qualified admission obtained. [1] Ambiguous statements are ineffective, both because of the invitation for explanatory comment or denial on the basis of a different interpretation from that you intend and because of uncertainty as to exactly what is admitted if you receive an affirmative reply.

You should consider the possibility of objection to the form of your statement. If you anticipate a dispute as to the propriety of a particular

---

1. See §11.18.

form of statement, you may be able to accomplish your purpose with another form of statement that would not be subject to the objection. If other forms are not as satisfactory from the tactical point of view, however, it is doubtful that you should include the less objectionable form of the statement in your request, since its being present for comparison with the form as to which you hope to get an admission would be an invitation to your adversary to raise an objection. A better method of proceeding, except in the rare instances when time does not permit, is to use the form you prefer, hoping that you will receive the desired admission without objection, but intending to submit another request for admission in the less favorable but clearly unobjectionable form if your original purpose is not accomplished.

§11.18 Making explanatory replies

CASE 85. *P* sues *D* on account of personal injuries suffered when their automobiles collided head-on, on a city street. *P* files a request for admission that, among other things, "*D*'s car was over the marked center line of the street at the time of the impact." In representing *D*, it is your position that *D* swerved sharply to the left to avoid striking *C*, a six-year-old child chasing a ball that rolled in front of *D*'s car, and that at the time of impact *D*'s car was at an angle with only the left front of the car over the center line, the maximum distance beyond the line being about one foot.

Should you make an argumentative or explanatory reply to a request for admissions?

Regulations concerning admissions pursuant to a formal request customarily provide for explanatory comment if the party requested to make the admission considers that he cannot properly deny the fact stated but has good reason for not admitting it. Comment other than mere denial or admission is sometimes used in other instances as well.

In the original federal rule on admissions no specific provision was made for responding to a request for admissions with a contention that it was improper. The federal rule has since been amended to provide for written objections on the ground that some or all of the requested admissions are improper. The manner in which you should meet objectionable requests in jurisdictions where there is no specific provision for objections to the propriety of the requests is a subject of disagreement. One method used is to reply with a refusal to admit or deny on the ground that the request is improper for a stated reason. Another and probably preferable method is to file written objections, exceptions, or a motion to strike objectionable requests, whatever form seems most appropriate under the local practice, and at the same time to seek an order extending the time to answer until a date after the ruling on the objections, exceptions, or motion.

Another situation in which comment is sometimes used arises when the statement in the request contains some element that makes it false, though that element is relatively immaterial and in material respects the statement is substantially true. The federal rule in original form, and that of some states patterned after it, left open the possibility of answering such a request with a mere denial, though that kind of response is obviously inconsistent with the spirit of the rule. As amended, the federal rule requires that a party deny only a part or a qualification of a matter of which an admission is requested when meeting the substance of the requested admission in good faith requires such an answer. This is another situation, therefore, in which explanatory comment is contemplated by the federal rule and has been used in practice under state rules not specifically requiring the qualified denial.

If the question or statement in the formal request for admissions is ambiguous or uncertain in meaning, it is obviously appropriate and usually desirable to respond with an explanatory answer rather than a categorical admission or denial.

In your reply to a request for admissions, should you limit your explanatory comment to such uses as those discussed above, or should you also make use of argumentative and explanatory comment as a means of incorporating your theory of the case into your reply, so that it is called to the attention of the jury if the admission is offered against you in the presence of the jury during trial? This question is affected by the practice of your jurisdiction with respect to whether admissions on file are automatically deemed part of the record of trial or intsead it is necessary that you formally offer them in evidence during trial. If the former practice is followed and the admission relates to some matter that will not be needed before the jury by way of explanation or background facts bearing on disputed issues submitted to them, then an argumentative admission is not likely to go before the jury. Use of the argumentative form may nevertheless be advantageous for the purpose of avoiding a reading before the jury of an unexplained admission that would be likely to fix an impression in their minds — an impression more difficult to remove by subsequent explanation than to avoid by explanation accompanying the admission. Disagreement exists as to the extent to which you are entitled to require that your explanation be presented to the jury, the formal admission practice being so much controlled by trial court rulings that authoritative opinions on the issue have not been developed. One position taken is that the fact admitted may be offered as an admission, without presenting the explanation, and that the party making the admission is not entitled to present this explanation in evidence since it is a self-serving, hearsay statement (though of course he may prove the explanatory facts and make the argument in other ways during the trial). On the other hand, some trial judges permit the explanatory comment to be offered simultaneously with the admission on the theory that a half-truth may be unfairly misleading to the jury, despite the opportunity to offer explanation at some other point in trial.

If there is doubt about the practices in your court with respect to use of admissions during trial, you should consider including explanatory comment in your reply to a request for admission of any fact that, standing alone, may be misleading and damaging. Such a reply should be argumentative in the sense that you should prepare it with thought to the effect it may have on persuasion of the jury, though you should avoid a contentious statement, if not for other reasons, because it is not generally a sound method of persuasion.

In Case 85, you are requested as D's lawyer to admit that "D's car was over the marked center line of the street at the time of the impact." The statement is ambiguous. It may be construed as meaning that the entire car was beyond the center line onto the left-hand side of the street from D's point of view, or it may mean that part of the car was directly above the marked center line. Even if the latter interpretation is accepted, the statement is still indefinite because it does not indicate how much of the car was over onto the left-hand side from D's point of view. Standing alone, it is misleading also because, in the absence of explanation of the reason the car was in that position, the statement is subject to being interpreted as implying fault (which would not be charged against one who, while proceeding carefully in other respects, suddenly swerved to avoid running over a child dashing into the street). You might reply to the request in a form such as this:

In reply to paragraph 4 of the request, D admits that the left front corner of his car was across the center line of the street, D's car being at an angle, with the part farthest to D's left being about eighteen inches across the center line, because D swerved to avoid striking a child, C, who suddenly dashed into the street in front of D.

It is more doubtful whether you should include further comment as to D's freedom from fault and as to the conduct of P at the time of this emergency. Should you add to the foregoing statement something such as the following?

D was acting with due care in so swerving his car, and if *P* had been equally alert to the emergency and had swerved likewise, rather than driving in a straight path near the center line of the street, the accident would have been avoided.

If any part of the admission were offered in evidence during trial, *P*'s lawyer would doubtlessly omit this latter part and contend that you should not be allowed to offer it even though *P*'s lawyer had offered the admission that the left front corner of the car was beyond the center line. Even if the former statement were permitted on the theory that it is essential to a description of exactly what is admitted, or is essential to avoiding a misconstruction by the jury of what is admitted, probably most trial judges would exclude the latter statement. The statement of the reason for swerving might also be excluded, but the explanation of the exact position of the vehicle is doubtlessly proper since the phrase in the request is an indefinite and ambiguous statement — and one that a party could not fairly be required to answer categorically.

§11.19 Admitting matters you might dispute

CASE 86. *P* brings suit against *D Bus Company* because of injuries sustained when the bus on which *P* was a passenger skidded into the rear of another bus, both buses being operated by servants in the scope of employment of *D Bus Company*. The accident occurred during a sudden ice storm, when visibility was low and the streets were slick. On the basis of the testimony of the bus drivers, a finding of unavoidable accident could be sustained by the courts as an inference not beyond reason. Several disinterested witnesses, as well as *P*, contradict the testimony of the bus drivers and indicate that the trailing bus on which *P* was riding was traveling at a speed of about thirty miles per hour despite the adverse weather and street conditions. *P* claims severe head injuries; as *D*'s lawyer, your investigation discloses evidence that many of *P*'s complaints had existed before the accident, and your principal medical witness is of the opinion that *P* sustained only minor injuries from which he recovered within two weeks after the accident.

Should you for tactical reasons admit matters that you might dispute under the evidence available?

Each contention that you make in trial is likely to influence the jury's consideration of your other contentions. The reaction of the jurors to any one of your points may influence their views as to the sincerity[1] and fairness[2] of your position in the trial generally. Inconsistent contentions

1. See §1.2.   2. See §1.3.

may be destructive of each other. Numerous contentions, even though consistent, may weaken the chances of jury acceptance of your best one through the loss of favorable emphasis when it is presented among a mass of others less well supported. It is often advisable to eliminate, by admissions, some of the possible contentions that you might make under the available evidence in order to improve your chances of success with contentions that are better supported or more important to your client in terms of effect.[3]

A special purpose for which it is sometimes tactically advisable to admit matters that you might dispute is the effect upon the right to open and close in the presentation of evidence and arguments to the jury. That right generally goes to the party with the burden of proof upon the case as a whole. Sometimes that burden can be shifted from one party to the other (usually from the plaintiff to the defendant) by an admission that the opposing party has a prima facie case and the assertion only that it is defeated by some affirmative reply.[4]

Another special purpose for which it is sometimes tactically advisable to admit matters that you might dispute is the effect upon admissibility of evidence. This use of an admission is illustrated by Case 86, in which, as counsel for the defendant, you anticipate that your client will be held liable and that the evidence concerning the conduct of your client's employees would be very damaging in its influence on the jury's attitude toward your client in general, though not actually relevant to the issue of damages. Negligence cases sometimes present this situation; cases of intentional wrong ordinarily do not present such a situation, since evidence of the nature of the wrong would be relevant to punitive damages and could not be excluded by an admission of the intentional wrong. As to ordinary negligence, however, or even "gross negligence" in those jurisdictions where such conduct does not support an award of punitive damages, you may use an admission of liability to forestall the plaintiff's proof of circumstances of the wrongful conduct that would inflame the jurors' minds against the defendant because of his conduct in committing the wrong, or because of his apparent effort in trial, with your blessing and help, to escape responsibility for his wrongful conduct. The extent to which such an admission can be effective depends both upon the facts of the case and upon the attitude of the trial judge, since the appellate courts generally allow the trial judge great leeway in rulings on objections to evidence as being either irrelevant or immaterial. The success of the tactics of admission to preclude evidence that would otherwise

---

3. See §7.16.
4. Case 61, discussed in §5.10, is an example.

be proper depends, of course, upon objections of irrelevancy and immateriality.

The usefulness of the admission of liability in Case 86 to keep out evidence of the circumstances of the accident is doubtful because of the dispute concerning the severity of impact and the relevancy of the circumstances of the accident to that issue. Even so, many lawyers would prefer to try the case under a stipulation of liability on the theory that the jury would be more inclined to agree with D on the question of extent of injury if D is not subject to the criticism of trying to defeat liability in a case in which D was obviously responsible for the accident.

§11.20 Requests for a medical examination

In a personal injury case, should the defendant's lawyer request a medical examination of the plaintiff?

Should the plaintiff submit voluntarily to a medical examination at the request of the defendant's lawyer?

Great conflict exists as to the right of the opposing party to insist upon a medical examination of one whose physical or mental condition is in issue in the case.[1] Specific provision is made in Federal Rule 35, and similar rules and statutes in some of the states, for a procedure by which one may be required to submit to an examination or suffer such severe penalties, within the court's discretion, as to make submission almost certain. In the absence of such a rule, some courts have held that they have inherent power to compel physical examinations as an aid to determining the reality of alleged injuries or abnormalities, and others have adopted the contrary view that there is a right of personal inviolability that precludes an order compelling a person to submit to physical examination.[2] In jurisdictions of the latter type, however, it is often possible for the adverse party to require physical examination after one exhibits his injury.[3]

If the case is on file in a jurisdiction where the rules, statutes, or decisions give the defendant an effective means of requiring a physical examination, as is true in the federal courts, the penalties that probably[4] will be suffered in the event of the plaintiff's refusal to submit are so

1. 8 Wigmore, *Evidence* §2220 (rev. ed. McNaughton 1961).
2. *Id.*
3. *Id.*
4. The trial judge generally has discretion in the matter; see *e.g.,* Federal Rules 26(c), 35, 37(b) (2) (D).

severe that there is rarely any occasion for doubt, from the point of view of the plaintiff's lawyer, whether he should advise his client to consent to the defendant's request for an examination. As a general rule, it would be better from the plaintiff's point of view to allow an examination by a doctor named by the defendant than to resist the defendant's request and finally submit to an examination by a doctor appointed by the court. The jury may think that reluctance to submit to an examination indicates insincerity in the claim and fear of the exposure of malingering, even though the reluctance is actually explainable on some other basis. Also a jury is much more likely to accept the findings and opinions of a court-appointed doctor than those of a doctor selected by the adverse party. This latter factor is so significant that it generally outweighs the disadvantage to the plaintiff, and the advantage to the defendant, that a doctor selected by the defendant is likely to be more conservative in his opinions of the extent of injury and disability than one selected by the court. For these same reasons, a defendant's lawyer normally should prefer an examination by a court-appointed doctor rather than one selected by himself. The court-appointed doctor's testimony also generally carries more weight with the jury than that of a doctor selected by "agreement of the parties," regardless of whether he is truly one selected by a joint choice or only one selected by one party, with the other exercising merely a veto power.

Even though the defendant's lawyer has available an effective rule, statute, or decision to compel the plaintiff to submit to a physical examination, it is not always to his advantage to demand it. If the plaintiff is apparently malingering and his doctor is fooled, or is deliberately winking at the situation, or is notoriously generous in his estimates of injury and disability, then it is to the defendant's advantage to get an examination by a competent doctor whose opinion will be reliable and whose testimony will probably carry weight with the jury. On the other hand, if it appears to the defendant's lawyer that the plaintiff is entirely honest and that his doctor is competent and reliable, little is to be gained by another examination that is likely to confirm the plaintiff's claims; in rare instances, the findings may even be more favorable to the plaintiff than those of his own doctor. Usually, however, the defendant's lawyer is at least skeptical of the plaintiff's claims. Arranging for an additional examination by a competent doctor or doctors has the advantage of aiding the defendant and the defendant's lawyer to become better satisfied as to what the plaintiff's true condition is, if they do not select the examining doctor solely for his testifying ability as distinguished from professional competency. For this reason, the additional examination is often an important factor both with respect to considering settlement [5] and with respect to assuring adequate preparation if the case is to be tried.

There is reason for not requesting a physical examination if the defendant is relying heavily upon a contention of nonliability and has reasonable hope of sustaining it. Too much attention to the extent of injury, strictly a damages problem, may be construed as a confession of lack of confidence in the contention of nonliability. [6] The choice between the risk of harm to the defense of nonliability and that to the defense on amount of damages often cannot be avoided and must be made upon a basis of choosing the lesser risk.

A problem frequently arises as to whether additional examinations should be requested or permitted, after one or more previous examinations have already been made at the request of the defendant. It is a great disadvantage to have medical testimony based upon a single examination compared with contradictory medical testimony based upon repeated observations and examinations over an extended period of treatment. It is also very disadvantageous to have only medical testimony based upon an examination long before trial compared with contradictory medical testimony based upon numerous examinations extending up to the time of trial. It is generally advisable, therefore, for the defendant to seek an examination at the time of trial, even though previous examinations have been made. Although the matter of additional examinations is generally discretionary with the court, even in those jurisdictions where provision is made for compelling the plaintiff to submit to examination, most trial judges are favorably disposed toward granting the additional examination near the time of trial. There is a greater reluctance to grant new examinations by additional doctors, however, and also greater doubt about the tactical advisability from the defendant's point of view of requesting such additional examinations. The answer to this problem will depend upon considerations relating to the effectiveness of the medical witnesses on each side, the number of witnesses on each side, and the possibility of unfavorable inferences because of the expense that the defendant is willing to incur in defense of the case. [7]

In those jurisdictions where there are no rules, statutes, or decisions compelling the plaintiff to submit to physical examination, the defendant nevertheless often has practical means available to obtain an examination. The plaintiff's refusal to submit to an examination, even though he has a right to refuse, may be proved in some jurisdictions, and supports a

5. See the latter part of this section, and see §9.22 concerning settlement.
6. See §7.18.
7. See §9.8 as to expense.

possible jury inference that the plaintiff is not hurt as seriously as he claims. Some plaintiff's lawyers customarily advise their clients to submit voluntarily to examinations because of this factor.

If the plaintiff refuses to submit to a medical examination, and proof of the refusal is permitted in your jurisdiction, as the defendant's lawyer you should consider making a written request for the examination by letter addressed to the plaintiff through his lawyer, explaining the terms of your request. Such a letter is useful in making your proof because it avoids any uncertainty or argument about the terms of your request. It is preferable that the letter name more than one physician satisfactory to you, giving the plaintiff an option; unless the practice is objectionable to the trial judge, it is also desirable to suggest that you will be willing to have the judge appoint a doctor to make the examination if the plaintiff is not willing to go to any of the doctors whom you name. From the point of view of the plaintiff's lawyer, if you represent a client who does not wish to have the examination or if for some reason you advise against it, it is sometimes possible to avoid unfavorable inferences (that the claim is exaggerated and that you are hiding contradictory evidence) by replying to such a request with the suggestion that you will consent to the examination if the defendant will be equally cooperative in supplying the names of all witnesses known to the defendant. This is particularly effective in cases in which discovery procedures are inadequate to force the disclosure and the defendant has made an investigation of the circumstances immediately after the accident, at which time it was possible to discover more witnesses than you could find in a much later investigation.

Examinations by doctors selected by the defendant often prove to be of material aid in settling cases in a manner satisfactory to both parties. Obviously, the defendant is more inclined to discount the meritorious nature of the plaintiff's claim when he refuses an examination than when he willingly submits and the findings of the examination tend to support his claim at least to some extent. The identity and character of the doctors making the examination and of the doctors who have seen the plaintiff at his or his lawyer's instance are very important in this respect. If each lawyer is relying upon doctors whose practice consists largely of examining claimants and appearing as witnesses in personal injury cases, on a certain side of the docket, their findings and opinions are quite likely to be so diverse as to be an obstacle to settlement. Rarely will both lawyers and their clients be able to view the situation with sufficient objectivity to appreciate the reasons for the differences.[8] On the other hand, if the doctors used by each party are thoroughly competent and reliable, there

8. As to the settlement appraisal generally, see §9.22.

is likely to be enough conformity in their views to improve the chances of settlement.

Sometimes the lawyers agree on an examination by a doctor selected by the defendant with the understanding that it will be used only in negotiations for settlement and not as evidence in trial. Whether you should make such an agreement will often depend on the exact terms. From the plaintiff's point of view, it is preferable to have an agreement that the fact that the examination was made shall not be referred to in trial, so as to avoid the unfavorable inference that the plaintiff is unfairly hiding evidence from the jury. From the defendant's point of view, such a provision in the agreement may make it inadvisable to accept the examination since it may deprive the defendant of an opportunity of proving the plaintiff's unwillingness to submit unconditionally to examination, supporting the argument that he is not hurt as seriously as he claims.

Other conditions in connection with the agreement or order for the examination may be significant. Should you, as plaintiff's lawyer, insist upon having a physician of your own selection present when the examination is made, or upon being present yourself? Provisions are made in some statutes and rules for a right to have someone present with the plaintiff, or for such discretion in the trial judge[9] that he may include this condition in the order for examination. Perhaps you are justified in insisting on being present if the doctor selected by the defendant is one you suspect of deliberate advocacy rather than merely an honest search for the truth with respect to the plaintiff's condition. There is a distinct tactical disadvantage to the plaintiff in having his own physician or lawyer present during the examination, however, unless he really needs protection from the possibility of unfair treatment. The fact that the plaintiff would not submit to examination without his adviser present, whether doctor or lawyer, may lead the jury to conclude that he fears discovery of malingering. Also, causing a physician selected by or for the plaintiff to be present places that physician in the position of a representative of the plaintiff — an interested party. If he is also to be a witness for the plaintiff, this may materially affect the jurors' views as to the weight his testimony deserves.

Another important condition regarding the examination concerns the disclosure by each party of reports of examinations. Some jurisdictions have statutes creating a patient-physician privilege, under the terms of which communications from the patient to the physician may be kept confidential at the instance of the patient.[10] The privilege is one that the

---

9. *E.g.*, see Federal Rule 35(a).

10. 8 Wigmore, *Evidence* §§2380–2391 (rev. ed. McNaughton 1961). In Federal Rules of Evidence, Rule 504, the privilege is limited to the psychotherapist-patient relationship.

patient may waive or forfeit. An express provision concerning "waiver" appears in Federal Rule 35. When an examination is made at the instance of the defendant, the plaintiff is entitled to a copy of a detailed written report of the examining physician setting out his findings and conclusions. As the plaintiff's lawyer, however, you should not make such a request unless you are willing to make a full disclosure of all medical reports in your possession. The rule provides that after such a request and delivery of the report of examination under order of the court, the defendant is entitled upon request to receive from the party examined a like report of any examination, previously or thereafter made, of the same mental or physical condition, and the plaintiff also forfeits any privilege he may have had regarding the testimony of every other person who has examined or may thereafter examine him in respect to the same mental or physical condition. This provision concerning reports applies also to the case in which the examination at the defendant's request was agreed to voluntarily by the plaintiff, rather than being made under order of court, unless the agreement expressly provides otherwise.

§11.21 Motions for continuance

CASE 87. *P* (a customer) sues *D Department Store* for personal injuries sustained by *P* when he was struck by a delivery cart loaded with packages. The cart was operated by one of *D*'s employees along a passageway between the shopping area of the store and a parking garage. There is a dispute as to whether *P*, who was attempting to pass two other customers, *C-1* and *C-2*, was within a lane marked for customers or suddenly stopped or was jostled out of that lane into one marked for employees only. *P* claims to have been struck from behind while walking within the lane for customers, though close to the edge, as he was passing *C-1* and *C-2*. *P* also claims that no warning of any kind was sounded by *S*, the servant of *D Department Store*, who was operating the cart. *S* says *P*'s body obscured his view so that he could not see whether *P* was jostled or voluntarily stepped away without being struck by *C-1*. *C-1* and *C-2* say that they were not scuffling and that *C-1* accidentally jostled *C-2* as *C-1* moved more to the right, away from the lane marked for employees only, when they heard the warning bell on the approaching cart. Both *C-1* and *C-2* say that they were not aware of *P*'s presence and that neither of them came in contact with *P* until *P* was struck by the cart, at which time *P* fell partially against *C-1*, injuring *C-1* slightly. Both *C-1* and *C-2* say that they do not know exactly where *P* was located with respect to the division between lanes when he was hit, but that he fell entirely in the lane marked for customers and the cart stopped at an angle with the right front corner slightly over into the customers' lane; they cannot say whether this is explained on the basis that the impact between P and that corner of the cart turned it from its direct course, or instead the cart was turned before striking P. There were no other witnesses to the accident. *C-1* and *C-2* have given written statements to both parties and have indicated willingness to testify voluntarily at trial. Their depositions have not been taken. Two days before trial, *C-1* is confined to a hospital because of a serious and contagious disease. *C-2* has left the jurisdiction in which the case is pending.

Should you move for continuance?
Should you oppose a motion for continuance filed by your adversary?

The granting or refusal of motions for continuance is generally a matter within the discretion of the trial judge, although there are in many jurisdictions statutes or rules that govern in particular situations. The manner in which motions for continuance are handled varies greatly with the attitude of the trial judge. Some judges customarily acquiesce in passing a trial setting if the parties desire it or if one urges it and the other acquiesces; other trial judges insist upon trial in the absence of valid grounds for continuance, even though both parties would prefer a continuance.

In the absence of conclusive proof of a special ground for continuance recognized by statute or rule, the possibility of obtaining a new trial because of an adverse ruling denying a motion for continuance is remote, and an adverse ruling granting the continuance is ordinarily not reviewable either immediately or after conclusion of the trial scheduled for a later date. Ordinarily, therefore, the only tactical considerations bearing on advisability of seeking or opposing a continuance are those with respect to the relative advantages and disadvantages of trying the case immediately as compared with trying it at a later date.

The factors recognized as grounds for continuance also have direct bearing on the tactical desirability of a delay and are usually more significant than other considerations; you should urge a continuance in the majority of cases in which you have adequate grounds to support the motion. You should consider other factors, however. In some instances it will be in the best interests of your client to have the case tried immediately, even though you have such support for a motion for continuance that the trial judge would probably grant it, and conversely it may be to your advantage to acquiesce in a motion for continuance urged by the other party though his grounds are of doubtful validity and the trial judge might overrule his motion.

It is sometimes stated that delay is one of the most effective weapons available to a defendant and that the lawyer representing the defendant should take every opportunity to have the case continued or to delay its final disposition in any other way.[1] Although it is typically true that (aside from exceptional situations such as may occur in proceedings for equitable relief or declaratory judgment) the plaintiff is more susceptible to pressure for settlement through delay and is the one who would be more harmed by indefinite continuance of the status quo, it does not follow that the temporary delays that can actually be obtained will benefit the defendant.

Developing a practice and a reputation for using every possible device to delay and escape trial necessarily harms a lawyer's standing with the judges before whom he practices and may thereby substantially affect the success with which he represents his clients, particularly with respect to matters within the discretion of the trial judge. Furthermore, it is often more difficult for a lawyer representing a defendant who is wealthy in comparison with the plaintiff to maintain the continued interest and co-operation of his witnesses than is the case with the plaintiff's lawyer whose client has the advantage of sympathies to aid him.

With respect to the possibility of very extended delays, you should consider the probable changes in money value and in size of verdicts. Cases delayed for years because of unavailability of witnesses in the armed services have illustrated the point; often such cases have resulted in higher verdicts because they were tried in a time of higher prices and continuing inflation.

Sometimes a special problem exists with respect to particular witnesses because of some factor such as an intended change of residence. Another type of special problem is likely to arise in Case 87, if C-1 is making a minor claim for his injuries and is willing to settle for a sum equal to his medical expenses, but D's lawyer prefers not to settle until after the trial of P's claim for fear that the settlement might be proved.[2] A delay because of his own illness, as in Case 87, would not be likely, however, to interfere with either the friendly relations between C-1 and D's lawyer or C-1's willingness to await termination of P's case before settlement of his claim, unless the illness results in an urgent need for funds.

Delays in litigation usually result in greater expense of trial to both parties, and the necessity for each lawyer's devoting substantially more time to the case. This is particularly true when the continuance is obtained so near the time of trial that each lawyer has necessarily done a part of the final trial preparation.

The question whether interest on any judgment in the case would run

---

1. This advice is probably contrary to the lawyer's ethical duties, if it is extended to the deliberate use of dilatory tactics to delay an admittedly just claim. See H. Drinker, *Legal Ethics* 82-84 (1953). Also compare §1.3.

2. See §2.17.

from the date of the wrong or only from the date of judgment may be quite material if the delay is an extended one. Obviously, if interest is collectible only from the date of judgment this factor makes delay more favorable to the defendant. On the other hand, if interest is collectible from an earlier date and is running during the delay, the delay may be an advantage to the plaintiff. This is especially true if a high contract rate of interest is applicable, as in the typical note providing 10 per cent interest on overdue amounts; it may also be true when a contract rate is not applicable, however, since in particular circumstances the legal rate of interest may be higher than the return on conservative investments.

Urging a motion for continuance sometimes involves the disadvantage of disclosing some of your evidence or a part of your plan of trial. In Case 87, for example, there might be doubt in the mind of each lawyer about calling C-1 and C-2 as witnesses and about whether the other is likely to call them.[3] Since their testimony is favorable to each party in some respects, it is conceivable that either party might successfully urge a motion for continuance on the ground that he intends to use the testimony of C-1 in trial, has used due diligence to arrange for his availability, and is prevented by C-1's illness from calling him as a witness or taking his deposition. Either party's filing of a motion in good faith would indicate his plan to use the witness and would suggest that the other party probably would have the benefit of favorable parts of the witness' testimony without accepting responsibility for him by calling him. Other factors you should consider are the possibility of arranging for C-2 to return to the jurisdiction for trial, the expense involved, and the comparison between his value as a witness and that of C-1. Your final decision in Case 87, whether you represent P or D, might well depend upon your judgment as to the relative persuasiveness of P and S — that is, what is the probable result of trial if the case is tried merely as a contest of credibility of the testimony of these two witnesses? If you consider that your witness is less likely to prevail in such a contest, you might improve your chances of success in trial by having C-1 present as a witness, even though his testimony is in some respects favorable to the adverse party.

§11.22 Consolidation and severance

CASE 78. As P's lawyer, you sue D for personal injuries suffered by P in a collision between cars of P and D. D counterclaims against P. As a defense to the counterclaim, P's insurer, *Liability Insurance Company*, represented by another lawyer, pleads a release obtained from D by one

3. See §2.2.

of its adjusters, acting in *P*'s name but without *P*'s personal participation in the transaction.

Should you move for consolidation of independent suits for trial?
Should you move for severance of independent claims or issues for trial?

Although the opportunity for consolidation of independent claims was more limited both at common law and under earlier codes (the codes being more liberal in some respects and less liberal in others than at common law), liberal rules for consolidation are now in effect in most jurisdictions. From the point of view of public interest, consolidation of as many claims as possible for simultaneous trial is advantageous when they involve common issues of fact and law. Disposition of all of the consolidated claims requires less time of the court and less public expense. The saving in time and expense may be important also for one or more of the parties. Consolidation or severance for trial may also make a substantial difference in the date of trial; customarily, consolidated cases are placed on the trial docket under the lower number, and in cities where the dockets are months or even years behind this may mean a much earlier trial for the suit filed later.

In addition to factors of convenience and expense, consolidation or severance may be tactically significant because of the probable influence of evidence and arguments concerning each issue upon the consideration of other issues. Case 78 presents an example of serious danger of harm to favorable consideration of *P*'s case if the fact of the settlement by *P*'s insurer, *Liability Insurance Company*, is made known to the jury. In these circumstances, it is obviously to *P*'s advantage to move for a severance of the claims for trial.[1]

If the controversies are claims of several plaintiffs against a single defendant, it is generally to the defendant's advantage to have the cases consolidated. Trial is less expensive and, if liability is established, the jury is likely to be influenced toward more conservative damages findings by consideration of the total sum they are awarding against the defendant. On the other hand, if the controversies are claims of a single plaintiff against several defendants, then it is generally to the plaintiff's advantage to have the claims consolidated or filed together as one suit.[2] If a fact issue must be resolved to determine which defendant is liable under some theories of the case, as in Case 70, it is obviously to the plaintiff's advantage to have the claims consolidated. It is probably also to the advantage of that defendant who has the best defense that the claims be tried in consolidation rather than separately, since there is more chance of his escaping liability if another defendant is readily available for the jury to saddle with responsibility.

1. See §10.15 as to other possible means of meeting the problem in Case 78.
2. See §10.2.

Conversely, that defendant who has the poorer defense probably has a better chance of escaping liability if the claim against him is tried separately and before the claim against the other defendant, leaving that claim outstanding but not fully developed before the jury. Furthermore, the presence of another defendant in the trial, against whom the plaintiff has a less satisfactory claim, creates a risk of harm from cooperation between the plaintiff and that defendant.[3]

§11.23 Initiating and participating in pretrial hearings

Although the procedure generally designated by the term "pretrial hearing" is a comparatively recent development from the historical point of view, procedures have long existed and now exist in every jurisdiction, regardless of whether they are called "pretrial hearing," for determining certain specific questions in advance of trial. For example, commonly there are special provisions for hearing such matters as pleas in abatement, motions regarding venue, objections or exceptions to allegations within the pleadings, motions for judgment on the pleadings or for summary judgment, objections or motions regarding formalities of taking and returning depositions, and motions for continuance. Even in jurisdictions where the procedure for "pretrial hearing" has been adopted, many individual matters may be heard by motion at a separate time, though the tendency is to hear all controversies of a preliminary nature at one time, simultaneously with a hearing designed to encourage settlement and, in the absence of settlement, stipulations to reduce the number of controverted issues for trial.

The extent to which the pretrial hearing is practiced largely depends upon the individual judge; the effectiveness of the procedure, likewise, largely depends upon the manner in which the trial judge exercises the discretion vested in him. For example, though operating under the same set of federal rules, some trial judges in the federal courts customarily go to the extreme of compelling disclosures at pretrial hearing that may be fairly criticized as improving the chances that a dishonest party will effectively avoid exposure (by traps that might otherwise have been laid for him through the use of documentary evidence that his opponent was required to disclose in the pretrial conference as one of his potential exhibits),[1] whereas other trial judges practice the opposite extreme of wholly ignoring the pretrial procedure, and still others (doubtlessly the majority) make use of the procedure to varying degrees between these extremes.

---

3. See §10.10 with reference to the danger of a so-called "gentlemen's agreement."
1. See §1.3. as to surprise generally.

In those courts where the trial judge does not customarily require pretrial hearings, it is rarely practicable for you to initiate such a hearing except by a motion upon some specific matter, in which case the hearing may be limited to the point raised by your motion. If, however, you have a reasonable basis for urging a motion for summary judgment, that motion often accomplishes essentially the same thing that would be accomplished by a pretrial hearing in that case. This is particularly true if the rule or statute under which the motion is presented provides, as is true of the federal rule,[2] that the trial judge's order at the conclusion of the hearing may designate the specific issues of fact remaining to be tried (rather than merely denying a motion for summary judgment because, for example, there is a genuine dispute as to a single fact issue material to decision of the case). Whether you should initiate such a hearing by motion for summary judgment depends upon a weighing of the chances that the motion will be sustained, possible limitation of the issues if it is not sustained, and the effect of disclosures of theories of law and fact that each party will be forced to make in the hearing on the motion. Unless the theory you urge is one depending entirely upon undisputed facts and subject to no possible response of confession and avoidance, you should be cautious about filing such a motion because of the certainty that you will educate your adversary concerning your own theories of the case in time to permit him to brief more exhaustively for legal theories and search more thoroughly for evidence to support some legal theory that would be a satisfactory answer to yours. In this respect, urging a motion for summary judgment is subject to the same disadvantages as urging an exception or objection to the sufficiency of pleadings because of allegations that might be changed or omissions that might be cured under the circumstancs of your case.[3] On the other hand, a motion for summary judgment may be an effective means of forcing more complete disclosure of your adversary's theory of the case; your motion may force your adversary to show at least some theories of fact and law and some supporting evidence, in order to rebut the prima facie showing of your motion that there is no genuine issue on any fact material to decision of the case.

Even though you have serious doubts that the motion for summary judgment will receive favorable consideration, filing such a motion is sometimes a sound tactical procedure for asserting a particular theory that in your judgment you cannot safely assert in trial before the jury because it may adversely affect consideration of other theories of claim or defense that you consider better. An example is a defense of settlement by an

2. Federal Rule 56.
3. See §10.16.

insurance adjuster of a negligence claim that you are defending, in a jurisdiction where you have a right to prevent disclosure of insurance coverage
ordinarily; asserting this defense of settlement in the presence of the jury
would probably result in disclosure of insurance coverage.[4]

Whether the trial judge should actively urge settlement of the case during
a pretrial hearing is a very controversial question. Some trial judges frankly
urge the use of the procedure for this purpose and customarily act as arbiters
in settlement negotiations, trying to get each lawyer to make concessions
for purposes of compromise. Others consider that such activity on the part
of the judge is inappropriate and also ineffective for the purpose intended
(delaying settlements that might be made earlier since each lawyer, knowing that the judge will urge settlement in this way, is more inclined to
withhold the intended best offer until the time of the pretrial hearing in
order to be able to make some concessions at that time in deference to the
judge's wishes). Participation of the judge in settlement negotiations is
also justly criticized because of the natural tendency of one in the judge's
role to assume that each party's position regarding settlement is unreasonably extreme. The judge's views regarding what would be a proper settlement may not be sound because of the comparatively sketchy knowledge
of the case the judge acquires in a pretrial hearing. If you consider that
the trial judge's views are not sound and that it is not in the best interests
of your client to compromise on a basis suggested by the judge, it is your
duty to your client to resist any pressure toward settlement used by the
judge. It is rare that any judge will actually penalize you or your client for
such a stand, though occasionally the judge will express or imply a threat
of penalty for refusal to take his suggestions regarding settlement.

With respect to the extent to which your participation in a pretrial hearing is guided by a principle of full and frank disclosure or the competing
principle of withholding information for surprise purposes,[5] the extent to
which your adversary will reciprocate either voluntarily or under pressure
from the court is material. Whether the trial judge should impose sanctions
to compel disclosures rather than merely soliciting the cooperation of lawyers
in full and frank disclosure is controversial. If it is apparent that he will
not do more than solicit cooperation, a pretrial hearing accomplishes little
with respect to disclosures by the lawyers, since it aids only in those cases
in which the lawyers would otherwise fail to discuss the case fully with
each other, a situation that is the exception rather than the rule among
experienced lawyers. If either lawyer is unwilling to make full and frank

4. See §7.16 for discussion of the advisability of using a motion for summary judgment in this situation.
5. See §1.3.

disclosures, the other lawyer is likely to understand that fact and to be equally reluctant to speak in the absence of a real threat of sanctions for noncooperation in the pretrial process. The controversy as to whether such sanctions should be imposed is basically the controversy concerning the element of surprise in the trial of lawsuits.[6]

6. *Id.*

INDEX